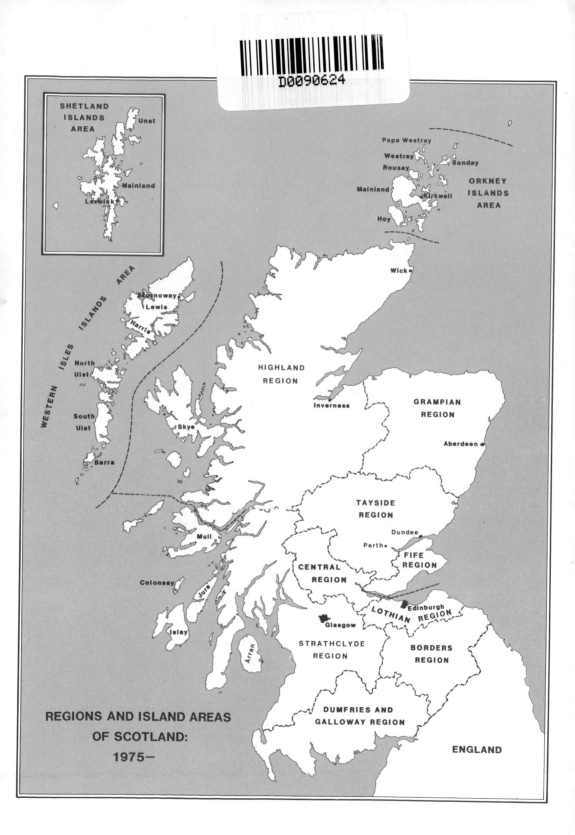

SHETLAND
ISLANDS
AREA

Unst

Mainland

Lerwick

Papa Westray
Westray
Rousay
Sanday
Mainland
Kirkwall
Hoy

ORKNEY
ISLANDS
AREA

Wick

WESTERN ISLES ISLANDS AREA

Stornoway
Lewis

Harris

North
Uist

South
Uist

Barra

Skye

Mull

Colonsay

Jura

Islay

Arran

HIGHLAND
REGION

Inverness

GRAMPIAN
REGION

Aberdeen

TAYSIDE
REGION

Dundee

Perth

FIFE
REGION

CENTRAL
REGION

LOTHIAN REGION

Edinburgh

Glasgow

STRATHCLYDE
REGION

BORDERS
REGION

DUMFRIES AND
GALLOWAY REGION

ENGLAND

REGIONS AND ISLAND AREAS
OF SCOTLAND:
1975—

THE
INTELLIGENT
TRAVELLER'S
GUIDE TO
HISTORIC
SCOTLAND

T · H · E
INTELLIGENT
TRAVELLER'S
GUIDE TO
HISTORIC
SCOTLAND

PHILIP · A · CROWL

CONGDON & WEED
New York • Chicago

Library of Congress Cataloging-in-Publication Data

Crowl, Philip Axtell, 1914–
　The intelligent traveller's guide to historic Scotland.

　Bibliography; p.
　1. Scotland—Description and travel—1981—Guide-
books.　2. Historic sites—Scotland—Guide-books.　3. Scotland—
Antiquities—Guide-books.　4. Scotland—History, Local.　I. Title.
DA870.C83　　1986　　914.11″04858　　86-2599
ISBN 0-86553-158-7

Copyright © 1986 by Philip A. Crowl
Library of Congress Catalog Card Number: 86-2599
International Standard Book Number: 0-86553-158-7
　　　　　　　　　　　　　　0-8092-2962-5 (Contemporary Books, Inc.)

Published by Congdon & Weed, Inc.
298 Fifth Avenue, New York, New York 10001
Distributed by Contemporary Books, Inc.
180 North Michigan Avenue, Chicago, Illinois 60601

Published simultaneously in Canada by Beaverbooks, Ltd.
195 Allstate Parkway, Valleywood Business Park
Markham, Ontario L3R 4T8 Canada

To my daughters:
Ellen Wood Crowl,
Catherine Pauline Crowl, and
Margaret Axtell Crowl

Contents

Acknowledgments

Many thanks are owed to the following for their part in bringing this book to completion: Libby McGreevy and Amy Teschner, for their skillful editorial work; Jack Murphy, Elizabeth Fee, and Bill Briendel of Cullen and Dykman, Brooklyn, New York, for their much-valued legal advice; Ross Sackett of Eureka Springs, Arkansas, for his sage counsel on matters relating to the publishing industry; Bill Clipson of Annapolis, Maryland, for drawing the endpaper maps; and the staffs of the Eisenhower Library, Johns Hopkins University, and the Chester W. Nimitz Library, U.S. Naval Academy, for their research assistance.

Gordon Donaldson, Professor Emeritus of the University of Edinburgh and Her Majesty's Historiographer in Scotland, painstakingly scrutinized the entire manuscript, called my attention to numerous errors of fact and interpretation, and shared with me invaluable insights gained from a lifetime's devotion to the writing and teaching of Scottish history. Mr. and Mrs. R. W. Munro of Edinburgh performed a like service. None of these scholars is to be held accountable for any residual flaws in the final product, for which the author, of course, bears sole responsibility.

Above all, tribute is due to the countless and nameless Scots who have so facilitated my own travels through their country by their courtesy, kindness, and good humor. The list is long and inclusive—personal friends, casual acquaintances, innkeepers, hotel porters, taxi drivers, ferry pilots, site and museum custodians, employees of the National Trust for Scotland and the Scottish Tourist Board, ministers of the Church of Scotland, even a duke or two. I hope that some of these anonymous benefactors will see this book and perhaps recognize their share in its production.

Philip A. Crowl
Annapolis, Maryland

Introduction

Foul weather . . . desolate landscape . . . backward and unfriendly natives!
These were the charges brought by the English historian Edward Gibbon
against the land that bordered his own country to the north. Writing of the
Roman legions' withdrawal from their frontier outposts in Scotland in the
second century A.D., the author of *The Decline and Fall of the Roman
Empire* explained: "These masters of the fairest and most wealthy climates
of the globe turned with contempt from gloomy hills assailed by the winter
tempest, from lakes concealed in a blue mist, and from cold and lonely
heaths over which the deer of the forest were chased by a troop of naked
barbarians." Such disdain was not uncommon among Gibbon's countrymen in the eighteenth century, nor has it completely disappeared. It has
seldom, however, checked the flow of distinguished visitors, English and
otherwise, into this land of "gloomy hills" and "lonely heaths." Many and
varied are the reasons that have drawn them there. Gibbon's own contemporary, Dr. Samuel Johnson, hoped nostalgically to get a glimpse of the last
remnants of a dying feudalism in the western Highlands and Islands. Queen
Victoria was enthralled by the wild and romantic landscapes along the
River Dee. Dwight David Eisenhower came for the golf.

Like other visitors before their time and after, all were captivated beyond
their expectations. Returning home by way of Iona, Dr. Johnson stood on
the site of St. Columba's ancient monastery and mused: "That man is little
to be envied, whose patriotism would not gain force upon the plain of
Marathon, or whose piety would not grow warmer among the ruins of
Iona." Victoria and Albert went back to build their sturdy summer palace at
Balmoral. And General Eisenhower was persuaded to accept the lifetime gift
of a guest flat in Culzean Castle on the Ayrshire coast.

Few visitors to Scotland can fail to be impressed by the grandeur of its
mountains, the stark beauty of its ruined abbeys, the gaudy charm of the
ubiquitous tartan, the poignant strains of distant bagpipes, the soothing
incomprehensibility of the broad Scots dialect, and the imperturbable
dignity of the Scottish people. Yet few, even among the English, know very
much of Scotland's history. A handful of names—William Wallace; Robert
Bruce; John Knox; Mary, Queen of Scots; Bonnie Prince Charlie—are of

course familiar to most English-speaking people of any education. But how many have heard of, or can identify, such noteworthy Scots as Andrew Moray, Andrew Melville, Lord George Murray, Henry Dundas, and James Keir Hardie? Or who recalls, without being reminded of it, that many centuries before Great Britain came into being, Scotland was an independent sovereign nation, as separate from England as Eire is today?

Scotland's history, and the still present traces of its storied past, form the subject matter of this book. These traces abound and are accessible to the modern traveller. Yet without some systematic study, no visitor could possibly understand the origin or significance of all these chambered cairns, hill-forts, castles, abbeys, tower-houses, village kirks, etc.—all mementos of six millenia of human occupation of the land.

At first glance, Scottish history may appear unusually melodramatic, even for Western Europe. Blood and thunder there are aplenty; endless brutal invasions by the English, relentless feuds among Scottish clans and families, treachery in high places, and rampant lawlessness everywhere. Throughout the story runs the sad recurring theme of disappointed expectations—of high ideals corrupted by fanaticism, of countless tragic ends to enterprises bravely undertaken, of honest toil rewarded by penury and dispossession. Thus Scotland's past lends itself easily to a romantic treatment. Sir Walter Scott of course is the best known exemplar of this tradition. But he is not alone. Indeed, the country's thriving modern tourist industry is steeped in it. Yet the known facts of Scottish history are colorful enough without the gloss of myth and fiction too often so thickly applied. But even the bare and unembellished record of events is apt to seem confusing—disjointed, paradoxical, chaotic, often all but incoherent. To bring some order out of this confusion—at least to the extent required by the interested traveller—is a major purpose of this book.

This is a companion volume to the author's previous publication, *The Intelligent Traveller's Guide to Historic Britain* (New York, London: Congdon & Weed, 1983), which covers England, Wales, and the Crown Dependencies.* Like it, the present book is part narrative history and part gazetteer, the two parts knit together by cross references. The purpose of the narrative history is to provide the intelligent traveller with sufficient historical information to understand the context of the sites he or she is visiting; the purpose of the gazetteer is to provide the necessary information as to how to get there and what to look for on arrival.

---

*Scotland was omitted from the earlier volume not out of lack of awareness that it too is British. The decision to devote a separate volume to Scotland was driven partly by considerations of space and partly out of recognition that it has a distinctly different history from that of England and Wales and therefore deserves separate treatment.

PART ONE: NARRATIVE HISTORY

This is a chronological account of Scotland's past, with emphasis on its visible and visitable remains. It is divided into nine chapters, each covering a period of Scottish history from the end of the Ice Age to the close of World War II. Wherever the name of a prehistoric or historic site appears—or of a museum, monument, church, garden, or distinguished piece of architecture—it is written in **bold print**, followed by a page reference to Part Two.

PART TWO: GAZETTEER

Here the same sites mentioned in Part One in chronological order are listed in the order of their geographical distribution. The following information is included in the heading for each site:

Location: The Gazetteer is divided into seven geographic regions, starting in the southwestern corner of Scotland and ending with the islands of the extreme North. Each region is subdivided into counties, also arranged in geographic order, from south to north and from west to east. With the exception of the Outer Hebrides, the counties are identified by the names in use before 1973 when the Local Government (Scotland) Act of Parliament replaced them with new administrative units called *regions*, *districts*, and *island authorities*. There are two reasons why the old county designations are retained in this book. First, Parliament notwithstanding, most people in Scotland still use the historic county names, as does the Post Office. Secondly, the old county boundaries, enclosing as they do areas of relatively small size, are better suited than those of the new, large administrative units for purposes of geographic orientation.

Within each county—or, in the case of the northern islands and the Outer Hebrides, within each island—the Gazetteer lists in alphabetical order the names of the population centers in which, or near which, are situated the sites mentioned in Part One. In deference to modern officialdom, the names of the new administrative regions are included in parentheses following each such place name. Thus, except for the island groups mentioned above, every city, town, and village listed is doubly identified: first, under the original county to which it belonged; secondly, with its present regional affiliation appearing in parentheses.

Under the place names so listed appear the names of sites in **bold print**, followed by the appropriate page reference, or references, to Part One. The site's exact location is then indicated. For most city and town sites, street names are given. For those situated in the country or in small villages or hamlets, the Gazetteer specifies the mileage and compass direction from the nearest population center—usually of a thousand or more inhabitants, though in the more remote and underpopulated parts of Scotland, sometimes the name of the nearest village must be used as a reference point. Also included are the route numbers of the main and/or secondary roads leading to the site in question.

Certain field sites are so remotely situated as to require even more precise pinpointing. This is especially true of prehistoric, Roman, and Dark Age sites, the great majority of which are classified as Ancient Monuments under guardianship of the Secretary of State for Scotland and maintained by the Scottish Development Department. For these, the Gazetteer provides grid references to the appropriate Ordnance Survey (OS) map in the 1:50,000 Series. Scotland is covered in its entirety in Sheets 1 through 85 of this series. Hence, the grid references appear as a number between 1 and 85, followed by two capital letters, followed by a six-digit number (e.g., 4 HU 457 236, which is the grid reference for Mousa Broch in Shetland). The first digit or two digits indicate the number of the appropriate OS map. The two letters identify the 100-square-kilometer grid of the National Grid System in which the site lies. They can be disregarded by users of the 1:50,000 Series. The six digits represent distances in kilometers and tenths of kilometers measured from the southwest corner of the map to the site in question. In locating a site on a 1:50,000 Series map, start at the lower left (southwest) corner and read right along the bottom edge to the figure indicated by the first two digits. Continue right to the number of tenths of a kilometer indicated by the third digit. From this point north is your longitude line. Starting again at the lower left corner, read up the left edge of the map to the figure indicated by the fourth and fifth digits. Continue up to the number of tenths of a kilometer indicated by the sixth digit. From this point eastward is your latitude. Where longitude and latitude lines intersect is the precise location of the site you are looking for. If it is an Ancient Monument under the care of the Scottish Development Department, it will be so designated on the map by a blue bar inside of which is written the name of the site.

Evaluation of Sites: The number of asterisks (or the absence of asterisks) in front of a site name in the Gazetteer is an indication of the author's evaluation of the site's historic or architectural significance and of its attractiveness to travellers. Attractiveness is measured in terms of the intrinsic interest or beauty of the site, of its convenience to visitors, and of the amenities provided. Convenience is measured by such factors as accessibility by car or public transport, the sufficiency and clarity of roadside signposts, and the frequency and duration of visiting hours. Amenities include car parks (parking lots), well-informed and courteous custodial staffs, and an adequate supply of on-site guidebooks or other informational material. With few exceptions, sites requiring regimented guided tours are downgraded as less than convenient to the time-pressed traveller. Also downgraded are sites (usually stately homes) that, though otherwise attractive and important, are open to the public fewer than three days a week.

The rating of three asterisks (***) means "outstanding" and not to be missed, if possible; two asterisks (**) means "very good"; and one asterisk (*) good. Where no asterisk at all precedes the site name in the Gazetteer, it is because the site in question, though of sufficient historic interest to warrant inclusion in the narrative, is either too difficult of access or not attractive enough to warrant most travellers' making any significant effort to search it out.

Site Descriptions: Under the heading of each site comes a paragraph or more explaining its historic origins and significance and describing its present appearance. These descriptions may duplicate some of the information contained in Part One, though they are usually more detailed and more specifically aimed at guiding the traveller through and around the site in question. They are not, of course, as detailed as the guidebooks that are often available for on-site purchase. For many travellers, however, they will provide all the guidance needed.

Sites Under the Care of National Organizations: In the site headings, immediately after the OS grid references or other indicators of the site's precise location, the letters *AM* or *NTS*, or sometimes both, will often appear. *AM* stands for Ancient Monuments under guardianship of the Secretary of State for Scotland and maintained by the Scottish Development Department. The letters *NTS* stand for The National Trust for Scotland. This organization, founded in 1931 and sanctioned by Act of Parliament in 1935, owns and manages more than eighty properties, including castles, stately homes, cottages, gardens, parks, nature preserves, etc. Founded to promote the preservation of fine buildings, historic places, and the natural wonders of the Scottish countryside, The National Trust for Scotland operates much like its older English counterpart, The National Trust. It is responsible for having rescued from probable oblivion a significant portion of the country's patrimony. Ownership of a property by the NTS is a guarantee that it will be well maintained, usually open to the public at convenient times, well signposted, supplied with readable guidebooks and other informational material, and staffed with courteous guides.

Visiting Hours and Price of Admission: Visiting hours at Ancient Monuments (AM) under the management of the Scottish Development Department are as follows:

April–September: Weekdays, 9:30 A.M. to 7:00 P.M.; Sundays, 2:00 to 7:00 P.M.

October–March: Weekdays, 9:30 A.M. to 4:00 P.M.; Sundays, 2:00 to 4:00 P.M.

At midday the custodians of these places often close shop for lunch. Otherwise these posted hours are usually observed, but not always. Unexplained absences of the custodians during posted hours are not, unhappily, as rare as one would hope. Also there are wide variations in the competence and helpfulness of the Ancient Monuments custodians. Some are courteous, well informed, and cooperative. Others display an indifference to the public, bordering on surliness.

Stately homes in Scotland ordinarily open their doors to visitors only in the afternoons and usually no more than four days a week. (The specific days vary, though Friday seems to be the favored weekday for staying closed.) Municipal museums almost always close for lunch and sometimes for entire days. Churches are often locked on weekdays, though keys can usually be obtained at the manse (minister's house), which is normally nearby and in any case easy enough to find on inquiry.

In short, the prudent traveller will take the precaution of ascertaining hours of admission before undertaking a visit. Since these change from time to time, they have been omitted from the Gazetteer for fear of giving misleading information. Readers are advised to consult one of several other publications that are produced annually and are therefore presumably up to date: the Scottish Tourist Board's *Scotland: 1001 Things to See*; the British Automobile Association's (AA) *Stately Homes, Museums, Castles & Gardens in Britain*; and two publications by ABC Historic Publications, entitled respectively *Historic Houses, Castles & Gardens* and *Museums and Galleries*. In the United States these can all be purchased directly or by mail from The British Travel Bookshop, Ltd., 680 Fifth Ave., New York, NY 10019. In London they can be obtained at the British Tourist Authority's Information Centre at 64 St. James St., SW 1; in Edinburgh, at the Scottish Tourist Board, 5 Waverley Bridge; and in Glasgow, at the Information Bureau in George Square.

Another important source of timely information for visitors to Scotland is the Scottish Tourist Board, whose central office is at 23 Revelston Terrace, Edinburgh. This organization maintains more than 140 Tourist Information Centres throughout Scotland. No town of any size is without one. They are well signposted and are not hard to find. Travellers need only look for a blue and white sign with the words *Tourist Information* followed by the small letter *i* in either black or bright red. Each of these centres contains a mine of information about local sites, tourist attractions, amusements, hotels, lodgings, restaurants, etc., and much of it is free.

Most sites in Scotland charge an admission fee, and of course these, like all other prices, are subject to change, usually upward. Serious travellers can save money by becoming members of the National Trust for Scotland for a fixed fee that guarantees free entry to all NTS properties. Membership can be obtained at the trust's headquarters at 5 Charlotte Square, Edinburgh; at

Hutcheson's Hospital, 158 Ingram St., Glasgow; or at any of the historic properties under NTS custody. An even better bargain is an "Open to View" ticket, which guarantees free admission to every Ancient Monument under the management of the Scottish Development Department *and* every National Trust Property, as well as some other places under private or Crown management. These tickets are good for only one month after first use. They can be purchased from the British Tourist Authority, 680 Fifth Ave., New York, NY 10019; the British Tourist Authority's Information Centre, 64 St. James St., London, SW 1; the Scottish Tourist Board, 5 Waverly Bridge, Edinburgh; or the Information Bureau, Prestwick International Airport outside Glasgow.

Visitors to the northern islands (Orkney and Shetland) and/or to the western isles (Inner and Outer Hebrides) will normally need to book passage by plane or boat. The Highlands and Islands Development Board publishes annually a "comprehensive guide for users of the area's transport system," entitled *Getting Around the Highlands and Islands.* This is obtainable from the Scottish Tourist Information Centres in Glasgow and Edinburgh or from the British Tourist Authority offices in London and New York (addresses above). Serving Orkney and Shetland is the P&O Ferries, PO Box 5, P&O Ferries' Terminal, Jamieson's Quay, Aberdeen AB9 8DL (Tel: 0224 572615). Travellers requiring car or passenger ferry service to the western isles must rely mostly on Caledonian MacBrayne, Limited, which enjoys a near monopoly of sea transport between the mainland and the islands off the west coast. The company's headquarters are in Gourock, and the telephone number is 0475 33755. Travellers to, from, and between these islands will appreciate the popular ditty (a paraphrase of the metrical version of the Twenty-Fourth Psalm):

> The earth belongs unto the Lord
> And all that it contains,
> Excepting for the Western Isles,
> And they belong unto MacBrayne's

Maps: There are only two maps in this book. The first, on the front endpaper, shows the names and boundaries of the counties of Scotland as drawn prior to the Local Government (Scotland) Act of 1973. The second, on the back endpaper, shows the names and boundaries of the new regions and island authorities established by the Act of 1973. Obviously these simple outline maps cannot be used as road maps. The latter are readily available in almost any book shop or stationer's establishment in Scotland and can also be obtained from the British Tourist Authority offices in New York and London at the addresses given above. For really serious travellers a road atlas is preferred, partly because it is easier to handle on the front seat of a car than a folding map, but especially because it can be counted on to contain an exhaustive index of place names. The author's preference is the *Automobile Association (AA) Great Britain Road Atlas* (Basingstoke, Hampshire: Farnum House, 1982). It too is easily obtainable at book shops in Scotland and in the cited locations in New York and London.

For extensive sight-seeing among prehistoric, Roman, and Dark Age field sites, travellers should procure the appropriate 1:50,000 Series Ordnance Survey (OS) maps mentioned above. These can be purchased at almost any book shop in the neighborhood of the site to be visited. John Smith & Sons, 57 St. Vincent St., Glasgow; and James Thin, 53–59 South Bridge, Edinburgh, usually have on hand the complete collection for Scotland. Travellers wishing to stock up on these maps before their arrival in Scotland can order them by mail from the above or from Hatchards, 187 Piccadilly, London W1V 9DA; or Cook Hammond and Kell, Ltd., The London Map Centre, 22–24 Caxton St., London SW1H OQU.

APPENDIX A: THE BEST OF SCOTLAND

This section lists, under a number of categories (e.g., ruined castles, military museums, etc.) those Scottish sites considered by the author to be the most attractive and interesting and therefore worthy of three asterisks (***) in the rating system described above.

SELECTED READINGS

This is not a complete bibliography, but rather a guide to further readings for those travellers interested in delving more deeply into the subject of Scotland and its history. Two types of books are included: (1) travel literature, including other guidebooks; and (2) general histories of Scotland as well as scholarly monographs of special interest.

INDEX

Page references in the Index appear in two types of print. Those in **bold print** refer to Part Two (the Gazetteer); all others to Part One (Narrative History).

HOW TO PREPARE AN ITINERARY

It is probably presumptuous to advise an intelligent traveller as to how to make the most of his or her trip, but the following suggestions may help visitors to Scotland to make the best use of this book and of their time while travelling. Non-British readers are doubtless in greater need of such guidance than are those from south of the Anglo-Scottish border or across the Irish Sea.

1. Study the county map on the front endpaper. Without a fairly good grasp of the distribution of these administrative areas, any reader or traveller is likely soon to get lost. Familiarity with the map on the back endpaper, showing boundaries of the modern regions and island authorities, is less important, though useful when employing a modern atlas.

2. Read Part One as needed. As already indicated, Scottish history can be confusing, and few strangers to it will be able to place the sites they visit in proper historical context without studying this narrative account.

3. After reading, or at least perusing, Part One, make a list of those sites or types of sites you most want to see. Appendix A (The Best of Scotland) may be helpful here. Then decide on which areas of Scotland you most want to visit. This is the place to begin exercising self-restraint. Scotland is not a big country by American or Australian standards, but road travel can be slow, and many places of interest require transport by boat. You can't see it all in three or four weeks.

4. Using the Index and Gazetteer, match your preferred list of sites with your preferred selection of areas to be visited. Eliminate those sites falling outside the areas chosen. They can await another visit.

5. Using the Gazetteer, check the other sites in the general area of those you have chosen. Though they were not included in your preferred list, you may want to visit some of them anyway while in the neighborhood.

6. Use the Gazetteer in conjunction with a road map or an atlas for the precise location of the sites you are seeking and the shortest routes by which they can be reached.

7. Before visiting any site, read the site description in the Gazetteer. This may save you the price of an on-site guidebook or brochure.

8. Do not crowd your itinerary excessively. A good rule of thumb for the motoring traveller is no more than six sites and no more than a hundred miles per day. Even this may prove too much for those who prefer long lunch breaks, early arrival at their evening's destination, and frequent stops to admire the magnificent scenery.

9. Finally, allow time for rest, recreation, and quiet observation of the Scottish scene. Play a round of golf on the Old Course at St. Andrews. Take a pony trek in the Trossachs. Spend a day at one of the Highland Games. Attend Sunday services at a village kirk. Take a guided tour through a single-malt distillery and sample the wares. Shop for woollens at a textile factory outlet. Buy a tartan scarf or necktie—but save it to wear at home. And last and best of all—especially if you are American or "colonial"—stop and talk to the local inhabitants. They like to listen to your funny accent and are bound to pay you close and courteous attention.

T · H · E
INTELLIGENT
TRAVELLER'S
GUIDE TO
HISTORIC
SCOTLAND

Part One

Narrative History

Chapter One
Prehistoric Scotland

In Scotland the traveller with an interest in paleontology will search in vain for such ancient human fossils as the skull of Swanscombe Man (ca. 200,000 B.C.) now in the British Museum in London or the ochred bones of the Red Lady of Paviland (ca. 16,500 B.C.) in the Oxford University Museum. All such traces of Paleolithic Man are missing from North Britain, probably because, during the hundreds of thousands of years known as the Ice Age, no human being dared venture into the territory later to emerge as Scotland. Four times during this era, ice sheets not unlike those found today in Greenland crept southward from the Arctic Circle to encase most of northern Europe. Between these periods of thick glaciation occurred long episodes of rising temperatures, known as *interglacials*, as well as shorter stretches of warmer climate called *interstadials*. During these periods of climatic amelioration, nomadic hunters and food-gatherers roamed the moors and forests of southern Britain in search of game. They left behind an amazing number of artifacts, including flint hand axes, scrapers, knives, and burins; spearheads and harpoons of bone and antler—the basic tool kit of a primitive society of big-game hunters. Today, no English museum of archaeology and local history is wanting in these relics of the Old Stone, or Paleolithic, Age.

Not so in Scotland—the reason being that no such artifacts have ever been discovered there. There is, in short, no evidence of human habitation in northern Britain before the melting of the last great ice cap. Possibly, of course, a few hunters did find their way into this inhospitable region during one or more of the Ice Age's intermittent thaws. If so, all traces of their presence were destroyed by subsequent glaciation. More likely, no one ventured that far north. The total absence of Paleolithic artifacts in Scotland can be taken to mean that, in all probability, no human being lived or even visited there during any part of the Ice Age.

Then, some time around the fourteenth millenium B.C., the last of the glaciers (called the Devensian) began to thaw. It was a slow process, but by 10,000 B.C. Britain was probably entirely free of ice. In Scotland, however, came three distinct glacial readvances that left huge deposits of clay and gravel, called *moraines*, as far south as Loch Lomond and the valley of the River Forth. After the last of these, the ice sheet rapidly dwindled, and by about 8300 B.C. it had virtually disappeared. Then emerged a bleak and craggy landscape, cruelly mountainous in the north and west, pocked with deep valleys between high hills in the south, and relatively level only in the midland valley, the broad basin of Strathmore, and the coastal region of the Moray Firth. Throughout the North and West the glaciers had dug deep declivities into which the newly released icy waters flowed to form innumerable inland lochs. Along the west coast the receding ice cap left great ravines to be filled by tidal waters to form long and narrow sea lochs. For, as the ice melted, the sea rose to unprecedented levels. The land bridge between southwestern Scotland and northern Ireland disappeared beneath it. New islands were formed: the Inner and Outer Hebrides along the Scottish mainland's western coast; the Orkneys off its northern tip. Then, probably no later than 6000 B.C., the last overland connection between Britain and the European continent disappeared under the waves. The British Isles were born.

A word should be said here about prehistoric dates. In 1949 the dating of ancient fossils was revolutionized by the discovery of a technique for measuring the residual radiocarbon substance (Carbon 14) of organic materials. This made it possible to determine the elapsed time since the death of the organism from which the material was derived. Thus the Carbon 14 content of a fossilized bone would indicate the time of the death of the man or animal from which it came; that of a piece of charred timber would tell approximately when the tree from which it was fashioned had been cut down. Radiocarbon testing could not, however, be employed to measure the age of such inorganic objects as pottery, stone implements, metal tools, etc. Moreover, the method was found not to work for samples older than 60,000 years, the residual radioactivity in such cases being too weak to measure. Then, in the 1960s, scientists compared the results of radiocarbon dating with those gained from counting the tree-rings of bristlecone pine trunks known to be at least 5,000 years old. This led to the discovery that all radiocarbon dates before 1000 B.C. fell short of their actual calendar equivalents by a considerable margin. Nevertheless, when radiocarbon dates are calibrated to take this probable error into account, a fair degree of precision can be achieved. Thus the dates given in this chapter can be presumed to be more or less accurate—at least until further scientific discoveries render them obsolete.

A word also needs to be said about prehistoric periodization. Reference has already been made to that long period of prehistory known as the Old Stone Age. It came to a close in Britain about 8300 B.C. The succeeding period, lasting until about 4000 B.C., is known as the Mesolithic, or Middle

Stone, Age. Next came the Neolithic, or New Stone, Age (ca. 4000 to 2000 B.C.); then the Bronze Age (ca. 2000 to 700 B.C.); and finally the Iron Age, which in Britain ran from about 700 B.C. until the first century A.D., when the conquering Romans appeared on the scene.

Needless to say, these dates are only approximate. Furthermore, the terms *Stone Age, Bronze Age,* and *Iron Age* imply a uniformity in the manufacture of artifacts (of either stone, bronze, or iron) and therefore a uniformity of culture over long periods of time. The fact is, however, that at any given time peoples of differing cultural levels might coexist in the same general area. Thus, while Lowland Britons might demonstrate all the characteristics of a Bronze Age culture, some of their Highland contemporaries could very well still be following the ways of their Stone Age ancestors. Such cultural lags are to be expected in a region as diverse as the British Isles, and particularly in such remote areas as the Scottish Highlands and Islands. Nevertheless, there is no reason to believe that, for most of the prehistoric area, North Britain was so very far removed from the mainstream as to require a different chronology from that normally applied to the island as a whole. The dates given above, as rough as they are, therefore provide a useful framework for the several thousand years of Scottish prehistory.

THE MESOLITHIC AGE: 8300–4000 B.C.

In the years immediately following the retreat of the ice, little but lichens and subarctic grasses could grow on the scarred tundra thus exposed. Over this wasteland roamed the wild horse, reindeer, bison, and mammoth— creatures of the steppe. Then, as temperatures rose still higher, came the trees—first birch, then pine, and finally deciduous species such as alder and oak. Unlike today, all of Scotland was forested—even the now almost barren Outer Hebrides. And into the forest came new woodland species: red deer, roe deer, wild oxen (aurochs), wild boar, squirrels, martens, and all manner of wood fowl. Now too the unfrozen seas began to teem with marine life: whales, dogfish, sturgeon, salmon, haddock, and an enormous variety of shellfish. And where such natural foodstuffs occurred in great abundance, man was bound to follow.

From what homelands and by what routes the first human pioneers entered Scotland is a matter of conjecture. Certainly some would have come north from England, where the earliest known megalithic site at Star Carr in North Yorkshire antedates the first known Scottish settlement by about a thousand years. Perhaps some crossed the narrow North Channel from

Ireland. Others may have built shallow boats of wood and hide and sailed across the North Sea from as far away as Denmark.

They settled nowhere permanently. Yet the sites of these first Scottish immigrants number close to a hundred. The oldest to have been identified is at Morton Farm in northern Fife near the mouth of the Firth of Tay. It dates possibly to about 6500 B.C. Whoever dwelt here in the seventh millenium B.C. left behind a hoard of tiny implements of flint and stone— scrapers, awls, and blades. These are called *microliths* to distinguish them from the heavier hand axes of the Old Stone Age. Some of these finds are now to be seen in the **University Museum** *(494)*, St. Andrews in Fife. On the north bank of the Tay, other temporary settlements have been detected at Stannergate and Broughty Ferry, both sites yielding flint microliths now on display at the **Central Museum and Art Gallery** *(510)* in Albert Square, Dundee. Further north, on the south bank of the River Dee near Banchory in Kincardineshire, lies another Mesolithic campsite, the occupants of which left behind a fine collection of microliths now housed in the **National Museum of Antiquities of Scotland** *(447)* in Edinburgh.

The National Museum is the most complete of all of Scotland's archaeological repositories; its showcases teem with artifacts from the entire span of Scottish prehistory. Its Mesolithic collection comes chiefly from the west coast from Wigtownshire to Argyll and the adjacent islands. This is the area where the great majority of Middle Stone Age Scottish sites have been discovered. Possibly these people migrated across the narrow North Channel from Ireland, for their artifacts closely resemble those discovered near Larne in County Antrim. Among the holdings of the National Museum are Late Mesolithic flint implements from the Sands of Luce in Wigtownshire; microliths and a beautifully shaped barbed point of red deer antler from Shewalton Moor in Ayrshire; a miscellany of microliths from Campbeltown on the Kintyre Peninsula; implements of bone and antler from the island of Oronsay, where huge middens of limpet and periwinkle shells mark the campsites of a littoral people known as "strand loopers"; and from Oban in Argyll, a great variety of bone and antler pins, awls, fish spears, flint blades and scrapers, and a number of curious scooped beach pebbles called "limpet hammers," thought to have been used to extract the meat of shellfish. These latter objects come from two of Scotland's most interesting Mesolithic sites: Mackay Cave and MacArthur Cave, both located near Oban on inshore "raised beaches" created by the isostatic uplift of the land following the disappearance of the heavy ice cap. These too were strand looper sites with the usual huge accumulation of seashells. Obanian and other west-coast Mesolithic artifacts are to be seen today not only in the National Museum in Edinburgh, but also in Glasgow at the **Glasgow Art Gallery and Museum** *(407)* in Kelvingrove Park and the **Hunterian Museum** *(408)* on the grounds of the University of Glasgow; at the **Stewartry Museum** *(381)* in Kirkcudbright; the **Campbeltown Museum** *(461)* in Argyll; and the **Buteshire Natural History Society Museum** *(395)* in Rothesay. Among the more fascinating discoveries from Mesolithic Scotland are the bones from whales stranded along the shores of the Carse of Forth in Stirlingshire. These fossils were accompanied by tools of antler, the most noteworthy being a perforated blubber mattock not unlike those still used by Eskimos.

THE NEOLITHIC AGE: 4000–2000 B.C.

While Mesolithic riparian savages were carving up the bodies of dead whales stranded in the Carse of Forth, other river valleys far to the east were witnessing the dawn of mankind's first true civilization. In the Fertile Crescent between the Tigris and the Euphrates, men and women, perhaps ten thousand years ago, began to grow cereal crops, maintain herds of domesticated sheep and goats, weave textiles, mold and bake clay into pots and other vessels, build permanent houses in nucleated villages, and exchange their nomadic way of life for the more settled occupations of farming and herding. This was the Neolithic Revolution, so named after the least significant of its innovations—the polished and hafted stone axe used for forest clearing.

Slowly the techniques of mixed farming spread westward, and by about the year 4000 B.C. immigrants from the European continent had introduced them into the British Isles. Their earliest known settlement in England—at Hembury, Devon—can be dated to the years 4210–3990 B.C. Almost the same dates are ascribed to the hearth remains in the forecourt of a Neolithic tomb on the Isle of Arran off the coast of Ayrshire. It can be presumed therefore that Scotland was not far, if at all, behind its southern neighbor in entering the New Stone Age.

Of the thousands of artifacts left by prehistoric peoples, to be discovered and collected by their distant descendants, two types are distinctly Neolithic. The first, as mentioned, is the stone axe-head, made of igneous or metamorphic rock, ground, sharpened, and polished. Oddly, considering its mountainous terrain, Scottish stone was unsuitable for this purpose, and most of the axe-heads discovered there had been imported from the "axe-factories" of Great Langdale in the English Lake District or from Tivebulliagh in County Antrim, Ireland. The second, and still more common, type of Neolithic artifact is the earthenware pot. The earliest such ware known in Scotland (from about 3800 B.C.) is called Grimston/Lyle Hills ware. It is plain and round-based. From about the same period, though less numerous, come round-bottomed pots with lugs. Of a later date is a series of round-bottomed carinated bowls, decorated with impressions of cord, fingernail, and bird-bone, called Beacharra, Hebridean, and Unstan ware. Finally, from the end of the Neolithic period comes a class of flat-based, grooved pottery known as Rinyo-Clacton ware, which has been discovered at sites as widely separated as Essex and the Orkneys. Samples of all these types of pots and bowls, as well as stone axe-heads without number, can be seen in all the museums of archaeology and local history mentioned above, plus numerous others, including the **Aberdeen University Anthropological Museum** *(535)*, Aberdeenshire; the **Dumfries Museum** *(383)*, Dumfriesshire; the **Elgin Museum** *(525)*, Moray; the **Hawick Museum and Art Gallery** *(412)*, Roxburghshire; the **Inverness Museum & Art Gallery** *(517)*, Inverness-shire; the **Paisley Art Gallery & Museum** *(396)*, Renfrewshire; the **Perth Art Gallery and Museum** *(505)*, Perthshire; **Tankerness House** *(558)*, Kirkwall, Orkney; and the **Shetland Museum** *(568)* in Lerwick. Happily these museums contain numerous artifacts from later prehistoric and historic periods as well, for the nonprofessional museum-goer can tire quickly of a redundancy of stone axe-heads and homely pottery.

Of far greater interest to most travellers are the two rare examples of Neolithic dwelling places, both situated in the northern islands of Scotland where deforestation at an early date had compelled their builders to use stone instead of timber. The first is **Skara Brae** *(563)*, north of Stromness on the main island of the Orkney group. Here is a Late Neolithic village of stone (ca. 2200 B.C.), sometimes dubbed the Pompeii of Britain, because, like the city at the foot of Mount Vesuvius, it was buried by a natural cataclysm. In this case, a violent storm from the sea apparently drove the villagers out of their homes and later covered the site with sand. Then, in the mid-nineteenth century, another storm stripped away part of a sand dune to reveal a cluster of seven roofless stone huts connected by meandering alleys. The huts are roughly square in shape with rounded corners; their internal measurements average about fifteen feet each way; the walls are from five to eight feet thick and are corbelled inward; the apex of the roofs (now open) were in all likelihood covered with heather or turf supported by whalebone rafters. At the center of each hut was an open hearth surrounded by an amazing collection of furniture made of flagstone; box beds, dressers, and shelves; privies with drains connected to an underground sewer: and little square "limpet boxes" to store live shellfish. The builders were pastoral folk, herders of sheep and cattle, with no apparent knowledge of agriculture. The finds from the settlement, now in the **National Museum of Antiquities** *(447)* in Edinburgh, include stone axe-heads; carved knobby stone balls used perhaps in some Stone Age game; little pots of stone and whalebone containing remnants of ochre, presumably for cosmetic application; awls, pins, and necklaces of sheep-bone and whales' teeth; and a few earthenware pots of the Rinyo-Clacton variety. Today, Skara Brae, overlooking the beautiful Bay of Skaill, is a fascinating sight with an excellent site museum where short, illuminating lectures are regularly given by the custodian.

Also of Late Neolithic (or possibly Early Bronze Age) construction is the small settlement of **Stanydale** *(569)* near the west coast of the main island of Shetland. Here are the ruins of two groups of houses, the best preserved of which is oval in outline and measures internally 30 feet by 15 feet within a wall 9 feet thick and up to 2½ feet in height. Of greater interest is the nearby ruin of a so-called temple, which is probably contemporary with the houses. It is an ovoid structure, measuring about 40 feet by 20 feet, built of undressed blocks of stone about 12 feet thick. Inside are six shallow recesses in the east wall and sockets for two massive posts of spruce—possibly driftwood from North America or timber imported from Scandinavia, since this species was not introduced into Scotland until the sixteenth century. Whether this remote ruin was in fact a sacred building, or a communal meetinghouse, or the hall of some Stone Age chieftain is unknown.

Skara Brae and Stanydale notwithstanding, Neolithic Man in general made better, or at least more durable, provision for the dead than for the living. Only a strong belief in an afterlife, coupled perhaps with a healthy fear of unpropitiated spirits of the dead, could account for the more than six hundred Neolithic funerary monuments known to have been raised in Scotland.

The generic term for most of these grave sites is *chambered tomb* or *megalithic tomb* after the Greek words *mega*, meaning "large," and *lithos*, meaning "stone." The chamber, or mortuary house, is usually walled with stone slabs, called *orthostats*, sometimes supplemented with dry-stone (mortarless) corbelling so that the upper courses of the wall are said to "oversail" to form a vault. Whether the walls are straight or corbelled, the roof normally consists of one or more huge flat capstones. After the chamber was built, it was covered with a huge mound. In Scotland this usually consisted of pebbles and rounded boulders and is called a "cairn." Sometimes, though not as often in Scotland as elsewhere in Britain, these mounds have disappeared, leaving only the megalithic infrastructure exposed to view. These bare stone skeletal remains are most frequently found in Wales and southwestern England, where they are known respectively as *cromlechs* and *dolmens*. In Scotland these terms are seldom heard, the preferred usage being *denuded cairns*. Sometimes the cairns are revetted with borders of boulders designed to hold the cairn material in place. These are called *curbs* (or *kerbs*), or, if they are of sufficient height, *peristalths*. Where the cairn material has disappeared around the edges, these curbstones are now freestanding and are therefore not always easily distinguishable from Bronze Age stone circles, about which more will be said below. Sometimes the cairns were indented toward the opening of the burial chamber to form a forecourt where fires were customarily lit in some kind of funeral rite. In almost all cases the tombs were used for collective, not individual, interments; that is, they were mausoleums to be opened again and again for the insertion of new bodies or cremated remains. Earthenware vessels, probably containing food and drink, were often lodged alongside the deceased, as were implements and weapons—stone axes, maces, flint knives, and arrowheads, for example. Such grave-goods, as these objects are called by archaeologists, have been found, however, to be far less plentiful in Scotland than elsewhere in Britain. Possibly the natives were less generous to their dead; possibly Scottish tombs were more frequently robbed by later generations.

Chambered tombs fall into two general categories, according to the architecture of the megalithic chamber and the entry into it. First is the gallery grave, usually elongated and parallel-sided and always entered directly from the outside. The second type is the passage grave, sometimes parallel-sided but more often round or polygonal and always entered through a walled and roofed passageway, usually both lower in height and narrower than the chamber into which it leads. Scottish chambered cairns can be further classified into five main groups, according to both architectural style and regional distribution. These are: (1) the Bargrennan group; (2) the Clyde (or Clyde-Carlingford) group; (3) the Clava group; (4) the Orkney-Cromarty-Hebridean group; and (5) the Maeshowe group. Sometimes a sixth category—the Shetland group—is added, but these cairns are so small, ruined, and remote as to be scarcely worth the attention of the nonprofessional traveller.

Archaeologists in the past have expended much time and energy trying to establish fine architectural distinctions among these various groups, chiefly in an effort to discover affinities between the chambered tombs of Scotland and those of England, Wales, Ireland, and the Continent. Thus, they reasoned, they might determine the ethnic and geographic origins of the various Neolithic peoples who colonized North Britain. This effort is now dismissed as largely irrelevant, since it appears that most of the chambers were composite, multiperiod monuments, remodelled so many times that their original architectural form is undiscoverable. Hence, it is believed, any similarities between Scottish tombs and those found elsewhere must be largely coincidental. Furthermore, common sense alone argues against imputing nice stylistic distinctions to such simple, primitive, and eminently functional structures. Nevertheless, the typology mentioned above does provide a useful frame of reference for the traveller as he moves from one Neolithic grave site to another.

Of the passage graves, probably the earliest in time are those of the Bargrennan group. There are only twelve of these, all located in southwestern Scotland. The chambers are small, trapezoidal or wedge-shaped, and were originally covered by round cairns. The approach passages are long and usually wider at the chamber than at the entry, so that there is no clear structural distinction between chamber and passageway. This is true of the type site, **Bargrennan White Cairn** *(383)* in Kirkcudbrightshire north of Newton Stewart. This tomb measures twenty-four feet from the end of the chamber to the passage entrance. Its side walls and end stone consist of split boulders that support two massive capstones rising about four feet above the floor. The upper part of the cairn has been removed so that the chamber is fully visible from above.

The distribution of the Clyde group extends for a distance of eighty-six miles along the western Scottish seaboard from the Solway Firth as far north as Loch Etive. These tombs are classified as gallery graves and were originally covered by cairns in a variety of shapes. Their chambers are roughly parallel-sided galleries built of stone slabs, many of them divided internally by transverse slabs or *septae* to form two or more compartments. The front of the cairn is often recessed to form a forecourt and is frequently edged by a curb of upright stones. Altogether, there are ninety-five sites in this group, of which the following four are recommended to the traveller as both representative and relatively easy of access.

In Kirkcudbrightshire, about five miles southwest of Gatehouse of Fleet, **Cairnholy I** and **Cairnholy II** *(381)* lie next to each other on a high hill overlooking Wigtown Bay. The cairn of the former was originally about 140 feet long by 33 feet wide, with a concave facade at the east end and a curb of spaced slabs around the edge. The chamber beneath was about 12 feet long, 2½ feet wide, and 6 feet high and was divided roughly in half by a transverse stone reaching to the roof. As seen today, most of the cairn material has been stripped away, leaving an exposed cluster of stones, which in England would be called a *dolmen.* The two highest (7½ and 9 feet respectively) formed the portal entrance to the grave. The 6-foot stone now lying prone in front of the portal originally stood upright and served to block the entrance after the most recent burial had taken place. On each side of the portal is a short arc of standing stones that constituted the facade of the tomb and the base of the forecourt. This would have been the backdrop for religious ceremonies associated with interments. For over 100 feet along the south side of the cairn runs a series of spaced slabs that were part of the peristalth or curb. The bipartite chamber itself, with its high septal stone, is roofless, thus permitting easy viewing of the interior. A little higher up the hill lies Cairnholy II. Here too the cairn (originally 70 feet by 40 feet) has all but disappeared. Like its counterpart, the chamber is divided into two parts by a high stone partition, but in this case the rear compartment is still covered by its original capstone. The front compartment, however, is unroofed, and its entrance is marked by the two tallest stones of the group, now leaning toward each other. The other tall stone in the ensemble apparently formed part of the chamber's side wall.

The greatest known concentration of Clyde-type gallery graves is in the southern half of the island of Arran. Most of them, however, are so remote from any passable road that only the most dedicated walker would venture to discover them. The one exception is the gallery grave called **Torrylin Cairn** *(395)* near Kilmory on the southern coast. It was originally divided by septal stones into four compartments. The roof and end stone are missing, but most of the two side walls enclosing the 21-foot chamber still stand to a height of up to 5½ feet, and three septal slabs are in place. They are shorter in height than the side walls, indicating that space was allowed beneath the roof for easy communication between compartments.

Finally, and most rewarding to the traveller, is **Nether Largie, South** *(470)*, situated near the center of a three-mile linear cemetery in the vicinity of the village of Kilmartin, Argyll. The other cairns in the cemetery cover cists (stone coffins) of a later date and will be treated below. At Nether Largie, South, the cairn has been mostly restored by the Scottish Development Department, so that the stony cairn material is heaped around the chamber to the level of its capstones. The chamber is twenty feet long and six feet wide and can be entered through a modern door. The original entrance was through a pair of tall portal stones set three feet apart. The chamber is divided into four segments by three low septal slabs, and the roof rises about seven feet above the present floor level. The side and end walls are constructed of huge blocks of schist supplemented by a considerable amount of drywalling. This is one of the best preserved and most instructive of all of Scotland's chambered tombs, easily accessible, and not to be missed.

Not far from the north end of Loch Ness, in the region around Inverness, and eastward into the Spey Valley are about a dozen passage graves, called the Clava group. These cairns are round, edged by heavy curbstones, and surrounded by circles of standing stones. Both curb stones and standing stones are graduated in height, the tallest two normally marking the entrance to the tomb passage, which invariably faces southwest. The passages themselves are low-roofed and fairly long, leading to round chambers walled by megaliths topped by dry-stone corbelling to form vaults capped by single massive stones. Several of the tombs show curious rock carvings called *cup-marks*—shallow circular depressions about three inches across, of which more will be said below. The best preserved of the Clava cairns is **Corrimony Chambered Cairn** *(520)* in Glen Urquhart, about eight miles west of Drumnadrochit, Inverness-shire. Here a circle of standing stones surrounds a curb consisting of upright slabs supported by large boulders. Two massive curb-stones, three feet apart, mark the passage into the tomb from the southwest. The cairn is in a good state of repair and consists of water-worn boulders and pebbles. The round corbelled chamber is about twelve feet in diameter. It is at present unroofed, so the visitor can peer within. The large cup-marked slab now lying on top of the cairn was probably the original capstone.

About six miles east of the town of Inverness, near Culloden Battlefield, lie two other passage graves of this class—the type sites, called **Balnuaran of Clava, Southwest**, and **Balnuaran of Clava, Northeast** *(519)*. At the former, the surrounding stone circle now consists of ten monoliths ranging in height from almost five feet to seven feet. The curbstones are much smaller. The cairn of boulders stands over nine feet high, with an entrance from the southwest. The passage is almost twenty feet long, two feet wide, and four feet high. The roofless chamber has an average diameter of about twelve feet and is not quite circular. Its present walls rise to almost seven feet in height. One of its orthostats displays about a dozen cup-marks. The northeastern Clava cairn is another passage grave. The surrounding stone circle consists of eleven stones, the two highest measuring six and nine feet. Inside it lies a curb of boulders. The cairn rises to a height of ten feet. The nineteen-foot passage is entered from the southwest, is about two feet wide, and, at the inner end, about four feet high. The roofless chamber is roughly circular with a diameter of twelve to thirteen feet, rises at the back to a height of seven feet, and is only slightly corbelled. Several of the boulders here display cup-marks. Between these two tombs lies **Balnuaran of Clava, Centre** *(519)*, which is not a passage grave at all but an associated type called a ring cairn. A ring cairn consists of a broad circle of cairn material around a vacant center, more or less in the form of a doughnut. Since there was no passage through the cairn, it is assumed that these graves, unlike the more common chambered tombs, were used for single burials, with the body or bodies left exposed to the elements. In other respects, however, the site resembles the Clava cairns. It is surrounded by a circle of standing stones (nine remaining), the tallest being seven feet high and situated in the southwest quadrant. There are two circles of curbstones—an outer one to keep the cairn material from sliding across the edges and an inner curb to keep the central area clear. As we shall see below, this type of cairn is affiliated with, and is probably the ancestor of, a later species of Bronze Age monument called the *recumbent stone circle*.

The next class of passage graves to be considered is the Orkney-Cromarty-Hebridean group, the largest of all in number, comprising about thirty-three sites scattered over a wide arc from the Outer Hebrides across the northernmost tip of mainland Scotland and on to the Orkney Islands. Within this group there are so many regional and individual variations that it is difficult for the layman to understand why archaeologists lump them all together. All, however, are passage graves; most are under round cairns; most of the chambers are polygonal; many are compartmentalized or "stalled" by pairs of large upright slabs projecting from opposite side walls of the chamber; and, in most, dry-stone masonry is profusely employed in combination with orthostats. In general it can be said that the tombs of this group especially give every evidence of having been enlarged and remodelled from time to time over centuries of use.

In the Outer Hebrides the most impressive of these tombs today is **Barpa Langass Cairn** *(556)* on North Uist. The cairn of stones forms a great dome rising to a height of fourteen feet and has been less disturbed than most. It is curbed by at least fourteen stones, the tops of which project above ground by as much as three feet. On the west side of the cairn is a funnel-shaped forecourt off which leads to a passage about twelve feet in length. The chamber, built of massive slabs, is oval-shaped and measures about thirteen feet by six feet. It is roofed by three large lintels and several additional flat stones. On the island of Lewis, **Steinacleit Cairn** *(558)* is in a much more dilapidated condition. Its most obvious feature is the curb, a circle of large stone blocks, surrounded by an oval setting of smaller stones. Inside is a considerable quantity of loose stones piled up in a mound about three feet high. At the center are several orthostats, but they are so widely spaced that the outlines of the chamber are difficult to make out.

Caithness, at the northeast corner of the Scottish mainland, is well endowed with passage graves. Among the most interesting are the two **Grey Cairns of Camster** *(554)*, about sixteen miles southwest of Wick. The so-called Long Cairn measures 195 feet along its major axis and is crescent-shaped or "horned" at each end. Underneath are two chambers, both entered by long, low passages. One chamber is polygonal with a diameter of about 6 feet; the other is "stalled" (subdivided by transverse slabs somewhat lower than the roof) into three compartments with curving walls. About 200 yards to the southeast is the Round Cairn, with a particularly fine chamber, also at the end of a low passageway. The cairn itself is about 60 feet in diameter and 12 feet high. It is virtually intact. The passage measures about 20 feet long by 2 feet wide and 3 feet high. The chamber is divided into two compartments, measuring about 4 feet square and 7 feet square respectively. The inner compartment is stalled by a pair of transverse slabs that stand somewhat lower than the roof, which stands about 10 feet above ground. A few miles to the southeast lies the **Cairn of Get (Garrywhin)** *(554)*, a horned cairn, 56 feet by 46 feet in dimension, 8 feet high, and now covered with turf and heather. The passage is only partly visible, but most of the chamber can be seen. It is divided into a rectangular outer compartment, 5 feet long by 6½ feet wide, and a circular inner compartment with a diameter of about 10 feet.

Crossing the Pentland Firth, the traveller comes to the Orkney Islands—a veritable wonderland of chambered tombs and other prehistoric sites. Among the several well-preserved Neolithic graves on Mainland, Orkney, is **Onstan (Unstan) Chambered Cairn** *(562)*, maintained by the Scottish Development Department and situated near the shore of the Loch of Stenness. Both passage and chamber have been reroofed, and the almost circular cairn, 43 feet by 45 feet in dimension, has been returfed. Windows in the concrete roofing provide a good view of the chamber's interior. It is roughly 11 feet long by 4 to 6 feet wide, and its walls survive to a maximum height of almost 7 feet. It is divided into five compartments or stalls by pairs of upright transverse slabs reaching almost to the roof. A small cell, measuring 5 feet by 3 feet by 4 feet high, leads off the main chamber. Two concentric retaining walls lie outside the chamber under the cairn. Of equal interest is the trio of cairns located on the south shore of Rousay Island, Orkney. Proceeding from east to west, the first is **Taversoe Tuack Chambered Cairn** *(565)*, a fascinating two-story tomb under a turf-covered cairn, 30 feet in diameter and edged by a curb of horizontally laid stone. A domed roof of concrete has been installed over the upper chamber. This room now stands only 3 feet high, measures about 15 feet by 6 feet, and consists of two compartments of unequal size with rounded ends stalled by a pair of slabs projecting from the walls. The lower, subterranean chamber is roughly oval, about 12 feet long by 5 feet wide by 5 feet high. It is divided into four compartments by vertical slabs opening from a central space. All compartments have shelves consisting of flat slabs projecting from the wall. This chamber was originally entered by a low-roofed passage from the north, while the passage to the upper compartment comes from the opposite direction. About a half mile to the west lies **Blackhammer Chambered Cairn** *(566)*, also under the care of the Scottish Development Department. The cairn, 50 feet long by 25 feet wide and 6 feet high at its maximum, has been returfed and reroofed over the chamber. The two sets of curbstones laid concentrically around the central chamber are invisible. The chamber is rectangular, measuring about 24 feet by 5 feet by 6 feet high. It too is stalled by upright slabs, none of which reaches the height of the roof. The third of the trio is the **Knowe of Yarso** *(566)*, a rectangular, stalled tomb, also reroofed and returfed. Three miles away, on Rousay's western shore, lies the most elaborate of all of the island's cairns. This is **Midhowe Chambered Cairn** *(566)*, now enclosed by a stone building. The cairn itself is rectangular with rounded corners, measures over 106 feet in length and 42 feet in width, and is bounded by a well-constructed curb with another smaller one inside.

The chamber is 76 feet long by 6 to 8 feet wide and is divided by pairs of transverse upright slabs into twelve compartments. The walls are of dry-stone masonry and survive to a maximum height of over 8 feet. Low stone benches, designed to hold corpses, can be seen on one side of the chamber.

The final category of passage graves to be considered is the Maeshowe group, consisting of only ten or eleven sites, all situated in the Orkney Islands. This group has closer architectural affinities with continental prototypes than do any of the other Scottish tombs, and the sites show less sign of having been remodelled over the centuries. Hence perhaps they do represent an imported architectural tradition and thus stand as an exception to the rule, noted above, that Scottish chambered tombs were in general the locally inspired products of multiperiod construction. The greatest of this group, and one of Britain's most impressive prehistoric monuments, is the type site, the **Maeshowe Chambered Cairn** *(563)*, located on the Mainland of Orkney northeast of Stromness. The large turf-covered cairn (124 feet by 105 feet) is surrounded by a broad berm outside of which is a wide ditch. The core of the mound is faced by a retaining wall reaching a maximum height of 14 feet. The entrance passage runs for about 50 feet to the main chamber, which is 15 feet square and topped by a high corbelled vault. The walls of the chamber survive to a height of 12½ feet, and the center of the roof is now capped by a modern concrete dome. At each corner is a substantial buttress of dry stone faced with a large slab. On three sides of the chamber, close to the floor, are windowlike openings leading to small cells, presumably used to house privileged corpses. On various stones runic inscriptions can be seen, along with three small engravings representing respectively a dragon, a walrus, and a serpent knot. (The runic alphabet developed, or was invented, in Scandinavia as early as the second or third century A.D. and survives chiefly as inscribed on memorial stones.) These inscriptions at Maeshowe were presumably executed by Viking grave-robbers hoping to find buried treasure.

Maeshowe is an altogether splendid mausoleum. None other can quite approach it in grandeur, though there are four additional tombs of the same type, all in the Orkneys, that are worth a visit. The first is **Wideford Hill Chambered Cairn** *(560)*, also on the main island. Its circular cairn, about 43 feet in diameter, contains three concentric retaining walls of flat stone, now partly exposed, thus giving the front of the mound the appearance of a stepped facade. The main chamber is roughly rectangular, about 10 feet by 4½ feet, and is now about 8 feet high with a modern roof. Surrounding it are three smaller connecting cells with oversailing walls, roofed at a height of about 7 feet. About three miles to the west is **Cuween Hill Chambered Cairn** *(561)*, another Maeshowe type of passage grave. The cairn here is turf-covered, about 55 feet in diameter and 8½ feet high. Access to the interior is to be gained only by crawling along a 17-foot entrance passage which is a mere 2½ feet wide and less than 3 feet high. The main chamber is an irregular rectangle, roughly 11 feet by 5½ feet and rising 7 feet to a corbelled roof. Four small cells open off the main chamber and are also corbelled. On the south shore of the outlying island of Sanday lies a third Maeshowe passage grave, called **Quoyness Chambered Cairn** *(567)*. The cairn is pear-shaped and is buttressed by three retaining walls, parts of which are exposed. The central chamber, entered today by steps leading through the outer wall, is rectangular (13½ feet by 6½ feet) between walls that are only slightly corbelled and rise to a roof 13 feet above the floor. Here are six small cells opening from the central chamber, arranged symmetrically around the walls. To the northwest of Sanday lies the island of Papa Westray, off the eastern shore of which is a tiny islet, site of the **Holm of Papa Westray Chambered Cairn** *(567)*. Here, under a long turf-covered cairn, is a 67-foot-long chamber, 5 feet wide and 9 feet high. Thick cross-walls with narrow portals divide the chamber into three parts, and from it open fourteen small mural cells. Just to the north lies a much smaller stalled cairn in a highly ruinous condition.

Finally, to the south of the Mainland of Orkney, lies the small island of Hoy, site of the strangest prehistoric tomb of all—the **Dwarfie Stane** *(564)*, unaffiliated architecturally with any of the five classes of chambered cairns described above. This is a huge block of red sandstone, pierced on one side by an entrance about 3 feet wide by 2½ feet high and hollowed out inside to form a central rectangular chamber flanked by two smaller chambers, one oval, the other semicircular. Outside the entrance is a large slab with a rounded projection that was used to seal the tomb. It is thought to be of Neolithic date, though it is possible that it belongs to the Early Bronze Age. The mystery surrounding the site not unnaturally attracted the attention of Sir Walter Scott, who immortalized it in his novel *The Pirate*.

THE BRONZE AGE: 2000–700 B.C.

Some time around the beginning of the second millenium B.C., a tall, heavy-boned people from the European continent began to enter the southern and eastern coasts of Britain from Sussex north to Aberdeenshire. They were more technologically advanced than the native Neolithic population and probably more given to the arts of war. They came from the Low Countries and the Rhine delta and were the first to introduce metalworking into the British Isles. Though they are considered precursors of the Bronze Age, there is no evidence that these immigrants had yet mastered the technique of smelting tin and copper together to produce that useful alloy. Copper they knew, and how to melt it in crucibles, pour it into molds of stone or clay, remove the casting, and hammer or grind the cold metal into tools and weapons of a desired shape and degree of sharpness. Their flat copper daggers and awls can still be seen in the **National Museum of Antiquities** *(447)* in Edinburgh and in many of the other Scottish museums cited above. Other contemporary artifacts include tanged and barbed arrowheads of flint, stone battle-axes, archers' wristguards of stone, and conical beads and buttons of jet.

The invaders are known by prehistorians as Beaker People after their distinctive pottery, also well represented in museums of archaeology throughout Scotland. These vessels, used probably for both food and drink, are characteristically flat-bottomed, wide-mouthed, six to eight inches high, S-shaped in profile, short-necked, and sometimes decorated with horizontal bands of lines or geometric figures. They were originally deposited as grave-goods under round cairns without chambers, sometimes in cists—those coffins of stone that the Beaker People first introduced to Scotland, where their usage continued for more than two thousand years.

Probably typical of the cairns of this period is **Memsie Cairn** *(540)* near Fraserburgh, Aberdeenshire, a well-preserved and very high mound of stones now under the care of the Scottish Development Department. Of cists dating from the Beaker period or from the succeeding Early Bronze Age, there is an interesting collection in the Kilmartin valley of Argyll, already mentioned as the site of the chambered tomb of Nether Largie, South. Approaching this prehistoric "cemetery" from the south, the traveller comes first to **Dunchraigaig Cairn** *(470)*, a pile of stones seven feet high alongside which sits a cist of boulders ten feet long by five feet wide, accompanied by its cover, a huge slab thirteen feet in length. Next is **Ri Cruin Cairn** *(470)*, a circular mound of loose stones that contains three cists. To the north lies **Temple Wood Stone Circle** *(470)*, consisting of a cist of four slabs and measuring five feet by three feet inside a circle of standing stones. Passing by Nether Largie, South, the next site in line is **Nether Largie Mid Cairn** *(471)*, which has two cists buried under a mound of loose stones. About 600 yards beyond it lies **Nether Largie, North** *(471)*, another stony cairn, this one built over a single central cist that today can be entered by a ladder descending from the top.

Probably the best-known Early Bronze Age cist is on **Cairnpapple Hill** *(431)* near Torphichen, West Lothian. Here, underneath a concrete dome, is a rock-cut pit with a standing stone at one end. When excavated, the cist contained a disintegrated body in the crouched position typical of Beaker inhumations. The site is on a hilltop a thousand feet above sea level with magnificent views in all directions. It has a long and complicated history and contains the remnants of a Neolithic cemetery, an Early Bronze Age henge and several other cairns and cists of both Bronze Age and Iron Age date. A small museum on the grounds provides useful guidance to what might otherwise appear as an incoherent conglomeration of rocks and stones.

In the thirteen centuries or so that followed the first arrival of the Beaker folk, there developed in Scotland, as elsewhere in the British Isles, a fairly stable society, probably aristocratic in structure, certainly skilled in the military arts and successful in developing a more sophisticated technology than had ever before been known. This was the Bronze Age proper. Funeral rites changed from inhumation to cremation, and with the change came new developments in ceramic styles. The early beakers gave way soon to conical shaped pots, called *food vessels*. Then, with the universal adoption of cremation came the production of a large variety of cinerary urns, often with heavy overhanging rims or collars, some barrel-shaped, others globular or conical. They were often decorated with various geometric designs encrusted in the clay before firing. Examples are to be observed, in more than sufficient number, in the various museums noted above.

Of greater interest, at least to most museum-goers, are the displays of a wide range of bronze objects, many of them discovered in hoards probably either left by itinerant bronzesmiths or deposited as votive offerings to some deity or deities. The earliest of these are flat axes, slightly curved at the sharp end and probably originally hafted to L-shaped pieces of wood. (The axe would have been inserted into the split short end of the L, which would then be bound by rope or leather thongs.) Also among surviving Bronze Age relics are stone molds in which the axes were cast. From the same period came halberds—heavy daggers mounted at right angles to a shaft; also tubular bronze beads and thick bracelets of the same material. During what is known as the Middle Bronze Age (ca. 1400 to 1000 B.C.), the flat axe was improved by hammering up flanges along the sides to prevent slippage in the haft and by casting a stop ridge along the middle to prevent the haft from being split by the backward pressure of the axe-head. Later came the palstave, an improvement over the flanged axe brought about by fusing the stop ridge with the flanges to form a sort of pocket on each side of the axe-head into which the split end of the haft could be snugly fitted. At the same time daggers developed into short rapiers, and socketed, bronze-looped spearheads appeared. From this period too came torcs of twisted gold ribbon, probably imported from Ireland. Then from the Late Bronze Age (ca. 1000 to 700 B.C.) came the socketed axe, the pommelled slashing leaf-shaped sword, and socketed spearheads with pegs instead of loops by which they could be bound to their shafts. From this period, too, came a variety of nonmilitary implements: tanged and riveted sickles; tanged and socketed knives; socketed hammers, chisels, gouges, and bronze razors. Sheet metal began to make its appearance in the form of great bronze buckets and cauldrons. A few round shields of embossed bronze are also known to date from the Late Bronze Age, as well as cart-fittings and harness rings. Clearly all this equipment implies a rising standard of living and the emergence of a society in which warfare was frequent if not endemic. It also implies the emergence of a superior military class.

It was no doubt this warrior aristocracy, reinforced by a priestly caste, that was responsible for organizing the sizable labor forces necessary for the construction of Scotland's most impressive Bronze Age monuments—the great circles of standing stones. Such monuments are unique to the British Isles. They had their origin probably as open-air sanctuaries built by Late Neolithic people in the form of circular ditches bounded by single embankments through which entrance was gained by one or two gaps opening onto causeways over the ditches. Sooner or later the circles came to be demarked additionally by placing large stones around their circumferences. Such sites are known as *henges*, the term derived from an Anglo-Saxon word meaning "hanging stones." This is an apt description of the huge lintels surmounting the uprights at the famous site of Stonehenge in Wiltshire, England. Stonehenge, however, is unique in this respect, as elsewhere in Britain no "hanging stones" surmount the circles of slabs or boulders still surviving in surprising number. At many of these the enclosing ditch and bank have disappeared, if indeed they were ever constructed in the first place. Most Scottish stone circles were never true henges in this sense. In this rocky soil, ditchdigging was more difficult than manhandling huge megaliths for purposes of marking off a circular enclosure.

From time immemorial it has been assumed that these circular settings of standing stones were centers of some sort of cult worship by the Late Neolithic and Bronze Age people who built them. In late years, however, a number of scientists, sometimes referred to as "archaeo-astronomers" or "astro-archaeologists," have set forth a different hypothesis. This is that these circles of standing stones were astronomical observatories built under the direction of astronomer-priests primarily for the purpose of calculating precise dates and of devising solar or lunar calendars. Buttressed by elaborate mathematical data, the argument runs that all these circles, as well as other megalithic alignments, were set out with their major axes pointing toward places on the horizon where significant celestial bodies rose or set on particular days of the year. Such axial orientations have been discovered in abundance—from one stone to another in the same circle, from circle centers to outlying stones, and even from standing stones to distant mountain peaks or notches between mountains.

One trouble with this hypothesis is that it is too clever by far. Leaving aside the unanswered question of how an illiterate people, possessing no known science of numbers, could have been capable of the refined astronomical calculations necessary for the preparation of a calendar, the fact remains that these thick, rough-hewn slabs or boulders could never have been suitable as sighting markers for making precise measurements of the movement of celestial bodies. Moreover, statistically, the odds are overwhelmingly in favor of a celestial sight-line occurring fortuitously in almost any known assemblage of megaliths. Significant astronomical alignments, therefore, can be claimed for almost any random settings of stones, wherever found.

This is not to say that many, or even all, stone circles were not oriented roughly to the movement of heavenly bodies, especially the sun. They were in all probability built to serve as temples to the gods of the sky, and the religious rites that took place there could well have been geared to the seasonal risings and settings of those celestial orbs to which divine attributes were attached. No very advanced knowledge of astronomy would have been needed to determine the approximate location of such recurring phenomena on any local horizon, and no very sophisticated grasp of geometry would have been required to arrange the settings of stones in such a way as to take advantage of these occurrences for ceremonial purposes. It is easy to imagine, for example, a Bronze Age religious rite climaxed by the setting of the sun at the summer solstice between the two highest stones in a sacred circle. And it would require far less scientific knowledge than is sometimes imputed to these prehistoric people for them to have arranged their megaliths in such a way as to bring this about. Indeed, as the archaeologist Richard Muir has pointed out, "the simple facts are as amazing as the astronomical speculations concerning stone circles." These are that, within a society no more technologically advanced than that of the North American Indians before Columbus, there were apparently tribal leaders and priests with sufficient imagination, authority, and organizational skill to assemble and direct the manpower and material necessary to erect these truly impressive monuments.

One of the best preserved of those in Scotland is **Torhousekie Stone Circle** *(377)*, a few miles west of Wigtown. This is a flattened circle, roughly seventy feet by sixty-five feet, consisting of nineteen granite boulders set on end, inside of which is a line of three additional upright boulders. The largest stone weighs six tons. Near the west coast of the Isle of Arran is **Auchagallon Stone Circle** *(394)* of fifteen standing stones inside of which is a round cairn. These stones may not have been freestanding originally, but rather served as a curb or peristalth around the cairn. South of here, just east of the village of Tormore, is a Bronze Age cemetery and ritual center consisting of at least five stone circles associated with numerous burial cairns and cists. Of these the most complete today is **Moss Farm Road Stone Circle** *(394)*, consisting of two concentric rings of granite boulders, the inner one circular, the outer ovoid. Looking from here to the northeast, one scans a somewhat confusing array of megaliths called the **Machrie Moor Standing Stones** *(394)*, representing the remains of four additional stone circles. In the Kilmartin valley of Argyll, close to the linear cemetery of Bronze Age cairns already mentioned, is **Temple Wood Stone Circle** *(470)*, a near perfect circle forty-three feet in diameter, around the circumference of which still stand thirteen of the original twenty earthfast slabs within a bank. Inside is the cist described above.

Near the western coast of the island of Lewis in the Outer Hebrides lies the most spectacular of all of Scotland's settings of standing stones. Indeed, next to Stonehenge and perhaps Avebury, here is the most interesting megalithic ensemble in all of Britain. This is **Callanish** *(557)*, a circle of standing stones from which extend the remnants of four avenues of megaliths, giving the site a cruciform pattern. Near the center of the circle is the tallest of the stones (15½ feet high) and next to it the remains of an unroofed small passage grave, probably installed some time before the standing stones were raised. The circle, somewhat flattened on the east, consists of thirteen megaliths spaced irregularly and 9 feet in height or more. The diameter is about 37 feet. To the southwest is a tall stone that may have belonged to an outer circle, uncompleted or destroyed. To the north-northeast stretches, to a distance of 270 feet, two parallel rows of stones, nineteen in all and spaced 27 feet apart between rows. This is the most complete of the four avenues. To the east-northeast a line of four stones probably represents all that is left of one side of a second avenue. Another similar line of four points is due west. These are also probably part of an original avenue. Still another line of five stones leads due south. The innermost of these is paired with a single stone that is probably the sole survivor of the western side of the original southern avenue. Astro-archaeologists, naturally, have had a field day with this site. Some among them claim that the northern avenue pointed to the appearance over the horizon of the bright star Capella and that the four stones to the east were directed to the rising of the star Altair. Both deductions seem farfetched as an explanation for the settings. A much more likely explanation is that the circle enclosed a sacred area for religious rites, and the avenues served as processionways to and from it.

Not so spectacular as Callanish, but still impressive enough, is the **Ring of Brodgar** *(562)* on the Mainland of Orkney, on the narrow neck of land between the Loch of Harray and the Loch of Stenness. This is a henge monument proper, surrounded by a ditch broken by a causeway at two points opposite each other. Of the original sixty stones placed in a circle of about 350 feet in diameter, twenty-seven upright slabs survive. They range in height from 9 inches to 15 feet, the average being 7 feet. Just to the west, on the shore of Loch of Stenness, lies the **Ring of Stenness** *(562)*, another henge, the original ditch and surrounding bank of which have been destroyed. All that remains of what was probably once a circle of thirteen standing stones is an arc of four megaliths measuring up to 17 feet in height. The curious stone bench here is a modern addition that somewhat mars the authenticity of the site.

Back on the Scottish mainland, Caithness is also rich in prehistoric monuments, including the **Achavanich Standing Stones** *(555)*, northwest of Lybster. Here about forty stones, some as high as six feet, form a U-shaped setting, picturesquely sited on the southern shore of Loch Stemster. In Aberdeenshire there is a concentration of stone circles, many with distinct regional characteristics. The most conventional of these to be named here is **Cullerie Stone Circle** *(536)*, west of the city of Aberdeen. Here, eight undressed boulders have been placed at almost equal intervals around the circumference of an almost perfect circle measuring thirty-two feet in diameter. On excavation, the site was found to have contained eight small burial cairns, most likely placed here after the circle had ceased to be used for its original ceremonial purposes.

The most interesting of this county's settings, however, lie north of here. They are the so-called recumbent stone circles, of which there are at least twenty-two. As the name suggests, the distinctive feature of these sites is the single large stone lying prone between the two highest standing stones of a circle. This recumbent stone and its two high flankers are always situated in the southwest quadrant of the circle. The settings generally have an internal cairn with a curb of small boulders not far inside the standing stones. Certain similarities between this group of Bronze Age circles and the Neolithic passage graves of the Clava group are immediately noticeable. Both consist of round cairns surrounded by a ring of stones; the number of standing stones in both was originally about a dozen; and in all cases the stones are graduated in height toward the tallest, which are always located in the southwest quadrant. The major difference, outside of the recumbent stone itself, is that in the Clava group the emphasis is on the cairns, while among the recumbent stone circles the emphasis is on the encircling megaliths. In any case, most archaeologists are convinced that the recumbent stone circles were built by immigrants from Inverness-shire, where the Clava cairns are largely found. Astro-archaeologists, naturally, make much of the uniform southwest orientation of the two tallest megaliths in both Clava cairns and recumbent stone circles. Some among them claim that the setting was deliberately designed so that the sun would set between them on the day of the winter solstice. Unfortunately for this argument, the axis of some of these cairns and circles, from the center to the two highest stones, is somewhat farther south of the point on the horizon where the midwinter sun sets in this region.

Easter Aquhorthies Stone Circle *(542)*, just west of Inverurie, is a typical example. Here nine stones stand in an almost perfect circle about sixty feet in diameter, and the recumbent stone with its two flankers lies on the south side just inside the circle. A few miles to the north lies **Loanhead of Daviot** *(542)*. Here too is a circle of nine stones with a diameter of about sixty-five feet plus a recumbent slab flanked by the southernmost of the nine on one side and on the other by a tenth stone just inside the circle. Within the circle of standing stones is a ring of curbstones about twelve feet in diameter, which probably enclosed the central area of a ring cairn. To the southwest lies **Tomnavarie Stone Circle** *(543)*, where the standing stones describe a circle fifty-six feet in diameter, and the interior circle of curbstones measures twenty-eight feet across. The huge recumbent stone lies in the southwest quadrant.

In addition to the conventional circular or quasicircular arrangements of Bronze Age megaliths, scattered throughout Scotland are a number of single stones (menhirs), irregular clusters of stones, and stone rows. The tallest single monolith (about twenty feet) is the **Trushel Stone** *(558)* on the island of Lewis near Balantrushel village. Probably the most complex stone alignment is the **Midclyth Stone Rows** *(554)* in Caithness, also known as the Hill o' Many Stanes. Here are about 250 stones, most no more than ankle-high, set out in twenty-two rows averaging 8 stones to each, the rows not parallel but converging toward the north to form a sort of fan. What purpose this pattern was meant to serve is impossible to say. Since many of the rows are out of line, they could not have been used for sightings on celestial bodies, though astro-archaeologists would like to think otherwise. The mystery remains not only unsolved but baffling.

Equally mysterious are the cup-and-ring marks unique to Scotland and the adjacent counties of England. They are to be found scratched on the sides of chambered tombs, on the surfaces of standing stones, or in random patterns cut into natural rock formations. They most often appear as small depressions surrounded by one or more concentric circular grooves and are probably of Early Bronze Age date. They have inspired more wild guess-work than almost any other prehistoric phenomenon. Claims have been made that they represent copper and gold prospectors' marks; that they are matrices that were filled with dyes from which star charts were printed onto skins; or that they served as the standard measure of the "megalithic inch," i.e., $\frac{1}{40}$th of a "megalithic yard," the unit allegedly used for laying out exact geometric patterns of standing stones for astronomical purposes. More probably they were nothing more than symbolic markings representing the sun, or possibly even purposeless graffiti. For those interested, good examples can be observed on flat, exposed rock-faces at **Drumtroddan** *(376)* and **Big Balcraig** *(376)* near Port William, Wigtownshire; at **Achnabreck** *(469)*, **Cairnbaan** *(469)*, and **Kilmichael Glassary** *(469)* near Lochgilphead, Argyll; and at **Ballygowan** *(470)* near the Kilmartin "linear cemetery" north of Lochgilphead.

Less mysterious and certainly more interesting are the remains of a Bronze Age settlement at **Jarlshof** *(569)* on the southern tip of the Mainland of Shetland. Actually the site shows evidence of use from at least 1500 B.C. to the late sixteenth century A.D., when the Stewart Earls of Orkney (Robert and his son Patrick) built a house here, rechristened Jarlshof by Sir Walter Scott in his novel *The Pirate*. The Bronze Age relics on the site consist of the foundations and side walls of four ovoid huts, the best preserved of which is now labelled Dwelling III. The various additions to the community by Iron Age inhabitants, Viking settlers, medieval farmers, and finally the Stewarts, will be described in greater detail below. No other site in Scotland offers such a splendid visual textbook of architectural history over so long a period of time.

THE IRON AGE: 700 B.C.–80 A.D.

From the northern Alpine region of Europe comes the first evidence of a cultural development so different from its Bronze Age antecedents as to signalize the beginning of a new and final prehistoric age. This was the Hallstatt culture, so-called after the village in northern Austria where its remains were first discovered. The people who lived here about the beginning of the seventh century B.C. knew how to smelt iron and forge it into all manner of tools and weapons. The process had first been discovered centuries before by the Hittites of Asia Minor and was to be much copied elsewhere because of the plenitude of iron ore in contrast to the relative scarcity of copper and tin. But iron-using was only one of the characteristics of the Hallstatt culture or of the more sophisticated La Tene culture that was to follow it. These Iron Age Europeans were above all a warrior race, dominated by military chieftains who rode to battle in horse-drawn carts or chariots, wielded long slashing swords of iron or bronze, carried heavily embossed shields, and sometimes painted or tattooed their bodies with fantastic designs to enhance their already fierce appearance. As conquest made them richer, they developed novel art forms, chiefly curvilinear, with which they decorated scabbards, helmets, shields, horse-trappings, etc., as well as pottery and such items of refinement as brooches, armlets, and bronze mirror-backs. Their style—developed fully in the La Tene period after about 300 B.C.—was characterized by asymmetrical undulating curves, flamboyant and naturalistic, and was distinctly different from the measured "classical" canon of contemporary Greece and Rome. Abstract and free-flowing, La Tene art has some affinities with modern art and great appeal to modern aesthetic tastes.

But the most distinctive and pervasive feature of the Hallstatt and La Tene cultures was the spoken language that these warlike people brought to all the lands they penetrated—to Galatia in Asia Minor, to Western Europe, and to the British Isles. It was an Indo-European tongue called Celtic. Some time in the first millenium B.C. the Celtic language split into two major linguistic groups, called Q-Celtic and P-Celtic. The former, also known by linguists as Goidelic or more commonly as Gaelic, still survives in Ireland, the Highlands and Islands of Scotland, and the Isle of Man. P-Celtic, called Brythonic, survives in Brittany and Wales and, until fairly recently, was sometimes used in Cornwall.

Though there is some argument as to when the iron-using Celts first appeared in Britain, it could not have been too long after the beginning of the seventh century B.C. that they first infiltrated southern England, and there is no reason to believe that Scotland was far behind. Because of their known addiction to war, it was long assumed that the Celts arrived *en masse* as invaders and then proceeded to conquer and rule the indigenous Bronze Age population. This theory is no longer widely held. It would seem instead that Celtic immigrants mostly crossed the Channel and the North Sea in small increments over a considerable period of time. It is probable that the majority of those who came to Scotland directly from the Continent spoke the Goidelic tongue, though some linguists maintain that the ancestors of the Late Iron Age people known as Picts were a Brythonic-speaking race. In any case, the Q-Celtic language prevailed as the native tongue, at least in the Scottish Highlands and Islands, where, as mentioned, it has survived in places to the present day.

Celtic pottery, of which a fair amount is currently displayed in archaeo-logical museums throughout the country, is not difficult to distinguish. From the first few centuries of settlement came bowls and buckets obviously modelled on metallic prototypes, some of them given a red coating in imitation of bronze. Later ware is usually black or dark brown, often burnished and decorated with incised patterns of typical La Tene curvilinear design. Ironware, most of it found in hoards presumably left by itinerant smiths or hidden in times of danger, consists of socketed hammers, axes, adzes, and gouges; miscellaneous items such as spades, sickles, ox-goads, pot-hook chains, bucket handles, etc., and, of course, spears and long swords in great number. Personal jewelry—bronze brooches, bracelets, and ring-headed pins, gold torcs, silver rings, jet armlets, and beads of glass— provides ample evidence of the Celts' notorious love of finery. Most interesting of all museum holdings from this period are the bronze horse and chariot fittings, of which the most justly famous is the so-called Torrs Chamfrein, a decorated pony cap to which two bronze drinking horns were later attached. This is one of the finest examples of La Tene art in Scotland and can be seen in the **National Museum of Antiquities** *(447)* in Edinburgh.

The Torrs Chamfrein calls to mind that characteristic for which the Celts are mostly renowned, that is, their martial spirit. According to almost all contemporary Roman commentators, the Celts were war-mad. The historian Polybius has left vivid descriptions of great hosts of these frightful barbarians, drawn up in battle array, their leaders mounted in horse-drawn carts or chariots, spears flying, swords clashing, horns blowing, warriors shouting, women screaming and pounding the sides of wagons disposed along the flanks of the battlefield. That such scenes took place in Scotland is probable, although there is no record of them until after the Roman invasions of the first century A.D. What was doubtless more common during the previous centuries of Celtic migrations was intermittent tribal warfare, sporadic raids, and habitual cattle-rustling. This, at least, would explain the prevalence in Scotland of that most typical of Iron Age field sites: the hillfort.

A hill-fort by definition is a prehistoric fortified enclosure so situated as to exploit the natural features of the terrain for defensive purposes, i.e., on a hilltop, or on the edge of a cliff, or on a rocky promontory surrounded by water on all sides but one. They may have numbered as many as fifteen-hundred in Scotland alone, though most of these were too small to have given shelter to more than a handful of households. The term *fort* itself is something of a misnomer, if it implies a stronghold manned chiefly by armed men. Most, if not all, of these sites were, on the contrary, nothing more than defended villages or, in a few cases, fortified towns. Many of them no doubt originated as Bronze Age settlements surrounded by wooden palisades for which earthenworks and stone walls were later substituted. Some appear to have been permanent settlements; others merely temporary refuges for men, women, and cattle during times of emergency.

Earth, stone, and timber were the basic materials used by Iron Age builders to construct their defensive works. First, they dug one or more ditches around the circumference of the area to be protected; then they piled the excavated material on the inner side to create one or more embankments. To prevent these ramparts from collapsing, they might install timber-facings both inside and out. Or, when stone was available in quantity, as it was in most of Scotland, they might build retaining walls of this material on both sides of the embankment. To prevent such revetments from being pushed outward by heavy rain or frost, beams of timber could be laid perpendicular to the axis of the walls, to tie these stone facings into the earthen body of the rampart. If these beams caught fire, the heat might become so intense as to reduce the stone to a glassy mass. Hence the famous Scottish "vitrified forts"—once thought to have been the product of the intentional effort of the builders to consolidate their walls, but now believed to have resulted from accidental burning or from deliberate arson by attacking enemies. The most vulnerable part of a hill-fort's defenses was the gateway, consisting of three parts: the gate itself, the adjoining guard chambers, and the passageway to the gate through the enclosing ramparts. Gate and guard chambers, being mostly made of wood, have of course disappeared without a trace. Some passageways, however, are still observable as breaks in the surrounding ramparts. Occasionally, a barbican or some other type of defensive works might be raised just outside the main entrance so as to impede a mass attack against the gate itself.

Hill-forts still abound in Scotland, especially in the southern borders and in the Northeast. They are much eroded, to be sure, robbed by time, weather, and human scavengers of their once-formidable aspect. Many, if not most, are remotely situated, accessible only by steep and narrow footpaths. The majority are on private land to which the public has no legal right of access without permission of the owners, who are not always easily identifiable. With these *caveats* in mind, the following representative selection can be recommended to those travellers hardy enough for an arduous climb and imaginative enough to reconstruct in their minds' eye these once mighty fortresses now reduced to banks of earth and rubble. Considering the large number of identifiable hill-forts, the sampling is small. But considering the difficulty of reaching them in the first place, and the lack of much to see once there, it should be sufficient for all but the most ardent of Iron Age buffs.

Southwestern Scotland offers two such forts of note. The first is **Barsalloch Point Fort** *(376)*, near Port William, Wigtownshire. This is a so-called promontory-fort, overlooking the wide expanse of Luce Bay. Its landward side is guarded by two substantial ramparts with a ditch in between. To the northeast, near Gatehouse of Fleet in Kirkcudbrightshire, lies tiny **Trusty's Hill** *(380)*. Outside its partially vitrified rectangular wall are stretches of ramparts and ditches that must have served as outworks. The entrance to the site is marked by two outcrops, one of which displays three interesting Pictish symbols inscribed in the rock. These presumably date from Scotland's post-Roman Dark Age which will be treated in the following chapter.

Coming eastward, just north of Duns in Berwickshire, lies **Edinshall Fort**

(424) on the northeast slope of the hill called Cockburn Law. The Late Iron Age hill-fort consists of a double rampart, each bank with an external ditch, enclosing an area about 440 feet by 240 feet. Inside are the remains of the circular walls (up to 5 feet high) of a massive dry-stone fort that has all the appearance of a first century A.D. broch—a type of fortification unusual for this part of Scotland and one to be described in some detail below. From a still later date (probably the second century) come the faintly discernible circular hut foundations of an undefended village. About fifteen miles to the west, also in Berwickshire, we come to **Haerfaulds Hill-Fort** *(424)*, the remains of which consist of a ruined wall of stone rubble, almost 15 feet thick, enclosing an oval-shaped area in which can be seen the circular foundations of a number of huts probably dating to the period of Roman occupation. Similar hut foundations can be seen at **Dreva Craig Hill-Fort** *(422)*, a few miles southwest of Peebles. The most interesting feature here, however, is the barrier of boulders set up outside the southwest side of the outer of the two concentric walls comprising the fort proper. There are about a hundred of these boulders still earthfast, with as many more lying loose around the grounds. They constitute a rare example of *chevaux de frise*, designed to break up cavalry charges much in the manner of a modern tank barrier. Coming northeast from here into East Lothian, a few miles south of Dunbar lies one of the better preserved of southern Scotland's hill-forts, called **The Chesters** *(454)*. This is a bivallate (two-walled) circular fort measuring up to 350 feet in diameter. Though robbed of much of their stone facings, the two thick earthen ramparts still survive to heights of 5 and 7 feet, each accompanied by an external ditch. Also observable are two entranceways through the outer wall. There are traces of other ramparts farther out, but these are scarcely visible to the naked eye.

Heading northward into Fife, the traveller comes to **Norman's Law Hill-Fort** *(486)*, near Cupar. Here the summit of a high hill overlooking the Firth of Tay is defended by a stone wall, now ruined, of undoubted Iron Age date. Outside, along the foot of the hill, runs another wall, possibly of a later origin. On the southwest side of the hill is a small oval enclosure with a wall twelve feet thick, which probably belongs to the period of Roman occupation or even to the later Dark Age. North of the Tay, in the county of Angus, is to be found perhaps the most impressive collection of hill-forts in all of Scotland. A few miles north of Montifieth lies **Laws Hill-Fort** *(514)*, consisting of a ruined ovoid wall of rubble faced with stone blocks, with outer defensive walls at either end. Inside can be seen the foundations of a broch of later date, similar to those to be discussed below. When the fort was excavated, considerable quantities of vitrified stone were found within the core of the main wall, indicating that it must have suffered severe damage by fire at one time. About sixteen miles to the north lies one of the largest and most heavily vitrified of all of Scotland's hill-forts. This is **Finavon Hill-Fort** *(512)*, near Forfar. Today it consists of a tumbled-down grass-covered single ruined vitrified wall, measuring in places more than six feet high, plus what appears to be a horn-work of vitrified rock projecting to the east of the wall's southern end. Inside is a rock-cut well, a comparative rarity among Iron Age hill-forts. Another ten miles or so to the north brings us to the best preserved of all of Scotland's hill-forts, the **White Caterthun** and the **Brown Caterthun** *(509)*, adjacent sites lying among the hills northwest of Brechin. The former is the larger and more elevated of the two. In plan it consists of five concentric elliptical defense-works. The outer two ramparts are now much eroded. Above them is a third ellipse formed by a ditch with a slight bank. Finally, the summit is enclosed by a huge bank of rubble that undoubtedly represents all that remains of two very large timber-laced walls, long since tumbled down after the interlaced wooden beams had decayed. Why the fort escaped the more common fate of fire followed by vitrification is unknown. Nor can it be determined why Iron Age builders saw fit to build a second fort only a mile away and on a lower elevation. This, the Brown Caterthun, is not so impressive as its neighbor. It consists of six concentric ramparts, the outer two very much eroded. Farther up the hill are two better preserved earthen ramparts with a ditch in between. The summit is encircled by a more substantial grass-covered bank that was probably originally faced with stone. Inside this are the more obvious ruins of a circular stone wall with a single entrance. Two other ramparts have either eight or nine entranceways—the most unusual feature of this site.

Aberdeenshire offers the interested traveller a fair number of Iron Age hill-forts, one of which is **Barmekin of Echt** *(536)*, about fourteen miles due west of Aberdeen. It is roughly circular in shape, surrounded by five concentric ramparts, now so eroded that about all that is observable to the naked eye are the partial remains of two concentric stone walls. Archaeologists have noted that the passages between these walls are out of line with the entranceways through the outer embankments. This asymmetrical arrangement was no doubt deliberate and was intended to protect the inner citadel by forcing any enemy who had broached the outer entrances to make a sharp turn before reaching the inner gateways. Some twenty-five miles to the northwest of the Barmekin, near the village of Rhynie, lies Scotland's second highest hill-fort, called **Tap o' Noth** *(541)*. It consists today of a single thick stone wall, much of it vitrified and mostly now covered with grass and heather. A row of detached boulders on the north and east sides of the hill probably indicates a second exterior wall.

Finally, on the southwest tip of Shetland, we have another example of an Iron Age promontory-fort, this one called the **Ness of Burgi** *(570)*. Here two ditches cut off the tip of a short, rocky promontory, and between them stands a substantial ruined wall about seven feet in height. Just inside the inner ditch is a stone "blockhouse," one end of which has been pruned away with the collapse of part of the cliff into the adjacent sea. The gap through the outer wall of this structure still shows evidence of its having contained a barred gate, on each side of which is a mural cell. It is evident that this was the gatehouse guarding the fort within, and it may be of somewhat later construction. Indeed, the Burgi blockhouse has close architectural affinities to two other types of Late Iron Age fortification unique to Scotland and among its most interesting prehistoric relics. These are the dun and the broch.

Though the word *dun* can be applied to almost any kind of premedieval fortification, as indicated by its frequent appearance in place names, in the strictest sense a dun is a small fortified enclosure consisting of a circular or ovoid defensive wall, ten to twenty feet in thickness, surrounding an interior space up to seventy feet in diameter. Sometimes the walls were solid, consisting of dry-stone masonry on each side of a core of rubble; sometimes they were concentric with mural galleries and passages inside the space between. Always the wall is pierced by one or two narrow entranceways with door-checks to prevent the door from swinging inward. Usually there is evidence of a housing for a door-bar, i.e., a hole and socket in the door-frame. Access to the top of the wall, where there was presumably some kind of a rampart, was either by way of a ladder inside the wall or by steps projecting from its inner face. Duns appear to be nothing more than fortified dwellings designed to accommodate a single family or family group. In function, therefore, they differ not at all from the smaller hill-forts, though they are of a somewhat later date of construction.

The broch is similar to the dun in ground plan, though the enclosed space is usually no more than twenty-five feet in diameter. It too had a narrow entryway with door-checks and bar-holes and sockets to hold a crossbar. The chief difference between the two is the height of their walls. The broch is essentially a tapered double-walled tower that originally rose as high as forty or fifty feet. There was usually a staircase within the cavity between the walls, winding up to the top of the tower, where there was probably a rampart walk. Around the face of the inner wall ran a ledge, presumably to support a second floor or a lean-to roof. So many brochs are located on or near the shore as to suggest that they were built primarily to defend their inhabitants and the neighborhood against sea-raiders.

Very little is known, however, about these unusual buildings, including why they were erected, and by whom. The present consensus among archaeologists seems to be that they made their appearance in Scotland during the Late Iron Age, perhaps around the second century B.C., and were abandoned some time after the first century A.D. The heavy concentration of

duns in the Highlands and Islands of western Scotland, and of brochs in the
extreme northern tip of the Scottish mainland and in the Orkney and
Shetland islands, suggests that they were built to defend their inhabitants
against incursions from the warlike hill-fort builders of the South and East.
It is possible, also, that the demise of brochs and duns can be attributed to
the penetration of Roman troops into southern Scotland toward the close of
the first century A.D. This may have had the effect, at first, of pacifying the
border tribes, and later, as Roman rule weakened, of diverting their
aggressiveness away from their northern and western neighbors and southward toward richer prey on the far side of Hadrian's Wall. In any case, the
era of the brochs and duns occurred in the three centuries straddling the
beginning of the Christian era. During this period about 350 of the former
and more than 400 of the latter were constructed. The following selection is
representative.

On the western coast of the Rinns of Galloway in Wigtownshire, looking
out on the Irish sea, stands **Ardwell Broch** *(375)*, a typical coastal fortification, fairly well preserved. Its walls are about thirteen feet thick, and its
interior courtyard is about thirty feet in diameter. The main entrance
passage faces the sea; the second entryway is on the landward side, possibly
cut through some time after the broch was built. In Kirkcudbrightshire,
overlooking Wigtown Bay, sits **Castle Haven Dun** *(381)*, now an ivy-clad
ruin. It is a D-shaped galleried dun, measuring internally sixty feet by
thirty-five feet, its hollow wall now nowhere higher than four feet and
pierced by a narrow doorway on the north and another on its southern,
seaward side. A few steps survive of what was once no doubt a staircase built
against the interior wall. Surrounding the fortification is another wall,
probably installed at a later date.

On the Kintyre peninsula, northeast of Campbeltown, is **Kildonan Dun**
(462). The enclosure here is somewhat egg-shaped; the wall is 12 feet thick
in parts, with a main entrance complete with door-checks and a bar-hole
and socket. Opposite the entrance is a small mural cell, and to the left of the
entry is a somewhat larger mural gallery. On the east coast of the island of
Lismore stands **Tirefour Broch** *(467)*, a dilapidated ruin about 20 feet high
in parts. In western Inverness-shire, near Glenelg across the Sound of Sleat
from Skye, lie three Iron Age fortifications especially worthy of the
traveller's attention. The easternmost of these is **Dun Grugraig** *(517)*. This
is a D-shaped fortification, halfway between a broch and a dun. The
unwalled straight side of the D runs along the edge of a cliff that drops
steeply to the burn below. The semicircular wall is 14 feet thick and still
stands to a maximum height of 8 feet, enclosing an area measuring 46 feet
by 38 feet. Mural chambers are discernible, as well as a blocked entrace
passage with door-checks and a bar-hole. Downstream about 1½ miles is one

of Scotland's best-preserved brochs, called **Dun Troddan** *(517)*. The dry-stone wall of this fort still stands to a maximum height of 25 feet. It surrounds a courtyard only 28 feet in diameter. Here can be observed all the features common to this type: a narrow, low entrance passage, mural cells and galleries, a staircase, and the remains of an interior ledge. Immediately downstream lies an even better-preserved example: **Dun Telve** *(517)*. The thick dry-stone wall of this broch stands to a maximum height of 33½ feet around a courtyard 32 feet in diameter. Mural galleries, stairs, passageway, and two inner ledges can easily be seen.

The Isle of Skye is well endowed with brochs, of which two are noteworthy: **Dun Beag** *(523)*, a dozen miles west of Portree; and **Dun Hallin** *(523)*, on the Vaternish Peninsula north of Dunvegan. The former is the more easily reached and is the better preserved of the two. It measures thirty-six feet in diameter, and its fourteen-foot-thick wall stands to a height of twelve feet. The measurements for Dun Hallin are approximately the same, though the site is badly signposted and not so easy to find.

In the outer Hebrides, the best preserved of several brochs and duns is **Dun Carloway** *(558)* on Lewis, about six miles north of the better-known prehistoric site of Callanish. Part of the wall surrounding the broch's courtyard, twenty-five feet in diameter, rises thirty feet above ground. The low entrance passage still retains its lintel; mural cells and galleries are clearly visible; so are the staircase and internal ledge. Almost identical to it is **Dun Donradilla** *(552)*, south of Loch Hope in Sutherland—the best preserved of the many brochs in this and the neighboring county of Caithness. Part of its external wall survives to a height of more than twenty feet, though the inner skin has mostly collapsed. Here too the entrance passage still retains its lintel.

Some of the best preserved of all surviving Iron Age brochs are to be found in the northern islands. On the northeast coast of Mainland, Orkney, overlooking Eynhallow Sound, is the ruined **Broch of Gurness** *(561)*. Its surviving walls rise to fifteen feet above high-water mark, and the broch displays the usual features: a narrow entrance passage with door-checks, two guard cells connecting with a mural gallery, a staircase in the wall, and a ledge running around the inside wall-face. Both inside and outside of this circular enclosure are the foundations of a number of dwellings, probably of a later date, perhaps from the period of Viking occupation. Across Eynhallow Sound on the island of Rousay stands **Midhowe Broch** *(566)*, adjacent to the chambered cairn of the same name. It measures thirty feet in diameter, inside a wall fifteen feet thick and still standing to a height of fourteen feet. The entrance passage is well preserved with lintels still in place, door-checks and bar-holes, two guard cells, galleries, and a staircase. Around the broch itself are the remains of massive outworks and a cluster of domestic dwellings of a later date.

On a little islet off the southeast coast of the main island of Shetland stands the best preserved of all the Scottish brochs. This is **Mousa Broch** *(569)*, still rising to a height of forty-three feet. Here the tapered characteristic thought to be typical of all broch construction is clearly observable; the tower measures fifty feet across at the base but only forty feet at the summit. The entrance passage is equipped with the usual door-checks and bar-hole; three large mural cells open off the central court; two ledges are preserved on the inside wall-face; the stairway rises clockwise inside the wall to the summit of the tower; and the upper portions of the broch still contain six mural cells. According to one archaeologist, Euan W. Mackie, this "ranks among the major archaeological monuments of Europe," and another, Richard Feacham, adds: "No other monument is better worth a visit." Travellers should be warned, however, that access to the island on which the broch stands is by private boat and subject to the vagaries of Shetland weather. About fifteen miles north, just outside the town of Lerwick, lies **Clickimin Broch** *(568)*, its highest surviving wall reaching about fifteen feet. The entrance passage lacks the usual door-checks; from the central court other narrow doorways lead into two mural chambers, both with corbelled roofs. The mural staircase starts above ground level and is now to be reached by a wooden ladder. On this site the subsidiary buildings are perhaps even more interesting than the broch itself. At the northwest corner of the site are the foundations of a Bronze Age "courtyard house." On the southeast is a semicircular "blockhouse." Around the entire site runs a massive stone wall, which, like the blockhouse, probably dates from the Early Iron Age. Inside the broch are the remains of a Dark Age "wheelhouse," possibly occupied by ninth-century Vikings. A similar sequence of building can be seen at **Jarlshof** *(569)* on the southern tip of Shetland. The Bronze Age remains of this site have been described above, and its later relics will be mentioned again. Superimposed on the southernmost of the Bronze Age ovoid huts and extending south from them are the foundations of three Early Iron Age circular dwellings, partly subdivided by radial walls projecting inward. In the Late Iron Age came the broch, so eroded by the sea that only half of it now remains on its foundations, and that not to any great height. It was surrounded by a wall, also now half destroyed, and between wall and broch later settlers in the second and third centuries A.D. built "wheelhouses," circular dry-stone huts with radial partitions like the cross section of a grapefruit. The foundations of three of these can still be seen.

From roughly the same period as these wheelhouses comes another type of structure, fairly common in the northeast of mainland Scotland and the northern islands, and among the most baffling of all archaeological phenomena. These are called *souterrains*, similar in character to the equally mysterious *fougous* of Cornwall. A typical *souterrain* is a long, curving, narrow underground passage about 8 feet wide and 6 feet deep. Some have lateral galleries and may assume quite complicated patterns. The county of Angus offers the most complete collection of these curiosities. **Tealing Souterrain** *(511)* is a stone-lined trench about 90 feet in length. **Carlungie Souterrain** *(514)* has a curving paved passage almost 140 feet long with a main entrance and three subsidiary ones. It is now roofless and looks like a sunken stone-walled trench. Of similar appearance is the nearby **Ardestie Souterrain** *(514)*, a subterranean, now roofless, stone-walled passage about 90 feet in length. Near Coupar Angus, Perthshire, lies **Pitcur Souterrain** *(500)*, with a main passage 190 feet in length and a side passage less than 60. About a quarter of the main passage retains its roofing lintels. Even more of the roof remains at **Culsh Souterrain** *(542)*, near Tarland, Aberdeenshire. Here the subterranean characteristic of these structures can be appreciated better than among those now exposed to the open air. The same is true of **Grainbank Earth House** *(560)*, just west of Kirkwall, Orkney. This is an underground chamber, not a covered trench like those in Angus. It is only 11 feet long by 5½ feet wide and 4 feet high, is lined with dry-stone walls, and is roofed with flat stones supported by four stone pillars. A couple of miles to the east is **Rennibister Earth House** *(561)*, another underground chamber. It is hexagonal in shape, about 11 feet long by 8 feet wide, lined with dry-stone walling and stone slabs, and roofed by overlapping flat slabs supported by four upright pillars. The room, now entered through a trapdoor, was originally approached by way of a low sloping passageway about 10 feet long.

As already suggested, the original function of these underground chambers and corridors is entirely a matter of speculation. Some prehistorians believe that they were merely stables for housing cattle in the winter. Others, more romantically inclined, see them as hideouts where defenseless natives sought refuge during times of raids and invasions. If so, their proximity in many cases to known Iron Age settlements would have led to easy discovery—a fact casting doubt on this hypothesis. Perhaps they were nothing more than winter dugouts—cozy shelters against the icy storms for which Scotland, and especially the northern islands, are famous. Against this theory can be set the sensible observation of a French archaeologist: that a people clever enough to have built these underground shelters would certainly have been clever enough to remain outside them.

In any case, about all that is certainly known of the *souterrains* is that they were built about the time of the Roman invasion or within the century or two thereafter. They stand, therefore, just on the dividing line between prehistory and history. The distinction, to be sure, is less precise for Scotland than for the rest of Britain, for the Romans never really conquered very much of the land north of the border, and Iron Age culture persisted there long after it had died out in the South. The *Pax Romana*, with its great public baths, its villas, and its amphitheaters, had little impact north of Hadrian's Wall and almost none at all in the Scottish Highlands and Islands.

Chapter Two

Roman and Dark Age Scotland

Scotland enters recorded history in the year A.D. 80 with an invasion of the southern Lowlands by an army of 20,000 Roman legionaries led by Gnaeus Julius Agricola. Their mission was to pacify the unruly northern tribes then threatening the Roman frontier, which had recently been established on a line running from the River Tyne to the Solway Firth. In a single season of campaigning, Agricola's veteran soldiers penetrated as far north as the River Tay, a distance of well over 150 miles. Their progress was presumably unopposed, though considering the nature of the terrain over which they had to march, it was a remarkable feat—even for the Romans.

It had been almost forty years since four legions of Roman troops had first landed on the shores of Kent to begin the conquest of *Britannia*, the westernmost province of the great empire created by Julius Caesar and his successors. During that time the English lowlands had been conquered, occupied, and, in the Roman fashion, civilized. Then, under the Emperor Vespasian (A.D. 69–79), Wales was conquered, followed by Brigantia, the territory lying between the Humber River and the Tyne. To the north lay an uncharted wilderness as yet unnamed but soon to be designated *Caledonia* by the Romans. Its turn was next.

Agricola was the third of Vespasian's fighting governors of Britain—all under orders to carry out the emperor's new strategy of forward defense. He is also the most famous—thanks to an adulatory biography written by his son-in-law, the historian Tacitus. To Tacitus is owed most of what is known of the first chapter of the history—as distinct from the prehistory—of Scotland.

The legions led by Agricola would have contained about five thousand infantrymen, divided into ten cohorts, each cohort further subdivided into six centuries of eighty men, each commanded by a centurion. The Roman legionary was normally garbed in a cloak, an armored vest or cuirass of overlapping metal strips, a tunic, and a helmet of bronze or iron shaped to cover the skull and rear of the neck. He was armed with a short, double-edged, sharply pointed sword called a *gladius* and with one or two *pila*, seven-foot javelins with an effective range of about forty feet. In battle he would first launch his javelins, then close with the enemy, sword in hand, to engage him in combat. In the **National Museum of Antiquities** *(447)* in Edinburgh is a tombstone depicting three typical legionaries, possibly a father and two sons. Though the monument dates from a generation later than Agricola's invasion, there is no reason to believe that the soldiers under his command would have been differently dressed and equipped.

Supplementing the legions were the *auxilia*, not Roman citizens like the legionaries, but recruited from pacified barbarian tribes, including Gauls and Britons. They were cavalrymen, archers, lancers, slingers, and light infantry, organized into cohorts of infantry and *alae* of cavalry. A cavalry-man, requiring greater reach, would carry a sword longer than the *gladius*, a lance rather than a javelin, and a round rather than a rectangular shield. Artillery consisted mostly of siege weapons—the *ballista*, which was a sort of outsized crossbow with a range of about four hundred yards, and the *onager* or "wild ass," a catapult that could lob a 175-pound stone ball to a distance of 200 yards. These weapons probably would not have been used in Agricola's march to the Tay, as there is no reference by Tacitus to siege operations during this initial campaign. Of greater utility on this occasion would have been the miscellany of engineering equipment that the Roman soldier on the march normally carried on his back or secured to his belt: an axe, a pickaxe, a mallet, tent-pegs, stakes for palisades, and possibly a wicker basket for hauling dirt. Several of such items can also be seen at the **National Museum of Antiquities** *(447)*.

Most of the Roman finds in this museum come from a single site: the camp at Newstead (*Trimontium*) near Melrose in modern Roxburghshire. It was first established by Agricola on Dere Street (now paralleled by the A 68), the main Roman road running north into Scotland from the fort at Corbridge, Northumberland. Unfortunately nothing remains above ground at Newstead, though for a century it served as the nodal point of Roman operations in Scotland. In general layout it would have resembled all other Roman camps, forts, and fortresses, whether built of earth and timber—as they mostly were in the first century A.D.—or of stone, as in the later centuries of occupation. Their outer ramparts formed a rectangle with rounded corners, more or less in the shape of a modern playing card. Each of the four sides was pierced by at least one gated entranceway from which a road led straight to the headquarters building (*principia*) in the center of the enclosure. Nearby were one or two granaries (*horrea*), a workshop (*fabrica*), and a hospital (*valetudinarium*); also inside the ramparts lay the barrack-blocks, latrines, stables, and storehouses; while outside stood the bathhouse, which not only served a hygienic purpose but was also a recreational center for the troops.

According to Tacitus, Agricola found time to plant a number of such military bases along the route of his first march northward to the Tay. The next summer (A.D. 81) he fortified the Forth-Clyde isthmus, i.e., the narrow neck of land between the headwaters of those two great estuaries, which penetrated farther inland then than now, almost cutting Scotland in two at its waist. The following year found this energetic soldier moving into the Southwest. Here in Galloway (roughly corresponding to the modern counties of Wigtownshire, Kirkcudbrightshire, and Dumfriesshire) "in repeated and successful battles [he] reduced tribes up to that time unknown" and contemplated conducting an amphibious operation against the nearby coast of Ireland. This was not to be, for word arrived of an organized "rebellion" among the northern tribes beyond the Tay under the leadership of a native chieftain, called by the Romans *Calgacus*—the first identifiable native name in Scottish history. Agricola rushed north.

By this time (early summer of A.D. 84) a new legionary fortress was taking shape on the north bank of the Tay, southwest of the present town of Blairgowrie, Perthshire. This place has since been dubbed **Inchtuthil** *(499)*, and it was from here that Agricola set forth by land and sea to subdue the fractious tribes of the Northeast whom the Romans called *Caledonii*. Under his command was a force of about eight thousand men; Calgacus had at his disposal perhaps as many as thirty thousand. Romans and Caledonians met at a place called *Mons Graupius*, still unidentified but probably situated in northeastern Scotland beyond The Mounth, the principal east-west mountain range that runs from south of Aberdeen west to Ben Nevis in Inverness-shire. Here, on the eve of the battle, Calgacus reportedly addressed his people in words made famous (and probably invented) by Tacitus:

> Here at the world's end, on its last inch of liberty, we have lived unmolested to this day, defended by our remoteness and obscurity. Now the uttermost parts of Britain lie exposed. . . . There are no other tribes to come; nothing but sea and cliffs and these more deadly Romans, whose arrogance you cannot escape by obedience and self-restraint. Robbers of the world . . . if their enemy have wealth, they have greed; if he be poor, they are ambitious. . . . To plunder, butcher, steal, these things they misname empire; where they make a desert, they call it peace (*ubi solitudinem faciunt, pacem appellant*)!

In the event, oratory proved no match for Roman arms. The invaders killed ten thousand Britons and routed the rest. "The night," reported Tacitus, "was jubilant with triumph and plunder for the victors. . . . The morrow revealed more widely the features of the victory; everywhere was dismal silence, lonely hills, houses smoking to heaven." Of Calgacus himself, no more is heard.

After the battle, Agricola sent his fleet north to overawe the natives along the shores of the Moray Firth and then across the Pentland Firth to the

Orkney Islands. With his victorious legionaries, he himself fell back on **Inchtuthil** *(499)*. Within a short time he was recalled to Rome. In A.D. 86–87 his still unfinished fortress on the Tay was torn down by imperial order. Its stone walls were pulled apart, timber buildings were disassembled, and 875,000 nails were deliberately buried to deny their iron to the barbarians. Rediscovered in the twentieth century, a few examples of this hoard are on display in the **National Museum of Antiquities** *(447)* in Edinburgh. The remains of the fortress from which they came are barely visible. On the east side of this forty-five-acre enclosure (now on private property) lies a fairly conspicuous ditch, and the earthen rampart on the south still stands to some height. Nothing else remains of Agricola's great endeavor. Reasons of state had nullified his gains. A Dacian uprising beyond the Danube required the dispatch of the Second Legion from its fort at Chester to Moesia (Serbia), so Agricola's Twentieth Legion had to be sent south from Inchtuthil to replace it. The Roman frontier was pulled back to the Forth-Clyde isthmus. In the words of Tacitus, "The conquest of Britain was completed and immediately let go."

Tacitus could only have been referring to that part of Britain north of the Forth-Clyde line. South of it the Romans remained, fortified key positions, and kept the native tribes more or less in order. Between the two isthmuses (Tyne-Solway and Forth-Clyde), there were four principal tribal groupings of Iron Age peoples, all speaking the Brythonic (P-Celtic) dialect, which has survived in modern Welsh. To the east, occupying modern Berwickshire and the Lothians, were the *Votadini*, who seem to have been the most peaceful and the least resistant to Romanization. Their tribal capital, or *oppidum*, was **Traprain Law** *(456)*, a huge hill rising high above the East Lothian plain, looking, as many have remarked, like a beached whale. Though this hill-fort has been badly eaten away on one side by quarrying and the archaeological remains *in situ* are scanty, there are signs here of occupation from the Bronze Age through the fifth century A.D. The fact that the Romans did not apparently capture the fort or otherwise molest its inhabitants indicates that the *Votadini* collaborated with their conquerors or at least put up no significant show of resistance. It was otherwise at **Eildon Hill, North** *(418)* in Roxburghshire, the largest of Scotland's Iron Age hill-forts. This was probably the *oppidum* of the *Selgovae*, who had controlled the area of the Upper Tweed basin before the arrival of the Romans. When the invaders came and set up their key fort at Newstead in the valley below, they apparently drove the *Selgovae* out of their capital, for there is no sign of subsequent native occupation, and a shallow ditch still observable at the summit of the hill marks the position of a Roman signal tower. The same fate befell **Woden Law** *(411)* near Jedburgh, Roxburghshire, also within the territory of the *Selgovae*. This place the Romans apparently emptied so as to use it as a practice ground for the troops stationed at the nearby temporary camp at **Pennymuir** *(414)*. Just outside the range of hand-thrown missiles from the native fort, they set up practice siege-works consisting of a double bank and three ditches and a flat-topped stone-based platform for their catapults. The same disposition was made of **Burnswark Hill-Fort** *(386)*, near the present village of Ecclefechan, Dumfriesshire. Close by lay a fort at **Birrens** *(386)*, called *Blatobulgium* by the Romans. Troops from this base were undoubtedly responsible for the practice siege-works at Burnswark, where three enormous mounds are still visible—built to support the catapults used in mock battles against a vacant native fort. Burnswark lay close to the vague borderline between two southwestern tribes, the *Damnonii* and the *Novantae*, and may have been occupied by either. The territory of the former stretched north and west of here into Ayrshire, Renfrewshire, Lanarkshire, Dunbartonshire, and Stirlingshire, while that of the latter lay to the southwest in Kirkcudbrightshire and Wigtownshire.

The first stage of Roman dominion over southern Scotland proved to be short-lived. Some time in the early years of the second century the forts along the border were burned, probably by the Romans themselves before they moved back to the Tyne-Solway line. Again, it was probably the war in Dacia that required the withdrawal of troops from Britain and the shortening of imperial lines of defense. Perhaps too the *Selgovae* and *Novantae* took to the warpath. It is certain that they did so in A.D. 117 when a native uprising in the area proved serious enough to bring the Emperor Hadrian to Britain. Then it was that he ordered the construction of the great stone wall that bears his name and stretches still across northern England between the Tyne and the headwaters of the Solway Firth.

Hadrian's Wall took six years (A.D. 122–128) to complete. The new frontier lasted for little more than a decade. Hadrian's successor, the Emperor Antoninus Pius, ordered a reinvasion of Scotland, which was undertaken in A.D. 140 by the new governor, Quintus Lollius Urbicus. In two years' time the Romans completed the pacification of the Scottish Lowlands and again penetrated to the River Tay. In the year 142 the emperor ordered a new line of defense to be built across the Forth-Clyde isthmus, to be known thereafter as the **Antonine Wall** *(476)*. Hadrian's Wall was demilitarized, and the Roman frontier was once more pushed forward deep into Scotland.

The Antonine Wall ran for thirty-seven miles from modern Bo'ness on the Forth west to Old Kilpatrick on the Clyde. It had a stone foundation, fourteen feet in width, on which turf was laid to a height of some nine feet. On top of this was a walkway, six feet wide, and possibly timber breastworks. On the northern side was a huge V-shaped ditch, forty feet wide and at least twelve feet deep. To the south ran a parallel military service road.

Eighteen or nineteen forts were attached to the southern side of the wall at approximately two-mile intervals. Except in two cases, these were built of turf rather than stone. The largest of them could have held a cohort of a thousand men. As segments of the wall were finished, the soldiers assigned to the task erected "distance slabs" of sculpted or incised stone to commemorate their labors. One of these, put up by the men of the Second Legion Augusta, is now on view at the **National Museum of Antiquities** *(447)* in Edinburgh. In addition to the inscription, the stone displays two contemporary scenes in clear relief: a Roman cavalryman riding over four naked Britons armed with swords and shields, and what appears to be a religious ceremony involving the sacrifice of a bull, a sheep, and a pig. All but one of the remaining extant distance slabs are on view in the **Hunterian Museum** *(408)* in Glasgow.

Impressive as it was as a feat of engineering, this wall of turf is not to be compared in magnitude with Hadrian's seventy-four-mile chain of forts and milecastles between the Tyne and Solway. Also the Antonine Wall is badly eroded, and much of it lies now in the most heavily industrialized part of Scotland, surrounded and obscured by factories, railways, and housing developments. Enough survives at a few places, however, to be worth the traveller's inspection, although it must be said that none of these is exactly spectacular.

Moving west from Falkirk, Stirlingshire, the first stop should be at **Watling Lodge** *(476)*, close to the B 816 about a mile southwest of its junction with the A 803. Nothing remains here of the wall itself, but the V-shaped ditch survives almost to its original dimensions of forty feet wide by twelve feet deep. Between Watling Lodge and the town of Bonnybridge to the west, the wall is especially well preserved and can be seen on the north side of the B 816. About a half mile southeast of Bonnybridge is **Rough Castle** *(476)*, the best preserved of all the wall-forts. Earthen ramparts and ditches enclose about an acre of ground extending south of the wall, which itself formed the northern side of the fort. A few traces of excavated stone buildings can be seen in the middle of the fort. North of the wall here, and about 20 yards beyond the ditch, lie a number of defensive pits called lilies *(lilia)* by the Roman soldiers. They are arranged in staggered rows and would have originally contained sharpened stakes covered with branches for camouflage—a type of ambuscade common to warfare in all ages. Finally, about a mile west of Bonnybridge on the south side of the B 816 lies **Seabegs Wood** *(477)*, another well-preserved section of wall and ditch, to the south of which lies the best surviving piece of the military way behind the wall. Along the thirty-seven-mile stretch there are a number of other relics of Roman work, but these are all too fragmentary to be of much interest to the ordinary traveller.

The Antonine Wall, like Hadrian's Wall and other comparable fortified frontiers throughout the Roman Empire, was not meant to serve as a barrier against massive attacks, in the manner of the Maginot Line of pre–World War II France. It was designed rather to separate the barbarians to the north from the more pacific tribes to the south, to serve as an early warning system against threats of infiltration, and to act as a base for mobile striking forces against concentrations of native troops beyond the frontier. Other forts within the hostile territory north of the Forth-Clyde line were still kept in operation. Chief among these was **Ardoch Roman Fort** *(504)*, initially founded by Agricola and later reinforced to serve as an outpost to the Antonine Wall. Situated just outside the present village of Braco north of Dunblane in Perthshire, it is today more impressive than any of the wall sites mentioned above. Though nothing remains of any of the original stonework, the earthen ramparts pierced by entranceways survive to a height of more than six feet in places, and their accompanying ditches are almost as deep as the originals.

Not much more than a decade after its completion, the Antonine Wall was abandoned and its forts burned by the Romans themselves to prevent their being used by the natives. Troubles with the *Brigantes* of northern England apparently required the presence of more troops in the area once guarded by Hadrian's Wall, which now underwent partial restoration. A few years later Roman soldiers were back in Scotland, and both walls were occupied until about A.D. 165, when the Antonine Wall was abandoned for good. Probably barbarian invasions in Parthia and Upper Germany had persuaded the central government in Rome again to withdraw troops from Britain and pull back to shorter lines. By the end of the second century, Scotland was free of Roman arms.

Then, late in that century, there occurred a major uprising of *Brigantes*, *Caledonii*, and a tribe called *Maeatae*. It was occasioned by the removal of most of the Roman garrison from Hadrian's Wall to the Continent by the then provincial governor, Clodius Albinus, in a bid to usurp the throne from the legitimate Emperor Septimius Severus. Severus defeated his rival in a great battle fought near Lyons in 197 and ordered Hadrian's Wall to be rebuilt. In the year 208 the emperor himself came to York, accompanied by his two sons, Caracalla and Geta. Together they launched a seaborne punitive expedition into Scotland, and in the course of their campaign reestablished **Cramond Roman Fort** *(452)* on the Forth as a forward operating base. Some of the remains of this important establishment are still visible in the pretty little village of Cramond, just west of Edinburgh. One stretch of the original wall still stands, and the outlines of most of the buildings are marked out with stones to give the visitor a good idea of the layout of a typical Roman fort.

Severus returned to die in York in 211, but Caracalla continued to campaign up the east coast of Scotland. By the time he returned to Rome, some sort of peace had been imposed on the *Maeatae* and *Caledonii*, and for most of the rest of the third century the frontier was quiet. Outpost forts north of Hadrian's Wall were restored, and new ones added, and a protectorate of sorts was extended over the tribes of southern Scotland to guard them against incursions from their more belligerent fellow-Celts further north.

Toward the end of the third century, a new threat appeared to disturb the tranquility of southern Britain. Saxon pirates operating out of the Rhine delta commenced to raid and pillage the eastern and southern coasts. A Belgian named Carausius was put in command of the Channel fleet at Boulogne to abate this nuisance; instead he rebelled, escaped to Britain, and defied the central government. Carausius was soon assassinated by his finance minister, Allectus, who himself continued the rebellion and stripped Hadrian's Wall of its garrison before suffering a decisive military defeat at the hands of the Emperor Constantius. Once again the northern tribes overran the unguarded wall. This is the first reported appearance of the historical Picts, about whom more will be said below. The Roman term *Picti* was new, but there is no reason to believe that these northern barbarians who attacked the wall in 296 were of a different breed from the *Caledonii* and *Maeatae* who had done the same in the reign of Severus. In any case, Constantius too campaigned in Scotland and, like Severus, returned in 321 to die at York, where his army proclaimed his son Constantine (known to posterity as "the Great") as emperor in his place.

Then, in 367, occurred a major disaster to Roman Britain—an alliance (*conspiratio barbarica*) among the Picts of the Scottish Highlands, the *Scotti* and *Attacotti* of Ireland, and the Franks and Saxons of the Continent, all of whom attacked simultaneously. Again Hadrian's Wall was overrun. Again order was restored, this time by Count Theodosius, the emperor's delegate, who rebuilt the wall for the fourth time. Signal towers were erected on the Yorkshire coast to warn against sea-raiders—Picts as well as Franks and Saxons. The frontier forts north of the wall were abandoned, and the Romanized Lowland tribes like the *Votadini* were left to defend themselves. It was possibly at this time or a little later that a *Votadini* chieftain at Traprain Law buried a huge hoard of the fragments of over a hundred silver vessels and other valuable objects, presumably to safeguard these riches from preying Picts and others. This so-called Traprain Law Treasure is now on view at the **National Museum of Antiquities** *(447)* in Edinburgh. It is thought to have been part of the payment the *Votadini* regularly received for cooperating with the Romans.

For the rest of the fourth century and beyond, Rome's grip on *Britannia* steadily loosened. In 383 another disaffected general, Magnus Maximus, rebelled and left for the Continent with a sizable part of the British garrison to defeat the Emperor Gratian in battle. It was probably he who invited a Votadinian chief called Cunedda to settle in North Wales to prevent that region from being overrun by Irish raiders and immigrants. (It was from Cunedda that the North Welsh princes of the Middle Ages claimed descent.) Then, in 396, the Romanized Vandal general Stilicho appeared in Britain to lead expeditions against Picts, Irish, and Saxons. But by 401 he was back on the Continent, taking with him still more troops from Britain for the defense of Italy. In 406–407 the army in Britain elevated in quick succession three would-be usurpers to the imperial throne, the last of whom took the field army and most of the remaining frontier garrisons to Gaul in an unsuccessful effort to make good his claim. In 410, in the face of barbarian threats from every quarter, city magistrates of southern Britain urgently appealed to the Emperor Honorius for military assistance. Faced with an imminent attack on the city of Rome itself by Alaric the Visigoth, the emperor could do no other than to advise the petitioners to look to their own defenses. It was the signal of the end of Roman rule in Britain.

DARK AGE SCOTLAND

It cannot be assumed that the final departure of Roman soldiers left Britain, or even that part of it lying north of Hadrian's Wall, in a state of total anarchy. For more than three hundred years, after all, North Britain had been mostly free of the presence of Roman troops except for sporadic punitive expeditions such as those of Severus and Constantius and the outpost garrisons just beyond the wall. Some sort of civil peace must have been maintained during that long period of time, and some degree of law and order enforced by tribal chiefs or "kings" with recognized authority within specific territorial limits. By the fifth century some of these rulers had been Romanized even to the extent of assuming Latin names, and some had been converted to Christianity at an early date. One such was called Corocticus by St. Patrick, who stoutly reprimanded him for allowing the massacre of some newly baptized Irish converts. Corocticus (or Ceredig Wledig, to use his British name) was the ruler of Strathclyde, a "kingdom" whose territory roughly corresponded to that of the ancient *Damnonii*. Its capital, or *oppidum*, was **Dumbarton Rock** *(475)* in modern Dunbarton-shire, an isolated volcanic plug of great height rising sheer above the River

Clyde. No remnants of Dark Age occupation have been discovered here (other than two tenth-century gravestones), but in the eighth century the English chronicler Bede described it as "the capital city of the Britons, most strongly fortified even today (*civitas Brettonum munitissima usque hodie*)."

South of Strathclyde, astride the Solway Firth and including perhaps most of the Pennine range, lay the kingdom of Rheged. Its legendary ruler was Coel Hen, or Cole the Old (the original Old King Cole of the nursery rhyme), whose Romanized name was probably Coelius or Coelestius. At a later date the capital of the kingdom was Carlisle at the western end of Hadrian's Wall, but within Rheged's fifth-century boundaries, on the opposite side of the Solway Firth in the modern county of Kirkcudbright-shire, lay a fortress known as the **Mote of Mark** *(380)*, a low coastal hill with a vitrified rampart, which has produced evidence clearly indicating Dark Age occupation.

To the east, around Lothian, lay the kingdom of the Gododdin, the name of which derives from the *Votadini* of Roman times. As already mentioned, the original tribal citadel was Traprain Law, but some time late in the fifth century the *Votadini* seem to have abandoned this place and concentrated around Dun Eidyn, the present site of Edinburgh.

All of these tribes of Brythonic-speaking Celts were known to their fellow Britons of Wales and southwestern England as *Gwyr y Gogledd*, "the Men of the North." And, like their southern fellow-countrymen who were being sorely pressed by encroaching Anglo-Saxons, they were the heirs of whatever was left of Roman civilization after the Roman soldiers had departed. Among other things, these Britons fought like Romans: they dressed in coats of mail, rode to battle on horseback, wielded swords and spears, and specialized in mobile tactics. (It will be remembered that the Roman cavalry was made up mostly of Romanized barbarians.) This too is the way the legendary King Arthur fought—not surprising since he too was a Roman-ized Briton. Arthur was probably not actually a king, but the leader of a cavalry band who fought for kings. Of his twelve battles listed in the *Historica Brittonum*, a collection of ninth-century Welsh chronicles, only one (the seventh) was located with any precision. It was fought *in silva Celidonis*, that is, "in the Caledonian forest," obviously somewhere in modern Scotland. What this cavalry captain from southwestern Britain was doing this far north, or against whom he was fighting, or on whose behalf, the record does not state. Scottish tradition, nevertheless, like that of Wales and Cornwall, embraces the Arthurian legend, citing as evidence of his one-time presence the name of **Arthur's Seat** *(435)*, the giant hill overlooking Edinburgh from the east.

King Arthur, of course, whether real or imaginary, is the symbol of fifth-century British resistance to the Anglo-Saxon tide that swept inexorably over the land in the wake of the Roman withdrawal. That tide pressed north as well as west, and in its path lay the land of the Gododdin, home of the most Romanized of Scottish Lowland tribes, the *Votadini*. The sequence of events from the fifth through the seventh centuries is very murky, but it appears that out of the turmoil incident to the evaporation of Roman power in the north of England, one of the native Anglo-Saxon kingdoms to emerge in the early sixth century was Bernicia. Its ruling aristocracy may have been descended from Germanic immigrants whom the Romans had settled in the north as a counterpoise to Pictish intrusions and/or from more recent Anglian immigrants from the north German coast. In 547 Bernicia's king was named Ida, and his capital was the newly fortified rock of Bamburgh on the Northumbrian coast. It was from this place that Anglian war bands began to venture into the territory of the Gododdin, looting, burning, and extracting tribute from the native Britons. In 598 the Men of the North retaliated by invading deep into Bernicia, but at Catterick, North Yorkshire, their forces were annihilated in a battle celebrated in the best known of early Welsh poems, the *Gododdin* by Aneirin. Of three hundred men sent out from Edinburgh, wrote the bard, only one returned. The rest were slain— "they never grew grey." Five years later the Bernicians encountered another war-band from the north at an unidentified place called Degsastan, this time led by Aidan, King of the Scots of Dalriada, about whom more will be said below. Again the English triumphed over their Celtic adversaries, and there was nothing remaining to impede their advance into Lothian. By 637 Edinburgh was in their hands. By that time the kingdom of Rheged had disappeared, overwhelmed by the military superiority of the English and finally absorbed by marriage into the new kingdom of Northumbria, formed by a union of Bernicia with its southern neighbor, Deira. Of all the British kingdoms of southern Scotland, only Strathclyde survived the Anglian onslaught. Indeed, its rulers on Dumbarton Rock, though sustaining many military defeats, retained their independence until Strathclyde was absorbed into the Scottish kingdom in the eleventh century.

Anglian settlers followed in the wake of their victorious war-bands, and by the end of the century the Lowlands were inhabited by a mixture of Anglo-Saxons and indigenous Celts, of whom the former were no doubt the dominant race. The degree of their domination is reflected in the language of the region: the Brythonic, or P-Celtic, tongue was submerged by an Anglian dialect that was eventually to develop into Broad Scots, familiar to readers of Robert Burns and still spoken in some parts of the country.

Anglian influences on native art forms were equally pervasive. More will be said on this subject below in connection with the sculptured stonework of Early Christian crosses. Perhaps the best example, however, of the amalgamation of Anglo-Saxon and Celtic artistic styles is the Hunterston

Brooch, one of the prize possessions of the **National Museum of Antiquities** *(447)* in Edinburgh. On the face of the brooch, the intricately designed beasts, birds, and reptiles, the eagle heads, and the ring of filigree animals are of Germanic origin; on the back, the spiral patterns of some of the decorative panels are Celtic, as is the overall shape of this masterpiece of craftsmanship. It was discovered in Ayrshire and is dated to about A.D. 700.

The Battle of Degsastan, in part responsible for English penetration of the Lowlands, was lost, as mentioned, not by indigenous Britons, but by Scots from Argyll. *Scotti* was the name the Romans and Romanized Britons gave to the barbarians who lived across the Irish Sea and who were almost as much of a menace in the fourth and fifth centuries as the Franks and Saxons. The Scots then, by origin, are Irishmen, and the Gaelic tongue still spoken in parts of the Scottish Highlands and Islands is the lineal descendant of the Goidelic, or Q-Celtic, language imported from Ireland.

In or about the year A.D. 500 a band of about 150 men sailed from County Antrim in northern Ireland to establish a permanent settlement on the west-central coast of Scotland in modern Argyll. They came from a place called Dalriada, and the new colony they established was known by the same name. Tradition has it that the band was led by three brothers: Fergus, Loarn, and Aengus, sons of Erc. Aengus and his immediate descendants apparently occupied the island of Islay. Loarn and his family settled in northern Argyll and built a stronghold at Dunollie, now the site of a much ruined castle (closed to the public) just north of Oban. Only Fergus and his successors were to have a substantial impact on the history of their adopted country. They settled in the Kintyre peninsula and neighboring Knapdale, and within a generation or two had occupied the ancient Iron Age hill-fort of **Dunadd** *(469)* on the Crinan isthmus between the Sound of Jura and Loch Fyne. This, the probable capital of the Scottic kingdom of Dalriada, is the most impressive Dark Age site to be seen today in all of Scotland. The huge rock rises abruptly from the once marshy Moss of Crinan and culminates in twin tops, of which the northernmost is conical and bare of signs of occupation. The southern top is a hog-backed ridge rising to a height of about 160 feet above the moor below. This was the Dalriadic citadel, defended by precipitous crags and a 12-foot-thick dry-stone wall. Looping out from this are lesser walls on the terraces below, forming a series of pendant enclosures. On the east flank of the hill, just below its summit, is a flight of steps cut into the cliff and leading to the top. Beside these steps is a large flat rock into which has been carved a human footprint, a cuplike depression 10 inches across, and the clearly incised figure of a boar. These are thought to have been connected with the investiture ceremony of the kings of Dalriada, although the boar may date from the period of Pictish occupation following the capture of Dunadd by King Angus MacFergus in 736.

It was presumably here at Dunadd that, in 574, King Aidan of Dalriada received the missionary St. Columba, who had been instrumental in his gaining the Scottic throne. It was this same Aidan who led the Scottish war-bands to defeat at the hands of the English at Degsastan. But the chief enemies of the Scots were the Picts into whose territory they had intruded. Intermittent warfare between Scots and Picts continued for almost 250 years, and at times Dalriada appears to have become a client state of Pictland. Then, in the middle of the ninth century, a Scottish king named Kenneth mac(son of)Alpin gained the Pictish throne; the two kingdoms became permanently conjoined under the rule of a Scottish royal family; and the political center of the new kingdom, called "Alba" or sometimes "Scotia," moved from Dunadd east to Perthshire.

Of all the many tribal groups and peoples populating Dark Age Britain, or migrating to, from, or within its shores, none is more mysterious than the Picts. The name *Picti* first appears in two different Latin sources in A.D. 267 to describe the tribes of the Far North, who were then invading the Roman province of Britain. Thereafter their name is frequently mentioned as among the fiercest of *Britannia*'s enemies, and indeed it was primarily to guard against the Picts that the Romans first established in England those colonies of Germanic settlers who were the forerunners of the great Anglo-Saxon migration to her shores.

The Latin word *Picti*, meaning "painted men," was once thought to have been applied by the Romans to these fearsome warriors because they tattooed their bodies or perhaps decorated them with applications of blue woad. It seems more likely, however, that the word is merely a Latinized version of the name by which these barbarians called themselves. (The Scandinavians, who were not Latin-speakers, called them "Petts" or "Pechts"—also probably an adaptation from the original.) That they were of Celtic strain there seems little doubt. Yet they were clearly different from the Brythonic-speaking Britons or the Goidelic-speaking Irish. Linguists suspect that they spoke a bastard form of P-Celtic closer to Gaulish than to Brythonic but not identical to either. It is possible that, in both language and customs, the Picts were originally an amalgam of Hallstatt-culture Celts with indigenous Bronze Age people, whose language, with Celtic variations, they adopted as their own. Uncertainty about the nature of the Pictish language is not resolved by the fact that a number of Pictish inscriptions do survive. They are incised on stone in Ogam, a linear cipher (translatable into Latin) probably invented in Ireland in the fourth century and brought thence into Pictland by intrusive Dalriadic Scots. When converted to Latin letters, these inscriptions turn out to be unintelligible in any known language. The mystery of the Picts remains unsolved.

There is no doubt, however, as to where Pictland lay. Though they raided far and wide and at times seized territories occupied by both Scots and Britons, the heartland of the Picts spread eastward from the Drumalban mountain range (the northwest Highlands) and north of the Firth of Forth at least as far as the Dornoch Firth and probably beyond to include Orkney and Shetland. At the end of the second century A.D., according to Latin sources, northeastern Scotland was divided among two dominant tribal confederacies—the *Maeatae*, who lived south of the east-west mountain range called The Mounth, and the *Caledonii*, who occupied the lands north of it as far as the Moray Firth. By the time the descendants of these two groups of barbarians came to be known as Picts, the division seems to have persisted, and even as late as the eighth century the chronicler Bede distinguishes between the northern and southern Pictish kingdoms.

The first king of the northern Picts known to history is Bridei (or Brude) (ca. 547–584), who was possibly converted to Christianity by St. Columba during a visit to his court near Inverness. Just west of that city, overlooking the Beauly Firth, is a vitrified Iron Age hill-fort called **Craig Phadrig** *(517)*, which has yielded archaeological evidence of Dark Age occupation. Local tradition holds this place to have been King Bridei's citadel, though there is no real evidence to support the claim. About thirty-five miles to the east, in Moray, on a narrow peninsula jutting into the Moray Firth, is another fort of undoubted Pictish association, also suggested as the possible site of King Bridei's court. This is **Burghead** *(530)* near Forres, which was a double fort divided by a huge rampart. Much robbed of its stonework in the nineteenth century, about all that is left of this once impressive citadel are the remains of the cross-rampart and a rock-cut well. On the premises were discovered about twenty-five slabs, each bearing the picture of a bull incised in the stone. These objects, some of which can be viewed in the **Elgin Museum** *(525)*, clearly indicate Pictish occupation of the fort, probably in the sixth century, when Bridei was king of the northern Picts.

The bull is but one of several stereotyped animal forms to be found incised on boulders or dressed slabs all over ancient Pictland and occasionally elsewhere in Scotland. The origins and meaning of Pictish art are as baffling today as is everything else about this once powerful people, who left no literary record for the edification of posterity. What they did leave, however, was, in the words of H. M. Chadwick, "a vast picture gallery of Pictish art, now surviving chiefly in stone sculpture of superb and mature quality . . . sculptured monuments of which there are over a hundred in existence."

Two types of symbols adorn these monuments. First are the animals: impressionistic pictographs executed with beautiful economy of line and a distinctive stereotyped style. They include, besides the bull, representations of the boar, the stag, the wolf, the salmon, the seahorse, the goose, the eagle, the snake, and a curious creature sometimes called the "swimming elephant," otherwise known as the "Pictish beast." Second is a series of abstract symbols, known by various descriptive names such as "Z-rod," "double-disc," "triple disc," "horseshoe," and "mirror-and-comb." What these symbols meant or what was the function of the stones they embellished is anybody's guess. The symbols might represent a pictographic alphabet, or clan badges, or signs of personal rank. The stones themselves might be funerary monuments or boundary markers bearing symbols of ownership. In addition to their symbol-markings, some of the stones bear carvings obviously representational in character: chiefly scenes of combat or of hunting or of processions of warriors or priests. These are perhaps monuments raised to commemorate notable events, such as battles or investitures or religious ceremonies.

Archaeologists classify the Pictish stones into three groups: Class I consists of natural boulders or roughly dressed stones that are incised, not carved in relief. These are thought to be the earliest in date, probably deriving from the fifth and sixth centuries. Class II are dressed slabs, carved in relief, each with a Christian cross on a field of interlace on one side and Pictish symbols on the other. They are usually dated to the seventh and eighth centuries. Class III stones, though found in Pictland, contain no Pictish symbols at all but are covered with crosses and other figures, often biblical, in high relief. They probably belong to the early ninth century or even later, after Pictland had ceased to exist as a political entity.

There are three major museum collections of Pictish stones in Scotland today, usually housed in company with Christian crosses in the Anglian and/or Celtic style. The first is in the **National Museum of Antiquities** *(447)* in Edinburgh. Here the most interesting example is the "Birsay Stone," found in Orkney, with engravings of numerous Pictish symbols and a row of three men wearing long coats, each carrying a spear and a small, square shield. Next is the **Meigle Museum** *(501)* near Coupar Angus. Here are thirty-four stones, of which perhaps the best is labelled Number 2: a huge Class III cross-slab in high relief with Daniel in the lion's den on one side and a cavalcade of horsemen on the other. Finally is **St. Vigean's Museum** *(508)*, just north of Arbroath, Angus. Of the thirty-two stones housed here, perhaps the most interesting is the "Drosten Stone," a Class II dressed slab with a cross, ornamented with interlace patterns flanked by beasts, and on the back a stag hunt with Pictish symbols. On the Drosten Stone are inscribed three Pictish-sounding names—a rarity.

Of individual Pictish stones still standing *in situ* there is an embarrassment of riches, especially in the counties of Perthshire, Angus, and Aberdeenshire. A short distance east of Crieff is the **Fowlis Wester Stone** *(502)* in the village of the same name. This is a much eroded Class II cross slab of red sandstone, twelve feet high, with horsemen, animals, foot soldiers, and Pictish symbols on one face and a cross with projecting arms on the other. Inside the parish kirk, in the north wall, is a smaller but better-preserved slab, carved on one side only with an elaborate wheel-headed cross flanked by strange animal and human figures. Also in Perthshire, near Pitlochry, is the **Dunfallandy Stone** *(507)*, a fine Class II Pictish stone just outside the churchyard. On the front is an interlace cross flanked by angels and various beasts, while on the rear are sundry Pictish symbols. Five miles east of the city of Perth, in the churchyard of Glencarse, stands **St. Madoe's Stone** *(000)*, another fine Class II stone with an interlace cross surrounded by fabulous beasts on the front, and on the back three cloaked horsemen and the usual Pictish symbols. Coming into Angus, a few miles west of Dundee, is the **Rossie Priory Stone** *(510)* inside the kirk. It too belongs to Class II but is unusual, having a cross carved on both faces, surrounded by fabulous beasts, horsemen, and a single Pictish symbol. In Glamis, at the east end of the village, is the **Glamis Manse Stone** *(513)*, a Class II example, nine feet high, incised on the back with a fish, a serpent, and a mirror symbol, while on the front is an interlace cross flanked by other symbols and mythical figures carved in relief. Just west of Glamis is the **Eassie Cross Slab** *(513)* in the village churchyard—a richly ornamented cross flanked by angels and other figures on the front, and on the back three priests carrying staffs, three cows, and a variety of Pictish symbols. The **Kirriemuir Pictish Stones** *(513)* in the village cemetery consist of Class II and Class III slabs with a variety of Pictish symbols and human figures. A few miles northeast of Forfar is a particularly fine group called the **Aberlemno Stones** *(511)*. In the church-yard here is a Class II slab with a handsome interlace cross flanked by intertwined beasts, and on the back a Pictish battle scene below a series of symbols. On the roadside nearby stands a particularly good Class I stone incised on one face with miscellaneous symbols, and next to it another Class II monument with a weathered cross flanked by angels and a hunting scene with symbols on the back.

In Aberdeenshire, northwest of Aberdeen in the vicinity of Inverurie, are to be found three excellent examples of Pictish art. First are the **Dyce Stones** *(535)*, standing inside the ruined church of St. Fergus just outside Dyce village on the road to Pitmedden. The Class I stone here has an incised "swimming elephant" as well as the usual abstract symbols, while the Class II slab beside it is sculpted on one face only with a wheel-headed cross accompanied by more symbols. Just north of Inverurie is the **Brandsbutt Stone** *(541)*, a Class I boulder reconstructed from broken fragments and incised with the customary symbols as well as with a line of Ogam markings that transliterate as *IRATADDOARENS* and are untranslatable. West of Inverurie, and just southeast of the village of Oyne, is the **Maiden Stone**

(542), a Class II stone with panels of sculpture around a carved cross on the front and a variety of beasts and symbols on the back.

Finally, perhaps the most magnificent of all Dark Age sculptured stones in Britain stands on the outskirts of Forres in Moray. This is the famous **Sueno's Stone** *(528)*, a Class III monument without Pictish symbols. It stands twenty feet high and dates probably from the ninth century, when Pictish power was on the wane. On the front is a wheel-headed interlace cross; on the back are four panels of horsemen, foot soldiers, and beheaded bodies; the sides are carved with Anglian vine-scroll. This is thought to be a cenotaph, commemorating a great battle fought near here, probably against Viking raiders. If so, it must have been one of the last great feats of Pictish arms.

Pictland in the seventh, eighth, and early ninth centuries had been the most powerful of the North British kingdoms. In 685 a Pictish king had badly defeated the Northumbrians at the Battle of Nechtansmere (Dunnichen) near Forfar, thereby saving the lands north of the Forth from being overrun by the English, as had the Lothians. Another king had captured Dunadd from the Dalriadic Scots in 736. Yet the Pictish monarchy, in the long term, was apparently incapable of capitalizing on its military superiority. For one thing, the Picts' failure, so far as is known, to develop a written language would have worked against the institutionalization of monarchical rule. For another, succession to the Pictish throne was governed by matrilineal descent, a custom that tended to produce dynastic warfare among eligible cousins and encouraged outsiders with Pictish mothers of royal blood to lay claim to the throne of Pictland. It was thus perhaps that Kenneth mac Alpin, king of the Dalriadic Scots, was able to establish himself as ruler of Pictland in the mid-ninth century, though it is likely also that he had to fight his way to the top. But the main reason for the decline and fall of the kingdom of the Picts is probably that they dissipated their strength in prolonged warfare with a new set of invaders from across the sea—the Vikings.

The term *Viking* comes from the Old Norse word *vikingr*, meaning "seafaring pirate." It was in this light that all Norwegians and Danes were viewed by the ninth- and tenth-century inhabitants of the British coastal regions and especially by churchmen, who had special reason to fear the approach of the long ships from Scandinavia, with their square sails and brightly painted figureheads. *A furore Normannorum libera nos, Domine* (from the fury of the Norsemen, O Lord, deliver us!) became a regular part of Church litany during these years, for, as one Irish chronicler wrote: "Neither honor nor mercy for right of sanctuary, nor protection for Church, nor veneration for God or for man was felt by this furious, ferocious, pagan, ruthless people"—the Vikings.

Yet the first Norsemen to arrive in the British Isles were probably peaceful enough. They came as farmers from western Norway to settle in Orkney and Shetland about the year 780. Land hunger drove them the short distance across the sea (about 200–250 miles) from their native country. Then came the long ships—some bearing peaceful traders, but others carrying fighting men bent on plunder. Armed invasion and pillage were no novelties in Dark Age Britain. What made the Vikings different and especially dangerous was their ships. Some time late in the eighth century these northern seamen perfected a new type of vessel—clinker-built, with heavy keels, about eighty feet in length, and propelled by oars and auxiliary sails. The combination made them strong and steady enough for ocean sailing, shallow-drafted enough for moving into inland waters, fast enough to make a landfall without detection, and maneuverable enough to make a quick getaway safe from pursuit.

At first the primary targets of these Norse pirates were Britain's many island and coastal abbeys—reasonable enough since these holy places were both undefended and rich in treasure. The monastery at Applecross opposite the Isle of Skye took the first onslaught in 793 or 794. St. Cuthbert's foundation at Lindisfarne off the Northumbrian coast soon followed. St. Columba's famous monastery at Iona was attacked and pillaged in 795, again in 803, 806, 825, and at frequent intervals thereafter throughout the ninth and tenth centuries.

Where fertile land was easily accessible from the sea, conquest and colonization followed piracy—or rather went hand in hand with it. By the late ninth century Shetland and Orkney were firmly under Norse control. Under the Norwegian kings a semi-autonomous earldom of Orkney came into being. The first known earl was Rognvald of More, whose brother Sigurd the Mighty moved south with an army to capture Caithness and much of the coastal areas of Ross and Moray before he died near Dornoch Firth. His successor was Turf Einar, who is credited with introducing peat-burning to the islands. Other Norse nobles established sway over the Inner and the Outer Hebrides and the Isle of Man. In southwestern Scotland, Galloway was overrun by Norse settlers from Ireland. Further north, the Earls of Orkney reached the summit of their power under Sigurd the Stout, who raided deep into Scotland and died in 1014 fighting the Irish. His son, Thorfinn the Mighty, ruled until about 1064. He was the lord of Orkney, Shetland, the Hebrides, and Man, and was said to have held nine Scottish earldoms, including Caithness, Ross, a part of Moray, and Galloway.

So thorough was the Scandinavian penetration of the northern islands that the native language (Brythonic, Goidelic, or Pictish) disappeared, and a Norwegian dialect called Norn remained the dominant tongue until the end of the Middle Ages. In both Orkney and Shetland most of the place names are of Scandinavian origin. Thus, the Old Norse word for "farm," *bolstadr*, appears as *-bister*, as in *Rennibister*; *kvi* ("cattle-pen") becomes *-quoy*, as in *Okraquoy*; and *vagr* (bay) is modernized as *-voe*, as in Sullom Voe, site of the new oil terminal in Shetland. On the mainland of Scotland, Scandinavian influences were less permanent, but the names of Wick (from *vik* meaning "bay") and Dingwall (from *thing-vollr*, meaning "place of assembly") are reminders that the Norse were once rulers of Caithness and Ross. In the Outer Hebrides, and especially on Lewis, the vast majority of place names are of ultimate Norse origin, and on Skye the proportion is as high as 60 percent.

A small number of artifacts from the Viking period are to be seen in the **Shetland Museum** *(568)* in Lerwick and at **Tankerness House** *(558)* in Kirkwall, Orkney. By far the largest and best collections, however, are in the **National Museum of Antiquities** *(447)* in Edinburgh. Here is the tenth-century Skaill hoard from Orkney, containing over a hundred silver objects, including necklets of twisted silver, armlets, and penannular brooches. (A penannular brooch has a gap in the hoop through which the pin passes.) Here also is a pair of ninth-century tortoise brooches from Reay, Caithness, and five late-twelfth-century chessmen of walrus ivory found on the island of Lewis.

Archaeological remains on the ground, unfortunately, are less common. The best-preserved relic of Scandinavian farm settlement is at **Jarlshof** *(569)* in Shetland. Most of the excavated foundations in the northern half of this long-occupied site date from the Viking Age, though there was so much rebuilding here that close attention to the official guidebook is required to make any sense at all out of this maze of low stone walls surviving from farmsteads of the ninth through the twelfth centuries. On the **Brough of Birsay** *(563)*, a tiny promontory off the northwest coast of Mainland, Orkney, is another fascinating complex of ruined buildings. The site includes the foundations of two Norse houses similar to those at Jarlshof and dating probably from the ninth century; a Norse cemetery of a later date; a pre-Norse Pictish cemetery in which the famous Birsay Stone was found; the remains of a church probably built in the eleventh century by Thorfinn the Mighty over the foundations of a Celtic church and monastery of the seventh century; and the ruins of a clerical residence dating from the twelfth century, as well as those of the great hall of the earls of Orkney. By the time the clerical residence was built, the Norse settlers of Orkney (and presumably of the other Norse colonies in Britain and Ireland) had been Christians for the better part of a century. Tradition dates the beginning of their Christianization to the year 995, when the Norse king Olaf Tryggvasson offered the reigning Earl of Orkney, Sigurd the Stout, a choice between instant death and conversion. The earl of course chose the latter. This would have been more than five centuries after Christian missionaries preaching the new gospel first made their way into southern Scotland.

EARLY CHRISTIANITY IN SCOTLAND

Christianity first came to Roman Britain in the third century A.D., if not before. By the time the Roman armies had departed in the early fifth century, the Christian Church in Britain had already produced three martyrs, one heretic, and three missionary saints. The martyrs were Aaron and Julius of Caerleon and Alban of Verulamium, all Roman soldiers allegedly put to death for adhering to the new faith. The heretic was Pelagius, who preached a doctrine of free will rejected by the early Church fathers in favor of the predestinarian teachings of St. Augustine of Hippo. The missionary saints were Iltud, Patrick, and Ninian (or Nynia). Iltud is credited with the conversion of the Welsh. Patrick was a Romanized Briton who was kidnapped by Irish raiders from his father's villa on the west coast, escaped, and was eventually sent back to preach among the northern Irish. Ninian, another Romanized Briton, was, according to The Venerable Bede, "a most revered bishop, trained at Rome," who made his way north of the Solway Firth in the early years of the fifth century to convert the southern Picts.

Historians reason that, contrary to Bede, a cleric of episcopal rank would not have made this expedition except to minister to an existing Christian community and that it was probably for the benefit of such people rather than the pagan Picts that Ninian established his episcopal seat at a place known, says Bede, "as Candida Casa, the White House, because he built the church of stone which was unusual among the Britons." Ninian's church was almost certainly on the site of the now ruined thirteenth-century **Whithorn Priory** *(377)* in Wigtownshire. At the east end of this medieval building, archaeologists have discovered the foundations of a seventh-century chapel, which was probably the successor to Ninian's church, as well as a Christian burial ground that dates to the saint's time or even earlier. In the adjacent museum are a number of Early Christian tombstones, of which the earliest is the so-called Latinus Stone, dating from the mid-fifth century. The inscription on it reads: "TE DOMINU(M) LAUDA-MUS (We praise thee, Lord!)," followed by the names "LATINUS ANNO-RU(M) XXXV ET FILIA SUA ANN(ORUM) IV (Latinus, 35 years of age and his daughter 4 years old)" and then the statement "HIC SI(G)NUM

FECERUT NEPUS BARROVADI (the nephew [or grandson] of Barrovadus made this memorial).'' Also in the museum is a collection of cross-incised boulders from **St. Ninian's Cave** *(378)*, which is located about two miles west on the beach south of Glasserton. Here crosses can be seen on boulders still *in situ* as well as on the walls of the cave. It is quite possible that the saint used this place as an occasional hermitage, but the crosses are probably the handiwork of pilgrims of a later date. Not far away is the Isle of Whithorn (approached by an artificial causeway), where the ruined **St. Ninian's Chapel** *(378)* is situated. This was a simple rectangular dry-stone building, now partially restored. It dates probably from the thirteenth century and may have served as an oratory for pilgrims disembarking here before proceeding inland to Ninian's church at Whithorn. Closer in time to the saint's own life are the three crosses called the **Kirkmadrine Crosses** *(376)*, now to be seen under glass on the outside wall of the Kirkmadrine church near Sandhead, Wigtownshire. The best preserved of these dates from the fifth century and bears the inscription "HIC JACENT S(AN)C(T)I ET PRAECIPUI SACERDOTES IDES VIVENTIUS ET MAVORIUS (Here lie the holy and principal priests, Ides, Viventius and Mavorius)." Another, dating from about 600, reads "INITIUM ET FINIS" (The beginning and the end)," a quotation from the Book of Revelations.

Whether Ninian went out from Whithorn to preach the gospel among the southern Picts is unknown, but about 470 St. Patrick wrote the already mentioned letter denouncing King Corocticus of Strathclyde for allowing his soldiers to seize Irish Christians and sell them as slaves to "apostate Picts." This clearly implies that at least some Picts had been converted in the fifth century and had then reverted to paganism. Ninian may have been responsible for this conversion, though there were other missionaries at work in southern Scotland. One of these of a later date was St. Kentigern (or St. Mungo). His field of operations was Strathclyde, and tradition has him setting up a bishopric at Glasgow in the 580s. By that time the Dalriadic Scots of Argyll were receiving the gospel from the greatest of Early Christian missionaries in Scotland: St. Columba.

Columba's preeminence in the history of the Early Christian Church in Scotland is attributable not only to his undoubted personal achievement, but also to the publication, a century after his death, of a biography by Adomnan, abbot of the saint's monastic foundation at Iona. Like all early hagiographies, this is a mélange of fact and myth, but there is no disputing that its subject was a remarkable man. Born in the mountains of Donegal in northern Ireland, Columba was the great-great-grandson, on his father's side, of Niall of the Nine Hostages, the high king who ruled at Tara; and on his mother's, a descendant of the royal house of Leinster. Choosing a religious life instead of the throne to which he had some claim, he founded monasteries at Derry, Durrow, Kells, and elsewhere in Ireland. Then, at the age of forty, despite his high connections, he found himself in deep trouble. Having purloined and copied a manuscript of St. Jerome's text of the Psalter and Gospels, Columba refused to deliver up his copy when ordered to do so by the reigning High King at Tara. Instead, he incited a rebellion of his kinsmen against the king. Facing excommunication by a synod of Irish monks for contumacy, Columba chose exile as an alternative; and in 563 he sailed with a dozen companions across the Irish Sea to take refuge in Scottish Dalriada. Seeking a home beyond the sight of their native land, the wanderers settled in Iona, a tiny islet off the coast of Mull. Here they founded **Iona Abbey** *(465)*, which, for almost three centuries, was the chief center of Celtic Christianity in Britain.

Very little remains on Iona today of Columba's early foundation. Unlike the abbeys of the Middle Ages, which typically consisted of an integrated collection of stone buildings surrounding a central cloistered garth, the early Celtic monastery normally took the form of a rectangular or oval earthen rampart, the *vallum monasterii*, within which were built, mostly of wood and wattle, a hut for the abbot, cells for the individual monks, a refectory (dining room) with kitchen, a guest house, and sundry work buildings. Such undoubtedly was the original version of the monastery at Iona. Thanks, however, to repeated ravaging by Vikings, all that is left of Columba's foundation are the scant remains of what may have been the saint's own cell or sleeping place on a low hill called Torr Abb. The existing abbey church is a restoration of the thirteenth- to fifteenth-century stone building raised by Benedictine monks on the site of Columba's defunct foundation. The ruined nunnery, close to the present pier, dates from the thirteenth century. Southwest of the abbey church lies St. Oran's Cemetery, reputed burial place of numerous Dark Age Scottish kings, as well as some from Ireland and Norway. The splendid collection of late medieval grave-markers from this place has been removed to the site museum. St. Oran's Chapel lies in the middle of the cemetery; it is of twelfth- or thirteenth-century date and has been restored. In front of the church stand three ninth- or tenth-century crosses, all examples of the amalgamation of Celtic and Anglian art forms, already mentioned in connection with the Hunterston Brooch. Of these, only St. Martin's Cross is in a good state of preservation. It is a single piece of granite, standing more than fifteen feet above its base; on one face is carved a representation of the Virgin and Child and another of Daniel in the lion's den; on the other face are Celtic spirals combined with Anglian interlace. The cross is wheel-headed, and its profile should be very familiar to Presbyterians in both Scotland and America, in whose churches it has been widely copied. Of St. Matthew's Cross, only the lower part of the shaft remains, but the stone-carving is excellent. St. John's Cross is a replica; fragments of the original can be seen in the site museum.

Before Columba and his party settled on Iona, they visited Dunadd, seat of Conall, king of the Dalriadic Scots, and kinsman of the saint. When Conall died, Columba intervened to secure the election to the throne of Aidan—he who later suffered disastrous defeat at the hands of the English at Degsastan. It was undoubtedly because of the patronage of the Dalriadic royal house that Iona prospered. Although The Venerable Bede was later to credit Columba with the conversion of the northern Picts to Christianity, it is more likely that most of his apostolic labors were among his fellow Scots of Dalriada. He did reportedly make one famous journey north among the Picts and visited King Bridei at his court near Inverness, possibly at **Craig Phadrig** *(517)* or at **Burghead** *(530)*. This trip was the occasion of the saint's confounding, with the sign of The Cross, a great water-beast encountered at the head of Loch Ness. The incident, related by Adomnan, is the earliest report of the famous Loch Ness Monster. Of great significance to the purposes of Columba's voyage, however, was his contest of magic with Bridei's court priests, which the saint won handily before sailing away, miraculously, against a contrary wind. Bridei may or may not have been converted, but it seems clear at least that thereafter Columba and other Irish missionaries were free to carry on their work in Pictland and to establish monasteries in its remotest parts. One of Columba's disciples, St. Cormac, who had accompanied him to the Pictish court, was given a safe-conduct to the Orkneys. A contemporary and rival, St. Moluag, settled on the island of Lismore in the mouth of Loch Linnhe and from there travelled deep into Pictish territory to become known as "Moluag of the Hundred Monasteries." Another Irish saint, though of a later generation, was St. Maelrubha, whose scene of operations included Kintyre, Arisaig, and Skye, and who founded a famous monastery at Applecross in Ross and Cromarty.

Unfortunately, archaeological evidence of all this missionary activity is scanty and not easily accessible to the traveller. On the island of Bute, just south of Kingarth, is a site identified with St. Blane, a younger contemporary of St. Columba. **St. Blane's Church** *(396)* itself has a ruined twelfth-century nave in the Romanesque style, but on the terrace below is a circular dry-stone wall or *vallum* standing two to three feet high, as well as the foundations of what are thought to have been monastic cells. Though these probably date from the eighth century, it is believed that they belonged to the monastery founded here two centuries earlier by St. Blane. Among the Garvelloch Islands at the mouth of the Firth of Lorne lies the **Eilach-an-Naoimh Monastery** *(462)*, one of the best preserved of all Early Christian sites in Britain, though not easy to reach. Here are three round dry-stone beehive cells, a plain rectangular dry-stone chapel, and a circular grave enclosure traditionally believed to be the burial place of St. Columba's mother, Eithne. One of the grave-markers displays an incised cross of the seventh-century type, and the island is reputed to have been often visited by St. Columba, who may have founded the monastery here. On a rocky, sea-girt promontory on the eastern edge of Mainland, Orkney, is the **Brough of Deerness Monastery** *(561)*, where the foundations of nineteen rectangular buildings can be seen under the turf around a stone chapel near the center. This too is considered to be the site of a seventh- or eighth-century monastery, possibly founded by Irish missionaries. Occupying a similar situation on the west coast of Shetland is **St. Ninian's Isle** *(570)*, reached by a narrow strip of sand from the main island. The only visible ruins here are the walls of the nave and choir of a twelfth-century church, but underneath it excavators found the wall of an earlier church, and more importantly, a hoard of twenty-eight pieces of ornamented silver, now known as St. Ninian's Isle Treasure and housed in the **National Museum of Antiquities** *(447)* in Edinburgh, with replicas on display in the **Shetland Museum** *(568)* in Lerwick. The hoard consists of a hanging bowl, seven other small silver bowls, a silver spoon, a single-pronged instrument that was probably a lobster fork, a silver-gilt sword pommel, two silver chapes that served as fittings to sword scabbards, three cone-shaped objects of unknown function, and twelve penannular brooches. The metalwork is Pictish, with motifs paralleling those found on Class II slabs. One of the bowls is decorated with a large cross, indicating a Christian association. Probably the owner of the hoard was a Pictish chief, though the possibility should not be ruled out that most or all of these objects belonged to the church where they were found buried. In any case they were doubtless hidden underground to prevent their being seized by Viking pirates. There is little doubt either that the church underneath which they were concealed suffered the same fate as Iona and Lindisfarne and countless other Celtic monasteries scattered along the vulnerable coastline of northern Britain.

Lindisfarne, off the Northumbrian coast near the old Bernician capital at Bamburgh, had been founded about 634 by St. Aidan and a company of monks from Iona. They had been invited there by King Oswald of Bernicia, who had been converted to Christianity during a period of forced exile in Scotland. When he returned to power in his native country, Oswald relied on Columba's successors to spread the gospel among the heathen English. His brother Oswiu, who became King of Northumbria after the amalgamation of Bernicia and Deira, continued the work of Christianization not only in his own realm but southward into the English Midlands and East Anglia. Thus by the 660s the influence of Iona had spread from Argyll south to the River Thames.

At this point, however, missionaries trained in the Celtic tradition fostered by Columba came into contact and conflict with other Christian clerics who owed allegiance to Canterbury. By happenstance the year of Columba's death (597) had coincided with the arrival on the shores of Kent of St. Augustine, whose church at Canterbury was eventually to become the ecclesiastical center of England. He came as the special envoy of Pope Gregory the Great to spread the faith in this pagan land—a task that he performed with remarkable success in spite of the hostility of preexisting Christian communities in southern Britain. Augustine and the churchmen who followed him at Canterbury were of course in close touch with Rome. The successors of Columba and Aidan were not. Though the Celtic Church of Scotland, Ireland, and Wales was orthodox in doctrine, it diverged somewhat in practice from the mainstream of Roman Catholicism. For one thing, its organization was far less centralized. The Roman church was divided into territorial dioceses, each headed by a bishop, who was normally responsible to a metropolitan archbishop, who in turn answered to the Pope in Rome—the Vicar of Christ on earth, heir of St. Peter the Apostle, and hence keeper of the keys to the kingdom of heaven. Bishops there were in the Celtic Church, but their powers were mostly limited to consecrating churches and cemeteries and ordaining other clergymen. Real leadership was vested in the abbots who were heads of the numerous monastic foundations that flourished throughout the Celtic fringe and especially in Ireland. These monasteries were independent of each other, and there were no archbishops to impose uniformity of practice upon them. So it was that, when the Church of Rome changed the method of calculating the date of Easter, most of the Celtic monasteries felt under no obligation to follow suit. Thus, throughout Britain and Ireland, this, the most important feast-day in the Christian calendar, was celebrated on different Sundays, sometimes weeks apart. This was no trivial matter. The Christian religion was founded on a belief in the historicity of the life, death, and resurrection of Jesus of Nazareth, and if the date of His rising from the dead were in doubt, the unconverted could more easily reject the entire case for His divinity.

To resolve this issue (and the less important matter of clerical tonsure) in Northumberland, King Oswiu held a synod of eminent churchmen at Whitby Abbey in 664. Roman and Celtic spokesmen argued the case. In the end the king decided in favor of the former—chiefly, it would seem, for fear that otherwise St. Peter might bar the gates of heaven to him. The Council of Whitby was a turning point. Thereafter the recalcitrant Celtic churches in Britain and Ireland gradually yielded on the question of Easter. In Strathclyde, the Roman usages were adopted about 688. In Pictland, King Nechtan decreed the expulsion from his realm of all nonconformists in 717, and soon thereafter the monks of Iona agreed to the new method for calculating Easter, thus bringing the Scottish church into line with Rome. It was probably about this time that Nechtan imported Northumbrian masons to build the church near Forfar, which was later incorporated into **Restenneth Priory** *(511)*. The ruined choir here dates from the twelfth century, but the lower half of the high tower was constructed probably in the early part of the eighth as the *porticus* of a church built in the Anglo-Saxon manner.

Parallel to the partial Romanization of the Church in Scotland, and possibly a reflection of it, was the spread northward, across the border, of Anglian art forms, especially manifest in monumental sculpture. Northumbrian stone-carvers in the seventh and eighth centuries developed a unique style that paralleled contemporary fashions in the field of manuscript art, as exemplified in the Lindisfarne Gospels now in the British Museum in London. Although the style contained some elements of Roman naturalism and Celtic curvilinear abstractionism, its chief inspiration appears to have been Germanic—as manifested in the frequent use of interlace patterns, either geometrical or naturalistic. Into the latter category falls the most typical of Anglian motifs—the "inhabited vine-scroll," an intricate design of intertwining foliage peopled with birds and beasts.

Freestanding stone crosses decorated in the Anglian manner are perhaps the handsomest of all Early Christian relics in Scotland. The most remarkable of these is the **Ruthwell Cross** *(385)*, which stands inside the parish church of Ruthwell in Dumfriesshire. Now restored after having been partially mutilated by Protestant fanatics in the seventeenth century, the cross stands fifteen feet high and is illuminated with floodlights. It is mostly covered with sculpted scenes from the Bible and the lives of the saints: Christ in Glory, Christ with Mary Magdalene washing his feet, Christ healing the blind man, Christ on the Cross, the Annunciation, the Visitation of Mary, John the Baptist, St. John the Evangelist, Saints Paul and Anthony in the desert. The sides are beautifully decorated with inhabited vine-scroll, and along the edges, in Scandinavian runic letters appear the first seventy-eight lines of the earliest known of English religious poems, "The Dream of the Rood." The date of the cross is late seventh or early eighth century. Also in Dumfriesshire, near the village of Thornhill, is **Nith Bridge Cross** *(387)*, of Anglian design dating from the late ninth century. It stands about eight feet high in an open field near the bridge. The cross arms have disappeared, but the shaft is decorated on all sides with intertwined foliage and animals, now somewhat difficult to trace because of the overgrowth of lichen. A finer specimen, though not easy to reach, is the **Kildalton Cross** *(466)* on the island of Islay, Argyll, near the village of Ardbeg north of Port Ellen. This, like St. Martin's Cross at Iona, is a wheel-cross; that is, the intersection of its vertical and horizontal members is enclosed by an open stone circle. This type of construction is incorrectly labelled "Celtic," whereas in fact it was common among English and Scandinavian standing crosses as well—

largely, one suspects, for the very practical reason that the four arcs of the wheel served as structural supports for the cross arms to prevent their easily breaking off. In this case both Celtic and Anglian motifs were employed by the stone-carvers: Celtic curves and spirals on the lower part of the shaft, Anglian interlace around the boss at the center, inhabited vine-scroll work on the back, and naturalistic representations of several biblical scenes—also on the back. For those travellers unwilling to undertake the ferry trip across to Islay, copies of the Kildalton Cross are to be seen at both the **National Museum of Antiquities** *(447)* in Edinburgh and the **Glasgow Art Gallery and Museum** *(407)*. Other repositories of Early Christian crosses in Scotland are the **Dumfries Museum** *(383)*, Dumfriesshire; **Govan Old Parish Church** *(400)*, near Glasgow; the **Meigle Museum** *(501)* in Perthshire; **St. Vigeans Museum** *(508)*, near Arbroath, Angus; and the site museum at **St. Andrew's Cathedral** *(491)* in Fife. At the last named is housed also the magnificent "St. Andrew's Sarcophagus." This probably dates from the tenth century, in spite of the tradition that it contained the relics of St. Andrew, allegedly brought to this place by St. Rule (St. Regulus) in the eighth century. (More likely the bones and their container were transferred here by Bishop Acca from his Church of St. Andrew in Hexham, Northumberland.) In any case, the stone sarcophagus with its fine carvings of the biblical hero David is a splendid example of Celtic *cum* Anglian artwork.

The site of the eleventh-century Church of St. Rule and the ancient cathedral ruin of a later date was, in the eighth century, occupied by a community of monks known as Culdees. Their name derives from the Gaelic term *Celi De*, meaning "servants of God." The order (if such a loosely organized body of clergymen can be called an order) originated in Ireland. Not much is known about the rules by which they lived, except that marriage was apparently permitted to the clergy and some of their rites differed from those authorized by Rome. In this sense, the Culdees represent a retrogression from the Romanization of the Scottish Church following the Council of Whitby. In any case, at several important religious centers in Pictland—Lochleven, Monymusk, Abernethy, Dunkeld, Brechin, St. Andrews, and elsewhere—they appear in the role of clerics soon after Kenneth mac Alpin's amalgamation of the Scottish and Pictish kingdoms about 841. It was around this time too that King Kenneth is thought to have brought to Dunkeld the relics of St. Columba, which had somehow been saved from the Vikings during their numerous onslaughts on Iona. Among these precious objects was the so-called Monymusk Reliquary, now to be seen at the **National Museum of Antiquities** *(447)* in Edinburgh. This is a small wooden box, encased in bronze and decorated with engraved silver and red and yellow enamel. It is probably the object referred to in ancient charters as the *Brecbennoch*, which was carried into battle by Scottish armies as a sort of totem as late as 1314 at the Battle of Bannockburn.

Kenneth mac Alpin's successors were no less supportive than he of the Celtic tradition in the Christian Church. Evidence of this can be seen in two great round church towers of probable tenth-century date—"outward and visible signs," says the architectural historian W. Douglas Simpson, "of the infiltration of the Columban Church into the ancient centers of Pictish Christianity during the period following the union of Pictland and Dalriada in 841 under the Scotic hegemony of Kenneth mac Alpin and his successors." Architecturally these round towers are affiliated with Irish prototypes of the same period, and functionally they served no doubt as refuges for clergymen and their possessions in times of threatened Viking incursions. The **Brechin Round Tower** *(508)* is attached to **Brechin Cathedral** *(508)* in Angus—a much restored thirteenth-century edifice now serving as a parish church. Originally the tower was probably freestanding. Its spire was added in the fourteenth century. The round-headed door is set some distance off the ground—an obvious measure of defense, since the ladder to it easily could have been pulled up once the occupants and their treasure were inside. Above the arch of the doorway is a sculpted relief of the crucified Jesus, the legs uncrossed in the manner of Irish stone-workers. On either side is the figure of a clergyman, presumably a bishop, and crouching beasts flank the bottom. The tower (not open to the public) is seven stories high, each floor originally connected to the one below by wooden ladders. The freestanding **Abernethy Round Tower** *(497)* in Perthshire lacks any sculptural decoration. Its upper parts are also a later addition.

More significant than these buildings, however, is the fact that clergymen trained in the Columban tradition brought literacy into Pictland in the ninth and tenth centuries. With the spread of both Latin and Gaelic, spoken language could be reproduced in writing, with incalculable effects not only on organized religion but also on the institutionalization of government. Though the successors to Kenneth mac Alpin could hardly be classified as enlightened rulers in the modern, or even medieval, sense, neither were they Dark Age barbaric chieftains scarcely distinguishable from their Iron Age predecessors. The kingdom over which they ruled was now called *Alba* (or *Albany*) by Irish annalists and usually *Scotia* by English chroniclers. By either name it was to become in the tenth and eleventh centuries the dominant political entity of North Britain.

THE KINGDOM OF ALBA: 841–1057

To the early kings of Alba must be given the same credit that historians have bestowed on Alfred the Great of Wessex. Like him, they saved their country from absorption by Scandinavian invaders in the ninth century and thus laid the foundation for its expansion in the tenth. The geographic center of their power was in Perthshire and Angus. Although they established no single "capital," they made of Scone, near the modern city of Perth, the ceremonial seat of royal authority. It was to this place, according to legend, that Kenneth mac Alpin brought from Dunstaffnage in Argyll the "Stone of Scone" upon which all Scottish kings were inaugurated until 1292, after which Edward I of England removed it to Westminster Abbey, where it still resides.

That the Vikings raided deep into the Alban kingdom in the ninth century is well known, but how often and to what effect is uncertain. By the end of the tenth century, at any rate, Scandinavian expansion onto mainland Scotland appears to have lost its momentum, and perhaps some sort of peace was established when Sigurd the Stout, Earl of Orkney, married the daughter of Malcolm II, King of Alba. Their son was Thorfinn the Mighty, who seems to have been on amicable terms with the kings of Alba. (He was probably an ally of King Macbeth, and his daughter [or widow] married Malcolm Canmore, Macbeth's successor.)

With Scandinavian pressure relaxing, the kings of Alba in the tenth and eleventh centuries devoted most of their energies to expanding their dominion southward into territories occupied by the Northumbrian English and the Strathclyde Britons. English dominance in Lothian (roughly the territory between the Tweed and the Forth) was checked and then reversed as the kings of Alba, and the Scotto-Pictish people over whom they reigned, began to move south. The process was probably gradual, though a few incidents are traditionally held to have been critical to the absorption of Lothian into the kingdom that would become known as Scotland. About the middle of the tenth century the fortress of Edinburgh was laid waste by an army from the North, and thereafter it remained in Scottish possession. King Malcolm I of Alba (943-954) is usually given credit for the conquest. It was he also to whom King Edmund of Wessex reportedly "let" Cumbria or at least that portion of it lying north of the Solway Firth. In 973 another English ruler, the powerful King Edgar, is supposed to have granted Lothian to the Alban king, Kenneth II (971-995) in return for some sort of acknowledgment of fealty. Then, in 1018, King Malcolm II won a battle against the English at Carham, Northumberland, and thereafter there was no doubt that the effective rule of the kings of Alba stretched at least as far south as the River Tweed. In the same year the King of Strathclyde died without heirs, and Malcolm, in effect, annexed the kingdom to his own.

It was the death of this Malcolm II that precipitated a succession crisis that brought about civil war in his kingdom. (Thus was set the scene for one of Shakespeare's greatest tragedies, and the one in which the Bard most shamelessly sacrificed the facts of history to dramatic license and the exigencies of Jacobean politics.) Malcolm's grandson Duncan II succeeded to the throne, only to be killed by Macbeth, Mormaer (or Earl) of Moray, whose own claim to the throne was reinforced by that of his wife Gruoch, daughter or granddaughter of Malcolm's predecessor. Macbeth held the throne for seventeen years and is thought to have been a worthy king. Duncan's son, another Malcolm, nicknamed "Canmore" or "Big-head," had been dispatched to his mother's homeland, Northumbria, for safekeeping. Grown to manhood, he returned with an English army in 1054 to claim his father's throne. He defeated Macbeth in a battle possibly near Dunsinane in Perthshire and killed him three years later in another foray at Lumphanan, Aberdeenshire. The following year (1058) he also killed Lulach, the son of Macbeth's wife by her first husband—thereby eliminating the chief rival contestant to the throne. He then, as Malcolm III, became uncontested ruler of the Scottish kingdom and progenitor of a long line of kings. It is significant, however, that only with English support had Malcolm Canmore gained his throne. Scotland thus entered the Middle Ages under the shadow of her southern neighbor. She would never fully emerge therefrom.

Chapter Three
The Early Middle Ages
War and Politics
1057–1296

The Scottish Succession: 1057–1290
Malcolm III (1057–1093)
Donald Bane (1093–1097)
Duncan II (1094)
Edgar (1097–1107)
Alexander I (1107–1124)
David I (1124–1153)
Malcolm IV (1153–1165)
William I (1165–1214)
Alexander II (1214–1249)
Alexander III (1249–1286)
Margaret, Maid of Norway (1286–1290)

On the grounds of **Scone Palace** *(506)*, a Georgian-Gothic mansion just north of Perth, stands the Moot Hill of Scone, probable site of the inauguration in 1057 of Malcolm III as King of Scots. The traditional ceremony, harking back to the ninth century, was more pagan than Christian. No crown would have been set on Canmore's (Big-Head's) brow. Nor would he have been anointed with holy oil—a right denied to Scottish kings by the Pope until 1329. Instead, the new king would have been "set upon the stone," that is, the Stone of Destiny, thought by some to have been the patriarch Jacob's pillow, long ago transported from the Holy Land to Spain, thence to Ireland, thence to Scottish Dalriada, and finally to this sacred mound in Perthshire. It is a block of coarse, red sandstone, later seized and carried off by King Edward I of England and now reposing in Westminster Abbey, where it is incorporated within the coronation chair of Britain's kings and queens. After his installation, the new King of Scots was probably approached by a Highland bard or *seannachie* and hailed in the Gaelic tongue as Malcolm, son of Duncan, son of Bethoc, daughter of Malcolm, son of Kenneth, and so on, back through a long line of real and mythical ancestors to Fergus, son of Erc, traditional founder of the Scottish monarchy. (Imaginary likenesses of these ancient kings, as well as portraits of their historic successors, were painted by Jacob de Wet in the seventeenth century and are still to be seen in the picture gallery of the **Palace of Holyroodhouse** *[442]* in Edinburgh.)

Malcolm Canmore would need whatever legitimacy these archaic rites could bestow. For, though he had disposed of his immediate rivals, Macbeth and Lulach, his grip over the land he claimed to rule was tenuous at best, and even its geographic boundaries were indeterminate. Orkney and Shetland off the north coast, and the Hebrides off the west, belonged clearly to the King of Norway, while Scandinavians of uncertain allegiance were well entrenched on the Scottish mainland as far south as the Cromarty Firth. The western Highlands, original homeland of the Dalriadic Scots, were too remote to be governed from Perthshire or from Malcolm's "castle" in Dunfermline, Fife, built upon a mound still visible in **Pittencrieff Park** *(487)*. In the extreme Southwest, and almost equally out of reach, lived a notoriously ferocious people of mixed Norse and Irish ancestry called the "foreign Gael," or *gall ghadil*, from whom this region of Galloway derived its name. South of Dumbarton lay the ancient British kingdom of Strathclyde, which Canmore's great-grandfather, Malcolm II, had annexed to Alba. South of Strathclyde lay Cumbria, and since none could say where the borderline between them lay, the King of Scots claimed lordship over the entire region as far as the modern English county of Lancashire. East of Cumbria and south of Scottish Lothian was the English earldom of Northumbria, where Canmore had spent his youth in exile and toward which his territorial ambitions ran.

A Northumbrian dialect of English was probably the dominant language in Lothian, the region between the Rivers Tweed and Forth. In central Scotland and much of the West Gaelic was the native tongue, but in the Far North and in the western isles Norse was widely spoken and in the northern islands it was universal, while the Welsh language (Brythonic) still held out in the Southwest. A common Christianity provided some degree of cultural unity to this conglomerate of disparate peoples, but the Church was still highly decentralized and incapable of imparting substantial coherence. If any sort of unity was to be imposed on the kingdom of Scotland, it would have to be the Scottish kings who did the job. This was to be the mission— and the great accomplishment—of Canmore and his successors.

The first duty of a medieval king—beyond that of mere survival—was to establish an undisputed hereditary succession. Not yet institutionalized in the eleventh century was the principle of primogeniture, whereby the eldest son of a king automatically inherited the kingdom. In Alba an altogether different rule of succession had obtained. By the custom known as *tanistry*, any adult male whose father, grandfather, or great-grandfather had been king was eligible for kingship, and the strongest and best among such claimants would normally succeed on the death of the reigning monarch. This practice had the advantage of precluding succession by minor children and of guaranteeing that the new king would be a fit military leader. It had the disadvantage of encouraging the assassination of reigning kings by their putative successors—which is, of course, what happened to both Duncan (Canmore's grandfather) and Macbeth. Prudence alone, therefore, would suggest that a king produce sons and that steps be taken to ensure that the eldest among them would succeed to the throne.

In this respect, Malcolm III was not remiss. By his first wife, Ingibiorg, daughter, or possibly widow, of Thorfinn the Mighty, Earl of Orkney, he had three sons, two of whom survived him. His second wife, Margaret, an Anglo-Saxon princess, bore him six sons. Nevertheless, after Malcolm's death in 1093 all his sons were at first set aside. Scottish magnates drove out the English followers of Queen Margaret and chose as king Donald Bane ("the fair"), Canmore's younger brother. Duncan, the king's eldest son by Ingibiorg—long a hostage at the court of King William the Conqueror of England and his son William Rufus—now came north with an army supplied by Rufus, ousted his uncle, and reigned for a few months as Duncan II before being slain by a follower of Donald Bane, who again came to the throne. The eldest surviving son of Canmore and Queen Margaret was Edgar, also a refugee in the court of William Rufus. With another army supplied by the English king, he too invaded Scotland, captured and blinded his uncle Donald, and ruled for ten years (1097-1107) as King Edgar.

From that time until almost the end of the thirteenth century, Scotland was ruled by a series of kings, all direct descendants of Malcolm Canmore and Margaret. Edgar died a bachelor and was succeeded by his brother, Alexander I (1107-1124), on whose death without legitimate issue the throne passed to the youngest brother, David I (1124-1153). During David's reign, rebellions broke out in the northern province of Moray, led by Earl Angus, son of Lulach's daughter, allied with Malcolm MacHeth, possibly an illegitimate son of Alexander I. Angus was killed and Malcolm captured and imprisoned. These threats to the principle of primogeniture were serious enough to induce King David to cause his eldest son, Henry, Earl of Huntingdon, to be declared "king designate." When Henry predeceased his father, David had his grandson, aged eleven, taken through Scotland at the head of an army to establish his claim to hereditary succession. This was Malcolm IV (1153-1165), nicknamed "the Maiden" because he never married nor showed any signs of wanting to. On Malcolm's death without issue, the throne passed to his next eldest brother, William, called "the Lion," probably because he was the first of Scotland's kings to display the heraldic device that came to be the royal arms of Scotland: a red lion rampant on a field of gold. In his and his successor's reigns occurred the last attempts to unseat the dynasty founded by Malcolm Canmore and Queen Margaret. They were led by the MacWilliams, progeny of a son of King Duncan, Canmore's son by Ingibiorg. All together there were three MacWilliam uprisings—all ruthlessly suppressed by the reigning monarchs. There were then no more pretenders to the Scottish throne in the twelfth and thirteenth centuries.

By the early thirteenth century, then, succession by primogeniture had been confirmed by custom. But as a guarantor of peaceful succession to the monarch, the principle was useful only so long as kings continued to produce legitimate heirs, preferably male. Unlike his brother, William the Lion was not remiss in the matter of paternity. But most of his children were bastards, and though he did sire four legitimate offspring by Queen Joanna, three of them were daughters. His only son by this marriage succeeded as Alexander II (1214-1249), and he in turn had only one son, who came to the throne as Alexander III (1249-1286).

It was the death of Alexander III and the circumstances surrounding it that demonstrated how very much the safety of the Scottish realm depended on the procreative abilities of its kings. Alexander lost his first wife, Margaret, in 1275; six years later their second son, David, died without issue; in 1283 their daughter Margaret, Queen of Norway, died giving birth to another Margaret, known as "the Maid of Norway"; the following year the heir apparent, Lord Alexander, died, also without issue. This rapid near-depletion of the royal line was a disaster that the king sought to repair by taking a new young bride—Yolande, daughter of the Comte de Dreux. On the night of 19 March 1286—only a few months after his marriage, Alexander, no doubt conscious of his royal responsibilities, hastened away from a late meeting of his council in Edinburgh Castle to rejoin Yolande at Kinghorn on the far shore of the Firth of Forth. He ferried across in a blizzard, then set out impatiently on horseback through the black night. Along the way his horse stumbled or reared, the king was thrown, his neck broken, and he died forthwith.

Six weeks later the magnates of the realm met at Scone; acknowledged Margaret, the infant Maid of Norway, as heir to the kingdom; and appointed a Committee of Guardians to govern the country until she could be properly inaugurated as queen. When the Maid also died—in Orkney en route to Scotland—the late king's bloodline ran out. In the ensuing contest for the throne, King Edward I of England seized the opportunity to assert his claim to feudal lordship over Scotland. The Scots resisted. And so began almost seven decades of intermittent English invasion that were to leave Scotland a devastated and impoverished country.

Malcolm III and his successors had shaped Scotland into an independent and viable nation. When the Canmore line gave out, the ensuing chaos was proof enough of the country's dependence on a self-perpetuating monarchy as an essential prop to a stable and secure society. After the event, men and women in Scotland looked back on the death of Alexander III as the end of a Golden Age. "Quhen Alysandyr our Kyng was dede," wrote an anonymous elegist in the earliest known piece of Scottish poetry, "That Scotland led in luve and le [law]/ Away was sons [abundance] of ale and brede/ Of wyne and wax, of gaymyn and gle/ Our gold was changyd in to lede." Then, on a final note of desperation:

> Chryst, borne in to Vyrgynyte,
> Succoure Scotland, and remede
> That stad is in perplexyte.

Here was the *cri de coeur* of a bereft nation: kingless, defenseless, and afraid.

THE FEUDAL KINGDOM

Of the three sons of Malcolm and Margaret who succeeded to the Scottish throne, only the last left an indelible impression on the country's history. This was David I, who reigned from 1124 to 1153. Most of his youth and young manhood had been spent in the English court after the marriage of King Henry I to his sister Edith (called Maud or Matilda by the Normans, who could not pronounce her name). Already endowed by his royal brothers with most of Lothian and Strathclyde, the young prince became one of the richest men in all of Britain when King Henry gave him in marriage to Maud, daughter of the Earl of Northumbria and grand-niece of William the Conqueror. Maud brought to her new (and second) husband a claim to the earldom of Northumbria and clear title to the honour of Huntingdon, which included extensive estates in Northamptonshire and other Midland counties. The homage owed for these lands to Henry I and his successors would in time greatly complicate relations between Scotland and England after David became King of Scots. The more immediate effect of his lordship over these English properties was to provide the new Earl of Huntingdon with a retinue of Anglo-Norman knights who accompanied him to Scotland when he inherited that kingdom from his brother, Alexander I. These were mostly the land-hungry younger sons of those land-hungry Norman warriors who had joined William the Bastard in his conquest of England. They now saw in Scotland opportunities for self-enrichment of the same sort that had induced their fathers to cross the English Channel in 1066 and the years thereafter. Thus began what some historians have called "the Norman Conquest of Scotland," although *penetration* or perhaps *infiltration* might be an apter term than *conquest*.

Thus Robert de Brus (Bruce), whose family came from the Cotentin Peninsula, was awarded the broad valley of the River Annan south of the present town of Moffat in Dumfriesshire; Robert Avenel received the Esk valley immediately to the east; Ranulf de Sules got Liddisdale in Roxburgh-shire; while he in turn had a neighbor to the northwest in Hugh de Morville who was also awarded the district of Lauderdale in Berwickshire. All of the above were Norman or of Norman extraction, as were William and Walter de Lindsey, David Olifard (Oliphant), William Comyn, and William de Graham. Among the most favored of the new arrivals in King David's entourage was Walter fitz Alan, younger son of a Shropshire baron born in Brittany. To him were given extensive holdings in Renfrewshire and East Lothian. David also endowed him with the office of high steward, which later became hereditary and to which the family's name of Stewart (or Stuart) is owed. Another Breton to be awarded land was Walter de Bidun; while from Flanders came one Freskin, who got lands in West Lothian and later in Moray, from which the family took the name de Moravia, later shortened to Moray or Murray.

The precedent set by David I was followed by his first two successors. Malcolm IV divided much of the valley of the upper Clyde among a group of Flemings, with names like Theobald, Finemund, Baldwin, Thankard, and Lambin. His brother, William the Lion, elevated the families of de Hay, de Berkeley (later Barclay), de Mortimer, and Gifford. By the beginning of the thirteenth century, then, a large share of the best real estate in Scotland (the Border counties, the Clyde valley, Lothian, Fife, Perthshire, Angus, eastern Aberdeenshire, and the coastal plain of the Moray Firth) had been parcelled out among large land-holders of Norman, Breton, and Flemish extraction by the process known as *feudalization*.

The word *feudalism* derives from the Latin *feudum*, translated as *fief* in French and *fee* in English. It is a word coined much later by lawyers and historians to describe an arrangement common to Western Europe in the Middle Ages, whereby kings, dukes, counts, and the like distributed lands to their vassals in return for services, chiefly military. Both the grants of land and the obligations incurred by the recipients (vassals) were heritable. In theory the king owned all the land in his realm and gave it out in return for services rendered and expected, mostly knight service in his feudal host (army). If heirs of the original grantee should fail, the land reverted (escheated) to the king. If the heir was a minor, the rights and profits from the estate returned to the king until the heir came of age. If the vassal died leaving an unmarried heiress, the king had the right to arrange her marriage on whatever terms were profitable to him. If a vassal rebelled or committed treason, his estates were forfeited to the king—a royal perquisite of great importance in Scottish history. A vassal could, however, subdivide his property among vassals of his own, in which case he became lord with the same rights vis-à-vis his grantees as the king enjoyed against him—except, of course, the right of forfeiture for treason.

In England King William I could plausibly claim to own all the land because he had conquered it. In short order he dispossessed the ancient Anglo-Saxon nobility, kept much of the best of their properties for himself, and redistributed most of the rest to his followers. The process of feudalization was therefore quick and thorough. In Scotland it was otherwise. Feudalism came gradually. There seems to have been no wholesale dispossession of the old Celtic nobility of Alba. Possibly David I settled most of his Anglo-Norman followers on royal demesnes in Lothian and Strathclyde. Not until the reigns of his grandsons, Malcolm the Maiden and William the Lion, was an active policy of colonization north of the Clyde-Forth line pursued.

Most of the Celtic mormaers kept their titles (eventually to be called *earls*) and much of their local power. Only gradually were they brought within the feudal system as the kings confirmed by royal charter the lands already possessed by inheritance from time immemorial. Many of the old earldoms remained with the ancient Celtic families: Lennox, Atholl, Strathearn, Fife, Mar, Ross, and Caithness. Others were taken over by the Anglo-Norman newcomers, often by marriage to native heiresses: Carrick by the Bruces; Buchan by the Comyns; Angus by the Umfravilles.

This slow fusion of Anglo-Norman and Celtic blood and institutions was to have a profound, if immeasurable, effect on Scottish history. In the more primitive Celtic society, rights and duties had tended to be defined in terms of blood relationship rather than territorial possession. Old habits die hard. So it was that the rigid distinctions between lords and vassals inherent in feudalism were to some extent in Scotland transcended by ties of kinship. Another significant difference between Scottish and English feudalism was the size of the average fief. Whereas south of the border the tendency was for the king to grant huge estates to his barons or tenants-in-chief in return for the services of sizable contingents of armed knights, the Scottish king quite often enfeoffed men with relatively small properties in exchange for a single knight's service or even a fraction thereof. This policy created a large class of barons or tenants-in-chief who, though equal in legal status to the greatest magnates of the land, were men of considerably less substance than their counterparts in England and were closer in wealth and status to freemen of lesser rank.

But similarities between England and Scotland in the twelfth century were more marked than differences. Like his English counterparts, David I fostered trade by granting charters to royal burghs. These were tiny agglomerations of houses and commercial establishments, not necessarily surrounded by walls, usually growing up around a marketplace designated by a mercat (market) cross, often situated in the neighborhood of a royal castle, and populated most likely with English or Flemish immigrants. Royal charters gave their inhabitants a monopoly of trade and manufacture within the burgh, as well as within extensive areas of surrounding countryside. (This custom accounts in part for the relative paucity of nucleated villages in medieval Scotland, at least in those regions where burghal charters had been granted liberally.) Burghs enjoyed the right to levy tolls on all commercial traffic; and from these tolls, as well as from rents from burghal lands, the king derived most of his money revenues. Burghers were outside the reach of feudal jurisdiction; if a man—even a former serf—lived there unchallenged for a year and a day, no lord could claim him as his man. David I, no doubt for fiscal reasons, was especially liberal in granting burghal charters. By the end of his reign, Berwick, Roxburgh, Edinburgh, Stirling, Rutherlgen, Dunfermline, and Aberdeen had all been incorporated, and to this list Dumfries, Ayr, and Dundee were soon to be added. Of all these early royal burghs, Berwick, Roxburgh, Edinburgh, and Stirling were the most important and acquired distinctive status as "The Four Burghs" with a special court to settle interburghal disputes, regulate weights and measures, etc. There were also ecclesiastical burghs, e.g., St. Andrews and Glasgow, founded by bishops or abbots acting under royal authority. Other burghs owed their charters to nobles—again acting with royal permission. (Later these would be called *burghs of barony*.)

By the end of David's reign too there had appeared the new royal office of sheriff, also derived from English models. The sheriff collected the king's rents, held court in the name of the king, and in general administered royal business from one of the king's castles, of which he was the chatelain. The area of his jurisdiction was called a *sheriffdom*, which eventually became the modern shire, or county, a unit of administration that remained in existence in Scotland until 1975. No royal castles, unfortunately, survive from this era, although the sites of some of them, Stirling and Edinburgh, for example, still contain castles of a much later date of construction. But each incoming Anglo-Norman baron also had his castle, and the sites of over two hundred are known. These are the so-called motte-and-bailey castles, and enough survives of several of them to warrant on-site inspection by the traveller.

The classic motte-and-bailey castle, probably a product of the Norman Conquest and certainly common in late-eleventh- and early-twelfth-century England, consisted of two parts: the motte or mound and the palisaded enclosure or bailey in which the motte was situated. The motte could be a natural hillock levelled at the top or an artificial mound of earth, circular or oval in plan and with a flat top of varying dimensions. At the summit of the motte, and within an encircling palisade, usually stood a wooden tower; around its base was a ditch, either dry or water-filled. A flying bridge of timber normally spanned the ditch. The bailey, within which the motte stood, was protected by its own palisade and exterior ditch. Stout gates would guard the entrance to the bailey and perhaps the motte end of the flying bridge as well. The tower rising above the motte would provide the elevation necessary for purposes of observing the surrounding countryside and launching or dropping missiles in case of attack.

Nothing, of course, remains of these timbered structures. But there are in Scotland, as already mentioned, a number of surviving mottes that are worth a visit. Among the best of these is the **Mote of Urr** *379)*, a few miles north of Dalbeattie, Kirkcudbrightshire. This is a conspicuous circular mound, more than thirty feet high and about eighty-five feet in diameter at the summit. Motte and bailey are each surrounded by a wide ditch. East of here, in Roxburghshire, is **Hawick Mote** *(412)*, situated in Mote Park in the town of Hawick. This is a truncated cone about twenty-five feet high with a flat top measuring about fifty feet across. The ditch around the base is barely visible, and there is nothing left to distinguish the bailey.

Aberdeenshire, though well north of the original Anglo-Norman colonization, contains some of the best of Scotland's motte-and-bailey sites. Moving from west to east, we begin with the **Doune of Invernochty** *(439)*, north of Ballater. It was the *caput* (headquarters) of one of the great feudal lordships of the province of Mar. Here the motte is sixty feet high, and its oval summit measures about three-quarters of an acre in area. A wide and deep ditch surrounds the motte, but again there is no observable bailey. The most interesting feature here is the stone wall (now mostly turf-covered) that girdles the summit. This is doubtless the ruin of a shell keep, common enough in England, but rare in Scotland. A shell keep is nothing more than a stone replacement for the timber palisades originally surrounding the motte. About 20 miles east is the **Peel of Lumphanan** *(542)*, north of Kincardine O'Neil and close to the spot where (Shakespeare to the contrary) Macbeth was overtaken and killed by Malcolm Canmore. Here is a large, circular earthen mound about thirty feet in height surrounded by a wide ditch contained by an earthen bank. There is a shallow outer ditch as well, which presumably encircled the original bailey. Again, a stone wall girdles the summit of the mound, no doubt a replacement for the original palisade. Inside are the foundations of a large stone hall, also presumably a later substitution for the original timber tower. Overlooking the River Don in the cemetery southeast of Inverurie is the **Bass of Inverurie** *(541)*, another example of a well-defined motte. It now stands fifty feet high with a summit diameter of about sixty feet.

In Moray, also colonized by David I, appears perhaps the most spectacular of all Norman mottes in Scotland. This is **Duffus Castle** *(528)*, near Elgin. Here, about 1150, Freskin, a Flemish immigrant who had settled first in West Lothian, built a castle, presumably of wood. About a century and a half later, his successor to the lordship of Duffus, Sir Reginald le Chen, raised the high stone keep whose ruins are still to be seen. Obviously the early motte was not solidly enough packed to bear the weight of such a heavy stone building. Some time after its erection, the earth subsided, and a considerable part of the keep broke off and slipped bodily down the slope toward the deep ditch surrounding the motte.

While the English in the twelfth century were almost universally substituting stone for wood in their new castles, the Scots for the most part seem to have stayed with timber. Explanations for this anomaly can only be hazarded. Scotland was a poorer and more sparsely populated country; neither its kings nor its barons were as rich as their English counterparts. Possibly its labor force was less easily mustered and disciplined than the Anglo-Saxon peasantry. Also, it should be noted, some stone castles may have been built and subsequently destroyed without a trace. In any case, it is noteworthy that in Scotland today, the only ruined stone castles of twelfth-century provenance are situated in areas that were then either not Scottish at all or beyond the effective control of its Normanized kings.

The first and probably the oldest of these is **Cubbie Roo's Castle** *(565)*, on the tiny island of Wyre off the coast of the Mainland of Orkney. There is good documentary evidence that this was built between 1143 and 1148 by a Norseman named Kolbein Hruga, whom the *Orkneyinga Saga* describes as "the most outstanding of men." The present ruins consist of the lower portions of a small tower, only twenty-five feet square, with walls five feet thick and rising to a height of seven feet. There is no entrance to the ground floor, so presumably there was a door reached by ladder to the now missing floor above. Possibly of about the same date and probably of Norse origin also is the **Castle of Old Wick** *(553)*, standing on a rocky promontory overlooking the North Sea just south of Wick in Caithness. Here too there is no visible entrance, though the walls rise to a height of thirty or forty feet. Beam holes for an intermediate floor, and scarcements for the two upper floors, can be seen in the interior faces of the walls. Still another twelfth-century coastal fortification is **Castle Sween** *(468)*, overlooking the Sound of Jura in Knapdale, southwest of Lochgilphead, Argyll. At first glance this looks like a "courtyard castle" of later construction, but it is more likely to have been instead a capacious Norman-style keep with a small round tower and a square tower inserted at two corners in the thirteenth and sixteenth centuries. The curtain walls are seven feet thick, rise to a height of some forty feet, and enclose an area measuring seventy feet by fifty. This may antedate the Castle of Old Wick; if so, it is the oldest standing castle ruin on the Scottish mainland.

TERRITORIAL EXPANSION

Castles were the fortified residences of kings, sheriffs, earls, barons, and perhaps of lesser men as well. They served as administrative centers where rents were paid (in kind); justice meted out; mill, smith, and brewery maintained; and family, servants, and retainers housed. They were not, however—at least not until the end of the thirteenth century—the primary strategic objectives of military operations. Warfare there was aplenty, but it consisted mostly of pillaging raids into hostile territory interspersed with the clash of armies in open-field combat. The core of the king's army under David I and his successors was the mounted cavalry of armored knights. Unfortunately no early medieval armor or armament survives, and the earliest known grave-slab depicting a knight in armor dates from the fourteenth century. By English analogy, however, and by a careful examination of a few extant twelfth-century seals, it can be deduced that a knight's armor in King David's reign consisted mainly of a hauberk, which was a short-sleeved hooded jacket of chain mail reaching to the knees and slit up the back and front for ease of body movement. He also wore a conical iron helmet, sometimes with a protective nose-piece, and carried on his left arm a large triangular shield, often with a curved top and a metal boss at the center. His weapons included a spear and a single-handed double-edged sword. His saddle was equipped with stirrups—probably a novelty in Scotland, but essential if the man behind the spear was not to be unsaddled. By the thirteenth century, the sleeves of the hauberks had become lengthened, and mail *chaussées* or leggings were worn to protect the legs. The conical helmet had given way to a cylindrical pot helmet completely enveloping the head, which in turn was to be discarded in favor of a round-top helmet flared at the sides to deflect blows.

Cavalrymen thus accoutred formed the nucleus of the armies employed by David and his successors against their untamed subjects in the lands bordering the Moray Firth and in Galloway, as well as for the purpose of extending their control over the western Highlands and Islands. The twelfth-century rebellions of the Macheths and MacWilliams have already been mentioned. Inspired in part by dynastic claims to the throne of

Scotland, these outbreaks can also be seen as separatist movements aimed at the secession of the northern region stretching from Moray to Caithness, possibly with a view to reuniting this once Norse-held district to the earldom of Orkney. Certainly, Harald Maddadson, Earl of Orkney and Caithness, was the instigator of northern rebellions against both Malcolm IV and William the Lion. In 1179 William took an army into Easter Ross and built two castles, one on the Black Isle and the other, called **Dunskeath** *(549)*, near the mouth of the Cromarty Firth across from the present town of Cromarty. This was no doubt a motte-and-bailey castle, and the green mound still observable here is in all likelihood what remains of the original motte. In the end the king established feudal lordship over Caithness, but not before castrating the son of Earl Harald for the father's mischief-making. Further uprisings occurred in Moray and in Ross in the reign of Alexander II (1214–1249), but in 1230 the last of the MacWilliams was put down. Thereafter the sovereignty of the Scottish kings in the far north was not subject to serious challenge.

Galloway—the land of the wild Gall-gaels—proved even less tractable. Galwegians, it is true, fought in the army of David I that invaded England and incidentally were in large part responsible for the Scots' reputation for barbarism there. Yet, three times, Fergus, Lord of Galloway, rebelled against the King of Scots before being put away as an Augustinian canon in Holyrood Abbey. His sons, Uchtred and Gilbert, took advantage of King William's capture by the English in 1174 to expel all royal officers from Galloway, kill as many Anglo-Normans as they could lay hold of, destroy their castles, and invite King Henry II of England to accept their allegiance. After his release, William succeeded in reestablishing nominal rule over the area. But it is some measure of the lawlessness of Galloway that in the fifty years after 1186 at least thirty-seven mottes were put up in the modern counties of Kirkcudbrightshire and Wigtownshire, illustrating, in the words of the historian A. A. M. Duncan, "the discomfort of incoming landlords in a province where blood feud was still permitted and which was still notorious for the barbarity of its men of war." The remains of a few of these, though small in comparison to the Mote of Urr in the same region, are worth observing: **Ingleston Motte** *(383)*, southeast of New Abbey, Kirkcud-brightshire; **Boreland Motte** *(380)*, near Gatehouse of Fleet in the same county; and, in Wigtownshire, **Druchtag Motte** *(376)*, north of Port William; **Droughdad Motte** *(375)*, a few miles west of Glenluce; and **Ardwell Motte** *(375)* and **High Drummore Motte** *(377)*, both south of Sandhead.

Not until the reign of Alexander II was the king's peace firmly established in Galloway. In 1234, on the death without legitimate male issue of the last lord, Alan of Galloway, the king insisted that the feudal law be observed and that the region be divided among the husbands of Alan's three daughters.

This provoked a rebellion in favor of the late lord's bastard son, but it was put down by a royal army. Thereafter, King Alexander empowered one of his leading barons, Walter Comyn, earl of Menteith, to enforce royal authority in the region. It was probably he who built **Cruggleton Castle** *(377)* on the western shore of Wigtown Bay. This place too can be visited, though not much more than the bare foundations of the thirteenth-century castle are now visible. Eventually, Devorguilla, one of Alan's daughters, acquired the entire lordship of Galloway as a result of her sisters' childlessness. She was the wife of John Balliol of Barnard Castle, County Durham; co-founder with him of Balliol College, Oxford; and mother of another John Balliol, who, as we shall see below, sat briefly and uneasily on the throne of Scotland.

Still more difficult to assimilate into the medieval Scottish kingdom were the western Highlands and Islands; that is, the area included in the modern counties of Argyll and western Inverness-shire plus the Outer Hebrides. For one thing, all the islands in this region belonged to Norway. This had been agreed to in 1098 by King Edgar of Scotland and Magnus Barelegs, King of Norway. Magnus was to possess all the western islands separated from the mainland by waters navigable by ship. The Norse king is alleged to have had his men pull a vessel, with himself at the helm, across the narrow isthmus between Loch Fyne and West Loch Tarbert. Thus was the peninsula of Kintyre converted into an island under the terms of the agreement.

Within fifty years, however, Kintyre and most of the western seaboard were under the control of neither Scotland nor Norway, but of a native chief named Somerled Macgillebrighe, a great warrior of mixed Norse and Celtic ancestry who had made himself Lord of Argyll. He then proceeded to mount a naval expedition against his brother-in-law, the King of Man, and from him wrested control of the islands of Islay, Colonsay, Jura, Mull, Tiree, and Coll—though not of Man itself or of the Outer Hebrides. Flushed with success, he next took on the King of Scots—technically his overlord, at least for his mainland possessions. Somerled mustered an army of Highlanders and Islemen against King Malcolm IV in 1164, but was defeated and slain near Renfrew.

Somerled's obvious intention had been to carve out an independent maritime empire based on sea power—certainly not an unreasonable geopolitical concept, given Scotland's much indented western coastline and the multitude of islands close to it. To support his bid, he had a fleet of as many as sixty-four galleys. These clinker-built oared sailing ships were the direct descendants of Viking long boats, and there was probably very little change in their basic design from the ninth century to the sixteenth except possibly for the substitution of stern rudders for steering oars. Sixteen to twenty-six oars was the usual complement, and in wartime each oar was manned by three men. The mast, stepped centrally and supported by shrouds and fore- and back-stays, carried a single square sail. No authentic early medieval representation of a Scottish galley survives, but simple incised sketches of these craft grace a number of the late-medieval western highland tomb slabs to be mentioned in the next chapter. The best—though late—specimen is to be seen on one of the decorative panels that adorn the early sixteenth century tomb of Alexander MacLeod in the church of **St. Clement's, Rodel** *(556)*, on the island of Harris. Though now somewhat damaged, the illustration of a galley is so precise in technical detail that it can be assumed that the sculptor worked from a real model. And though four centuries had passed since Somerled's rise to power, there was probably not very much difference between the ship depicted here and those led by the lord of Argyll up the Clyde to meet his death at Renfrew. Skilled as his men were in sea battles and amphibious operations, they were probably no match for the well-armed and armored knights of King Malcolm IV's feudal army.

After Somerled's death, his vast territories were parcelled out among his three sons: Dugall, Angus, and Ranald (Reginald). The line of Angus eventually failed of male issue, and its lands (mostly in Bute) went by marriage to the Stewarts. The other two lines survived and proliferated and in later years were to emerge as Clan Donald and Clan MacDougall.

The western Highlands still, however, remained outside the effective control of the Scottish king. In 1221 Alexander II mounted an expedition into Argyll to enforce the allegiance of the mainland chiefs. Then, in 1249, he assembled a large fleet for the purpose of subduing the western isles, whose chiefs were vassals of the King of Norway—to the extent that they acknowledged any monarch's overlordship. Alexander died, however, at Kerrera (opposite modern Oban), and the mission aborted. His son and successor, Alexander III, sent an embassy to King Hakon of Norway to negotiate for a peaceful cession of the isles, but this gambit also failed.

Taking alarm at the obviously aggressive Scottish designs against his empire, Hakon in 1263 assembled a large fleet that sailed around the North of Scotland and dropped anchor off the Isle of Arran in the Firth of Clyde. En route a detachment put ashore on Bute and stormed **Rothesay Castle** *(395)*, where the east side of the curtain wall still bears signs of reconstruction at the spot where Norsemen could have broken in on this occasion. It was the end of September when King Hakon's fleet sought shelter in the lee of the Cumbrae Islands off the Ayrshire coast. As usual at this time of year, a heavy storm came up and drove a number of the Norse ships ashore near Largs. There they were set upon by Scots. Rescue troops were dispatched from the fleet, and on 2 October 1263 the king himself came ashore with a sizable expeditionary force. A skirmish ensued (known and magnified in

Scottish history as the Battle of Largs); the Norse withdrew; their fleet set sail for Orkney; and there in December their king died at Kirkwall in the **Bishop's Palace** *(559)*. Alexander then prepared an expedition against the Isle of Man, which its king anticipated by coming to Dumfries to surrender his kingdom. The new ruler of Norway, Magnus IV, now decided to come to terms. By the Treaty of Perth, concluded on 10 July 1266, Magnus surrendered to the King of Scots all claim to the western isles (though not to Orkney and Shetland) in return for a large lump sum payment plus an annual rent. The Scottish mainland and all the islands to the west were finally under Scottish sovereignty.

THE AULD ENEMY: ENGLAND

Without question, the most intractable problem facing medieval Scottish rulers and their subjects was that of coping with the English. Since the days of Agricola, if not before, Scotland had been the natural prey of land-hungry, defense-minded, or merely adventuristic invaders from the South. Not that the Scots, any more than their Caledonian ancestors, were mere passive victims of naked aggression. The exchange of incivilities between North and South Britons was about equally balanced. For every burnt-out Lothian homestead in the wake of an English army, there was usually one or more to match it south of the Tweed. Geography, however, favored the English. The main invasion route from the South lay along the east coast and opened onto the most fertile and most heavily populated part of Scotland. The same route taken south led only to the sparsely peopled moors and mountains of the English north country. Nature had loaded the dice against the Scots.

At the heart of the dispute between the two countries in the Middle Ages lay two separate but related issues. First was the exact location of the border between the two kingdoms—not settled until 1237. Secondly, and never resolved in the period covered in this chapter, was the question of the exact nature of the feudal relationship between the kings of Scotland and England. Or, to put it more precisely: Were the kings of Scotland lawful vassals of the English kings, owing homage and fealty for their Scottish realm? The answer was complicated by the fact that for much of the twelfth and thirteenth centuries the Scottish kings did indeed pay homage to their English counterparts for extensive estates held in England proper. The kings of England were bent on extending this relationship to cover the whole realm of Scotland as well. Another complication was that many of the leading Scottish nobles, like their king, held lands on both sides of the border and were thus under conflicting legal obligations. In a society held together by a network of nicely defined feudal relationships, such ambiguities were bound to cause serious trouble.

When Malcolm Canmore came to the throne in 1057 there was no recognized border between Scotland and England. On the west, Cumbria, stretching from the Solway Firth perhaps as far as the English Lake District, had for more than a century been considered part of the kingdom of the Scots. On the east, Northumbria, though claimed by the Anglo-Saxon kings of England, was in fact a country without rule and with no clear demarcation between it and Scottish Lothian. Malcolm invaded it five times. On the fifth occasion he and his son Edward were killed at Alnwick, the first of a long series of disasters attending Scottish military expeditions into northern England. Meanwhile, in 1072 William the Conqueror had invaded Scotland. His motive, aside from reprisal for Malcolm's own incursions, had to do with the recent marriage of the King of Scots to Margaret, sister of Edgar the Atheling, scion of the ancient Anglo-Saxon royal house, with a valid claim to the throne of England now occupied by William the Bastard. Edgar had fled to the Scottish court with his two sisters and a number of disaffected Northumbrian nobles. Malcolm's marriage to one of the sisters inevitably incurred the Conqueror's wrath. He crossed the border with an army, put Canmore to flight, and at last cornered him in Abernethy, where Malcolm acknowledged his vassalage to the King of England and agreed to give no further shelter to William's enemies. The oath of Abernethy notwithstanding, Malcolm invaded Northumbria three more times, while Anglo-Norman armies ravaged Lothian and Cumbria. More importantly, the English built two great castles to guard their northern border—one at Newcastle-upon-Tyne, the other at Carlisle. Then, for more than a generation after the death of Malcolm III, the border was quiet. Both Duncan II and Edgar owed their thrones to English armed assistance, and both acknowledged the feudal superiority of the English king. Peace was further cemented by the marriage of Edith (Maud/Matilda), King Edgar's sister, to Henry I of England.

It was this marriage that brought David, the youngest of Canmore's sons, to the English court, where he was known as "brother of the queen," not "brother of the King of Scots." There the young man won the favor of his royal brother-in-law and was rewarded with a profitable marriage to Maud, widow of Simon de Senlis, and grandniece of William the Conqueror. With the marriage, David received the vast complex of estates in the eastern Midland counties of England known as the honour of Huntingdon, plus his wife's hereditary claim to the ancient earldom of Northumbria. For these properties he of course rendered homage to the King of England, which enormously complicated relations between the two kingdoms once David succeeded his brother as King of Scots.

After the death of Henry I, two rival claimants to the throne of England—

Stephen of Blois and Henry's daughter Matilda—threw that country into prolonged civil war. King David shifted his support from one side to another and back again. Defeated at the Battle of the Standard in 1138, he lost the honour of Huntingdon, but nevertheless succeeded in wringing from King Stephen the concession of Cumbria as well as most of the earldom of Northumbria for his son Henry. This was the high-water mark of Scottish expansion southward. Carlisle Castle and its dependent province of Cumbria were David's; and, practically speaking, so was Northumberland, except for the castles at Bamburgh and Newcastle.

Then, in the summer of 1157, the situation was dramatically and permanently reversed. The greatest of England's medieval rulers, Henry II, had come to the throne. He now summoned the youthful Malcolm IV to Chester, where the King of Scots was compelled to restore Cumbria and Northumberland to the English Crown in exchange for the return of the honour of Huntingdon. Worse was to come. In 1174 King William the Lion invaded England in support of a foolish rebellion engineered by Henry II's eldest son. Captured at Alnwick, the King of Scots was brought before Henry at Northampton, his feet ignominiously shackled beneath the belly of his horse. Thence, still a prisoner, he was carried across the Channel to Falaise, where the English king was campaigning against the French. There William agreed to a treaty surrendering Huntingdon and his claim to Northumbria as well as the castles of Roxburgh, Berwick, Jedburgh, Edinburgh, and Stirling. (Huntingdon was later awarded to David, the King of Scots' younger brother.) More importantly, William was forced to render homage to the King of England "for Scotland and all his lands." In other words, Scotland was once again a fief of the English Crown.

Scottish fortunes recovered again, however, soon after the death of Henry II. His son, King Richard I, bent on financing a crusade to the Holy Land, in effect sold Scotland back to the King of Scots. In 1189 the two kings met at Canterbury, where William was "made quit" of the promises extorted from him at Falaise, and for the payment of ten thousand marks, the *status quo ante* was restored. In the next reign, however, King John of England was able to reimpose a degree of subjection on the Scots, and at Norham in 1209, with a large army at his back, the English king forced William the Lion and his heir apparent Alexander to pledge their fealty to the King of England and pay a sum of fifteen thousand marks "for having the king's good will." The pledge did not deter Alexander II in 1215 from joining the rebellious barons who forced Magna Carta on King John at Runnymede. The following year found Alexander again in the field, this time in league with Prince Louis, Dauphin of France, who had landed in England with an expeditionary force bent on conquest. Meanwhile, King John had marched north, threatening to "smoke the little red fox [meaning the red-haired Scottish king] out of his den." He invaded Lothian and burned Haddington, Dunbar, Coldingham Priory, and Berwick. Alexander retaliated by capturing Carlisle and plundering Cumbria. Then he marched south to join Prince Louis at Dover—farther into England than a Scottish expeditionary force was ever again to penetrate. The affair came to nothing, however; the Pope excommunicated both Louis and Alexander; the former returned to France and the latter to Scotland, making no further effort to hold on to Carlisle.

For eighty years thereafter, no armed incursions from either side took place. Alexander II married Joanna, daughter of King John and sister of Henry III of England. Alexander's sister was married to Hubert de Burgh, justiciar of England. In 1237 a papal legate conducted negotiations at York, which ended in Alexander's yielding his claims to the northern counties of England in exchange for minor holdings in Cumbria and Northumberland. In effect the Treaty of York implicitly established the line between the Solway Firth and the River Tweed as the Anglo-Scottish border.

In the next reign, the child king Alexander III was married to Princess Margaret, daughter of Henry III. When her brother, Edward I, ascended the throne of England in 1272, the question of fealty owed to the King of England by the King of Scots came up again. According to Scottish accounts, Alexander responded to his brother-in-law's demand for homage with the words: "I became your man for the lands which I hold of you in the Kingdom of England, for which I owe homage, saving my kingdom. . . . No one has the right to homage for my kingdom of Scotland save God alone. . . ."

Thus matters stood between the two countries when, on the stormy night of 19 March 1286, Alexander III, King of Scots, fell from his horse and broke his neck. Guardians were appointed to oversee the realm until his acknowledged successor, the three-year-old Margaret of Norway, could be safely brought to Scotland. In July 1290 the Guardians concluded a treaty at Birgham in Berwickshire with representatives of the English king, whereby the latter's son, Edward of Caernarvon (later King Edward II), was to be betrothed to the Maid of Norway. This was a statesmanlike arrangement, joining the two kingdoms under one royal house but with the proviso that the kingdom of Scotland was to remain separate from England and not subject to its laws. Unfortunately, a few months later, while en route to Scotland, Margaret died.

Thirteen contenders soon appeared to lay claim to the now vacant Scottish throne. Guardians and claimants alike turned to King Edward to decide the contest. An assembly of Scottish magnates met with the King of

England at Norham, Northumberland, in May and June 1291. There all the competitors swore to accept Edward as superior lord of Scotland with lawful cognizance of the case. In desperation the Scots thus conceded what all their kings since 1189 had tried to deny: that the King of England was their rightful feudal overlord. The realm was resigned to Edward, who reappointed the Guardians, who swore fealty to him.

Hearings before the king were held at Berwick Castle in October and November 1292. By then the selection lay between the two most eligible competitors: Robert Bruce and John Balliol. Both claimed by right of descent from David, Earl of Huntingdon, younger brother of Malcolm IV and William the Lion. Balliol was the grandson of Earl David's eldest daughter; Bruce the son of his second daughter. (See chart, *The Scottish Succession: 1057–1329.*) Consistent with the rule of primogeniture, King Edward declared in favor of Balliol, who immediately swore fealty to the King of England for the realm of Scotland. On the last day of November, Balliol was installed as King of Scots at Scone, and at Newcastle the following month he did homage to the English king.

Edward lost no time in asserting his feudal rights as overlord. King John was summoned to appear before the English Parliament to answer charges brought against him by his own subjects. Denying the authority of the high court of Parliament at Westminster, he was treated as a defaulting debtor and sentenced to lose his three chief castles until he made amends. In 1294 he and his chief earls and barons were ordered to join Edward I's impending expedition to France. In King John's absence, a council of Scottish magnates agreed to a treaty of mutual assistance with King Philip IV of France. Though by no means the first instance of Franco-Scottish cooperation against England, this agreement, when ratified by the Scottish king and parliament in 1296, was to prove the formal beginning of a long-lasting entente between the two countries, which came to be known as "the Auld Alliance." It was also tantamount to a declaration of war against England.

Edward I retaliated by sacking Berwick with a thoroughness and ferocity remarkable even for the thirteenth century. The English then laid siege to **Dunbar Castle** *(454)* in East Lothian, now nothing more than a picturesque stone fragment barely distinguishable from the rocky promontory on which it stands. There they were attacked by the main body of King John's feudal host—with disastrous results for the Scots, who suffered so many casualties and lost so many distinguished prisoners that their army virtually ceased to exist. King John was brought to Brechin Castle in Angus and stripped of his crown, of his sword and sceptre, and even of the blazon of royal arms from his tabard, or surcoat. Then, as "Toom [Empty] Tabard," he was taken away to England, where he spent three years as a prisoner before being allowed to depart in exile for his family estate in Picardy.

THE SCOTTISH SUCCESSION: 1057–1329

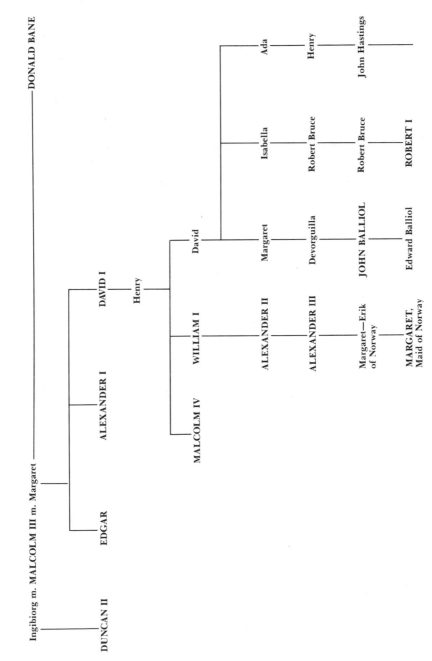

Meanwhile, King Edward had taken forcible possession of Scotland as far north as Elgin. On his return he picked up the Stone of Destiny from Scone, and from Edinburgh he "liberated" a large quantity of Scottish records, plate, jewels, and a portion of the True Cross (the "Black Rood") brought to Scotland by Malcolm Canmore's sainted Queen Margaret. By August 1296 he was back in Berwick, where he collected about two thousand Scottish oaths of fealty, afterward entered in what came to be known as the Ragman Rolls.

Scotland's subjection was now complete. Or so it seemed to the King of England. The most renowned soldier of Europe could not have guessed that this backward country, leaderless and divided against itself, would prove unconquerable. Three more invasions of Scotland had still not convinced the doughty "Hammer of the Scots." King Edward I died at Burgh-on-Sands in Cumbria on 7 July 1307 at the head of still another mighty army poised to enforce English rule on this stubborn and fractious people who would have none of it.

THIRTEENTH-CENTURY CASTLES

Enforcing English rule on a country of Scotland's size and character required more than capturing its king, routing his army, and exacting oaths of fealty from his nobility. Permanent occupation and pacification of such a large and hostile territory required the garrisoning of troops, either English or pro-English, in scattered locations throughout the country. Such garrisons had to be housed in castles—fortified residences of sufficient size and strength to provide security to contingents of armed men charged with maintaining local law and order and putting down insurrection.

No one among his contemporaries was more familiar than Edward I with the requirements of castle construction and defense. While on crusade in the Middle East, he had observed the elaborate fortifications produced by sophisticated Byzantine engineers. On his return home to assume his kingly duties, he had tarried awhile at the Castle of St. Georges d'Esperanche in Savoy, where he met James the Mason, who followed him back to England and for thirty years served as the king's chief architect. After Edward's conquest of North Wales, James of St. George and other masons constructed a chain of magnificent stone castles—nine in all, at a cost of 93,000 pounds—to keep that contumacious land in thrall. These have rightly been called "the climax of European military architecture in the Middle Ages"

(Stewart Cruden). With elaborate gatehouses and curtain walls studded with projecting towers, the inner citadels of these mighty fortresses were virtually impregnable.

No such complex fortifications were ever erected in Scotland. Although King Edward is known to have brought with him on his northern campaigns some of his most highly skilled carpenters and masons (including possibly James of St. George), there is no documentary evidence that he built any castles there. In all likelihood he did not, if for no better reason than that by the close of the thirteenth century there were plenty of sturdy castles already strategically positioned throughout that country. Unlike North Wales, which was mostly barren of stone fortifications when Edward's armies arrived on the scene, all parts of Scotland were studded with strongholds easily converted to English use once surrendered by their original owners.

It is customary to classify British castles according to four main categories: (1) the isolated stone tower or keep; (2) the simple courtyard castle or castle of *enceinte*, which was defined by an enclosing wall of stone; (3) the courtyard castle with curtain walls reinforced by mural towers, usually at the corners; and (4) the courtyard castle with a massive frontal gatehouse keep, usually flanked by twin towers. It should be noted that this classification would have been meaningless to contemporaries and that these categories do not, for the most part, imply preconceived architectural styles. Though contemporary French or English influences can be inferred in a few cases, Scottish castles were mostly the indigenous products of local masons, were shaped to match the contours of the terrain on which they stood, and were fashioned primarily to meet the requirements, whims, and purses of their builders. Moreover, it is impossible to date these buildings with any degree of precision; furthermore, it cannot be assumed that the more complex structures are later than those of simpler design. About all that can be said of those ruined castles described below is that they probably date from the thirteenth century, most from the second half of it. This is not to deny, however, that subsequent repairs and renovations have significantly altered the originals, so that much of what remains standing today may be of a still later period of construction.

It is well to remember that castles were built both for defense and for comfort, although in their present ruined condition the second of these considerations is sometimes hard to discern. Their chief defensive features, and the functions they were meant to serve, are as follows:

The Keep: This was the residence of the lord and his family, his domestic servants, and possibly some or all of his armed retainers. The word *keep* itself is a modern substitute for *donjon* or *turris* which were the medieval words used to describe the tall, quadrangular or circular stone tower of three or four stories that constituted the heart of a castle.

Curtain Walls: These are the high walls enclosing the castle courtyard. Their protective function is obvious.

The Parapet: Both keep and curtain walls might be topped by parapets, i.e., breastworks of at least man height, often divided into alternate solid and empty squares, the former known as *merlons*, the latter as *crenelles*. Such a "crenellated" parapet was also known as a *battlement*. It was the main defensive feature of any castle. The merlons provided protection for a defending archer or crossbowman when he was not shooting through the crenelles. The profile of the parapet is perhaps the most typical and best known feature of a castle, as indicated in the design of the chess pieces called by that name.

The *Bretasche* (Hoarding) and Machicolations: The *bretasche* or hoarding was a wooden platform projecting out from the face of either keep or curtain wall, usually at the base of the parapet. Putlog holes might be left in the masonry for insertion of the timber beams on which the platform rested. Alternatively, or in addition, stone braces, called *corbels*, might be built into the wall for undergirding the platform. Openings in the base of this projecting gallery allowed stones, quicklime, and burning material to be dropped on attackers below. The next stage was to build the gallery of stone or to move the parapet itself outward to rest on stone corbels. The open spaces left between the corbels were called *machicolations*—again used for dropping lethal objects on unfriendly folk below. In Scotland there are no known cases of machicolation until the fifteenth century—about the time guns were being introduced and high parapets were no longer a necessity for castle defense. Thereafter, machicolations became chiefly decorative—designed to give all sorts of buildings a fake military appearance.

Mural Towers and Bartizans: Small round towers projecting from the corners of castles or curtain walls and resting on corbels were, in Scotland, called *rounds* or *roundels*. The word, *bartizan*, is modern, but nevertheless is now the term most commonly used to describe these appendages. There is some doubt as to what purpose they were supposed to serve. A common assumption is that, when pierced by narrow windows, they provided bowmen an advantageous position for enfilade fire along the axis of the adjacent wall. On closer examination, it appears doubtful that many were well suited for such purposes, and it is more likely that bartizans were installed primarily to provide additional living space.

Gate and Gatehouse: The entrance to the castle was inevitably its weakest point and therefore the object of special precautions. If a ditch or moat (dry or water-filled) surrounded the establishment, it would be crossed by a drawbridge leading to the gate and operated by a windlass situated in the room above. Also worked from the same room would be the *portcullis,* a heavy wooden grating shod with iron that slid up and down in grooves. The portcullis chamber floor might have a hole in it, called a *meurtrière* or murder hole, through which dangerous objects could be dropped on attackers passing through the entryway below. Sometimes a second gate, known as the *yett,* was installed behind the portcullis. This was formed of iron bars penetrating each other horizontally and vertically in alternate sections. It is unique to Scotland. An outer gateway connected with the main gate by parallel walls is known as a *barbican.* In larger castles, it was usual to have a small secondary gate, known as the *postern,* to be used as an escape route in time of siege or as a sally port for troops bent on engaging the besiegers outside the castle walls. In the later Middle Ages the function of a gatehouse and keep might be conjoined so that the same frontal building served as both the defensive and residential headquarters of the castle.

It is easier for today's visitor to visualize a ruined medieval castle as a fortress than as a royal or baronial residence—the best-appointed living accommodation available to medieval laymen of high degree. Gone are the roofs, the wooden floors between stories, the furnishings, carpets of rushes, brightly painted walls, tapestries, fireplaces ablaze, and all the other accoutrements that made these places habitable, if not exactly luxurious by modern standards. The center of life in the castle was the hall—usually on the first floor above ground level and now most easily distinguished as the room with the most elaborate fireplace. Here the lord and his family ate at the high table set upon a dais near the fireplace and at the opposite end from the screens passage that separated hall from kitchen, pantry, and buttery. Private rooms, known as *chalmers* (chambers) or *solars,* might open off the dais end of the hall. Sleeping quarters would normally be on the upper floors, interconnected by stone stairways, either straight or spiral (turnpike). Here also would most commonly be the latrines or *garderobes,* usually mural chambers with flues discharging the effluvia into the surrounding moat. The kitchen, located on either the ground floor or the first floor, is always recognizable by its cavernous chimney, and the bakehouse by its ovens. The capacious vaulted apartments on the ground floor are cellars where food supplies were kept in bulk—the most important being the larder where meat was stored after being salted or larded with fat to keep it over the winter. Legend to the contrary, these were not "dungeons" where helpless prisoners were commonly manacled and tortured. If there was a prison in the basement level, it would normally be a small chamber, set in the wall or within an empty space between vault and the floor above, perhaps with a slit window for air and entered only through a hatch in its ceiling. This is called a *pit prison* and is rare in England but fairly common among Scottish castles and later tower-houses. Slit windows also occurred at higher levels and are usually now referred to as *arrow-slits* or *arrow-loops*. In fact, it is not at all certain that they were used for purposes of defense. A glance at the splayed recesses into which they opened on the inside should be enough to convince any thoughtful observer that a man with a crossbow would have a hard time taking aim and firing through these narrow apertures. Anyway, the field of fire that his weapon could cover would be too small an arc for effective defense. The parapet was the proper station for bowmen, not the inside of the castle. Windows were made narrow to keep out the wind while letting in some light and air.

No visitor to Scotland should neglect to inspect at close quarters at least some of the country's mighty, though ruined, medieval castles. Coming across the border from Carlisle, the first stronghold of any size to be encountered is **Caerlaverock Castle** *(384)*, about seven miles southeast of Dumfries. It was probably built between 1290 and 1300, though whether by the Scots to block the passage of an English army from the south or by the English as a bridgehead for such an invasion is unclear. In any case, it was in Scottish hands in 1300 when it was besieged and captured by King Edward I. With the invading army was one Walter of Exeter, who penned a rhyming narrative of the operation. The castle he described as "in shape . . . like a shield, for it had but three sides round it, with a tower at each corner, but one of them was a double one, so high, so long and so wide, that the gate was underneath it, well made and strong, with a drawbridge and a sufficiency of other defenses . . . and good walls, and good ditches filled right up to the brim with water." Except for the absence of the drawbridge, the description is almost as accurate today as when it was written, and most modern visitors would agree with the writer's added comment that "I think you will never see a more finely situated castle." What we have here is a courtyard castle with its defenses concentrated in the twin-towered gate-house keep, an early example of the fourth category of castellar construction mentioned above—unusual only in that the ground plan is triangular. It was partially destroyed and rebuilt several times after 1300, so that, of the original building seen by Walter of Exeter, only the northwest gatehouse tower, the lower courses of the west curtain wall, and the base of the southwest corner tower survive. Still, except for the machicolated parapets added in the fifteenth century, the front face of Caerlaverock cannot look much different from the way it appeared to the approaching English army in 1300.

In a far greater state of dilapidation is **Lochmaben Castle** *(386)*, also in

Dumfriesshire, south of the town of Lochmaben. The ruin is situated at the end of a promontory extending into Castle Loch and was guarded at the landward end by a series of ditches cut across the neck of the promontory. So little is left standing that it is hard to make out what this building looked like in its original state, except to say that it was a courtyard castle with high curtain walls and an entrance in the middle of the south curtain. The date of construction is uncertain, though it was probably built late in the thirteenth century, possibly by the Robert Bruce who was to compete unsuccessfully for the Scottish crown and was the grandfather of King Robert I of Scotland. Probably of about the same date of construction was another Bruce stronghold, **Loch Doon Castle** *(390)*, on the western shore of the loch of that name in Ayrshire. It was originally situated on an island in the middle of the loch, but was dismantled and reerected on its present site when the waters were raised. It is an eleven-sided courtyard castle, so built to conform to the shape of the island on which it originally stood. Its most interesting features today are the arched entryway (minus the original portcullis chamber above) and the postern gate, a pointed barrel-vault passage through one side of the curtain.

Of a slightly earlier date is **Bothwell Castle** *(410)*, overlooking the upper Clyde Valley near Hamilton in Lanarkshire. This, in the words of the late W. Douglas Simpson, distinguished Scottish architectural historian, "is the grandest piece of secular architecture that the Middle Ages have bequeathed to us in Scotland." The castle—or at least the great moated circular *donjon* with its adjoining wings—probably was built in the third quarter of the thirteenth century by Walter de Moravia of the powerful northern family descended from Freskin the Fleming. Of about the same vintage is **Dirleton Castle** *(453)* in East Lothian, built by the de Vaux family. This is a courtyard castle with the heaviest defense works concentrated near the front gate. Here, in the southwest corner, is a cluster of two high round towers with a square building in between, the three together representing the major surviving portion of the original stronghold. This is not, however, a gatehouse keep like Caerlaverock, for the main entrance is in the center of the south curtain wall, where it is marked by two massive jambs projecting outward. Though much modified by later owners (Halyburtons and Ruthvens), the strong defensive features of the original castle are clearly discernible in this splendid ruin, rising above a charming garden in one of the prettiest villages in Scotland. Less than six miles to the south lies **Hailes Castle** *(455)*, approximately contemporary with the original buildings at Dirleton and Bothwell. Constructed probably by an Earl of Dunbar and March, it was enlarged at the end of the fourteenth century by the Hepburns, who owned the castle for two centuries. The oldest parts of today's ruin are the lower courses of the rectangular keep, the curtain wall extending eastward from it, and the vaulted stairway leading to a well. Interesting to architectural historians chiefly because of the substantial amount of its thirteenth century masonry, Hailes was not a place of any great strategic significance.

Rothesay Castle *(395)*, on the other hand, was for centuries one of the most important strongholds on Scotland's west coast, standing as it does on the island of Bute, overlooking the upper reaches of the Clyde estuary. There was a castle here in the thirteenth century that was stormed by Norsemen who chopped their way through the curtain wall with axes—perhaps on the east side of the present curtain wall where there are signs of rebuilding. This too is a courtyard castle, but circular in plan rather than the more usual quadrangular shape. The original gateway was replaced in the fifteenth or sixteenth century by the still-standing barbican stretching into the moat, but the four drum towers, spaced at equal distances around the curtain's circuit, are of thirteenth-century provenance. Taken over by the Stewarts in the fourteenth century, this is one of the best preserved medieval castles in Scotland. Roughly contemporary with it, on the other side of the Sound of Bute, is **Skipness Castle** *(474)* near the head of Kintyre Peninsula. This is really an early-thirteenth-century hall house enlarged later in the century into a courtyard castle, with an arched entrance above which is a small portcullis chamber. Also dating from the early thirteenth century is **Dunstaffnage Castle** *(472)*, situated on a rocky knoll on a low-lying promontory jutting into the mouth of Loch Etive a few miles north of Oban, Argyll. Probably built by Ewen MacDougall, this is a four-sided courtyard castle with drum towers rising from three corners and an entrance passage in the fourth, the latter now surmounted by a tower-house built in the seventeenth century. Lancet windows, of undoubted early-thirteenth-century date, are to be seen in the east and northwest curtain walls, as well as in the roofless chapel lying about two hundred yards from the castle.

Rock formations like that at Dunstaffnage are not unusual in the western Highlands and provided ideal foundations for courtyard castles whose curtain walls could in effect be more than doubled in height by being built along the edges of precipitous cliffs. Two of special interest are to be found on or near the Ardnamurchan Peninsula of Argyll, both constructed in the thirteenth century, probably about the time King Alexander III was freeing the area from Norse control after the Battle of Largs. **Mingary Castle** *(460)*, at the western end of the peninsula on the shore overlooking the Sound of Mull, has a high curtain wall rising from the rocks on the seaward side and is approached from landward over a deep, wide, dry ditch. The wall-heads are crenellated, and there are putlog holes that once supported a *bretasche*. The original keep inside the curtain has unfortunately disappeared, though an eighteenth-century barracks block still stands. Not far away, at the eastern neck of Ardnamurchan Peninsula on a spit of land jutting into Loch

Moidart, is **Tioram Castle** *(460)*, another courtyard castle adapted to the rock on which it stands, occupying the whole of it. The well-preserved and crenellated curtain walls rise about thirty feet from their base and about sixty from the waters below. Again, the main entrance is on the landward side. Here the keep inside the curtain still stands, as does a high tower with corbelled angle turrets erected about 1600. Both Tioram and Mingary occupy sites of spectacular scenic beauty. So does **Kisimul Castle** *(555)*, on its rocky islet in Castlebay on Barra in the Outer Hebrides. The crenellated curtain walls, pierced with putlog holes to support a *bretasche*, seem to rise straight out of the sea. Inside is a four-story square keep that may date from as early as the twelfth century. The curtain walls were probably erected in the thirteenth, though it was not until the fifteenth that the castle is known to have been occupied by the MacNeills, one of whose American descendants has recently restored it. Twice a week it is open to visitors who come by boat from the nearby town of Castlebay. Nothing could be more picturesque.

Coming back to the mainland—and more accessible to today's visitor than any of the three previously mentioned sites—**Inverlochy Castle** *(516)*, near Fort William, Inverness-shire, is roughly contemporaneous with them. Built by the Comyn family and now a rather ill-kept ruin, this is a courtyard castle of the third category mentioned above; i.e., it is surrounded by curtain walls with mural towers at the four corners. This is a type common in England and Wales but not in Scotland. Three sides of the curtain are surrounded by a wide ditch and outer bank; the River Lochy runs at the foot of the fourth side. The courtyard has arched entrances, one on each side, and one of the corner towers is considerably larger than the other three, suggesting its employment as the castle *donjon*. Three other ruined Comyn strongholds, all in the north, are **Castle Roy** *(529)*, near Nethybridge, Inverness-shire; **Lochindorb Castle** *(529)*, north of Grantown-on-Spey, Moray; and **Balvenie Castle** *(531)*, near Dufftown, Banffshire. Castle Roy is a rather simple structure—a square enclosure bounded by high curtain walls with a slightly projecting rectangular corner tower. Lochindorb, though less accessible, is more interesting. Built on an island in the middle of a loch, this is a courtyard castle with comparatively thin curtain walls and small corner towers. The castle dates from the second half of the thirteenth century and was owned by John Comyn, Lord of Badenoch. This is one of the castles of the North known to have been visited by Edward I while campaigning in Scotland. Another is Balvenie Castle. Here is a spacious quadrangular enclosure surrounded by a thick but uncrenellated curtain wall some thirty feet in height.

None of these Comyn fortalices can compare in size and strength, however, to the greatest of all northern strongholds—**Kildrummy Castle**

(537), west of Alford, Aberdeenshire. Almost all of it was built in the thirteenth century, but on a most unusual ground plan, in that the castle incorporates both a powerful frontal gatehouse keep and a tall circular *donjon* to the rear. The twin-towered gatehouse at the southeast corner is now no more than a stubby ruin, and very little more remains of the *donjon* at the northwest corner. The northeast tower, however, stands almost to its original height, and projecting from the east curtain wall are the substantial remains of a chapel still containing the framework of three lovely lancet windows.

Of the eighteen castles mentioned above, at least six—Caerlaverock, Bothwell, Dirleton, Dunstaffnage, Inverlochy, and Kildrummy—were to undergo siege during the protracted War of Independence that followed soon on John Balliol's abject surrender to King Edward I. The English monarch had expected Scotland to be another Wales—untamed but tamable, rebellious but ultimately submissive to *force majeure*. This great warrior king, who gloried in his reputation as the "Hammer of the Scots," would discover, however, as the Romans had before him, that Scotland was unconquerable.

Chapter Four

The Later Middle Ages
War and Politics
1296–1488

THE WAR OF INDEPENDENCE

Interregnum: 1296–1306
Robert I (the Bruce): 1306–1329
David II: 1329–1371

On the summit of the Abbey Craig northeast of Stirling stands the **Wallace Monument** *(480)*, a massive stone tower 220 feet in height and topped by a pinnacled lantern (crown steeple) visible for more than twenty miles on all sides. Outside the building is a larger-than-life statue of William Wallace clothed in mail; inside is a 5½-foot two-handed, double-edged sword allegedly taken at the time of his capture in the year 1305. In all likelihood, the sword, of a type known in Scotland as a *claymore* (Gaelic: *cleadheamh-mor*), is not authentic. Weapons of this sort did not come into use until the sixteenth century. Nor does the tower itself authentically reflect the architectural styles prevalent in Wallace's lifetime. It is in fact a mid-Victorian "Scottish baronial" fantasy. Though not unimpressive in its commanding position, the monument is both pretentious and overpowering. Scotland's greatest national hero deserves a more appropriate memorial than this.

William Wallace was the younger son of an obscure knight from Elderslie in Renfrewshire, a vassal of James the Steward. Some time in May 1297, as a result of a private quarrel, he slew the English sheriff of Lanarkshire and shortly thereafter drove the English justiciar out of his court at Scone. What appeared at first to be a minor uprising led by a common outlaw soon escalated into a major revolt against the oppressive government of King Edward I. The resistance movement was supported by Robert Wishart, Bishop of Glasgow, and by a number of nobles and gentry, including James the Steward and his brother John, Sir William Douglas, Sir Alexander Lindsay, and the twenty-two-year-old Robert Bruce, Earl of Carrick and grandson of the Robert Bruce who had failed in his bid for the throne of Scotland against the superior claim of John Balliol—in whose cause

Wallace was fighting. Both in numbers and in strength, however, William Wallace drew his chief support not from the nobility or even from the knightly class, but rather from the "horseless classes" of peasants, herdsmen, and the like, who had historically comprised the Scottish army (*exercitus Scoticanus*). This was the "common army" of bowmen and spearmen that had survived in Scotland long after its English counterpart had been replaced by mailed knights and mercenary foot soldiers.

While men of all degree flocked to Wallace's standard in the South of Scotland, an uprising of comparable size and strength was also taking place in the North. It was led by Sir Andrew Moray, scion of one of the great families of that region. By the close of the summer, Moray had cleared the English out of the entire area between the Rivers Spey and Dee, and the two resistance fighters joined forces near Stirling, the military nodal point of Scotland. Only here, between the marshy headwaters of the Rivers Clyde and Forth, was the land high and dry enough to permit the passage of an army moving north into the Highlands. To force such passage, an English army led by John de Warenne, Earl of Surrey, and Sir Hugh Cressingham, treasurer of Scotland, appeared on the scene in the first week of September 1297.

Wallace and Moray had drawn up their motley band of archers and spearmen on the slope of the Abbey Craig, looking southward toward a narrow wooden bridge across the Forth—probably a short distance above the present stone **Stirling Bridge** *(480)*, not to be erected for another hundred years or so. To the English demand to surrender, Wallace replied: "We are not here to make peace but to do battle to defend ourselves and liberate our kingdom. Let them come on, and we shall prove this in their very beards." The English did in fact come on—slowly, across the narrow bridge that formed a sort of bottleneck. When a sufficient number had crossed, Wallace and Moray sent their spearmen rushing down the hill to cut them off from their fellows still on the far side of the river. Nearly a hundred English knights were slain, including Cressingham, whose body was flayed by the victorious Scots. (Pieces of the skin were later put on display at sundry places around the country.) The Earl of Surrey barely escaped to Berwick. But Moray was so badly wounded that he died before the end of the year.

This left Wallace the undisputed leader of the Scottish resistance. He was knighted, assumed the role of Guardian of the Realm in the name of the absent King John, and conducted a punitive raid into Northumberland. In March 1298 King Edward I returned from campaigning in Flanders and personally led an army of some two thousand four hundred horse and twelve thousand foot soldiers (mostly Welsh archers), across the border. One detachment under Anthony de Bec, Bishop of Durham, captured **Dirleton Castle** *(453)* after a long siege. The king himself moved on to Falkirk to confront Wallace's much smaller army. Deluded perhaps by his easy success at Stirling Bridge, Wallace stood his ground and arranged his spearmen in four great *schiltrons,* or hedgehogs, each a thickly packed circle of foot soldiers, their long spears slanting obliquely toward the circumference. King Edward's knights and Welsh archers made short work of these human fortresses; the battle became a slaughter, and Wallace himself barely escaped to live as a fugitive until a fellow Scot betrayed him into the hands of the English in August 1305. He was carried off to London; tried at Westminster Hall for treason, murder, and sacrilege; inevitably convicted; dragged on a hurdle to Smithfield; and there hanged, cut down while still alive, disemboweled, beheaded, and hacked into quarters. His head was set on a pike above London Bridge, and parts of his dismembered body were put on public view in Newcastle-upon-Tyne, Berwick, Stirling, and Perth. Lacking both the military genius and personal ambition that was soon to distinguish the young Robert Bruce as one of the great guerilla leaders of history, William Wallace was above all else a patriot. As such, he was an anomaly in a feudal age, when most men's loyalties were personal, provincial, dynastic, or familial. In Wallace's mind and heart dwelt a vision of *national* self-determination such as medieval Europe would not see again until Joan of Arc appeared before Orleans in 1429.

Meanwhile, King Edward I completed the subjection of Scotland. As already mentioned, **Caerlaverock Castle** *(384)* in Dumfriesshire was besieged and captured in 1300. In September 1301 **Bothwell Castle** *(410)* fell after a long siege, for which the English built a massive wooden tower or "belfrey" and hauled it all the way from Glasgow to be emplaced against the castle walls. **Stirling Castle** *(477),* under the command of Sir William Oliphant, held out until July 1304, when the royal standard of Scotland—the red lion rampant on a field of gold—was finally lowered. By this time almost every Scottish noble, high churchman, and man of note had renewed his oath of fealty and homage to the English king. In March 1305 Edward decreed the "establishment of our realm of Scotland" and issued detailed orders for its governance. Within less than a year, however, Scotland was afire again—set this time by Robert Bruce, Earl of Carrick.

Up to the year 1306 Bruce had followed a tortuous path through the minefield of Anglo-Scottish affairs. Like many of his noble countrymen with large estates subject to forfeiture, he had much to lose by ending up on the wrong side. Tergiversation, therefore, seemed the better part of valor. In 1296 he had sworn fealty to the English king at Berwick and had his name recorded in the Ragman Rolls. Two years later he announced to the knights of Annandale: "No man holds his own flesh and blood in hatred and I am no exception. I must join my own people and the nation in which I was born." Thereupon he joined forces with Wallace and Moray and probably fought alongside them at Falkirk. Shortly thereafter, he replaced Wallace as Guardian of Scotland, along with John Comyn of Badenoch, called "the Red Comyn." It was an uneasy partnership, owing in part to the fact that Comyn was John Balliol's nephew and therefore hostile to Bruce's own claim to the throne of Scotland, inherited from his grandfather. In any case, Bruce resigned the guardianship in 1302 and later defected to Edward I. His reasons may have been that King Philip IV of France was rumored to be about to send to Scotland an army to restore Balliol to the throne. When the French king instead went down to defeat at the Battle of Courtrai, the danger of a Balliol restoration subsided; now it was Edward I who stood between Bruce and the Scottish throne.

Such was the situation on 10 February 1306, when Comyn met Bruce at the latter's invitation in the Greyfriars' Church (not the present building) in Dumfries. Exactly what words were exchanged is unknown. Probably Comyn, who also had sworn fealty to Edward I, rejected Bruce's request for help in a bid for the throne. Whatever took place, a blow was struck, and Comyn fell wounded at the high altar. "I doubt I have slain the Red Comyn," Bruce is reported to have said. "Doubt ye?" answered one of his henchman. "I mak siccar [sure]" and then proceeded to dispatch the bleeding Comyn. (This famous dialogue in Lowland Scots probably never took place, if for no other reason than that Bruce and his knights are likely to have spoken to each other in Norman French.) In any case, Bruce had committed a terrible sacrilege for which he was promptly excommunicated. He had also invoked a blood feud with the powerful Comyns and all their kinsmen and connections, including the MacDougalls of Lorne; Alexander MacDonald, Lord of Islay; and the MacDoualls of Galloway. Civil war within Scotland and retribution at the hands of Edward I were alike inevitable. Bruce promptly seized the initiative by having himself crowned King of Scots at Scone. Countess Isabella of Buchan, sister of the Earl of Fife, whose family (the MacDuffs) had traditionally installed the King of Scots on the Stone of Scone, placed a gold circlet on the new king's head.

Disaster quickly followed. King Robert's little army was routed at Methven and again at Dalry near Tyndrum. He sent his wife and daughter Marjorie under escort of his brother Neil and the Earl of Atholl to **Kildrummy Castle** *(437)*. The Prince of Wales (later King Edward II) laid siege to this place and captured it after a traitor inside had set fire to the stores. The queen and Marjorie Bruce had already left but were later captured and put under confinement. Neil Bruce was executed; so also were two other brothers, Thomas and Alexander, as well as the Earl of Atholl. Simon Fraser, another Bruce supporter, was hanged, drawn, and quartered and had his head impaled beside that of William Wallace on London Bridge. Bruce's sister Mary and Isabella, Countess of Buchan, were confined in cages of iron and timber in Roxburgh and Berwick castles respectively. Bruce himself, probably with the help of Neil Campbell, along with Angus Og, younger brother of the hostile lord of Islay, managed to escape from western Scotland by boat and disappear for the next four and a half months.

Bruce returned to the mainland in February 1307, won a victory over the English in May at Loudon Hill in Ayrshire; and in July received the welcome news that King Edward I had died at Burgh-on-Sands on his way north to crush this latest and most serious of Scottish rebellions.

The old king's death and the new king's (Edward II's) preoccupation with personal pleasures and domestic troubles gave Bruce the opportunity to prove his consummate skill at guerilla warfare—quick raids, small engagements, scorched earth; capturing castles by stealth rather than siege and then destroying them to preclude reoccupation by the enemy. Herein lay the Scottish king's real genius—his willingness to forsake the conventional massed cavalry tactics so dear to the hearts of his knightly contemporaries in favor of a more appropriate strategy of irregular warfare. In November 1307 he captured **Inverlochy Castle** *(516)*; then moved up the Great Glen to take **Urquhart Castle** *(520)* on the western shore of Loch Ness; and on to Inverness and Nairn. Moving eastward into Aberdeenshire, he won a brief engagement at Inverurie, laid waste the Comyns' territory of Buchan, and captured Aberdeen. His trusted captain, James Douglas (known as "the Good Sir James"), devastated Galloway, putting down the MacDoualls. In the autumn of 1309 Bruce invaded Argyll, where John (MacDougall) of Lorne had emplaced soldiers on the heights of Ben Cruachan to roll boulders down on the king's troops as they filed through the Pass of Brander. Bruce turned the tables by sending Douglas and a contingent of archers higher up the mountain to foil the ambush from the rear. This battle broke the power of the MacDougalls, and shortly thereafter Bruce took their stronghold, **Dunstaffnage Castle** *(472)*. Dundee fell in the spring of 1312, and Perth and Dumfries in the early months of 1313, after which Bruce may have taken ship to reduce the Isle of Man.

In the early morning hours of Ash Wednesday, 1314, Douglas and his men broke into Roxburgh Castle and took the revelling garrison by surprise. Three weeks later, Bruce's nephew, Sir Thomas Randolph, captured **Edinburgh Castle** *(436)* by sending a party of intrepid rock climbers up the steep north cliff (the side now facing Princes Street) to storm the outer defenses from the rear. Like Roxburgh, the stronghold was razed to the ground—not to be rebuilt until the following reign. Only **Stirling Castle** *(477)*, on its high rock overlooking the valley of the upper Forth, remained in the hands of English supporters. It had been under siege by the king's brother, Edward Bruce, who had foolishly agreed to allow its garrison to postpone surrender until Midsummer Day (24 June) of 1314, on condition that no English army should appear before that date within three miles of the castle. This typically chivalric gesture might have cost Robert Bruce his kingdom. It gave King Edward II ample time to summon the English feudal host for the relief of Stirling. King Robert could do no other than come to the aid of his brother. Thus he could no longer avoid a pitched battle with the main body of the English army—a type of warfare for which his mobile, lightly equipped, irregular troops were ill suited.

The English king and his soldiers came up the old Roman road from Falkirk (now the A 9) on the afternoon of 23 June 1314, reaching a point about 2½ miles south of the castle, where they camped on the south side of the stream known as the Bannock Burn. The English army consisted of about fifteen thousand foot soldiers and twenty-five hundred mounted knights. King Robert's force, consisting of about sixty-five hundred infantry (mostly spearmen) and a mere five hundred light cavalry, was drawn up in the area of the New Park about 2 miles south of the castle, approximately where the National Trust of Scotland now maintains its **Bannockburn Heritage Centre** *(479)*. The English knights, mounted on huge war-horses, called *destriers*, were doubtless clothed in hauberks of mail (i.e., linked metal rings) over aketons (sleeved tunics) of padded linen, their legs covered with mail stockings and their heads and shoulders with mail coifs or aventails (i.e., open-faced hoods) over which their flat-topped barrel-shaped helms could be fitted. A knight, English or Scottish, would carry into battle a lance for charging his opponent, a sharp double-edged sword, and a short-hafted battle-axe for close combat. The infantry on both sides would most likely be clothed in leather or padded linen, though the English might also have been protected by mail shirts. The main strength of the English infantry lay in its archers, especially the Welsh longbowmen. Bruce, on the other hand, had relatively few archers, and these armed only with short bows of lesser range. Most of his foot soldiers carried eighteen-foot-long spears and were arrayed in *schiltrons* as at Falkirk. The Scottish cavalry would have been mounted on smaller horses (palfreys) because Scotland did not produce sufficient fodder to feed the heavier *destriers*. Scottish knights also wore mail, but their heads were normally covered with pointed helmets called *bascinets*.

No authentic mail armor of the fourteenth century survives in Scotland. (The elaborate suits of plate armor on display in various museums are of a later date and are imports from the Continent.) A few grave-slabs of the late fourteenth and early fifteenth centuries, however, depict fashions in knightly gear that had probably not changed much since 1314. Good examples are the effigies of Bricius MacKinnon in the abbey museum at **Iona Abbey** *(465)*; John Drummond at **Inchmahome Priory** *(497)* on an island in the Lake of Menteith; John Menteith in the roofless choir of **St.**

Mary's, Rothesay *(396)* in Bute; and several knightly effigies among the three fine collections of western highland stone carvings in Argyll—at **Kilmartin Church** *(471)* near Lochgilphead; **Kilmory Knap Chapel** *(468)* in Knapdale; and the **Kilberry Sculptured Stones** *(469)*, also in Knapdale.

The battle between Scots and English, one of the few fought on British soil that could be called strategically decisive, took its name from the Bannock Burn, which defined the southern edge of the main field of combat. Thanks to the epic poem *The Bruce* by John Barbour, Archdeacon of Aberdeen (d. 1395), the course of the action is known in some detail (making allowances, of course, for the author's literary license). On the afternoon of 23 June a small party of English knights advanced across the burn and encountered the solitary figure of King Robert himself, astride a gray palfrey and easily identifiable by the crown he wore over his bascinet. The leader of the party, Sir Henry de Bohun, immediately lowered his lance and charged. Bruce pulled aside, so that, in Barbour's words, "Schir henry myssit the nobill kyng," who then rose up in his stirrups and, with his hand axe, split his assailant's head in two. The English then withdrew. That night Edward II made the mistake of separating his cavalry from his bowmen by sending the former across the Bannock Burn. At daybreak on the 24th the Scottish spearmen, arrayed in *schiltrons*, attacked. The field of battle was probably not on the site of the **Bannockburn Heritage Centre** *(479)* but on lower ground about a mile to the northeast on the outskirts of the present village of Bannockburn. The English and Welsh archers were out of range, and Edward's cavalry alone could not break up the Scottish *schiltrons*. Bruce's spearmen, as ordered, concentrated first on the horses and then played havoc with the knights thus grounded. At the climax of the battle, Bruce himself came up with a brigade of Highlanders and Islemen. At this point a great array of unarmored peasants came into view. The English mistook them for a second Scottish army and fled, many of them to be drowned in the burn. Edward II left the field in haste and eventually made his way back to Berwick. Sir Philip Mowbray surrendered **Stirling Castle** *(477)*, and Bruce, as was his custom, razed it to the ground, so that today little or no trace is left of the walls and towers that looked down upon his splendid victory.

Secure at last on his throne, King Robert could now turn to the task of tightening his grip on his kingdom. Strong centralized government in the modern sense was beyond the reach of a medieval Scottish ruler. The best he could do was to secure the loyalty and cooperation of local magnates upon whom the maintenance of law and order devolved. In this connection Bruce had the advantage of having at his disposal vast territories forfeited by the Balliols, Comyns, and their followers. These could be parcelled out among his own supporters. Thus a large portion of the estates of the Balliol faction in the Southwest went to Sir James Douglas and to James the Steward, whose son Walter received as well the hand of the king's daughter Marjorie in marriage. In the West, Angus Og of Islay got most of the former Comyn lordship of Lochaber, as well as the districts of Glencoe, Morvern, and Ardnamurchan and the islands of Mull, Tiree, and Coll. In Argyll most of the lands of the MacDougalls went to Sir Neil Campbell and his relatives, thereby founding a dynasty to compete with the MacDonalds for dominance in the western Highlands. Tarbert, the strategic position at the head of the Kintyre Peninsula, the king kept in his own hands. It was probably he who rebuilt **Tarbert Castle** *(474)*, now a sparse ruin overlooking the town of the same name. To his nephew Thomas Randolph, Bruce gave the Isle of Man and the great earldom of Moray, including the former Comyn property of **Urquhart Castle** *(520)*, now a much damaged but highly picturesque ruin overlooking Loch Ness. The Comyn earldom of Buchan was dismembered and distributed among a number of Bruce's followers including the Rosses, Keiths, Gordons, Frasers, Grants, Setons, Hays, Roses, and Irvines. It was one of the last named who was given, or possibly himself built, **Drum Castle** *(535)*, about ten miles west of Aberdeen—today a well-preserved early-fourteenth-century granite tower-house adjacent to a seventeenth-century mansion, until very recently occupied by descendants of William de Irwin, armor-bearer to King Robert.

Paying off his Scottish friends and enemies was easier for the king than reaching a lasting settlement with the English. Edward II's escape from Bannockburn, no matter how ignominious, made it possible for his countrymen to nullify the verdict of the battle. Not for fourteen years did an English government recognize the independence of Scotland and the sovereignty of its king. Meanwhile, the Scots raided freely over the border—burning, pillaging, and extracting as much as £20,000 in protection money over a ten-year period. In 1318 the English garrison at Berwick surrendered, although in the same year the king's brother, Edward Bruce, lost his life in a futile campaign to establish Scottish sway over Ireland. In 1326 King Robert renewed the alliance with France, whose rulers had been distressingly unhelpful throughout the recent conflict. The following year Edward II was deposed and murdered by his own people. In 1328 the newly appointed English regents, Queen Isabella and her lover Roger Mortimer, agreed to peace with Scotland. According to the treaty, concluded at Edinburgh and ratified at Northampton, the English king (now Edward III) renounced all claim to suzerainty over Scotland; King Robert promised an indemnification of £20,000; his son and heir, David Bruce, was to marry Joan of the Tower, Edward III's sister; and the English government would do what it could to have the papal sentence of excommunication against the King of Scots repealed.

Bruce's long quarrel with the papacy, to which the final clause of the treaty alluded, dates from his sacrilegious murder of the Red Comyn on the high altar of the Greyfriars' Church in Dumfries. Excommunication inevitably followed. It was renewed from time to time partly as a result of English influence at the papal curia. Bruce, however, enjoyed the support of most of the prelates of the Scottish Church—traditionally anti-English if for no other reason than their fear of domination by the archbishops of York and Canterbury. In 1319 Pope John XXII had cited four leading Scottish bishops to appear before the curia for contumacy. When they ignored the summons, they too were excommunicated. In response, Abbot Bernard of Arbroath composed a defiant letter to the Pope, to which a group of leading Scottish earls and barons set their seals. This is the so-called Declaration of Arbroath, an original version of which is on display at the **West Register House** *(446)* in Edinburgh. The magnates declared their devotion to King Robert Bruce as "the person who hath restored the people's safety in defense of their liberties," and warned that, should this king desert the cause of Scottish independence, they would endeavor to expel him and "make another king who will defend our liberties." Then came the ringing challenge—in noble words borrowed freely from the Roman historian Sallust and sacred still in the hearts of all true Scots:

> For as long as one hundred of us shall remain alive we shall never in any wise consent to submit to the rule of the English, for it is not for glory we fight, nor for riches, nor for honors, but for freedom alone, which no good man loses but with his life.

Sometimes referred to as the "Scottish Declaration of Independence," this document ranks high—along with Magna Carta and Thomas Jefferson's Declaration of 1776—among the world's classic pronouncements in the name of liberty. In the end the Pope gave way and released Bruce and the others from the dire penalty of excommunication. In 1328 he went even further by conceding the privilege, long denied to Scottish kings, of being anointed on the occasion of their coronation. By the time word of this last concession reached Scotland, however, Robert the Bruce was dead. His body was interred in **Dunfermline Abbey** *(488)*, where it still lies beneath the pulpit in the choir. His embalmed heart he hoped to have laid to rest in the Church of the Holy Sepulchre in Jerusalem, and "the Good Sir James" Douglas was entrusted to conduct it there. En route to the Holy Land, Douglas was himself killed in Spain battling the Moors. Bruce's heart was brought back to Scotland to be buried in **Melrose Abbey** *(417)*, though whether it is still there is uncertain. Sir James's bones were taken to **St. Bride's Chapel** *(399)*, in Douglas, Lanarkshire, where his illegitimate son, Archibald the Grim, erected a splendid alabaster tomb, still to be seen. In memory of his failed expedition, Sir James's descendants still display the heart of Bruce on the Douglas family arms.

A child of five now inherited the throne. This was David II, sole legitimate son of King Robert. War broke out again between Scotland and England, whose king, Edward III, unilaterally voided the Treaty of Edinburgh/Northampton on the grounds of his having been underage when it was signed. Under English sponsorship and supported by various nobles "disinherited" for defecting from the Scottish cause, Edward Balliol, son of the late King John, returned to press his claim to the throne. He was crowned at Scone. Berwick surrendered to Edward III after the disastrous defeat of a Scottish army at Halidon Hill in Northumberland. The young King David and his English queen were sent to France for safety's sake. Balliol did homage to Edward III and surrendered in perpetuity most of the southern counties of Scotland. The war dragged on. The English occupied most of the important castles in the South, though **Dunbar Castle** *(454)* in East Lothian (now a very dilapidated ruin) resisted capture, owing to the determination of its remarkable chatelaine. This was Agnes Randolph, wife of the Earl of March and known as "Black Agnes," who made history with her mocking defiance of the besieging army. (The conventional method in the Middle Ages of ridiculing the English was to threaten to cut off their tails, thus reminding them of the popular myth that nature had endowed every Englishman with the hindquarters of a dog.) The unsuccessful siege of Dunbar marked a turning point in the war. The same year (1338) Edward III set sail for Flanders in a campaign that proved to be the beginning of the Hundred Years War between France and England. In his absence, the Scots recouped most of their losses.

David II and Queen Joan returned in 1341, but five years later the king was captured at Neville's Cross, County Durham, during a raid across the border. He was held prisoner in England for eleven years, while the business of royal government was carried on by his nephew, Robert the Steward, son of the king's older sister Marjorie. It was rumored that the Steward had deliberately engineered the childless David's capture at Neville's Cross so as to advance his own progress toward the throne to which he was next in line. If so, his expectations had to be deferred when David was set free in 1356 on the promise to pay 100,000 marks (about £67,000) in ten installments—all of which but 24,000 marks was in fact paid off. It was no bargain for Scotland, except that the Treaty of Berwick, which ratified the agreement, implicitly recognized the right of the King of Scots to his throne, with no obligation to the English monarch other than the payment of the ransom. Though hostilities between Scotland and England were to continue for another two centuries, the War of Independence was over.

King David ruled for another fifteen years. Politically, they were uneventful—at least by comparison to Scotland's recent tumultous past. Yet slowly the country recovered from its long ordeal of invasion and civil war. Though Berwick and Roxburgh were lost to the English, other towns on the east coast began to prosper—Haddington, Dunbar, North Berwick, Edinburgh, Dundee, and Aberdeen in particular. With the development of new port facilities at Leith, Edinburgh was able to capture much of Berwick's former overseas traffic. This town was by no means yet the "capital" of Scotland, nor even the principal residence of its peripatetic monarch. Still, its strategic importance was recognized again when the king rebuilt **Edinburgh Castle** *(436)*, destroyed by his father after Thomas Randolph's men had scaled the rock to capture it in 1313. "David's Tower" still stands in part, though mostly obscured today by the Half Moon Battery. The king who had it built died in 1371, still childless. His nephew, Robert the Steward, now aged fifty-four, at last came into his own.

THE EARLY STEWART KINGS

Robert II: 1371–1390
Robert III: 1390–1406

While the Bruces derived their surname from the village in Normandy from which their ancestors had emigrated to England, the Stewarts owed theirs to their hereditary position in the royal household of Scotland from the time of David I, who had appointed Walter fitz (son of) Alan to be his *dapifer*, or high steward. In *Macbeth*, written as a compliment to the Scottish King James VI, who had recently succeeded to the throne of England as James I, Shakespeare traced the Stewart ancestry back to the murdered Banquo. On being shown by the weird sisters a vision of the latter's royal descendants, his companion Macbeth exclaims: "What, will the line stretch out to the crack of doom?" (Act IV, Scene 1). In fact, the line (from which the present queen is descended) can be traced no further back than to one Alan, steward to the count of Dol in Brittany in the eleventh century. His son Flaald settled in Monmouthshire in the reign of Henry I of England. Flaald produced a son, also named Alan, who in turn had sons, one of whom became the ancestor of the English earls of Arundel and another of whom (Walter) migrated to Scotland with David I to become baron of Renfrew and the king's high steward. The office became hereditary, and its holders expanded their estates to include Bute and Cowal, while a junior branch acquired the earldom of Menteith and large holdings in Arran and

Knapdale. James, the fifth high steward, joined Bruce's rebellion, and his son Walter received the hand of Bruce's daughter Marjorie in marriage. It was their son who succeeded his uncle, the childless David II, on the throne of Scotland. But, though Robert II might be recognized as King of Scots, none of his contemporaries could forget his earlier status as the steward, only one among several of the chief barons of Scotland. Neither he nor his successors would ever quite overcome the handicap of being considered only *primus inter pares* (first among equals). They were, after all, *parvenus* to royalty, and it was a long time before their mere baronial origins would be forgotten.

By medieval standards, Robert II was an old man when he inherited the throne. He is described as being somewhat ordinary in appearance, with "red bleared eyes, the color of sandalwood." His reputation as a warrior was sullied by his conduct at Neville's Cross, where he had retreated from the field of battle leaving his uncle, King David, a prisoner of the English. Robert Stewart's major accomplishment up to the time of his succession had been to sire a huge brood of children—at least twenty in number—legitimate, illegitimate, and of doubtful legitimacy. In this last category were three sons by Elizabeth Mure, all born before their mother and father had been married. These were John, Earl of Carrick; Robert, Earl of Fife and later Duke of Albany; and Alexander, Earl of Buchan, known as "the Wolf of Badenoch." All were retroactively legitimatized by papal dispensation, but enough doubt remained as to their legal status to give encouragement to the dynastic ambitions of others among the king's numerous progeny. Included in this category were the undoubtedly legitimate earls of Strathearn and of Atholl, sons of the second wife, Euphemia of Ross. Also, waiting offstage, as it were, stood the sons of Robert's numerous daughters whom he had married off to sundry great nobles. Under a stronger king, this "Stewartization" of the Scottish nobility might have been a source of strength to the monarchy. As it was, it only served to create an aristocratic caste that, by virtue of its kinship with the royal house if for no other reason, waxed arrogant and ungovernable.

Moreover, the reign of Robert II witnessed the full emergence of two great baronial dynasties that eventually bade fair to split the kingdom asunder. The first of these was headed by Archibald the Grim, third Earl of Douglas, an illegitimate son of "the Good Sir James." His vast estates included not only his father's properties in the Border counties, but all of Galloway, plus that part of Lanarkshire dominated by **Bothwell Castle** *(410)*, which he held by right of his wife. This he restored to something of its previous glory; his handiwork can be seen today in the ruined north and east curtain walls. At the center of his lordship in Galloway he built **Threave Castle** *(378)* on an island in the River Dee, upstream from the burgh of Kirkcudbright. This is today a splendid and well-preserved ruin—a five-story tower-house, later reinforced with a surrounding curtain wall, its corner towers pierced with gunports. Threave's builder, called "the Grim" allegedly because of his "terrible countenance in warfare," was also called "the Black." His descendants were known as the Black Douglases as distinct from the Red Douglases, whose progenitor was George Douglas, first Earl of Angus, and bastard son of Archibald's cousin William, first Earl of Douglas. It was this William who probably was responsible for the building of **Tantallon Castle** *(458)* on a rocky promontory jutting into the Firth of Forth just east of North Berwick, East Lothian. This massive stronghold of red sandstone is today one of Scotland's most spectacular ruins. With a curtain wall fifty feet high and twelve feet thick, a great gatehouse keep in the middle, and a strong tower at each end, Tantallon was almost impregnable.

On the other side of the country lay the seat of another powerful family that was to be for several generations a thorn in the side of the kings of Scotland. These were the MacDonalds, who, among the many heirs of Somerled, emerged in the fourteenth century as the most powerful clan in the western Highlands and Islands. In the reign of Robert II, their chief was John of Islay, son of Angus Og, who had sided with Bruce in the War of Independence and who had been amply rewarded with extensive land grants on the west coast and in the Inner Hebrides. It was this John who first assumed the title Lord of the Isles. Later he married Amy MacRuari, who brought to her husband lordship of several of the islands of the Outer Hebrides, as well as additional territories on the mainland. The MacDonald chief and his successors had at least two castles on Islay, both now very much ruined. Only one of them is today easily accessible to visitors. This is **Dunyveg Castle** *(466)*, a tower standing above the shore a short distance east of Port Ellen. The other is an island stronghold whose ruins are visible from the adjacent shore of the loch in which it is situated. This is **Finlaggan Castle** *(466)*, off the north shore of Loch Finlaggan west of Port Askaig. It was apparently more of a fortified residence or hall house than a castle and seems to have been the chief administrative center of the Lords of the Isles.

On the mainland, the principal stronghold of the Lords of the Isles was **Ardtornish Castle** *(467)*, on the Morvern (north) shore of the Sound of Mull, just east of Loch Aline. The scanty ruins here consist of the lower walls of a small rectangular tower only seventy-five by fifty feet in plan. It is hard to imagine this place as the site of the great feastings, complete with Celtic bards and harpists, which Scottish tradition, reinforced by the writings of Sir Walter Scott, associates with the Lords of the Isles. There is no doubt, however, that John of Islay regarded himself, and was regarded, as something more than a mere baron. The quasi-regal status he enjoyed in his own domain was enhanced when he divorced Amy MacRuari to marry Margaret, daughter of Robert the Steward. Thus he became, in time, the son-in-law of one King of Scots and the brother-in-law of another when Robert III ascended to the throne.

That event took place in 1390, when the old king, aged seventy-four, drew his last breath at his favorite residence, **Dundonald Castle** *(393)* in Ayrshire, now a picturesque ruin rising from the hill above the village of the same name. His eldest son succeeded as King Robert III, though his Christian name was John. The switch can probably be attributed to the belief that John was an unlucky name for a king, given the experience of Balliol, to say nothing of King John of France, who in 1356 had been taken prisoner by the English at the battle of Poitiers. Also, for a new king of Scotland to have assumed the title of John II would have, by implication, retroactively endorsed Balliol's claim to the throne as John I—a proposition hard to swallow by the Stewart heirs of Robert Bruce.

The newly crowned Robert III, at the age of fifty-three, was almost as old as his father had been at the beginning of his ineffectual reign. Furthermore, for the previous few years he had been a chronic invalid, still suffering from a kick received from a horse. Hence the actual reins of government were taken in hand by his next younger brother (confusingly christened Robert), the Earl of Fife and later Duke of Albany. More ambitious than able, Albany proceeded to solidify his position as Governor of the Realm by building a magnificent new palace, called **Doune Castle** *(502)*, in Perthshire. This is a courtyard castle of the gatehouse keep variety, with its major defensive works and its principal residential quarters both concentrated at the main entrance. Roofed and still standing mostly to its original height overlooking the lovely River Teith, Doune Castle still speaks to today's visitor of the power and glory of its builder.

Far to the north, another ruin speaks just as clearly of the unruliness of another member of the king's family, his younger brother Alexander Stewart, Earl of Buchan, justly called the "Wolf of Badenoch." In the first year of Robert III's reign, this high-born bandit let loose a gang of "wild wykkyd Heland-men" on **Elgin Cathedral** *(526)* in Moray and burned it down. The Bishop of Moray had discontinued the blackmail payments to which the earl had grown accustomed, and this was his revenge. He was, of course, excommunicated, but later made his peace with the Church and was buried in **Dunkeld Cathedral** *(504)*, where his recumbent effigy can still be seen. His illegitimate son, also named Alexander Stewart, later carried on the family tradition by seizing **Kildrummy Castle** *(537)* and forcing its chatelaine, Isabella Douglas, to marry him so as to acquire her right to the earldom of Mar. Small wonder that a chronicler wrote of the reign of Robert

II: "In those days there was no law in Scotland, but he who was stronger oppressed him who was weaker, and the whole kingdom was a den of thieves; murders, herschips [ravagings] and fire-raising, and all other misdeeds remained unpunished; and justice, as if outlawed, lay in exile outwith the bounds of the kingdom."

The most notorious slaughter of the reign took place in 1396 under official auspices. This was the so-called "battle of the clans"—a staged melee between representatives of Clan Kay and Clan Chattan on the North Inch of Perth, presided over by the king himself. (A fictionalized account of the affair is to be found in *The Fair Maid of Perth* by Sir Walter Scott.) When the dust had cleared, there were only twelve survivors of the original sixty combatants.

The origin, nature, and *raison d'être* of Scotland's clans are subjects of endless controversy among historians, ancestor-worshippers, genealogists, and promoters of Scottish tourism. The word itself derives from the Gaelic *clann*, meaning children; but the idea that all clan members, even when they bear the same surname, derive from a common ancestor is fanciful. So is the theory that Scotland's "clan system" owes its origins to ancient Celtic custom imported from Ireland by the first settlers of Dalriada. In fact, there is no evidence of such continuity. Indeed, the absence of any but the most fragmentary documentary references to clans in the Early Middle Ages suggests that coherent kindred groupings of this sort were of little or no significance in Scotland until the close of the fourteenth century. Then, in the general anarchy characteristic of the reigns of the first two Stewart kings, it was natural for lesser men to seek protection from the more powerful and for the latter to surround themselves with loyal dependents who would work and fight for their lord or chief. If, as was sometimes the case especially in the western Highlands and Islands, there were actual ties of consanguinity between lord and tenant, so much the better. If not, fictitious ties of kinship could be, and were, created. Thus, the Gordon Earls of Huntly are known to have required their tenants to assume the surname Gordon. In other cases the adoption of a chief's family name was a voluntary act. The fact is that it was not so much kinship as the geographic isolation of self-sufficient communities coupled with their urgent need for protection in a turbulent society that gave birth to the Scottish clans. They survived until the coercive power of the central government became strong and pervasive enough to render them obsolete.

If the clans were to some extent the product of neglect by the royal government, the continuation of hostilities with England can be attributed simply to misguided policy. Scotland at the end of the fourteenth and for most of the fifteenth century might have enjoyed protracted peace with its southern neighbor. Preoccupied with the renewal of the Hundred Years War in France, and later with the Wars of the Roses at home, the kings of England were not anxious to take up arms again against the Scots. By reaffirming the "auld alliance" with the French in 1371, 1390, and six more times throughout the fifteenth century, the Stewart kings left the English little choice but to do so. When a French expeditionary force of more than a thousand men-at-arms joined the Scots in a raid on Northumberland in 1385, King Richard II retaliated by burning Edinburgh and laying waste the border countryside, including **Melrose Abbey** *(417)*, Roxburghshire, which was devastated. (As an act of contrition, the English king later sent masons north from York to rebuild the abbey church in the late Decorated and early Perpendicular styles then fashionable in England.)

Soon the Scots and their French allies redeemed their honor by putting much of Cumbria to fire and sword. Meanwhile, private warfare raged between the great magnates from both sides of the border. In 1388 the Earl of Douglas and March encountered Harry Hotspur, son of the Earl of Northumberland, at Otterburn, North Yorkshire. Hotspur was taken prisoner, but Douglas was killed. His dying words, as reported by the contemporary French historian Froissart, perfectly expressed the chivalric ideal of the later Middle Ages: "Thanked be God there hath been but a few of myne aucytours [ancestors] that hathe dyed in their beddes. . . . I praye you rayse up agayne my baner, which lyeth on the grounde. . . . But syrs, shew nother to frende nor foe in what case ye se me in, for if myne enemyes know it they wolde rejoyse." Thus spoke James, the second Earl of Douglas. Fourteen years later, his kinsman Archibald, the fourth earl (son of Archibald the Grim), was defeated by the same Hotspur near Homildon Hill in Northumberland and taken prisoner—along with more than two dozen other Scottish nobles, including Murdoch, son of the Duke of Albany.

The Duke meanwhile continued to rule Scotland, his ailing brother Robert III serving in name only. The latter's eldest son and heir apparent had been created Duke of Rothesay and was preparing to succeed to the throne. Instead, he was imprisoned by his uncle Albany at Falkland, where he died, perhaps by enforced starvation. The old king rallied his wits enough to hurry his surviving son James out of the kingdom. En route to France, the boy was captured at sea by English pirates and taken to the court of the King of England (Henry IV), who is reported to have jested: "If the Scots were grateful, they would have sent this youth to be taught by me, for I too know the French language." Thus began a captivity of eighteen years. When news of the event reached Scotland, the old king grew despondent and died at that ancient Stewart stronghold, **Rothesay Castle** *(395)*. He is said to have told his queen: "Bury me, I pray in a midden, and write for my epitaph—'Here lies the worst of kings and the most wretched of men in the whole realm.' "

THE FIFTEENTH CENTURY

James I: 1406–1437
James II: 1437–1460
James III: 1460–1488

The final chapter in the history of medieval Scotland is distinguished for melodrama but notably lacking in coherence. Murders, abductions, vendettas, and bloody reprisals follow each other with melancholy regularity and with no apparent end in sight. Significant gaps in the evidence render even the bare chronology of events all but impossible to follow. In the words of the historian Gordon Donaldson: "It is all rather like watching a play in an unknown language, and watching it, too, by a rather fitful light." The plot is exciting enough, to be sure, but weak on the score of plausibility. Yet, out of the confusion emerges one constant theme: the failure of the kings of Scotland to impose order on their realm. Unlike their immediate predecessors, however, the first three Jameses were not weak in character or resolve. Rather, they were victims of bad luck and of circumstances mostly beyond their control. Among these circumstances, four can be singled out as primarily responsible for the disturbed condition of Scotland for most of the fifteenth century: (1) the recurrence of royal minorities; (2) the unruliness of Scotland's "overmighty subjects"; (3) the inherited enmity of England, exacerbated by the Auld Alliance with France; and (4) the fiscal weakness of the central government. Scottish history in this turbulent period can best be understood in the light of these four factors.

Royal Minorities

From 1406 to 1460 three kings in succession were underage when they succeeded to the throne: James I when he was eleven; James II at six; and James III at eight years of age. During their minorities, Scotland was ruled by regents or governors who took advantage of their temporary hold on the reins of government chiefly to aggrandize themselves, their families, and their connections at the expense of the Crown and to the detriment of good government. When at last each king came of age, he proceeded to retaliate against those who had governed in his minority, to try to recoup the Crown's financial losses, and to reassert the royal prerogative against the pretensions of a fractious nobility grown arrogant in the absence of a strong central government. James I and James III died in the attempt. James II was more successful against his domestic enemies, only to come a cropper in an engagement with the ancient foreign foe.

James I was not only a minor when his father expired, but a prisoner of England's King Henry IV. Even so, considering the fate of his older brother, the Duke of Rothesay, he was safer in the Tower of London and his various other places of confinement than he would have been in Scotland. His uncle, the Duke of Albany, was Governor of the Realm. He was also next in line to the throne and in no hurry to ransom the boy-king, although he did succeed in rescuing his own son Murdoch out of the custody of the English. Not that the life of the royal Scottish prisoner was altogether unpleasant. He was given a proper education in a court far more civilized than that of his own country; was knighted and made a member of the Order of the Garter by King Henry V; and, on his release, was given the hand in marriage of the English king's cousin, Joan Beaufort, who had inspired the ardent King of Scots to write a lengthy poem in the Chaucerian manner (*The Kingis Quair*). But he was not returned to Scotland until 1424—eighteen years after his capture.

Meanwhile, the Dukes of Albany, father and son (Robert and Murdoch), ruled, or rather misruled Scotland. The endemic lawlessness of Robert III's reign continued unabated. Civil war broke out in the North when the elder Albany's nephew, Donald, Lord of the Isles, invaded the mainland in an effort to seize the earldom of Ross. At Harlaw, near Inverurie, Aberdeen-shire, he was turned back by a full-sized army led by another of the duke's nephews, Alexander Stewart, Earl of Mar, the bastard son of the "Wolf of Badenoch." The battle, known as "the Red Harlaw," was bloody in the extreme. (One of the casualties was Sir Gilbert de Greenlaw, whose tomb slab is to be seen at **Kinkell Church** *[541]*, not far from the battlefield.) But Harlaw was not decisive. The Lord of the Isles continued to exercise quasi-legal powers in his own widely scattered domains and declined to renounce his claim to Ross. In the South, the fourth Earl of Douglas enjoyed full rights of regality over Annandale by express grant from Albany. Similar agreements between the governor and sundry other great nobles removed large areas of land from the jurisdiction of the Crown.

In 1424 James I was freed at last on the promise to pay more than £30,000 to cover the "costs and expenses" of his long involuntary stay in England. He was thirty years of age, strong, athletic, experienced in warfare from fighting with the English army in France, accomplished in poetry and music, and endowed with a much-prized wife, the great-granddaughter of

King Edward III of England and granddaughter of John of Gaunt, Duke of Lancaster. On his return to Scotland, he is reported to have vowed: "If God grant me but the life of a dog, I will make the key keep the castle and the bracken-bush the cow." His first step toward restoring law and order was to destroy his faithless relatives, the Albany Stewarts. Murdoch, his two sons, and his father-in-law, the Earl of Lennox, were summarily seized and executed. By the time of the king's own death thirteen years later, he had gone far to keep his vow and to humble the nobility of Scotland. His reign was too short, however, for him to have produced a fully grown heir. When his only son succeeded to the throne as James II, the new king was only six years of age.

Once again a royal minority produced a power vacuum into which ambitious nobles rushed. First on the scene was Sir William Crichton, member of a prominent Midlothian family, whose seat at **Crichton Castle** *(432)*, southeast of Dalkeith, is still among the more attractive ruins in the country. Here, to an earlier plain three-story tower-house, Sir William attached a powerful gatehouse keep, later expanded by subsequent owners. Crichton was keeper of Edinburgh Castle and later Chancellor of Scotland. In league with his former rival, Sir Alexander Livingston of Callander, he won custody of the boy-king's person, and together the two nobles managed to control the government and to enrich themselves for almost thirteen years. It was Crichton who engineered in 1440 the famous "Black Dinner" at Edinburgh Castle. This was the occasion of the murder of the youthful sixth Earl of Douglas and his younger brother, whom Crichton had invited to dine, then seized, and had summarily executed. (The story that he placed a black bull's head on the table after dinner to announce his intentions is a later fictitious embellishment—a gilding of the lily, so to speak.)

At the age of nineteen, James II married Mary of Guelders, niece of the Duke of Burgundy, and at the same time became king in fact. A contemporary portrait by Jorg von Ehingen (in the *Würtenbergische Landesbibliothek* in Stuttgart) shows him to have been a slim young man with a red birthmark covering the left side of his face. In the *Ballade des Seigneurs de Temps Jadis*, François Villon described this disfigurement as *"vermeille comme une amatiste, depuis le front jusq'au menton"* (bright red, like an amethyst, from forehead to chin). This deformity won him the sobriquet of "James of the Fiery Face," and the same adjective could have been applied to his temperament. Although Crichton remained chancellor and his family continued to enjoy the royal favor, the Livingstons were promptly struck down. The king had two of them beheaded and others imprisoned and their property forfeited. For the rest of his reign, however, he was chiefly preoccupied with hunting bigger prey than the Livingstons—in the persons of the eighth and ninth Earls of Douglas and the Lord of the Isles (see below). And, though in general successful as a monarch, he died at the age of thirty, leaving a child of eight to inherit the throne.

Queen Mary of Guelders took over the regency in the name of still another royal minor, James III, but in 1466 he was abducted and carried off to Edinburgh Castle by a party of nobles led by Robert Boyd of Kilmarnock, Ayrshire. (The Boyd family seat, now known as **Dean Castle** *[390]*, is a fourteenth-century tower-house, much enlarged in the fifteenth century by Robert Boyd and more recently fully restored and surrounded by a lovely public park.) During the young king's captivity, he was compelled to agree to the marriage of his sister to Lord Boyd's son Thomas, who was then created Earl of Arran. But once again the tables were turned when James came of age. The Boyd properties were forfeited; the Earl of Arran survived only by escaping to Denmark; his uncle was captured and beheaded. Thus for the third time in succession a king of Scotland took revenge on noble opportunists who had enriched themselves at the Crown's expense during a royal minority.

Overmighty Subjects

Control of the central government or the person of a royal minor was not the only avenue open to ambitious members of the Scottish nobility. Land was the major source of wealth in the Middle Ages, and in its acquisition lay the road to power. Drawing on their extensive estates, great nobles could put into the field private armies sometimes numbering into the thousands. These men-at-arms were sometimes kinsmen, sometimes tenants, sometimes simply lesser men tied to a lord by bonds of "manrent." This was an arrangement whereby a great man's dependents, other than his tenants, agreed to support him in his quarrels in exchange for protection. Thus the feudal obligation of military service owed to a king by his tenants-in-chief could be counterbalanced by extrafeudal ties between great magnates and their "followings." Against such arrogation of power by his own subjects, the king had but one major weapon: forfeiture for treason.

James I used this device, as well as other arbitrary measures, to good effect. By the attainder of Albany and his sons he obtained for the Crown the entire earldoms of Fife and Menteith. After the execution of Murdoch's father-in-law, the Earl of Lennox, he annexed all of his estates. The earldom of Buchan he took when the old earl was killed in France, and the earldom of Mar on the death of the incumbent. The earldom of March was seized from the Dunbar family. On a flimsy pretext, he deprived Malise Graham (a descendant of Robert II by Euphemia of Ross) of the earldom of Strathearn. In 1428 he summoned his northern tenants-in-chief to a parliament at

Inverness, seized and imprisoned fifty of them, and executed several. Then he took arms against Alexander MacDonald, Lord of the Isles, defeated him in battle at Inverlochy, and imprisoned him for a while in **Tantallon Castle** *(458)*.

In the end, however, the king was hoist with his own petard. His furious campaign against his overmighty subjects eventually drove a few of them to regicide. The instigator of the plot to kill the king was Walter Stewart, Earl of Atholl, senior surviving representative of the line of Euphemia of Ross and therefore next in line to the throne after James I's only son. The chosen place of execution was the Dominican friary at Perth, where the king and queen had come to celebrate the feast of Christmas. The assassins, including Atholl's grandson, Sir Robert Stewart, broke in upon the royal couple, wounded the queen, and set upon the king with swords. Though now grown corpulent, James fought back manfully before being hacked to death. When the conspirators were caught, they were handled roughly—especially Atholl, upon whose brow was pressed a crown of red-hot iron. "The fiendishness of the punishments" inflicted on the regicides, says the historian Ranald Nicholson, "on this unique occasion even surpassed English practice."

In the next reign, King James II, after disposing of the Livingstons, turned his attention next to the Black Douglases, who, along with the Lords of the Isles, were the mightiest of Scotland's overmighty subjects. In February 1452 the king issued an invitation to William, the eighth earl, to come to **Stirling Castle** *(477)* along with a written safe-conduct to assure his acceptance. After dinner James ordered Douglas to break a bond recently sealed with the Earls of Crawford and Ross, presumably in derogation of royal authority. When Douglas refused, the king promptly stabbed him, while his courtiers rushed in to finish the job, throwing the gory corpse out of the window into the garden below. After the murder, James Douglas, ninth earl and twin brother to William, forswore his fealty and declared war on the king. Two years later James II invaded Douglas territory. The earl fled to England and was declared guilty of treason. The king captured **Threave Castle** *(378)* with the help of a great bombard, thought to be "Mons Meg," the 6½-ton gun still to be seen at **Edinburgh Castle** *(436)*. All the Black Douglas lands were forfeited and annexed to the Crown. James II was now master of his own realm and confident enough of his own power to create new "honorific" earldoms and bestow them on his loyal supporters. Thus Colin Campbell was made Earl of Argyll; George Leslie, Earl of Rothes; James Douglas of Dalkeith, Earl of Morton; and William Keith, Earl Marischal. Already the earldom of Huntly had been created for Alexander Gordon, the king's most trustworthy vassal in the North. It was he who began construction of **Huntly Castle** *(540)* in Aberdeenshire. This was a large rectangular stone palace or hall house with a high round tower at the southwest corner. All that remains today of the fifteenth-century construction is the basement, with its three vaulted cellars in the main building, and a dome-vaulted "dungeon" in the great tower. The castle was completely rebuilt above ground in the sixteenth and seventeenth centuries, but the ground plan must be attributed to the original builder, Alexander Gordon. In later reigns the earls of Huntly would prove troublesome enough to James II's successors. But, like other medieval Scottish rulers, his solution to baronial disloyalty was to replace insurgent nobles with others whom he felt he could trust. Thus, as a counterpoise to the Black Douglases he raised up the Red Douglases, earls of Angus and custodians of **Tantallon Castle** *(458)*. The king's son and grandson would have cause to regret James II's choice of allies.

James III's problems with the Boyds have already been mentioned. But these were nobles of middling rank and easily disposed of once the king came of age. The more powerful barons, including the king's own brothers, were not so amenable to discipline. During the royal minority, the exiled Earl of Douglas concluded the so-called Treaty of Westminster/Ardtornish with John MacDonald, Lord of the Isles, and his kinsman Donald Balloch. The signatories agreed to become vassals of King Edward IV of England in return for an annual money payment and English assistance in their scheme to conquer Scotland and divide it among themselves. After James III came of age, he took decisive action against the conspirators; forced the Lord of the Isles to surrender Ross, Knapdale, and Kintyre to the Crown; and later captured the Earl of Douglas and sent him to confinement in Lindores Abbey, Fife. Against the ambitions of his younger brothers, James III was equally effective. These were Alexander, Duke of Albany, and John, Earl of Mar, both more popular among the nobility than their royal brother and both disposed to treason against him. Mar was seized by order of the king, imprisoned in **Craigmillar Castle** *(450)*, Midlothian, convicted of witchcraft, and later moved to the Canongate near Holyrood Abbey, where he died in circumstances suggestive of murder. The castle where he had earlier been confined is today a handsome ruin on the outskirts of Edinburgh. As it appeared at the time of Mar's imprisonment, it was a tall L-shaped tower-house with a courtyard enclosed by curtain walls adorned with corner towers.

As to Albany, he was imprisoned in Edinburgh Castle in 1479, escaped to his own castle of Dunbar, then fled to France. He then sold out to King Edward IV of England, who recognized him as Alexander IV of Scotland and promised assistance to his scheme to usurp the Scottish throne by dispossessing his brother. Albany did in fact return to Scotland to be restored to his lands; but in 1483, under charges of treason, he escaped back to England; invaded Scotland in league with the exiled Douglas; escaped again, this time to France; and there was accidentally killed in a tournament.

Disposing thus of his brothers did not endear James III to his barons, especially the great feudatories of the South, including Archibald, fifth Earl of Angus and lord of **Tantallon Castle** *(458)*. The major complaint of these malcontents seems to have been against a group of courtiers who had apparently displaced the hereditary Scottish baronage in the counsels of the king. Unlike most of the hard-bitten, battle-scarred nobility of Scotland, James III was a man of sensitivity and refinement, as indicated by his portrait in the Trinity Alterpiece by Hugo van der Goes, now in the **National Gallery of Scotland** *(444)* in Edinburgh. According to the tradi-tional story, the king's "familiars" at court, loathed by the barons, included a musician, a fencing master, a tailor, and an architect. A handful of these low-born courtiers were allegedly hanged on Lauder Brig in Berwickshire by a lynching party of nobles, led by the Earl of Angus, who thus won the sobriquet of "Bell-the-Cat" (after a fable by Aesop) for being the only person brave enough to risk the king's displeasure by the performance.

In any case, about the time the incident at Lauder is supposed to have taken place, James III was taken to Edinburgh Castle to be temporarily confined. Within a year he was restored to power, but in 1488 open insurrection broke out, again led by the Lowland nobility, this time joined by James, Duke of Rothesay, the king's son and heir. James III, leading an army composed mostly of northerners, was put to flight after losing a battle at Sauchieburn near Stirling. Allegedly, he fell from his horse, was carried to the nearby mill, asked for a priest, and was stabbed in the heart by the false cleric who answered his call. Parliament took note of the event by referring to Sauchieburn as "the unhappy field in the quhilk the King our soverane lord, happinit to be slane." Along with his Danish wife, Queen Margaret, he was buried at nearby **Cambuskenneth Abbey** *(479)*, where the royal bones were discovered almost four hundred years later and reinterred under a suitable memorial stone set up by a distant descendant, Queen Victoria.

Scotland-England-France

Intermittent warfare with England continued throughout the fifteenth century, as before, to drain Scotland of its manpower and resources. So long as Roxburgh and/or Berwick remained in English hands, there were seemingly good reasons of state for keeping the ancient enmity alive.

Furthermore, high-ranking Scottish clergymen, always fearful of the hegemonial designs of the English Church, condoned it. Moreover, the great southern nobility profited from it by looting expeditions across the border. Most of all, the Auld Alliance, renewed in 1407, 1423, 1428, 1448, and 1484, legitimatized it. These pacts committed both France and Scotland to mutual assistance against English aggression, but it was the French who benefitted mostly, while the Scots were the more faithful in meeting their treaty obligations.

In the reign of James I, John Stewart, Earl of Buchan, and Archibald, fourth Earl of Douglas, sailed with a force of some six thousand men to fight for the French King Charles VII in the second phase of the Hundred Years War. The former was made Constable of France and the latter Duc de Touraine before both were slain at the Battle of Vernueil in 1424. Thereafter, command of the Scottish forces in France was in the hands of John Stewart of Darnley, lord of Concressault. In 1436 the King of Scots' daughter Margaret, aged eleven, was married to the thirteen-year-old Dauphin of France, but died before her husband came to the throne. Scottish troops were organized as the French king's *Garde Ecossaise*, later romanticized by Sir Walter Scott in *Quentin Durward*.

These mounted knights would undoubtedly have been garbed in plate armor, which by the mid-fifteenth century had generally replaced mail. The only authentic evidence of what these warriors looked like is to be found, again, in the stone carvings decorating western Highland tombs. A good example is the effigy of Alan MacDougall at **Ardchattan Priory** *(473)* on Loch Etive, northeast of Oban, Argyll, showing this Highland knight's body encased in plate armor worn over a haubergeon (tunic) of linen, while his legs are sheathed in plated greaves and his knees protected by poleyns of the same material. (The nearby effigy of Alan's father Somerled, by contrast, is covered with old-fashioned mail.)

The year before his death, James I laid unsuccessful siege to Roxburgh Castle—an inglorious failure that hastened his own downfall. His son, James II, was equally determined to drive the English out of Roxburgh and Berwick. In August 1460 he again laid siege to the former, but was killed instantly when a wedge used to tighten the iron hoops around one of the new Scottish bombards flew off and struck him. As the sixteenth-century chronicler, Lindsay of Piscottie, put it: "This Prince, mair curieous nor became him or the majestie of ane King, did stand neir hand by the gunneris quhen the artaillezerie was dischargeand." Despite their loss, the Scots did at last take and keep Roxburgh, though they destroyed the castle for fear of its falling again into English hands. The site of this once famous bastion is now marked by the almost denuded **Roxburgh Castle Mound** *(415)* outside of Kelso. As to Berwick, it was surrendered to Scotland in 1161 during the minority of James III as the price of the Scots' support for the Lancastrian cause during England's Wars of the Roses. Twenty-one years later, the Yorkist King Edward IV sent an army north to recapture it. Thereafter, Berwick was to remain a part of England, though the county of Berwick-shire north of the Tweed was retained by Scotland. The border between the two countries had at last been stabilized.

Royal Revenues and Central Government

As mentioned previously, after his return from captivity in England, James I's first priority, he said, was to reestablish law and order in his kingdom—"to make the key keep the castle and the bracken-bush the cow." These were brave words but impossible of accomplishment, either by this king or by any of his successors for more than a century and a half. The Crown simply lacked the tools of law enforcement to impose order throughout the realm. Though there was an embryonic system of royal courts comparable to that which had been developing steadily in England since the twelfth century, royal jurisdiction had been steadily alienated along with the many territorial concessions to various nobles in exchange for their dubious loyalty. Courts of regality held by the greater barons had jurisdiction over all types of cases except treason; courts of barony, presided over by nobles of lesser stature, had power to deal with a myriad of criminal and civil cases and to enjoy the profits therefrom. Even the sheriffs, theoretically agents of the king, were mostly great magnates who could and did act independently of him. Their positions were hereditary, and their custodianship of royal castles gave them a degree of autonomy seldom enjoyed by their counterparts in England.

The fact is that the early Stewart kings lacked the financial resources to establish an effective infrastructure of government, even had they been able to impose it on their noble subjects. In the fourteenth century, Scottish kings were poor. Royal revenues were no more than a tenth of those of contemporary English monarchs. Land, of course, was the chief source of income, and so much of it had been alienated, first by Robert I and then by his grandson Robert II, as to leave James I with little more than the patrimony of the Bruces and Stewarts in the Southwest. The first two Jameses of course added considerably to the royal demesnes by forfeiting their Stewart relatives, the Douglases, Livingstons, and others. In the reign of James III, the MacDonald Lords of the isles were forced to relinquish the earldom of Ross, as well as Knapdale and Kintyre. Already during this king's minority, the islands of Orkney and Shetland had in effect been transferred to Scotland by a marriage treaty with King Christian of the united kingdom of Denmark and Norway. King Christian's lands, rights, and revenues in the two northern islands were pledged as security for the dowry of the Danish Princess Margaret, who was to be wed to the young Scottish king. Subsequently, the Earl of Orkney, William St. Clair, was persuaded to resign his lands and rights to James III in exchange for estates in Fife, including **Ravenscraig Castle** *(489)* in Kirkcaldy. When the Danish king failed to redeem his pledge, Orkney and Shetland effectively became Scottish. Thus the royal demesne by the third quarter of the fifteenth century had been both restored and enlarged.

Rents from land, however, were normally paid in kind, not in money, and the Scottish kings were perennially short of cash. Some revenues, especially from the royal burghs, were fixed in perpetuity, and their real value was declining with inflation. Royal revenues, to be sure, were being somewhat enhanced by the practice of "feu-ferming"; that is, making hereditary grants of land in return for fixed annual cash payments in lieu of feudal service, military or otherwise. General taxation, however, was seldom resorted to, and then only in extraordinary circumstances, such as to pay the ransoms of David II and James I.

Why the Kings of Scots were unable or unwilling to levy taxes—a practice long established in England—is not at all clear. The reason may be found in the stunted development of the Scottish parliament. Parliaments of tenants-in-chief and high churchmen had been called with some frequency since the Early Middle Ages to advise the king and, among other things, declare war, confirm treaties, ratify forfeitures, and serve as a high court of justice. From the early fourteenth century, representatives of the royal burghs had also been invited to sit with the assembled nobles and prelates. James I, having observed during his enforced stay in England the development of the House of Commons, tried to induce his lesser barons and free tenants to elect their own representatives to parliament and even to select a common speaker to act as their spokesman. His purpose may have been to broaden the tax base by trading political concessions to the commons for grants of supply, as the kings of England were accustomed to do. If so, the plan failed. County representatives were not elected, and there was never a speaker. Parliament in Scotland remained unicameral and entirely dominated by the great magnates, lay and ecclesiastical.

In spite of their relative poverty, however, the Scottish kings were great spenders—luxury-loving and extravagant, at least in the eyes of their subjects. High on the list of their expensive outlays were the moneys paid for the purchase of artillery. In 1430 James I imported a "huge bombard of brass'' from Flanders. More commonly, these guns were made of wrought iron rods encircled with iron hoops. In the last years of his reign he is known to have spent some £590 for gun manufacture. "Mons Meg," already mentioned and still on display at **Edinburgh Castle** *(436)*, is probably typical. It weighs 6½ tons and could fire a stone shot of 550 pounds or 1,125 pounds of iron shrapnel to a distance of two miles. It was expensive to build and expensive to use, requiring huge teams of men and oxen to move from one place to another. James II was of course an ardent gun buff and used artillery pieces in his successful siege of **Threave Castle** *(378)* in 1455. In the end, as mentioned, his enthusiasm was his undoing when he stood too close to an exploding bombard at Roxburgh.

Domestic comfort, as well as martial glory, was a preoccupation of the royal Stewarts in the fifteenth century. The castles of their forefathers were gloomy places, fashioned far more for defense than for amenity. James I began the rebuilding of **Linlithgow Palace** *(426)* in West Lothian as a suitable residence for himself and his English bride, Joan Beaufort. He spent more than £4,500 on the project and completed the eastern wing of the present four-sided building surrounding a central courtyard. This lovely and well preserved ruin of gray and yellow sandstone is one of Britain's finest surviving examples of a late medieval palace. As such, it was by definition a residence, not a stronghold, and its defensive features are limited to the gunports in the main gateway added in the sixteenth century. Though greatly enlarged by later kings and adorned with neoclassical features, the most impressive part of the building is still the Great Hall or Lyon Chalmer built by James I and now constituting the eastern range of the quadrangle. It was, and remained for several generations, a most suitable residence for royalty.

Also built as a residence for royalty, but of a completely different character, is **Ravenscraig Castle** *(489)*, on the coast of Fife at Kirkcaldy. It was begun in 1460 by James II as a gift to his wife, Mary of Guelders, and was ready for her brief occupation as a widow three years later. This was the first castle built in Scotland expressly for the purpose of withstanding and returning gunfire. Its walls are pockmarked with inverted keyhole gunports and its parapet with widemouthed embrasures, both designed to afford the castle's defenders as wide a field of fire as possible against an army approaching from its landward side. (Attack up the cliffs from the sea was not, apparently, seriously considered to be a possibility.) Though ample provision was made inside for the comfort of Mary of Guelders, Ravenscraig was designed primarily as an artillery fortress, unique in medieval Scotland and not to be duplicated for another two centuries. It is thus a fitting memorial to the king whose passion for gunfire was so ardent that it killed him. To the master mason who designed it, James II paid the not inconsiderable sum of £600. Such an expenditure can be viewed on the one hand as typical royal extravagance, but on the other as an indication of the increasing solvency of the Scottish Crown despite its manifold financial difficulties.

DOMESTIC ARCHITECTURE

According to the conventional view of Scottish history, the Late Middle Ages was a period of almost unrelieved turbulence, bloodshed, anarchy, and economic privation. "The Scots," wrote the Spanish Ambassador Don Pedro de Ayala at the end of the fifteenth century, "are not industrious and the people are poor. They spend all their time in wars, and when there is no war they fight with one another." The ambassador's judgment was as simplistic as it was harsh. In fact, violence was the exception rather than the rule in the lives of most men and women as they went about their daily business. Scotland did recover, though slowly, from the War of Independence. Trade with France and the Low Countries flourished. The east-coast towns—Aberdeen, Dundee, Perth, and especially Edinburgh—grew in population. In the countryside, landholders of middling rank—later to be known as *lairds* as distinct from *lords*—were beginning to prosper. Even the failure of James I to organize these people into a house of commons is an indication of their growing independence, at least to the extent that they were able to resist pressure from the Crown to submit to the financial burden and inconvenience of attending parliament. More enduring evidence of their development as an incipient "middle class" of landed gentry is to be found in the proliferation of residential country seats—substantial houses of stone, less grandiose than the royal and baronial castles of the thirteenth century, but far more imposing than the modest homesteads of the ordinary run of agrarian tenants.

In England, men of moderate wealth were building fortified manor houses—simple stone dwellings usually consisting of an undercroft, a spacious first-floor hall with a well-defended entranceway, and sometimes an adjacent wing or angle tower. In Scotland, these are called *hall houses*, and they are comparatively rare. The best surviving example is **Morton Castle** *(388)*, near Thornhill, Dumfriesshire, built around the turn of the thirteenth and fourteenth centuries. It is now roofless and floorless, but the walls still stand to the original height. It consists of a typical medieval long hall over an unvaulted undercroft. A large and defensible arched entrance led to the screens passage of the hall, where no doubt once stood a tall wooden screen to hide the serving tables from the hall itself. At the other end was the dais where the owner and his family would have dined. A hooded fireplace marked this end. Beyond it is a rounded tower containing private compartments, latrines, etc. The approach from the landward side of the lakeside promontory on which it stands is guarded by a twin-towered gatehouse, now much ruined.

Far more typical of Scottish residential building in the fourteenth and fifteenth centuries is the so-called tower-house, which continued to be the most popular form of domestic construction until the end of the seventeenth century and is today one of the most characteristic features of the Scottish landscape. The tower-house provided about the same amount and type of accommodation as the hall house, but was vertically disposed rather than horizontally. It consisted simply of a series of apartments built on top of one another to a height of at least three or four stories. The ground floor, often vaulted, was the storage cellar, usually entered by a door at ground level and connected with the floor above by a ladder leading up to a hatch. The hatch opened onto the first floor, which was entered from the outside by a wooden stair or ladder. Here was the hall, arranged in the same way as in any manor house or castle. In the corner, set into the wall, was a spiral stone staircase or turnpike leading to the floors above. These were usually subdivided into compartments serving as bedrooms, withdrawing rooms, etc. Garderobes or latrines would normally be mural chambers. Sometimes within the basement wall might be a subterranean chamber used for a pit prison and accessible only through a hatch in the first floor.

Variations on this basic rectangular plan were many, but in the fourteenth and fifteenth centuries the most common of these was the L-plan house, with a wing or "jamb" at right angles to one end of the rectangle. Architectural historians once thought that the purpose of this arrangement was primarily defensive; that is, to allow the entrance, which was often situated at the inner angle of the L (the reentrant angle), to be covered by fire from both the central block and the jamb. The present consensus among experts, however, seems to be that considerations of domestic amenity outweighed military factors in determining tower-house design. An additional wing might provide more space for living quarters or for a turnpike staircase; offered greater convenience in the positioning of service facilities; and served as demonstrable evidence of the wealth and status of the builders. Tower-houses relied mainly on their own thick walls for defense. They might have machicolated parapets, yetts to guard the doors, and barmkin walls around their courtyards. But they are not to be thought of as true castles. They were, for the most part, manor houses, built strong enough to keep out robbers and fend off sudden raids, but not normally to house large bodies of retainers or withstand long sieges. The distinction is well to keep in mind, especially since many tower-houses are today labelled "castles."

No visitor to Scotland can fail to notice the multitude of tower-houses dotting the rural landscape, their solitary silhouettes etched against the sky. Some are ruined, some roofed, and some even still (or again) inhabited. Representative examples dating from the fourteenth and fifteenth centuries are listed below, roughly in geographic order from west to east and south to north.

Cardoness Castle *(380)*, just south of Gatehouse of Fleet, Kirkcudbright-shire, is typical. It is a well-preserved ruin, dating from the fifteenth century, is four stories high above the vaulted basement, and is laid out in the manner described above. It was the home of the McCullochs, not one of the great baronial families of Galloway. In the same county, southeast of Castle Douglas, is **Orchardton Tower** *(379)*, built in the mid-fifteenth century by the local laird, one John Carnys. Though ruined, it still rises to its original three-story height above the ground-floor storage basement, but is uniquely circular, rather than rectangular, in plan. North of here, in Renfrewshire, are two tower-houses very different from each other. **Newark Castle** *(397)*, in Port Glasgow on the south bank of the River Clyde, is a very well-preserved fortified residence consisting of three connecting parts: (1) a typical rectangular tower-house built some time after 1478 by George Maxwell of a powerful county family; (2) a two-story gatehouse contemporary with it; and (3) connecting the two, a Scottish Renaissance mansion installed by Sir Patrick Maxwell at the end of the sixteenth century. **Crookston Castle** *(397)*, just east of Paisley, is a much ruined mid-fourteenth-century tower-house built by Alan Stewart of Darnley, progenitor of a constable of France and of the second husband of Mary, Queen of Scots. It is unusual in plan, in that a small square tower projects from each of the four corners of the rectangular central tower, thus providing greatly amplified living space.

Crookston is sometimes said to be the twin of a much better-known and better-preserved tower-house, **Hermitage Castle** *(413)*, south of Hawick, Roxburghshire. The similarity is far from apparent to the naked eye, however. This grim border stronghold lying athwart one of the major routes of access to and from England, though technically a tower-house, looks like a mighty fortress and bears some resemblance to a courtyard castle. Construction here began in the mid-fourteenth century, when English owners, the Dacres, built a manor house of two rectangular blocks connected by screen walls to enclose a small open court. About 1371 the estate came into the hands of William, first Earl of Douglas, and it was he or his immediate successors who were responsible for the rebuilding to which the structure's present appearance is mainly due. The manor house was elevated into a tower-house, and to each corner of the rectangular central block was added a quadrangular tower of the same height. On the east and west faces of the building, the projecting towers were linked together at the top by filling up the upper portion of the space between them with an added layer of masonry, interrupted near the lower edge by a wide arch. Putlog holes and stone corbels around the wall-head supported hoardings. Hermitage, more than most tower-houses, was built for defense.

Coming north to the town of Peebles, the traveller will encounter **Neidpath Castle** *(421)*, overlooking the River Tweed. This is an L-plan tower-house built in the fourteenth century by the Hays of Yester, ancestors of the earls and marquises of Tweeddale. It was much remodelled in the seventeenth century, altered again in the eighteenth, and reroofed and restored in the twentieth. These various renovations changed considerably the internal appearance of the tower, but externally it remains not too different from the original. **Borthwick Castle** *(432)*, a dozen miles southeast of Edinburgh, has been described by the architectural historian Stewart Cruden as "one of the finest late medieval castles in Britain." "Castle" it is called, and "castle" it appears to be, but architecturally speaking, it is a tower-house—a tall, rectangular central block with a jamb advancing from each end of the west side, thus forming a double-L or U-shaped ground plan. The curtain wall and gatehouse were added in the late fifteenth century. Still in use as a guest house and conference center, Borthwick's interior displays a magnificence unusual for an early fifteenth-century tower-house. Yet it was built not by one of the great hereditary barons of Scotland, but by a mere laird, Sir William Borthwick, not yet elevated to his ultimate status of "lord of parliament."

Cutting across to the opposite side of the country to Loch Awe in Argyll, we come to **Kilchurn Castle** *(464)*, seat of the Campbells of Glenorchy, afterward the earls and marquises of Breadalbane. Built probably late in the fifteenth century (with seventeenth-century additions), it is badly dilapidated but now under restoration by the Scottish Development Department. Standing close to the northern shore of one of Scotland's lovelier inland lochs, it is a fine and picturesque ruin—romantic enough in appearance to have inspired a poem by William Wordsworth. Moving southeastward from here, the traveller will encounter **Clackmannan Tower** *(481)* on the outskirts of the town of the same name. Partly collapsed, but otherwise a well-preserved ruin, this is a fourteenth-century tower-house to which a still taller jamb was added in the fifteenth, giving the building an L-shaped ground plan. Still farther to the east, in Kinross-shire, is **Loch Leven Castle** *(482)*, historically famous as the prison from which Mary, Queen of Scots, escaped in 1567. Situated on an island in the loch, this is a late-fourteenth-century tower-house, almost square in plan and five stories in height. A few miles to the north, also in Kinross-shire, lies **Burleigh Castle** *(482)*, seat of the Balfour family. Here is a ruined tower-house dating from about 1500, adjoined by the remains of a barmkin wall and a gatehouse of the late sixteenth century with roof and windows still intact and walls bristling with gunports.

All of these tower-houses were solidly built, secure against robbers and raiding parties, though not powerful strongholds like most early medieval castles. Also, they are very plain houses. They boast little in the way of embellishment and are undistinguished as to aesthetic refinement. Yet Scotland suffered no dearth of talented masons and stone-carvers in the Middle Ages. To view their workmanship, the intelligent traveller must turn aside from purely secular architecture and look to the plethora of ecclesiastical buildings still standing, in whole or in part, throughout the length and breadth of Scotland.

Chapter Five

Medieval Religion, Art, and Learning
1057–1560

Within the precincts of **Edinburgh Castle** *(436)*, on the highest point of the great basaltic rock overlooking the city, stands St. Margaret's Chapel, a tiny edifice consisting of a nave that holds no more than twenty people, and a semicircular apse at the east end, divided from the nave by a typical rounded Norman or Romanesque arch incised with chevrons. Though much restored (including the unfortunate installation of stained glass in the round-headed windows), this altogether charming little place of worship dates probably from the late eleventh or early twelfth century, not long after the death of the queen (and later saint) for whom it is named.

This pious Anglo-Saxon princess, sister to Edgar the Aetheling who had been deprived of the English throne by William the Conqueror, became the second wife of Malcolm Canmore about 1070. She had been reared as a child in the intensely religious royal court of Hungary and then in the equally Christian household of the English King Edward the Confessor. Her biographer, Turgot, a Benedictine monk who rose to become prior of Durham and later bishop of St. Andrews, described her as an intensely devout woman, given to constant prayer, fasting, scriptural study, alms-giving, and other good works. Queen Margaret's gift to Scotland was to arouse that country from its spiritual lethargy and to commence the process by which the Scottish Church was brought into conformity with the Church of Rome and Western Christendom.

Scotland was, of course, a Christian nation. At St. Andrews there was a bishop who claimed some sort of primacy over other bishops, and there were communities of Culdees at Loch Leven, Monifeith, Brechin, Muthill, Monymusk, Abernethy, and Iona, as well as at St. Andrews. It was to the last named place that St. Rule (Regulus) had allegedly brought the bones of the Apostle Andrew, whose cult was to replace that of St. Columba at Iona and who would in time become the patron saint of Scotland. Here in the eleventh century was built the **Church of St. Rule (Regulus)** *(492)*, a splendid architectural monument in the Anglo-Saxon style. Its substantial remains today consist of the roofed 24-foot-long choir (chancel) and, at the west end, the great 108-foot tower that rises above the ruins of Scotland's preeminent Cathedral of St. Andrew (see below). Roughly contemporary with it are the tall towers of **Muthill Church** *(501)* and **St. Serf's, Dunning** *(497)*, both in Perthshire. The former stands 70 feet high and was incorporated into the adjacent fifteenth-century kirk, now in ruins. The latter is a few feet higher, and its attached church is of early-nineteenth-century construction, though the doorway leading into the tower from the nave is Transitional—a Gothic pointed arch mounted on Romanesque cylindrical columns.

The queen did nothing to disturb these established institutions. Indeed, she endowed the church at St. Andrews, gave generously to the Culdees of Loch Leven, and may have been responsible for the building of St. Oran's Chapel at **Iona Abbey** *(465)*, though that island was not yet within the dominion of the King of Scots. What is more certain is that she enlarged the church on the site now occupied by **Dunfermline Abbey** *(488)* and to it invited three Benedictine monks from Canterbury, selected by the great Archbishop Lanfranc himself for what was obviously intended to be a missionary enterprise.

When these three arrived, Queen Margaret convened a conference of Scottish churchmen in an effort to induce them to follow established Roman practices on the timing of Lent, partaking of the Sacrament on Easter Day, and particularly the rites to be followed in celebrating the Mass, which she found in Scotland to be "barbarous." Whether the Scottish clergy immediately mended their ways is unknown, but it can be said that the queen's insistence on a stricter observance of the Lord's Day set a precedent for the strict Sabbatarianism for which Scotland later became famous. And the Benedictines stayed to found a priory at Dunfermline.

MONASTERIES

These monks belonged to the oldest of the Roman Church's monastic orders. In 529 at Monte Cassino in Italy St. Benedict had founded a monastery where the residents took vows of chastity, poverty, and obedience and lived under a strict rule prescribed by the founder. (The Latin word for *rule* is *regula*; hence, monks were called "regular" clergy as distinct from parish priests and cathedral canons, who were known as "secular.") The sixty-sixth chapter of St. Benedict's Rule ordains that the monastery should be self-contained; that is, enclosed within precincts beyond which the residents would normally not stray. If such an establishment was ruled by an abbot, it was called an *abbey*; if of lower status and ruled by a prior or prioress (in the case of a nunnery), it was referred to as a *priory*. Although monks and nuns might be charged with manual or intellectual labors, their main business was to glorify and worship God and especially to pray for forgiveness for their own sins, for those of the benefactors of their houses, and for mankind at large. Worship took the form of prescribed choral services conducted seven or eight times daily from midnight until about nine in the evening the following day. Collectively, these were known as the *Opus Dei*; sequentially, they were designated Vigils (or Nocturns), Matins (or Lauds), Prime, Tierce, Sext, None, Vespers, and Compline. In addition, High Mass was celebrated in the morning and special masses might be said at other times of the day. This left about eight hours for sleep, and the rest of the time was spent in work, at meals, attending the daily chapter meeting, in silent meditation, or in communication with one's fellows.

Such austerity was hard to maintain over long periods of time, especially as monasteries grew wealthy from large endowments and expanding revenues from their estates. From time to time, therefore, individual monasteries in Western Europe undertook to restore the rigors of early Benedictine monasticism; these in turn founded "daughter houses," thus giving rise to several "orders" of reformed Benedictines. Four of these were to found houses in Scotland. (A fifth, the Carthusians, had a single priory— at Perth—but no part of it has survived.) The oldest among the reformed orders was that first established in the tenth century at Cluny in Burgundy, which became the motherhouse of a large number of abbeys on the Continent and in Britain. An even more austere order was that of the Cistercians, which had its beginnings at Cîteaux, also in Burgundy, in the early twelfth century. These monks settled mostly in remote places and invited lay brothers to share their monasteries and work their usually extensive lands. In the early days of the order's existence, they insisted on architectural simplicity in their buildings and from the beginning wore nothing but robes of undyed wool—hence, they became known as the White Monks. Similar in the severity of their rule were the Brown Monks, the Tironensians, originating at the abbey of Tiron near Chartres. An even stricter order was that of the Valliscaulians, who in the early thirteenth century sent out colonies to Scotland (but not England) from their mother-house in the Val des Choux (*Vallis Caulium*) in Burgundy.

Of a somewhat different nature were the Augustinians (the White Canons) and Premonstratensians (Black Canons). Though they too lived in cloistered communities; took vows of poverty, chastity, and obedience; and lived under a rule; they moved in the world outside the monastery walls, held themselves responsible for the cure of souls (i.e., served as parish priests), and in general lived less secluded lives than their monkish brothers. Indeed they were not monks at all, but "canons regular," though their abbeys and priories differed in no important respect from those of the other regular orders. Out of Palestine in the aftermath of the First Crusade came the military orders—the Knights Templars, following the rule of St. Benedict, and Knights Hospitallers, following that of St. Augustine. Both were to found establishments in Scotland. Finally came the female orders—both Benedictine and Augustinian—although only the latter has left any visible trace in Scotland.

The medieval monastery, whether abbey, priory, or nunnery, was above all functional; that is, it was a complex of buildings designed specifically to meet the particular requirements of its residents. The life of the monk, nun, and (to a lesser extent) canon was a communal existence, centered around the celebration of the Mass, choral worship, prayer, and strict obedience to the Rule under the authority of abbot, prior, or prioress. The architectural plan of almost any monastery was ideally suited to these needs. The central building was of course the church, usually cruciform, with the high altar at the eastern end in the presbytery. At this end also were sedilia (stone seats) for officiating clergy against one presbytery wall; a piscina for rinsing the chalice on the other; and aumbries (wall recesses) for storing the sacred vessels. Immediately to the west of the presbytery was the choir or chancel with facing rows of stalls for the monks or canons. Still further to the west was the nave (aisled or aisleless), sometimes used as the local parish church, sometimes assigned to the lay brothers. The nave was usually separated from the monks' choir by a screen of wood or stone, called the *pulpitum*. Finally, projecting north and south from the main axis of the building and opening into the crossing underneath the tower, were the transepts, usually with chapels and altars aligned along their eastern sides.

Abutting the church, usually on the south side, was the cloister—three ranges of buildings laid out around a grassy "garth," with the side of the church forming the fourth side of the quadrilateral enclosure. Here the monks or canons lived, ate, slept, studied, worked, and communed with one another. The east range was normally an extension of the south transept. The entire first floor above the ground floor was given over to the residents' sleeping quarters. It was called the *dorter*, and abutting it was the *reredorter*, which contained the latrines. From the dorter a night stair led into the east end of the church for the convenience of the monks who had to bestir themselves around midnight for the nocturnal service. On the ground floor, the room immediately next to the transept usually contained the sacristy, which was entered from the transept. Next to it was the library; then an inner parlor where conversation was permitted; then the chapter house, where the monks met daily for a reading of a chapter of the Rule and to discuss sundry items connected with the business of the monastery; then a day stair leading up to the dorter; then possibly a slype, or open passageway through the building; and finally a basement room containing a drain beneath the latrines above. The south range contained the dining facilities—frater or refectory with an attached kitchen, buttery, and pantry. The west range in most monasteries contained a *cellarium* for storage on the ground floor and above it quarters for the abbot or perhaps for guests. Outside the cloister proper, but within the monastic precincts, might be an abbot's house, a gatehouse, an infirmary, a cemetery, and sundry domestic buildings—malt house, smithy, and the like.

Although there were minor variations in this ground plan, the similarities among abbeys and priories are more noticeable than the differences. One difference, however, was in the occasional setting of the cloister north of the church instead of in the sunnier southern location. In this case, the ground plan was simply a mirror image of the more conventional arrangement. Another difference is to be found among Cistercian monasteries. Here the west range, instead of being used for storage and guest quarters, was reserved for the lay brothers, whom these monks invited to live within the cloister and to whom was assigned the task of tilling the monastic fields, tending the sheep, etc. These *conversi* had the use of the west end of the church nave; they might have had their own infirmary and their own cemetery. Another Cistercian variation was the positioning of the frater at right angles to the cloister so that it projected well beyond the main walls of the south range. Next to it might be a warming room with open fireplace, which served as a common gathering place.

Travellers intending to visit any number of ruined Scottish abbeys—and they should certainly do so—are encouraged to study the paragraphs above. Otherwise the scant remains of most of the claustral buildings will appear as little more than a meaningless clutter of stones and masonry. With the ground plan firmly in mind, however, it requires no great act of imagination to re-create in the mind's eye the original appearance of these once-thriving Christian communities.

The ground plans of medieval monasteries were more or less uniform. Less so was the architectural design of the monastic buildings, especially the churches. Here, at least in the twelfth and thirteenth centuries (i.e., before the War of Independence), architectural styles tended to follow those of England, possibly because the masons were English or English-trained. And as in England (and France too), fashions in ecclesiastical architecture changed, and as they changed became standardized until succeeded by still another stylistic mode. For the twelfth and thirteenth centuries, the names assigned by architectural historians to these succeeding styles are: (1) Norman or Romanesque; (2) Transitional; (3) early Gothic, which in England is called "Early English" but in Scotland "First Pointed"; and (4) middle Gothic, known in England as "Decorated" and in Scotland as "Second Pointed."

Norman or Romanesque churches mostly date to the twelfth century and are distinguishable by their massiveness and roundness—semicircular arches above doors, windows, and interior passageways; very thick exterior walls; heavy cylindrical pillars, if any. Decorative carving is simple but of high quality and consists mostly of chevron and zigzag incisions on the surface of the arches. Transitional buildings display both round and pointed arches. The latter was a discovery of French masons and spread to Britain about the mid-twelfth century. In the eighteenth century, when classicism was in the ascendant, architects derisively referred to the pointed arch and associated elements of medieval architecture as Gothic, meaning "barbarian." The word stuck, though not the pejorative connotations. Functionally, the pointed arch was an improvement over the semicircular (round-headed) arch because the weight of the roof was carried more downward than outward, thus permitting thinner exterior walls; and because the height of all vaulted portions of a building could be kept uniform by the simple process of varying the angle at the apex of the arch so that any width of space beneath could be covered without raising or lowering the roof level. Another Gothic innovation, though not so common in Scotland as elsewhere, was the ribbed vault over the nave, replacing a flat wooden roof with a curved roof of stone supported on the underside by stone ribs stretching from pillars or corbels at the side to the apex in the middle. Still a third feature of this style was the flying buttress—a quarter arch of stone emplaced against a wall so as to counteract the lateral thrust of the weight from above. All three features were probably introduced into Scotland during the heyday of Transitional architecture (the last half of the twelfth century), though the most distinguishing characteristic of the period is the mixture of round and pointed arches. The First Pointed style of the early thirteenth century is pure Gothic and is, in addition, characterized chiefly by narrow lancet windows, single or double. It is less common in Scotland than is Early English south of the border. It was succeeded by Second Pointed, distinguishable mainly by its wider pointed windows, divided vertically by narrow stone bars called *mullions* or *munions* (Scottish), and featuring in the arch a pattern of stone tracery of geometric or curvilinear design, the latter usually indicating a later date of construction than the former. To this period, if not earlier, also belongs the introduction of huge circular windows, sometimes called "rose windows"—also filled with stone tracery of intricate design.

To the reigns of the three younger sons of Malcolm Canmore and Margaret is owed the introduction of Western monasticism into Scotland. In inviting members of the established orders into their country and endowing them richly with lands and other goods, it can be assumed that all three were devoutly concerned with the welfare of their own souls and were, in a sense, buying insurance for eternity through the expected intercessionary prayers of the incoming monks. But there was another motive—especially apparent in the case of the youngest of the three, David I. That was the desire to integrate the Scottish state and Scottish society under the monarchy along the lines already successfully attempted by William the Conqueror and his immediate successors. The establishment of monasteries, along with the episcopal and diocesan organization of the Church to be discussed below, was the ecclesiastical counterpart of the feudalization and "Normanization" of Scotland.

There had formerly been a Celtic monastery at St. Abb's Head in Berwickshire. In 1098 King Edgar (1097–1107) gave the land here to the Benedictine monks of Durham Abbey, who subsequently established **Coldingham Priory** *(424)*. Of the stone church and claustral buildings raised by these original settlers, only fragments are still visible above ground, though excavations have revealed considerable quantities of masonry now buried. The north and east walls of the priory choir, built about 1216 after a devastating raid by King John of England, are now incorporated into the parish church. Lancet windows combined with Norman arcading indicate the Transitional style. Inside this lovely pink stone building, the Gothic arcading under the lancets and along the north wall are especially appealing, though the modern organ is somewhat overwhelming. Sparse as these relics are, they far outnumber the remains of the priory of Augustinian canons imported to Scone, Perthshire, at the invitation of Alexander I (1107–1124), probably from Nostell in Yorkshire. They have left almost no trace of their long occupation beyond a few fragments of masonry in the grounds of **Scone Palace** *(506)*. The same king brought another colony of Augustinians to found **Inchcolm Abbey** *(483)* on a tiny island in the Firth of Forth where, tradition has it, Alexander had been shipwrecked and given shelter by a hermit, in gratitude for which he established a new monastery on the site of an earlier Celtic establishment. A visit here (by boat from Hawes Pier in South Queensferry) can be most instructive to the student of medieval monastic architecture. The tiny stone cell with a "beehive" roof is alleged to be the dwelling place of the hermit who gave succor to Alexander I. The ruined church dates from the thirteenth century, though with many subsequent alterations up to the fifteenth. The cloister walks, however, lying underneath the abbey's frater, dorter, and guest hall, are the most complete in Scotland. The central tower of the church still stands to its original height, and the octagonal chapter house with fine rib vaulting is an outstanding example of late-thirteenth-century work.

Of King David I, Saint Margaret's youngest son, a disgruntled successor, James I, is said to have remarked that he was "ane sair sanct for the croun," meaning that he had been excessively prodigal in the alienation of crown lands to the Church. Certainly this English-bred and thoroughly Normanized prince was not remiss in pious generosity to the monastic orders. Even before he succeeded to the throne, on lands allotted to him by his royal brothers, he had brought monks from Tiron to Selkirk to found an abbey. Later they moved about twenty miles east to be closer to the king's castle of Roxburgh and there established **Kelso Abbey** *(415)* in 1128. Though almost nothing is left here of the claustral buildings, the ruins of the abbey church constitute one of the most splendid examples in Scotland of Romanesque architecture with Transitional features. This was a double-transepted church, unusual in Britain. All that remains are the towering west end—a "Galilee porch," where great processions forgathered before marching into the church; the north and south transepts; and, adjoining the latter, an outer parlor, which is the only surviving portion of the west range of the cloister. The attractive, and somewhat incongruous, mixture of massiveness and delicacy, which is the essence of the Romanesque style, is nowhere better illustrated than at Kelso.

After he became king in 1124, David's benefactions to the monastic orders became a central feature of his program of deliberate Normanization of his newly acquired realm. To Melrose in Roxburghshire he invited Cistercians from Rievaulx Abbey in Yorkshire to found the first of the eleven houses of that order eventually to be established in Scotland. **Melrose Abbey** *(417)*— thought by many to be the country's most romantic ruin—was to be ravaged so many times by English armies that nothing remains of the original buildings except the lower courses of the west wall of the abbey church. The east end, however, is a gorgeous ensemble of English Late Gothic (called Perpendicular) and French Flamboyant (curvilinear Second Pointed) design, unique in Scotland. Especially attractive are the great Perpendicular east window erected by Yorkshire masons sent north by King Richard II to repair the desecration committed by his own army in 1385, the curvilinear chapel windows of French design piercing the south wall, the flying buttresses positioned on the outside of the same wall, and the marvelously carved bosses and gargoyles both inside and out. Less visually exciting, but in a way more instructive, are the foundations of the claustral buildings, here situated north of the church so as to take advantage of the River Tweed for purposes of drainage. A trace of the dorter abutting the north transept can still be observed in the door high up in the gable through which the monks filed to descend the night stairs for nocturnal services. Some of the original tiles of the chapter house floor remain *in situ*; north of it are the foundations of a parlor, then the warming house, and in the northeast corner the day stair to the dorter. As was the custom in Cistercian houses, the frater projects perpendicularly from the north range. Because of the large number of *conversi* at Melrose, the lay brothers' range on the west is extra long and, like the monks' frater, projects north of the north range; also, there is an additional cloister for their special use to the west. Across the great drain (still visible) is the commendator's house, a product of fifteenth- and sixteenth-century construction, now housing the site museum. Nowhere in Scotland can today's traveller get a better understanding of the living arrangements of a medieval Cistercian monastery.

From Melrose, in King David's reign, Cistercians went out to establish another foundation in the north of Scotland. This was **Kinloss Abbey** *(528)* in Moray, of which very little remains standing—part of the south transept and an adjacent vaulted chamber; an arched entrance on the south side of the cloister; a rare example of the monks' washing trough (lavatory); and the ruins of the abbots' house of late medieval construction. **Dundrennan Abbey** *(382)* in Kirkcudbrightshire is another matter. Colonized, like Melrose, by monks from Rievaulx who came here in 1142, the present ruin provides a better illustration of the severity of early Cistercian architecture than any other of their monasteries in Scotland. "No other abbey," says Stewart Cruden, "so eloquently expresses the ideals of Cistercian brotherhood." The simple round-headed west doorway is still intact, but the walls of the nave are all but gone. The north and south transept walls, and part of those of the presbytery, however, still stand high and are splendid examples of Transitional architecture, with round-arched and pointed-arched windows and doors intermingled. The cloister lies to the south. The *cellarium* of the west range is in a good state of preservation. In the east range the most notable surviving feature is the chapter house, of much later construction than the church—with thirteenth-century Second Pointed windows and doorway and, to support the vaulted roof (now gone), fine molded clustered columns, some of whose lower sections are still to be seen.

To Edinburgh David I brought Augustinian canons from St. Andrews to build, at the foot of Canongate, **Holyrood Abbey** *(443)*, so named apparently in commemoration of the holy rood (cross) of ivory and ebony brought to Scotland by his mother and later, it is said, taken from David II at the time of his capture by the English at Neville's Cross. (A charming medieval legend has it that the king was shamed into founding the abbey when a vision of the Holy Rood appeared between the horns of a white stag that he was irreverently hunting on the day of the Feast of the Elevation of the Holy Cross.) English pillage in the sixteenth century, Protestant desecration after the Reformation, the encroachment of the seventeenth-century Holyroodhouse Palace, inadvertent damage incident to rebuilding, and general neglect and decay have reduced this once magnificent establishment to a shambles, albeit a very attractive one. Hardly anything remains of the claustral buildings. A thirteenth-century rebuilding of the church destroyed the original Augustinian edifice, leaving only a blocked eastern doorway leading into the former cloister to the south. This second building was

Transitional in character, as indicated by the round-headed arcading in the north wall in contrast to the pointed arches of the south-wall arcade. The imposing west front, with its deeply recessed main doorway, belongs to this period of construction. So does the great tower to the north of the entrance, though remodelled in the seventeenth century, at which time also a new east window was inserted. The north door into the nave and the buttresses on the outside were added in the fifteenth century. Indeed, so many structural changes have taken place on this site that its architectural history is extremely confusing to any but the most expert eye.

Jedburgh Abbey *(413)*, Roxburghshire, a far more substantial ruin, is also more comprehensible. Another Augustinian house, founded by David I in 1138, it was peopled by canons from Beauvais who built one of the finest Romanesque and Transitional abbey churches left in Scotland. The west end (opening from the present street) is of late-twelfth-century date and was built in the Transitional manner. The Romanesque round-arched recessed doorway is particularly fine. The nave belongs to this period as well. The east end is mostly earlier, the choir being purely Romanesque on the west and Transitional to the east, the junction between the two styles clearly visible. The north transept has been heavily restored for use as a mausoleum for the earls of Lothian. The south transept is mostly the product of a fifteenth-century rebuilding following the usual English depredations. The claustral buildings to the south are badly ruined, but the layout is clearly traceable, and the Scottish Development Department handbook available on the site provides easy identification of the component parts of the cloister.

Cambuskenneth Abbey *(479)*, just outside of Stirling, is another Augustinian house founded by David I, but, though less exposed to English fire and sword than the great Border abbeys, it is today in a far more advanced stage of ruination. About all that is left of the abbey church, built by the founding canons from Arrouaise or their successors, is the western doorway. The only architectural legacy here is the high (sixty-seven feet) detached bell tower built in the First Pointed style of the thirteenth century. Of historical interest, of course, is the restored tomb of King James III and Queen Margaret, already mentioned in the previous chapter. Somewhat less fragmentary are the remains of **Torphichen Preceptory** *(431)*, near Linlithgow, West Lothian. This was a foundation of the Knights Hospitallers of the Order of St. John of Jerusalem, chartered by David I in 1153, the year of his death. About all there is to see here are the transepts, crossing, and a small section of the north wall of the nave of the Transitional priory church, restored and reconstructed in the fourteenth and fifteenth centuries. Upstairs in the tower above the crossing is an excellent museum maintained by the Scottish Development Department, with a highly instructive display showing the history of the military orders.

To King David's reign also belongs the foundation of **Dryburgh Abbey** *(418)* in Berwickshire, just across the county line from Melrose, Roxburgh-shire. This was the first of the Premonstratensian houses in Scotland, founded, with the king's blessing, by his Norman constable, Hugh de Moreville, in 1140 and colonized by canons from Alnwick, Northumber-land. Occupying a bend in the River Tweed, this place is considered by some to be the most attractive monastic ruin in Scotland. Certainly, the claustral buildings are the most complete of all. Proceeding south from the splendid round-arched heavily recessed processional doorway at the east end of the nave, one passes, in order, the roofed library, vestry, parlor, chapter house, and warming room, all in the east range, which then stretches still farther south to include the novice's dayroom. Above all this was the dorter. The south range is less complete, consisting mostly of the undercroft, but the west gable of the frater above still stands high and is pierced by a lovely rose window. The west side of the cloister is enclosed simply by a wall—an unusual arrangement. The abbey church is in a more ruined condition. The west doorway, though round-arched, dates from a fifteenth-century rebuild-ing—an example of late medieval anachronism peculiar to Scotland, about which more will be said below. The walls of the nave are just about levelled to the ground. The fine east end is Transitional, with both Romanesque round arches and First Pointed lancet windows. The high north transept contains the tombs of Field Marshal Earl Haig, distinguished soldier of the First World War, and of Sir Walter Scott, whose interment in this romantic and very medieval setting could not be more appropriate.

The implantation of monastic communities, so fervently encouraged by David I, continued throughout the succeeding reigns of his two grandsons. Malcolm IV (1153–1165) founded the Augustinian **Restenneth Priory** *(511)* in Angus on the site of the Pictish King Nechtan's earlier church distin-guished by a high square tower. In the thirteenth century a new church was built around the tower; its nave has all but disappeared, but the roofless choir with fine lancet windows still survives. Also in the reign of Malcolm IV (1153–1165), Hugh de Morville, in a second outburst of piety, founded **Kilwinning Abbey** *(391)* in Ayrshire for Tironensian monks who built there another double-transepted church (like Kelso's) with the usual claustral attachments. Not much is left, and the Scottish Development Department has been slow to set up a site museum for the enlightenment of the curious visitor. The style of the ruin is predominantly First Pointed, with enough round arches surviving to indicate Romanesque or Transitional beginnings. The most attractive feature at Kilwinning is the high gable wall of the south transept of the abbey church with three lancet windows surmounted by a small circular opening. Much of the south wall survives, as does enough of the west end (next to the modern clock tower) to indicate that there was a second pair of transepts here. The claustral remains contain round-arched doorways, suggesting a twelfth-century date of construction. Of the east range, the ruined chapter house is the most substantial part; the west range is very much ruined, and the south range consists of foundations only. Not far away—in Renfrewshire—another of King David's Anglo-Norman household, Walter the Steward, set up a priory for Cluniac monks from Wenlock, Shropshire, where the ancestors of the royal Stewarts had settled after the Norman Conquest. This daughterhouse was later raised in status to become **Paisley Abbey** *(396)*. Paisley suffered severely from those traditional enemies of Scottish monastic architecture: faulty construction, the English, accidental misfortune, neglect, and to some extent Protestant desecration (although the latter factor has been greatly exaggerated). In 1307 an English army burned it to the ground—partly, no doubt, because of the fifth High Steward's close association with Robert Bruce. In 1498 the abbey was badly damaged by fire and the central tower collapsed, destroying most of the north transept, crossing, and choir. After the Reformation, the nave was walled off for use as the new parish church. Restoration began in the mid–nineteenth century and was continued in the twentieth, so that most of what is to be seen today, though authentically medieval in appearance, is in fact modern. The oldest part of the abbey church is the Romanesque processional door at the east end of the south wall. Within St. Mirren's chapel is a fine and rare early medieval sculptured frieze depicting the life of this little-known Celtic holy man. The west gable, including the great doorway, is in the First Pointed style of the early thirteenth century. The rest of the nave dates mostly from a fifteenth-century restoration. The handsomest single part of the church is, however, the great Second Pointed eastern window with its modern stained glass. The cloister garth has been converted into a charming garden.

In the next reign, King William the Lion (1165–1214) continued the family tradition. It was he who established a colony of Tironensian monks from Kelso at **Arbroath Abbey** *(507)* in 1178. The house was dedicated to St. Thomas of Canterbury, perhaps as a deliberate affront to King Henry II of England, author alike of Thomas à Becket's murder and the Scottish king's humiliation at Falaise. The great red sandstone ruin standing in the center of this coastal town in Angus is one of the ecclesiastical marvels of Scotland. The deeply recessed west doorway is Romanesque, as is the unusual tribune or Galilee porch above it. Flanking the west front are the ruins of two massive towers. The outstanding architectural feature here, however, is the First Pointed south transept with lancet windows and a large circular window in the pediment of the gable. The vaulted sacristy is of fifteenth-century construction. Not much is left of the claustral ranges except for a late-twelfth-century vaulted undercroft at the west end of the south range, on top of which was later raised the abbot's house, now the site museum. The huge fortified gatehouse was built in the late thirteenth century west of the church and is entered from the High Street of the town. A second Tironensian foundation of King William's reign was **Lindores Abbey** *(490)* in Fife, endowed by his younger brother, David, Earl of Huntingdon. Unlike Arbroath, it is a badly depleted ruin, obviously looted by owners of the neighboring farmstead. The few scattered fragments of masonry still to be seen *in situ* represent parts of the precinct wall and an archway that may have covered a slype leading through the claustral east range.

Other great nobles besides the king's brother were equally active in encouraging monks to settle within their territories. The great Somerled himself is credited with having brought Cistercians to Kintyre to found **Saddell Abbey** *(462)*, now so badly ruined as to defy comprehension of its layout, though worth a visit because of the fine collection of west Highland sculptured stones now housed under a roof. Somerled's son Reginald was probably responsible for the establishment of an Augustinian nunnery and a Benedictine monastery on the site of Columba's ancient **Iona Abbey** *(465)*. The church belonging to the former is a solid Transitional building (now roofless) with interesting architectural features of Irish origin. All that remains of the monks' church, now encased within the much restored abbey kirk, are fragments of masonry from the original thirteenth-century building and portions of the fifteenth-century walls. The present cloister is entirely the work of twentieth-century restorers. In the Southwest, Fergus of Galloway is credited with bringing about the reestablishment of the bishopric of Galloway (under the jurisdiction of the Archbishop of York) and of importing Premonstratensian canons to serve as the chapter of the new cathedral situated on St. Ninian's ancient site at **Whithorn Priory** *(377)* in Wigtownshire. The present ruins consist of the roofless rectangular nave of the priory church and, some distance to the east, portions of a lady chapel and another chapel, as well as a now restored crypt. The nave was rebuilt so many times that it is difficult to piece its history together. The oldest portion, dating from the twelfth century, is the Romanesque doorway inserted at a later date into the south wall. The eastern portion of the side walls appear to date from a thirteenth-century restoration, and to this period belongs the single lancet window in the south wall. Most of the remainder of the church is the product of eighteenth-century rebuilding. **Glenluce Abbey** *(375)*, also in Wigtownshire, was the product of the beneficence of Roland, a successor to Fergus as lord of Galloway. Here the Cistercians came in the last decade of the twelfth century. Not much remains of their thirteenth-century church except the lower portions of the west front, the south wall, and the high-standing south transept. The cloister, rebuilt in the fifteenth century, is in a better state of preservation—especially the fine vaulted chapter house with a central pillar and two barrel-vaulted apartments. The foundations of the rest of the east range can still be seen, as well as of the frater, jutting southward of the south range in the Cistercian manner.

In the final year of King William's reign (1214) monks from Paisley colonized **Crossraguel Abbey** *(392)*, in Ayrshire, on lands granted about 1214 by another powerful noble, Duncan, Earl of Carrick, ancestor of Robert Bruce who inherited the title as well as the abbey's patronage. This is today a fascinating ruin, but very little of it dates to the thirteenth century. The abbey church, originally cruciform, was rebuilt in the fourteenth century after an especially rough handling by the English, owing, no doubt, to its connection with Bruce. To the same period of construction are owed the east and south ranges of the cloister and the abbot's house and court southeast of the cloister. In the following century the choir of the church was rebuilt with a three-sided apse at the east end—a feature more common in Scotland than in England. In the sixteenth century, for reasons not clear, a gable wall was installed between choir and nave, cutting the church in two. About the same time a four-story tower-house was erected alongside the abbot's house, an outer parlor built along the west side of the cloister, a formidable gatehouse raised still farther to the west, and a row of tiny cottages built to house the abbey's pensioners, called *corrodiars*. Altogether, at least from an architectural viewpoint, Crossraguel is the most unusual monastic establishment in Scotland.

In the following reign—that of Alexander II (1214–1249)—benefactions to the monastic orders continued, but at a slower pace. Malcolm, Earl of Fife, founded the Cistercian house of **Culross Abbey** *(485)* in 1217, inviting monks from Kinloss to settle there. Almost nothing is left to see of this establishment. The nave of the monastic church has disappeared except for a small portion of the twelfth-century south wall to the right of the present front door of the parish kirk, which was built over the monastic choir. The west end, incidentally, through which this doorway passes, was originally (probably late fourteenth century) the pulpitum separating choir from nave. The claustral remains are even more fragmentary, though part of the lay brothers' west range stands fairly high. Also from Kinloss came other Cistercians to colonize **Deer Abbey** *(544)*, Aberdeenshire, founded in 1219 by William Comyn, Earl of Buchan. Even less is visible here than at Culross. The church was totally demolished in the nineteenth century, and all that is left of the cloister are the walls of the south range and foundation stones of the other ranges. Not much more remains to be seen of **Balmerino Abbey** *(490)* in Fife, founded about 1226 in honor of King William the Lion by his widow, Queen Ermengarde, and colonized by Cistercians from Melrose. About all that is to be seen here today are the ruins of the vaulted chapter house and adjacent parts of the east range, here, as at Melrose, set north of the church.

King Alexander II himself was responsible for first bringing to Scotland representatives of the Valliscaulian Order, who were, along with the Carthusians, the strictest of the reformed Benedictines. In or about the year 1230 these monks from the Val des Choux in Burgundy set up three separate houses. **Pluscarden Abbey** *(527)* in Moray is today the most interesting— chiefly because in this century the much ruined monastery (originally a priory as were all the houses of this order) was reoccupied by English Benedictines, who have restored it and put it back into operation as a functioning abbey. Although the original nave is gone (if it was ever built), transepts and central tower have been reroofed and restored for use as the abbey church, where white-robed monks can again be seen at worship. The architectural style is generally First Pointed, with fine modern stained glass lancets surmounted by a circular window in the north transept. The choir to the east is still roofless and awaiting reconstruction. A tiny lady chapel abuts the south transept, and south of this is the completely restored east range of the claustral buildings (no admittance to visitors), consisting of chapter house, a slype converted into a library, and the kitchen/refectory, which was probably originally the monks' warming room. Forty miles west of here, in Inverness-shire, another colony of Valliscaulians under the patronage of Sir John Bisset settled at the head of Beauly Firth and built **Beauly Priory** *(518)*, now a handsome ruin in the center of the village of the same name. The cloister has disappeared, and only the roofless priory church remains standing. It is an interesting architectural amalgam, a good example of the eccentric paths followed by late medieval Scottish masons, to be discussed at greater length below. The walls of nave, choir, and transepts still stand to roof height. Choir, south transept, and the eastern end of the nave are of thirteenth-century construction, with later modifications dating from the fourteenth through the fifteenth century. The windows are atypical—especially those in the nave shaped like curved equilateral triangles with cusped trefoils. Also, several of the lancets are unusually wide. The north transept, now sealed off from the church, is a modern restoration. Much less than this survives at the third of the thirteenth-century Valliscaulian houses—**Ardchattan Priory** *(473)*, situated on the north shore of Loch Etive in Argyll and founded by Sir Duncan MacDougall. Except for a few fragments of the choir, the buildings have all been destroyed or incorporated into the private house that now occupies the grounds. A small section of the east wall retains an aumbry; another aumbry is in the north wall; opposite is a piscina surmounted by an arch. Only the armed and armored stone effigies of the MacDougalls (noted in Chapter 4) are of interest here.

Of an entirely different order of magnitude and beauty are the ruins of **Inchmahome Priory** *(497)*, an Augustinian house founded in 1238 by Walter Comyn, fourth Earl of Menteith, on a tiny islet near the north shore of the Lake of Menteith in Perthshire. Although the bell tower at the southwest corner of the church is of late medieval date, most of the architecture is pure thirteenth-century First Pointed. An array of five tall lancets fills most of the east gable of the choir, where triple sedilia, a piscina, and a wall aumbry can still be seen. Though the surviving claustral buildings are fragmentary, the layout of the cloister can easily be traced, and still standing are the arched doorways that once led into the chapter house, parlor, reredorter, and frater, and the spiral stair to the upper story of the west range, where the guest house and prior's lodging were located. Fine knightly effigies of medieval date are to be found in both the choir and chapter house. This is a charming spot as well as instructive and is very much worth the boat ride. On another island, although of much later foundation, is **Oronsay Priory** *(462)*, separated by water (except at low tide) from the southern tip of Colonsay. An Augustinian house, probably founded by John, first Lord of the Isles, in the early or mid-fourteenth century, the ruined buildings here are of less interest than the splendid fifteenth- and sixteenth-century sculptured crosses and grave-slabs housed on the site.

Oronsay Priory notwithstanding, by the end of the thirteenth century the impulse for monastic foundation had largely spent itself. Kings and rich nobles alike had, as we shall see below, found other and somewhat less expensive means for advertising their piety and ensuring perpetual prayers for the well-being of their souls. The last great monastery to be founded in Scotland was established in 1273 in Kirkcudbrightshire under the patronage of Devorguilla, daughter of Alan, Lord of Galloway; wife to John Balliol of Barnard Castle; co-founder with him of Balliol College, Oxford; and mother of King John of Scotland. This was the Cistercian foundation (colonized from Dundrennan) of **Sweetheart Abbey** *(382)* or the Abbey of *Dulce Core,* so named because its founder, at her request, was buried there along with the embalmed heart of her husband encased in a casket of ivory bound with enamelled silver. Almost nothing is left of the claustral buildings, though the precinct wall stands remarkably high. The cruciform abbey church, however, in spite of periodic damage by fire and lightning, is a remarkably well-preserved ruin—partly, no doubt, because it escaped English destruction first by virtue of its abbot's loyalty to Edward I and later because it lay outside the main route of northbound English armies in the fourteenth through sixteenth centuries. The most attractive feature here are the well-preserved window openings, some First Pointed, others Second Pointed, in style. The restored tombs of Devorguilla and of John, the first abbot, are in the south transept. The central tower, of mellow red sandstone like the rest of the church, stands high. Its roof line is battlemented, a vernacular feature found in no other abbey, but not rare among other types of Scottish ecclesiastical buildings.

ARCHITECTURAL STYLES

Up until the War of Independence, Scottish ecclesiastical architecture imitated, with only slight modification, the changing styles prevailing south of the border. Probably most of the masons were English or English-trained. Certainly most of the abbots and bishops who supervised church building, at least in the eleventh and twelfth centuries, were Anglo-Normans or direct immigrants from France, which had the same architectural tradition. Thus, in all three countries the massive Norman style of building gave way to experimentation with the pointed arches, ribbed vaulting, and flying buttresses that characterized the Transitional period, and then to the unalloyed early Gothic of the mid-thirteenth century. In England the evolution continued with the introduction of the Decorated and Perpendicular Gothic styles in the mid-thirteenth and mid-fourteenth centuries respectively. Standardization in each case came so rapidly that, as the historian A. J. P. Taylor puts it (with only slight exaggeration), "when you enter a medieval building [in England] you can date it or the varied sections of it within a few minutes." Such is not the case in Scotland.

For reasons that can only be guessed at, Scottish masons, after the War of Independence, went off on their own tack—or rather tacks, so that no sequential stylistic traditions prevailed, nor was there any uniformity in style among buildings erected in the same time frame. Today's visitor, unless extremely expert, simply cannot tell by looking at an arch or a column or a decorative device just when a particular church or any part of it was built. By English standards anyway, much Scottish architecture of the fourteenth through the sixteenth century is anachronistic: semicircular arches and heavy cylindrical pillars, for example, reappear long after they have become elsewhere obsolete. In other instances, French Flamboyant influences, especially in window tracery, predominate over the more conservative English Decorated style. On the outside some churches come to resemble contemporary vernacular buildings, castles and tower-houses in particular. By the fifteenth century, English influences seem to have disappeared almost entirely. (The Perpendicular choir of Melrose Abbey is a rarity and is known to be the handiwork of stonemasons from Yorkshire.) Late medieval Scottish ecclesiastical architecture in short is individualistic and eccentric. This *caveat* should be born in mind by travellers as they inspect Scotland's cathedrals and other large churches of medieval foundation.

CATHEDRALS

A cathedral, by definition, is the seat of a diocesan bishop. Bishops there had been in the ancient Celtic Church, but their status was below that of the abbots, and their duties seem to have been confined mostly to the ordination of other priests and the consecration of churches and cemeteries. Certainly, they had under their jurisdiction no clearly defined episcopal territories or dioceses; the Celtic Church was not organized on a regional basis. At St. Andrews there was a "high bishop," sometimes styled Bishop of Alba or Scotia, and before 1100 there were several other episcopal sees. In the twelfth century, especially under David I, sees that had fallen into decay were renewed and perhaps one or two new ones established. A complete system of dioceses was organized: St. Andrews, Glasgow, Dunblane, Dunkeld, Brechin, Aberdeen, Moray, Ross, Caithness, and, before 1200, Argyll. Thus, by the twelfth century, there were ten episcopal sees in Scotland, not counting Galloway, which was under the jurisdiction of the Archbishop of York, and Orkney and The Isles, which, still being within Norwegian territory, were under the Archbishop of Trondheim.

The immediate successors of Malcolm Canmore were, of course, concerned with more than the propagation of the Christian gospel throughout their already Christianized realm. Like the great abbeys, these episcopal sees were the ecclesiastical counterparts of royal castles and county sheriffs in these kings' efforts to feudalize Scotland and establish some semblance of central government over its diverse and mostly autonomous parts. Moreover, bishops, like abbots, almost alone among the king's subjects, had the education and experience to carry out the administrative duties required of effective royal government. On the king's council, in his parliaments, and within his personal household, the clergy, high and low, performed the function of a modern civil service.

Church buildings, chapter houses for the conduct of business, and residences for bishops and cathedral clergy were largely the product of the late twelfth and thirteenth centuries. Though subject to many later alterations, **St. Andrews Cathedral** *(491)* in Fife, which also served as the priory church for the Augustinian canons who constituted the chapter, was begun about 1160; the choir was completed by 1238; the original west end was so severely damaged that it had to be rebuilt about 1280; the new church was consecrated by Bishop Lamberton in the presence of King Robert Bruce in 1318; a great fire in the 1370s gutted the building, and the damage was not fully rectified until about 1440. Thus, the present "toothy" ruin of what was once Scotland's longest church represents more than three centuries of construction and reconstruction. Briefly, the oldest parts are the east end of the choir, with its three round-arched window openings constructed in the twelfth century (but not the upper pointed-arched window, which is a fifteenth-century insertion), and the eastern portion of the nave's south wall, also distinguishable by round-headed windows in the Transitional style. The rest of the south wall and the west front, with its fine, though small, Gothic dog-toothed arched doorway, is of late-thirteenth-century construction. The surviving part of the south transept, with the remnant of a stairway leading to the canons' dorter, dates from the early fifteenth century. The rest of this splendid edifice is mostly gone, its stones scattered throughout the town of St. Andrews, embedded in the walls and foundations of domestic dwellings. Of the Augustinian priory cloister, the east range is represented by a ruined slype and parts of two chapter houses built consecutively, plus the warming house and the reredorter. Of the south range, only the undercroft remains, and the west range is represented only by a much ruined barrel-vaulted cellar. West of the cathedral stand the substantial remains of the fourteenth-century precinct gatehouse, called The Pends, and around the thirty-acre priory precinct runs a fine sixteenth-century wall built upon fourteenth-century foundations. Beyond the east range of the cloister is the prior's lodging, now the site museum. Northwest of the cathedral, at the edge of a steep cliff falling down to the North Sea, is the ruined **St. Andrews Castle** *(492),* once the residence of the bishop and after 1472 of Scotland's primate, the Archbishop of St. Andrews. The first castle was built about 1200 by Bishop Roger, but of this phase of construction, only the cross-wall within the foretower survives. A stronghold as well as a residence, it changed hands several times between Scots and English during the War of Independence; was repaired in the early fourteenth century by Bishop Lamberton; was rebuilt again by the English, who occupied it in behalf of Edward Balliol; was almost totally destroyed in 1337 by the Scots; was rebuilt by Bishop Walter Traill at the end of the fourteenth century; was repaired in the sixteenth by Cardinal David Beaton, who was to be assassinated by Protestant rebels and have his corpse hung from the castle wall; was rebuilt again in the 1550s by Archbishop John Hamilton after much destruction by French besiegers; was surrendered to the Crown after the Reformation (though sometimes still the archepiscopal residence);

and in the seventeenth century was dismantled by the Town Council of St. Andrews, its walls to be used as a quarry for building a new harbor. The medieval portions of the existing ruin consist of the fourteenth-century foretower, with its early-thirteenth-century cross-wall (part of the original bishop's palace); and the late-fourteenth-century curtain wall, sea tower with a "bottle dungeon," and kitchen tower, with a few sixteenth-century additions. It is to this last period that belong the sunken mines and countermines, which will be described in the next chapter in connection with the siege of the castle in 1548.

As a sacred Christian site, Dunkeld in Perthshire is probably even more ancient than St. Andrews. It was to this place that Kenneth mac Alpin is held to have brought some of the bones of St. Columba from Iona, and there was a bishop at Dunkeld as early as 865, though the continuous history of the see may not have begun until the reign of King Alexander I (1107–1124). **Dunkeld Cathedral** *(504)*, as it now stands, however, is of a much later date. The earliest part of the aisleless rectangular church is the choir of thirteenth-century construction, altered in the fourteenth when the sedilia and cinquefoil-headed arches were added. This last was the work of Bishop William Sinclair, whose headless alabaster effigy is still to be seen. This area is roofed and now serves as the parish kirk. West of it is the roofless nave. It dates from the fifteenth century and is a good example of the anachronistic and eccentric trends of Scottish architecture mentioned above. Huge round pillars and semicircular window arches surmounted by twin-lighted Gothic openings combine to suggest an imitation of the Transitional style of two hundred years before. One of the builders was Bishop Robert de Cardeny, whose recumbent effigy still rests in a mural tomb. His successor was Bishop Thomas Lauder, who was responsible for building the chapter house on the north side of the choir and beginning the erection of the northwest tower. In the choir is an effigy believed to be that of Alexander Stewart, the "Wolf of Badenoch"; in the tower are the remnants of a medieval wall painting, rare in Scotland. When not occupied with building and other episcopal duties, Lauder's chief concern appears to have been with defending himself and his cathedral from neighboring Highlanders, who on at least one occasion invaded the church and drove the bishop out during the celebration of High Mass.

Such sacrilege was minor compared to what had been suffered at **Elgin Cathedral** *(526)* two generations earlier. A bishopric of Moray probably existed before 1100, though its seat was not finally settled at Elgin until 1224. The earliest parts of the now ruined cathedral—the "lantern of the north" and one of great medieval feats of architecture in Scotland—date from about the time of this move. These are the north and south transepts,

Transitional in style with lancet windows surmounted by round-headed openings. From the same period dates the lower two-thirds of the north wall of the choir. Some time in the thirteenth century the west facade with splendid portal flanked by two towers was raised. This is a fine example of Scottish First Pointed style. In 1270 the church was burned and a great rebuilding took place. To this period is owed the First Pointed presbytery, with two rows of lancets topped by a huge circular window; also the first version of the chapter house. In 1390 the church was burned again—this time by the "Wolf of Badenoch," and his "wyld wykked Heland-men." In the reconstruction that followed the inner screen of the portal was erected in the Second Pointed style and the great wide, pointed-arched window was inserted in the west facade above the main portal. At the same time, the splendid octagonal chapter house was remodelled with the introduction of the still extant central pillar of stone and rib-and-panel vaulting. The church contains a number of fine grave-slabs and effigies, including one of a knight wearing typical fifteenth-century armor: camail and long shirt of chain mail, arm pieces and greaves of plate, a pointed bascinet, and a dagger and long sword. Why this cathedral should be in a state of ruin when none other in Scotland, save those at Whithorn and St. Andrews, was permitted to suffer such degradation is a complicated story. The last bishop, Patrick Hepburn, sold off most of the episcopal lands, leaving nothing for the church's upkeep. As there was already an adequate parish church in Elgin, the cathedral was never taken over as a place of Protestant worship, as were most of Scotland's churches after the Reformation. In 1567 the government stripped off the lead roofing, which of course exposed the area below to the elements. In the seventeenth century Covenanters did more damage, and during the Civil War Cromwell's soldiers were guilty of more destruction. Then, in 1711, the central tower fell in, taking with it much of the nave. What was left is basically what is to be seen today—a noble skeleton and an eloquent testament to Bishop Alexander Bur's boast (in 1390) that his church was "the ornament of the realm, the glory of the kingdom. . . ." Equally magnificent in its own way was the bishop's own residence, at nearby **Spynie Palace** *(527)*, though not until the fifteenth century did it receive its ornate gateway with portcullis and murder holes and the adjacent high tower house called "David's Tower"; and not until the sixteenth did Patrick Hepburn pierce the walls of this house with gunports to complete its militarization.

The bishopric of Glasgow, which already had a long history, was restored by David I when he was still Earl of Huntingdon and effective ruler of Strathclyde. After he became King of Scots, a cathedral was built on the site of an ancient Celtic monastery, founded, according to tradition, by St.

Kentigern (or St. Mungo) in the early seventh century. Almost nothing of this structure remains. The building of the present **Glasgow Cathedral** *(406)* began in the early thirteenth century under Bishop William de Bondington (1233–1258), and it is his church, with later additions and revisions (but minus the original two western towers) that is seen today. The predominant style is First Pointed, with numerous lancet windows, high pointed arches, ribbed vaulting, and clustered piers. In shape it is unusual, owing to its having been built on ground that sloped abruptly downward toward the east. For this reason the eastern end consists of two stories; the western of one only. The lower church, miscalled the "crypt," has a slightly raised platform in the center within which stand four slender pillars that once enclosed the shrine of St. Kentigern. To the east of this is the Chapel of the Blessed Virgin, with magnificent vaulting and sculptured bosses. At the extreme east end is the Chapel of the Four Altars; in one of these, the Chapel of St. Andrew, is the recumbent stone effigy of Bishop Robert Wishart, who supported Bruce in his time of need, absolved him of excommunication for the murder of the Red Comyn, and assisted in his installation as King of Scots at Scone. At the northeast corner of the lower church is the chapter house begun by Bishop William de Bondington in the thirteenth century but not completed until early in the fifteenth. In it is a fifteenth-century dean's seat and stone benches around the walls for the secular canons who comprised the chapter. Above the lower church is the choir, built about the same time and architecturally distinguished for its great east window of four lights and unusual for its ambulatory, which circles around the high altar near the square east end. To the west is the nave, probably not built until after the War of Independence and somewhat inferior architecturally. Between choir and nave is a rare stone pulpitum dating from the end of the fifteenth century, installed by Archbishop Blacader. Of a slightly earlier date is the sacristy, opening off the choir and situated immediately above the chapter house. The heavy oak door is original. A flight of steps down from the south aisle of the nave leads back to the lower story and to Blacader's Aisle, built in the late fifteenth century by the archbishop of that name, apparently with the intention of adding a two-story south transept to the church, which is otherwise rectangular. The second story was never completed, but, as it now stands, this ground floor chapel with its fan vaulting and brightly painted bosses is the most charming part of the cathedral. The word *cathedral* is, to be sure, an anachronism, for this place now serves as the parish kirk of Glasgow, where worship is conducted according to the Presbyterian rites of the Church of Scotland. Before leaving the cathedral precincts, and as a reminder of the chapter of canons that once served it, the visitor should stop outside the main gate and inspect **Provand's**

Lordship *(405)*, the oldest house in Glasgow (1471) and once but one of the thirty or more manses of canons and prebends attached to the cathedral. Of about the same vintage is **Provan's Hall** *(409)* on the eastern outskirts of the city—once the bishop's summer residence and now the property of the National Trust for Scotland.

Until the eighteenth century, Glasgow was little more than a village overshadowed by its great cathedral. Aberdeen on the east coast, by contrast, developed into a thriving seaport in the Middle Ages. There was already a bishopric in the area before the see was established at Aberdeen in 1136 on the site traditionally associated with a missionary church established by St. Machar, a contemporary of St. Columba. A cathedral was raised in the twelfth century, of which no part remains but a piece of a square pier, now on display in the Charter Room of the present church. A second cathedral went up in the late fourteenth century, but, except for two great cylindrical piers of red sandstone that originally supported a central tower and now stand at the east end of the existing church, nothing remains of this second building either. To Bishop Henry Lichton (1422–1440) is owed the main fabric of today's **St. Machar's Cathedral** *(533)*. The great granite church was originally cruciform, with a central tower added by Bishop Elphinstone in the early sixteenth century. In 1688, however, this tower collapsed, carrying with it the east end and the transepts, so that what is left today is the west end and nave, now serving as a parish kirk of the Church of Scotland. Here is the best example of all of the eccentric nature of Scottish ecclesiastical architecture in the later Middle Ages. The west front is dominated by heavy square twin towers, very military in appearance, with machicolated parapets. On the southern exterior is a porch with a crowstepped gable, typical of contemporary Scottish vernacular building. Inside, heavy cylindrical pillars support the pointed arches of the arcades dividing nave from aisles. This combination of Romanesque and Gothic is vaguely Transitional in appearance, but not quite. Architecturally speaking, the most remarkable feature of the church is the great west window—a huge arch under which appears a row of *round*-headed lancet windows of equal height. The arrangement is original and probably unique. One later, and quite felicitous, addition to the nave was the flat oak ceiling with forty-eight splendid painted heraldic devices, installed by Bishop Gavin Dunbar about 1520. Aberdeen's cathedral cannot be said to be a graceful building. But in its solidity it *is* impressive.

The bishopric at Dunblane in Perthshire possibly owed its origin to the local rulers of Strathearn. There is supposed to have been some association of the church here with the seventh-century missionary St. Blane. The lower part of the square tower of **Dunblane Cathedral** *(503)* is of eleventh-century date. However, most of the church—to which the tower is rather awkwardly attached—was built in the thirteenth century. The interior is the product of two nineteenth-century restorations, mostly in the First Pointed manner with some florid additions meant to simulate the French High Gothic of the late fifteenth century. Also mostly the product of modern restoration is **Brechin Cathedral** *(506)*, center of the episcopal see embracing much of northern Angus created by David I. The style is First Pointed, presumably a faithful duplication of the original, with the standard lancet windows, clustered columns, etc. The two transepts have been not restored but rebuilt. The square cathedral tower (not to be confused with the adjacent tenth-century round tower) was probably built in the fourteenth century and required less reconstruction than the church, which now serves as a parish kirk.

Of the two northernmost sees on the Scottish mainland, only traces of the medieval buildings can be seen today. **Dornoch Cathedral** *(551)* in the modern county of Sutherland served the see of Caithness. The original thirteenth-century church, much damaged in 1570, was rebuilt in the nineteenth century and is now the parish kirk, of which the choir and lower portions of the transepts retain the Transitional features of the original construction. Across the road, the Castle Hotel incorporates the remains of the original bishop's palace. Of **Fortrose Cathedral** *(548)*, seat of the Bishop of Ross, only a little more survives of the thirteenth- and early-fourteenth-century building—part of the Second Pointed south aisle, now a roofless ruin. The attached fifteenth-century polygonal tower contains the original bell. The see of Argyll, created about 1180, had its episcopal seat on the island of Lismore, where **Lismore Parish Kirk** *(467)* contains all that remains of the earlier cathedral: traces of the thirteenth- or fourteenth-century walls of the choir, sedilia, and a piscina. The see of The Isles was, in the eleventh century, part of the Norwegian Church, with a cathedral on the Isle of Man. Some time after that island was lost to England, however, the church of **Iona Abbey** *(465)* was designated the cathedral for the southern islands. **Whithorn Priory** *(377)* in Wigtownshire, as already indicated, served as the cathedral of the bishop of Galloway, its Premonstratensian canons constituting the chapter. (This and St. Andrews were the only monastic cathedrals in Scotland; the rest were secular.) Not until 1472 was it definitively removed from the jurisdiction of the Archbishop of York and declared to belong to the national Scottish church (the *Ecclesia Scotticana*) under the newly elevated Archbishop of St. Andrews.

This leaves only the bishopric of Orkney to be accounted for. Its early history properly belongs to that of Norway, because only in the reign of James III (1460–1488) did these islands come into the possession of the

Scottish Crown, and, again, not until the papal bull of 1472 giving metropolitan status to the archbishop of St. Andrews was the see of Orkney made formally subject to the Scottish Church. Long before this, however, a fine cathedral had been built on the Mainland of Orkney. In the mid–eleventh century, on the **Brough of Birsay** *(563)*, Earl Thorfinn the Mighty had erected a church after his return from his "most famous" visit to Rome where, according to the *Orkneyinga Saga*, he received papal absolution for his sins, which were probably manifold. This church, somewhat enlarged by a Bishop William in the early twelfth century, is today represented by the lower courses of a small rectangular nave and a narrower, almost square, choir with a rounded apse at the east end. To the north of it lie the foundations of what is thought to have been a clerical residence. In the church came to rest the body of Earl Magnus, murdered in 1117. After miracles were reported at his tomb, his bones were removed to Kirkwall to be enshrined in the splendid new **St. Magnus Cathedral** *(559)*, which commenced building in 1137 under the direction of Earl Rognvald, the saint's kinsman, and with the assistance of masons from Durham. Choir and transepts are Romanesque; the crossing and eastern portion of the nave, Transitional; most of the rest is thirteenth-century Gothic, though the tower was not completed until the fourteenth century, and the west end until the fifteenth. Of special interest on the interior are the interlaced round-arched Romanesque blind arcades in the nave. In the nineteenth century two wall burials were discovered, encased within piers in the choir. They proved to be the remains of St. Magnus and St. Rognvald the builder. This massive building of weathered red and honey-colored sandstone, it can be argued, is the most authentic and most aesthetically pleasing of all early medieval buildings in Scotland (Glasgow Cathedral possibly excepted). Certainly nowhere else does the surprising airiness and grace of the Romanesque and Transitional styles of architecture show up so well. The cathedral has belonged to the town of Kirkwall since 1468 and now serves as its parish kirk.

Across the street are the ruins of another fine building—the **Bishop's Palace** *(559)*, where King Hakon died in 1263 and probably also the seven-year-old Maid of Norway in 1290. Like the cathedral church, it was first built in the twelfth century, then completely reconstructed by Bishop Robert Reid (1541–1558), and finally revised again around 1600 by Earl Patrick Stewart. The original masonry can be seen in the lower courses of the walls and undercroft; the three buttresses on the west face were put up by Bishop Reid, as well as the three-story tower on the northwest corner and the great hall. Earl Patrick divided the latter into four rooms and added the southern extension with its fine oriel windows. The bishops of Orkney, like their fellow prelates in mainland Scotland, lived well. The same cannot be said for the medieval parish clergy.

PARISH KIRKS

The parochial system in Scotland, like much else pertaining to the ecclesiastical establishment, developed under King David I, who made the collection of teinds to local kirks enforceable by royal sheriffs and landowners. Teinds (in England called *tithes*) were defined as that fraction (about a tenth) of the year's production of grain and dairy products and of the offspring of domestic animals to which the parish kirk was entitled. Other revenues collectible by the local priest included offerings or oblations that were expected on such occasions as baptism, marriage, burial, and the celebration of the Mass, especially at Easter.

Altogether about nine hundred parish kirks were built in Scotland in the Middle Ages (as compared to almost eleven thousand in England), and Church statutes of the twelfth century declared that in every parish there should be a stone-built kirk, the nave of which should be maintained at the cost of the parishioners, while the chancel at the east end should be paid for by the parson. That such a small number remains to be seen today requires some explanation—especially to travellers acquainted with the great wealth of parish churches of medieval foundation in England. The main reason for the relative sparsity of such edifices in Scotland is the fact that, by the end of the Middle Ages, about 85 percent of the parish kirks in that country had been "appropriated" by monasteries, cathedrals, or colleges. That is to say, the bulk of the teinds had been diverted from local use to the support of these great ecclesiastical foundations, which then technically became kirk parsons. Kelso Abbey, for example, was supported by the teinds of thirty-seven appropriated parishes; Holyrood, twenty-seven; Paisley, twenty-nine; and Arbroath, thirty-three. The actual cure of souls was farmed out to vicars (from the Latin *vicarius*, meaning "substitute") to whom a much smaller share of teinds was assigned. Thus the Scottish parochial clergy were notoriously underpaid and, as a result poorly educated, lax in the performance of their duties, and usually no more morally upright than the parishioners whose spiritual lives and ethical standards they were supposed to edify.

Since the parsons who drew the teinds were also charged with the physical upkeep of the most important part of their churches (the chancel or choir) and since, as absentees, they were mostly neglectful of this responsibility, it is no wonder that Scottish kirks suffered such decay. Other reasons, of course, operated to explain the relative scarcity of surviving medieval kirks in Scotland. Endowments by nobles, lairds, or rich merchants (responsible for so many of England's most beautiful churches) tended to be diverted first to monasteries and later to collegiate churches or burghal churches. Scotland was never as rich a country as England. The War of Independence and its aftermath constituted a serious drain on the limited national resources. English armed incursions did untold damage to parish kirks as well as to the richer monasteries, especially in the Lowlands. The Highlands were never well supplied with churches to begin with; the spiritual needs of the vast mountainous and watery region north and west of the Highland line had never been adequately addressed by the medieval Church. And besides, church buildings frequently fell victim to the scourge of clan warfare. As Professor Gordon Donaldson concludes, "the romantic fiction of a pious Catholic population who maintained their faith" in the Highlands and Islands before and after the Reformation is without factual foundation.

Given all these factors, it is surprising that as many parish kirks of medieval foundation survive at all—at least in part. Most of these, it must be said, date from the twelfth or early thirteenth century before the parochial system had degenerated to its ultimate state of inanity. It is natural then that Romanesque and Transitional architectural styles are disproportionately represented among the medieval parish kirks still visible today.

The best-preserved Romanesque church in Scotland is **Dalmeny Church** *(429)* in West Lothian. Here is a simple rectangular nave, a slightly narrower chancel, and a rounded apse at the east end. The semicircular arch between nave and chancel is covered with chevron ornamentation, as is the arch leading into the apse. Outside, the lofty south entrance is covered by a round arch with interesting grotesque carvings. The south wall contains a fine blind arcade of interlaced round arches. The west tower is modern, and though some restoration has taken place here, none of it departs from the Romanesque style of the original.

The county of Fife boasts a fair assortment of churches with Romanesque and Transitional features. Of these the most attractive is **Leuchars Parish Church** *(495)* near St. Andrews. Most of the nave is modern, but the round arches over chancel and apse are fine late-twelfth-century Romanesque, and the outer walls are ornamented with good round-headed arched arcading. The octagonal turret with stone cupola is a later insertion. **St. Fillans, Aberdour** *(483)*, next to the ruined castle, though restored and reroofed, is a typical early medieval Scottish kirk in plan—a simple two-chambered building consisting of a rectangular nave and a somewhat smaller and narrower chancel at the east end. The south porch and south isle are additions probably of the fifteenth century. At least part of the west gable, much of the north wall of the nave, and most of the chancel, including its round-arched windows, are original. **Crail Parish Church** *(485)* has basically the same layout with the addition of a high square tower at the west end. Nave and chancel belong to the thirteenth century, though the latter was later reduced to half its original length. Chancel arch and pillars are in the Romanesque style. The church also boasts a good eighth-century Pictish cross-slab.

A good though ruined example of Romanesque architecture is **Auchindoir Church** *(538)* in Aberdeenshire south of Rhynie. Rectangular in plan, the roofless though almost complete little church has a fine Romanesque round-arched doorway on the south. North of here near Elgin, Moray, is **Birnie Church** *(527)*, Romanesque in appearance and built in the twelfth century. It claims to be the oldest church in continuous use in Scotland. Not in use, but in a good state of repair, is **Cruggleton Church** *(377)*, far to the southwest overlooking Wigtown Bay. Chancel arch, doors, and windows are all round-headed in the Romanesque manner, and the church is thought to have been built in the twelfth century.

Among the most interesting church ruins of probable twelfth-century date are several in the Orkneys—that archaeological treasure house unexcelled in Britain. Of these the most curious is **Orphir Round Church** *(562)* on the Mainland of Orkney, overlooking Scapa Flow. Here is the only medieval circular church in Scotland. (There are three in England, not counting the chapel at Ludlow Castle.) It is believed to have been built about 1120 by Earl Hakon Paulsson, who had gone on pilgrimage to Jerusalem after his murder of St. Magnus. In any case, it is obviously modelled on the Church of the Holy Sepulchre in Jerusalem, though, looking at the site today, it is difficult to imagine the similarity. Here only the barrel-vaulted apse and fragments of the adjacent wall remain standing, enough to indicate that the circular nave was about twenty feet in diameter. Much more remains of **St. Magnus Church** *(565)* in Egilsay, an islet just east of Rousay. This church probably dates to the eleventh century and would therefore be the one in which St. Magnus was killed. Its most distinctive feature is the round tower at the west end, rising still to a height of almost fifty feet. The nave typically is rectangular with a smaller barrel-vaulted chancel at the east end, above which is an upper chamber. Most of the round-arched doorways and window openings are original. Further to the north, on the island of Westray, **Cross Kirk** *(567)*, though smaller and more ruined, is probably of about the same date. Again nave and smaller chancel are rectangular. The chancel arch is semicircular; the original door and window remain in the south wall of the nave; the eastern end, however, is the product of a later extension.

Parish kirks with First Pointed features are rare in Scotland, probably because the dates of this style's *floruit* coincided with the War of Independence or perhaps because Scotland already had a sufficiency of parish churches. There are lancet windows in evidence in the chapels of **Kil-**

drummy Castle *(537)*, Aberdeenshire; **Dunstaffnage Castle** *(472)* near Oban; **Skipness Castle** *(474)* on the Kintyre Peninsula; and elsewhere, but, compared to England, they are few in number.

Middle-to-Late Gothic (loosely speaking, Second Pointed) features are somewhat more common. They are to be found, for example, at **The Church of St. Monan** *(495)* in St. Monanace, Fife, originally built in the mid-fourteenth century and paid for by King David II, allegedly in gratitude for recovery from wounds received at the Battle of Neville's Cross. The church was in the next century turned over to Dominican friars, who were responsible for the four Second Pointed windows in the south wall of the nave. (The other pointed-arched openings are presumed to be originals, except for one nineteenth-century insertion.) In the nineteenth century the kirk was renovated for Presbyterian use by the Edinburgh architect William Burn. Today, with its whitewashed walls and pulpit in the south transept, it is very much a Presbyterian kirk, but medieval traces still linger in the ground plan, the pointed arches, the vaulted roof of the choir, and the sedilia, piscinas, and aumbry in the choir and transepts. To about the same date of construction is ascribed the nave of the cruciform church of **St. Mary's, Whitekirk** *(455)*, in East Lothian. The choir was built in 1439. This was at a time when there was a well here, thought to be responsible for miraculous cures, which of course brought many pilgrims to the church, including King James I. Burned by suffragettes in 1914, the church has been completely restored, and only its fabric speaks of the later Middle Ages when it was first built. In Berwickshire, the church known as **Ladykirk** *(423)*—originally the Kirk of Our Lady of the Steill—also allegedly owed its being to a miracle, i.e., King James IV's escape from drowning in a steill (pool) of the River Tweed in 1496 or 1497. Built after 1500, the church is cruciform and consists of an aisleless nave with a western tower, a three-sided chancel, and short transepts. The style is simple Scottish Late Gothic and it is still a place of worship.

ECCLESIASTICAL ARTWORK

Although all three of these churches just mentioned have attractive and well-adorned interiors, the visitor to Scotland today cannot help being struck by the simplicity and plainness of most parish kirks, especially when compared to their English counterparts. Scotland, it must be remembered, was relatively poor to begin with, and the drawn-out hostilities with its southern neighbor exacerbated that condition. Also, almost all decorative features that may once have embellished its medieval churches have disappeared. There are no known monumental brasses in the entire country. The only surviving medieval stained glass window is to be found in **Magdalen Chapel** *(433)*, Edinburgh, and it dates to the sixteenth century just before the Reformation. The fine heraldic roof of oak at **St. Machar's Cathedral** *(533)* and the beautiful woodwork in nearby **King's College Chapel** *(534)* are noteworthy. So are the dimly colored wall paintings at **Dunkeld Cathedral** *(504)* and the tomb paintings at **Inchcolm Abbey** *(483)*. At **Dunblane Cathedral** *(503)* are the "Ochiltree Stalls," among the best and very few surviving examples of medieval wood carving. At **Fowlis Easter Collegiate Church** *(510)* in Angus is a fifteenth-century carved oak door and, best of all, several paintings on oak panels, dating from the fifteenth and sixteenth centuries—a busy Crucifixion scene and another of the entombment of Christ. This is just about the total inventory of Scottish medieval church art still *in situ*. Compared to England and the Continent, there was probably not an abundance in the first place—owing no doubt to the poverty and/or parsimoniousness of parishes and their priests. Much of what there was fell prey to English vandalism, Scottish thievery, Protestant iconoclasm, and neglect. Hence, the austerity of so many Scottish church interiors today.

The one exception to this general aesthetic impoverishment is stone sculpture-work. Late in the Middle Ages, there appeared in the western Highlands a flourishing body of Freemasons who left a rich legacy of sculptured stone monuments—more than six hundred in all—to delight the eye of any observer willing to seek them out in the remote places where they are usually to be found. About 90 percent of them are situated south of the Ardnamurchan Peninsula as far as Kintyre, though some are to be found as far north as the island of Lewis. They are richly carved freestanding crosses, grave-slabs, and effigies to Highland chiefs and church dignitaries, dating from about the mid–fourteenth to the mid-sixteenth century. There were four principal schools of carving: on Iona, the Kintyre Peninsula, the little island of Oronsay, and in the vicinity of Loch Awe. Each enjoyed the patronage of the leading local churchmen and of the Highland chiefs, among whom was certainly John of Islay, son of Angus Og, Lord of the Isles, and chief of Clan Donald, who died in 1387. Though there are distinctions among these schools, the dominant decorative motif of all is the plant scroll with either a single parent stem, two intertwined stems, or a combination of stems and leaves in a rich pattern of folaceous interlace, as in Anglo-Saxon art. Figures, divine and human; animals, real and mythical; ships, weapons, targes (round shields), tools, and liturgical accoutrements are carved in low relief. Standing crosses are disc-headed; i.e., the crossing is encircled by solid stone, as distinct from the wheel-headed cross (mistakenly called the Celtic cross), where the space between the outer stone rim and the crossing is open.

One of the best of the standing crosses is **MacLean's Cross** *(465)* on the path leading up to **Iona Abbey** *(465)* from the ferry landing. It stands about ten feet high, is disc-headed, and is carved with a figure of the crucified Christ, underneath which, on the shaft, is an effigy of an armed warrior, presumably the chief of Clan MacLean. In the abbey museum itself is the largest single collection of fourteenth- to sixteenth-century grave-slabs and effigies—more than eighty altogether, of which the best are the memorials to Bricius MacKinnon and Prioress Anna MacLean. At Campbeltown in Kintyre, in the park adjacent to the quay, stands **Campbeltown Cross** *(461)*, dated about 1480, about ten feet high on a modern base, disc-headed, and erected by Ivor MacEachern, priest of Kilchoman, on behalf of his father and himself. The intricate carving includes figures of St. Mary, St. John, St. Michael slaying the dragon, a mermaid, a sea monster, a griffin, and plant scrolls with interlaced foliage. Farther up the peninsula, **Saddell Abbey** *(462)*, though a very scant ruin, has on display a good collection of grave-slabs and effigies. At the ruined **Oronsay Priory** *(462)*, as already noted, is probably the best preserved of all late medieval western Highland crosses. Disc-headed and about eleven feet in height, it is carved in high relief with a very naturalistic Crucifixion. Parts of two other crosses stand nearby and in the prior's house some thirty effigies, grave-slabs, and cross fragments. On Islay, in addition to the famous Early Christian Kildalton Cross described in Chapter 2, there is the splendid fifteenth-century **Kilchoman Cross** *(466)*—disc-headed with interlaced foliage and on the shaft a carving of an armed man on a rearing charger. Of the Loch Awe school of sculptured stones, numbering about a hundred in all, the best collection is at **Kilmartin Church** *(471)* near Lochgilphead, Argyll, and has been described in Chapter 4. In Knapdale, to the southwest, are three important repositories. At the bottom of the narrow peninsula between Loch Sween and the Sound of Jura is **Keills Chapel** *(468)*, with a high standing cross, carved on one side only with linear patterns devoid of foliage and strange animals and a representation perhaps of Daniel in the lion's den. At **Kilmory Knap Chapel** *(468)* on the east side of Loch Sween is MacMillan's Cross, a splendid disc-headed rood with a Crucifixion on one side and a hunting scene on the other; plus numerous grave-slabs, both ecclesiastical and knightly. Finally, about fifteen miles southeast of here, are the **Kilberry Sculptured Stones** *(469)* of the same genre.

This considerable investment by Highland chiefs and others in funerary and memorial monuments might be explained as a practical alternative, in this remote and inaccessible region, to the more conventional methods of buying soul-insurance by material demonstrations of piety. In all the western Highlands and Islands there were only four monasteries: Iona, Saddell, Oronsay, and Ardchattan. At Kilmun on the north shore of Holy Loch was the area's only collegiate church (a subject to be treated below). And of friaries there was none.

FRIARIES

By the end of the twelfth century in Western Europe the religious enthusiasm that had drawn countless men and women to the monastic life and had inspired countless rich laymen to unprecedented generosity toward these religious foundations was beginning to wane. Or, rather, it was moving into new channels: the orders of mendicant friars. The first of these, founded, with papal permission, by St. Francis of Assisi about 1209, was called the *fratres minores*, the minor brethren (in French, *frères* from which came the English word *friars*). The Franciscans (the Grey Friars) were at first dedicated to Christlike poverty, begging where no other means of supporting themselves was available (hence mendicant), and, above all, to preaching the word of God, not to each other in cloistered retreats, but to the multitudes of laymen deprived of spiritual food by the growing indifference of both regular and secular clergy to their religious needs. This meant that their mission took them primarily to urban population centers. A second order, recognized by the Pope in 1216, was that of the "preaching brethren" founded by St. Dominic of Castile originally to counteract the Albigensian heretics of Provence. The Dominicans (Black Friars) were more intellectually inclined and tended to gravitate to centers of learning, but they too were primarily preachers. They first came to England in 1221 and promptly established themselves at Oxford. The Franciscans followed three years later. By 1231 both orders were in Scotland. They were followed first by the Augustinian friars; then, in mid-century, by the Carmelites, or White Friars; and at the end of the century by the Trinitarians, or Red Friars, who are more properly designated canons regular and who devoted themselves to raising funds for ransoming captive Christians from the Saracens. A reformed order of Franciscans, called Observantines, established their first Scottish settlement at Edinburgh in the mid–fifteenth century.

That the friars filled a genuine need, not satisfied by the cloistered monks or by the impoverished and ignorant parish priests, is demonstrated by the avidity with which kings, nobles, and especially burgesses welcomed them onto their lands and into their burghs. Considering their emphasis on preaching, it is not surprising that they tended to build their churches and cloistered communities in or on the outskirts of the towns. And it is for this reason, primarily, that so little remains to be seen today of the fairly modest buildings they erected. Like other Catholic religious foundations, apart from those required for parish worship, they were done away with (sometimes violently) by Protestant reformers in the sixteenth century. Since then urban growth has all but obliterated their traces.

In Kirkcudbright a tiny Scottish Episcopal chapel calls itself **Greyfriars' Church** *(382)* and is thought to contain fragments of the medieval Franciscan establishment in this city. In Fife, the small **Inverkeithing Museum** *(489)* is housed in the *hospitium*, once part of the medieval Franciscan establishment. (This is signposted as a Dominican friary, which must be a mistake.) Dominicans came to St. Andrews in 1275, and a fragment of **Blackfriars Chapel** *(495)*, built in 1525, survives in front of Madras College in South Street. **The Church of St. Monan** *(495)* in Fife (mentioned above) was turned over to Dominicans by James III, but the extent of their remodelling is not clear. In Peebles, **Cross Kirk** *(421)* became an establishment of the Trinitarian Friars in the mid–fifteenth century. It is now a fairly substantial ruin, consisting of a west tower of about this date attached to the remains of a thirteenth-century nave. The Carmelites had a house in Queensferry, West Lothian, on property donated in 1441 by James Dundas. Here, still serving as an Episcopal church, is the **Priory Church of St. Mary of Mount Carmel** *(428)*, one of the two surviving friary churches in Scotland (though much restored in the nineteenth century). Of the original building what remains today are the choir, the tower, and the south transept, which was originally a chapel. The second extant friary church is that of the Franciscan Observantine Order at Elgin, Moray, called today (with disregard for correct nomenclature) the **Church of the Greyfriars Monastery** *(527)*. It was completely restored at the end of the nineteenth century by the third Marquis of Bute (more famous for his restoration of Cardiff Castle and Falkland Palace). Now serving a convent of the Sisters of Mercy, the interior of this truly lovely little church is believed by some to have recaptured, better than anywhere else in Scotland, the authentic spirit of a medieval place of worship.

COLLEGIATE CHURCHES

By the mid–fifteenth century, friaries, like monasteries before them, were, for reasons unexplained and perhaps unexplainable, going out of fashion as prime recipients of benefactions from the rich. Votive masses in behalf of the souls of the dead, present and future, came to be regarded as more efficacious than the prayers of monks or friars. Secular priests could be hired to say a stipulated number, or, better still, a college of priests, headed by a dean or a provost and assisted by trained choristers, could be endowed to celebrate Mass in perpetuity for the patron and anyone else he might designate. A private chapel then might be turned over to the use of such a college; or a parish church might become "collegiate" by incorporation; or an especially designed collegiate church might be built *de novo*. No unique architectural features were required, so long as sufficient space was made available in aisles and/or transepts for altars before which masses could be said. Patrons were a mixed lot: kings, nobles, lairds, and merchants all joined the throng of benefactors.

The oldest of the collegiate churches in Scotland was founded well in advance of the others. This was the **Church of St. Mary's of the Rock** *(493)*, whose bare foundations can still be seen overlooking the harbor of St. Andrews just north of the ruined cathedral. It belonged to a body of clergy known as Culdees because they drew the ancient revenues of the original Culdee foundation. It received its corporate charter as a collegiate church in 1250. More than a century later (1389) **Lincluden College** *(384)* on the outskirts of Dumfries was founded by Archibald the Grim, third Earl of Douglas, on the site of a Benedictine nunnery suppressed for alleged disorderly conduct. The collegiate church and the associated living quarters for provost and canons were in fact built in the early fifteenth century by the fourth earl, called Archibald the Tyneman (the loser), who was created Duc de Touraine by King Charles VII of France and died fighting the English. It was this earl's wife, Margaret, daughter of King Robert III and sister of James I, who is buried in the magnificent tomb that is the main attraction of the present ruined church. Situated in the north wall of the choir, it is a splendid example of Scottish stone carving, as is the pulpitum separating choir from the now all but nonexistent nave. Opposite the tomb are the remains of a piscina and triple sedilia. Also extant are the south transept and sacristy; of the cloister, only the undercroft of the provost's lodgings is still in evidence.

To the fifteenth century belong more than half of the forty collegiate foundations known to have been established in the later Middle Ages. Among the earliest of these was the collegiate church of St. Nicholas, founded by Sir James Douglas in 1406 and now incorporated into the much restored **Dalkeith Parish Church** *(431)* in Midlothian. The most interesting features here are the late-fifteenth-century effigies of James Douglas, first Earl of Morton, and his wife Joanna, mute daughter of King James I. They are to be seen in the ruined and unroofed apse of the church. Southeast of Dunbar in East Lothian is the **Collegiate Church of St. Mary, Dunglass** *(455)*, founded in 1423 by Sir Alexander Hume with a provost, two chaplains, and four boy choristers. The existing church is a substantial ruin, still roofed. It is cruciform in plan, with a central tower, the choir being slightly narrower than the nave, the transepts serving as burial vaults for Humes and Halls of Dunglass. In the choir is the fragment of a piscina and well-preserved triple sedilia. A sacristy lies north of the choir. Windows are in the Second Pointed style, with some flamboyant tracery still evident. Another foundation of the same kind, though larger and still in use as a parish church on the western outskirts of Edinburgh, is **Corstorphine Collegiate Church** *(452)*, incorporated as a college by Sir John Forrester in 1429. This is a fine example of Scottish late medieval architecture, now serving as a parish kirk (unfortunately, like many of its kind, locked up most weekdays). The considerable number of aisles and chapels testifies to its original use as a collegiate foundation.

Not currently in use, but in almost perfect structural condition, is **Tullibardine Chapel** *(502)*, located near Crieff, Perthshire. Founded in 1446 by Sir David Murray as a family chapel, it has remained substantially unaltered since completion. Another cruciform building, it has typically Scottish crow-stepped gables; a western tower accessible only from the aisleless nave; a south doorway with a round-headed arch in the pseudo-Romanesque style fashionable in fifteenth-century Scotland; and square-headed windows that are few and narrow, giving the interior a gloomy appearance. The Scottish Development Department has posted inside a series of very helpful and instructive wall placards. Another private chapel, converted to collegiate status in 1449, is **Crichton Collegiate Church** *(433)* in Midlothian, founded by Chancellor Sir William Crichton of "Black Dinner" fame and rebuilder of Crichton Castle up the hill from the church. Like most other collegiate churches, it was never finished, so that the present parish kirk is naveless, making it unintentionally T-shaped in the manner of post-Reformation churches, which were thus designed so as to make the pulpit visible and the minister audible throughout the building.

Unlike the Crichton church, **Seton Collegiate Church** *(459)* is no longer in use, though roofed and in a good state of preservation, thanks to the Scottish Development Department. Begun by George, third Lord Seton, who died circa 1478, the church was established as a collegiate foundation by his son, the fourth lord, who died in 1508. The nave was never finished, so what we have here is a vaulted choir ending in a three-sided apse, a central crossing surmounted by a square tower with an unusual truncated broach spire, transepts north and south, and a two-story sacristy adjoining the choir. Inside are piscinas, sedilia, and interesting funerary monuments. Of about the same original date, and founded by King James IV, is **Restalrig Collegiate Church** *(435)*, now a parish kirk in the eastern outskirts of

Edinburgh. In 1560 it was largely destroyed as a "monument of idolatrie," and what remains is mostly the product of a nineteenth-century restoration. Of the same date of incorporation as a collegiate foundation (1487) is the church of **St. Dutho's, Tain** *(549)*, in Ross and Cromarty. It is a good example of Scottish Decorated architecture and in the fifteenth century attracted many pilgrims, including James IV.

The impulse for establishing collegiate foundations continued into the sixteenth century—indeed, to the very eve of the Scottish Reformation. In 1501 King James IV, possibly still conscience-stricken over being the indirect cause of his father's assassination, won the Pope's approval to establish a college of secular priests headed by a dean at the Chapel Royal in **Stirling Castle** *(477)*. It was replaced in 1594 (probably on the same site) by King James VI on the occasion of the birth of his first son, Prince Henry, by a Renaissance neoclassical building with three pairs of round-arched lancets within arched frames on each side of a round-arched doorway flanked by Corinthian pillars. Inside, under the timbered roof, is a fine set of wall paintings executed in 1628 by Valentine Jenkin. James VI himself had been crowned a short distance down the Castle Wynd from here in the **Church of the Holy Rude** *(479)*, a collegiate establishment since 1546. This is a large Second Pointed rectangular church with a high western tower and the original open timber roof still in place. The nave was begun about 1415; the choir, with a splendid three-sided apse, dates from about a century later.

Fowlis Easter Kirk *(510)* in Angus near Dundee has already been mentioned in connection with its rare fifteenth- and early-sixteenth-century paintings on oak. Other interesting furnishings here include a medieval octagonal baptismal font, the fifteenth-century oak doors of the rood screen, an aumbry adorned with a painting of the Annunciation, and a set of seventeenth-century jougs (a collar used for restraining and publicly humiliating sinners among the congregation). There is a fine Second Pointed window in the west gable, but none at all in the east. It was made collegiate in 1538 under the patronage of the first Lord Gray. Of a somewhat earlier date in neighboring Perthshire, near Crieff, is **Innerpeffray Chapel** *(501)*, founded in 1508 as a collegiate church by Sir John Drummond. Now under the care of the Scottish Development Department, there is not much to see here beyond an original altar stone and the original painted ceiling. One of the last of the collegiate foundations before the Reformation was **Kirk Cullen** *(531)*, in Banffshire. Established in 1543 and now serving as the parish kirk, here is a particularly good aumbry in the north wall and next to it an elaborate sculptured monument to the founder, Sir Alexander Ogilvy, for whose use the ornate laird's loft was built against the south wall.

Perhaps the most famous of all of Scotland's late medieval collegiate churches, and certainly the most visited today, is **Rosslyn Chapel** *(452)* in Midlothian, founded as the Collegiate Church of St. Matthew in 1446 by Sir William Sinclair, third Earl of Orkney. This is a small building, consisting only of the barrel-vaulted choir and lady chapel of what was originally intended to be a full-sized church. The style is essentially Second Pointed, with strong French, and possibly Iberian, influences evident in the Flamboyant tracery of the windows. Rosslyn's chief distinction, however, is the elaborate stone carving, inside and out. Pinnacles, buttresses, arches, pillars, corbels, bosses constitute a veritable forest of intricate sculpture featuring an exotic display of animals, plants, bagpipers, sailors, saints, and religious symbols. The most elaborate of all is the so-called "Apprentice Pillar," so named by Sir Walter Scott, who apparently invented the fiction that it had been carved by a stonemason's apprentice whom his master later murdered out of jealousy. Rosslyn is certainly a sculptural *tour de force*. The Victorians loved it. Whether its rococo fanciness is indeed beautiful or merely bizarre is a matter of personal taste. Today it is a place of Scottish Episcopal worship.

A subspecies of the late medieval collegiate church is the burgh church, a Scottish specialty not commonly duplicated elsewhere in Britain, perhaps because in Scotland, unlike in England, each town formed a single parish requiring a larger than average church. Usually constructed, or at least enlarged, under the aegis of burghal councils, these tended to be cruciform in plan, adorned with one or more towers, and, when finished, filled with altars and side chapels endowed by merchants, craftsmen, guilds, and local nobility. The best-known, and most magnificent is the **St. Giles Kirk** *(439)*, Edinburgh (mistakenly called a cathedral—a status it enjoyed only briefly in the seventeenth century). There was a twelfth-century cruciform church here that was burned by the English under Richard II in 1385, but unlike Melrose Abbey, not the beneficiary of that king's uneasy conscience. Restoration did take place, but at the expense of the King of Scots and certain nobles and Edinburgh merchants. Now began that filling in of the four angles of the crossing so that, both inside and out, the church lost its cruciform appearance and became virtually rectangular. In 1460 the choir was lengthened to the east and the roof raised to approximately its present height above a vaulted ceiling supported by heavy polygonal columns. In 1467 the church became collegiate. More chapels and altars were added. During the reign of James IV (1488–1513) the great open-crown steeple rose to become one of Edinburgh's most famous landmarks. After the Reformation the church (like many other medieval houses of worship) was split up for separate Protestant congregations—a situation that continued into the nineteenth century in spite of King Charles I's temporary conversion of the kirk to cathedral status. Following the well-advertised visit to Edinburgh of

King George IV in 1822, overeager restorers squared off the exterior and encased it in new masonry. In time, however, the interior was cleared of its clutter and today presents a handsome, if somewhat sombre, appearance— and one recognizably medieval in the Second Pointed style.

Another burghal church is **St. Mary's, Haddington** *(456)*, cruciform in plan and built in the late fourteenth and early fifteenth centuries. It suffered severe damage during the Franco-Scotto-English wars of the sixteenth century, was radically altered in the nineteenth, and was restored in the twentieth to something like its original magnificence. More authentically medieval is **St. Michael's Church** *(427)*, in Linlithgow, West Lothian, a burghal church, served by a provost and chapter under the terms of a charter granted by King James V in 1540. There was a church on this site before the War of Independence, but it appears to have been mostly destroyed during the English occupation of Linlithgow, and the present cruciform building is the product of about two centuries of construction (ca. 1320–1531) with major restorations undertaken in the nineteenth and twentieth centuries. (An unfortunate by-product of the latest restoration was the installation of a hideous modernistic "open crown" on top of the battlemented western tower.) The interior is splendid. Worth special attention are the aisle vaulting, the flamboyant tracery of the Second Pointed windows, the nineteenth-century Burne-Jones stained glass, the relic of a stone-carved retable in the vestry, the blocked door to the north aisle through which the Stewart kings and their families entered from the nearby palace, and the polygonal apse added in 1531 with English-style Perpendicular windows, the only known example in Scotland outside of Melrose Abbey. One of the bells in the tower is original, dating from the reign of James IV.

UNIVERSITIES

The word *college* is seldom used anymore in its original ecclesiastical sense, but almost always with an academic connotation. This is an accident of history, stemming from the fact that masters and students in medieval universities were usually members of collegiate foundations established for the dual purpose of celebrating Mass in the name of the founders and making provision for the higher education of the clergy. After the Reformation, the only colleges to survive were those connected with education. Hence the word came to have an exclusively academic definition.

Before the War of Independence, a number of Scottish clerks bent on intellectual pursuits went to England—chiefly to Oxford, where John and

Devorguilla Balliol had in the late thirteenth century founded a college partly for the benefit of their own countrymen. Even while hostilities were in progress, this migration did not cease altogether, but throughout the fourteenth century most Scottish scholars gravitated instead to France—to the University of Paris or to Montpelier. Then, in 1378 began the great schism between rival popes in Rome and Avignon, with England, Germany, and Italy supporting the former and France, Spain, and Scotland the latter. In 1408, however, the University of Paris abandoned the Avignon papacy and the French king exiled Pope Benedict XIII to Pensicola in Aragon. This event, plus the outbreak of civil war between Burgundians and Armagnacs, made the position of Scottish scholars in Paris precarious since their country still acknowledged Benedict. Out of this predicament was born the **University of St. Andrews** *(493)*, first incorporated in 1412 by Bishop Henry Wardlaw in his cathedral city and in the following year established as a *studium generale* in theology, canon and civil law, arts, and medicine by the exiled Benedict XIII—"Scotland's Pope."

Typically, there were at first no university buildings, and masters and students lived, studied, gave and attended lectures, and participated in academic ceremonies wherever room could be found. At an early date, however, a chapel and college of St. John the Evangelist was established on South Street, and soon thereafter, in the same vicinity, a "pedagogy" was founded by Bishop Wardlaw with a house for the faculty, whose members were to celebrate masses for the founder's soul at neighboring St. John's. Nothing now remains of this house or any of the other of these first buildings. Wardlaw's successor as bishop was James Kennedy. It was he who was responsible for the first permanent building at the university. In August 1450 he issued the charter of foundation to a new college dedicated to the Holy Savior (confirmed by papal bull the following year) and to consist of four masters and six poor scholars charged with glorifying God publicly as canons and choristers of the collegiate church and with teaching and studying as members of the university community. Bishop Kennedy's chapel of the **College of St. Salvator** *(493)* still stands on North Street in front of a quadrangle of buildings of later construction now part of the United College of St. Salvator and St. Leonard. It is a fine Late Gothic building, though the original vaulted roof and window tracery have disappeared. Still to be seen, *in situ*, however, are Bishop Kennedy's splendid tomb and the ornate college mace donated by the founder. Some sixty years later a second college was established at St. Andrews by Archbishop Alexander Stewart in conjunction with Prior John Hepburn of the local Augustinian monastery. This was St. Leonard's College, whose students were originally under the jurisdiction of the priory and therefore obliged to conform to strict monastic regulations, including short haircuts, fasting, frequent chapel attendance, and *no* football. All that remains of the medieval college buildings is **St. Leonard's Chapel** *(494)*, a tiny place of worship restored and reconsecrated in 1951. The third of the pre-Reformation university foundations was **St. Mary's College** *(494)*, begun in 1525 by Archbishop James Beaton, specifically for the teaching of theology—which is still St. Mary's specialty. Although greatly altered, the college buildings on the north and west sides of the present quadrangle date to the early sixteenth century.

Scotland's second university was at Glasgow, founded by Bishop Turnbull of that city's cathedral in 1451. No traces of the early college buildings were left standing after the university moved in 1870 to Kelvingrove Park northwest of the city center to become the great Victorian showpiece described later in Chapter 9. The third of Scotland's great pre-Reformation centers of learning was the **University of Aberdeen** *(534)*, founded by Bishop William Elphinstone with the consent of Pope Alexander IV (the Borgia pope) in 1494. Most of the university buildings here are of a later date, but **King's College Chapel** *(534)*, built for thirty collegiate canons with mixed religious and academic responsibilities, dates from the year 1505. Like St. Giles, Edinburgh, this fine Gothic building is noted especially for its open-crown spire. Inside is a splendid display of medieval woodwork—stalls, misericords, rood screen, and wooden vaulted roof. The stained glass windows, of course, are a modern restoration.

It was clearly not the intention of the founders of these three universities to promote a flowering of Scottish literature. Colleges were places of prayer and worship, and those established within a university setting were different only in the sense that the collegians were expected to be masters and students. Yet out of these three universities came most of the writers who endowed the fifteenth and early sixteenth centuries with the distinction of being considered a "golden age" of Scottish literature. None was so vigorous perhaps as John Barbour, author of that noble epic, *The Bruce*, and none certainly rivalled Chaucer. But the later Middle Ages did witness in Scotland a literary flowering of no small consequence and one that arguably excelled its richer neighbor to the south.

Of the prose writers, however, no such claim can be made. Those who were not theologians wrote mostly chronicles. These protohistorians were John Fordoun (d. ca. 1385), compiler of the *Scotichronicon*; Walter Bower (d. 1449), who continued the latter's work; Hector Boece (1465–1536), author of *Scotorum Historiae*; and John Major (d. 1550), who wrote *The History of Greater Britain*. Of these, two are known to have been associated with Scottish universities: Boece was Principal of King's College, Aberdeen; Major was provost of St. Salvator's College, St. Andrews. They all wrote in Latin. Not so the poets, to whom is owed whatever literary reputation

Scotland's "golden age" enjoys. Theirs was the vernacular language of their country—that Anglian dialect that was inexorably replacing Gaelic or "Ersche" (Irish) and was first known as "Inglis" and, after the end of the fifteenth century, as "Scots." Their works, though not always intelligible today without a glossary, have a pungent, earthy quality that admirers of Robert Burns will at once recognize and appreciate.

The first of these was Robert Henryson (ca.1425-1506), author of *The Morall Fabillis of Esope the Phrygian* and of *The Teastament of Cresseid*, meant to be a sequel to Chaucer's *Troylus and Criseyde*. He was a lecturer at the University of Glasgow. Next among the major poets was William Dunbar (ca. 1460-1520), who received both his Bachelor's and Master of Arts degrees from St. Andrews University and was something of a court favorite in the reign of King James IV (1488-1513). His best known poem is "Lament for the Makaris," an elegy for a number of deceased Scottish poets (makars), none of whose works have survived. Dunbar's contemporary was Gavin Douglas (ca. 1475-1522). He was the third son of Archibald ("Bell-the-Cat") Douglas, fifth Earl of Angus, had also been a student at St. Andrews and later Paris, and served as Provost of St. Giles in Edinburgh. After his nephew, the sixth Earl of Angus, married James IV's widow (Margaret Tudor), he became deeply involved in court politics on the side of the Angus faction and was eventually forced into exile in England, where he died. His reputation is based chiefly on his translation into Scots of Virgil's *Aeneid*—a rendition (in historic couplets) that Ezra Pound found superior to the original, but that most readers today will value more for the naturalistic "prologues" added by the author than for his Scots rendition of the familiar tale of a Trojan hero's seduction and betrayal of a Carthaginian queen.

Finally, and best of all, comes Sir David Lindsay of the Mount (1486-1555), a student at St. Salvator's who later held office in the court of James IV; tutored the young prince who, after his father's death at Flodden (1513), became King James V; and served as Lyon King of Arms, the chief Herald of Scotland. After publishing a number of poems, including two anticlerical diatribes, "The Testament and Complaynt of Our Sovereign Lord's Papyngo" and "Ane Dialogue betwix Experience and ane Courteour," he produced his best-known work, a poetic drama called *Ane Pleasant Satyre of the Three Estaitis*, which was performed before the royal court at Linlithgow at the Feast of Epiphany in 1540; again at the author's hometown of Cupar in Fife in 1552; and a third time, in 1554, before the Queen Regent and a huge audience on the lower slopes of Calton Hill in Edinburgh. Though designated a "pleasant" satire, it could not have been so viewed by the representatives of the clergy who witnessed it. While glorifying the "common man" in a manner much approved of by modern "proletarian" writers, and ridiculing the nobility and bourgeoisie, Lindsay levelled against the clerical estate a barrage of invective so bitter and unmitigated as to warrant amazement that the play was not banned and its author excommunicated. Lechery, greed, incompetence, deceit, and fraud are only some of the charges brought. Neither the lowly ignorant village priest, extorting the poor man's last groat for a mortuary fee, nor the rich bishop, in his splendid palace surrounded by fawning sycophants and expensive mistresses, was spared. Yet both court and populace applauded. The Holy Church, bulwark of royal government in the Early Middle Ages, bastion of civilization, center of culture and learning, nursery of Scottish patriotism, had become, by the mid–sixteenth century, an object of general condemnation. Why this had happened is a complex story that can be examined only briefly here.

THE CHURCH IN DECLINE

Until 1192, despite the best efforts of Scotland's kings and prelates, the English Church and particularly the Archbishop of York laid claim to metropolitan jurisdiction over the Church of Scotland. In that year, however, in the bull *Cum Universi*, Pope Celestine III declared the Scottish Church to be the "special daughter" of Rome "with no intermediary." Special daughter or no, most of Scotland's bishops broke with Rome over the matter of national independence when Edward I claimed suzerainty over their country. Robert Wishart, Bishop of Glasgow, and William Lamberton, Bishop of St. Andrews, supported Sir William Wallace's rebellion from the outset. Even after Robert Bruce suffered papal excommunication for the murder of the Red Comyn in the Greyfriars' Kirk of Dumfries, most of the country's leading clergymen rallied to his standard. The Bishops of St. Andrews, Glasgow, Dunkeld, Aberdeen, and Moray all loaned more than moral support to the patriotic cause, and several of them suffered excommunication along with Bruce. After the English government at last recognized Scottish independence at Northampton, however, the papal see, never blind to the realities of war and politics, released Bruce from his excommunication and even conceded that the King of Scots could be crowned and anointed according to the rites of the Church.

Rome was less willing, however, to allow the Scottish Church its own metropolitan archbishop, though every other national branch of the Western Church enjoyed that privilege. Not until 1472 was the episcopal see of St. Andrews elevated to the rank of an archbishopric, though twenty years later the authority of the "primate" of the Scottish Church was diminished by the grant of similar metropolitan rank to Glasgow. As a result of this unusual arrangement, until 1472 appeals from the judgment of a bishop's court had to go directly to Rome, as did ecclesiastical office seekers in search of preferment to higher positions in the Church. In the fourteenth century, papal appointment to such benefices was common and often cost the nominee a fee equal to one-third of the annual revenue to which his new office entitled him. To the civil government, this outflow of scarce money to Rome represented a serious fiscal threat, as did the popes' insistence on the right of "provision," i.e., appointment to all bishoprics, abbacies, and other lucrative posts within the Church. Thus ensued a running fight between papacy and kings, which, though represented by the latter as being in defense of the right of free election of bishops and abbots by the chapters of monks and canons whom they were to head, was in fact no more than a sordid scramble over ecclesiastical revenues. For the Church of Scotland— even by comparison to that of more prosperous countries—was rich. By the middle of the sixteenth century Church lands were assessed at half of the taxable value of all real estate in Scotland, and the papal envoy to the court of James V reported that the clergy far surpassed the laity in wealth.

It is little to be wondered at then that the Stewart kings were anxious to control appointments to the higher positions in the ecclesiastical hierarchy and thus to dispense largesse to members of their own family and to nobles whose support they sought to purchase. In the long run they were successful—especially after the defection of King Henry VIII of England from the Church of Rome made popes more amenable to Scottish persuasion. As early as 1487 King James III won a papal indult, later renewed, which in effect gave the monarch control over appointments to all bishoprics and abbacies. James V was even more successful; he extorted from Rome a tax of three-tenths of all ecclesiastical revenues for the years 1530 to 1533 and from all Scottish prelates another heavy imposition for the support of a new royal college of civil justice so long as the king and his successors remained loyal to the faith.

Thus the Church of Scotland, with few exceptions, fell under the management of materialistic and greedy prelates, often holding plural benefices, whose primary qualification for their positions was royal favor. To the archbishopric of St. Andrews, James IV appointed first his brother, aged twenty-one, and then his illegitimate son, aged eleven. James V divided the abbeys of Kelso, Melrose, St. Andrews, Holyrood, and Coldingham among four of his illegitimate sons. To favored noble families these kings were likewise generous: Hamiltons, Erskines, Homes, Gordons, Campbells, Douglases, and Kennedies all partook of the royal munificence in the form of grants of commendation to the nation's many abbeys.

The grant of an abbey *in commendam* to a beneficed churchman had originally been a device to provide for the temporary administration of a particular house during a vacancy. In time grants were made in perpetuity and often to a favored layman whose primary interest was in extracting quick revenues from the monastic estates. By the mid–sixteenth century there were forty-six such commendatories. Matters grew worse after James V instituted the new tax levy authorized by papal decree. To raise revenues, commendators took to feuing monastic lands, in effect granting heritable leases in perpetuity for a fixed sum of money, part of it due immediately and the balance payable in annual installments. Thus a large number of monastic properties fell into lay hands long before the Reformation abolished the monasteries. It is no wonder that James V rejected Henry VIII's suggestion that he follow the English example and confiscate these establishments. The King of Scots had found an easier, and probably only slightly less lucrative, alternative.

Thus in its last decades the medieval Church of Scotland, once singled out as Rome's "special daughter," had reached a sorry state of decadence. Rich and worldly prelates held its highest offices; the Crown milked it of its revenues; nobles and lesser lairds carved private estates out of monastic lands; Church properties (especially abbeys and priories) deteriorated from wanton neglect; and all the while the general populace was starved of spiritual food for want of an informed and dedicated priesthood in the appropriated parishes.

In his "pleasant satire," David Lindsay merely recognized the obvious. At one climactic moment in that play, one of his allegoric characters (Veritie) complains to God himself:

> Get up, thow sleipis all too lang, O Lord,
> And make sum reasonabill reformatioun.

Reformation was indeed about to come, though not from on high. (True Protestant believers, to be sure, will think otherwise.) Reformation came from abroad—at the hands of Scottish exiles imbued with the radical teachings of Luther, Zwingli, and Calvin. It came from within—out of the dissatisfaction of some monks and lesser secular clergy with the sad spiritual condition of the country. It came from a wide cross section of the laity— from craftsmen envious of the alleged wealth of the friars, from peasants oppressed by teinds and rising rents, and from lairds and nobles anxious to confirm their acquisition of monastic lands. And most of all, it came as the by-product of the complicated interplay of dynastic politics, foreign wars, and international diplomacy that was to characterize the history of Scotland in the sixteenth century.

Chapter Six

Renaissance and Reformation

1488–1625

THE MONARCHY: 1488-1542

James IV: 1488-1513
James V: 1513-1542

When King James III "happinit to be slane" on the "unhappy field" of Sauchieburn, his only son and heir, though less than sixteen years of age, was promptly crowned at Scone as James IV, King of Scots. Thus was avoided that recurring curse of Scotland—a protracted royal minority. Instead, a short minority, followed by an exceptionally long reign of an energetic and able king, precluded the usual baronial grab for power that had so often emasculated the central government of Scotland. With the accession of James IV began a gradual, if halting, enlargement of royal authority that, though hardly comparable to the "Tudor despotism" of contemporary England, was marked by a distinct shift in the balance of power between the Crown and the nobility in favor of the former.

In some respects, the new king was firmly rooted in the Middle Ages. He was, for instance, obsessively pious—a frequent pilgrim to such holy places as **Whithorn Priory** *(377)*; the shrine of **St. Dutho's, Tain** *(549)*; and the miraculous well of **St. Mary's, Whitekirk** *(455)*. He was, moreover, unusually strict in his observance of Sundays and fast days and was given to wearing an iron chain around his waist as penance for his participation in the baronial rebellion that had resulted in his father's death.

On the other hand, James IV came as close to the ideal of the Renaissance prince as Scotland was to see. He was, in the words of the Spanish Ambassador Pedro de Ayala, "of noble stature, neither tall nor short, and as handsome in complexion and shape as a man can be." He was a superb athlete—at archery, tennis, and bowling and especially on horseback. As a military leader he was fearless—too fearless, thought de Ayala, who considered him "not a good captain because he begins to fight before he has given orders." His intellectual attainments were considerable, and his scientific and cultural interests varied. He spoke Latin, French, German, Flemish,

Italian, and Spanish, as well as Scots—an offshoot of Northumbrian English that had replaced French as the language of the court and had long been the tongue of the generality of the Lowland population. He even spoke some Gaelic—"the language," said the Spanish ambassador, "of the savages who live in some parts of Scotland and on the islands." He was a patron of poets, William Dunbar and Sir David Lindsay in particular. He was responsible for setting up the first printing press in Scotland under the management of Walter Chepman and Andrew Myllar of Edinburgh. He encouraged the founding of the new university at Aberdeen, where **King's College** *(534)* was named in his honor. He issued the original charter for the Royal College of Surgeons in Edinburgh. In his reign, and presumably with his support, Parliament passed an act requiring all barons and freeholders of substance to educate their oldest sons and heirs. His own illegitimate sons, Alexander and James, he sent to Italy to be tutored by the great Renaissance humanist, Desiderius Erasmus.

As to architecture, the modified classicism of fifteenth-century Italy and France slowly made its way into Scotland at the hands of master masons (many of them French) hired to restyle and refurbish the royal palaces. James IV was responsible for the first permanent building at the **Palace of Holyroodhouse** *(442)*, then on the outskirts of Edinburgh, which was gradually assuming the de facto rank of the country's capital. The northwest tower of the present palace was begun probably between 1498 and 1501 and completed in the following reign (James V) as a freestanding rectangular building, four stories high, with a gabled roof rising within a crenellated parapet. The same sequence of events took place at **Stirling Castle** *(477)*, which in these two reigns was converted from a massive, stark, and drafty medieval keep into something resembling a luxurious Renaissance palace. To James IV can be credited the great defensive forework across the main approach to the castle as well as the completion of the great hall. To his successor is owed the erection of the imposing palace in the upper square, with its classical facade imitating the Renaissance chateaux of contemporary France, its fine array of statuary, and the famous Stirling Heads— splendidly carved roundels affixed to the ceiling of the king's apartments.

At **Falkland Palace** *(488)* in Fife, it was again James IV who began the renovation of an ancient castle built by his ancestors, and again his son James V who completed it. The now ruined north range of what was meant to be a three-sided building laid out around an inner court belongs to the first period of reconstruction. So probably does the fabric of the south range. The twin-turreted and battlemented gatehouse and the courtyard facade of the south range were built by James V to impress his two successive French brides. It is here that contemporary architectural influences from the Continent are best to be seen. This "Renaissance screen which hangs in front of an unaffected Gothic range, a corridor's breadth behind," is, in the words of Stewart Cruden, "window-dressing, a two-dimensional exercise in Renaissance design." At **Linlithgow Palace** *(426)* in West Lothian James IV added passages, galleries, and stairs. But again, it was James V who must be credited with the Renaissance features of the present ruined building. He converted the existing palace into a quadrangle surrounding a courtyard, added the south range and shifted the main entry to this part of the castle from the original east wing; built an elaborate outer gateway; and installed an elegant fountain at the center of the inner courtyard as a present to his second wife, Marie de Guise. This cultured lady, familiar with the palaces of Fontainebleau and Blois in France, is reported to have declared on first visiting Linlithgow that it was as fine as any castle in her native land.

More tactful than truthful, Queen Marie's statement served no doubt as balm to her husband's sensitivity about his status among the crowned heads of Europe. That his country was relatively poor and backward there could be no question. Yet James V, by virtue of his father's marriage to Margaret Tudor, was the grandson of King Henry VII of England and therefore the nephew of King Henry VIII; moreover, by his short-lived first marriage to the Princess Madeleine, he had been son-in-law to King Francis I of France. In such distinguished company it behooved the King of Scots to surround himself with all the trappings of Renaissance regality. This may explain his heavy expenditures on palaces. It may also account for his refashioning the crown and scepter of his ancestors. (Some of the Scottish Regalia now on display at **Edinburgh Castle** *[436]* probably date to James V's reign and are thus more than a century older than the Crown Jewels in the Tower of London.)

All these palaces and baubles cost money—a commodity not easily available to Scottish kings in the absence of any machinery to levy and collect general taxes on a regular basis. James IV was able to tap a relatively new source of revenue by feu-ferming some of the royal estates, that is, granting heritable leases in exchange for cash. His marriage to Margaret Tudor of course brought him a substantial dowry. His son did even better by acquiring two well-endowed wives in quick succession. The first—Madeleine, daughter of the King of France—died shortly after her arrival in Scotland; the second—Marie, daughter of the powerful Duc de Guise—was also richly dowered. From the Church, James V was able to extract large sums by the simple act of remaining loyal to Rome at a time when England had succumbed to Protestantism and even France seemed likely to do the same. In 1531, as already mentioned, Pope Clement VII issued a bull declaring that the Scottish prelates were all to provide £10,000 annually to the Crown as long as James V and his successors remained faithful. The pretext for the gift was the king's declared need to finance the establishment of a College of Justice—a permanent high court of law that was to sit in Edinburgh. In fact, the new "college" was little different from the already functioning Court of Session, so the Crown, not the judiciary, was the chief beneficiary of the Pope's largesse.

The dispensation of justice was of course an important potential source of royal revenue, as English kings had long since discovered with the development in that country of the Common Law. A common law for Scotland, however, was virtually impossible, so long as the nobles kept control of their private courts of barony and regality and so long as the king's law was virtually unenforceable in the outlying regions of the Highlands and Islands and in the Borders adjacent to England. To quell these turbulent regions, rife with clan feud and general lawlessness, two recourses were open to the Crown. One was to undertake punitive military expeditions against the major troublemakers; the other, especially suitable to the Highlands and Islands, was to issue letters of fire and sword to a loyal clan authorizing military action against its offending neighbors and to delegate responsibility for the general maintenance of law and order to a few favored Highland chiefs from whom cheerful cooperation in putting down their own local rivals could be expected. The central government used both methods. After forfeiting John of Islay, fourth and last of the MacDonald Lords of the Isles, James IV conducted six naval expeditions to the western isles between 1493 and 1496. At **Mingary Castle** *(460)* on the Sound of Mull, the chiefs of several of the clans formerly subordinate to the Lord of the Isles made their submission to the King. These included MacLean of Mull, whose stronghold was the now restored **Duart Castle** *(472)*; MacNeil of Barra, whose seat was **Kisimul Castle** *(555)* (also now much restored); and MacDonald of Sleat, with two major castles on Skye—**Dunscaith** *(522)* and **Duntulm** *(524)*, both now in a very ruined condition. (On the site of another property belonging to this branch of the clan is Armadale Castle, housing the **Clan Donald Centre** *[521]*, mostly a collection of weapons, tartans, and other Highland mementos.)

These MacDonalds of Sleat were at almost constant feud with their neighbors, the MacLeods of **Dunvegan Castle** *(522)*. In 1498 James IV granted to the clan's eighth chief, Alasdair (Alexander) Crotach ("Humpbacked") a charter for the lands he held in northern Skye and on the island of Harris. It is this MacLeod whose magnificent tomb at the church of **St. Clement's, Rodel** *(556)* on Harris, has been described (Chapter 3). He lived in splendor at Dunvegan, where he added the "fairy tower" to the existing keep of this massive, sprawling castellated mansion which is *the* showpiece of Skye. He was a great patron of harpers and bards and, above all, of pipers.

By the beginning of the sixteenth century the bagpipe had replaced the harp as the favored musical instrument of the Highlanders when engaged in warfare, mostly because it could be heard above the din created by the large armies now being mustered to follow their chiefs into battle against other chiefs. The origins of the instrument are too ancient to be traced with any certainty. There is, however, documentary evidence that the *chorus* (Latin for *bagpipe*) was used in Wales and Scotland in the twelfth century. Chaucer mentions it in *The Canterbury Tales*, and James I of Scotland (1406–1437) is reported to have been an accomplished player. Toward the end of the fifteenth century, it was not uncommon for the burghs of Lowland Scotland to employ a town piper to play through the streets at dawn and dusk.

By the sixteenth century, when the great Highland bagpipe had reached its maturity, the instrument consisted of four major parts: the blowpipe; an inflatable bag of skin; the chanter; and one or more drones. The art of bagpipe playing has not changed much since. The player fills the bag with air by exhaling through the blowpipe; under the pressure of his arm, the air then passes through a double reed in the chanter, thus producing a high, thin sound; melody is achieved by the player's fingering the holes along the length of the chanter; rudimentary harmony is produced by the drone or drones (long pipes, each with a single hole, sounding a single note.)

The hereditary pipers of the MacLeods were the MacCrimmons, and to them is attributed the origin of the *ceol mor* or *piobaireachd* (pibroch), the wonderfully intricate and stylized classical music of the Highland pipes. Donald Mor MacCrimmon (born 1570) is usually accepted as the inventor or originator of the *piobaireachd*. Alexander MacLeod is credited with the founding of a college of piping at or near the site of the present **Borreraig Piping Centre** *(523)* not far from Dunvegan, where the MacCrimmons taught the MacArthurs (hereditary pipers of the MacDonalds of Sleat), the MacIntyres (pipers to the chief of Clan Menzies), the MacKays (clan pipers to the MacKenzies), and others. This is a fascinating tiny museum not to be missed by devotees of this uniquely haunting style of music. Better still in this connection are Scotland's famous Highland Games, more than forty in all, held sequentially every summer and culminating in the great Braemar Highland Gathering on the first Saturday in September (normally attended by Queen Elizabeth and other members of the royal family). Featured on these occasions (along with caber-tossing, Highland dancing, and other uniquely Scottish sports and arts) is a pibroch competition among the most accomplished pipers of Scotland and elsewhere.

The MacLeods of Dunvegan remained mostly loyal to James IV and did not join an uprising led by Donald Dubh, grandson of the fourth and last Lord of the Isles, and Torquil MacLeod of Lewis—not put down until 1505 when the king took the field in person and sent his navy against the western islands. Thereafter for the rest of his reign, the Highlands remained relatively quiet, but after James IV's death at Flodden in 1513 (see below), the islanders again rose in revolt, this time joined by Alasdair Crotach, who used the occasion to capture **Dunscaith Castle** *(522)* from his hereditary enemies, the MacDonalds of Sleat. By about 1518 the uprising subsided, but some twenty years later there was a resurgence of disorder provoked by Donald Gorme of Sleat (of Clan Donald), which prompted James V to sail around the North of Scotland on a pacifying mission. He visited the Orkneys; landed at Skye (where the name of the principal town, Portree—King's Haven—commemorates his visit); touched down at Coll, Tiree, Mull, Arran, and Bute; and ended the expedition at Dumbarton. At almost every stop he took aboard Highland chiefs as hostages, and after his return formally annexed the Lordship of the Isles to the Crown by act of Parliament.

It cannot be said, however, that either James IV or James V succeeded in permanently pacifying the Highlands and Islands. In the end the net result of their policy was to replace the dominance of the MacDonald Lords of the Isles with three other families, who were elevated to a new eminence in the decades surrounding the turn of the fifteenth and sixteenth centuries. These were the Campbells of Argyll, the Gordons of Aberdeenshire, and the MacKenzies of Ross and Cromarty.

Chief of Clan Campbell (or Clan Diarmaid) was the Earl of Argyll, with a stronghold on the islet of Innis Chonnel in Loch Awe and another on the site of the present (mostly eighteenth-century) **Inveraray Castle** *(463)* on the northwest shore of Loch Fyne. Over a long period of time, by dint of conquest, marriage, and royal favor, the family established a wide network of influence, not only in the western Highlands, but in central Scotland and on the shores of the Moray Firth as well. From the Crown the Earl of Argyll received custody of **Castle Sween** *(468)* in Knapdale and the **Castles of Tarbert** *(474)* and **Skipness** *(474)* at the head of the Kintyre Peninsula. In the fifteenth century Colin Campbell of Glenorchy built **Kilchurn Castle** *(464)*, later a seat of the Campbell earls of Breadalbane and now a romantic ruin overlooking Loch Awe. Toward the end of the same century the first Earl of Argyll (another Colin Campbell) acquired by inheritance a former Stewart estate near Dollar in Clackmannanshire and raised a tower that comprises the oldest part of the magnificently sited present ruin of Castle Gloom, renamed **Castle Campbell** *(481)* and much enlarged in the sixteenth century. In 1498 the posthumous daughter of the Thane of Cawdor was abducted and married off to a son of the Earl of Argyll, thus bringing into Campbell possession **Cawdor Castle** *(525)* in Nairnshire—a fourteenth-century keep, crenellated a century later, to which buildings were added in the seventeenth century to create a splendid stately home.

As to the Gordons, the Crown's chief agents in the northeastern Highlands, their main seat was **Huntly Castle** *(540)* in Aberdeenshire, also known as Strathbogie Castle. Here the first Earl of Huntly in the late fifteenth century began construction of an oblong castle with a round tower at its southwest corner, which was to be completely rebuilt from the ground upward by the fourth earl in the sixteenth century and further embellished by the fifth earl in the early seventeenth. Though ruined, it remains today a stunning example of Renaissance architecture.

The original home of the MacKenzies was in Kintail at the foot of Loch Duich just east of Skye. Gradually throughout the fifteenth and sixteenth centuries the clan occupied Lewis and expanded north and east to win a dominant position in Ross and Cromarty. In 1623 its chief, already enjoying the title Lord MacKenzie of Kintail, was elevated to the earldom of Seaforth. By this time, the seat of the clan was Castle Brahan near Dingwall—since gone. The MacKenzies' original stronghold on Loch Duich was **Eilean Donan Castle** *(548)*, which in consequence of their migration northward they turned over to the MacRae chiefs to serve as constables. Subsequently destroyed by British naval artillery (see below), the castle was rebuilt in the twentieth century as a memorial to Clan MacRae and in its romantic island setting is probably the most photographed of all of Scotland's medieval castles—even though not exactly authentic.

As indicated, King James IV's forfeiture of the Lordship of the Isles brought neither law nor order to the Highlands and Islands. Indeed, if anything, it created a power vacuum into which rival clans promptly moved, and, in their competition for land and power, brought about a condition of constant warfare, terrorism, forced migrations, and general unrest. Strong kinship and tribal ties, in a society that had never been entirely feudalized, aggravated and perpetuated the strife. Wrongs inflicted on an individual, especially if he was high in the clan hierarchy, came to be viewed as affronts to the honor of the clan itself and therefore grounds for revenge. Clan feuds, in short, became a way of life.

It was not much different on the Borders, though this region was free of the clan system proper, with its paraphernalia of dubious genealogies, bards, pipers, lavish hospitality, and filial pietism directed toward the chief. Instead, kinship groups bearing the same surname and usually geographically separated from each other by the rugged hills that lay between the short river valleys in this region vied for power and property in much the same manner as the Highland clans. (In the Borders, unlike the Highlands, surnames had become stabilized by the sixteenth century and were universally used as labels of personal identification.) Feud was endemic here also: Elliots versus Pringles and Scotts; Scotts versus Kerrs as well as Elliots; Armstrongs versus Johnstones, Turnbulls, and Bells; Bells versus Irvines as well as Armstrongs; Irvines versus Maxwells as well as Bells; and, most deadly of all, Maxwells versus Johnstones. Occasionally, the English Crown, intent on weakening or distracting the central government of Scotland by provoking domestic turmoil, would subsidize one feuding clan against another—both Scottish.

On their part, the Scots, when not engaged in internecine warfare, habitually raided across the border, stealing cattle, burning homesteads, kidnapping hostages, and extorting blackmail. English borderers, with such surnames as Graham, Charlton, Fenwick, and Nixon, did likewise. These border reivers normally rode in bands, wearing helmets of iron (miscalled "steel bonnets") and quilted coats of leather and metal called "jacks"; carrying lances, swords, and sometimes bows, but more often arquebuses or "dags" (a kind of pistol). They made their forays mostly in the winter months, when nights were long and cattle and their owners had returned to permanent valley homesteads from their scattered summer pastures in the hills.

In an effort to maintain some semblance of order in this wild and turbulent region, both Scottish and English governments established administrative areas called *marches*, three on each side of the border, placing wardens over each. In peacetime their job was to try to put down local crime and to cooperate with their opposite numbers across the border so that criminals of either nationality might be brought to book for felonies committed on the other's side. Thus over the years a kind of international law developed that was administered by pairs of wardens, Scottish and English, when they met jointly during "days of truce" held periodically at specified spots near the border. For the most part, the system was ineffective, if for no other reason than that the wardens themselves were often guilty of the kinds of transgressions they were charged with deterring or punishing. On the Scottish side the Home (or Hume) family traditionally held the wardenship of the East March. Their principal seat was **Hume Castle** *(416)*, north of Kelso, Roxburghshire, later reduced to ruins and then in the eighteenth century converted into a sham antique by the addition of new battlements to the crumbling walls of the original medieval keep. Wardenship of the Middle March alternated between the Kerrs of Cessford or of Ferniehurst and the Scotts of Branxholm. The West March was mostly under the titular control of the Maxwells, who held the **Castles** of **Caerlaverock** *(384)* and **Lochmaben** *(386)*. Between the East and Middle March was the particularly ungovernable region of Liddesdale, where **Hermitage**

Castle *(413)* was, in the words of one Border historian, "the guard house of the bloodiest valley in Britain." For most of the period under consideration it was held by the Hepburn earls of Bothwell, who enjoyed the title of Keepers of Liddesdale.

Perennial breakdown of the wardens' control over the areas they were supposed to administer led to frequent intervention on the Scottish side of the border by the king himself. James IV on one occasion accompanied the English warden, Lord Dacre, on a punitive raid through Eskdale. Royal "justice ayres" ("eyres" in England) were periodically held in Dumfries and Jedburgh, the latter becoming famous for "Jeddert justice" by which prisoners were brought before the bar with nooses already around their necks; i.e., condemned first, tried later. Supplementary to such proceedings, "judicial raids" were commonly carried out by the monarch himself at the head of a conventional feudal army called up for such occasions. On one of these, led by James V in 1529, occurred the execution of Adam Scott of Tushielaw and Piers Cockburn of Henderland—an incident that inspired "The Lament of the Border Widow," one of the most poignant of the Border ballads, with its complaint:

> There came a man, by middle day,
> He spied his sport, and went away;
> And brought the King that very night,
> Who brake my bower, and slew my knight. . . .
>
> Nae living man I'll love again,
> Since that my lovely knight is slain;
> Wi' ae lock of his yellow hair
> I'll chain my heart for evermair.

A year later the same king was back in the Borders, this time intent on breaking the power of the Armstrongs, probably the most turbulent family in the area. Inviting Johnnie Armstrong of Gilnockie to meet him at Carlinrigg about ten miles from Hawick, James V had the notorious reiver seized and hanged on the spot. Again the incident produced a splendid Border ballad, often cited as evidence of this king's legendary ruthlessness. "I have asked grace at a graceless face," Johnnie Armstrong is quoted as complaining, "but there is nane for my men and me!" **Gilnockie Tower** *(386)*, which may have been the Border stronghold from which Johnnie rode jauntily out to his death, lies on the east side of the A 7 just north of Canonbie and has recently been restored and put to use as a private residence.

A "graceless face" was not the only unattractive feature of King James V.

Cruel, vindictive, and excessively greedy even for a king are the characteristics usually attributed to him. "He must have been," says the historian Gordon Donaldson, "one of the most unpopular monarchs who ever sat on the Scottish throne." A troubled childhood might explain some of his personality disorders. Only seventeen months of age when his father, James IV, was killed at Flodden, he quickly became the prize pawn in a complicated struggle for power involving his mother, the widowed Margaret Tudor; her second husband, Archibald Douglas, sixth Earl of Angus; and John Stewart, Duke of Albany, first cousin to James IV and Regent of Scotland for nine years during the young king's minority. In the years 1525–1528 James was a virtual prisoner of Angus, for whom he developed an undying hatred and who is sometimes held responsible for the king's paranoia as well as for his precocious lechery. Angus was eventually overthrown and escaped to England along with other Douglases after the loyal Earl of Argyll had successfully captured the family stronghold of **Tantallon Castle** *(458)*.

Though sometimes represented in popular folklore as a "poor man's king" (possibly because Angus had encouraged in him a taste for low company), James V was held in terror by most of the nobility. And for some reason. In 1537 Angus's sister Jonet, Lady Glamis, was burned in Edinburgh on trumped up charges of conspiring against the king (not for witchcraft, as is commonly alleged). James V then temporarily repossessed for the Crown **Glamis Castle** *(512)* in Angus, a fifteenth-century L-plan tower-house, much expanded and altered in the seventeenth, eighteenth, and nineteenth centuries and today one of Scotland's most attractive stately homes. Shortly after Lady Glamis met her fiery fate, another Douglas relative, the Master of Forbes, was executed on charge of plotting to shoot the king. Punitive proceedings (often turning out to enhance the royal treasury) were brought against the Earl of Bothwell, Walter Scott of Branxholm, the heir of the Earl of Crawford, the Earl of Morton, and sundry lesser nobles and lairds.

The most shocking case of royal vindictiveness was that of Sir James Hamilton of Finnart, illegitimate son of the first Earl of Arran. Finnart had been an early favorite of the king, the master of works for the reconstruction of Stirling Castle and Linlithgow Palace, and for himself the designer of **Craignethan Castle** *(411)* near Lanark, which, after his death, was completed by his half-brother, the second Earl of Arran, later Duke of Chatelherault. (Still later this place became the model for Sir Walter Scott's "Tillietudlem Castle" in his novel *Old Mortality*.) This impressive stronghold, now a substantial ruin, consists of a tower-house built upon a spur of land formed by a bend in the River Nethen, surrounded on the three sides overlooking ravines by conventional stone walls flanked by rectangular towers and on the fourth, the approach side, by a thick masonry rampart rising from a broad ditch across the spur with provision for artillery emplacements. The most unusual feature of this defense-work was a "caponier" built across the north end of the ditch—a vaulted stone gallery with loopholes facing inward through which hand-gunners could fire at any attackers trying to cross the ditch. Craignethan was, in the words of the architectural historian Charles Knightly, "perhaps the most comprehensively defended private castle of its day." If so, it served its builder little purpose. In August 1540 Finnart was executed on a charge of plotting to kill the king in collaboration with the exiled Douglases; his lands and goods (including a hoard of gold) were confiscated. This act seems to have severed the few remaining threads of baronial loyalty to the Crown. Yet James V had military designs against England that required the cooperation of the nobility. Hoist on the petard of his own ruthlessness, this "graceless" prince could not muster sufficient support from his leading barons to ward off utter humiliation at the hands of the "auld enemy."

FOREIGN RELATIONS: 1488–1542

As in the past, Scotland's major problem in the reigns of James IV and V was how to defend itself against the hostility of its southern neighbor without subordinating its national interests entirely to those of France, the "auld ally." No escape from or through the horns of this dilemma was to be found in these years. At the beginning of his reign, James IV foolishly lent support to the harebrained scheme of the pretender Perkin Warbeck to wrest the throne of England from King Henry VII, who only recently, as Henry Tudor, Duke of Richmond, had overthrown King Richard III at Bosworth Field. Warbeck, a low-born fraud, claimed to be the younger of the two Yorkist princes done to death in the Tower of London by their uncle Richard. The imposter succeeded in attracting much encouragement and some support from the English king's Continental enemies, but by the time he reached Scotland in November of 1495, he had already been expelled from the French court, driven off the Kentish coast after a bumbling amphibious landing, and suffered a decisive defeat in his effort to capture Waterford in Ireland. The King of Scots, however, welcomed him as a visiting prince, married him to his own kinswoman, Lady Katherine Gordon, and even mounted a shortlived and futile expedition across the border before becoming disillusioned with Warbeck and shipping him out of the country.

After another failed military sortie into England, James IV reversed himself, concluded a seven-year truce with Henry VII, and in 1502 agreed to marry his daughter, Margaret Tudor. This princess, only twelve years of age at the time, developed into an ill-tempered, headstrong, and stupid woman with few redeeming features. But it was through her bloodline that the Stewart dynasty eventually ascended to the throne of England. It was also in preparation for her arrival in Scotland that James IV built the new tower at the **Palace of Holyroodhouse** *(442)*, already mentioned.

A peace of some duration with England might nevertheless have been the product of this marriage had not the Scottish king been lured into another self-defeating military adventure on behalf of France. When, in 1511, Pope Julius II organized a "holy league" against France to be joined by Henry VIII, England's newly ascended king, James IV was induced by the reigning French monarch, Louis XII, to renew the "auld alliance" and make war against the Scots king's brother-in-law across the border. Thus it was that in August 1513 the Scottish national army, with its eager king in the van, crossed the Tweed. Simultaneously, the Earl of Surrey (in the absence of King Henry VIII, who was across the Channel, laying siege to Tournai) was coming up from Newcastle-upon-Tyne with an army of twenty thousand men, mostly infantry. The two forces came within sight of each other at Flodden Hill in Northumberland a few miles across the border from Coldstream.

The ensuing battle was a major disaster for the Scots. They too were mostly infantrymen—armed, as at Bannockburn, with fifteen-foot spears and deployed in great diamond-shaped formations like the ancient *schiltron*. The English carried "bills"—eight-foot halberds with heavy jagged blades designed for cutting and slashing. When Surrey moved northwest of the Scots' encampment to occupy the nearby hill of Branxton, thus cutting off their retreat back home, James took the offensive—a major tactical error since the *schiltrons* were, as Bruce had proven, best suited for defense. The Scots in consequence were slaughtered—their long spears shattered by the English bills, their swords useless too against these longer-shafted weapons. Their king, on foot, died early in the forefront of the battle. So too did perhaps ten thousand others, including reportedly two bishops, two abbots, eleven earls, fifteen lords, and the king's own illegitimate son Alexander, Archbishop of St. Andrews. Of this young man, his former tutor Erasmus wrote: "What hadst thou to do with fierce Mars . . . thou that were destined for the Muses and for Christ?" Of the common soldiers who were buried in great pits after the battle, their chief memorial was that most poignant of Scottish ballads, "The Flowers of the Forest":

I've heard them lilting, at the ewe-milking,
Lasses a' lilting, before dawn of day;
But now they are moaning on ilka green loaning;
The flowers of the forest are a' wede awae. . . .

Dool and wae for the order, sent our lads to the Border!
The English, for ance, by guile [sic] wan the day:
The flowers of the forest, that fought aye the foremost,
The prime of our land, are cauld in the clay. . . .

On display in **Halliwell's House Museum and Gallery** *(419)* in Selkirk is the much worn "Flodden Flag," allegedly captured by a Scottish soldier who survived the massacre to return here to his native town. In Edinburgh, when news of the battle arrived, the citizens began construction on a wall against the expected English invasion. A short stretch of this **Flodden Wall** *(433)*, with arrow-loops and crenellation, can still be seen in the Vennel leading up from the Grassmarket. But the English never came, and Scotland was spared the normal retribution for her most popular king's most egregious act of folly.

His successor, when he came of age, was far less popular, but just as foolish in the matter of foreign policy. Inveterate hatred for his captor, the Earl of Angus, possibly colored his attitude toward England, which had given refuge to this noble exile. James's two French marriages, first to the Princess Madeleine, daughter of King Francis I, and second to Marie de Guise, sealed his attachment to France. In 1540, when Henry VIII, in fear of a hostile European coalition inspired by the Pope's bull of excommunication for having separated the English Church from Rome, arranged for a meeting at York with his Scottish nephew, James V agreed but failed to appear. An English army under the Duke of Norfolk made a brief but damaging foray across the border. James sought to retaliate, but his barons, remembering Flodden and disgruntled with his high-handed treatment of the nobility, refused to cross the Tweed. Two new forces were raised to invade England, each by a separate route. The king intended to lead the western army, but stopped instead at Lochmaben and turned command over to his current favorite, Oliver Sinclair. At Solway Moss in late November 1542 the Scots were routed. But there were few casualties, and the English capture of fifteen hundred prisoners, many of them high-born, suggested collusion with the enemy. The king made his way back to **Falkland Palace** *(488)*, where he received news of the birth of a daughter, Mary. This was slight consolation for the previous death of two male children. "It came with a lass, it will pass with a lass," said he, referring to the fact that the Crown of Scotland had come to the Stewarts by virtue of the marriage of

Margery Bruce to Walter, the high steward. And with this false prophecy, James V died in his thirty-first year—out of despair, it was generally believed at the time.

RELIGION, WAR, AND DIPLOMACY: 1542–1560

Governor, 1542–1554: James Hamilton,
second Earl of Arran, Duke of Chatelherault
Regent, 1554–1560: Marie de Guise

The lass in question was the six-day-old princess, Mary, born in **Linlithgow Palace** *(426)* and to become famous in both history and romantic legend as Mary, Queen of Scots. After a brief struggle for power, a new Governor of the Realm was appointed to assume direction of affairs during the royal minority. This was the infant queen's closest male adult kinsman, James Hamilton, second Earl of Arran.

The Hamilton family had achieved eminence mainly through the marriage of James, Lord Hamilton, to Mary, daughter of James II. The second earl was the grandson of this couple and therefore next after the newborn queen in succession to the throne of Scotland. (See table: "The Scottish Succession 1437–1649.") Their close association to the reigning house had naturally brought the Hamiltons much power and wealth. The original family seat was Cadzow Castle (since gone) located in the High Parks of the present town of Hamilton. But they were extensively endowed with other estates and noble residences as well. One was **Brodick Castle** *(393)* on the island of Arran, which went to the Hamiltons in 1503 and was rebuilt by the second earl about 1558. Of this now magnificent and sprawling stately home, the southeast tower and that part of its adjacent wing containing the dining room date from this period of construction. At an earlier date Arran commenced building **Kinneil House** *(425)* near Bo'ness, West Lothian. It consisted of a conventional, rectangular, five-story Scottish tower house to which the earl attached a more refined "palace" at the northeast corner. Though partially demolished, the house, roofed but unoccupied, stands today in a good state of preservation and is especially notable for the Renaissance wall paintings in the palace built by the second earl. **Craignethan Castle** *(411)*, already described, was another of the second earl's

THE SCOTTISH SUCCESSION: 1437–1649

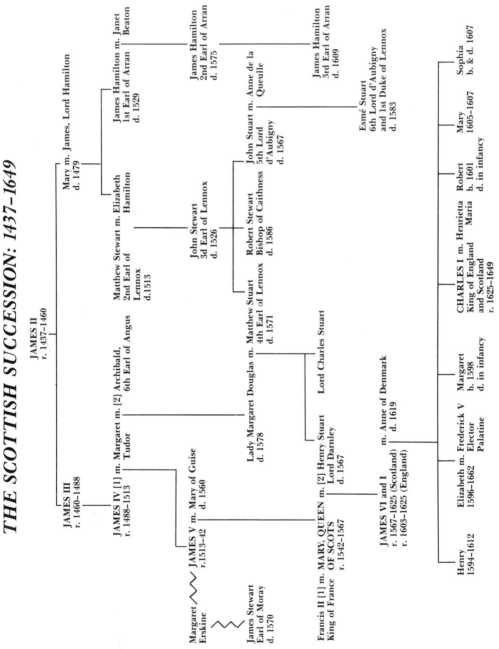

properties—acquired after the death of his bastard half-brother, Hamilton of Finnart, who had all but completed the major works here before his execution by James V.

The first years of Arran's governorship were troubled by the return to Scotland of the exiled Earl of Angus and of sundry prisoners captured by the English at Solway Moss and released on condition that they agitate on behalf of a treaty that would commit the infant queen to marry Henry VIII's young son, Edward (later King Edward VI). Arran at first agreed, but such an obvious power play on the part of the English king was too much for the Scottish Parliament to swallow; the treaty with England was denounced and the "auld alliance" with France reconfirmed. Henry retaliated by sending the Earl of Hertford across the border to "put all to fyre and swoorde, burne Edinborough town, so rased and defaced when you have sacked and gotten what ye can of it, as there may remayne forever a perpetual memoray of the vengeaunce of God"; sack Holyroodhouse and as many towns and villages about Edinburgh "as ye may conveniently; sack Lyte [Leith] and burne and subverte it and all the rest, putting man, woman and child to fyre and swoorde without exception"—and much more of the same. This the Scots, with typically sardonic humor, have referred to ever since as "the Rough Wooing." Twice (in 1544 and 1545) Hertford swept over the border with "fyre and swoorde." Though the devastation was perhaps not as frightful as Henry VIII had wished for, it was adequate, as evidenced still in the ruins of the Border monasteries—**Kelso Abbey** *(415)*, **Melrose Abbey** *(417)*, **Dryburgh Abbey** *(418)*, and **Jedburgh Abbey** *(413)*, as well as **Holyrood Abbey** *(443)*, near Edinburgh, and even as far north as **Balmerino Abbey** *(490)*, on the south bank of the Tay.

But even before the appearance of English troops came the English Bible—deliberately "let slip amongst the people" by English Protestants and pro-English Scots. Parliament in 1543 made it lawful for men to read the Bible in English or Scots, an act the Reformer John Knox later declared to have been "no small victory for Christ Jesus" as "then might have been seen the Bible lying almost upon every gentleman's table" and "the New Testament . . . borne about in many men's hands." The incendiary nature of this great book, translated into English by William Tyndale in 1515–1529, can hardly be overestimated. The very reading of it by laymen was a challenge to the exclusive authority claimed by the Church of Rome to interpret the word of God to all Christians. Its publication was the essential prerequisite for the realization of a reformed Church that, in Luther's phrase, would be "a priesthood of all believers."

Martin Luther, a German Augustinian monk, had nailed to the main door of the castle church of Wittenberg on 31 October 1517 his famous ninety-five theses denouncing the current papal practice of selling indulgences (i.e., blanket exemptions from penances imposed on confessed sinners). From here he rapidly moved to more radical positions, culminating in his denouncing the claim of the Pope to be the supreme head of the Church of Christ on earth and urging the German princes of the Holy Roman Empire to cast off the yoke imposed by the Roman "Antichrist." Those who followed his advice and protested against the emperor's continued loyalty to Rome were called "protestants," a term soon applied to all who declared their independence of the Catholic Church. The main theoretical, or theological, foundation of Protestantism was the doctrine of "justification by faith," derived from St. Paul and St. Augustine. It was by God's grace alone, bestowed on those who lived in faith in Christ, that sinful man might be saved from eternal perdition. Thus the mediation of the Church of Rome—its Masses, prayers for the dead, auricular confession, penances, and indeed most of the functions performed by its clergy—were supererogatory. Not by such "works" was man to be saved, nor by the exercise of his own free will, but by the grace of God bestowed upon the faithful.

Gradually these heresies travelled to Scotland, chiefly by way of trade between the Baltic and the east coast ports, and by 1525 had received sufficient currency to provoke an act of Parliament banning Luther's books. This did not prevent young Patrick Hamilton, a descendant of James II on his mother's side and related to the Earl of Arran on his father's, from travelling to Marburg to study them at their source and returning to his native land to teach and preach the radical new doctrines. Summoned by the Archbishop of St. Andrews, James Beaton, to recant, Hamilton refused and was burned publicly before the front gate of **St. Salvator's College** *(493)* in 1528. It was a raw, windy day and the fire had to be rekindled several times, so that the martyr's suffering was protracted and the audience disgusted. One of the archbishop's henchmen reportedly commented: "My Lord, if ye burn any more, except ye follow my counsel, ye will utterly destroy yourselves. If ye burn then, let them be burned in how [deep] cellars, for the reek of Master Patrick Hamilton has infected as many as it blew upon."

Neither heresy nor heresy hunting made fast progress in Scotland, however, and the next notorious burning did not take place for another seventeen years, when George Wishart was condemned to the fire by Cardinal David Beaton, the old archbishop's nephew. Wishart, son of an Angus laird, had come north from England in the early years of Arran's governorship and may have been a paid agent of Henry VIII. He had been much influenced by Swiss reformers at Zurich who, even more than Luther, rejected all religious beliefs and practices for which warrant was not expressly given in the Scriptures. Such strict interpretation of the Bible was to become a hallmark of Scottish Protestantism—so much so as to give some color to the charge of bibliolatry levied against the Reformers.

Wishart's martyrdom was shortly followed by an even more spectacular event; namely, the murder of his persecutor, Cardinal Beaton, in his own episcopal residence of **St. Andrews Castle** *(492)*. This was accomplished by a tiny band of Protestant conspirators who entered the castle by stealth, did away with His Eminence, and hung his body from a wall-head for the edification of the townspeople. For a year these "castilians," with some assistance from Henry VIII, withstood a siege whose marks can still be seen in the mine and countermine tunnelled through the rock. Government forces, with significant help from a French fleet, eventually overcame the defenders, who were then seized and dispatched, some to imprisonment in France, others to serve as galley slaves. Among the latter was John Knox, a disciple of Wishart who would shortly return to Scotland in a role far more dangerous to the established order than that of preacher to the captors of St. Andrews Castle.

The intervention of both English and French in this affair was symptomatic of the political and diplomatic implications of the Reformation in Scotland. That there were profound and deeply felt religous differences between Protestants and Catholics there can be no doubt. But religious sentiments were colored by, and in some cases rooted in, differences of opinion over foreign policy. In general, Catholics preferred strong ties with France—a continuation of the "auld alliance." Protestants, on the other hand, tended to look to England as a natural and necessary ally, notwithstanding the ancient enmity reinforced recently by Henry VIII's brutal tactics. These two countries, for their part, naturally exploited religious differences in Scotland to forward their own ambitions in the wider arena of European politics. In each case, troops were dispatched to Scotland in the name of the "true faith." Thus, after the death of Henry VIII and the accession to the throne of his minor son, Edward VI, under the regency of the ardently Protestant Duke of Somerset (formerly Earl of Hertford), an English army in September 1547 again came over the border. It was led by Somerset himself, who routed the badly led Scots at Pinkie Cleugh near Musselburgh, inflicting heavy casualties and capturing about fifteen hundred prisoners. Somerset withdrew, but English garrisons remained in Haddington and at **Broughty Castle** *(511)* near Dundee. The Earl of Arran, now weaned from his earlier Protestant leanings, arranged for a new treaty with France, agreeing to the eventual marriage of the infant Queen Mary to the French Dauphin. For this he received the Duchy of Chatelherault. French troops were invited to garrison **Dunbar Castle** *(454)* and **Blackness Castle** *(428)*, a royal fortress overlooking the Forth between Queensferry and Bo'ness. The young Queen Mary was meanwhile dispatched to the safety of **Inchmahome Priory** *(497)* in the Lake of Menteith, where she stayed for only three weeks before being brought back to Stirling, then transferred to **Dumbarton Castle** *(475)* and thence to France. She was in her sixth year on her arrival and was to spend the next thirteen years of her life in the country that was more home to her than Scotland could ever be.

In 1554 Chatelherault was persuaded to resign his governorship, and the queen mother, Marie de Guise, became Regent of Scotland in her daughter's absence. This tall, auburn-haired, handsome, and intelligent woman was of course wholly committed to the "auld alliance" and the French interest. Four years later, Mary, now sixteen years of age, married the Dauphin in Notre Dame Cathedral, Paris. By a secret treaty she agreed that, if she died without issue, the King of France would inherit Scotland. Shortly thereafter, she and her husband began quartering the arms of England, thus in effect denying the legitimacy of the newly crowned Queen Elizabeth and asserting Mary's right to the English throne by virtue of her descent from Margaret Tudor. (See table: "The English Succession 1485-1625.") By this act alone, Mary, Queen of Scots, assured the undying suspicion and enmity of her English royal cousin.

With the French marriage (even though the terms of the secret treaty remained unknown), Francophobia in Scotland took a new turn. Already the presence of so many French troops and French officials in the government of the regent had alienated a significant section of the Scottish nobility. In December 1557 the Earls of Argyll, Glencairn, and Morton, with sundry others, known as the Lords of the Congregation, signed a band to promote "the true [i.e., the Protestant] religion." Next year the French king died, to be succeeded by the Dauphin as Francis II, whose queen of course was Mary, Queen of Scots. Fear of total French domination reached new heights among Scottish Protestants. And in 1559 John Knox, the ex–galley slave, returned to Scotland.

Knox had spent the better part of his exile in Geneva and had fallen under the influence of the French refugee lawyer and Reformer, John Calvin. Calvin's major contributions to the evolution of Protestant doctrine were two: First, unlike Luther, who hedged on the matter, he denied the "real presence" of the body and blood of Christ in the elements (bread and wine) of the Catholic sacrifice of the Mass and denounced the rite as idolatrous. Second, he maintained (somewhat legalistically) that, since God was infinitely wise, He must have known and decreed before the beginning of time just which human beings, born and unborn, would receive the blessing of His saving grace. The first doctrine had the practical effect in Calvinist churches of substituting for the priestly celebration of the Mass the corporate act of Communion by clergy *and* laity alike in commemoration of the Last Supper, where Christ had enjoined his disciples to eat the bread and drink the wine "in memory of me." The second doctrine—known as

THE ENGLISH SUCCESSION: 1485–1625

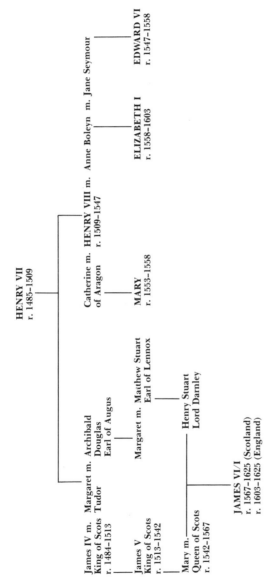

HENRY VII
r. 1485–1509

James IV m. Margaret m. Archibald
King of Scots Tudor Douglas
r. 1484–1513 Earl of Augus

Catherine m. **HENRY VIII** m. Anne Boleyn m. Jane Seymour
of Aragon r. 1509–1547

James V
King of Scots
r. 1513–1542

Margaret m. Matthew Stuart
Earl of Lennox

MARY
r. 1553–1558

ELIZABETH I
r. 1558–1603

EDWARD VI
r. 1547–1558

Mary m.
Queen of Scots
r. 1542–1567

Henry Stuart
Lord Darnley

JAMES VI/I
r. 1567–1625 (Scotland)
r. 1603–1625 (England)

predestination—distinctly separated the "elect" from the damned, made short work of the Catholic doctrine of free will, and imbued those Protestants who felt assured of their election with a sense of self-worth that was to be the source of tremendous inner strength. If the dark side of Calvinism was characterized by spiritual arrogance, intolerance, and fanaticism, it was also the source of inspiration for great steadfastness of purpose, courage, probity, sobriety, respect for the written word, and, most importantly, the conviction that the elect were equal before God regardless of worldly distinctions of power and status. Egalitarianism—a salient characteristic still of Scottish society—is partially rooted in that country's Calvinist tradition.

Fired with this heady spiritual brew, and secure in his knowledge of strong support among the lairds, burgesses, and even nobility of Scotland, Knox mounted the pulpit of **St. John's Kirk** *(505)* in Perth on 11 May 1559 and preached a thunderous sermon against the idolatrous practices of the Church of Rome. The congregation then proceeded to loot the nearby Carthusian monastery and the houses of the Dominican and Franciscan friars. Similar episodes occurred in several other towns and cities, but it would be a mistake to attribute too much of the ruination of medieval church buildings in Scotland to iconoclastic Reformers. The friaries suffered the most—chiefly because they were located in urban centers where unruly mobs were most likely to assemble. Otherwise, the greatest damage done during these first years of the Reformation was not to church fabrics, but to their furnishings—altars, vestments, statuary, and the like. Few parish churches suffered much destruction, and the ruins of Scottish monasteries and cathedrals can mostly be attributed to English depredations, stone quarrying by greedy neighbors, and neglect both before and after the Reformation. It was, after all, in the interest of the Reformers to occupy churches and convert them to the uses of the true religion—not to destroy them.

The incident at Perth touched off a series of armed movements and encounters between the Lords of the Congregation and the French and Scottish forces raised by Marie de Guise. June found Knox at St. Andrews, where he preached another inflammatory sermon at **Holy Trinity Kirk** *(494)*—his first there since the days when his fellow "castilians" were in occupation of the nearby castle. By July the Protestant army was in Edinburgh. In August a thousand French reinforcements arrived to support the regent, who had captured Leith. In September Chatelherault changed religions again and joined the Congregation. In November the Protestants were driven out of Edinburgh to Stirling. In January 1560 an English fleet appeared in the Forth to prevent a new French landing. Late in February the Protestant James Stewart (later the Earl of Moray), illegitimate son of James

V and therefore half-brother to Mary, Queen of Scots, negotiated with the English the Treaty of Berwick, which was essentially a mutual defense pact against France. In early April an English army, eight thousand strong, joined forces with the Congregation and commenced the siege of Leith. In June Marie de Guise died of natural causes, no doubt aggravated by the burden of her cares. In July the French and English agreed to the Treaty of Edinburgh, whereby both would evacuate Scotland. In December the young French King Francis II died, and Mary, Queen of Scots, announced her decision to return to her native land.

Meanwhile, "in the name of Francis and Mary," a Scottish Parliament had been called. It was attended, as never before, by more than a hundred lairds or lesser barons. Named by historians "the Reformation Parliament," it convened in Edinburgh in August 1560. It abolished papal jurisdiction over Scotland, repealed the laws against heresy, and forbade the saying or hearing of Mass on pain of death for the third offense. It adopted *The Scots Confession of Faith*, prepared in four days' time by Knox and five collaborators—a thoroughly Calvinist document, setting forth the doctrines described above. Parliament also charged Knox and his cohorts to produce a treatise on church government; this became known as "The First Book of Discipline." It was never enacted into law, but did become the basis on which the first Reformed Church in Scotland was organized. Members of kirk congregations were to elect their own ministers; also elders and deacons—to be chosen annually. In place of bishops, superintendents were to be appointed to oversee the kirks within their provinces, which had more rational boundaries than the old episcopal dioceses. Sermons and prayers were to be offered daily in larger towns and once a week besides Sundays elsewhere. Children were to be examined publicly on the catechism, and adults once a year. To assure an educated ministry and a laity at least literate enough to comprehend the Bible, a three-tiered system of national education was recommended: a school to be established in each parish for the instruction of children "in their first rudiments" and in the catechism; colleges to be set up in every "notable town" for instruction in Latin, Greek, logic, and rhetoric; and at the top the existing Scottish universities (and others that might come into being) to be devoted to education in the learned professions—law, medicine, and, above all, the ministry. The catechism referred to was contained in Knox's *Book of Common Order*, a compendium of the order of worship drawn up for his congregation of English exiles in Geneva with Calvin's express approval. It included, in addition, forms for the election of ministers, etc.; procedures for ecclesiastical discipline; the Lord's Prayer, Apostle's Creed, and Ten Commandments; and the metrical psalms for congregational singing.

Leaving aside fine points of doctrine, the major accomplishment of the

Reformation Parliament was to diminish the power of the clergy and enhance the role of the laity in Christian worship and church government. The new emphasis on preaching and Bible-reading required that education be spread among the people; ministers, elders, and deacons were to be selected by the congregations over whom they presided; the celebration of the Mass by priests was discarded in favor of Communion—a commemoration of the Last Supper in which ministers and laymen alike assembled around a table and partook of the symbolic bread and wine.

But as yet no settlement had been made in respect of the vast amounts of property held by the medieval Church. No move had been taken officially to dispossess bishops, abbots, lay commendators, or even parish priests. Knox and his brothers had firm ideas about diverting ecclesiastical revenues toward the payment of salaries to the reformed clergy, supporting the poor, and endowing schools, colleges, and universities. But all this required governmental action. And nothing substantial could be done in this connection until the arrival of Mary, Queen of Scots.

MARY, QUEEN OF SCOTS: 1561–1567

On Tuesday, 19 August 1561, the recently widowed Queen of Scots set foot again on her native soil at the port of Leith after an absence of almost thirteen years. It was a foggy, rainy day, a day, wrote Knox, when "the very face of heaven . . . did manifestly speak . . . [of the] sorrow, dolor, darkness, and all impiety" she brought with her to the country. At the age of nineteen, she was a tall (five feet, eleven inches), slender, pale-complexioned, auburn-haired, swan-necked, attractive woman—not outstandingly beautiful perhaps, but of compelling grace and charm. Her courtly accomplishments included a smattering of Latin and Italian (besides her fluent French), adequate command of Scots, none yet of English, facility in dancing, great skill in hawking and horsemanship. Unfortunately, she was deficient in common sense, though it took a while for this to become apparent.

Stopping briefly in Leith, she was then escorted to what became her favorite Scottish residence—the **Palace of Holyroodhouse** *(442)* outside Edinburgh. The first Sunday after her arrival she held a private Mass in the chapel. A riot ensued. The Queen then issued a proclamation that no one was to introduce alterations in the existing (i.e., Protestant) religious settlement, but that no one either was to molest her servants or French courtiers in the practice of their religion. John Knox, now occupying the pulpit of **St. Giles Kirk** *(439)* a mile away, complained that "one Mass was more fearful . . . than ten thousand armed enemies." The queen summoned him to Holyroodhouse for the first of their several tumultous interviews. At the last of these, when Mary asked who was *he* "within this Commonwealth" to censor the conduct of a *queen*, the preacher answered: "A subject, Madam, born within the same. And albeit I neither be earl, lord, nor baron within it, yet has God made me a profitable member within the same." These were Calvinist words, spoken with the self-assurance vouchsafed only to one of the elect.

Mary's Catholicism posed a problem for Knox and the Protestants, notwithstanding her hands-off policy toward their Church. In England, a "godly prince" (first Edward VI and later Elizabeth I) acted as supreme governor of the Reformed Church. Obviously, a queen who continued to attend Mass could not serve in that capacity, and a substitute had to be found. Thus was born the General Assembly of the Church of Scotland—a governing body organized along the same principles as Parliament, i.e., representing the three estates: clergy, nobility (including lesser barons), and burgesses. The ministers were at first far outnumbered by the lay members— another indication of the anti-clerical tenor of the early Scottish Reformation.

But without support from the Crown, and not at one among themselves, the General Assembly was unable to follow up the break with Rome with a complete reorganization of Church government and Church finances. Driving the priests from their parish kirks proved mostly unnecessary, since gradually enough of them converted to Protestantism to fill the greater part of the existing pulpits. As to the bishops, three of them changed religions, and in the remaining dioceses superintendents were appointed. Among these was John Carswell for Argyll—later made bishop. The Campbell earls were his patrons, and he became famous for his translation into Gaelic of *The Book of Common Order*. His residence was **Carnasserie Castle** *(471)*, north of Lochgilphead, today a stately and substantial ruin. Superintendents, assisted by commissioners, were supposed to exercise general supervisory functions over individual kirks, only much more aggressively than had been the case with the Catholic bishops. As to those among the latter who remained faithful to the old religion, as well as the abbots, priors, and lay commendators of the religious houses, they were permitted to hold on to their properties and most of their income for the duration of their lives. It was the same with monks, who continued to receive their "portions" of monastic revenues. Nor were feuars of Church lands to suffer any cancellation of their heritable leases—often recently acquired. Thus was the consent of many nobles and lairds to the new religious dispensation assured.

As to the Protestant parish clergy, those who had previously been benefice-holders kept two-thirds of their former incomes plus a fraction of the remaining third, which was to be shared with the Crown. Newly ordained ministers, however, were to receive only that part of the one-third that did not go to the royal treasury. This settlement displeased Knox greatly. He was sure that "the Spirit of God is not the author of it, for first I see two parts freely given to the Devil, and the third must be divided betwixt God and the Devil." Among other things, it made no provision for his scheme for universal education. Even so, the parish clergy were probably better off financially than they had been under the old religion. And it should be noted that the spirit of compromise that informed the Scottish Reformation produced a minimum of social and economic disruption and, in contrast to contemporary England, almost no heresy hunting.

Much of the credit for Scotland's easy transition from Catholicism to Protestantism must be awarded to the queen's first principal adviser, her half-brother James Stewart, whom she elevated to the earldom of Moray, with its principal seat at **Darnaway Castle** *(528)* near Forres. His preeminent role in the government was shared in the early years by William Maitland of Lethington, a representative of the new class of lairds whose social and economic status had been steadily rising in the sixteenth century. One of the Maitlands' family seats was Lethington Tower near Haddington, East Lothian—later renamed **Lennoxlove House** *(457)* and today, with many modifications, a fine stately home in possession of the Duke of Hamilton. Maitland, though Protestant, was primarily a *politique*—so dedicated to secular objectives and so ruled by *raison d'état* as to earn the sobriquet "Mitchell Wylie," a Scotticization of Machiavelli. His prime concern, while serving as Mary's secretary of state, was to assure her right of succession to the English throne.

His mistress naturally shared this ambition. By the rule of primogeniture, Mary was undoubtedly next in line if Queen Elizabeth I died without issue, which even in 1561 seemed likely. The Queen of Scots was, after all, the eldest surviving grandchild of Margaret Tudor, sister to Henry VIII. In the view of the papacy, she was already the rightful English sovereign on the grounds that Henry VIII's marriage to Anne Boleyn had been unlawful and therefore their daughter Elizabeth illegitimate. Mary herself appeared to endorse this position by refusing to ratify the Treaty of Edinburgh, which stipulated that she should renounce the inclusion of the arms of England in her own coat of arms. Small wonder then that Elizabeth declined to name the Queen of Scots as her rightful successor, especially since to do so would have been an invitation to rebellion among her own subjects, always, as she put it, "more prone to worship the rising than the setting sun."

It was soon after this impasse that Mary's cousin, Henry Stuart, Lord Darnley, arrived in Scotland. He too was a grandson of Margaret Tudor—by her second marriage to Archibald Douglas, sixth Earl of Angus. (See table:

"The Scottish Succession: 1437-1649.") His branch of the family had adopted the spelling of their name preferred in France, which eventually prevailed over the original, at least so far as the royal house was concerned. He too had a claim to the English succession reinforced by the fact that, unlike Mary, he had been born in England and was moreover a nominal Protestant. From a dynastic standpoint then, he was the ideal choice as the Queen of Scots' second husband.

There was, moreover, another reason for a marriage between these cousins; i.e., the queen fell in love with him. He was a year or so younger than she, tall (six feet, one inch), slender, blonde, beardless, polished in manner, skilled in playing the lute, and somewhat brainless. When he fell ill with measles, Mary nursed him back to health and in the process fell in love. Male invalidism seems to have had an aphrodisiac effect on this strange woman. Her first husband's sickliness was apparently at the root of her genuine fondness for him; she became enamored of her third husband on seeing him laid up with serious body wounds (see below). In any case, they were soon married (by Catholic rites) and Darnley became King of Scots, though not given the "crown matrimonial" that would have entitled him to succeed the queen in the event of her prior death without issue.

This marriage was her first major political blunder. Moray and other nobles rebelled, were put down, escaped to England, and began to plot their new king's overthrow. Darnley turned out to be a disaster: vain, drunken, vicious, and obsessed with resentment over not being granted the crown matrimonial. When Mary came to prefer the company of David Riccio, an Italian musician whom she made her private secretary, her husband became insanely jealous. He was therefore easily persuaded to join a conspiracy of Protestant lords to murder Riccio, apparently so as to restore their influence at court. The plotters may have contemplated the death of the queen herself, perhaps hoping she would not survive a possible miscarriage of the six-months-old fetus then in her womb. In any event, the murder took place in Mary's presence at the **Palace of Holyroodhouse** *(442)*. Riccio was torn from his grip on the queen's skirts and stabbed to death by many hands. She and her unborn child, however, escaped. The foolish Darnley was persuaded to join her flight to **Dunbar Castle** *(454)*. A group of loyal lords, including James Hepburn, Earl of Bothwell, rallied to the queen. The leading conspirators, including James Douglas, Earl of Morton, fled to England. Moray returned and was readmitted into the queen's counsels. Her son (later James VI of Scotland, James I of England) was born in **Edinburgh Castle** *(436)* in one of the rooms now known as Queen Mary's Apartments within the building called The King's Lodging. And with the succession thus secured, Darnley's minimal usefulness came to an end.

Back to the business of royal government, the queen went to Jedburgh in

October 1566 to hold justice ayre, i.e., a judicial session for the enforcement of peace in the Borders. She stayed at a fortified town house, known as a "bastel," which still stands as a museum in the center of Jedburgh under the name of **Mary Queen of Scots' House** *(414)*. While there, news came that James Hepburn, Earl of Bothwell, had been seriously wounded in a Border foray and was lying in danger of death at **Hermitage Castle** *(413)*, about twenty-five miles away. The queen, accompanied by the Earl of Moray and others, rode there and back in one day. It was probably then that she fell in love again with a stricken man, this time as inappropriately as the last. Bothwell was at the time about thirty years of age, a battle-hardened adventurer, ambitious and unscrupulous, yet polished enough from having been in the service of the King of France. He had already proven his loyalty to the Queen at the time of the Riccio murder. As owner of the **Castles** of **Borthwick** *(432)*, **Crichton** *(432)*, **Hailes** *(455)*, and **Dunbar** *(454)*, as well as **Hermitage** *(413)*, he was a useful ally.

When Mary returned to Jedburgh, she fell violently ill from unknown causes, but November found her recovered enough to move to **Craigmillar Castle** *(450)* near Edinburgh. Here she was advised of a bond signed by a group of nobles, including Bothwell and Maitland of Lethington, to get rid of Darnley in some manner yet unspecified. Mary was soon persuaded to pardon the exiled Earl of Morton, who later also signed the bond. In January 1567 Darnley fell ill in Glasgow, probably from syphilis. Mary went there promptly and persuaded her husband to return to Edinburgh and take up lodgings in an outlying house attached to the old collegiate Church of St. Mary in the Fields, known as the Kirk o' Field. On the night of 9–10 February the house was blown up and Darnley was smothered or strangled to death in his nightgown in the garden outside. Three months later the queen was married by Protestant rites to the Earl of Bothwell, who was generally, and probably correctly, believed to have been instrumental in Darnley's assassination. She was by this time probably pregnant with twin children by Bothwell, conceived presumably in late April, when the queen had collusively submitted to being "abducted" to Bothwell's stronghold of **Dunbar Castle** *(454)*.

As a result of the marriage, Mary was inevitably accused of having joined the plot to kill her late husband in order to marry one of his murderers. Whether she was actually guilty of complicity is perhaps the most contested issue in all of Scottish historiography. The case for or against the queen's guilt rests primarily on the estimate of her motives for persuading her husband to leave the safety of Glasgow and take up residence at the Kirk o' Field. Three explanations suggest themselves, in descending order of probability: (1) Knowing of the Craigmillar bond and fully aware of the violent character of some of the nobles who signed it, she deliberately put her husband's life at risk by bringing him back to Edinburgh. (2) As early as her visit to Glasgow, Mary believed herself to be pregnant by Bothwell and, wanting to assure her unborn child's claim to legitimacy, lured Darnley back to court in order to recommence marital relations with him. (3) Affected as usual by compassion for an invalid, the queen forgot her grievances against Darnley and honestly hoped for a reconciliation.

Whatever her motives, the hasty marriage to Bothwell was a political blunder of major proportions. It immediately provoked another baronial rebellion—this one led by James Douglas, Earl of Morton, who, as a signer of the Craigmillar bond, was also no doubt partially responsible for Darnley's death. Armies were mustered; Mary and Bothwell fled Edinburgh to **Borthwick Castle** *(432)*. The rival forces met, but did not fight, at Carberry Hill near Musselburgh. Mary surrendered on condition that Bothwell be allowed to escape. He went to **Dunbar Castle** *(454)*, then to Moray and the Orkneys, and finally to Denmark, where he eventually died insane in prison. The queen was carried back to Edinburgh, assailed by cries of "Burn her, burn the whore!" She was imprisoned in **Loch Leven Castle** *(482)*, a Douglas island stronghold, where her half-brother Moray coerced her into abdicating in favor of her infant son. In July she miscarried twins, doubtless Bothwell's. The following May she escaped from Lochleven by boat and made her way to the Southwest, where friendly forces, led by the Hamiltons, rallied to her support. At a battle fought at Langside outside Glasgow, the queen's little army was routed; she herself fled the field in panic. After two days of flight, she decided to throw herself on the mercy of Queen Elizabeth and hired a boat to take her across the Solway Firth into England.

This was Mary's third great error of judgment—matched only by her two disastrous marriages. She might have encouraged her allies to regroup and then resumed the battle. She might have waited for a ship to France. Instead, she put herself at the mercy of an unsympathetic English government that could neither risk returning her to Scotland nor allow her to proceed to France. Queen Elizabeth ordered a hearing to determine whether her cousin had been unjustly deprived of her throne. The Earl of Moray, then regent, produced the famous "casket letters," intending to prove Mary's complicity in the murder of Darnley out of illicit love for Bothwell. (A silver box purporting to be the original casket containing the letters is now on view at **Lennoxlove House** *[457]*.) There is little doubt that these were forgeries or, if not, so manipulated as to be the equivalent of forgeries. The "trial" at York and Westminster was inconclusive. Moray was sent back to Scotland; Mary to confinement. For the next nineteen years she was moved from one English castle-prison to another until finally beheaded for having given encouragement to a feckless Catholic conspiracy (the Babington Plot) to assassinate Elizabeth. The enduring romantic legend that thenceforth formed around the name and memory of Mary, Queen of Scots, cannot erase her almost infinite, and fatal, capacity for folly.

JAMES VI AND I: 1567-1625

King in Name: 1567-1585

At the age of thirteen months, King James VI was crowned at the **Church of the Holy Rude** *(479)* near the entrance to Stirling Castle. John Knox preached a sermon; the crown was held over the infant's head by the hereditary keeper of the castle, John Erskine, Earl of Mar, whose own house, known as **Mar's Wark** *(479)*, stood nearby. The king's half-uncle Moray was chosen regent, but Queen Mary's partisans, led by the Hamiltons, refused to acknowledge his right to rule in the name of a king whose possession of the throne they considered premature. Civil War ensued for about eight years. Moray was assassinated by a Hamilton while riding through Linlithgow. His tomb (restored) is still to be seen in the Moray Aisle of **St. Giles Kirk** *(439)* in Edinburgh, where Knox preached his funeral sermon. Moray was succeeded by the king's paternal grandfather, Matthew Stuart, Earl of Lennox, who soon died from mortal wounds during a raid on Stirling Castle. The Earl of Mar replaced him briefly. Finally, James Douglas, fourth Earl of Morton, took over the regency in 1572. He had inherited the earldom in the right of his wife, and among his residences was **Aberdour Castle** *(482)* in Fife, a typical fourteenth- to fifteenth-century tower-house much expanded in the sixteenth by this earl and today a well-preserved ruin. He was a hard, obstinate, and ruthless man, and it was he at last who put down the rebellion. After placating the Hamiltons, he laid siege to the last remnant of the "queen's party" (including Maitland of Lethington) in **Edinburgh Castle** *(436)* and, with the help of English artillery, compelled the beleaguered rebels to surrender in May 1573. Thereafter, he undertook a major rebuilding of the castle, as evidenced today in the Half Moon Battery and the Portcullis Gate. For the five years of his regency, Scotland enjoyed an unwonted interval of peace and steadily increasing prosperity.

Meanwhile, the king was growing up. At the age of four, his formal education began under the tutelage of George Buchanan, a staunch Protestant who was also a poet, historian, satirist, and Latinist. "They gar [made] me speik Latin ar [ere] I could speik Scottis," wrote the king later. He also learned Greek and French to perfection and Italian adequately. But theology was his main interest, and Buchanan made sure that he was thoroughly grounded in an orthodox Calvinism from which the king never wavered. That he became a pedant is well known; the French King Henry IV later was to dub him "the wisest fool in Christendom." On the other hand, he developed into a fine horseman who excelled at, and was addicted to, hunting. In appearance he grew into middle height with brown hair, heavy-lidded eyes, a long nose, and a small mouth. Except on horseback, he was somewhat ungainly and walked with a pronounced shuffle—owing probably to childhood rickets.

That his personality was warped by too much childhood discipline and too little affection goes without saying. Buchanan taught him to detest his Catholic mother and to suspect all women. Thus he was ill prepared for adolescent sexuality, and when an older cousin, Sir Esmé Stuart, seigneur d'Aubigny, arrived at court from France in 1579, the thirteen-year-old lad fell in love with him. This was the first of his many passionate attachments to handsome men. Whether these liaisons were more than platonic cannot be proved or disproved. What difference they made, as far as concerns James's effectiveness as king, is arguable. Certainly, he was more than generous to his favorites, showering them with gifts, estates, and titles. But other kings did the same with their mistresses, so the net charge on the royal treasury may have been no greater than if James VI had been more conventionally amorous. Clearly, his homosexual inclinations did not inhibit his performance of the kingly duty of procreation. He did, after all, sire six legitimate children, which is more than can be claimed for most of his royal ancestors or successors, including that notorious womanizer Charles II. And if, toward the end of his reign as King of England, his emotional attachment to George Villiers, Duke of Buckingham, warped his political judgment, his choice of advisers up to that time was on the whole coolheaded and judicious. Too much, in other words, should not be made of James VI's unorthodox sexual preferences.

D'Aubigny's regime was profitable to himself, but short. The infatuated young king elevated him to the earldom and later the dukedom of Lennox. But by 1582 he was banished from the kingdom. Meanwhile, he had spearheaded a coup d'état against the Regent Morton, who was convicted on trumped up charges and beheaded on a guillotinelike contraption he had himself invented. This was called "the Maiden" and is still on view at the **National Museum of Antiquities** *(447)* in Edinburgh. Within a year, some of Morton's former Protestant allies, in the traditional Scottish manner, kidnapped the king. At their head was William Ruthven, Earl of Gowrie, in whose castle near Perth James VI was held prisoner for eight months. Later renamed **Huntingtower Castle** *(506)*, this was a handsome residence of two towers then connected by a curtain wall (subsequently replaced by a central apartment). The building still stands to its original height and is distinguished for its rare mural paintings and early plasterwork. From this place the king escaped in June 1583. Next year another Protestant coup overthrew Captain James Stewart, Earl of Arran, who had replaced d'Aubigny in the king's favor. His premier position at court was then taken by a coalition of nobles more or less headed by John Maitland of Thirlestane, younger brother of Queen Mary's secretary, Maitland of Lethington. (**Thirlestane Castle** *[425]* in Lauder, Berwickshire, today a stately home open to the public, was mainly built by James VI's chief minister though later enlarged by his grandson, the first Duke of Lauderdale.)

The appearance at court of Maitland and his elevation to the chancellorship coincided with James VI's finally assuming chief responsibility for the conduct of government. He was now nineteen years of age. Together king and chancellor reorganized the institutions of the Scottish state, curtailed the power of the more rambunctious nobility, brought into the central government an increasing number of professional lawyers and others of the lairdly class to create a sort of proto-civil service, and completed the redirection of foreign policy toward firm friendship with England. Maitland held the chancellorship for ten years, to be replaced not by the usual palace revolution led by discontented nobles, but by a coalition of eight (hence known as the Octavians) who, though aristocratic, were predominantly lawyers and administrators. Until the overthrow of Arran and the rise of Maitland, says the latter's biographer, Maurice Lee, "the king had not been the most important person in the government; after Arran's fall he undoubtedly was. . . . Before 1585 James had been king in name; now he became king in fact."

King in Fact: 1585-1625

The first major step in asserting the king's authority was taken in 1586 when James accepted the English offer of an alliance, along with a respectable annual pension from Queen Elizabeth. This not only gave him a greater degree of financial independence but also cut off the traditional flow of money from Westminster into the pockets of dissident Scottish nobles willing to destabilize their own government to promote the English interest—and their own. It also increased the likelihood of James's peaceful succession to the English throne in the now almost certain event of Queen Elizabeth's dying without issue. So anxious was the King of Scots for such a consummation that, when his mother was finally executed in 1587, his protests to the English government were feeble at best. His marriage in 1589 to Princess Anne of Denmark enhanced his dynastic attractiveness to the

English, especially when the new queen produced six children, of whom three (Henry, Charles, and Elizabeth) survived to adulthood. England had not been blessed with such an abundance of royal issue since the reign of Henry VIII, and James VI's fruitfulness was as welcome to a country weary of uncertain royal succession as were his Protestantism and the undoubted legitimacy of his claim to the throne by descent from Margaret Tudor. As to the King of Scots himself, he was so pleased with the birth of his first son, Henry, that, for the baptism, he rebuilt the Chapel Royal at **Stirling Castle** *(477)* in its present form.

Notwithstanding the central government's improved solvency and efficiency, the king's problems with his "overmighty subjects" did not altogether cease. Two great lords proved especially troublesome—George Gordon, sixth Earl of Huntly, and Francis Stewart, fifth Earl of Bothwell. Both were involved in a harebrained plot to induce the Spanish Duke of Parma to send a landing force from the Netherlands to Scotland preparatory to an English invasion. This foolish scheme was exposed; the king overawed the schemers with a show of force; and the two earls and their confederates submitted. Huntly, a Catholic except when he thought it politic to abjure his religion, then precipitated a crisis by coldly murdering his hereditary enemy, James Stewart of Doune, Earl of Moray, at the latter's castle of Donibristle. The young earl was a Protestant and particularly popular in Edinburgh, where his assassination caused an uproar and produced a famous ballad, lamenting the foul murder of "the bonny Earl of Moray." Another, though less-known, relic of this *cause célèbre* is the contemporary painting on wood of Moray's bleeding corpse, now on view at **Darnaway Castle** *(528)* near Forres.

King James—reluctantly because he was fond of Huntly—led two expeditions against him, the second one of which resulted in the destruction of **Huntly Castle** *(540)*, the Gordon family seat in Aberdeenshire. The earl was banished from Scotland, but within a year returned, made formal submission to the king, and in 1599 was created a marquis, after which he remained docile and law-abiding. It was during this last period of his life that he restored his castle in the grand Renaissance manner, adding to his ancestral home the still extant row of oriel windows, the grand doorway with its armorial bearings, and the splendid carved fireplace.

These decorative features vie for architectural distinction with the unusual diamond-faceted north range facing the courtyard of **Crichton Castle** *(432)* in Midlothian—the handiwork of Francis Stewart, Earl of Bothwell. Son of one of Queen Mary's illegitimate half-brothers and nephew of her third husband, Bothwell was far more hateful than Huntly to King James VI. This was because of testimony offered at a much publicized witchcraft trial in North Berwick to the effect that Bothwell was himself a wizard and had instigated a hellish plot to raise a mighty storm in the North Sea while the king was en route to Denmark. James, who was later to write a learned treatise on "demonology," was convinced of the truth of the allegations. Bothwell poured fuel on the fire by twice raising armed rebellion against the king and on another occasion breaking into his bedroom at Holyroodhouse. Failing either to overawe the monarch or extract from him a pardon, this strange, talented, highly cultivated, headstrong, and erratic nobleman finally, in 1595, left Scotland, never to return.

Subduing the Highlands and Islands was not so easy. There, as on the Borders, feud was endemic and the very nobles and chiefs of clans who were supposed to repress disorder were among the main culprits. "They bang it out bravely," wrote the king, "he and all his kin against him and all his." Another problem was the growing number of "broken men," i.e., members of smaller clans who had lost their lands to their more aggressive neighbors and lived by brigandage and blackmail. Such was the notoriously "wicked Clan Gregor" who had been driven out of their ancestral homes by the powerful Campbells of Glenorchy. When, in 1589, some MacGregors killed the king's forester in Glenartney and took his severed head to their chief in Balquhidder, Perthshire, King James issued letters of fire and sword against them. And when a band of MacGregors slaughtered about three hundred Colquhouns at Glenfruin, the privy council outlawed the offenders, hanged their chief, and proscribed the very name, MacGregor.

This clan, however, was not the only offender, and the government tried to solve the more general problem of lawlessness by requiring landlords to arrest all broken men upon their lands and chiefs to give pledges for the good conduct of all their followers. In 1597 Parliament passed an act requiring landlords and clan leaders to produce their title deeds and to find security for the regular payment of His Majesty's rents and for the peaceful behavior of their tenants and dependents. Under the provision of this act, the lands of Lewis, Harris, Dunvegan, and Glenelg (across the Sound of Sleat from Skye) were forfeited, although only the first was retained by the Crown and settled by a colony of Lowlanders from Fife who founded the town of Stornoway but failed to make a go of the venture. In 1608 Andrew Knox, the Protestant Bishop of the Isles, was instructed to tame his diocese by Christian persuasion. He complied by inviting a number of the principal chiefs aboard ship to hear a sermon, then took them prisoner and delivered them for further confinement in the royal **Castles** of **Blackness** *(428)*, **Stirling** *(477)*, and **Dumbarton** *(475)*. A year later, MacDonald of Dunyveg, MacDonald of Sleat, MacLeod of Dunvegan, MacLean of Duart, and others assembled at Iona and signed the Statutes of Icolmkil (i.e., Iona) by which the chiefs agreed to accept responsibility for the behavior of their kinsmen and for the maintenance of law and order within the areas under their control. Six years later a rebellion led by the MacDonalds of Islay was ruthlessly suppressed by the Earl of Argyll on behalf of the Crown. The following year the signatories of the Statutes of Icolmkil agreed to support the Reformed Church, send their eldest sons to school in the Lowlands, expel their bards, establish inns, and restrict the production of alcoholic beverages.

Nevertheless, these measures failed to bring permanent stability to the Highlands and Islands. The lasting result of all of James VI's policies toward these regions was the ruination of a few clans but the further aggrandizement of others: Gordons, Mackenzies, and Campbells in particular and, to some extent, the less powerful clans of MacLeods, MacLeans, Camerons, several branches of Clan Donald, a variety of Stewarts, and the rising family of Murray.

In the northern isles, James VI did better. His mother had feued all of the royal estates in Orkney and Shetland to her half-brother, Robert Stewart, who became Earl of Orkney in 1581. For forty years he and his son, Earl Patrick, earned abominable reputations for greed, tyranny, and maladministration. At last King James reestablished royal rule in the islands, appointed Bishop James Law as his commissioner there, and in 1615 beheaded first Earl Patrick's rebellious natural son and then the earl himself, whose name was so odious that the event gave birth to a popular canard that his execution had to be postponed a day for him to be taught the Lord's Prayer.

To these two Earls of Orkney, however, are owed some of the finest sixteenth-century buildings in Scotland. Robert Stewart built the **Earl's Palace, Birsay** *(563)*, near the northwest corner of Mainland of Orkney. Though much ruined, enough remains to indicate a substantial building of four sides built around an inner court. Far more elaborate, however, was Patrick's **Earl's Palace** *(560)* in Kirkwall, only a short distance east of the Bishop's Palace mentioned in the last chapter. This place has been described as "possibly the most mature and accomplished piece of Renaissance architecture left in Scotland." Though today it lacks a roof, it is otherwise almost complete—two long ranges of buildings set at right angles, and at the northwest corner of the eastern range a large square tower. Corbelled turrets and oriel windows, an elaborate classical frontispiece, and an elegant fireplace in the great hall suggest an architectural influence emanating from the chateaux of the Loire Valley. Corbelled turrets also adorn the chief Shetland seat of Earl Patrick—**Scalloway Castle** *(568)*, west of Lerwick. Built in 1600, it is an L-plan tower-house, four stories high, well preserved still, though open to the sky, and distinguished for its numerous shot-holes, both round and quatrefoil in shape. Another Shetland residence of Earl Patrick lay among the prehistoric and Viking ruins of **Jarlshof** *(569)*, where the foundations and walls of his house, built in 1604–1605, can still be seen lying just east of the Iron Age broch. On Westray Island, Orkney, stands another stronghold once occupied by Earl Patrick, though originally built by Gilbert Balfour, one of the ringleaders in the plot to murder Darnley. This is **Noltland Castle** *(567)*, now a ruined, though well preserved, Z-plan tower-house consisting of a main building with a square tower at each of two diagonally opposite corners and still displaying as many as seventy-one gunloops. Such protective devices also adorn **Muness Castle** *(571)* on the island of Unst in the Shetland group, the most northerly castle in Great Britain. Another now ruined Z-plan tower-house, it was built in 1598 by Laurence Bruce, half-uncle to Earl Patrick.

At the other end of his kingdom, James VI was determined to establish the rule of law on the Borders, if for no other reason than to avoid trouble with the English, which might lessen his chances of inheriting Queen Elizabeth's throne. Thus in 1587, when some two thousand Scots swept over the border, their king promptly ordered them to release all English prisoners, denounced Robert, Lord Maxwell, as a rebel, and descended on Dumfries with a military force to impose order. Nine years later, however, another party of Scots—about eighty strong under the leadership of Walter Scott of Buccleuch—conducted a commando raid against Carlisle Castle and freed a notorious Scottish reiver, William Armstrong of Kinmont. The episode, celebrated in the famous "Ballad of Kinmont Willie," was the final chapter in the long history of international strife along the border. In 1603 King James VI in fact did inherit Queen Elizabeth's kingdom as James I of England. Thereafter, the border no longer existed—at least in the old sense as a line of demarcation between two hostile kingdoms. The Marches became the "middle shires" of what King James liked to think of as the united kingdom of Great Britain. English and Scottish officials at last acted in unison; cross-frontier thieving was made punishable by death; borderers were forbidden to carry weapons or own fast horses; mass public hangings were staged in Dumfries, Carlisle, and Newcastle. The days of the reivers were soon gone.

"This I must say for Scotland, and I may trewly vaunt it," wrote James VI/I late in his reign. "Here I sit and governe it with my Pen, I write and it is done, and by a Clearke of the Councill I governe Scotland now, which others could not doe by the sworde." The boast was not without foundation. Though he promised otherwise when he left his native land for a new and richer realm, in fact he only returned once to Scotland—in 1617. Government there was carried on by the privy council assisted by a handful of civil servants. Parliament was controlled by the Lords of the Articles.

The two men to whom the king assigned the day-to-day task of administering his northern realm were George Home of Spott, Earl of Dunbar, and

Alexander Seton, Earl of Dunfermline. Dunbar died in 1611 and was commemorated with a splendid tomb in **Dunbar Parish Church** *(454)* (see Chapter 7). Thereafter, Dunfermline, as Chancellor of Scotland, became the dominant power in that country's government. His seat of operations was Edinburgh, but his country residence was **Fyvie Castle** *(545)* in Aberdeenshire, which he had purchased in 1596. As a Roman Catholic, he had been educated in Italy and France, and with this background it is not surprising that he would convert this late-medieval crenellated courtyard castle into an imposing Renaissance palace. His major innovations were to convert the south range into a splendid turetted show-front and to reconstruct the west range as sumptuous living quarters. (Further remodelling was undertaken in the seventeenth, eighteenth, and nineteenth centuries, and in 1984 the National Trust for Scotland acquired this noble building with the intention of opening its doors to the public.)

Dunfermline's success in governing Scotland can be attributed in some measure to King James's absence. The Scots nobility, robbed of the person of a king who might be kidnapped, cozened, terrorized, or otherwise manipulated, lost much of their sting. Only the Protestant clergy remained to be tamed, and this the King of England and Scotland almost succeeded in accomplishing.

CHURCH AND STATE: 1567–1625

John Knox died in November 1572 and was buried in the graveyard at the back of his own **St. Giles Kirk** *(439)* in Edinburgh. The Regent Morton was among the mourners and at the graveside pronounced the great preacher's epithet: "There lies one who neither feared nor flattered any flesh." Less than two years later, Andrew Melville came home from a long sojourn in Geneva, first to be principal of Glasgow College, then of St. Mary's College at the University of St. Andrews. If Knox is to be regarded as the patron saint of Scottish Calvinism, Melville can justly be claimed as the father of Scottish Presbyterianism.

As probable author of the *Second Book of Discipline* approved by the General Assembly in 1578, and as the unchallenged leader of that body for at least twenty years thereafter, Melville's chief aim was to establish a Reformed Church that was both independent of state control at the highest level of Church government and free of interference from laymen in the conduct of Church affairs at all levels from the smallest parish kirk up through the General Assembly. What he desired for Scotland was, in short, a sort of clerical oligarchy, not unlike that established at Geneva by Calvin's successor, Theodore Beza. To achieve these ends, three major changes were required: (1) the abolition of the office of bishops appointed by the Crown; (2) the substitution of permanent presbyters of quasi-clerical status for the annually and freely elected lay elders of the kirk as authorized by Knox's *First Book of Discipline*; and (3) the establishment of a hierarchical system of Church government. In this hierarchy, the individual kirk sessions of permanent presbyters (also called elders) were at the lowest level; above them were representatives of several kirk sessions meeting together in committees called *presbyteries*; still higher, at the regional level, were synods with jurisdiction over an entire province; and at the top was the General Assembly, made up of ministers and permanent elders and dominated by the former.

In defense of this revolutionary scheme, Melville developed a novel political theory, which he explained in person to James VI: "There is two kings and two kingdoms in Scotland. There is Christ Jesus the King, and his kingdom the kirk, whose subject King James the Sixth is, and of whose kingdom not a king, nor a lord, nor a head, but a member." The kirk, on the other hand, through the voice of its clergy, was free, and indeed obliged, to "teach the magistrate" how to exercise his civil jurisdiction, i.e., to instruct the king in matters of government and admonish him when his performance was wanting. Not surprisingly, James VI was outraged by such lèse majesté especially when Melville plucked him by the sleeve and called him "God's silly vassal." (The fact that the word *silly* then meant "weak," not "foolish," did little to mitigate the offense.) Small wonder that James later pronounced that Presbyterianism "as well agreeth with a monarchy as God and the Devil. . . . No bishop, no King." Indeed, so alarmed was he over Melville's subversive notions that he penned a treatise called *The Trew Law of Free Monarchies*, arguing for the divine origin of the institution of monarchy and claiming that kings were not only God's lieutenants on earth and sat upon God's thrones, but even by God Himself were called gods.

It was not on theoretical grounds, however, that the issue between James VI and Melville was mainly fought out. Rather, as suggested in the king's remark about presbyteries and bishops, it centered on the question of the internal government of the Church of Scotland, i.e., whether bishops appointed by the Crown or courts (committees) of clergymen and permanent elders answerable only to God should have the controlling voice. In 1592 the Presbyterians could claim a victory with the passage of an Act of Parliament ("the Golden Act"), establishing a system of church government based on kirk sessions, presbyteries, synods, and General Assembly. But there were loopholes in this legislation. Episcopacy was not expressly abolished. The king, moreover, was given the authority to fix both time and place for meetings of the General Assembly. James saw his chance and took it. By choosing such meeting places as Dundee, Perth, and Montrose, he was able to stack the General Assembly with north-country ministers more amenable to royal wishes than Melville and his fellow clergymen from the southern counties.

After he moved to London, the king grew bolder. In 1604 he postponed a scheduled meeting of the General Assembly for a year. Two years later, he summoned Melville to London, where this doughty Scot outraged his Church of England colleagues by denouncing the vestments worn by the Archbishop of Canterbury as "Romish rags." He was sent to the tower and then exiled for life. The Scottish bishoprics were now filled by royal nomination, and their landed properties, of which they had earlier been deprived, were restored. Three of these nominees, including John Spottiswoode, Archbishop of Glasgow, received consecration from the Anglican bishops of London, Ely, and Bath. In 1607 a docile General Assembly agreed to the appointment of "constant moderators" of presbyteries—later extended to synods. These looked very much like diocesan bishops. Two years later, consistorial jurisdiction was restored to the bishops by Act of Parliament, and certain powers, including the admission of ministers, were transferred from the presbyteries to the bishops. In short, James VII succeeded in grafting an Anglican-style episcopate onto the existing Scots Presbyterian Church structure.

Yet these changes made little difference to the ordinary kirk member who continued to worship according to the forms established in the *First Book of Discipline*, the *Book of Common Order*, and the *Scots Confession of Faith*. Sunday services were long and drawn out. In the morning they began with a reading from the Scriptures by the lay reader, who then led the congregation in prayer and in the singing of metrical psalms. These were found in the Genevan psalter republished and enlarged in Scotland in 1561—a work that contained, among others, the still familiar "Old Hundredth" with its exuberant lines:

> All people that on earth do dwell
> Sing to the Lord with cheerful voice,
> Him serve with mirth, his praise forth tell
> Come ye before him and rejoice!

This part of the service lasted about an hour, after which the minister entered the pulpit, prayed, led another psalm, prayed again, preached a sermon, prayed again, led the congregation in the Apostle's Creed, prayed again, and pronounced the Benediction. In the afternoon was held a second service that consisted of more prayers and catechizing the congregation.

Periodically, Communion was served—at long narrow tables set lengthwise along the church and covered with white cloth, around which the congregation gathered in relays to receive the bread and wine distributed by minister and elders. Those who wished to communicate had to present tickets or tokens, obtained previously from the elders. Moral turpitude, failure to pass examinations on the catechism, or neglect to contribute to the poor were sufficient reasons for withholding tokens. (Collections of these flat, stamped metal objects are on display at the **National Museum of Antiquities** *[447]* in Edinburgh and at many local museums throughout Scotland.) The long tables have mostly disappeared, but there are representative examples at the **Howmore Parish Kirk** *(556)* on South Uist and **Reay Parish Kirk** *(553)* in Caithness.

Although no statistics are available, church attendance was undoubtedly higher after the Reformation than before. Community pressures in such strongly Protestant areas as the Southwest, Fife, and the Lothians would have accounted for some of this increase. But other compelling reasons were the gradual substitution of a truly educated Protestant clergy for the ignorant parish priesthood of the old establishment and, especially, the active, corporate nature of the Reformed worship in contrast to the largely passive role assigned to the laity in the traditional medieval service. Psalm singing, partaking of the Lord's Supper, congregational praying, public catechising, and even the act of listening to the finely spun scriptural exegesis of the presiding minister required a degree of lay participation then unknown in the Roman Catholic Church.

These radical changes in form of worship demanded a remodelling of existing church interiors to meet the new requirements. No longer was the focal point of worship the chancel at the east end, site of the altar before which the ritral sacrifice of the Mass was performed. Instead it was the pulpit, usually placed in the center of the long south wall of the nave, standing high above the stools or benches arranged around three sides facing the minister. Sometimes the pulpit might be equipped with an auxiliary desk for the lay reader, and it was usually furnished with a bracket for holding the basin used in public baptisms.

Typical examples of medieval parish churches adapted in this way are **Duddingston Kirk** *(450)*, on the outskirts of Edinburgh, and **Stobo Kirk** *(422)*, west of Peebles. To accommodate the growing congregations, it sometimes became necessary to add lofts or galleries at the west and east ends (if one would fit in the now unused chancel), and sometimes an aisle (projecting wing—from the French word *aile*) was added on the north side to hold a loft for the local laird with a burial vault for his family underneath. From this practice developed the T-plan kirk—a uniquely Scottish architectural form often employed in new church construction in the late seventeenth and eighteenth centuries. The oldest of such laird's lofts is that of the Ogilvies in **Cullen Kirk** *(531)*, Banffshire, dating from 1602. In some cases, medieval churches were too large to be adapted to the more intimate needs of the Reformed service, and they were simply divided into separate compartments for two distinct congregations. This is what happened in the case of the **Church of St. Nicholas, Aberdeen** *(534)*, once the largest parish kirk in Scotland. The nave became the West Kirk and the choir the East Kirk, and although both were rebuilt, in the eighteenth and nineteenth centuries respectively, the division between them dates from the Reformation.

Only a handful of new Reformed churches were put up in the late sixteenth and early seventeenth centuries. The earliest of these was **St. Columba's, Burntisland** *(484)*, in Fife. This is a square building with a central tower over a central pulpit around which the pews and galleries are arranged on all four sides. Built soon after the Reformation, no provision for altar space was required. In Edinburgh the first new Protestant church to be built was **Greyfriars Kirk** *(433)*, later made famous as the scene of the signing of the great National Covenant of 1638 (see Chapter 7). Built on the grounds of a former Franciscan friary that had been converted into the town burial yard, the original church here was completed in 1620. It was rectangular in plan, with a square tower at the west end, while inside, the pulpit stood against the mid-south pier and lofts were installed at the east and west ends. An explosion of gunpowder in 1718 and a fire in 1845 required much rebuilding in each instance, so that little more than the foundations of the seventeenth-century kirk remain, though the present interior arrangement (minus lofts) conforms to the original.

Greyfriars is, and probably originally was, designed in a Gothic style. So was **Cawdor Kirk** *(525)* in Nairnshire, built in 1619. In both cases, the choice of styles reflected a typically Scottish architectural conservatism and not, as is sometimes claimed, an Episcopalian reaction against the Presbyterian form of worship. It was otherwise with **Dairsie Kirk** *(495)* in Fife, built by Archbishop Spottiswoode in 1621 and now the property of nearby St. Andrews University. Its Gothic windows, with their unusual tracery of cinquefoil design, were an architectural expression of the archbishop's Anglican leanings. So was the chancel screen, since gone along with all the other interior furnishings of the church.

Spottiswoode was doing no more than his master James VI/I would have wanted. The king, though never wavering in his Calvinist convictions, had been seduced by his long sojourn in England, where Protestant worship was somewhat more formalistic than in Scotland. In 1617, during his only visit to his native land after the union of the crowns, he presented to the General Assembly the "five articles of Perth," which would have introduced into the

Church of Scotland the English practice of kneeling at Communion, as well as certain other innovations, including the observance of the church calendar. To strict Scots Presbyterians, this was backsliding in the direction of Rome. Though agreed to a year later, the articles were in practice largely ignored, and James VI was canny enough not to push his stubborn countrymen too far. As we shall see in the next chapter, his son and royal successor proved disastrously incapable of such discretion.

In the year of his return to Scotland (1617) King James also entertained representatives from **Edinburgh University** *(435)* at Stirling Castle. In 1582, at the behest of the town council, he had granted a royal charter to this institution, the fourth university in Scotland. After listening to, and joining in, an elaborate debate staged by the masters, the king was so pleased that he agreed to be "godfather" to the university and have it called "the College of King James." By that time classes were being held in a house built by the second Earl of Arran on part of the site occupied by the ruined Collegiate Church of St. Mary of the Fields, where Darnley had been murdered a few years before. None of these buildings remains, however, and the earliest construction on the present university grounds dates from the late eighteenth century. But in the reigns of Queen Mary and King James VI and shortly afterward, the town of Edinburgh began to take on the appearance that its oldest parts still show.

TOWN HOUSES AND TOWER-HOUSES

Edinburgh in 1560, though by far the largest town in Scotland, could boast a population of probably no more than twenty thousand. To call it the nation's capital would be an anachronism, but at least since the reign of James IV it had become the principal seat of government. Never as central to the political and commercial life of Scotland as London was to England, the city nonetheless grew rapidly in the late sixteenth and early seventeenth centuries, as evidenced by the number of buildings still standing along the Royal Mile from the castle to Holyroodhouse, which date in part at least from those years.

Coming eastward from Edinburgh Castle, one first encounters on the south side of Castle Hill **Cannonball House** *(437)*, the south wing of which dates from 1630. Across the street is the **Outlook Tower** *(437)*, whose bottom stories are of early-seventeenth-century provenance, though the upper part was added in the mid-nineteenth century. Proceeding eastward to the Lawnmarket is the well-preserved narrow six-story tenement called **Glad-**

stone's Land *(438)*, dating from 1617 to 1620, though parts of it were built even earlier. Thomas Gladstone, who bought the property in 1617, lived only on one floor; the others were rented out to tenants—a typical arrangement for Edinburgh town houses, which was to persist for another two centuries and more. Next to it is **Lady Stair's House** *(438)*, originally built in 1622, though "medievalized" in the late nineteenth century. Across the street and through two arched pends (covered passages) to Riddle's Close is **Bailie MacMorran's House** *(438)*, which is known to have been the scene of a royal banquet in 1598. In the High Street, across from St. Giles Kirk in Byer's Close, is **Adam Bothwell's House** *(441)*, a tall thin building named after the Bishop of Orkney. Farther along, on the same (north) side of the street, are a sixteenth-century four-story town house called **Mowbray House** *(441)* and the nearby **John Knox's House** *(441)*, which in fact belonged in the late sixteenth century to a goldsmith named James Mossman. Further eastward, still on the south side of Canongate, stands the **Moray House** *(441)*, built about 1628 and probably the finest private mansion to survive from this period of Edinburgh's history. Next to it is **Huntly House** *(442)*, a sixteenth-century building now housing a fine museum of local history. Across the street is the **Canongate Tolbooth** *(441)*, dating from 1592, now also a museum of local history. It was originally, of course, the town hall of the independent burgh of Canongate, where the Augustinian canons of nearby Holyrood Abbey once resided.

Aberdeen was the third largest town (after Edinburgh and Dundee) in Queen Mary's reign, with a population of perhaps seven thousand. The city still boasts two town houses of sixteenth-century origin. The oldest part of **Provost Skene's House** *(534)* is the west wing, dating from 1545. Sir George Skene himself did not acquire the property until 1669, when he added the east wing. Now restored, the house is used as a municipal museum, noteworthy chiefly for its several rooms furnished in different period styles. **Provost Ross's House** *(535)*, also much restored and now a maritime museum, was built in 1593.

Contemporary with the Aberdonian merchants who built these houses was the greatest of all Scottish entrepreneurs of the reign of King James VI—George Bruce of Culross in Fife. This tiny burgh on the north bank of the Forth was already famous for its coal mining and salt manufacture when Bruce took over the local colliery in 1575, developed new machinery for draining the mines, and drove new shafts, at least one extending out under the waters of the estuary. In 1617 James VI visited the mine, knighted its owner, and stayed at his house in Culross, called **The Palace** *(485)*. Built in stages between 1597 and 1611, this is a great rambling complex of two disconnected buildings adjoined by walls surrounding two courtyards. Restored and preserved by the National Trust for Scotland, it is noteworthy above all for its fine wall and ceiling paintings in tempera and oil. Nearby are other sixteenth- and seventeenth-century buildings: **Bessie Bar's Hall** *(485)*, a malt house; the **Culross Town House** *(485)*, the burgh tolbooth or town hall built in 1626; **The Study** *(485)*, built about 1610 and the grandest residence in Culross after the palace; and sundry other contemporary or near contemporary smaller houses and cottages. In 1625 a great storm destroyed Sir George's underwater mine workings, and he died the same year. Gradually, coal mining and salt panning petered out, and Culross became a ghost town. The buildings survived, however—probably because there was no economic motive for replacing them to keep up with the times. Consequently the National Trust, with some assistance from private individuals and other organizations, has been able to capture and preserve a unique historical artifact—an almost entire Scottish burgh as it looked in the seventeenth century.

In other towns as well, the Trust has had remarkable success in preserving important examples of Scottish vernacular architecture of both seventeenth- and eighteenth-century provenance. Especially noteworthy are the "little houses" situated in the string of towns along the coast of Fife. In Dysart near Kirkcaldy is a row of houses (now privately occupied) called **Pan Ha'** *(491)*. Up the coast in St. Monans is another group stretching along the **West Shore** *(496)*, facing the harbor. In Pittenweem are the restored sixteenth-century houses called **Kellie Lodging** *(490)* and **Gyles House** *(490)*. Further east in Anstruther is an L-shaped eighteenth-century group, called **The White House** *(484)*. Finally, in Crail are the seventeenth-century **Customs House** *(484)* and sundry other small houses of about the same date or a century later.

No such humble dwellings from the reign of James VI remain to be seen in the Scottish countryside. The wholesale feuing of Church and Crown lands, both before the Reformation and after, enriched the nobility and the lesser barons or lairds, but, if anything, diminished the security of those agrarian tenants not able themselves to become feuars. The majority of Scottish peasants held their tiny properties at the will of the landlord or by short-term leases and thus had no reason to erect dwelling places of any permanence. And they did not.

It was otherwise with the lairds and merchants whose wealth and status were steadily mounting from about the middle of the sixteenth century. Like their contemporaries, the English landed gentry so favored by the Tudor monarchs, they adorned the land with houses. Unlike their counterparts across the border, however, Scottish lairds and would-be lairds built up instead of out. Vertical, not horizontal, construction remained the fashion in Scotland long after it had ceased to serve any urgent military purpose. The late medieval tower-house persisted into the seventeenth century as the preferred model for domestic architecture. Though such features as yetts and gunports were often still in evidence, considerations of comfort and refinement gradually took precedence over those of defense, as internal strife in Scotland slowly subsided. Architectural plans became more complex. The simple three- or four-story rectangular block had already in the Late Middle Ages begun to give way to the L-plan tower with a "jamb" at right angles to the main building. In the late sixteenth century a new form emerged, called the Z-plan, with towers placed at diagonally opposite corners of the central block. Gunfire from these wings could of course command all four faces of the main building, but the main functional purpose of the Z-plan design seems to have been to provide increased living space.

No traveller through Scotland can be unaware of the omnipresence of these tower-houses—usually called "castles." Many of them date from the late sixteenth and early seventeenth centuries—of which the following are examples:

Smailholm Tower *(416)*, near Kelso, Roxburghshire, is a plain rectangular, five-story building of rubble masonry, raised mostly in the first half of the sixteenth century, though the top story was added probably in the seventeenth. It was owned by the Pringles, a well-known Border family and, unlike some later tower-houses, was designed primarily for defensive purposes—not surprisingly in this turbulent and much fought over region. Of probable mid–sixteenth century date is the still roofed and well-preserved **Elcho Castle** *(507)*, built by John, Earl of Wemyss, on the south side of the Tay, a few miles below Perth. Here the rectangular block is adjoined by towers at three of the corners and on one side. That on the southwest is battlemented; some of the windows are iron-grated; and gunloops guard the approaches to the building. Elcho may have been originally a Z-plan tower to which additional wings were added. **Castle Menzies** *(496)*, near Aberfeldy, Perthshire, was definitely of this design, though in the nineteenth century another wing was built onto the west. This is a fine and well-preserved tower-house, completed in 1577 by Sir James Menzies and now in the process of restoration as the Clan Menzies headquarters. Smaller, and of simpler design, is the L-plan **Greenknowe Tower** *(417)*, not far from Kelso, built in 1581 for Sir James Seton. This is another well-preserved Border castle with the original iron yett still guarding the main doorway. More complex in plan is **Maclellan's Castle** *(381)*, in Kirkcudbright (ruined but standing to the wall heads), consisting of a rectangular block adjoined by two projecting towers. Here residential (versus defensive) considerations prevailed when the house was built in 1582 by Sir Thomas Maclellan out of stones quarried from the nearby ruins of the local Franciscan friary. **Haggs Castle** *(400)*, now situated on the outskirts of Glasgow and converted into a children's museum, was originally an L-plan tower-house constructed in the 1580s by Sir John Maxwell.

Near St. Andrews in Fife stands **Earlshall Castle** *(495)*, a mid-sixteenth-century five-story Z-plan tower-house with a smaller house attached. The interior was embellished in the seventeenth century with a splendid painted ceiling, and the house was restored in the late nineteenth by Sir Robert Lorimer. Also in Fife, not far from Cupar, is **Scotstarvit Tower** *(486)*, built probably between 1550 and 1579. It is a four-story, parapetted building with a cap-house on the roof. The ground plan is rectangular with a small wing containing the turnpike stair. In a fine state of preservation, and not much remodelled in the three centuries since its construction, Scotstarvit is one of the best surviving examples of its kind in Scotland.

North of the Tay, tower-house building in the decades surrounding the turn of the sixteenth and seventeenth centuries took a more sophisticated turn than in the southern Lowlands. **Claypotts Castle** *(510)*, east of Dundee, is a classic Z-plan tower-house, but with a difference. It was built by Sir John Strachan, probably between 1569 and 1588. In plan it consists of a central rectangular block with round towers at two of the diagonally opposite corners, but its striking appearance is due to the square garret chambers corbelled out over the corner towers. Obviously designed to provide more and better living space, these unusual chambers, looking like cliffside cottages, are symptomatic of the changing emphasis in tower-house construction from functional defense toward greater comfort and convenience. Not that military considerations were altogether overlooked. The English, after all, had invaded this shoreline as recently as 1544 and captured nearby Broughty Castle. Thus there are ten widemouthed gunports at Claypotts—positioned low and cleverly arranged so as to provide a maximum field of fire. Another Z-plan tower-house, begun in 1567, was **Brodie Castle** *(529)*, near Forres, Moray. Now a stately home open to the public, the original ground plan has been largely obscured by later additions. More elaborate still is the now ruined **Tolquhon Castle** *(543)*, near Oldmeldrum, Aberdeenshire. Starting with a fourteenth-century rectangular tower, Sir William Forbes, in 1584–1589, created a Z-plan castle built around an inner court—an open square with towers at diagonally opposite corners. Each tower with its gunloops (some of them with three holes pointing at different angles) commands two sides of the central structure. The approach is guarded by a forecourt, also with triple gunloops, and the main entrance lies between drum towers with heavily grated windows. But the rooms are spacious and well lighted through wide windows, and the residence is graced with a long gallery containing an arched book press—a refinement not likely to be found in this remote area at an earlier date. Also in Aberdeenshire, west of Alford, stands the more conventionally designed **Glenbuchat Castle** *(538)*, a Z-plan building with a square tower at each of two diagonally opposite corners. Now a roofless ruin recently restored by the Scottish Development Department, the castle was built in 1590 by Sir John Gordon. Here, a series of enfilading gunloops, fittings for an iron yett, and the original outer wooden door remind today's viewer that the Gordons were a fighting clan, not yet entirely tamed by the central government. Indeed, only twenty years before Glenbuchat was built, a party of Gordons, ostensibly fighting in the name of Queen Mary, set fire to nearby **Corgarff Castle** *(532)* and burned to death its chatelaine, Margaret Forbes, along with twenty-six of her family and servants.

The year 1603, when James VI of Scotland made his way to Westminster to be crowned James I, marks the beginning in England of the Jacobean era—so-called from the Latin rendition (*Jacobus*) of the new king's Christian name. By coincidence, Sir Alexander Burnett of Leys at about the same time completed his tower-house near Banchory, Kincardineshire, and called it **Crathes Castle** *(545)*. Though enlarged with additional wings in the early eighteenth century, this is essentially a Jacobean house—comfortable, commodious, attractive living quarters encased in a pseudo-medieval shell. Turreted bartizans there are aplenty, some of them sprouting fake stone cannon. Above the main door with its original yett is a decorative version of a *bretasche*, installed no doubt to reinforce the illusion of formidability, where none in fact existed. Crathes is not a defensible castle. With its present gorgeous yew-studded garden, long gallery, and original painted ceilings, this is one of Scotland's more attractive stately homes. **Edzell Castle** *(509)*, near Brechin, Angus, would no doubt also qualify as such had it not been despoiled in the eighteenth century and reduced to ruins. Here an early-sixteenth-century L-plan tower-house was enlarged about 1580 by the addition of an uncompleted quadrangular mansion to which the owner David Lindsay, Lord Edzell attached, in 1604, a walled garden, or "pleasance." It is this last that gives the place its chief distinction—as restored and maintained by the Scottish Development Department. In the center is a raised mound surrounded by short-cut topiary and flowering shrubs. The surrounding redstone wall is pierced on three sides with square niches arranged in a checkerboard design and filled with pots of flowers. Between the niches are sculptured panels representing gods and goddesses, the sciences and virtues. At one corner of the garden is a summer house; at another the foundations of a bathhouse. "Taken as a whole," reads the official guidebook, "the pleasance with its sculptured wall and adjuncts forms one of the most remarkable artistic monuments that Scotland can show,"—a product of the peace that followed the union of the crowns that permitted "a rapid spread of the Renaissance, which up till now had gained but a tardy and halting foothold in Scotland." A less formal but equally attractive walled garden graces the precincts of **Kellie Castle** *(491)* in Fife. Here, to a fourteenth- or fifteenth-century tower, the fourth Lord Oliphant, between the years 1573 and 1604, added another tower and a long hall between the two, thus converting a vertical tower-house into a T-plan mansion, beautified in the later seventeenth century with the installation of some fine plastered ceilings. Leased in 1870 by James Lorimer, father of the prominent architect Robert Lorimer, the house was restored and converted into the showpiece that it now is.

Far less pretentious is **Muchalls Castle** *(547)*, north of Stonehaven. This is a harled (Americans would say "stuccoed") L-plan house, originating in a late medieval tower and enlarged, between 1619 and 1627, to its present dimensions by Alexander and Thomas Burnett, owners of nearby Crathes Castle. Its chief attraction to today's visitors lies in its exceptionally elaborate Jacobean plasterwork. More or less contemporary with it, but much more castlelike in appearance, is **Castle Fraser** *(536)*, a dozen or so miles west of Aberdeen. It was built by Sir Michael Fraser and his son between 1575 and 1636 as a high Z-plan tower-house with added wings. Like Crathes, it is much turreted, with blind machicolations and batteries of stone cannons. Finally and perhaps the masterpiece of Jacobean Scottish domestic architecture, is **Craigievar Castle** *(537)*, south of Alford, Aberdeenshire. Here, in 1626, William Forbes, an Aberdonian merchant (nicknamed "Danzig Willie" or "Willie the Merchant") completed the building of a pink-granite, six-story, much turreted and gabled, L-plan tower-house that has survived intact and without significant changes—the epitome of the Jacobean Renaissance in Scotland. Here in perfect balance, such medieval features as yett and groined vaults harmonize with elegant plastered ceilings of strap-work and decorative pendants, as well as medallion portraits of biblical heroes and Roman worthies. Here too, above the fireplace in the great hall, is a plaster representation of the heraldically correct Scottish version of the royal arms of the United Kingdom of Great Britain, with two of the quarters accorded to Scotland and one each to England and Ireland.

This fine "achievement" was of course meant to be a tribute to James VI/I, dead only a year when the final touches were applied to Craigievar. And the union of the crowns was indeed his greatest achievement—brought about by the luck of inheritance combined with his own discreet handling of the English and their temperamental queen. The pity was that James VI/I could not pass on his supple political sense to his son and heir, Charles I. Before that monarch's reign wound down to its sorry end, he had succeeded in provoking a rebellion in Scotland and civil war in both Scotland and England. The fatal Stuart inclination to folly had not died out with Mary, Queen of Scots.

Chapter Seven

Civil War, Restoration, and Union

1625–1746

CHARLES I: 1624-1649

When James VI married Anne of Denmark, he gave her as a bridal present the guest house of **Dunfermline Abbey** *(488)* in Fife, which had been converted into a royal palace (now a ruin southwest of the abbey church) and was to become the favorite residence of the royal couple before their departure for England. It was here in 1600 that Prince Charles was born—the second of their sons to live to manhood. He was scarcely more than an infant when James VI/I moved the royal family south to Westminster in 1603, and it was in the English court that Charles was raised and educated. Thus, when, by virtue of the death of his older brother, Prince Henry, he became king of both England and Scotland in 1625, he knew almost nothing of the land of his birth.

James VI, by contrast, had been reared among the cantankerous Scottish nobility and the hardheaded clergy of the Reformed Church. He had survived repeated threats to his life, his dignity, and his rule by persistence coupled with timely compromise and especially by avoiding action that might unite Scotland's powerful clerical and aristocratic factions against the Crown. In short, James VI knew his fellow Scots. Charles I did not.

But there were other flaws in this king's makeup to compound his ignorance of Scotland and the Scots. Though kindly by nature, courteous, brave, faithful to friends and family, and a discriminating judge of art, he was aloof, uncommunicative, obtuse, and devious. Above all, he was stubbornly doctrinaire. Persuaded, as was his father, that kings ruled by divine right, he lacked James VI's intuitive understanding that politics was the art of the possible and that, in the real world, rectitude—even in a king—was not enough.

Coupled with his blindness to political realities was an undeviating devotion to the religious tenets and liturgical practices of the Church of England, or rather to that branch of it that today would be called High Church or even Anglo-Catholic. In these convictions he was encouraged by William Laud, whom he was to elevate from the bishopric of London to the

archepiscopal see of Canterbury. Laud was an Arminian, i.e., a follower of
the Dutch theologian Jacobus Arminius, whose doctrines of free will and
salvation by good works seemed papistical to orthodox predestinarian
Calvinists. So too did Laud's emphasis on liturgy at the expense of
preaching and his modifications of the Church of England's Communion
service toward a closer approximation to the Roman Mass. James VI, who
had learned from his Scottish experience the danger of attempting radical
liturgical changes, recognized the folly of Laud's tactless innovations. "He
hath a restless spirit and cannot see when matters are well," the king warned
the Duke of Buckingham. "Take him to you, but on my soul you will repent
it." Buckingham did not live to see the old king's prophecy fulfilled. But
Charles, to his sorrow, did.

Like his father, Charles I tried to rule Scotland "by the pen," that is, with
the advice of a secretary of state resident in London and through the Scots
privy council in Edinburgh. From 1626 until his death in 1640, the secretary
of state was Sir William Alexander, later Earl of Stirling. A poet and
courtier, he had won the favor of James VI, who granted him the charter to
the vast territory in North America lying between New England and
Newfoundland. After the failure of two efforts to found a colony in this land
called Nova Scotia, a tiny settlement was finally established at Port Royal,
only to be surrendered to the French in 1632. Meanwhile, to encourage
colonization, the king had offered to sell a baronetcy to any Scots gentleman
willing to pay £150 for the honor, and the space in front of **Edinburgh
Castle** *(436)*—now covered by the Esplanade—was declared to be a part of
Nova Scotia so that the new barons could lawfully take "sasine" of their
overseas possessions. The sale continued in the reign of Charles I, and the
coats of arms of forty-five of these baronets are now on display in the
Commemoration Room of **Menstrie Castle** *(480)* in Clackmannanshire.
This now restored sixteenth-century tower-house was Alexander's birthplace. He was later to remodel his house in nearby Stirling into a
sumptuous courtyard residence in the Scottish Renaissance style—a building that the architectural historian John G. Dunbar ranks as "the finest
surviving example of its class in the country." Today, serving as a youth
hostel, it bears the name of **Argyll's Lodging** *(479)*—after the ninth Earl of
Argyll, who completed the construction in 1674. Lord Stirling could not
have spent much time here, however, as his chief residence was in London,
where he remained as out of touch with Scottish affairs and attitudes as the
king himself.

Between 1636 and 1641, Charles I's chief instrument for managing the
privy council was the Lord Treasurer, John Stewart, Earl of Traquair, a man
of no firm convictions whose salient characteristics appear to have been
arrogance, tactlessness, and timidity in the face of danger. His only lasting
accomplishment was to convert the family tower-house near Peebles into an

elegant French-style mansion. **Traquair House** *(420)* remains today one of Scotland's most attractive stately homes.

Lord Traquair, however, was not responsible for Charles I's first great mistake in dealing with Scotland. This was the Act of Revocation, promulgated in the first year of his reign. Enlarging on an ancient custom whereby Kings of Scots, on coming of age, revoked grants made in their names during their minorities, Charles issued a sweeping revocation of all grants of both royal and church property made since 1540, i.e., sixty years before his birth. Most of the church lands involved had long since been taken up by laymen, many of them nobles. So had the rights to the collection of teinds (tithes), only a fraction of which went to the support of the parish clergy. The king's intentions were reasonable enough: to systematize the collection and distribution of church revenues and to siphon off for the use of the Crown a fair share of Church income alienated at the time of the Reformation and later. In execution, the Act of Revocation proved not to be confiscatory. In the end, the nobles lost little except certain feudal superiorities over former kirk lands they had feued out, and even in such cases they received compensation. But the king's intentions were not originally made clear; the provisions of the act were highly complex and not easily understood (nor are they yet); and the net result of the act was to set in motion a great wave of anxiety among both nobility and lairds as to the security of their landed estates and residual feudal rights.

Nor was this the end of the threat, especially as perceived by the nobles. Reversing precedents established in the reign of Queen Mary, the king began to fill the privy council with bishops, even elevating John Spottiswoode, Archbishop of St. Andrews, to the position of Chancellor of Scotland. Bishops, moreover, were given considerable influence in the selection of the Lords of the Articles, the steering committee by which the Kings of Scots had traditionally managed their parliaments. Objections were registered to this episcopal aggrandizement as well as to a number of perceived threats to the independence of the Scottish Church. One of the objectors, James Elphinstone, second Earl of Balmerino, was tried and convicted of treason. Though pardoned by Charles I, the lesson was clear: refractory nobles had more to lose at the hands of this king than their mere property rights. Alarm spread also among the burgesses, especially in Edinburgh. When Charles paid his first visit to that city in 1633, he used the occasion to designate **St. Giles Kirk** *(439)* as the cathedral church of a newly erected bishopric. This involved not only extensive renovation of the church fabric and furnishings, but also the building of a new kirk nearby—the **Tron Kirk** *(440)*—to serve the needs of the parish. This cost the city of Edinburgh dearly, as did the king's decision to erect a new **Parliament House** *(439)* with an elaborate hammerbeam roof that was as expensive as it was (and is) magnificent.

Early in 1636 the king, with Laud's encouragement, proclaimed a new book of canons for the Scottish Church. It made no reference to presbyteries, synods, or general assembly; enjoined the clergy to preach the antipredestinarian doctrine of good works; prohibited extempore prayer during church services; and announced the king's intention to promulgate a new prayer book for required use in church services. Thus, in one stroke, Charles I struck at the doctrinal foundations of the Church of Scotland; demanded radical changes in the modes of public worship to which two generations of Scots had become accustomed; and threatened the substitution of the rule of bishops for the existing mixed presbyterian-episcopalian form of church government—a happy compromise worked out during the preceding reign. In so doing, the king resurrected the old specter of *English* religious imperialism directed from Canterbury; fed popular fears of a Catholic reaction, already heated up by the ongoing Thirty Years War on the Continent; and provided all classes in Scotland—nobility, lairds, burgesses, and others (at least in the Lowlands)—with a common cause around which to rally. And most importantly, because the Scottish bishops, in consultation with the king and Archbishop Laud, took so long to prepare the promised prayer book, the opposition was given ample time to organize.

The new version, based on the English Book of Common Prayer, was first employed in all church services under the jurisdiction of the Bishop of Edinburgh on Sunday, 23 July 1637. At **St. Giles Kirk** *(439)*, the congregation that morning included the two Scottish archbishops, eight or nine of the bishops, and numerous lay dignitaries. It also included a large assemblage of townspeople, well primed for protest. As soon as the cathedral dean began to read from the new prayer book, he was shouted down and pelted with stools. (This was before fixed pews were in common use in Scottish churches.) Tradition has it that the first stool was thrown by one Jenny Geddes, and although there is no documentary proof that a person of that name did in fact initiate the uproar, there is no doubt that a riot did take place and that a number of women took part in it. There is no doubt either that it was not a spontaneous outbreak of outraged worshippers, but a well-planned and well-organized demonstration.

Rebellion succeeded riot in short order. Petitions against the prayer book, the book of canons, and the bishops poured into the privy council. Unauthorized elections were held to choose commissioners to meet in Edinburgh. These in turn selected permanent committees of nobles, barons (lairds), burgesses, and Protestant ministers, who met regularly in the new **Parliament House** *(439)* and came to be known as "the Tables." Among the many nobles involved in the movement was James Graham, sixth Earl of Montrose. Other ringleaders included Alexander Henderson, minister of Leuchars in Fife, and Archibald Johnston of Wariston, a rising young advocate. When the king refused to back down, these last named two were selected to draw up a band pledging its prospective signers to mutual support. This was the National Covenant, read to a concourse of nobles and barons and signed by them in **Greyfriars Kirk** *(433)*, Edinburgh, on 28 February 1638. Copies were then carried throughout the country for additional signatures, which were added in large numbers, although not in the Northeast or the western Highlands and Islands north of Argyll. Surviving examples are to be seen today in the session house of **Greyfriars Kirk** *(433)*, the **West Register House** *(446)*, and the **National Museum of Antiquities** *(447)*, all in Edinburgh, and at **Blair Castle** *(498)* in Perthshire.

In substance, the National Covenant was a conservative, not a revolutionary, document. It did not condemn episcopacy or attack the monarchy as such. It republished the so-called Negative Confession of Faith signed by James VI in 1581, which was little more than an abjuration of Roman Catholicism, and it summarized the Acts of Parliament that had established the Reformed Church of Scotland. The signers then pledged themselves to defend their religion against all innovations not sanctioned by Parliament and general assemblies and also asserted their loyalty to the king. But there were phrases included in the document that had revolutionary implications. The undertaking was described as "a public covenant of the collective bodie of the kingdom [of Scotland] with God." Johnston of Wariston, one of the authors, described the occasion of its promulgation as "the glorious marriage day of the Kingdom with God." This was no mere hyperbole. Churchgoing Scots had long been thoroughly familiar with the story of God's covenant with the children of Israel, as recounted in the Genevan version of the Holy Bible as well as in King James VI/I's authorized version, first published in 1611. It was easy for them to imagine themselves as the spiritual heirs of the Israelites, a persecuted nation to whom Jehovah had promised great things, but on condition that they remained faithful in their worship and obedient to His commandments. This perception of themselves as a chosen people would strongly fortify these self-styled Covenanters and their successors in their coming struggles with enemies of all descriptions—the king, English parliamentarians, Irish and Scottish Catholics, and fellow Protestants whose interpretation of the Word of God might differ from their own. It also inclined them to a righteous, and eventually self-defeating, fanaticism.

In any event, the signing of the National Covenant set in motion a train of events that culminated in a religious and constitutional revolution in Scotland, a Scottish invasion of England, and civil war in both countries. As a temporizing measure, Charles I agreed to calling a General Assembly of the Church—the first to be held in twenty years. It convened in the **Glasgow Cathedral** *(406)* and was dominated by lairds and nobles, elected as elders. Among others in attendance was Archibald Campbell, eighth Earl of Argyll, who from this time forward took a leading position in the Covenanting party. The assembly condemned the book of canons, the new prayer book, and the Five Articles of Perth; it then proceeded to depose all the Scottish bishops and archbishops. A year later, a second assembly meeting in Edinburgh confirmed these decisions. Shortly thereafter, Parliament ratified these acts and ordered the National Covenant to be signed by all Scots. The following year, it met again and passed an "act rescissory" nullifying all previous legislation in favor of bishops. Thus was presbyterianism unequivocally established as the official system of government of the Scottish Church. At the same time, Parliament carried through what amounted to a constitutional revolution by abolishing the clerical estate, doing away with the Lords of the Articles, and passing a Triennal Act requiring parliamentary sessions to be held at least every three years. In August 1641 King Charles himself came to Edinburgh, capitulated to the demands of the Covenanters, and rewarded several of their leaders with honors—Argyll was made a marquis and Alexander Leslie was created Earl of Leven.

Leslie's elevation was in recognition of his military leadership, demonstrated recently against the king himself. This seasoned veteran of the Thirty Years War, as well as many other Scottish soldiers in service abroad, had come home to put teeth into the Covenanters' quarrel with King Charles, who had summoned the trained bands of northern England to Newcastle in preparation for an invasion of Scotland. Forced to abandon his plans in the face of Leslie's superior army, the king had agreed to most of the Scots' demands; summoned an English Parliament (the Short Parliament) for the first time in eleven years in the vain hope of persuading it to finance a second campaign against Scotland; dissolved this meeting when it proved recalcitrant; and then proceeded without parliamentary assistance to organize an invasion. Seizing the initiative, a Scottish army under Leslie then crossed the Tweed, occupied Newcastle, and held the town and surrounding countryside at ransom. In desperation, Charles then summoned Parliament again to meet at Westminster—the so-called Long Parliament, which proved to be his undoing when its Puritan majority demanded concessions of the king that he could neither successfully resist nor agree to without serious impairment of the royal prerogative.

Charles and the English Parliament now entered into a contest for Scottish support. The king, as mentioned, came to Edinburgh and conceded most of the Covenanters' demands. He went back to England prepared to face down the opposition at Westminster. Failing to intimidate the Puritans in Parliament, he summoned an army and raised his standard at Nottingham on 22 August 1642. Civil War in England thus began. Parliament proposed a military alliance with the Scots, who responded by presenting the Solemn League and Covenant, which was accepted in September 1643. Under the terms of this second covenant, it was agreed that episcopacy in England would be abolished and popery in Ireland extirpated, and that the churches in all three kingdoms would be brought "to the nearest conjunction and uniformity in Religion, Confession of Faith, Form of Church government, [and] Directory for Worship and Catechizing . . . according to the word of God and the example of the best Reformed Churches." This meant primarily that the English Church was to conform to the Scottish Presbyterian model. The Scots' insistence on these terms as the price of their cooperation was partly motivated by missionary zeal, but also by a recognition that the establishment of Presbyterianism in both kingdoms would serve as a deterrent to future conflict between them, which could only end to Scotland's disadvantage.

Pursuant to the covenant, the English Parliament summoned the Westminster Assembly to work out the details of the new religious settlement. Only eight Scots were invited, out of a total attendance of more than 120 ministers and laymen. The assembly produced a confession of faith based on Calvinist principles; a "larger catechism," a "shorter catechism," and a directory of public worship to replace the English Book of Common Prayer. In the event the Westminster documents were approved by the General Assembly of Scotland and have remained the official standards of the Church of Scotland ever since and of the Presbyterian churches of the United States. (Hence so many American Presbyterian churches bearing the name "Westminster.") In England, however, Presbyterian influence in Parliament soon declined, and the Westminster resolutions were shelved. By a curious irony then, the Church of Scotland, as it still exists, owes its standards and practices to a conference held in London and completely dominated by Englishmen.

But the Solemn League and Covenant had a significance beyond its immediate impact on the religious settlement in either Scotland or England. It hardened the Covenanters' commitment to Presbyterianism as the only "true religion," incorporated Presbyterian dogma into the imagined covenant between God and the nation, and legitimatized and sanctified an uncompromising Presbyterian orthodoxy. The attempt to enforce a rigid conformity of course bred nonconformity and dissension, and thus for another half century or more Scotland was to be a nation riven with religious controversy. Moreover, the Solemn League and Covenant, contrary to the intention of its authors, served to exacerbate traditional hostilities between Scotland and England and to delay effective union between the two countries.

On the military side, the dispatch of two Scottish armies into England in 1644 did not prove as decisive as either the king or Parliament had anticipated. At the critical battle of Marston Moor, to be sure, though the Earl of Leven fled the field, the Scots infantry stood fast and the Scots horse under David Leslie joined Oliver Cromwell's cavalry to turn the tide of battle in favor of the parliamentarians. Thereafter, however, Scottish forces in England were mostly engaged in siege operations, while in September 1645 Leslie took about six thousand of his men back to Scotland to deal with the Marquis of Montrose and his Irish allies.

James Graham of Montrose had been among the first of the Scots nobles to sign the National Covenant. His disillusionment followed soon after Archibald Campbell, Earl (later Marquis) of Argyll, with some hesitation, had cast his lot too with the Covenanters. Land hunger was endemic among the Campbells and this (the eighth) earl was no exception. Having acquired legal claims to extensive estates in Lochaber, Badenoch, and Angus, he spread havoc among the clans and families in those areas under the pretense of serving the cause of the Covenant. Campbell imperialism produced a reaction in the form of a bond signed at Cumbernauld near Glasgow by Montrose and seventeen other nobles and lairds in opposition to Argyll and his self-aggrandizement in the name of religion.

Imprisoned briefly by the Covenanters, Montrose made his peace privately with King Charles and, with the new rank of marquis, agreed to undertake a counterrevolution in Scotland. He was to be joined in this endeavor by one Alasdair MacDonald, a wild Irishman of Scots descent who had invaded the Ardnamurchan Peninsula with a force of about sixteen hundred men. Alasdair promptly captured the ancient MacDonald stronghold of **Mingary Castle** *(460)* and proceeded to ravage the surrounding countryside with fire and sword, paying particular attention to the Campbells, hereditary foes of his own family. He then joined Montrose near Blair Atholl, Perthshire, and the combined army of about twenty-five hundred to three thousand Highlanders and Irish set out to terrorize central Scotland.

After a battle fought and won at Tippermuir near Perth, this motley gang of royalists proceeded to capture and sack the city of Aberdeen, where Alasdair and his men were allowed three days of pillage and butchery—a stain on Montrose's reputation for gallantry that even the admiring novelist Sir Walter Scott could not entirely erase. From here, in spite of frequent desertions by both Irish and Highlanders, Montrose piled one victory on another in a brilliant guerrilla campaign unmatched in Scotland since the days of Bruce. He routed the enemy at Fyvie; captured **Inverlochy Castle** *(516)* (a Campbell stronghold); ravaged Stonehaven; and won battles at Auldearn, Alford, and finally, in August 1645, at Kilsyth, near Glasgow. The Lowlands were now defenseless, and the Covenanters' cause in Scotland seemed undone. But strategically, Montrose's military genius made little difference. The previous June Charles I had suffered decisive defeat at the hands of Oliver Cromwell's new model army at Naseby in Northamptonshire. The issue of the war was no longer in doubt.

Montrose decided nonetheless to move south across the border. By the time he set out from Bothwell near Glasgow, his army had disintegrated. His Irish and Highland followers were more interested in ravaging Argyll territory than in coming to the rescue of a distant king. When the remnant reached Philiphaugh near Selkirk on the afternoon of 12 September 1645, they were obviously no match for the six thousand fresh troops brought up from England by David Leslie. The next day's battle was of course a rout. (Weapons taken from the field of Philiphaugh are on display at **Halliwell's House Museum** *[419]* in Selkirk.) Montrose escaped the battlefield and sought refuge at **Traquair House** *(420)* near Peebles. There King Charles's former Lord Treasurer barred the door to the fugitive, who then fled north. The Scottish Parliament, recovering from its fright, convened in the new "public school" in St. Andrews (because of the plague in Edinburgh) and tried and condemned a number of Montrose's supporters. (Now called Parliament Hall, this building serves today as the **University Museum** *[494]*, housing historic treasures of St. Andrews University and of the town and its environs.) Montrose himself was eventually provided with a safe conduct overseas and on 3 September 1646 set sail for Bergen on a Norwegian ship.

Not all of his supporters were so lucky. At Philiphaugh, those Irish soldiers not killed in the battle had been lined up and shot in the courtyard of nearby **Newark Castle** *(420)*. Also, about five hundred camp followers, cooks, and horseboys were massacred (as compared to the two hundred citizens of Aberdeen, who had suffered like fate at the hands of Montrose's troops). That the victims were mostly Irish, and therefore Roman Catholic, seemed adequate justification in the minds of those who had perpetrated the atrocity and probably of most other Covenanters as well.

Eight months after Philiphaugh, Charles I, in the face of certain defeat at the hands of Cromwell, turned himself over to the Scottish army camped near Southwell in Nottinghamshire. The Scots took the king to Newcastle, tried unsuccessfully to persuade him to agree to the Solemn League and Covenant, then turned him over to the English in return for a partial payment of the £400,000 still due the Scots for their armed assistance. They then marched home.

By this time, many of the Covenanters had become more fearful of Cromwell than of the king. Increasingly sympathetic with those self-styled Independents in his new model army who opposed all forms of enforced religious conformity, the victorious general was soon to lend his powerful support to the principle of toleration of all law-abiding Protestant denominations. Such a solution was, of course, in total contradiction to the covenants. There could be only *one* true religion. To admit otherwise would raise doubts about the very majesty of God Himself. When, a few years later, Cromwell challenged the General Assembly with his famous plea, "I beseech you, in the bowels of Christ, think it possible you may be mistaken," the Scots' shocked answer was inevitable: "Would you have us be skepticks in our religion?" Hoping vainly to convert the king, three Presbyterian nobles—William Hamilton, Earl of Lanark; John Campbell,

Earl of Loudoun; and John Maitland, Earl of Lauderdale—made their way to his place of imprisonment at Carisbrooke Castle on the Isle of Wight. There at the end of December 1647 they signed the "Engagement" whereby the Scots promised military assistance to Charles I in return for his agreement to establish Presbyterianism in England for three years and to suppress all "heretics [i.e., Catholics], schismatics [presumably including Episcopalians], and Independents [meaning Cromwell's party]."

The Engagement cut the fragile cord that for more than a decade had bound most of the Scots nobility and clergy in a common endeavor. With the exception of Argyll and a few others, the nobles supported it. Against it were arrayed most of the clergy and a growing number of lesser laymen, especially in the Southwest. Here was the beginning of a social and ideological cleavage that would tear Scotland asunder for the rest of the seventeenth century.

After Cromwell had soundly defeated an army sent by the Engagers into Lancashire, a group of radicals from the Southwest—about a thousand strong—invaded central Scotland in what became known as the Whiggamore Raid. (Whiggamores were Galwegian cattle-drovers who would have been astonished to know that their nickname would one day, in a shortened form, be the proud label of political parties in both Britain and the United States.) The rebels captured the government in Edinburgh and, with the tacit support of Cromwell, raised the Marquis of Argyll to a position of supreme power. They then proceeded to pass the Act of Classes, excluding from public office all "malignants" who had supported the Engagement or Montrose.

Thus Charles I, by entering the Engagement, had at last succeeded in fracturing the Covenanting party, which his own wrongheadedness had brought into being in the first place. He also thereby snapped the patience of Oliver Cromwell, who had him beheaded at Whitehall on 30 January 1649.

THE INTERREGNUM: 1649–1660

The summary execution of a King of *Scots* by an *English* Parliament under the control of an anti-Presbyterian military dictator was more than the Covenanters had bargained for. The late king's eldest son was proclaimed King Charles II by Parliament in Edinburgh, though coronation was made contingent on his giving satisfaction concerning the covenants. Commissioners were then sent to Holland, where Charles was in residence. While negotiations were still in progress, the king commissioned the Marquis of

Montrose to invade Scotland in an effort to achieve by force what Charles had yet to accomplish by persuasion: i.e., an acknowledgment of his unconditional right to the Crown of Scotland without prior agreement to the covenants. The king instructed Montrose to "proceed vigorously" so that his actions would "either dispose those who are otherwise minded to make reasonable demands to us in a treaty, or be able to force them to it by arms, in case of their obstinate refusal." In other words, Montrose's expedition was conceived by Charles II as a "bargaining chip." Montrose himself, however, was promised royal protection in the event the king came to terms with the Scots commissioners.

In April 1650 Montrose, with an army of about twelve hundred men, landed near John o' Groats on the Pentland Firth and advanced rapidly as far south as Carbisdale near Bonar Bridge in Sutherland, where his troops were routed by Colonel Archibald Strachan. The marquis, however, escaped and made his way westward across the barren northern Highlands to **Ardvreck Castle** *(552)*, which still stands in a ruined state on the shore of Loch Assynt. The owner of this stronghold was Neil MacLeod, who is said to have clapped the fugitive in a cellar prison and then turned him over to General David Leslie in exchange for twenty-five thousand pounds Scots, twenty thousand in coin, and the balance in oatmeal. Already condemned to death, Montrose was bound and taken to Edinburgh and carried in an open cart along the Royal Mile to the tolbooth, to suffer the ignominy of hanging. En route the prisoner passed **Moray House** *(441)*, a recently built mansion considered to be the most elegant of its kind in the city. Inside, watching the sorry parade to the gibbet, were the Marquis of Argyll and Johnston of Wariston, both of whom would, within little more than a decade, suffer a similar fate. Montrose's body was cut down and mutilated, head and limbs then placed on exhibition in Edinburgh, Stirling, Glasgow, Perth, and Aberdeen. The trunk was interred beside the public gallows, to be reburied in 1661 with great fanfare in **St. Giles Kirk** *(439)*, where it still lies beneath the floor of the Chepman Aisle on the south side of the church. This posthumous recognition was the work of the restored Charles II, who had neglected to insist on a clear guarantee of Montrose's safety when he signed the Treaty of Breda with the Scottish commissioners on 1 May 1650.

On 24 June the new king landed at Garmouth, where the River Spey runs into the Moray Firth. Just before coming ashore, he signed the covenants, thereby committing himself to uphold the "true religion" and the Presbyterian form of worship and church government in both Scotland and England. On 1 January 1651 he was crowned at Scone, the Marquis of Argyll himself performing the act of coronation.

Meanwhile, on 22 July, Cromwell had crossed the Tweed with an army of about sixteen thousand to put down what was, in his eyes, a royalist counterrevolution. On 3 September he met a much larger Scottish army under David Leslie at Dunbar and routed it, killing some four thousand Scots and taking ten thousand others prisoner. "The enemy's horse and foot were made by the Lord of Hosts as stubble to our swords," reported the victorious general, by then generally known as "Old Ironsides." Extremist Covenanters among the Scots held a like view, maintaining that the debacle at Dunbar was God's vengeance on Scotland for not purging its army of Engagers and other "malignants." Moderate Covenanters of royalist hue were, on the contrary, convinced that the defeat was attributable to the Act of Classes, which had robbed Leslie of too many seasoned officers on purely ideological grounds. This growing rift between strict covenanting Presbyterians (especially the clergy) and pragmatic compromisers (especially the nobility) was greatly to facilitate Cromwell's coming conquest of Scotland.

The English entered Edinburgh on 7 September, and Cromwell established his headquarters in **Moray House** *(441)*. Two of his lieutenants, George Monck and John Lambert, took **Dirleton Castle** *(453)* in November. It had been a nest of royalist "moss-troopers," threatening the line of communications to the south. In December **Edinburgh Castle** *(436)* finally surrendered. In late February 1652 Monck captured **Tantallon Castle** *(458)* and the next month **Blackness Castle** *(428)*, thus consolidating English control of the south shore of the Forth. In July Monck and Lambert crossed into Fife to win the north shore. Cromwell himself then took the bulk of his army across the river and marched on Perth, which capitulated on 2 August. Charles II, then in Stirling, seeing the way into England open before him but not realizing that Cromwell had set a trap, marched south. Cromwell and Lambert took off in pursuit and at Worcester virtually destroyed the royalist army and drove Charles into his second exile on the Continent.

Monck stayed behind to lay siege to **Stirling Castle** *(477)*, which fell on 13 August, then stormed Dundee on 1 September and allowed his troops to plunder the town. At Alyth, three days earlier, a detachment of his army had taken prisoner a number of members of the General Assembly and of the Committee of Estates (the standing committee of Parliament) and shipped them off to England. Aberdeen was occupied during the second week of September; Inverness was garrisoned with English troops; and **Dumbarton Castle** *(475)* surrendered to Lambert in January 1652. In April **Brodick Castle** *(393)*, on the Isle of Arran, succumbed and was garrisoned and refortified by English troops. The following month **Dunnottar Castle** *(546)*, south of Stonehaven, capitulated after a long siege. Inside had been hidden the private papers of Charles II and the Regalia (crown, scepter, and royal sword) of Scotland, but the English failed to seize them. Before the castle fell, they had been smuggled out by the wife of the minister of nearby **Kinneff Church** *(547)*, where they lay buried beneath the floor until the king's restoration. This act of bravado could not disguise the fact that Scotland was a conquered nation. Next month the Marquis of Argyll agreed to submit to English rule and opened five of his strongholds to Cromwell's garrisons, including **Dunstaffnage Castle** *(472)* and **Tarbert Castle** *(474)*.

Under the rule of Cromwell, Scotland would enjoy for a brief span the most efficient government it had ever experienced. Scotland and England were declared to be one commonwealth. Cromwell was designated Lord Protector in December 1653, and subsequently an Ordinance of Union admitted 30 Scottish members (out of a total of 460) to a new Commonwealth Parliament. George Monck, with the help of a mixed Anglo-Scottish council of state, served as the Protector's alter ego in Scotland. New forts were built at Ayr, Inverlochy (later Fort William), Leith, Perth, and Inverness, the last of which is believed to have been constructed out of stones taken from **Fortrose Cathedral** *(548)*, **Kinloss Abbey** *(528)* and **Beauly Priory** *(518)*. An improved system of justice was established: barons' courts were abolished and justices of the peace appointed in every sheriffdom. In the Highlands, chiefs were made legally responsible for the conduct of their clansmen. Such unaccustomed law and order inspired one contemporary to comment: "A man may ride Scotland all over with a switch in his hand and £100 in his pocket, which he could not have done these five hundred years."

The Protectorate, however, was of too recent origin and unpopular in too many quarters to survive much beyond the Protector's lifetime. When Cromwell died in September 1658 to be succeeded by his son Richard, the fabric of his rule began to disintegrate. George Monck was to play the decisive role in the resolution of the crisis. Having been seduced by Charles II with the promise of a munificent pension contingent upon the king's restoration, Monck, on 1 January 1660, set out for London from Coldstream, where he had established headquarters in a building now housing the **Coldstream Museum** *(423)*. With him went his personally commanded regiment, later known as the Coldstream Guards. The English parliamentarians were overawed; Charles II was recalled to his patrimony; and George Monck, who was the first to greet the royal fugitive as he stepped ashore at Dover, was made Duke of Albemarle.

CHARLES II: 1660–1685

When news of the king's return reached Edinburgh, a day of thanksgiving was declared; fountains ran with claret; trumpets, drums, and cannon resounded; and a great display of fireworks on Castle Hill showed Cromwell chased by the devil and then blown to pieces. One who did not rejoice, however, was Archibald Campbell, Marquis of Argyll. Though he himself had previously crowned the king at Scone, he was seized and clapped into the Tower of London. Sent back to Scotland, he was tried for treason, convicted, imprisoned in **Edinburgh Castle** *(436)* (perhaps in that part of it now called Argyll's Tower), and beheaded at the market cross, though later commemorated with a splendid funereal monument in **St. Giles Kirk** *(439)*, opposite the burial place of his enemy Montrose. Facing death, Argyll proclaimed from the scaffold a commitment to the Covenanting principle not always demonstrated in a lifetime of political equivocation: "God hath laid engagements on Scotland," he declared, "we are tyed by covenants to religion and reformation . . . and it passeth the power of all Magistrates under heaven to absolve a man from the oath of God."

Such sentiments would have been altogether incomprehensible to the newly crowned thirty-year-old king in London. Years of deprivation, flight, exile, and the misfortunes of war had rendered him cynical, worldly, and unprincipled—except in a steadfast determination not to go on his travels again. His earlier and unhappy sojourn in Scotland had made that country and its inhabitants loathsome to him, and he was determined never to go back. Though he spent a large sum restoring and enlarging the **Palace of Holyroodhouse** *(442)* (see below), he never visited it or any other place in Scotland during the twenty-five years of his reign. The northern kingdom was again made constitutionally separate from England. Its government was delegated to a secretary of state, resident in London, who carried out the king's policies through the privy council in Edinburgh, headed by a commissioner. The first secretary was John Maitland, elevated to the dukedom of Lauderdale; the first commissioner, General John Middleton, on whom the king bestowed the rank of earl. Parliaments were held in Edinburgh, but under the close rein of the Lords of Articles, the Crown-appointed standing committee, now restored after its abolition in 1639.

The Covenants, to which Charles II had sworn allegiance before his Scottish coronation, were promptly set aside. Presbyterianism, he had told Lauderdale, was not a fit religion for a gentleman. In 1661–1662 it was abolished; archbishops and bishops were restored to their former positions of authority in the Church of Scotland; and, most significantly, lay patronage was reestablished. This last measure, which returned to the owners of great estates the right of nominating parish ministers, succeeded, as was intended, in driving a wedge between the nobility and the covenanting faction of the clergy. Charles I and Archbishop Laud had united these two powerful elites in an unnatural alliance against the Crown. Charles II restored their mutual hostility.

James Sharp, formerly minister of Crail, was appointed Archbishop of St. Andrews; Alexander Burnet, an extreme anti-Covenanter, Archbishop of Glasgow; Robert Leighton, a moderate compromiser, Bishop of Dunblane. But there was no restoration of the Anglican sacerdotalism that had precipitated the rebellion of 1637. Though bishops, subject to royal and parliamentary control, replaced the General Assembly at the apex of church government, kirk sessions, presbyteries, and synods were retained. Church worship remained much as it had been—no kneeling to receive Communion, no surpliced clergy, and no compulsory prayer book, though the Lord's Prayer, the Doxology, and the Apostle's Creed were reintroduced. In short, the Restoration religious settlement approximated the mixed Presbyterian-Episcopalian order that had prevailed in the middle years of James VI's reign—a pragmatic solution that would probably have proved generally acceptable if left alone.

But the king and his episcopal advisers would not leave it alone. Clergymen were additionally required by law, at risk of deprivation of their livings, to take an oath of allegiance to the king, to celebrate his birthday, to attend diocesan meetings held by the bishops, and to refrain from attending any meetings not so authorized. More importantly, those ministers who had not been "presented" to their parishes by lay patrons, and who failed to correct the omission within a specified time, were to be deprived of their livings and compelled to move outside the bounds of their respective presbyteries. A total of 262 ministers—roughly one-fourth to one-third of the total number in Scotland—refused to comply and were ejected. Disobedience was most widespread in the Southwest (Wigtownshire, Kirkcudbrightshire, Dumfriesshire, Ayrshire, Lanarkshire, and Renfrewshire) and in Lothian. In many places, laymen followed their ministers out of the established church, unlawfully declined to attend kirk services, and gathered instead to listen to the preaching of the "outed" ministers in private homes or in open fields. These gatherings, called *conventicles*, were proclaimed illegal, and to prevent their taking place, the government resorted to coercion. In retaliation and self-defense, conventiclers took up arms against the government. Reprisals followed, and once again a civil war of sorts broke out in Scotland.

Under the symbolic banner of the Covenants (and calling themselves "Covenanters"), these dissidents stood not for religious toleration, but for a single and uniform religious establishment, organized according to Presbyterian principles, free of bishops, and immune from state interference or from the dominance of lay patrons, meaning the nobility. Their principal leaders were the "outed" clergy, and their intentions were to serve God and guard the "true religion" against internal corruption and external enemies. Yet the fact that this was largely an uprising of underprivileged tenants (primarily in the Southwest) suggests that there may also have been elements of class struggle involved. The economic and social grievances of the peasantry, for the first time in Scottish history, were to find expression in an organized armed revolt, though in the guise of a religious crusade. On the other side, the government viewed the uprising not primarily as a religious protest, but as a seditious threat to the established order of society.

Troops were raised and sent into the Southwest under the command of Sir James Turner, a venal and brutal mercenary soldier. In November of 1666 he was seized at Dumfries by a handful of Galloway peasants, who then raised the standard of revolt in Ayrshire and Lanarkshire, where perhaps as many as three thousand men began the march toward Edinburgh in what came to be known as the Pentland Rising. At Rullion Green in the foothills south of the city, this poorly armed band, now much diminished by desertion, was intercepted by General Thomas ("Tam") Dalyell in command of the king's forces in Scotland. This hard-bitten soldier had fought for Charles II at Worcester, been taken prisoner and confined to the Tower of London, escaped to the Continent, and for a time served as general officer in the army of the Czar of Russia—hence called by Covenanters "the Bluidy Muscovite." He had returned to his native country not long before the Pentland Rising and established himself at his father's country house in West Lothian, **The Binns** *(428)*—today a pleasant mansion owned by the National Trust for Scotland. Dalyell's troopers killed about fifty insurgents at Rullion Green; another eighty were taken prisoner and shut up in "Haddo's Hole" above the north porch of **St. Giles Kirk** *(439)*, Edinburgh. Of these, some were tortured and some hanged. Still others were confined in **Blackness Castle** *(428)* in West Lothian. Altogether there were thirty-six executions: about eighty were transported to Barbados, Virginia, or Tangier. In August 1667 Dalyell's forces, which had been terrorizing the Southwest for nine months, were disbanded by government order. The Duke of Lauderdale had decided to try persuasion in lieu of repression in dealing with the Covenanters. In July 1668 an act of indulgence was proclaimed, and forty-two of the "outed" ministers were readmitted to their parishes. Conventicling continued. The government reverted to sterner measures with the "clanking act," increasing penalties for attending conventicles, for assaulting ministers who had returned to the established church, and other like offenses. A second act of indulgence was passed. Conventicling increased. Troops from the Highlands were brought into the Southwest and quartered on the conventiclers. Then, in May 1679, Archbishop James Sharp was dragged out of his carriage by a gang of Covenanters on Magus Muir near St. Andrews and hacked to death in the presence of his daughter. (He is commemorated by an ornate marble monument erected in the 1680s in **Holy Trinity Kirk** *[494]*, St. Andrews.)

The incident marked a turning point both for the government and for the Covenanters. The more moderate among the latter recoiled at the barbarity of the act, but the extremists, including the assassin David Hackston, and two "outed" ministers, Richard Cameron and Donald Cargill, rejoiced in the killing. The privy council responded with heavier reprisals. John Graham of Claverhouse ("Bluidy Clavers" in the lexicon of the Covenanters) was dispatched to the Southwest with a troop of horse. He was met by an armed conventicle at Drumclog east of Kilmarnock and surprisingly routed. The rebels then occupied Glasgow, but soon split among themselves over fine points of doctrine.

The king's bastard son James, Duke of Monmouth, was now sent north to deal with the insurgents, and at Bothwell Brig near Hamilton his army of ten thousand killed about four hundred, captured twelve hundred, and routed the remainder of a rabble mob of about four thousand. Relics of the battle are to be seen today in the **Cameronians Regimental Museum** *(410)* in Hamilton. Among them is the parish of Shotts banner, secreted away from the battlefield, and the "bluidy banner" carried by William Cleland and inscribed with the words "For Christ and His Truths" and "No Quarter for ye Active Enemies of ye Covenant." Monmouth, by marrying Anne Scott, heiress of the Earl of Buccleuch, had been created Duke of Buccleuch and Earl of Dalkeith. In the magnificent mansion of **Bowhill** *(419)*, near Selkirk, built by their descendants in the early nineteenth century, is the Monmouth Room, containing numerous memorabilia of the victor of Bothwell Brig.

The duke, associated as he was with Protestant dissenters in England, was inclined to lenity in dealing with the Covenanters of Scotland. The majority of his prisoners, after having spent the summer of 1679 confined in the yard of **Greyfriars Kirk** *(382)* in Edinburgh, were allowed to go home, though more than two hundred were designated for transportation to Barbados and drowned when their ship went down off the Orkney coast. Only five were executed, and those for alleged complicity in the murder of Archbishop Sharp.

Bothwell Brig spelled the end of Lauderdale's influence in Scotland, and James, Duke of York, the king's Roman Catholic brother, came north to serve as commissioner. Repression again was the order of the day, especially since the most extreme of the Covenanters, under the leadership of Richard Cameron and Donald Cargill, had disowned the king as a tyrant and formally declared war against him at the market cross of Sanquhar. Cameron was later killed in battle with Claverhouse's dragoons, and Cargill caught, hanged, and dismembered. His last night before capture was spent in a house now located in Biggar, called the **Greenhill Covenanters' Museum** *(398)*. Hackston, the murderer of Archbishop Sharp, was finally apprehended and executed in the usual grisly manner. This was "the killing time," so labelled by Robert Wodrow in his *History of the Sufferings of the Church of Scotland from the Restoration to the Revolution*, published in 1721-1722, though in fact probably no more than a hundred were executed. Among the victims were the "Wigtown martyrs," commemorated with the Martyrs' Monument in the **Wigtown Parish Kirkyard** *(377)*. A hundred yards beyond the kirk is the **Martyrs' Stake** *(377)*, a stone replica of the wooden stake to which two local Covenanting women were bound so as to be drowned by the incoming tide, though there is no proof positive that the sentence was carried out. For want of sufficient space to house those taken into custody, the privy council designated **Dunnottar Castle** *(546)* as a state prison. This was a grim fourteenth-century tower (now a spectacular ruin) rising above sheer cliffs falling off to the North Sea south of Stonehaven. Here more than 150 men and women were packed into two vaults with little food and hardly any drinking water. Most were later transported; some died of exposure and disease while still confined; others fell to their deaths while trying to escape down the precipitous cliffs. Their memorial is a simple slab in nearby **Dunnottar Kirkyard** *(547)* incised with these words:

HERE LYES JOHN STOT: JAMES ATCHISON: JAMES RUSSEL: & WILLIAM BROUN: AND ONE WHOSE NAME WEE HAVE NOT GOTTEN: AND TWO WOMEN WHOSE NAMES ALSO WEE KNOW NOT: AND TWO WHO PERISHED COMEING DOUNE THE ROCK: ONE WHOSE NAME WAS JAMES WATSON: THE OTHER NOT KNOWN: WHO ALL DIED PRISONERS IN DUNNOTTAR CASTLE: ANNO 1685 FOR THEIR ADHERENCE TO THE WORD OF GOD AND SCOTLANDS COVENANTED WORK OF REFORMATION

Fanatics the Covenanters certainly were. But their courage, self-sacrifice, and steadfast service to a transcendent ideal cannot be denied. They were mostly peasants who left few tangible relics of their mark on history. Only here and there in kirkyards such as this are they memorialized—their names, in the words of the novelist Lewis Grassic Gibbon, "graved in tragedy."

REVOLUTION AND UNION

One reason for the overcrowding of Dunnottar Castle was that a new shipment of prisoners had arrived after the quelling of a rebellion by the ninth Earl of Argyll. The occasion for this outbreak was the succession to the throne in February 1685 of James, Duke of York, as King James II of England and VII of Scotland. The new king's adherence to Roman

Catholicism was alone sufficient to cause alarm. Yet there was no general uprising when Argyll returned to Scotland from the Continent with a small band of armed followers in May. In the event, he was easily defeated, captured, and, like his father before him, beheaded for treason in Edinburgh. A like fate met the Duke of Monmouth who had tried to organize a Protestant revolt in southwestern England and seize the throne for himself.

Until the accession of James VII, "prelacy" had been perceived as the major threat to the "one true religion" in Scotland. Now it was Roman Catholicism. Adherence to the National Covenant was declared treasonable and attendance at a conventicle made punishable by death. Jesuits were brought to Edinburgh to teach their hateful doctrines and even to establish a printing press. The nave of **Holyrood Abbey** *(443)* was converted into a Roman Catholic chapel. It was doubtless cold comfort to the Protestant congregation thereby displaced to be endowed with the new **Canongate Kirk** *(442)*—a handsome church with a baroque front pierced by a Doric portico. With its cruciform ground plan and semicircular apse, its appearance would doubtless have been more pleasing to Archbishop Laud than to John Knox or Andrew Melville.

Though persecution of conventiclers continued, the king sought to win the support of other Presbyterians to a policy of religious toleration that would protect Catholics as well as dissenting Protestants. By a proclamation issued in June 1687 all denominations were allowed to worship in private houses or chapels. This outraged clergy and laity of the established Episcopalian church, and though it allowed moderate Presbyterians to open meeting houses, it failed to reconcile them to the legalization of Catholicism.

Thus discontent with the new regime was on the rise when news came of the landing of William of Orange in Devon, his march toward London, the flight of King James to France, and the enthronement by the English of Protestant "Dutch William" and his wife Mary, Protestant daughter of the now exiled king. A convention of estates was called in Edinburgh. Lairds and nobles raised troops of horse and companies of foot to put down rebellious Catholics or other "Jacobites." (From *Jacobus*, the Latin version of *James*, this term henceforward was used to describe supporters of the exiled Stuart king and his successors.) In Lanarkshire the Earl of Angus raised one such regiment among the Covenanters—later to be known as "the Cameronians" in memory of the radical conventicler, Richard Cameron. (The **Cameronians Regimental Museum** *[410]* in Hamilton houses numerous mementos and memorabilia of this unit, which served in the British Army for many years with high distinction.)

In April the convention of estates resolved that James VII had forfeited the Scottish crown and offered it to William and Mary conditionally on their agreeing to the terms of two documents called the Claim of Right and the

Articles of Grievances. Taken together, these established the two main features of the revolutionary settlement in Scotland: (1) the independence of the Scottish Parliament, which was to be assured by the abolition of the Lords of the Articles, the requirement for frequent parliaments, and the prohibition against the king's raising supply (i.e., levying taxes) without prior parliamentary consent; and (2) the abolition of episcopacy in favor of a Presbyterian form of church government. The first would prove short-lived; the second was to become permanent.

Three commissioners—the tenth Earl (later first Duke) of Argyll for the nobles, Sir James Montgomerie of Skelmorlie for the lairds, Sir John Dalrymple for the burgesses—were chosen to go to England and tender the Crown of Scotland to William and Mary. The monarchs accepted the terms imposed by Parliament and were duly proclaimed king and queen. They would have preferred to retain the Episcopal form of church government, but the pronounced Jacobitism of the Scottish bishops drove the king and queen into the arms of the Presbyterians. The General Assembly was recalled in 1690 for the first time in thirty-seven years. Parliament abolished lay patronage. An oath of allegiance to William and Mary was required of all clergymen. A large number of ministers of doubtful orthodoxy were forced out. Those of Episcopalian leanings who took the oath were allowed to retain their churches, but many (especially in the Northeast) did not, and as "nonjurors" were deprived. Into this category fell all the former Scottish bishops whose enduring loyalty to "the king over the water" brought them many hardships.

Jacobitism was strong also in the Highlands, where Graham of Claver-house (now Viscount Dundee) promptly repaired to raise the clans. Many of the chiefs pledged allegiance to the exiled king, though probably less from a sense of loyalty to the House of Stuart than out of hatred of the Campbells, now led by the tenth Earl of Argyll, firmly committed to King William. The government sent Major General Hugh Mackay of Scourie into Perthshire: an armed clash occurred at the Pass of Killiecrankie near **Blair Castle** *(498)*, which Mackay was trying to recapture; the Jacobites won the day, but "Bonnie Dundee" lay dead on the field of battle. (Near the site of the battle, the National Trust for Scotland maintains today the **Killiecrankie Visitors' Centre** *[499]* with a fine array of explanatory exhibits.) The victorious Highlanders then made for Dunkeld to do battle with the Earl of Angus's regiment of Covenanters from Lanarkshire led by Lieutenant Colonel William Cleland, a veteran of Bothwell Brig. The clansmen were routed, but Cleland was killed. His burial site is marked by a simple gravestone in the southwest corner of the now roofless nave of **Dunkeld Cathedral** *(504)*. During the battle, most of the town was burned, to be replaced in the decades following 1689 by the **Dunkeld Little Houses** *(505)*, recently restored by the National Trust.

Mackay then pushed westward into the Great Glen and, near Inverlochy, built Fort William, putting it under the command of Colonel John Hill, who had served in Cromwell's outpost on the same site. (The fort was torn down in 1864, but the **West Highland Museum** *[515]* in the town that rose around it contains a room transferred here from the commanding general's quarters.) But more than a fort was required to pacify the neighboring clans. The government threatened to go after them with "utmost severity" unless their chiefs swore to submit to King William no later than 1 January 1692. Though released of their previous pledges of allegiance by James VII, many of them procrastinated. Among those who delayed until the very last minute was Alasdair MacIain, head of a tiny sept of Clan Donald that occupied the valley of the little River Coe flowing westward into Loch Leven in Argyll.

These MacDonalds of Glencoe were notorious for their habitual banditry and were a perennial bane to their neighbors, especially the Campbells. MacIain arrived at Fort William to take the required oath on the night of 30–31 December only to be told by Colonel Hill that he had reported to the wrong place. Directed to Inveraray, he arrived there on 2 January but had to wait for the deputy sheriff to return; therefore, it was not until the sixth of the month that he was tendered the oath.

The aging chief's venial dereliction (by six days) would doubtless have been overlooked, had it not served the purpose of the government to intimidate all the Highland clans with a terrifying act of exemplary punishment. The most forceful advocate of such a policy was the Scottish secretary of state in London, Sir John Dalrymple, Master of Stair. Acting under instructions that he himself had persuaded King William to sign, he ordered Hill to "cut off that nest of robbers who have fallen in the mercy of the law now . . . and by all means be quick." To Sir Thomas Livingston, the king's commander-in-chief in Scotland, he wrote: "I am glad that Glencoe [i.e., MacIain] did not come in within the time prescribed . . . I believe you will be satisfied it were of great advantage to the nation that [that] thieving tribe were rooted out and cut off."

Execution of the intended punishment was assigned to Robert Campbell of Glenlyon, an impecunious and alcoholic captain of the Earl of Argyll's regiment. Glenlyon had already brought two companies of troops into Glencoe to be quartered among the MacDonalds—ostensibly because there was no room for them at Fort William. MacIain had bade the soldiers welcome, in keeping with the Highland code mandating hospitality to strangers. Thus, when Glenlyon received orders "to fall upon the rebels the MacDonalds of Glencoe and to put all to the sword under seventy," he was obliged to commit the crime of "murder under trust," a heinous and unnatural offense in the view of most contemporary Scots.

The massacre was committed in the early morning hours of 13 February 1692. It was a botched job. MacIain was shot to death and thirty-seven of his clansmen butchered, but the majority escaped into the snow-covered hills. In Edinburgh, members of Parliament demanded an investigation, and the king complied by appointing a commission of inquiry. The commission of course exonerated His Majesty but fixed the blame chiefly on Dalrymple—not surprisingly since the Master of Stair had many political enemies. As a result he lost his secretaryship but otherwise went unpunished, though his primary responsibility for the atrocity is hard to deny.

Legend has taken over the gruesome affair, however, and assigned a heavy share of guilt to Clan Campbell. The case against these hereditary foes of the MacDonalds is weak. True, Glenlyon was a Campbell, and so were some of his troops, but he and they were executioners, not judges. John Campbell, Earl of Breadalbane, may have had some knowledge of the plan in its early stages but was not a principal actor. Even less involved was Archibald, tenth Earl of Argyll. The fact is that the Glencoe massacre was not, as is often assumed, just another incident in the perennial feud between Campbells and MacDonalds. It was an act of government terrorism and a very ugly one. Perhaps in Scottish lore its historic significance has been exaggerated, but as drama—or melodrama—the tragedy of Glencoe ranks high in Scotland's romantic tradition. Visitors to this gloomy valley flanked by lowering and majestic mountain ranges (today easily accessible over the A 82) cannot help but brood over the bloody events that took place here almost three hundred years ago. For further information they can stop at the **Glencoe Visitors Centre** *(460)* and the **Glencoe and North Lorn Folk Museum** *(460)*, both a few miles east of Ballachulish.

The Glencoe massacre served the immediate purpose of persuading some of the remaining laggard chiefs to submit to *force majeure* and swear allegiance to King William. In the long run, however, it was probably a boon to the Jacobites, alienating many Highlanders who might otherwise have been friendly to the government or at least neutral. And Jacobitism had by the beginning of the eighteenth century acquired significant and dangerous international implications.

William of Orange, Stadholder of Holland, had seized the throne of England in the first place so as to commandeer that country's military and economic resources in his ongoing war against the hegemonial ambitions of King Louis XIV of France. In 1689 England entered the War of the League of Augsburg (an anti-French coalition) and from that time until 1814 was engaged intermittently in large-scale military and naval operations against the French kingdom, republic, and empire—the so-called Second Hundred Years War. It is in this context alone that the threat to the English government of the dynastic pretensions of the exiled Stuarts is to be understood. In 1701 James II/VII died at St. Germain-en-Lay. France immediately recognized his thirteen-year-old son (the "Old Pretender") as King James III of England and VIII of Scotland. In the same year war broke out again between France and England (the War of the Spanish Succession). Thus the Jacobites of Britain could reasonably be regarded as a Francophile "fifth column" and the royal Stuarts as tools in the hands of Louis XIV. That they were Roman Catholic of course magnified the threat. So did the fact that William and Mary had no issue and that their successor, Mary's younger sister Anne, had lost all her children and was too old to produce any more. Faced with the certain depletion of the reigning Protestant dynasty, the English Parliament in 1701 passed the Act of Settlement, bestowing the right of succession to the throne of England on the Protestant heirs of James I's daughter Elizabeth and her husband, the Elector Palatine. This meant in effect that Elizabeth's daughter Sophia, Electress of Hanover, or her heir would be England's next monarch after the death of Queen Anne. (See table: "The English Succession: 1603–1760.")

For the Scottish Parliament not to do likewise would mean an end to the union of the crowns and the possibility of England's once more becoming exposed to the danger of hostile attack by, or by way of, her northern neighbor. The Scots, however, dallied. They were still smarting from the recent disastrous failure of the so-called Darien Scheme—a fatuous and expensive undertaking to found a Scottish colony on the Isthmus of Panama, the undoing of which they wrongly blamed on English obstructionism. There were Jacobites in Parliament at Edinburgh, and some Presbyterians feared that continued union with England on any level would expose the "true religion" to the dangers of corruption by the Anglican Church.

Not until 1704 did the Scottish Parliament legislate on the matter of succession, and then to declare that Scotland would *not* accept the Hanoverians as monarchs except on condition that the Scottish government, religion, and trade be secured from subordination to England. In London this quasi-declaration of independence was received with alarm, and Parliament passed the Alien Act, which declared that, unless Scotland adopted the Hanoverian succession by Christmas Day 1705, Scots would be treated as aliens and a virtual embargo on Scottish trade to and from England would go into effect. The law was subsequently repealed, but its passage served the purpose of persuading the Scottish Parliament to appoint commissioners to meet with English counterparts and work out a treaty of union between the two countries.

What emerged from these deliberations was the Act of Union passed by both parliaments in 1707. Under its terms, England and Scotland were to be united as Great Britain with one parliament and under one monarch as already decreed by the English Act of Settlement. The number of Scottish representatives to the House of Commons was fixed at 45, as compared to 513 for England and Wales; and 16 peers were to sit for Scotland in the House of Lords, as against 190 English. There was to be complete freedom

THE ENGLISH SUCCESSION: 1603–1760

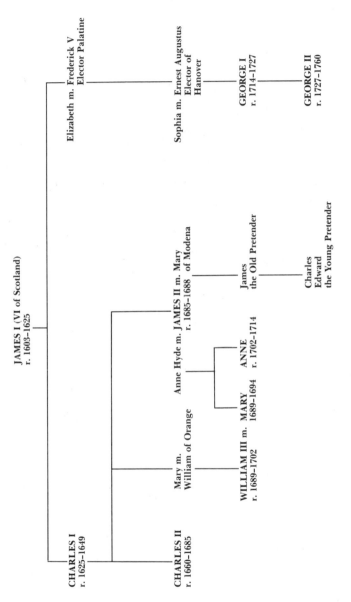

JAMES I (VI of Scotland)
r. 1603–1625

Elizabeth m. Frederick V
Elector Palatine

Sophia m. Ernest Augustus
Elector of
Hanover

GEORGE I
r. 1714–1727

GEORGE II
r. 1727–1760

CHARLES I
r. 1625–1649

CHARLES II
r. 1660–1685

Mary m.
William of Orange

Anne Hyde m. JAMES II m. Mary of Modena
r. 1685–1688

James
the Old Pretender

Charles
Edward
the Young Pretender

WILLIAM III m. MARY
1689–1694
r. 1689–1702

ANNE
r. 1702–1714

of trade and navigation within the new united kingdom and its colonies. Uniform (English) coinage, weights, and measures were to be established. The Scottish legal and judicial systems were to remain unaltered, though appeals to the House of Lords were not expressly barred and were in fact later carried out. The sum of £400,000 sterling was to be paid to Scotland, part of it to be devoted to paying off the unlucky investors in the Darien Scheme (an inducement that undoubtedly brought some influential Scots around to support the Act of Union). Finally, by later legislation incorporated into the treaty, the Presbyterian establishment of the Church of Scotland was guaranteed.

In the parliament that sat in Edinburgh on 16 January 1707 the treaty was ratified by a vote of 110 to 67. "Now there's ane end of ane auld sang," James Ogilvie, Earl of Seafield, is reported to have remarked. If the reference was to the legislative independence of the Scottish Parliament, the statement needed qualification. Only since the Revolution of 1689–1690 had that body been very much more than a rubber stamp. But in a more general sense, Seafield was right. Though Scotland had seen little of its kings since James VI went southward in 1603, now it was no longer even a kingdom. Not only did it lack a parliament, but after 1708 it also lost its privy council. Always inferior to England in population, wealth, and power, Scotland within the union became more and more subordinate.

In his novel, *The Heart of Midlothian*, Walter Scott has one of his characters complain, "When we had a king and a chancellor and parliament-men o' oor ain, we could aye peeble them wi' stanes when they werena' guid bairns. But naebody's nails can reach the length o' Lunnon." London was indeed more than ever the principal locus of authority over Scotland and its people. It was the principal residence of a handful of rich and powerful Scots to whom the English government entrusted general management of the affairs of their homeland. Between 1707 and 1746 a number of them served as secretaries of state, charged with Scottish business. The most important among them were James Douglas, second Duke of Queensberry; John Ker, first Duke of Roxburghe; and John Hay, fourth Marquis of Tweeddale. Though thoroughly anglicized, they all retained great estates and noble mansions in Scotland—Queensberry at **Drumlanrig Castle** *(387)* in Dumfriesshire; Roxburghe at **Floors Castle** *(415)* near Kelso, Roxburghshire; and Tweeddale at Yester near Gifford, East Lothian. But by far the most powerful of the London-based managers of Scotland, at least in the period 1725–1761, were John Campbell, second Duke of Argyll, and his younger brother Archibald, Earl of Ilay and subsequently third Duke. Ilay, especially, worked in close association with Sir Robert Walpole (prime minister of Britain in all but name) and, after Walpole's fall from power, with his successor, Sir Henry Pelham. The "work" consisted of lobbying in behalf of Scottish interests in the bureaucratic maze of Whitehall and keeping Scottish members of the House of Commons and Scottish peers in the House of Lords lined up behind the English ministry. The Campbell estates in Scotland were, of course, immense, and the third duke was responsible for the creation of a costly new residence in Argyll, called **Inveraray Castle** *(463)*.

The day-to-day governing of Scotland, of course, could not be handled as far away as London. After the abolition of the Scots privy council in 1708, supervision over local government became the responsibility of resident agents, serving in the capacity of "subministers" answerable directly to the lordly Scottish "managers" in London. These men were charged with maintaining their patrons' interests and those of the Crown, chiefly by means of distributing patronage and keeping a watch over the army of officeholders who enjoyed it. The Campbell brothers relied most heavily on the Lord Advocate, Duncan Forbes of Culloden, and the Lord Justice Clerk, Andrew Fletcher, Lord Milton.

Surprisingly perhaps, the system (if such it can be called) worked reasonably well. Edinburgh bustled with placemen of all descriptions. As seat of the Court of Session and the Court of Judiciary, the town teemed with lawyers. The General Assembly, brought back to life in 1690, met there annually. Lairds and nobles built, bought, or leased town houses along the Royal Mile. Among those still standing are **Mylne's Court** *(438)*, 513–523 Lawnmarket, built by the busy master mason, Robert Mylne, in 1690, eight stories high and arranged around an inner court; **Numbers 3 and 5 James Court** *(438)* at 501 Lawnmarket; **Numbers 312–328 Lawnmarket** *(438)*, a six-story row built between 1726 and 1752; **Number 199 High Street** *(441)*, a fine seven-story tenement at the corner of Cockburn Street; **Tweeddale House** *(441)* at 14 High Street, originally a sixteenth-century dwelling, enlarged in the seventeenth by Sir William Bruce, reconstructed in the eighteenth for the marquis, and much admired by Daniel Defoe during his visit of 1724; and **Queensberry House** *(442)*, 64 Canongate, built in 1682 to a design by James Smith, also responsible for the Queensberry country residence, **Drumlanrig Castle** *(387)*.

The living arrangements in these high tenements reflected the Scots' traditional carelessness about social distinctions. Within the same residential building, a merchant would normally have his shop on the noisy lower floor; nobles, judges, or lawyers would occupy the choice positions in the middle; and poor laboring families the top stories, overcrowded and hard to reach. All would use the common narrow stone staircase. Since the town did not expand laterally, residential class distinctions, such as they were, were thus arranged vertically. Household refuse emptied from above onto the streets, to the traditional cry of "Gardy loo" (i.e., "*Gardez l'eau*"), accounted for Edinburgh's notoriety as probably the worst-smelling city in all of Britain.

Glasgow was still small by comparison, but growing. The Act of Union had opened the English tobacco colonies to Scottish merchants, and the Glaswegians were among the first to break into the former English monopoly. Shipbuilding on the Clyde began in 1718, and before long the city's favorable location near the Atlantic trade routes began to pay off, to the substantial enrichment of its merchant class.

Glasgow and Edinburgh both were the scenes of famous eighteenth-century riots. The so-called Shawfield riot took place in June 1725, when Glaswegians ran amok in response to a new malt tax and looted and razed the house of Daniel Campbell of Shawfield, the local member of parliament. More serious, or at least more celebrated, was the "Porteous riot" in Edinburgh, eleven years later. (A good account of this incident is contained in Scott's *The Heart of Midlothian.*) After "Black Jock" Porteous had opened lethal fire on a city mob that was protesting the hanging of a famous smuggler, he was put to trial and condemned but granted a reprieve. A few months later, in a well-concerted operation, he was kidnapped from his place of confinement in the tolbooth and promptly lynched. News of the affair was ill received at Westminster, and severe reprisals against the city of Edinburgh were thwarted only by the intervention of the Duke of Argyll.

The Porteous riot was a reminder that organized violence in Scotland was not altogether a thing of the past. It would recur too in the form of Jacobite insurrections throughout the early eighteenth century (*see below*). But after 1690, religious warfare died out. More importantly, the nobility (outside of the Highlands) grew tame. Factionalism among rival families had been the source of much of the endemic disorder in Scotland. Now, after the union of the parliaments, many of the nobles left for London; others joined the British Army to fight abroad. Those who stayed no longer had the arena of the Scottish Parliament to play out their hostilities. They were fast becoming anglicized and comfort-loving. Nowhere was this more evident than in their growing attention to the refinements of aristocratic living, as expressed in luxurious dwelling places beautified with surrounding parks and gardens.

DOMESTIC ARCHITECTURE AND GARDENS

In 1670 Patrick Lyon, third Earl of Strathmore and Kinghorne, began the reconstruction of his ancestral home in Angus, **Glamis Castle** *(512)*. By the time he was finished, he had completely remodeled the place, converted the medieval great hall into an elegant drawing room, redecorated the chapel, and in sum metamorphized a fourteenth-century L-plan tower-house into the splendid stately home that Glamis still is. "There is no man," wrote Strathmore in his record book, "more against these old fashions of tours and castles than I am, for who can delight to live in his house as in a prison? . . . Such houses truly are worn quyt out of fashione, as feuds are, which is a great happiness, the cuntrie being generally more civilized than it was."

This was the voice of a Restoration Scots noble—civilized, luxury-loving, and sophisticated in matters of art and architecture. Moreover, neither his opinions nor his tastes were idiosyncratic. Since the reign of James VI, master masons of sufficient imagination and skill to be labelled *architects* had been embellishing town and country with buildings and houses in a style of mixed ancestry known today as Scottish Renaissance. Of these the most representative was William Wallace, whose masterpiece was **Heriot's Hospital** *(434)*, Edinburgh, begun about 1628, though not completed until 1659 by Robert Mylne, a mason of equal skill. Here the symmetrical courtyard plan is of French or Italian provenance; the battlemented corner pavilions hark back to the traditional Scottish late medieval tower-house; the chapel looks Gothic; the ornamental detail Flemish, and Mylne's cupola baroque. Wallace may also have drawn the original plans for **Drumlanrig Castle** *(387)* in Dumfriesshire, judging from its close similarity to Heriot's Hospital, except for the lack of battlements and for the spectacular classical frontispiece (front porch) with its ascending horseshoe staircase, Corinthian pilasters, and central clock tower surmounted by a ducal coronet. It was built between 1679 and 1681 for William Douglas, first Duke of Queensberry, and the architect was probably James Smith or his father-in-law, Robert Mylne.

Mylne was also one of the master masons engaged in the reconstruction of the **Palace of Holyroodhouse** *(442)*, ordered by Charles II and directed by Sir William Bruce, the King's Surveyor and Master of the Works. Preserving the original sixteenth-century tower erected in the reigns of James IV and James V, Bruce raised another matching tower and joined the two by a low building with a Doric gateway in the center. Behind this facade he built three new ranges around an inner courtyard whose facing walls were decorated with pilasters of the classical orders—Corinthian above Ionic above Doric. The end product was a medieval castle encased in a Renaissance mold, sturdy yet classically elegant—and very Scottish. The king also took the trouble of commissioning Jacob de Wet to paint likenesses of all the long line of Scottish monarchs, legendary and real. These were duly hung in the new palace gallery, but Charles II never saw them. He never came to Edinburgh.

Sir William Bruce, son of a Fife laird, was both architect and garden designer. It was he, according to the architectural historian J. G. Dunbar, "who must be accounted the founder of the classical school in Scotland." He was active in the negotiations leading to Charles II's restoration, was knighted by the grateful king, and became a protégé of the Duke of Lauderdale. For his noble patron Bruce (again assisted by Robert Mylne) remodelled the Matilands' sixteenth-century tower-house, **Thirlestane Castle** *(425)* in Berwickshire, adding the classical front that (with nineteenth-century alterations) still graces this palatial mansion. For himself Bruce built a splendid residence in Kinross-shire, overlooking Loch Leven and its historic castle where Mary, Queen of Scots, was sequestered. Viewable from the outside only, this is a purely classical building, rectangular in shape, symmetrical in its fenestration, and ornamented with Ionic pillars and Corinthian pilasters. Behind the house in the direction of Loch Leven, Bruce also laid out the **Kinross House Garden** *(481)*, which *is* open to the public. How much of the present layout (created early in the twentieth century) is faithful to Bruce's original design is open to question. In any case, the grounds of Kinross House are well worth a visit. Even more so is **Hopetoun House** *(430)*, close to the south shore of the Firth of Forth west of Queensferry, West Lothian. Here too Bruce was the original architect of what became one of Scotland's grandest stately homes, begun in 1699 for Charles Hope, first Earl of Hopetoun. In plan it is a huge U-shaped central block, flanked by squarish outbuildings or "pavilions" connected to the main house by curved wings or screens. The garden front, which remains much as Bruce left it, is clearly of seventeenth-century French provenance. About twenty years after Bruce was finished, Lord Hopetoun commissioned William Adam to remodel the house, both outside and in—a work that was not completed until 1767 by Adam's two more famous sons, Robert and John. Most of William Adam's structural changes are observable on the entrance front and reflect the infuence of the English architect, Sir John Vanbrugh. Here, in contrast to Bruce's reserved classicism on the other side, Adam's curvilinear forms and exuberant ornamentation more closely resemble the baroque than the Palladian style then fashionable in England.

The senior Adam hailed from Kirkcaldy, made a small fortune in Edinburgh in a variety of business enterprises, and rose rapidly in reputation as an architect, thanks in part to the patronage of John Dalrymple, second Earl of Stair, son of the author of the Glencoe massacre and himself a Field Marshal in the British Army and Ambassador to France. In 1728 Adam obtained the government post of Clerk and Storekeeper of the Works, and two years later he received the more important appointment of Mason to the Board of Ordnance in North Britain. These appointments followed shortly on the building, between 1721 and 1726, of **Floors Castle** *(415)* near Kelso, for John Ker, first Duke of Roxburghe and Secretary of State for

Scotland. How much Adam had to do with designing this house is uncertain, but there is little doubt that he made some contribution, perhaps as assistant to Sir John Vanbrugh. Of the great baroque palace visible today, only the central block was finished at this time, the flanking wings being the work of the Edinburgh architect, William Playfair, in the 1840s.

Whatever the extent of Adam's responsibility for Floors, there is certainly no doubt that it was he who designed **Duff House** *(530)*, in Banff, begun in 1730 for the very wealthy William Duff, later Earl of Fife. Though he planned to re-create the symmetrical, classical style of Hopetoun House with a central block flanked by pavilions attached by shallow wings or screens, Adam spent so much of his patron's money on the main part of the house that, rich as he was, Duff took alarm, and the additions on the two sides were never built. The upshot is a tall, massive, rectangular block with four corner towers, serenely classical in detail, but nonclassical in its distinctly vertical appearance. More typical of the eighteenth century, and the most distinctly Palladian of all of the senior Adam's works, is **Haddo House** *(539)* in Aberdeenshire, built (1732–1735) for William Gordon, second Earl of Aberdeen. Again the architect was William Adam, though he consulted the eminent Scottish Palladian, Sir John Clerk, at every stage of design and construction. As at Hopetoun House, there is a large central block with a pavilion on each side. Though later modified, the main entrance was on the first story above the ground floor, reached by a double curving flight of steps.

Finally, only two years before his death in 1748, the elder Adam was commissioned by the third Duke of Argyll to supervise the construction of **Inveraray Castle** *(463)*. He was assisted by his sons John and Robert, but the architect was Roger Morris, renowned in England for his Palladian houses. For Argyll, however, Morris designed a Gothic Revival mansion, based on plans drawn originally by Vanbrugh but modified to conform to the new craze for "gothick" ornamentation started at Strawberry Hill near London by Horace Walpole. The interior was drastically modified in the 1770s by the fifth duke, and the exterior again remodelled after a fire in 1877 when Anthony Salvin raised the main roof and added conical caps to the corner towers. Today's visitor to Inveraray Castle will be hard put to detect traces of William Adam's influence, but when the most powerful noble in Scotland was ready to begin construction of a country seat suitable to his dignity, it was inevitable that he would turn for help to the country's most renowned architect.

Country houses without matching "policies," i.e., parks and gardens, were unthinkable, so it is no surprise that gardening also took a forward leap in the seventeenth and eighteenth centuries. In the Early Middle Ages each monastery doubtless had a garden, but, like the monastic orchards, these were largely utilitarian and devoted to vegetables and medicinal herbs. In the fifteenth century there were probably "knot gardens" in Scotland. These were formed of geometric patterns of low clipped evergreen hedges mixed with herbs of grey tint—box, lavender, and rosemary being the most common plants in use. None, of course, has survived, but on the grounds of **Haggs Castle** *(400)* near Glasgow there is an authentic reproduction. Knot gardens were made to be seen from above, as is evident from the "King's Knot" lying to the west of **Stirling Castle** *(477)* and viewable from that part of the upper square known as the "Lady's Hole." Today the geometrically patterned earthen mound is grassed over, but it probably once displayed shrubs and herbs, possibly with various colored earths or gravels intermixed.

The garden at Stirling may have existed as long ago as 1450, though the present remains probably date from the mid–seventeenth century. By this time the fashion for French and Italian parterres had reached Scotland. The parterre was very similar to the knot garden, but more elaborate. Probably the earliest were those installed at the royal palaces of Holyrood and Falkland, but of these nothing remains. (The present charming garden of **Falkland Palace** *[488]* is a creation of the 1940s and not a reproduction of the original parterre.) The "pleasance" of **Edzell Castle** *(509)* in Angus (described in Chapter 6) dates from the first decade of the seventeenth century. Its central, geometrically arranged plantings are typical of the period, but the intricate brickwork of the enclosing walls is unique. Not at all unique, however, is the concept of the walled garden. These exist in all parts of Britain, but nowhere in such numbers as in Scotland, probably because weather conditions in the north required greater-than-average protection for any but the hardiest plants.

Pitmedden Garden *(543)* in Aberdeenshire is not only walled but sunken—doubtless so that the designs of the parterre could better be seen from above. This is today one of the most magnificent horticultural sights in Britain. It was first laid out in 1675 by Sir Alexander Seton and his wife Dame Margaret Lauder and may have been copied from the French-style parterre at Holyroodhouse Palace installed by Charles I. That, at least, was the assumption made by the National Trust for Scotland when it restored Pitmedden according to a drawing of a "bird's eye view of Edinburgh" executed in 1647. Six miles of clipped box form the outlines of the designs here, and no fewer than thirty thousand annuals are incorporated within these patterns. The employment of such modern plants as alyssum and begonia is somewhat anachronistic, to be sure, but the result is more colorful and probably more aesthetically satisfying than the original— except perhaps to purists.

Pitmedden is French in provenance and appearance. **Drummond Castle**

Garden *(501)* near Crieff is now distinctly Italian, though probably not always so. The garden lies in a deep valley behind the much rebuilt fifteenth-century tower house (not open to the public), and the view of it from the upper terrace is breathtaking. In the center is a multifaceted sun dial designed by Charles I's master mason John Mylne, and it seems likely that the original garden was laid out about the same time. In 1830, however, the parterre was Italianized with the addition of a variety of classical statues, urns, etc., and the plantings arranged in the form of a St. Andrew's Cross or saltire. A more modest parterre of about the same date lies at one side of Tyninghame House in East Lothian (not open to the public). An older part of **Tyninghame House Gardens** *(455)*, however, dates from about 1660. This is the walled garden with its splendid high hedges of yew.

More great yew hedges are to be seen at **Crathes Castle** *(545)* in Aberdeenshire (described in Chapter 6), arguably the most impressive in Scotland. The remainder of the gorgeous array of shrubs and herbaceous plants at Crathes, however, dates from the twentieth century. Roughly contemporary with the equally fine lime trees of Tyninghame House and Crathes was the great arboreal garden of John Dalrymple, second Earl of Stair, at **Castle Kennedy Gardens** *(376)* in Wigtownshire. Field Marshall, veteran of the Duke of Marlborough's campaigns, and Ambassador to France, he laid out the grounds of the old (now ruined) family castle in the form of a giant wheel, with avenues of trees forming the spokes and a large circular lily pond the hub. The inspiration was French (probably William le Nôtre's great garden at Versailles), but the avenues were named after battles fought by the British against the French. For this gigantic job of landscaping, Stair commandeered the services of two regiments of dragoons—the Royal Scots Greys and the Inniskilling Fusiliers. Such were the privileges allowed to favored grandees of Scotland under the rule of the Hanoverian kings.

RELIGIOUS ART, ARCHITECTURE, AND WORSHIP

Great houses and noble "policies" were not the only means available to Scottish magnates intent on advertising their wealth and status. As in the past, heavy expenditures on funerary art offered a splendid opportunity to combine piety with conspicuous consumption. Marble and alabaster, as well as native stone, were used as raw material, and sculptors versed in the exacting requirements of baroque statuary could be found locally or imported from abroad. Among the more magnificent of the seventeenth-century aristocratic tombs is that of George Home, first Earl of Dunbar, and Treasurer of Scotland under James VI. In **Dunbar Parish Church** *(454)*, East Lothian, where he was buried in 1611, his memory is honored by a truly splendid kneeling effigy of the earl in his Garter robes beneath a busy baroque canopy of brown and white marble. Another is that of David Murray, first Viscount Stormont, who died in 1631 and is commemorated in the chapel atop the Moot Hill at **Scone Palace** *(506)* with a fine alabaster monument showing the deceased kneeling at prayer along with his friends, the Marquis of Tullibardine and the Earl Marischal. In Largs, Ayrshire, the **Skelmorlie Aisle** *(391)* is even more elaborate. Originally attached to the parish kirk, which has since disappeared, this is a mausoleum built in 1636 by Sir Robert Montgomery of Skelmorlie for his deceased wife. An elaborate canopied tomb of carved stone rises from a sunken well and presumably once held the recumbent effigies of Lady Montgomery and, after his death in 1651, of the founder himself, both of whom lie buried underneath. (It was their son, Sir James, who was a member of the delegation sent to London in 1689 to offer the crown to King William.) On the barrel-vaulted ceiling above are paintings of the four seasons, the signs of the zodiac, various biblical characters, and, incredibly, the coats of arms of the twelve tribes of Israel. In the north transept of the church of **Culross Abbey** *(485)* in Fife is the fine tomb of the wealthy entrepreneur, Sir George Bruce (d. 1642), builder of **The Palace** *(485)*, knighted by James VI for his success in Culross in developing the nearby coal seams. Below the recumbent effigies of Sir George and his wife are the kneeling figures of their three sons and five daughters, their hands clasped in prayer. The **Durisdeer Parish Kirk** *(388)* in Dumfriesshire contains a still more elaborate monument to James Douglas, second Duke of Queensberry, Scottish Secretary of State and owner of nearby **Drumlanrig Castle** *(387)*. The monument in the "Queensberry Aisle" would look more at home in Rome than in this tiny hamlet in southwestern Scotland. In the center of a checkered marble floor a baldachino with twisted columns stands above the entrance to the burial vault where lie the effigies of the duke and duchess, the latter prone, the former recumbent but leaning on one elbow. All is white marble except for the panel behind the effigies, which is black. The sculptor was John van Nost; the date of execution, 1713. Within this rather simple village kirk the effect of all this magnificence is startling.

   Less elaborate but more functional is the "Hopetoun Aisle" in **Abercorn Church** *(430)* near South Queensferry, West Lothian. Here is no tomb but a prettily decorated gallery where the occupants of nearby **Hopetoun House** *(430)* could enjoy seclusion while attending Sunday services and even have a cold lunch in the adjoining suite of panelled rooms between morning and afternoon sessions. "Laird's lofts" of this sort were common in post-

Reformation Scottish kirks. They account in part for the large number of T-plan churches, so-called because they were built with an aisle projecting at right angles from the center of the long axis, thus forming a T. Within this aisle, which directly faced the pulpit standing in the center of the opposite long wall, might be a gallery for the local grandee, and perhaps his family's burial vault below.

Sometimes such an aisle would be added to a preexisting rectangular church; sometimes the T-plan was incorporated into new construction. In the first category is **Pencaitland Church** *(458)* in East Lothian. Built on medieval foundations, the nave here is probably of early-sixteenth-century (pre-Reformation) date, but the sacristy on the north side of the east end (the Winton Aisle) was built in the thirteenth century. After the Reformation, a laird's loft (since removed) was installed in the sacristy; and in the seventeenth century another aisle was projected north from the middle of the nave, a tower was added to the west end, and inside it a new loft entered by an external staircase was installed. What we have here then is a T-plan church with one angle of the T partially filled in by the original medieval church around which the present building was constructed.

More characteristic of post-Reformation churches is **Yester Kirk** *(457)* in Gifford, East Lothian, built in 1708–1710, possibly by James Smith, who designed nearby Yester House for John Hay, second Marquis of Tweeddale. Here the pulpit stands in the center of the long (west) wall of the nave, and facing it is the laird's loft at the base of the T. Designated "the Tweeddale Gallery," this was, of course, reserved for the marquis and his family. It was entered by a staircase from the outside and has an anteroom that once had a fireplace. (At the foot of the staircase is the grave of James Witherspoon, father of the one-time President of Princeton University and signer of the American Declaration of Independence, John Witherspoon, whose nearby birthplace is marked with a bronze plaque.)

The Far North of Scotland is well supplied with T-plan kirks of late-seventeenth and early-eighteenth-century date. **St. Andrew's Kirk** *(552)* in Tongue was built by Donald MacKay, Lord Reay, in 1680 and rebuilt in 1729. Here the pulpit stands at the center of the crossbar of the T, faced by pews in the long arm, with the laird's loft at the back. The original Reay Loft was removed in 1951 and placed in the custody of the **National Museum of Antiquities** *(447)* in Edinburgh. In Caithness, the **Reay Parish Kirk** *(553)* is small, but remarkably pretty, thanks partly to recent restoration. Built about 1740, the canopied pulpit (probably original) again stands in the middle of the south wall of the church's long axis and is faced by a laird's loft in the north aisle, in front of which is the elders' pew and a long communion table. At **St. Andrew's Golspie** *(551)*, completed in 1738, a high canopied central pulpit stands in the middle of the south wall, facing the

Earl of Sutherland's richly decorated loft and retiring room in the north aisle, and at both ends of the long axis of the nave are additional galleries.

The ground plan and seating arrangements of all these churches were adapted both to the requirements of Presbyterian worship and the demand of Scotland's "upper class" for deference. Notwithstanding the Protestant clergy's efforts to free themselves from lay interference, nobles and lairds had played a leading role in Church affairs from the very beginning of the Reformation. The restoration of lay patronage by Act of Parliament in 1712 tightened their grip over kirk business at the parish level, and, in a sense, the proliferation of country kirks with the best seats in the gallery reserved for the local magnate was a symbolic recognition of that fact.

Yet the overriding factor determining the layout of Protestant churches was the requirement for a single-chambered building in which people could easily hear the preacher and take part in the celebration of the Lord's Supper. The T-plan kirk answered this need and was the most commonly used. But a church building so constructed that seats and galleries could be grouped around a central pulpit would also serve the purpose. Such was the thought that lay behind the design for **Lauder Kirk** *(424)* in Berwickshire, built by Sir William Bruce for the Duke of Lauderdale as a sort of appendage to nearby **Thirlestane Castle** *(425)*. The building was laid out on the plan of a Greek cross, with four arms of equal length extending from the center, which is topped by an octagonal steeple. The pulpit is attached to a pillar under the central tower, and its occupant is clearly visible and audible from the seats and galleries facing it on all sides. The logic of this arrangement is so obvious, given the requirements of the Presbyterian service, that it is surprising that many churches of this shape were not so constructed.

Mention has been made of the parliamentary act of 1712 restoring the right of patronage (i.e., nominating parish ministers) to the laymen who had been deprived of it by the Revolutionary settlement of 1690–1691. The fact that the Crown was the patron of about a third of all the parishes in Scotland lay behind the passage of the legislation, but made it no more palatable to those staunch kirkmen who regarded it as a subversion of Presbyterian principles. When in 1732 the General Assembly compounded the offense by further restrictions on congregational rights, a number of congregations, following the lead of Ebenezer Erskine, seceded from the established church to form an "Associate Synod." This was only the first of the many schisms within the Church of Scotland that fragmented its unity and produced within its ranks more than a century of bitterness and factionalism.

Such continuous wrangling was, of course, testimony to the centrality of religious worship in the lives of most Scots, at least well into the nineteenth century. A covenanted people did not take lightly their personal and societal obligations implicit in the bargain struck between God and the Scottish nation. On the more mundane level, the role of the kirk in the lives of most parishioners was all-encompassing. It was, first of all, the community social center—the most convenient, if not the only place where neighbors might regularly forgather. Secondly, in the absence of any effective local police force, especially in the rural areas, the kirk's moral sanctions and exemplary punishments, such as assigning sinners to the "repentance stool" during Sunday services or chaining them in jougs to the church wall outside the door, were about the only means available for maintaining law and order. Thirdly, with no newspapers in general circulation, the pulpit was almost the only mechanism by which public information could be circulated. Finally, the kirk sessions supervised those elementary schools that each parish had been required to establish and maintain under a series of parliamentary acts passed between 1633 and 1696. Although this legislation was not uniformly enforced, the Lowlands of Scotland in the early eighteenth century could boast a rate of literacy superior to that of England or of almost any other country except for certain other strongly Calvinist areas of Western Europe and the North American colonies. Visitors to Scotland were constantly amazed at the sight of mere peasants' closely following, in their own well-worn copies of the King James version, the Sabbath reading of the Bible from the pulpit.

Scotland, however, did not provide an especially fertile ground for the evangelism of such spellbinders as George Whitfield and John Wesley, both of whom came north on more than one proselytizing mission. Methodism never made significant inroads into the established religion as it did in England and Wales. Perhaps Sir Walter Scott (in *Rob Roy*) had the answer: "The Scotch, it is well known, are more remarkable for the exercise of their intellectual powers than for the keenness of their feelings; they are, therefore, more moved by logic than by rhetoric and more attracted by acute and argumentative reasoning on doctrinal points than influenced by . . . enthusiastic appeals to the heart and to the passions. . . ."

But not all Scots were Presbyterians. In the Highlands and Islands there were still pockets of Roman Catholics, mostly among the MacDonalds. Episcopalianism was much more prevalent, especially in the northeast. After the Revolution of 1688–1689 none of the Scottish bishops would take the oath of allegiance to King William, and thus, as nonjurors, were deprived of their livings, as were those among the parish clergy who joined them in their recalcitrance. In 1712 Parliament passed the Act of Toleration, which permitted freedom of worship to Episcopalians in Scotland who would recognize the Hanoverian succession. Those who did so were permitted to set up "qualified" meeting houses where services were conducted according to rites of the Church of England. But many refused the offer, including those bishops still alive who had received their consecration under the authority of the late King James VII. They, and those who continued to follow their lead, remained nonjurors. Thus these Scottish Episcopalians found themselves in the anomalous position of adhering to a Roman Catholic pretender while refusing to swear allegiance to a Protestant monarch and supreme head of the Church of England whose doctrines and forms of worship they emulated. To the government in London this was sheer Jacobitism and all nonjuring Scottish Episcopalians therefore suspect. When sympathy for the exiled Stuarts ripened into open rebellion, Episcopalianism in Scotland inevitably became equated with sedition.

JACOBITISM: 1690–1746

On 10 April 1707 a Jacobite agent, Nathaniel Hooke, arrived at **Slains Castle** *(544)* on the Aberdeenshire coast, seat of John Hay, twelfth Earl of Erroll. He came armed with promises of French assistance to those dissident Scottish nobles who would join an insurrection in favor of the exiled James VIII/III ("the Old Pretender") (See table: "The English Succession: 1603–1760"), now residing at St. Germain en Laye under the protection of King Louis XIV of France. For five years the War of the Spanish Succession had been in progress; the armies of France had suffered serious setbacks at the hands of the Duke of Marlborough at Blenheim and Ramillies. French strategy required a diversionary action that might compel the British to pull their forces back from the Continent, and Scotland was the obvious place for such a maneuver. Hooke took back with him a memorial signed by several nobles promising to raise thirty thousand Scots in rebellion if Louis XIV would furnish six thousand men plus arms. The Sun King agreed. The Pope promised money. James VIII/III left for Dunkirk to head a landing operation on the Scottish coast, but fell sick with measles, so that the expedition was delayed until March 1708, when it finally sailed. Arriving off the mouth of the Firth of Forth, the French commander, on hearing of the approach of an English fleet, decided to run for home without disembarking his troops. Thus the danger passed, though the British government was sufficiently alarmed to improve the defensive works at **Stirling Castle** *(477)*. In retrospect, the episode can be seen as a preview of the next four decades of Jacobite adventurism in Scotland: extravagant expectations of local support for the exiled Stuarts; false hopes of massive aid from France (and/ or Spain and/or the Papacy); faulty organization and timing of overseas expeditions; and effective naval and military resistance on the part of the British government. In sum: wishful thinking, poor planning, inept execution, and superior opposition—all spelling almost certain failure.

French encouragement, however, could not be blamed for the next failed Jacobite enterprise—called in Scotland "The Fifteen" after the year in which it broke out. The War of the Spanish Succession had ended in 1713, leaving France in a worse position than before the fighting started. The Peace of Utrecht required Louis XIV to recognize the Hanoverian succession in Britain, and the Old Pretender accordingly was forced to take up residence elsewhere in Europe. Rebellion in Scotland commenced when John Erskine, sixth Earl of Mar, disgruntled with his treatment by the first Hanoverian king, George I, repaired to his family estate in Aberdeenshire and at Braemar raised the standard of revolt on 6 September 1715. Mar's call to arms was answered by about twelve thousand recruits—from the strongly Episcopalian northeastern counties and the anti-Campbell clans of the central and western Highlands. At Sheriffmuir near Dunblane on 13 November this ill-sorted but eager horde encountered a smaller army led by the second Duke of Argyll. The ensuing battle was a draw, but at the end of it Argyll held the field and Mar's undisciplined troops began to melt away. One of the participants (in a manner of speaking) was Rob Roy MacGregor, a notorious outlaw who had for years lived off the plunder of his neighbors in the region between Loch Lomond and Loch Katrine. Ostensibly pledged to the Jacobites, MacGregor in fact kept his people out of the battle until the end of it and then set them to robbing the baggage and dead of both sides. Celebrated by Sir Walter Scott as Scotland's Robin Hood, this dedicated scoundrel lived to a ripe old age and died in bed. His grave in **Balquhidder Kirkyard** *(500)*, near Lochearnhead, Perthshire, is today a minor shrine for visitors who share Sir Walter's view of Scottish history, as well of course for many bearing the surname of MacGregor. Personal effects belonging to Rob Roy can be seen at **Inveraray Castle** *(463)* and at **Abbotsford** *(419)*, Sir Walter Scott's house near Melrose, Roxburghshire.

In October another detachment of Jacobites had invaded England but, the day after Sheriffmuir, was intercepted and defeated by government troops at Preston in Lancashire. The Old Pretender, characteristically tardy, landed at Peterhead in late December and, seeing that the game was up, reembarked for France six weeks later. The Earl of Mar went with him. Government recriminations against the rebels were less severe than might have been expected. **Kildrummy Castle** *(537)*, which had served as Mar's headquarters, was dismantled. Nineteen Scottish peers were forfeited, but only one (William Gordon, sixth Viscount Kenmure) lost his head. Some of their followers were transported to the British plantations overseas. A few Episcopalian meeting houses were closed down. Legislation was passed to disarm the Highland clans, but only those already inclined to loyalty to the government seem to have turned in their weapons.

In the event, lenity produced meager results and Jacobitism continued to flourish. A little more than three years after James VIII/III had fled back to France, a tiny Spanish force was landed on the northwest coast of Scotland to support another Highland rising. The Spaniards succeeded in capturing and garrisoning **Eilean Donan Castle** *(548)* on Loch Duich until three British frigates arrived and all but blew away this ancient stronghold of the MacKenzies and MacRaes. Soon thereafter, in June 1719 at Glenshiel, a dozen miles away, government troops easily overwhelmed a rebel band of Highlanders. For another quarter of a century Jacobitism in Scotland remained quiescent.

A major reason for this unusual state of affairs was the dispatch to Scotland in 1725 of Major General (later Field Marshal) George Wade, as commander-in-chief. One of his first steps in the pacification of the Highlands was to recruit from among the clans loyal to King George (chiefly Campbells, Grants, Frasers, and Munros) six independent companies of soldiers (about five hundred men in all) to "watch among the braes," i.e., to patrol the areas where disaffection was most likely to reappear and to enforce the disarming act. In 1739 four more companies were added, and in May 1740 the 42d regiment of regulars (later the 43d) was officially mustered at Aberfeldy, Perthshire, at a site now commemorated by the **Black Watch Memorial** *(496)*. This is a bigger-than-life-size statue (erected in 1887) of a Highland soldier armed with a basket-hilted broadsword, dirk, pistol, musket, bayonet, and cartridge belt. The regiment's distinguished history is memorialized in the **Black Watch Museum** *(505)* in Balhousie Castle in Perth, one of the best of its kind in Scotland.

"Black Watch" was the unofficial name attached to this regiment because of the sombre colors—dark green, navy blue, and black—of the belted plaids worn over the soldiers' regulation scarlet jackets and waistcoats. The belted plaid, or *feileadh mor*, had been the basic outer-garment worn by male Highlanders since at least the early seventeenth century. It was about twelve to eighteen feet in length, five feet in width, and woven of wool. To put it on, a man would lay it on the ground with the belt underneath and fold it partially into vertical pleats; then he would lie down in it lengthwise with the lower edge level with his knees; seize the two outer edges and wrap the cloth around his waist; fasten the belt, stand up, and then drape the upper part over one shoulder or wear it as a hood. The lower part of the plaid then fell to his knees as a pleated skirt. When not worn as a garment, the *feileadh mor* could be unbelted and used as a blanket or ground cover. Some time in the eighteenth century the belted plaid began to give way to the *feileadh beag* or kilt. This simple knee-length pleated skirt was nothing more than the *feileadh mor* with the top two-thirds cut off. Less multi-purposed than the belted plaid, it was also less cumbersome and became the standard item of apparel where easy body movement was called for. Neither of these garments, however, entirely replaced the trews, which were tight-fitting trousers incorporating hose, more suited than plaid or kilt for riding horseback.

In the Highlands the fabric out of which plaids, kilts, or trews were cut was often woven in a checked or striped pattern that was called *breacan*, meaning parti-colored or speckled. If different-colored yarns were used in a fixed design (known as a *sett*) the woven cloth would resemble what came to be called *tartan*. In the eighteenth century, however, only vegetable dyes were available, and the material, even when new, would not have been as brightly hued as the chemically dyed modern product. (A few authentic eighteenth-century tartans are on view at the **Museum of Scottish Tartans** *[500]* in the village of Comrie west of Crieff, Perthshire, and at the **Canongate Tolbooth** *[441]* in Edinburgh.)

Because the Black Watch was a military unit, the sett of the tartan issued to its members was uniform. This was a novelty in Scotland. It had not been customary, and was not to be until the late eighteenth century at the earliest, for Highlanders to wear distinctive tartans as insignia of their clan affiliation. The development of clan tartans as such did not take place generally until the early nineteenth century under circumstances to be described in the next chapter. The tartan as uniform dress originated with the Black Watch and was thereafter copied, with slight modifications, by other independent Highland companies and regiments. The point is important only because of the common, persistent, and erroneous belief that the colors and setts of the clan tartans sold and displayed everywhere in Scotland today are of ancient origin and were once worn to distinguish one clan from another in the heyday of internecine Highland warfare. Highlanders at war carried badges of heather, bog-myrtle, etc., in their bonnets as clan insignia; they did not wear tartan of uniform design.

The government in London was not so fatuous as to believe that Highlanders garbed in His Majesty's uniform were sufficient to police the Highlands. Companies of British Army regulars were sent north to permanent stations, there to stand on guard against repetitions of The Fifteen. One of Wade's jobs was to prepare the way by restoring old forts in Scotland and building new ones. At **Dumbarton Castle** *(475)*, the ruined north curtain wall was repaired, the old south defenses were replaced by King George's Battery, and the Governor's House was built. As a companion to Fort William, a new installation was constructed at the head of Loch Ness on the site of the present Benedictine Abbey in Fort Augustus. Near the town of Kingussie, **Ruthven Barracks** *(521)*—now an attractive ruin—was enlarged and strengthened. Its near-twin was **Bernera Barracks** *(516)*—also ruined—in Glen Elg overlooking the Sound of Sleat and the Isle of Skye. At Inverness, on the site of the castle to be built in the nineteenth century, Wade constructed his northernmost fort and named it after the reigning monarch, George I.

To connect these nodal points and to establish permanent lines of military communication throughout the Highlands, the general then began the greatest road-building scheme to have been undertaken in Britain since the Roman occupation. Like the Romans before him, he used soldiers as his primary labor force, and even his techniques of road construction were not dissimilar to theirs. Topsoil was dug out to the required depth of the foundations; large stones were levered by crowbars, small stones were smashed with sledgehammers; at least two feet of gravel was tipped into the trench thus dug and beaten with shovels; over boggy land, embankments would be built on top of timber rafts; milestones were set in place, as well as marker stones to guide the traveller in winter months; and finally, bridges were put up across rivers too deep to be forded. In this manner, Wade built altogether about 250 miles of road between 1725 and 1732. There were three basic routes: the first had two branches running north from Dunkeld and Crieff respectively to connect at Dalnacardoch (now on the A 9 about 19 miles northwest of Pitlochry) and thence as a single track through Dalwhinnie and on to Inverness. The second (the Great Glen road) connected Inverness with Fort Augustus and Fort William. The third ran from Dalwhinnie northwestward across the formidable Corrieyairack Pass to Fort Augustus.

Except for the last named route, modern roads parallel or in some cases overlie those set out by Wade, and the really diligent traveller can still find numerous traces of this truly remarkable feat of engineering. Mentioned here are only those most easily identifiable (though now turf-covered) and least likely to require arduous walking and climbing. On the Dunkeld to Inverness road, three sites bear investigation. At Calvine on the east side of the A 9, and plainly signposted, a steep climb of a quarter of a mile leads to a stretch of **Wade's Road** *(499)* running northwest along the east side of the motorway. About seven miles northwest of Calvine on the east side of the A 9 stands **Wade's Stone** *(499)*, an eight-foot-high marker bearing the date 1729, moved to its present position beside the southbound lane of the dual carriageway. About half a mile north of Dalwhinnie, where the A 889 bears left, a section of the **Wade's Road** *(521)* lies straight ahead. On the old route from Crieff to Dalnacardoch there is a good section of **Wade's Road** *(502)* veering left off the A 822 just north of Faulford Inn about five miles from Crieff; also another stretch, parallel to and west of the A 822 from just north of the bridge crossing the River Almond; and still another from Corrymuckloch west of the A 822 north to Amulree. At Aberfeldy, adjacent to the Black Watch Memorial already mentioned, the River Tay is crossed by **Wade's Bridge** *(496)*, the only one of this species to have been built of ashlar and ornamented at both ends with obelisks. Wade's **Tummel Bridge** *(497)* crosses the River Tummel alongside the modern iron bridge carrying the B 846.

Along the route connecting Inverness with Fort Augustus and Fort William, Wade made a false start in 1726, laying his road too far to the east over mountains impassable in the winter. In 1732 he put down a new stretch hugging the southeastern shore of Loch Ness, which became the permanent road. The 1726 road roughly corresponds to today's B 862, but where the B 852 branches westward south of Dorres, **Wade's Road** *(520)* of 1732 begins and continues south along the loch until it rejoins the B 862. Though modernized and passable by automobile, this single-track road probably looks as much like the original as is possible, given the passage of more than 250 years. At Inverfarigaig on the B 852 and, about six miles south, at Whitebridge on the B 862, there are **Wade Bridges** *(515, 520)* upstream of those now in use. More impressive than these, however, is **Wade's High Bridge** *(524)*, across the River Spean between Fort Augustus and Fort William. It stands about two miles west of the present Spean Bridge and about a mile north of the A 82 on a signposted minor road.

By 1732, Wade's network of military roads was essentially complete. British army regulars stood guard in the new and expanded forts in the Great Glen and elsewhere, and four independent companies of loyal Highlanders patrolled the hinterlands. Then international events once more intruded themselves upon the Scottish scene, stopping, and then reversing, the government's program of pacifying the Highlands. In 1739 war broke out between Britain and Spain (the War of Jenkin's Ear). That year King George II ordered the formation of the 42d Highland Regiment of Foot (the Black Watch). The war with Spain soon escalated into a more widespread conflict, with Britain, Austria, and Sardinia lined up against France, Spain, Prussia, Saxony, and Savoy in the War of the Austrian Succession. In March 1743 the Black Watch was ordered to march to London, ostensibly for a review by the king, but actually to be shipped to Flanders. More than a hundred of the men mutinied on the grounds that they had been "levied only to guard the Highlands and not to be employed elsewhere." The mutineers were subdued and dealt with harshly, and the regiment was dispatched to the Continent on schedule. It would have been better for the British government had they never left Scotland. Though small in number, their presence had helped deter a resurgence of Jacobitism. Now, with France once more at war with Britain, Scotland again became a target of opportunity for French diversionary tactics, and the nuisance value of the exiled Stuarts soared.

By this time James VIII/III had come to rest in Italy, old and discouraged by a lifetime of failure and repeated betrayals by one European ruler after another. His twenty-four-year-old son, Charles Edward Stuart ("the Young Pretender"), was, however, of a different mettle. Nurtured on the nostalgic fantasies of a court in exile, he inevitably yearned to return to a homeland he had never known. With the French preparing a massive invasion of England from Dunkirk, Charles Edward made his way from Rome to France to join the expedition. On 24 January 1744, however, a violent storm destroyed the French transports and the invasion was called off. The prince was not dismayed. Somehow he managed to organize a landing force of two French ships, about seven hundred men, fifteen hundred muskets, and eighteen hundred broadswords and set sail for Scotland in early July 1745. The ships were intercepted by *HMS Lion* off the Lizard, and the French vessel carrying the troops and weapons was so badly mauled that she had to return home. But the *Du Teillay*, aboard which rode Charles Edward Stuart, escaped to carry the Young Pretender and a small company (the "seven men of Moidart") to Eriskay in the Outer Hebrides, where they went ashore on 23 July. Two days later the prince was on the mainland, near Arisaig in southwestern Inverness-shire.

Meanwhile, British forces in Flanders had been faring badly. In May at Fontenoy the French commander, Marshal Saxe, had soundly drubbed the army led by another young man of twenty-four years—William Augustus, Duke of Cumberland, younger son of George II. (Notwithstanding the outcome, the Black Watch performed valiantly on this occasion.) Saxe then led his armies into the Austrian Netherlands (modern Belgium), capturing Tournai, Ghent, Oudenarde, and, on 12 August, Ostend. The Dutch Republic stood in grave danger. It was in the wake of these disasters that Cumberland received word of the Young Pretender's landing in Scotland as well as orders from George II to send Sir John Ligonier home with ten battalions to meet the Jacobite challenge. The duke complied, but not cheerfully. His heart was set on a return match with Marshal Saxe.

On 19 August Charles Edward arrived at Glenfinnan at the northern end of Loch Shiel and unfurled the Stuart standard. (The site is now marked by the **Glenfinnan Monument** *[516]*, a high pillar of stone with the statue of a Highlander on top, beautifully silhouetted against the loch. Across the road is the National Trust's **Glenfinnan Visitors' Centre** *[516]* with both audio and visual aids describing the rebellion.) "The Forty-five," traditionally celebrated as the most romantic episode in Scottish history, had begun.

The prince's little army was at first made up chiefly of Clan Cameron of

Lochiel and the Clanranald and Kinlochmoidart MacDonalds. As he pushed into the central Highlands and beyond, he picked up volunteers mainly among the Stewarts of Appin, MacLeans, MacDonnells, various septs of MacDonalds, the Atholl men (Murrays and Robertsons), MacIntoshes, MacPhersons, Gordons, Farquharsons, Frasers, and sundry other small contingents. But the total number who rallied to the Stuart cause in 1745 was small—probably never more than about eight thousand and more often closer to five thousand, i.e., less than half the size of the Jacobite army that had "come out" during The Fifteen. Against this figure must be placed the equal or greater number of Highlanders who either fought for King George or in effect supported his government by declining to aid the prince. In this category were the MacDonalds of Sleat, the MacLeods of Dunvegan, most of the Grants and MacKenzies, the northern clans of MacKays and Munros, and, of course, the Campbells. Indeed, it would probably be fair to say that hatred of the Campbells, at least among their neighbors in the central and western Highlands, was a stronger motivating factor in bringing these people out to the aid of Prince Charles Edward than was any residual loyalty to the House of Stuart.

The clansmen who fought for the prince (and most of those on the other side as well) would have been armed with single- or double-edged basket-hilted swords (sometimes mistakenly referred to as "claymores"); nail-studded, leather-covered, circular wooden shields called targets or targes; dirks (long daggers without guards); occasionally a Lochaber axe (a broad blade backed by a hook and mounted on a long pole); and smooth-bore, muzzle-loading muskets without bayonets. Gunpowder was carried in horns fashioned for the purpose, and bullets were stored in sporrans, i.e., leather pouches worn on a tight belt around the waist—not over the genitals, as was later fashionable when Highland dress became stylish. (The best collections of eighteenth-century Highland weapons to be seen today are in the **National Museum of Antiquities** *[447]* in Edinburgh, the **Glasgow Art Gallery and Museum** *[407]*, and the **West Highland Museum** *[515]* in Fort William.)

The Highlanders were ferocious fighters, though undisciplined and unversed in the formal infantry tactics of eighteenth century armies, which relied most heavily on massed volleys of musket-fire. Instead, these doughty warriors normally surged onto the battlefield; discharged one round from their muskets and then dropped them to the ground; fired their pistols and then threw them at the heads of their opponents; and finally rushed against the enemy lines with nothing but their swords. It was an unnerving experience for their foes, as the government troops would soon discover.

The clansmen also moved rapidly on the march. Driving up the Great

Glen, they crossed over the fearsome Corrieyairack Pass; occupied **Blair Castle** *(498)*, property of the Hanoverian John Murray, second Duke of Atholl; moved on through Dunkeld, Perth, and Stirling; and occupied Edinburgh on 17 September, slightly less than a month after the prince had first raised the standard of rebellion at Glenfinnan. Four days later the Jacobites, in a battle at Prestonpans outside the city that lasted no more than ten minutes, routed government forces commanded by Sir John Cope, who fled the field and fetched up, like Edward II after Bannockburn, in Berwick. Edinburgh society rejoiced in the good fortune of this handsome, charming, and victorious young prince, now beginning to be referred to as "Bonnie Prince Charlie" (an undignified title that Queen Victoria would one day forbid to be used in her presence). Poor Sir John, however, became a laughingstock; subject of a derisory ballad, commencing, "Hey Johnie Cope are ye wauking yet?"; and victim of a widely circulated canard that he was the first general in Europe to have served as the courier bearing the initial tidings of his own defeat in battle.

On 1 November the prince, with an army of about five thousand men, marched for England. By 4 December the Jacobites had penetrated as far as Derby, only 127 miles from London. They had met little resistance but had gathered few reinforcements from English Tories, whom the prince had expected to join his cause. These disgruntled squires who had so often toasted "the king over the water" were less than anxious to risk their lives and fortunes on his behalf. As one of them said of his fellow English Jacobites, "No people in the universe know better the difference between drinking and fighting." On 6 December Prince Charles Edward reluctantly agreed to turn back—persuaded by one of his officers, Lord George Murray (the Duke of Atholl's brother), and by threats of desertion among the Highlanders. It was a sensible decision. By now, not only had Ligonier's ten battalions been brought back to England from Flanders, but the Duke of Cumberland himself had come home with five regiments of Dutch and British troops. The King of France had made a good investment. For the price of two ships, a small amount of arms and money, and the loan of about a thousand regular troops (mostly Scots and Irish in French service), Louis XV had succeeded in drawing most of the British army off the Continent.

On 17 January 1746 the Jacobites scored one more victory—at Falkirk against General Henry Hawley. Then, with Cumberland known to be heading north, Charles Edward led his army of about five thousand back into the Highlands and to Inverness, which the Jacobites captured on 21 February. By mid-February the Hanoverian duke had established headquarters at Aberdeen. In the same month the rebels burned **Ruthven Barracks**

(521) and captured Fort Augustus, and in mid-March Lord George Murray laid siege to **Blair Castle** *(498)*, his brother's house in Perthshire then garrisoned by Cumberland's troops. By the end of the month, however, Jacobite fortunes began to falter. Murray decamped from Blair and went back to Inverness; the prince's forces called off their siege of Fort William; a British naval patrol intercepted a French sloop carrying badly needed money to Charles Edward and forced it to run aground on Melness Sands near Tongue in Sutherland, where a band of loyal MacKays took it into custody; a relief force of fifteen hundred men was sent north by the prince to recover the treasure, but was intercepted and defeated by loyal clans under the Earl of Sutherland and Lord Reay. On 4 April Cumberland moved out of Aberdeen, reaching Nairn in time to celebrate his twenty-fifth birthday on the eve of the final showdown between the House of Hanover and the House of Stuart.

In the early morning hours of 16 April Cumberland's troops—about nine thousand strong—marched out of Nairn westward toward Inverness. At about 11:00 A.M. they sighted the Jacobite army—less than five thousand in number—drawn up in two parallel lines across Drummossie Moor south of Culloden, the estate of the absent Lord President of the Court of Session Duncan Forbes, a Hanoverian sympathizer recently in command of the progovernment forces driven out of Inverness by the Jacobites. Prince Charles Edward himself had chosen the battle site—against the advice of Lord George Murray, who would have preferred hillier ground across the River Nairn as more suitable to the Highlanders' style of fighting. Overconfidence born of his easy victories at Prestonpans and Falkirk persuaded the prince to risk an orthodox battle in the eighteenth-century formal fashion against an army of mostly seasoned regular troops, more than twice the size of his own.

The battle commenced at one o'clock in the afternoon. Within an hour the Jacobites were finished. Against the superior gunfire, better discipline, and sheer numbers of the government's troops (including Campbells), Charles Edward's brave and reckless clansmen had no chance. Retreat became a rout. The prince escaped, but hundreds of his men, including the wounded and dying, were mercilessly cut down by English dragoons as they charged the fleeing Highlanders. "I never saw a field thicker of dead," said one eyewitness, a veteran fusilier. On Cumberland's personal orders, no mercy was to be shown. All the way to Inverness the rebels were pursued and slain, no nice distinctions being drawn between battlefield fugitives and civilian bystanders—including women and children. Wounded men who had sought shelter in nearby cottages were shot, bayonetted, or burned to death. Small wonder that even in London the Duke of Cumberland soon came to be known as "The Butcher." Yet in his own mind, and that of many contemporary Englishmen and Lowland Scots, these Highlanders deserved no better. They were considered vermin, wild animals worthy only of extermination—an attitude not unlike that of many American frontiersmen toward the hostile Indians. Moreover, because of these rebels, the Duke of Cumberland had been robbed of his chance of glory in civilized combat with the armies of France.

Today **Culloden Battlefield** *(518)* has been cleared of trees and is undergoing restoration that promises to re-create the scene as it probably appeared on 16 April 1746. Nearby, the National Trust's **Culloden Visitors' Centre** *(518)* contains a good display of explanatory placards and offers a fifteen-minute audiovisual presentation of the battle, the events leading to it, and its aftermath.

Part of the aftermath was the trial and punishment of those rebels taken at Culloden and elsewhere. Three Jacobite peers—Simon Fraser of Lovat; Arthur Elphinstone, sixth Lord Balermino; and William Boyd, fourth Earl of Kilmarnock—were executed for treason. One hundred thirty Jacobites of lower status were also put to death. About two thousand were transported to the plantations or died in the filthy and disease-ridden prisons and prison ships in which they were confined. Close to thirteen hundred prisoners were eventually set free.

But it was the latent military power of the Highland chiefs that was the real threat to domestic peace and security from foreign invasion in Scotland. Accordingly, many of those who had come out for the Stuart cause were forfeited. To prevent the rest from organizing their tenants and clansmen into private armies, Parliament renewed and strengthened the laws against carrying arms in the Highlands, banned the wearing of tartan as an incitement to rebellion, and forbade the bagpipe as an instrument of war. Further to loosen the ties between chiefs and tenants, the Abolition of Heritable Jurisdictions Act (Scotland) of 1747 did away with courts of regality and reduced the competence of courts of barony. To enforce the peace, garrisons were quartered at numerous places throughout the Highlands, including **Braemar Castle** *(539)* and **Corgarff Castle** *(532)* in Aberdeenshire. A fine new fortification was raised on the shore of Moray Firth just east of Inverness and called **Fort George** *(519)*. But the most important contribution of all to the destruction of the clans as military units was the total defeat at Culloden of the clansmen themselves and the campaign of terrorism that followed. Cumberland completed what Dalrymple had so unsuccessfully begun at Glencoe a generation before. But, contrary to one of Scotland's most persistent myths, it was not "Gaeldom" as such that the government was set on destroying. It was the independent military power and juridical authority of the Highland chiefs who for centuries, had enjoyed a quasifeudal autonomy at odds with the claims to sovereignty of the central government, whether in Edinburgh or London.

The young duke, on his way back to England, paused at Fort Augustus and Fort William long enough to set in motion a scorched-earth policy, never to be forgotten in the Highlands for its thoroughness. Castles and cottages were burned, plows broken, cattle driven off, crops confiscated, Roman Catholic and Episcopalian meeting houses destroyed, men killed, women raped. Cumberland returned to London in July to a special thanksgiving service at St. Paul's Cathedral and an anthem, "See the Conquering Hero Comes," composed for the occasion by George Frederick Handel. Next year he was back on the Continent fighting Marshal Saxe, who bested him a second time, at Lauffield. The duke suffered a third disastrous military defeat at Hastenbeck in 1757, after which he came back to England in disgrace.

As to the young prince whose dreams of a Stuart restoration came to an end at Culloden, he escaped the field of battle, and with a price of £30,000 on his head, began five months of wandering "in the heather." Dodging his pursuers with the connivance of many Highlanders, he made his way back to Loch nam Uamh near Arisaig, where he had first come ashore, then to the Outer Hebrides, then back "over the sea to Skye," then to Raasay, then again to Skye, then across to the mainland and into Glen Moriston, then on to Badenoch, and finally back again to Loch nam Uamh to be picked up at last by a French ship, providentially named *L'Heureux*.

For the rest of his life (i.e., until 1788), Charles Edward Stuart moved restlessly throughout France and Italy, took a mistress who left him because of his habitual drunkenness, and then a wife who did likewise. His younger brother Henry took holy orders, was created Cardinal York by the Pope, was driven into exile when the French Republican army occupied Rome in 1798, and was awarded a pension by the British government with the approval of his distant cousin, King George III. Henry's death in 1807 brought to an end the male line of the Royal Stuarts. It did not bring an end to a sentimental nostalgia for the Jacobite cause, which has flourished ever since in Britain, and which, in Scotland, centers mostly around the romantic figure of Bonnie Prince Charlie. Jacobite relics can still be seen there in numerous castles and stately homes, notably **Traquair House** *(420)* in Peeblesshire, and **Blair Castle** *(498)* in Perthshire, and in many museums, especially the **West Highland Museum** *(515)* in Fort William.

On Skye, near the north end of the Trotternish peninsula, stands the **Flora MacDonald Monument** *(524)* in the Kilmuir churchyard, where this remarkable woman is buried. It was she who risked her life by rescuing the Young

Pretender and bringing him back in an open boat from North Uist to Skye—the prince disguised as her Irish serving maid, Betty Burke. *"Flora MacDonald,"* wrote Dr. Samuel Johnson thirty years after the event, "is a name that will be mentioned in history, and if courage and fidelity be virtues, mentioned with honour." Honour is due also to those mostly nameless Highlanders who joined The Forty-five at the behest of their chiefs; fought at Culloden; suffered death, imprisonment, transportation, and persecution by Cumberland's brutal troopers; and, like Flora MacDonald, refused to betray their prince in spite of dire threats and generous monetary inducements. As to the quixotic adventurer who had made all these things possible, it would have been far better for Scotland had he never set foot in the country.

Chapter Eight

Improvement, Enlightenment, and the Industrial Revolution

1746–1832

THE HIGHLANDS

"There was perhaps never any change of national manners so quick, so great, and so general," wrote Samuel Johnson, the great savant and lexicographer, "as that which has operated in the highlands, by the last conquest [of 1746], and the subsequent laws. We came thither too late to see what we expected, a people of peculiar appearance, and a system of antiquated life. . . . Of what they had before the late conquest of their country, there remain only their language and their poverty. . . ."

These words were written shortly after Dr. Johnson had returned from his ten-week tour of the western Highlands and Inner Hebrides in the company of his young friend James Boswell, Edinburgh advocate (lawyer) and diarist *par excellence.* Johnson arrived in Edinburgh on 14 August 1773; lodged at Boyd's Inn in **White Horse Close** *(442)* at the foot of the Canongate; was entertained by Boswell at his quarters at **James Court** *(438)*; hobnobbed with a number of the city's famous *literati*, including the historian William Robertson, principal of the university; but seems to have been more impressed by Edinburgh's notorious stench than by its culture or its amenities. The two men left for the north on the 18th, travelling by post chaise (a closed carriage drawn by two horses) as far as the state of the roads would permit. They stopped to look at the sights of St. Andrews, Arbroath, and Aberdeen; were entertained by the Countess of Errol at **Slains Castle** *(544)*; proceeded through Banff, Cullen, Elgin, and Nairn to **Fort George** *(519)*, where they dined with the commandant, Sir Eyre Coote; and left their carriage at Inverness as they prepared to enter the Highlands. From here they travelled on horseback—no mean feat for Dr. Johnson, who was sixty-four years of age, overweight, and suffering from palsy. They went by way of Wade's Road to Fort Augustus; then westward to Glen Elg over the military road recently laid out by Wade's successor, William Caulfeild; crossed the Sound of Sleat to Skye, where they spent their first few nights at Armadale House (on the site of the present **Clan Donald Centre** *[521]*) as guests of Sir Alexander MacDonald of Sleat; visited the island of Raasay; enjoyed the hospitality of Lady MacLeod at **Dunvegan Castle** *(522)*; and departed from Skye on 3 October. They then visited Coll, sailed to Tobermory on Mull, stopped briefly at the tiny islands of Ulva and Inch Kenneth, and made a pilgrimage to **Iona Abbey** *(465)*, where Johnson pronounced his famous apothegm about patriotism and piety, quoted at the beginning of this book. Back on the mainland on 22 October, the travellers made their way to Inveraray, where they lodged at the inn now called the Argyll Arms Hotel and dined with the fifth Duke of Argyll at **Inveraray Castle** *(463)*. Finally, before returning to Edinburgh on 9 November, they stopped to visit Boswell's father at his house at Auchinleck in Ayrshire near the site of the present **Boswell Mausoleum and Museum** *(388)*. When one of Lord Auchinleck's guests asked Johnson how he liked the Highlands, the doctor's quick retort was: "Who can like the Highlands? I like the inhabitants very well."

What Dr. Johnson did *not* like about the Highlands were the barren, treeless landscape; the universal poverty and ignorance of the Gaelic-speaking peasantry; their primitive living conditions and unproductive agriculture; and their eagerness to be gone to North America. Their open friendliness he did appreciate, and even more he immensely enjoyed the hospitality of the leading families (MacDonalds, MacLeods, MacLeans, etc.) in whose homes and castles he discovered an astonishing degree of "southern elegance." Yet for all the amiability and good manners of his hosts, Johnson deplored their degeneration "from patriarchal to rapacious landlords." The former clan chiefs, he observed, "divested of their prerogatives, necessarily turned their thoughts to the improvement of their revenues, and expect more rent as they have less homage. . . . The tenant . . . refuses to pay the demand and is ejected, the ground is then let to a stranger."

Here in a nutshell was the Highland problem: a barren soil worked by antiquated and inefficient methods yielding little more than a meager subsistence, let alone a sufficient surplus to be applied against rent; a luxury-loving landlord class no longer requiring a large body of military retainers and being rapidly assimilated into the sophisticated culture of the South with its expensive sumptuary standards; and an expanding peasant population with no long-term legal rights to the land they occupied and therefore liable to eviction whenever an alternative and more productive method of land use presented itself. The problem was only beginning to become acute at the time of the visit of Johnson and Boswell. It would become more so over the next two generations.

In the last half of the eighteenth century most of agrarian Scotland— Lowland as well as Highland—continued to be farmed in the traditional medieval manner. At the center of each agricultural unit was the Highland clachan or Lowland "fermtoun," in either case a small cluster of huts. Sometimes referred to as "black-houses," these tiny dwellings were built of unmortared fieldstones with roofs of heather or straw thatch, often anchored to large exterior stones by means of plaited-straw ropes. Inside lived both cattle and humans, their quarters separated only by a wattled partition. The floor was bare earth; there was seldom a window. Heat was provided by a peat fire on the stone hearth in the center of the hut, the smoke escaping through a hole in the roof.

At the **Auchindrain Museum of Country Life** *(464)* near Inveraray can still be seen a number of these houses, dating from the eighteenth and early nineteenth centuries, though "modernized" with corrugated iron roofs and gable-end fireplaces. A reconstructed black-house is to be found in **Highland Folk Museum** *(521)* in Kingussie, and a life-sized model is on view at the **Old Byre Heritage Centre** *(472)* on the island of Mull.

The land surrounding these settlements was normally divided into three separate parts, each managed communally. Close by was the "infield," that is, the arable, which was regularly manured with the droppings of the cattle that were let loose here after the annual crop of oats or barley had been harvested. Seed was sown broadcast in "rigs," that is, long S-shaped ridges of plowed soil between which lay shallow trenches of unplowed land to serve for drainage. Each tenant was allotted a fixed number of these rigs scattered through the infield, and periodically they were reallocated so as to preserve equity of distribution. The plow was communally owned. In the Highlands this was an unwieldy single-handled implement that cut a very narrow and shallow furrow and required at least four horses and three men for operation. In spots too rough or stony for the plow team to reach, the *cas-chrom* or crooked spade was used. This had a long shaft attached at an obtuse angle to an iron-tipped wooden blade and was a useful tool to lever out heavy stones or dig between them. Examples of this curious implement are still to be seen in numerous Scottish museums of local history. Beyond the infield was the "outfield," which was seldom manured and on which the standard cereal crops were grown for four or five years successively until the yield became so poor that the land was then allowed to go fallow. Beyond this was the *muir*, where sheep were pastured in the summer and cattle in the winter. In the summer months Highland cattle would normally be dispatched to mountain grazings some distance away, to be tended by women and children who found shelter in temporary dwellings called *shielings*.

This was a very inefficient system of agriculture, even by contemporary standards, and especially so in the Highlands, where weather conditions were frequently cruel and crop failure fairly common. When this happened, famine occurred, as it did with particular severity in the years 1782–1783.

But even in 1803, which was not considered to be a famine year, James Hogg, the "Ettrick Shepherd" *(see below)*, reported after visiting the western Highlands that "there are many thousands in these countries whose conditions cannot be worsened unless they are starved to death." Indeed, many would have starved to death in that year and others had it not been for the earlier introduction from America by way of Ireland of the potato. Cultivated as a field crop in the Outer Hebrides in the 1740s, it quickly spread to the mainland and became a major source of food supply. It proved to be (until the arrival of the great potato blight of 1845) a sturdy and dependable crop; was easily grown in the thin, peaty soil of the Highlands; and provided far more nutriment per unit of measurement than either oats or barley.

Even so, Highland agriculture never rose much above the level of bare subsistence and was certainly insufficiently productive to allow tenants to pay the rents demanded by landlords or by the "tacksmen" who held large pieces of property under lease or "tack" from the great landowners to whom they were often related by blood. Rents, in most cases, were paid out of the sale of black cattle, possibly two or three per year by each tenant. Late in the summer these rugged but scrawny beasts would be gathered into herds by drovers and driven to the great annual cattle tryst at Crieff in Perthshire or, later (after about 1770), to the tryst held three times a year near Falkirk. Certain traditional routes—the so-called drove roads—converged onto one or both of these centrally located entrepôts from all parts of the Highlands and Islands. (From the Outer Hebrides the cattle normally went by open boat to Skye, where they were roped in tandem and forced to swim across Kyle Rhea to the mainland.) By 1723 as many as 30,000 beasts a year were being driven south to the great fair of Crieff, and, before the traffic ended in the mid-nineteenth century, an estimated 150,000 head were sold at Falkirk. The buyers were mostly English, who then drove the cattle farther southward to the rich grazing grounds of Northumberland or Yorkshire for fattening before final butchery. High on their list of consumers were the British Army and Navy, with their virtually insatiable demand for salted beef. From 1739 to 1815, Britain was involved in an almost continuous series of wars with France and her allies, and the steady rise in the price of cattle was in direct proportion to the expansion of the armed forces. And far away from the battlefields of Europe or from the distant seas where the Royal Navy fought its many engagements, the simple Highland peasant year after year turned over a fraction of his tiny herd to the drover, pocketed a few pounds in exchange, and paid the rent.

Cattle, however, were not the only Highland product that brought otherwise scarce cash into the region. Beginning in the 1760s, a growing demand for kelp opened new opportunities for profit-making in the

Hebrides and along the western seacoast. Kelp is a form of seaweed that, on being reduced to ash, produces an alkaline compound (also called *kelp*) formerly used in the manufacture of soap and glass. Wartime interruptions in the supply of barilla from Spain cleared the way for the development of the Scottish kelp industry. The market value of the product trebled between 1770 and 1810. But the rise in price was not accompanied by an advance in the wages of the Highland peasants who were employed in gathering the seaweed and incinerating it for shipment south. Profits went to the owners of estates bordering the shore, that is, to the great landed proprietors of the Highlands and Islands. Among the most successful of these were Sir Alexander MacDonald of Sleat (Dr. Johnson's host at Armadale), the Earl of Seaforth, the Duke of Argyll, and the chief of Clanranald, who in a single year (1809) grossed more than £14,000 from the sale of kelp. As to their tenantry, who performed the onerous work of collecting and burning the seaweed, their lot was if anything worse than ever. Compelled in many cases to leave their native clachans in exchange for tiny land allotments (crofts) along the coast, they exchanged a poverty-stricken existence to which they had grown accustomed for one as bad or worse in a setting both unfamiliar and alien. Except for the potato, they would have suffered destitution, as well as deracination.

Whatever the poor kelpers may have thought of their altered circumstances, there is no doubt that the introduction of an alternative industry into the Highlands was consonant with the new ideology of improvement that was fast becoming fashionable in Scottish aristocratic and intellectual circles as the eighteenth century progressed. Improvement, as applied to the Highlands, meant diversification of industry through the introduction of fisheries, trades, and manufactures; the laying out of roads and canals to encourage interregional commerce; the promotion of advanced agricultural techniques; and the conversion of the natives from Gaelic-speaking clansmen to English-speaking peasants and artisans. Improvement theory was in fact not far removed from the doctrines of modernization and development applied in recent times by Western economists and statesmen to the problems of the underdeveloped Third World. In reference to Scotland after The Forty-five, it was reinforced by the general belief in government circles that the endemic lawlessness of the Highlanders could be cured only by their conversion into English-speaking, Presbyterian, industrious, and sober counterparts of the more or less pacific Lowland Scots. Thus the Act of Parliament of 1752 annexing forfeited Jacobite estates to the Crown declared that all rents and profits derived therefrom were to be used for "Civilizing the Inhabitants upon the said Estates and other Parts of the Highlands and Islands of Scotland, the promoting amongst them the Protestant religion, good Government, Industry and Manufactures and the Principles of Duty and Loyalty to his Majesty, his Heirs and Successors, and to no other Use or Purpose whatsoever." This pretty well sums up the objectives of improvement as far as the Highlands were concerned.

The Commissioners of the Forfeited Estates—constituting a vast, though not always contiguous, swath of land some 30 to 40 miles broad and stretching from north of Stirling to Inverness, plus territories in the western Highlands and Cromarty—had good intentions of stimulating industrial development and persuading their tenants to adopt improved methods of agriculture. But they largely failed, if for no other reason than their inability to gain control over all the estates until 1770 or to keep them past 1784, when the properties were returned to the heirs of the original owners.

Greater progress was made by progressive Highland proprietors acting on their own initiative. Their attempted improvements took several forms: (1) getting rid of the tacksmen as intermediate tenants on the assumption that they had a vested interest in the traditional modes of land use; (2) shifting from communal to individual farming by consolidating the scattered rigs into discrete, enclosed (fenced) blocks of land let out to tenants on long-term leases conditional on their adopting modern methods of agriculture; (3) encouraging such cottage industries as flax spinning; and (4) founding model villages on their estates to serve as regional centers of industry and commerce. The fifth Duke of Argyll took the lead in such reforms, and others among the country's great landowners followed close behind—the Earl of Breadalbane, the Duke of Hamilton, and the Duke of Gordon, to name a few. Each of the latter three was responsible for the creation of model villages on his estate, including Kenmore, Brodick, and Tomintoul respectively—all still in existence. The most conspicuous surviving memorial to Argyll's improving efforts is the village of Inveraray, laid out a short distance from the ducal castle of the same name. The duke's architect was Robert Mylne, scion of the famous family of Scottish stonemasons, who did most of his work in the mid-eighteenth century and was responsible for the still-standing **Old Town House** *(463)*, the inn (now the Argyll Arms Hotel) where Johnson and Boswell lodged; the handsome arches on either side of it; and several other buildings. **Inveraray Parish Kirk** *(463)* at the head of the square was not completed until 1806 and was divided by a central wall into an "English end," with a laird's loft for the ducal family, and a "Gaelic end," now used as an arts and crafts center. Paradoxically, only a few miles from Inveraray, is the deserted Highland clachan of Auchindrain, now being restored as part of the excellent **Auchindrain Museum of Country Life** *(464)*. Although situated on the Argyll estate, this tiny township continued to function on the antiquated communal run-rig, infield-outfield system until late in the nineteenth century, long after it had become extinct elsewhere in Scotland.

The most ambitious of the improvement projects, however, were those sponsored by the British Fisheries Society, a semi-philanthropic organization chartered in 1786 with the Duke of Argyll and the Earl of Breadalbane as governor and deputy-governor respectively. It was empowered to collect capital, buy land for lease to fishermen and curers, build houses and sheds, and even establish towns. Four fishing communities were indeed laid out: Tobermory, Ullapool, Lochbay (in Skye), and Pultneytown on the southern edge of Wick. Of these only the last worked out as planned. Unpredictably, the herring shoals ceased to frequent the west coast. As a result, the projected fishing "station" at Lochbay failed; the tenants of Ullapool were unable to pay their rents, although the village itself survived; and Tobermory, situated strategically between Glasgow and the western isles, took on new life as a center of communications after the arrival of the steamboat. Only Wick flourished as a fishing port, and some of the docks and buildings associated with the herring industry can still be seen at the **Wick Heritage Centre** *(553)* near the town harbor.

Of even greater significance to the history of Highland development, however, was the British Fisheries Society's bringing Thomas Telford back to Scotland. Born in Dumfriesshire in the valley of the Esk in a tiny cottage by Megget Water, the son of a Border shepherd, Telford apprenticed as a stonemason in Langholm; left for London, where he worked for Sir William Chambers on the construction of Somerset House; went to Shropshire, where he designed and built more than forty bridges between 1790 and 1796; and, as general manager, agent, and architect of the Ellesmere Canal Company, designed the two splendid aqueducts at Chirk and Pont Cysyllte in Wales. At this point in his career (1801) he was chosen by the British Fisheries Society to supervise the construction of the new fishing harbors. In that capacity, he was also commissioned by the Treasury to survey the potential need for road and canal construction in the Highlands. Telford's report resulted in the establishment of two parliamentary commissions: one for the building of roads and bridges, the other for the construction of a canal to connect the west coast of Scotland with the Moray Firth through the Great Glen. Telford was put in charge of both projects, as well as of the building of about forty "parliamentary churches" in the Highlands.

Between 1723 and 1740 General Wade had already constructed nearly 250 miles of military roads, and another 800 miles or so had been laid between 1740 and 1767 by his successor, Major William Caulfeild. But these had had no significant impact on the economic life of the Highlands and, indeed, were avoided by the drovers because, they said, the gravel hurt their cattle's feet and the hard surfaces wore down their hooves. Also, none of the military roads penetrated the great mountain wilderness north of Inverness. Under Telford's supervision, between 1803 and 1821, 980 miles of new roads were built in the Highlands, and in addition 280 miles of the old military roads were realigned and remade. Modern roads now overlie or run more or less parallel to Telford's creations, including the now numbered A 830 from Fort William to Arisaig; the A 87 and A 887 from Loch Ness through Glen Moriston to Kyle of Lochalsh; the A 834, A 832, and A 8901 from Dingwall to Loch Carron; the A 836 and A 9 from Dingwall to Bonar Bridge; the A 9 and A 836 from Bonar Bridge to Tongue; and the A 9 and A 892 from Bonar Bridge to Wick and Thurso, the last crossing the head of Loch Fleet by a great embankment named **The Mound** *(551)*. Small wonder that his friend, the poet Robert Southey, named Telford the "Colossus of Roads." For his equally impressive feats of bridge-building, Southey coined another sobriquet: "Pontifex Maximus." More than a thousand (mostly very small) were built in the Highlands, of which the best survivors are the restored cast iron **Craigellachie Bridge** *(527)* in Moray and the graceful six-arched **Dunkeld Bridge** *(504)* in Perthshire, which still carries the A 923 across the River Tay. Of the many churches built by Telford or to his design, three surviving examples are **Strathy Parish Kirk** *(553)* in Sutherland; **Croick Church** *(550)* near Ardgay, Ross and Cromarty; and the little parish kirk close to **Iona Abbey** *(465)*.

Telford's most spectacular engineering achievement in Scotland, however, was the **Caledonian Canal** *(515)*. Parliament's objectives in ordering its construction were (1) to enable shipping to avoid the dangerous passage around the north coast of Scotland and through the Pentland Firth; (2) to facilitate the passage of ships of war from the Atlantic to the North Sea; and (3) to provide employment in the Highlands and thus discourage emigration, which in the eighteenth century was considered bad for the commonweal. Work began in 1803. Not until 1822 did a ship make the entire transit from Fort William to Inverness. Instead of costing £350,000, as Telford estimated, total expenditures came to over a million. By the time the canal was completed, most oceangoing vessels had already outgrown it, and, with the advent of steam power, the passage through the Pentland Firth had lost much of its terror. It was in short a white elephant—"an expensive highway," in the words of Alexander Youngson, "going from nowhere to nowhere." It was, nevertheless, an impressive engineering feat, as can still be appreciated by a visit to **Neptune's Staircase** *(515)*, the series of eight locks near the southern terminus of the canal at the head of Loch Linnhe just outside Fort William. Another white elephant was the **Crinan Canal** *(469)*, which cut across Knapdale between the Sound of Jura and Loch Fyne west of Lochgilphead. Instigated by the Duke of Argyll, and surveyed by another Scottish engineer, John Rennie, it was opened to traffic in 1801 but never paid its way. Today, it is used mostly by pleasure yachts and is a very picturesque sight.

The concern about emigration from the Highlands, which Dr. Johnson shared with many of his contemporaries and which partially inspired the decision to build the Caledonian Canal, dated from about 1760. Before that time, to be sure, Scottish emigrants had settled in Georgia, New Jersey, and Pennsylvania, and, after the two Jacobite rebellions, perhaps as many as fifteen hundred prisoners had been transported to Maryland, Virginia, and the Carolinas. The exodus accelerated in the early 1760s, and by 1775 an estimated twenty thousand people had left the Highlands for America. This was the "epidemick" that Johnson noted—and deplored—on Skye. It was, he believed, the product of post-Culloden rack-renting by landed propri- etors, instigated in many cases by their own tacksmen, who found them- selves unable or unwilling to raise the rents of their subtenants, while being compelled to disgorge more and more to their superiors. Tacksmen and tenants together boarded the emigrant ships and sailed off to America, the greatest number, before the War of Independence, heading for North Carolina. There they often found the tidewater plantation owners and western land speculators no less grasping than their former landlords at home; and, since these colonial grandees generally sided with the American rebels against the government of George III, most of the recent Scots settlers became loyalists and many fought for His Majesty. After the conclusion of the War of Independence, a few, like Flora MacDonald and her husband, returned to Scotland. Many more, however, reemigrated to Canada, which also became a powerful magnet for direct migration from Scotland after 1783. Canada indeed had already attracted a fair number of Scottish settlers—chiefly veterans of Scottish regiments who had been engaged in campaigns in America during the Seven Years War (1756–1763). The Black Watch fought at Ticonderoga in 1758; the Royal Scots at the capture of Louisburg in the same year; while Fraser's Highlanders bled and died with Major General James Wolfe on the Plains of Abraham (Quebec) in 1759. Some of these soldiers, discharged at the end of the war, accepted land grants in Canada from a grateful government, thus forming a nucleus of Scotsmen around which many more of their countrymen were soon to gather.

The recruitment of Scottish soldiers for service overseas was a more-than- century-old practice by the time the Seven Years War with France broke out. The first regular unit of Scots infantry was the Royal Scots Regiment, authorized by Charles I in 1633 and raised by John Hepburn to fight in the service of King Louis XIII of France. "Restored" to Charles II in 1662, it soon became a permanent part of what would become the British Army establishment. The record of its three centuries of military service is on view at the regimental museum in **Edinburgh Castle** *(436)*. The Royal Scots Fusiliers was first called up in 1678 by Charles Erskine, fifth Earl of Mar, to assist in the suppression of the Covenanters of the Southwest. Some of its mementos can be seen at the **Royal Highland Fusiliers' Regimental Museum** *(405)* in Glasgow. Ten years later, in defense of the Glorious Revolution, the Covenanters of Lanarkshire formed a unit of their own, later to be called the Cameronians, whose history is on view at the **Cameronians (Scottish Rifles) Regimental Museum** *(410)* in Hamilton. In 1739 came the Black Watch, already described in the previous chapter and lovingly commemorated in the **Black Watch Museum** *(505)* in Perth.

Lowlanders, as well as Highlanders, were thus to be found in His Majesty's service, fighting on the Continent under the command of William III, or Marlborough, or Cumberland. But it was not until after The Forty-five that the British government embarked on a policy of wholesale recruitment in the Highlands. The government's object was threefold: (1) to fill the ever-expanding ranks of the army as Britain became increasingly involved in foreign wars; (2) to rid Scotland of a potentially seditious element in the event of a resurgence of Jacobitism; and (3) to promote the assimilation of the Highlands into the rest of Britain. The scheme incidentally appealed to heirs of former Highland Jacobites as an opportunity to regain the estates forfeited by their fathers. And to any male member of the Highland aristocracy, the grant of authority to raise a regiment among his tenants or his neighbors' tenants gave promise of enhanced prestige, favor with the government, and patronage in the form of junior officers' commissions. As to the recruits themselves, appeals to clan loyalty, tempting money rewards, cajolery, blatant deception, and threats of eviction seem to have been the most common devices used to fill the ranks. When some of these men later mutinied rather than serve overseas, they claimed to have been misled with promises of exemption from duty abroad. Once fully integrated into the British Army, however, Highland soldiers quickly won renown as fierce fighters the world over.

Altogether more than twenty regular regiments of the British Army and twenty-six regiments of fencibles (home guard units) were raised in the Highlands between 1739 and 1800. One estimate puts the number of men so recruited during the wars with France and her allies (including the rebellious British colonies and the United States of America) at more than seventy-four thousand men. William Pitt the Elder claimed credit for first exploiting this great reserve of manpower. "I sought for merit wherever it could be found," he told the House of Commons. "I was the first minister who looked for it in the mountains of the north. I called it forth, and drew into your service a hardy and intrepid race of men . . . who . . . served with fidelity, as they fought with valor, and conquered for you in every quarter of the world." Pitt's example was copied by succeeding ministers during the War of American Independence, the Wars of the French Revolution, and the Napoleonic Wars. Among the "hardy and intrepid race of men" were Lord

MacLeod's Regiment, the 73d (renumbered 71st) Highlanders, first recruited in 1778, and now commemorated in the **Royal Highland Fusiliers' Regimental Museum** *(405)* in Glasgow, along with the 74th Highland Regiment, organized in 1787; the Seaforth Highlanders, the 78th (renumbered 72d) Regiment of Foot, also dating from 1778 and today memorialized in the museum at **Fort George** *(519)*, which also houses mementos of the Queen's Own Cameron Highlanders and the Ross-shire Buffs, both dating from 1793; the 75th Highland Regiment of Foot, first organized in 1787 and later amalgamated with the Gordon Highlanders (recruited in 1795) with whom they now share the **Gordon Highlanders Museum** *(535)* in Aberdeen; the Argyll Highlanders, dating from 1794 and afterward joined with the Sutherland Highlanders, first recruited in 1793, both well represented at the fine Argyll and Sutherland Highlanders Museum at **Stirling Castle** *(477)*; and the 90th Perthshire Light Infantry, born in 1794 and later amalgamated with the 16th Cameronian Regiment, whose museum at Hamilton has already been mentioned.

At Waterloo, on 18 June 1815, soldiers of the Black Watch who had two days before stood off the French at Quatre Bras, lined the Flemish hedges, shouting "Scotland Forever!" as the Royal Scots Greys and Gordon Highlanders made their famous and decisive charge against the last desperate remnant of Napoleon's once unconquerable army. Those Highlanders who survived these final battles of the Second Hundred Years War with France and received their discharge papers came home to a surprising welcome. The land they and their fathers once had tilled was fast being given over to sheep and their native clachans disappearing. The great Highland clearances were in full progress.

The year 1815, which saw the end of the war, saw also the collapse of the wartime economic boom. Cattle prices collapsed. The market for kelp, already diminished, began to disappear entirely with the reopening of trade in barilla with the Continent. Tenants could no longer pay their rents. Landlords, with mounting expenses, grew embittered at the contemplation of permanent loss of rental income. Famine struck in 1806–1807, again in 1811, and still again in 1816–1817, and tenants turned to landlords for emergency rations of meal and seed, thus incurring additional and unpayable debt. Expectations that coastal fishing would provide an alternative food supply proved illusory. The only marketable staple that did not drop in price, and indeed rose in value, was wool.

As early as the 1760s, it had been discovered that the black-faced Linton and white-faced Cheviot sheep of Lowland Scotland could survive the much colder winters of the Highlands. Shepherds from Dumfriesshire and Ayrshire began to move their flocks into Argyll and Perthshire, where they found desperate landlords more than willing to lease large portions of their debt-burdened estates to men with ready cash. In the proprietors' view, they had no choice. James Hogg, the "Ettrick Shepherd," who toured the western Highlands in 1803, described in a few words the landlords' dilemma there. George MacKenzie of Dundonnel asked Hogg what he thought the Dundonnel estate would bring annually if let out in sheep walks. The Ettrick Shepherd's answer was, "not below £2,000." Mackenzie then remarked that his people would never pay him half of that. He was loathe to chase them all away to America, but at present they did not pay him £700.

The story was the same all over the Highlands, and sheep herding gradually spread north: from mainland Argyll to Inverness-shire, to Ross and Cromarty, to Sutherland, and west into the Inner and Outer Hebrides. (Exhibits and audiovisual shows at the **Great Glen Exhibition** *[515]* in Fort Augustus and the **Landmark Visitor Center** *[515]* in Carrbridge, Inverness-shire, offer succinct accounts of this movement.) And where the sheep came the tenants had to go. The southern graziers were men of capital. They insisted that sheep raising could be profitable only on a large scale. They maintained that their breed of animal required a diet consisting of various kinds of grasses and therefore had to be pastured not only on the hills but also in the glens, where most of the clachans and infields were located. They wanted no Highlanders on the premises for fear of sheep stealing or, more likely, illicit sheep slaughter. Tending the flocks required few hands, and the graziers usually brought their own shepherds from the South and set them up in tidy cottages, contrasting starkly with the hovels of the natives. (The contrast is spelled out dramatically in the exhibition shown at the **Old Byre Heritage Centre** *[472]* on Mull.) And with ample funds to sweeten their demands, the graziers mostly had their way.

Though the ordinary Highlander might have imagined that his rights to the land he occupied were firmly sanctioned by custom and tradition and that the lands belonged to the clan and were inalienable, the truth was that in law he was a tenant-at-will or at best a short-term leaseholder. Hence, if the landlord so decided, the tenant had no choice but to leave. Some, with the encouragement and sometimes even financial assistance of their landlords, boarded the emigrant ships bound now mostly for Canada or Australia. Some settled on small crofts on the nearby seashore or on vacant moorland, where they could subsist on potatoes and whatever else they might earn through casual labor or fishing. Some (usually in second or third moves) made their way to the Lowlands to swell a labor force already being absorbed by the growing industries of Glasgow and its surrounding towns.

Of all the Highland clearances, none received more public attention at the time and since than those that took place in Sutherland, mainly between 1811 and 1821. None, it might also be said, were less typical. Elizabeth,

Countess of Sutherland in her own right and owner of about two-thirds of the county, was married to the second Marquis of Stafford, who in 1803 inherited the largest fortune in England. The Staffords were high-minded Whigs, dedicated improvers, and true believers in the newly fashionable economic doctrines of Adam Smith. The Sutherland estates were typically debt-ridden and unprofitable; the tenants long in arrears; the proprietors on occasion forced to supply meal and cereal seed to prevent general starvation. With good intentions buttressed in liberal dogma, the Staffords decided to introduce large-scale sheep farming and move the displaced tenants to prepared crofts on the seacoast, there to devote themselves to fishing and other trades. This was social engineering on a grand scale: rural slum clearance to be accompanied by relocation in a new environment where economic opportunities abounded.

The plan failed. The glens of Sutherland indeed were cleared of several thousand tenants who were resettled on crofts in such new coastal communities as Strathy, Brora, and Helmsdale. But they were unversed in the skills of deep-sea fishing and, accustomed as they were to communal farming and cattle raising, inept at crofting, which was an individual enterprise. Many gave up, drifted southward to become squatters and casual labor, or took ship for Canada or Australia or even the Cape of Good Hope. In the end the scheme proved a financial failure even for the Marquis of Stafford (made Duke of Sutherland in 1833, the year of his death). Moreover, its execution brought unforgettable infamy to his name.

Partly because the Sutherland clearances took place on such a grand scale, and partly no doubt because their perpetrator was an Englishman, this particular episode in Highland history has attracted a disproportionate share of the calumny heaped on the heads of evicting landlords in general. Another reason for its notoriety is that the agents chosen to execute the scheme were unnecessarily brutal. The most opprobrious of these was Patrick Sellar, an entrepreneur from Moray, who was eventually brought to trial, though acquitted, for causing the death of several elderly people whose houses he had allegedly ordered to be burned during the evictions. His portrait—a dour, stony visage—is on view in the **Strathnaver Museum** *(550)* in Bettyhill, a former church that still contains the pulpit from which the reluctant minister, David MacKenzie, announced the names of those of his parishioners who were scheduled for eviction. Here also are a few fragments of broken pottery, glass, etc., found in nearby **Rossal Township** *(550)*, where thirteen families were evicted by Sellar in 1813. Excavated in 1962 by archaeologists from the University of Glasgow and situated within grounds maintained by the Forestry Commission, here are the scattered foundations of a typical preclearance clachan. Elsewhere throughout the Highland glens are the meager remains of many other such deserted settlements, but they are mostly unmarked and undistinguishable by any but the most practiced archaeological eye. What these places looked like shortly after the departure of their inhabitants was reported in 1825 by one Alexander Sutherland, recently returned from a tour of the northern Highlands: "All was now silence and desolation. Blackened and roofless huts, still enveloped in smoke—articles of furniture cast away, as of no value to the houseless—and a few domestic fowls, scraping for food among hills of ashes, were the only objects that told us of man."

THE LOWLANDS

Improvement and Enlightenment

At the beginning of the eighteenth century, agricultural management and techniques in the Lowlands of Scotland were almost as backward as in the mountainous regions of the North and West. Almost everywhere the run-rig/infield-outfield system, described above, prevailed. Even in this more fertile soil, acid conditions, poor drainage, primitive equipment, and tradition-bound communal farming kept yields of the ubiquitous oats and bere (barley) at a low level. When weather conditions worsened—as in the last seven years of the seventeenth century ("the seven ill years" or, as the Jacobites would have it, "King William's years")—famine was the result. The peasantry, clustered in tiny fermtouns, were either tenants-at-will, enjoying no legal security at all, or at best leaseholders whose tenure was short and subject to frequent renewal on terms dictated by the landlord. Thus they had no incentive to improve the land they tilled and on which they lived. Over and above their normal work in the fields, they were compelled to perform numerous labor services for the local lord and were "thirled" to the local baronial mill, i.e., required to have their meal ground there exclusively and to pay an additional fee. (One of these, the **Preston Mill** [454] in East Lothian, still survives from the seventeenth century and is maintained in an operating condition by the National Trust for Scotland.) Pastoral farming was equally primitive. Hay was scarce, and no other special cattle food was grown. The English called the cattle coming from north of the border "Scotch runts."

After the Union of 1707, the stream of Scots nobles and gentry southward swelled to a flood. Some went as members of the House of Lords or House of Commons; others to vie for commissions in the army or lucrative posts in the civil service; still others simply to seek their fortunes in the more prosperous environment of southern England. As Dr. Johnson put it: "The noblest prospect that a Scotchman ever sees is the high road that leads him to England." Whatever their motives, en route to and from London they must have been made aware of the changes taking place in English farming—changes amounting to what historians have called an "agrarian revolution." Crops were being rotated on a scientific basis, turnips grown for feeding cattle in the winter, clover and artificial grasses planted to enrich the soil as well as to provide additional cattle food. Trees were abundant, in contrast to the bleak Scottish countryside that moved Dr. Johnson to remark that "a tree might be a show in Scotland as a horse in Venice." New farm implements were being invented: Jethro Tull's drill, permitting seed to be planted in straight lines so as to allow deep cultivation by horse-drawn plows between rows; and the Rotherham triangular plow, requiring only two horses instead of the traditional six or eight. And most importantly, large areas of open fields, common holdings, and wasteland were being consolidated and enclosed with ditches and hedgerows, so as to keep out wandering cattle, encourage experimentation with new crops, increase the quantity of arable land under cultivation, and in general raise the level of productivity.

It was from England then that Scottish "improving" landlords derived their inspiration for the revolution in agriculture that, by about 1830, had transformed the face of the southern Lowlands, Perthshire, Angus, Kincardineshire, the counties bordering the Moray Firth, and even parts of Argyll. Their task was made easier than that of their English counterparts by the fact that Scottish tenants, unlike English copyholders, had no long-term legal rights in the land. Thus Scottish improvers required no special parliamentary enclosure acts as was the case in England. Agrarian improvement began simply with the arbitrary redistribution and consolidation of the scattered rigs into separate land units, followed later by enclosing dykes or fences of unmortared fieldstone. There was no general displacement of people in favor of sheep. Evictions of redundant tenants there were, but, contrary to the Highland experience, it was not customary to destroy whole fermtouns and drive the people off. Normally, the more efficient tenants would be offered long-term leases (nineteen years was standard) on condition that they adopt approved agricultural practices. The rest might become casual agricultural laborers or engage in cottage industry or drift to the nearby towns where mills were springing up. Thus turnips, clover, and artificial grasses came to Scotland; stone fences went up, farms of a hundred or two hundred acres became commonplace; bogs were drained; and the sickle gave way to the scythe.

Other more complex pieces of farm machinery also appeared. Early in the eighteenth century, James Meikle invented a winnowing machine; in 1763 James Small of Berwickshire demonstrated his "swing plow," a vast improvement over its time-hallowed predecessor; Andrew Meikle, son of James, produced the first threshing machine in 1786; and in 1818 Patrick

Bell perfected a mechanical reaper, the principles of which seem to have been incorporated into the world-famous McCormick machine produced in Chicago a few years later. (Illustrations of Scotland's agrarian revolution can be seen at The Border Country Life Museum in **Thirlestane Castle** *[425]*, Lauder, Berwickshire.)

Afforestation too became a favored project of the improvers. The Dukes of Atholl planted more than four thousand acres, mainly larch and Scots pine, on the grounds surrounding **Blair Castle** *(498)* and beyond. At **Tyninghame House Gardens** *(455)*, East Lothian, Thomas Hamilton, sixth Earl of Haddington, laid out a forest (still visible) and published a book called *Some Directions About Raising Forest Trees.* One of the most influential of Scotland's pioneer tree enthusiasts was Sir James Naesmyth, a pupil of the great botanist Linnaeus, who began the plantings at **Dawyck House Gardens** *(422)*, in Peeblesshire, still considered perhaps the most impressive collection of trees in Scotland, in spite of the loss of about fifty thousand to the great storms of 1968 and 1973.

Enthusiasm for improvement grew apace in Scotland as the eighteenth century wore on. As early as July 1723, three hundred members of the nobility and gentry formed themselves into the "Honourable Society of Improvers in the Knowledge of Agriculture in Scotland," which functioned as a clearinghouse of information for landlords interested in modernizing their estates. In 1755 the Select Society of Edinburgh *(see below)* formed an auxiliary called "The Edinburgh Society for Encouraging Arts, Sciences, Manufactures and Agriculture," which offered prizes for tree planting, new machinery, new breeds of cattle, superior seed grain, and written essays on farming. Among the individual landlords most active in the movement were John Cockburn of Ormiston, who went bankrupt in 1747 as a result of his excessive enthusiasm for improvement; Henry Home, Lord Kames, who was among the first to grow turnips in drills and drained a vast acreage of bog in the Carse of Stirling; and Sir Archibald Grant, who reclaimed the badly run-down estate of Monymusk near Aberdeen. To such as these and to the Honourable Society of Improvers, the poet Allan Ramsay, Senior, wrote:

> Continue, best of clubs, long to improve
> Your native plains and gain your nation's love.
> Rouse every lazy laird of each wide field
> That unmanured not half their product yield.
> Show them the proper season, soils, and art,
> How they may plenty to their lands impart,
> Triple their rents, increase the farmers' store,
> Without the purchase of one acre more.

Ramsay's name, of course is most often associated with that other great outburst of the progressive spirit in eighteenth-century Scotland, called simply "The Enlightenment." Son of a lead-mine overseer in Leadhills, Lanarkshire, this enterprising and talented young man came to Edinburgh in the early years of the century; established himself as a wig maker; helped to found a literary society called "The Easy Club"; became a bookseller, publisher, and poet (some would say "versifier"); wrote a Scots ballad-opera, *The Gentle Shepherd*; published an anthology of old Scots songs, *The Tea-Table Miscellany*; and, on the High Street of Edinburgh, set up the first lending library in Scotland in 1728.

It was not long after this that a similar service was established in Ramsay's hometown. **The Leadhills Library** *(399)*, founded in 1741 by the local minister, schoolmaster, and twenty-one miners, had by 1821 increased its holdings to fifteen hundred books. At the **Innerpeffray Library** *(501)* near Crieff, the borrowers' ledger, dating from 1747, includes the names of a barber, a dyer, a flaxdresser, a mason, a miller, a shoemaker, and a weaver and other craftsmen and tradesmen. The apparent popularity of all these institutions is a good indication of the broad base of literacy and intellectual curiosity among the people of Scotland. This was the infrastructure on which were founded the country's flourishing universities, its publishing business, and its remarkable literary outburst of the late eighteenth century. In the words of Anand C. Chitnis: "If William Robertson's *History of Charles V* was regularly read by artisans in Perthshire [as the list of Innerpeffray's borrowers indicates], the intellectual elite of Scotland were not operating in a sphere totally above that of their fellow countrymen."

William Robertson, Principal of the University of Edinburgh and Moderator of the General Assembly of the Church of Scotland, was author not only of the *History of the Reign of the Emperor Charles V*, but also of the *History of Scotland During the Reign of Queen Mary and of King James VI till his Accession to the Crown of England* and a *History of America*. He was, as well, a member of the Select Society, founded in Edinburgh in 1754 by Allan Ramsay, Junior, a distinguished portrait painter, whose *oeuvre* appears today to be of somewhat higher quality than his father's *(see below)*. The society's roster (fifteen members, growing to ninety-five) constituted an intellectual elite that no other provincial city in the West could equal. Meeting together regularly to match wits and share ideas in the congenial all-male atmosphere of this and other similar organizations were judges, lawyers, medical doctors, writers, artists and architects, clergymen, improving landlords, and university professors. Though Glasgow and Aberdeen could boast their own like-minded clubs and their own progressive universities and intelligentsia, Edinburgh was the primary seedbed of that remarkable flowering of intellectual and cultural endeavor known as the "Scottish Enlightenment."

There were many contributors to this great philosophic, scientific, artistic, and literary effusion, and a few are still well remembered, chiefly through their writings. Robertson has already been mentioned, though his reputation as a historian was soon to be, perhaps unfairly, overshadowed by that of his English contemporary, Edward Gibbon. The greatest of the Scottish philosophers was David Hume, author, *inter alia*, of a *Treatise on Human Nature*, the *Philosophical Essays Concerning Human Understanding*, and the *Inquiry Concerning the Principles of Morals*. Too skeptical in matters of religion for most of his contemporaries, he is considered to be the forerunner of the great utilitarians, Jeremy Bentham and John Stuart Mill, and the progenitor of the Logical Positivists of the twentieth century. Hume's antithesis, philosophically speaking, was Thomas Reid, author of the *Inquiry into the Human Mind* and *Essays on the Intellectual Powers of Man*. His "commonsense" philosophy was far more acceptable than Hume's to orthodox Christians, and his influence on academic philosophical teachings was especially strong in America, thanks mostly to the mediation of John Witherspoon (see below). Reid was Professor of Moral Philosophy at Marischal College, Aberdeen, and then at the University of Glasgow where he succeeded Adam Smith, author of the *Theory of Moral Sentiments* and later of the seminal *Inquiry into the Nature and Causes of the Wealth of Nations*. Close friend to Hume and, like him a cofounder of the Select Society, Smith was to have the longest-lasting influence of any of the Scottish "moral philosophers" of the eighteenth century. His *Wealth of Nations* became the bible of nineteenth-century liberal economics in Britain and elsewhere and is still revered for its persuasive defense of free enterprise against state intervention in economic affairs. If Smith can be considered the father of the discipline of economics, Adam Ferguson probably deserves the same credit as sire or grandsire of modern sociology. Author of the *Essay on Civil Society*, the *Institutes of Moral Philosophy*, and *Principles of Political Science*, this Perthshire-born, Gaelic-speaking, ex-chaplain to the Black Watch focussed his attention on the societal origins of law and morality and was concerned with the dangers to community values of unbridled individualism. He too was a Professor of Moral Philosophy—at the University of Edinburgh.

The role of the Scottish universities—Edinburgh and Glasgow especially—as fountainheads of enlightenment can hardly be exaggerated. Scotland had five such institutions as compared to England's two: in order of their founding, St. Andrews; Glasgow; King's College, Aberdeen; Edinburgh; and Marischal College, Aberdeen. All had benefitted by the abolition of the ancient custom of rotating regents, that is, assigning each class for all four years to the exclusive tutelage of a single master, irrespective of his special field of knowledge. Increased specialization of instruction was obtained by the founding of professorial chairs in a variety of subjects, including moral philosophy, history, mathematics, chemistry, natural history, medicine, and public law. Enrollments rose at a steady rate—except at St. Andrews, which, like the two English universities, Oxford and Cambridge, sank into a century-long period of intellectual decay. The other four Scottish institutions flourished—partly no doubt because lectures were now given in English instead of Latin. The practice had been started by Francis Hutcheson, Professor of Moral Philosophy at Glasgow, and proved so popular that it was quickly emulated elsewhere. Popularity was much sought after by eighteenth-century Scottish professors because their stipends came out of student fees—a practice that no doubt accounted in part for the universities' vitality and their avoidance of that brand of mandarinism to which academia is especially prone.

In any case, the universities of Scotland rose to international eminence, and in the teaching of medicine and related natural sciences, to *pre*eminence. In the lead was Edinburgh, which replaced the University of Leyden as Europe's most distinguished medical school and where no less than eleven chairs of medicine were established between 1685 and 1807. The best known of these professors were the three Alexander Monros (father, son, and grandson), who held the chair of anatomy in unbroken succession from 1720 to 1846. Glasgow, with Dr. William Cullen as Professor of Medicine, was not far behind, and the two universities shared the services of Joseph Black as Professor of Chemistry, first at Glasgow and after that at Edinburgh.

Auxiliary to both medical schools were the botanical gardens. Edinburgh's dates as far back as 1670, when Dr. Robert Sibbald, the university's first Professor of Medicine, and Dr. Andrew Balfour began to grow medicinal plants in a small plot of land near the Palace of Holyroodhouse. After two subsequent moves, the site of the present **Royal Botanic Garden** *(450)* at Inverleith was selected in 1820 and the garden's contents gradually moved thereto under the supervision of William McNab, Britain's leading horticulturist. The present site of the **Glasgow Botanic Garden** *(409)* at Kelvinside dates only to 1842, but as early as 1705 there had been a "physic garden" associated with the university, and in 1817, at the west end of Sauchiehall Street, the Royal Botanic Institution of Glasgow founded a garden that grew to horticultural eminence under the ministration of Sir William Hooker, the university's Professor of Botany from 1821 to 1841. To the University of Glasgow also went the contents of the anatomical collection, paintings, antiquities, and books of Dr. William Hunter, who had left his native city to become an eminent London physician and personal attendant to Queen Charlotte. The original bequest of 1807 included £8,000 to erect a building to house these items—the original

Hunterian Museum *(408)*, whose contents were moved after 1870 to the new university campus on Gilmorehill.

Scottish education was a commodity for export, as the British colonies in North America learned to their advantage. As early as 1693, James Blair, a graduate of Marischal College, Aberdeen, and of the University of Edinburgh, was instrumental in the founding of William and Mary College in Virginia and served as its first president until his death in 1743. William Smith, who had attended King's College, Aberdeen, from 1743 to 1747, emigrated to New York and then to Philadelphia, where he helped to found, and became first provost of, a college later to be designated the University of Pennsylvania. The university's justly famous medical school originated with the creation, in 1765–1771, of a medical faculty consisting of four graduates of the University of Edinburgh: William Shippen, John Morgan, Adam Kuhn, and Benjamin Rush. Finally, the flowering of what was to become Princeton University began with the appointment to the presidency of the College of New Jersey of the Reverend John Witherspoon in 1768. Born in the manse of **Yester Kirk** *(457)* in Gifford, East Lothian, where his father was the minister, John Witherspoon himself preached at Paisley before accepting a call to head the college, founded in 1746 by American Presbyterians from the middle-Atlantic colonies. A graduate of Edinburgh University, he was identified with the conservative, evangelical wing of the Church of Scotland (see below) and was a spokesman in America for the "commonsense" philosophy of Thomas Reid. Soon after his arrival in America, he became involved in the political agitation that led to the rebellion of the thirteen colonies and was in 1776 to put his signature to the Declaration of Independence. In 1788 he became first Moderator of the General Assembly of the Presbyterian Church in the United States.

Presbyterianism, of course, was another exportable commodity. Wherever Scots settled in America in any numbers—in New York, New Jersey, eastern Pennsylvania, the Shenandoah Valley of Virginia, the Piedmont region of North Carolina—they established kirks on the familiar pattern and chose ministers of like persuasion. What is perhaps more surprising is that the hierarchy of the Protestant Episcopal Church of America had Scottish origins. Unwilling to take the oath of allegiance to King George III after American independence had been declared and won, and unable therefore to obtain episcopal consecration of one of their own clergymen from the Archibishop of Canterbury, Americans who had formerly adhered to the Church of England were at an impasse. Appeal was therefore made to the nonjuring Scottish bishops, who until the death of Prince Charles Edward in 1788 were in a like position. Thus it was that Samuel Seabury was consecrated Bishop of Connecticut in Aberdeen in 1784.

As to the Scottish Presbyterians, in keeping with tradition dating back at least to the reign of Charles I, they were bitterly divided among themselves. The expulsion from the General Assembly of Ebenezer Erskine and his associates in 1733 had led to the latter's formation of the "Associate Presbytery," which by 1760 had grown from four congregations to almost a hundred. At issue had been the right of lay patrons of parish kirks to nominate the ministers thereof, as legalized by the Patronage Act of 1712. Lay patronage was condoned by the majority of the General Assembly but was strenuously objected to by Erskine and like-minded Presbyterians of the Covenanting tradition. The same issue rose again in the General Assembly of 1752 and led to the expulsion of Thomas Gillespie of Garnock who, with others, then formed the "Relief Presbytery."

These secessions from the Church of Scotland, coupled with subsequent fission of the Associate Presbytery into several factions and factions within factions (Burghers, Anti-Burghers, New Lichts, Auld Lichts), strengthened the hand of the Moderate Party within the General Assembly in their continued controversy with a vociferous group of so-called Evangelicals. Lay patronage was still the ostensible issue between the two, although the rift in fact lay much deeper. The Moderates, led by Principal William Robertson, were mostly worldly men, cosmopolitan in their attitudes and interests, receptive to the new ideas of the Enlightenment (even, in some cases, those of David Hume), somewhat permissive in matters of personal morality, authoritarian in respect to the subordination of presbyteries and kirk sessions to the General Assembly, and not unhappy with the principle of lay patronage since most patrons tended to nominate ministers of the Moderate persuasion. The Evangelicals, on the other hand, heirs to the Covenanting tradition, were shocked at the doctrinal latitudinarianism of their Moderate brothers, adhered to a literalist interpretation of the Holy Bible as the revealed Word of God, opposed encroachments of both lay patrons and the General Assembly on the autonomy of kirk sessions, deplored the creeping secularization of religion, and were scandalized at the moral laxity demonstrated when a Moderate minister, John Home, produced a stage play (*Douglas*) whose performance in Edinburgh was attended by other Moderate ministers. The strength of the Moderates lay chiefly in the cities and among the aristocracy, the legal profession, and the intellectual elite of the universities. That of the Evangelicals was based in the small towns and villages, where ministers and elders were accustomed to impose a strict Calvinist discipline on their communities and stand guard against the wickedness of the ungodly. It was such as these that the Ayrshire poet, Robert Burns, had in mind in the opening lines of his "Address to the Unco Guid."

O ye wha are sae guid yoursel,
Sae Pious and sae holy,
Ye've nought to do but mark and tell
Your neebours' fauts and folly.

Burns was born on 25 January 1759 in a two-room ("but-and-ben") cottage in Alloway, a few miles south of Ayr. The **Burns Cottage**, to which the **Burns Museum** *(389)* was subsequently appended, was an "auld clay biggin," built, with his own hands, by the infant's father, William Burnes (sic), who lies buried in the yard of **Alloway Old Kirk** *(389)*, already a ruin when the poet used it as the scene of the witches' dance in the best of his narrative poems, "Tam O'Shanter":

When glimmering thro' the groaning trees,
Kirk-Alloway seemed in a bleeze,
Thro' ilka bore the beams were glancing,
And loud resounded mirth and dancing.

William Burnes, though a poor man, had the Scot's traditional respect for learning, and saw to it that Robert and his brother Gilbert received more than minimal tuition in letters and numbers. The year 1781 saw the family on a miserable boggy farm near Tarbolton, Ayrshire, where young Burns, now in his early twenties, became a Freemason and also helped to found the **Bachelor's Club** *(391)*, a debating society and social club. A year later he was studying flaxdressing in Irvine, then a thriving seaport, where a friendly sailor encouraged him in his poetry writing and also introduced him to the joys of fornication. Burns was an apt pupil. After leaving Irvine for a rented farm near Mauchline, he sired on a servant girl, Bess Paton, the first of the eleven illegitimate children he was to admit to. Another affair with a Mauchline lass, Jean Armour, produced twins. (The **Burns House Museum** *[391]* in Mauchline contains the room Burns rented for Jean.) In 1786 he persuaded a Kilmarnock printer to publish a book of poems containing such now familiar titles as "The Twa' Dogs," "To a Mouse," "The Cottar's Saturday Night," and "To a Louse."

Here, in the words of the literary historian David Daiches, was "a new Scottish poet, of astonishing liveliness and verve, whose genius was nourished by the poetic traditions of his own people." His "own people" spoke Lowland Scots, and Burns's great accomplishment was to fold this native dialect gracefully into English verse of superb lyrical quality. The *literati* of Edinburgh were impressed, thanks in part to a review by the novelist Henry Mackenzie, who dubbed his new discovery "the heaven-taught ploughman." On the heels of the sellout of the Kilmarnock edition,

Burns, on a borrowed pony, drove to Edinburgh and instantly became the social and literary lion of the season. Among his patrons and admirers were the popular university professor, Dugald Stewart; the Dean of the Faculty of Advocates, Henry Erskine; the Earl of Glencairn; the Duchess of Gordon; and Mrs. James M'Lehose, with whom he later carried on a lengthy and platonic correspondence, he signing his name "Sylvander" and she "Clarinda." Burns's *succès fou* was well deserved, but merit alone cannot account for it. Jean Jacques Rousseau and other French *philosophes* had idealized the "natural man" uncorrupted by civilization, and here was one in the flesh: a genuine rustic with an unmistakable genius for polished versification. And in this society there were few to object to the poet's jaundiced view of conventional Calvinist piety, as expressed in "The Holy Fair" and "Holy Willie's Prayer."

Burns stayed long enough in Edinburgh to publish an expanded edition of his collected verse; returned to Mauchline and married Jean Armour; moved to **Ellisland Farm** *(384)* near Dumfries; transferred to the town itself, where he served as an exciseman; and continued to write poetry, concentrating now on Scottish songs (e.g., "Auld Lang Syne" and "O My Luve's Like a Red, Red Rose"). He died at **Burns House** *(384)* in Dumfries in 1796 and was buried in St. Michael's Kirkyard, where the elaborate **Burns Mausoleum** *(384)* was later erected in his memory. Besides those already mentioned, other memorials to Scotland's greatest poet include the **Land o' Burns Centre** *(389)*, the **Burns Monument**, and **Brig o' Doon** *(389)* in Alloway; **Souter Johnnie's Cottage** *(391)* at Kirkoswald; the **Burns Monument and Museum** *(390)* in Kilmarnock; and the **Tam o' Shanter Museum** *(389)* in Ayr. Of these the last named, crowded and untidy, reflects perhaps best of all the disordered quality of the heaven-taught ploughman's private life.

The Ayrshire poet was not the only Scottish writer of plebeian origin to be honored by Edinburgh's *literati*. Another was James Hogg, born in 1770, son of a shepherd in a remote part of Ettrick Forest in Selkirkshire. Befriended by Walter Scott *(see below)*, he published his first poem in 1801 and, with the subsequent appearance of "The Queen's Wake "(1813), was hailed as "The Ettrick Shepherd" and given a place on the staff of *Blackwood's Magazine*, where he came to associate with Wordsworth, Byron, and other literary luminaries. Not until 1824, however, did his true genius come to maturity with the publication of *The Private Memoirs and Confessions of a Justified Sinner*. This short novel is, quite simply, a masterpiece. Whether viewed as a Scottish variation on the theme of Faust, a devastating attack on Calvinist theology, a psychological study of a schizophrenic religious fanatic, or a simple tale of horror, this is a gripping and disturbing story that deserves far more attention in the English-speaking world than it has received. Its author is commemorated in his native village of Ettrick with the **James Hogg Monument** *(420)*.

Hogg's first introduction to the literary world came about as a result of his having helped Walter Scott assemble a collection of Border ballads that were published in 1802 as *The Minstrelsy of the Scottish Border*. Scott had been born in Edinburgh of a middle-class family, educated at the university there, and admitted to the bar. As a child suffering from infantile paralysis, he had been sent to his grandfather's farm near Kelso, where the gaunt ruins of **Smailholm Tower** *(416)* and other relics of the Border's turbulent past excited his imagination and imbued him with an abiding passion for the romantic aspects of Scottish history. After publishing the ballads, he turned his hand to writing narrative poetry and in quick succession (1805–1810) produced *The Lay of the Last Minstrel, Marmion*, and *The Lady of the Lake*—all well received in spite of Samuel Coleridge's criticism that Scott had done no more than to reduce to verse the standard formulae of the typical Gothic novel. His poetry was certainly easy to read and easy to memorize, and such lines as "O what a tangled web we weave/ When first we practise to deceive!" *(Marmion)* rapidly achieved the status of cliché.

In 1814 he turned to fiction, and, with the publication of *Waverley*, his career as a novelist began. From then until his death in 1832, Scott cranked out twenty-five historical novels, sometimes as many as three a year. Such an accelerated production schedule was necessary if the author was to meet the heavy expenses incurred in enlarging his estate near Melrose and building thereon, after 1822, the pseudomedieval manor called **Abbotsford** *(419)*. As Thomas Carlyle was to put it, "Scott's career consisted of writing impromptu novels to buy farms with." Another spur to his busy pen was the bankruptcy in 1826 of the Ballantyne press with which Scott was associated. Feeling morally obligated, he worked for the next five years for no other return than the satisfaction of seeing the partnership's accumulated debt paid off.

Immensely popular in his own day, Walter Scott's fiction has not withstood the test of time. His plots, though ingenious, seem contrived and often unbelievable. His genteel heroes and heroines are uninteresting and two-dimensional, their language absurdly stilted, and their motivations obscure. Yet it must be said that Scott was a master of suspense, and as E. M. Forster remarked, "We do just want to know what happened. And keep turning the pages eagerly to the end." Paradoxically, considering the author's Toryism, his plebeian characters are much better drawn than his aristocrats, and their dialogues in Broad Scots are pungent, often witty, and seemingly authentic. The decided superiority of *Old Mortality* and *The Heart of Midlothian* over all the rest of Scott's *oeuvre* is doubtless explainable, therefore, by the fact that both novels are concerned in large measure with the lives of peasants. Jeanie Deans (*The Heart of Midlothian*) and Cuddie Headrigg (*Old Mortality*) still come across as real people caught up in serious moral dilemmas; Edgar Ravenswood (*Bride of Lammermoor*) and Rose Bradwardine (*Waverley*) seem made of papier-mâché.

Scott's real genius lay not in the delineation of plot or character but in his sympathetic re-creation of the historical setting of his works. Indeed, it can be said that he invented the historical novel, and such subsequent writers as Count Tolstoy, Victor Hugo, and Alexandre Dumas were, in a sense, mere followers. Most of the novels dealing with Scottish history concern conflicts of cultures: Highland versus Lowland; peasant versus aristocrat; Calvinist orthodoxy versus secularism; and, most of all, past versus present. The painful birth of new manners, beliefs, and values and the accompanying resistance to change of the old order constitute together the major recurring theme of Scott's abundant fictional works. In this respect he stood outside the contemporary mainstream of improvement and enlightenment. The costs of modernization, and not its hoped-for benefits, were his chief concern. He was, after all, by his own admission, "a Jacobite at heart." The conspicuous **Scott Monument** *(444)* in Edinburgh, raised in his honor in 1840, is therefore a singularly appropriate memorial. Rising to a height of 180 feet above Princes Street, this anachronistic Gothic fantasy stands in marked contrast to the severe neoclassical elegance of Edinburgh's New Town (*see below*). Behind it is the railway track, but Sir Walter's statue, beneath a crowded canopy of pinnacles and crockets, faces, fortunately, in the opposite direction.

The author's baronetcy was the gift of King George IV, who paid a splendid royal visit to Edinburgh in 1822—the first of his family to do so since his great-uncle, the Duke of Cumberland. Scott was chosen master of ceremonies, and the climacteric of the event was the grand levee at the Palace of Holyroodhouse, where His Majesty appeared kilted in something called the Royal Stuart tartan, which, with the rest of his "Highland" wardrobe, cost slightly more than £1,354. The occasion marked the official beginning of the cult of the Highlands, which has ever since been a central feature of Scotland's projected image and which owes much to the popularity of Scott's novels and narrative poems.

The growing fashionability of the tartan proved a boon to the Lowland woollen industry, which was struggling to stay alive against the competition of the more efficient Yorkshire mills (*see below*). Soon there was a demand for clan setts, which at least one manufacturer, Messrs. William Wilson of Bannockburn, satisfied by the simple device of assigning clan names to patterns previously identified only by number. The publication in 1831 of *The Scottish Gael; or Celtic Manners as Preserved Among the*

Highlanders by James Logan seemed to authenticate at least fifty-five setts (some of them obtained from Wilson's pattern book). About a decade later, two brothers, calling themselves the Sobieski Stuarts and claiming falsely to be legitimate heirs of Prince Charles Edward, published the *Vestiarum Scoticum*, with seventy-five color plates illustrating the tartans of that many clans and families. Allegedly based on a sixteenth-century manuscript, the publication was a fraud, but so great was the frenzy among Lowlanders as well as Highlanders to garb themselves in ancestral tartan that the hoax was overlooked. As Lord Cockburn remarked: "The affectation of Celticism was absurd and rather nauseous. Hundreds who had never seen heather had the folly to array themselves in tartan." Today, an objective view of the history of the entire subject of Highland dress can best be obtained at the excellent **Museum of Scottish Tartans** *(500)* in Comrie, Perthshire.

"Celticism" was also kept alive by the Highland Society of London, formed in 1778, and by that of Edinburgh, founded in 1784 under the presidency of the Duke of Argyll. Emigration, both internal and overseas, spawned innumerable offshoots, among which various clan organizations proved to be the most tenacious. Clan museums abound today in Scotland. Among them are the **Clan Donnachaidh Museum** *(499)* near Blair Atholl, Perthshire; the **Clan MacPherson House and Museum** *(521)* in Newtonmore, Inverness-shire; the **Clan Donald Centre** *(521)* on Skye; and the Clan MacKay room in the **Strathnaver Museum** *(550)* in Bettyhill, Sutherland. Others are housed in various castles and stately homes: **Castle Menzies** *(496)* near Aberfeldy, Perthshire; **Duart Castle** *(472)* (Clan MacLean) on Mull; **Dunvegan Castle** *(522)* (Clan MacLeod) on Skye; and **Eilean Donan Castle** *(548)* (Clan MacRae) near Kyle of Lochalsh, Ross and Cromarty.

Artists and Architects

Another son of Scotland to be knighted by King George IV was the portrait painter Henry Raeburn. The ceremony took place during the king's visit of 1822 at **Hopetoun House** *(530)*, where several Raeburn portraits are still to be seen—one, of the second Earl of Hopetoun, copied from the original by Allan Ramsay, Junior. Both men were talented and popular portraitists. Ramsay (1713–1784), son of the famous poet and bookseller, maintained his studio in London, where he was eventually to be appointed Painter-in-Ordinary to King George III. Less renowned today than his contemporary Joshua Reynolds, Ramsay, in his own time, enjoyed almost as distinguished a patronage as his younger competitor. He was a friend of Dr. Johnson, corresponded with the French *philosophe* Diderot, and was admired by Voltaire. Cofounder of the Select Society, he was, in spite of his frequent absences in the southern capital, one of the moving spirits of the Scottish Enlightenment. Two of his best, and most famous, portraits are those of David Hume and Jean Jacques Rousseau, now hanging respectively in the **Scottish National Portrait Gallery** *(448)* and the **National Gallery of Scotland** *(444)*, both in Edinburgh. Others grace numerous of Scotland's stately homes, including one of Norman, twenty-second Chief of MacLeod, in **Dunvegan Castle** *(522)*, and one of Archibald Campbell, third Duke of Argyll, in **Inveraray Castle** *(463)*.

Raeburn, born near Edinburgh, opened his studio in that city in 1786 and remained there until 1810, when he too departed for London. More colorful than Ramsay, he painted portraits that somewhat resemble the flushed visages painted by his English contemporary, Sir Thomas Lawrence. His *oeuvre* is scattered through Scotland's stately homes and galleries. Among the best known are his portraits of Walter Scott at **Bowhill** *(419)*; the third Earl of Rosebery at **Dalmeny House** *(429)*; General Alexander MacKenzie at **Castle Fraser** *(436)*; Major General Norman MacLeod, twenty-third chief, and his wife at **Dunvegan Castle** *(522)*; James Ker, fifth Duke of Roxburghe, at **Floors Castle** *(415)*; Sir Charles Hope at **Hopetoun House** *(430)*; numerous Edinburgh personages, including Professor Dugald Stewart and the publisher William Creech, in the **Scottish National Portrait Gallery** *(448)*; and the spectacular Colonel Alastair MacDonnell of Glengarry in the **National Gallery of Scotland** *(444)*. (Also here is the famous painting of Reverend Robert Walker skating on Duddingston Loch, which a family tradition claims to be by Raeburn, but which is so different in style from his usual work that the attribution is probably mistaken.)

Another Scottish painter who pleased King George IV was David Wilkie (1785–1841), whose portrait of the sovereign in tartan hangs at **Bowhill** *(419)* and whose crowded painting of the same king's entry into Holyrood in 1822 is in the **Scottish National Portrait Gallery** *(448)*. Son of a Fife minister, Wilkie is chiefly noted for his many genre paintings of Scottish peasant and village life—a subject that became increasingly attractive to artists as sentimentalism came to dominate the public taste of the Victorian era. In 1804 he painted *Pitlessie Fair* which hangs in the **National Gallery of Scotland** *(444)* along with *Distraining for Rent* and *The Irish Whisky Still*. Among his most typical productions, and probably the best known, is *The Village Politicians*, commissioned by Lord Chief Justice William Murray, first Earl of Mansfield, and now hanging in **Scone Palace** *(506)* outside Perth.

If Scottish painters of the late eighteenth and early nineteenth centuries were somewhat eclipsed by their English contemporaries (William Hogarth, Sir Joshua Reynolds, Sir Thomas Lawrence, Thomas Gainsborough), the same cannot be said of Scottish architects. Indeed, since the publication in 1717–1725 of *Vitruvius Britannicus* by Colin Campbell, a Scots lawyer turned London designer, a disproportionate share of the most lucrative architectural commissions in Britain fell to Scotsmen. Campbell is credited with the reintroduction into Britain of Palladianism, an extremely severe form of neoclassicism that had gone out of fashion after the death of Inigo Jones in 1652.

Of a different school was James Gibbs—an Aberdonian Jacobite whose architectural style can best be described as a mixture of baroque and Italian mannerist. Known chiefly for his church of St. Martin-in-the-Field on Trafalgar Square in London, Gibbs's only surviving work in Scotland is the West Kirk of the **Church of St. Nicholas** *(534)* in his native city. With its central pulpit and galleries on all four sides, this is a very Protestant-looking "preaching-box"—obviously more suited to the tastes of its worshippers than to those of its Roman Catholic architect. Closer in style to St. Martin-in-the-Field is **St. Andrews Parish Church** *(402)* in Glasgow, begun in 1739 but not completed until 1756 because of the interruption of The Forty-five, during which time Prince Charlie on one occasion stabled his horses in the unfinished church nave. The architect here was Allan Dreghorn, but the inspiration was clearly Gibbs, and the pedimented portico, elegant steeple, and rusticated architraves are distinctly reminiscent of the Aberdonian's masterpiece on Trafalgar Square.

Also Scottish, at least by descent, was Sir William Chambers, born in Sweden, the son of a Scottish merchant, who served as architectural tutor to Frederick, Prince of Wales, and later as chief architect to King George III. In that capacity he designed Somerset House, a mammoth neoclassic public building overlooking the Thames in London. He came seldom to Scotland, but in Edinburgh in 1771–1774 he did build for Sir Lawrence Dundas a fine neoclassical town house on St. Andrew Square in the New Town *(see below)*. Now the head office of the **Royal Bank of Scotland** *(447)*, the building is mainly remarkable for the startling cast iron dome of the "Banking Hall," added in 1858. With its glazed star-shaped coffers through which daylight filters into the room below, this is arguably the handsomest interior in the city.

More fashionable and therefore more successful than any of the above were William Adam's sons, John and Robert (and later James), who took over their father's business on his death in 1748 and in time developed a large clientele in both England and Scotland. Their first important Scottish commission was to complete the elder Adam's work at **Hopetoun House** *(430)*. The Earl of Hopetoun seems to have relied mostly on Robert, and it is he who was responsible for the delicate plasterwork and moldings in the hall, dining room (now the "yellow drawing room"), and "red drawing room"—all done with the airy elegance always associated with the name of

Adam. A second of their father's unfinished stately homes was **Pollok House** *(400)* near Glasgow, property of Sir John Maxwell of Blawarthill, who commissioned John and Robert to complete the construction and decorate the interior. Now chiefly famous for its art collection, this place too bears unmistakably the Adam stamp. At **Mellerstain** *(416)* near Kelso, Robert Adam once again took up an uncompleted work of his father. The death of the owner, George Baillie, in 1738 had brought an end to the construction of a great house planned in the Hopetoun style with a central block flanked by pavilions. William Adam had begun the work in 1725 but was never able to complete more than the two wings, which for forty years lay unconnected. Then, in 1770, his son Robert was commissioned by a new owner, George Baillie-Hamilton, to put up the missing central block and complete the original plan. The result is a great sprawling but symmetrical mansion whose classical proportions are concealed under oddly crenellated parapets, false machicolation, and hooded windows. The interior decorations are as graceful and elegant as any of Robert Adam's work. His next and final country-house commission in Scotland was for the rebuilding of **Culzean Castle** *(392)* on the Ayrshire coast. The owner was David Kennedy, tenth Earl of Cassillis, who had inherited from his brother a modified sixteenth-century tower-house. By the time Adam was finished in 1792 (the year of his death), Culzean had flowered into a parapeted Italianate palace, wildly romantic on a bluff overlooking the sea. Inside, however, all is ordered, cool, and classical—one of Robert Adam's major masterpieces of interior decoration.

Classicism was on the wane by the time of Robert Adam's death. With the new century, fashions began to change again—this time in the direction of Gothicism, that is, toward a fanciful imitation of medieval art forms that was eventually (late in the century) to culminate in the most bizarre forms of "Scotch baronial." The trend is often associated with the Romantic movement in literature and, in Scotland certainly, bore some relation to the tremendous popularity of Walter Scott's poems and novels. But it was an English architect, William Atkinson—a student of the better known James Wyatt—who was responsible for the earliest Scottish essays in what came to be known as Georgian Gothic. **Scone Palace** *(506)*, which he built (1802-1813) for David William Murray, third Earl of Mansfield, on the grounds of the ancient abbey near Perth is a restrained example of the style. Constructed of red sandstone, it is a rather sedate, symmetrical building whose chief "Gothic" characteristics are the battlemented towers and parapets and the small double pointed-arched windows. The interior is both Gothic and Georgian, with plasterwork reminiscent of Robert Adam in company with a vaulted gallery and chandeliers meant to look medieval. In 1812 Atkinson went to work for Charles Scott, fourth Duke of Buccleuch, to enlarge his eighteenth-century house of **Bowhill** *(419)* near Selkirk into something grander and more fashionable. Twenty years later, further additions were made under the direction of the Scots architect, William Burn, and the chapel was added in 1875–1877 by David Bryce, Burn's partner and a prolific builder of country houses in the by-then-very-popular Scotch baronial style. Here in the study hangs the famous portrait by Raeburn of Walter Scott, which is not surprising in view of the close friendship between the writer and the Duke of Buccleuch. No doubt this association had something to do with Scott's choosing Atkinson as architect for his storybook manor house of **Abbotsford** *(419)*. Here the crenellated tower, conical turrets, fake machicolation, and portcullis definitely pre-shadow the baronial fashions of the Victorian era. Scott stuffed the place with Scottish "antiquities," still on view: Rob Roy's sporran, dirk, and sword; a pocketbook worked by Flora MacDonald; a lock of Prince Charlie's hair; Bonnie Dundee's pistol; etc. It is a splendid monument to the author of *Waverley*—and just as appropriate as the Gothic shrine later raised in his honor on Princes Street, Edinburgh.

More restrained and more authentically Tudor in style is **Dalmeny House** *(429)* near Queensferry, West Lothian, built after 1815 by Archibald Primrose, fourth Earl of Rosebery. His architect was William Wilkins of London, but it was Rosebery himself who insisted on this more or less faithful reproduction of an East Anglia country house. As one commentator has put it, here is "a piece of England transported north of the Border to the shores of the Firth of Forth." **Lauriston Castle** *(451)*, just west of Edinburgh, is more authentically sixteenth century—at least in part. To the tower-house erected by Sir Archibald Napier some time before 1600, the Scottish architect William Burn, in 1827, attached a new range in the then fashionable neo-Jacobean style. The north facade overlooking the Firth of Forth—except for minor changes made in the late nineteenth century—remains almost entirely as Burn designed it.

Urban Growth: Edinburgh and Glasgow

Between 1755 and 1821, the total population of Scotland rose from a probable 1,265,000 to about 2,091,000. Edinburgh, by comparison, grew in the same period from 52,720 to 128,225, representing a much higher rate of increase, while Glasgow went from 24,451 to 147,043, which was higher still. Already Scotland was beginning that process of urbanization that, by 1871, would see two-thirds of its people living in cities.

At the midpoint of the eighteenth century most of the population of Edinburgh was still hived in the tall, crowded tenements off the Royal Mile, with some spillover down the steep slope to the south into the nether region called the Cowgate. To the north, residential expansion was blocked by the Nor' Loch (site of the present Princes Street Gardens); to the south by the Cowgate, which lay in a deep hollow accessible only by narrow wynds leading down the steep inclines from each side. The Old Town was overcrowded, busy, noisy, colorful, odiferous, and dirty. Edinburgh was still the headquarters of the law courts and the General Assembly of the Church of Scotland and, with its port of Leith nearby, a commercial center of some importance. It was not primarily an industrial city, but what manufacturing there was—breweries, tanneries, printing works, etc.—lay concentrated among the high tenements of the Canongate and the High Street, adding their smoke to that of the thousands of coal-burning domestic hearths to give the town its deserved nickname of "Auld Reekie." And in the short span of about twenty years all this was changed. The city burst its bonds to north and south, and if the Royal Mile showed little improvement as a result, it was now possible at least for citizens of means to escape it.

Credit for this remarkable feat of urban renewal must go chiefly to George Drummond, six times Lord Provost of Edinburgh. It was at his instigation that a set of proposals "for carrying on certain Public Works in the City of Edinburgh" was published in 1752 and, for the most part, actually put into execution. Three major propositions were submitted: (1) to build a merchants' exchange on the north side of High Street; (2) to erect a new building for the law courts and town council next to the old Parliament House; and (3) to extend the town northward by turning the Nor' Loch into a canal and opening new streets on the far side.

The first of these recommendations was acted upon promptly, and John Adam was commissioned to design a new Royal Exchange, on the High Street, since converted into the **City Chambers** *(439)*. Severely neoclassical with Corinthian pilasters, a pedimented frontispiece, and a rusticated piazza, the building would look out of place were it not for the reconstructed **Parliament House** *(439)* and **High Court of Justiciary** *(439)* across the street. Rather than raise a new edifice, as suggested in the second of the 1752 proposals, the city fathers ordered the old Parliament House and the adjacent court building to be remodelled. The architect chosen was Robert Reid, a rather unimaginative neoclassicist, who finished the work in 1807, replacing what must have been a rather interesting, turreted, "Jacobean" facade with a somewhat ponderous neoclassical front of Ionic pillars, pedimented windows, and roof-line balustrades. Reid was later (1802) to raise a new classical building for the **Bank of Scotland** *(439)*. Later modified along baroque lines, the bank still stands in a prominent position at the top of the Mound leading from the Old Town down to the new suburb built according to the third recommendation of the 1752 proposals.

Almost immediately after their publication, operations were begun to drain the Nor' Loch, although, instead of canalizing it as suggested, a public park (the Princes Street Gardens) was eventually installed on the dry bed. And in 1763 Provost Drummond laid the foundation stone for the North Bridge connecting the ancient city with Edinburgh's New Town.

The plan for this urban development had been drawn up by James Craig, about whom little is known save that he won the competition organized by the city fathers for designing a suburb on the far side of the new bridge. Craig's plan, possibly derived from the layout of the French provincial town of Nancy, consisted of two squares joined by a straight central east-west street (George Street), flanked by two others (Princes Street and Queen Street), and intersected at regular intervals by streets running north and south—in short, a grid.

Here was a potential bonanza for Scotland's architects, and a number seized this unusual opportunity to help build a new town *de novo*. Among them, of course, was Robert Adam; also Robert Reid, the last to enjoy the title of King's Architect for Scotland. Other contributors were William Burn, Thomas Hamilton, and Archibald Elliot. Finally, William Henry Playfair (1789-1857), working well into the nineteenth century, added what can be regarded as the finishing touches to James Craig's grand plan. But none—not even Adam—was allowed complete license. Strict municipal controls were maintained over building heights, window sizes, and many other details of construction. The canons of Greece and Rome were to be strictly observed, and, with the exception of the rounded pillars of the classical orders or the occasional dome or statue, a rigid rectangularity was to prevail. Not everyone was (or is) entirely pleased with the result. Henry Cockburn (1779-1854), Whig Solicitor General and Lord of Session, was not. In his *Memorials* (posthumously published) he complained: "Our escape from the old town gave us an unfortunate propensity to avoid whatever had distinguished the place we had fled from. Hence we were led into the blunder of long straight lines of street, divided to an inch, and all to the same number of inches, by rectangular intersections, every house being an exact duplicate of its neighbour." Admittedly, the prospect of George Street, especially looking eastward on a rainy day, can seem depressingly dull. But there is an austere elegance about it, and, in any case, it was to the taste of the enlightened elite of Edinburgh, who in short order vacated the Old Town for dwelling places in the New (as in fact did Cockburn himself).

The first building to go up in the New Town was Sir Lawrence Dundas's mansion (now the **Royal Bank of Scotland** *[447]*, already mentioned). Meanwhile, Robert and James Adam had been appointed architects for a new building to house the Scottish archives. Started in 1774 and in use by

1778, the **Register House** *(445)* on Princes Street is arguably Edinburgh's finest classical building, with its projecting Corinthian portico, Venetian windows in the corner pavilions, and flat central dome modelled on the Pantheon. Next to appear was St. Andrew's Church, now the parish **Church of St. Andrew and St. George** *(446)*, originally intended to be built on St. Andrew Square but shouldered out to a nearby location on George Street by Sir Lawrence Dundas who had co-opted the more favored site for his personal residence. The architect was Major Andrew Frazier, and the building was completed in 1784. It is oval in plan, with a pedimented front porch in the Corinthian order, a tall delicate spire added in 1789, and superb plasterwork on the interior ceiling in the manner of Robert Adam. The latter was commissioned in 1791 to produce a plan for Charlotte Square at the west end of George Street. He died before more than a beginning was made on the north side, but the monumental elegance of this very handsome four-sided oasis in the city center can be attributed to Adam and to the fidelity of his successors to the original plan, albeit with some departures. It is, in the words of A. J. Youngson, "symmetrical without needless duplication; full of variety yet harmonious and devoid of fussiness." On the north side is situated Number 7 Charlotte Square, maintained by the National Trust for Scotland as **Georgian House** *(446)*, decorated and furnished in the manner of the late eighteenth century, and today open to visitors. At the west end of the square stands the **West Register House** *(446)*, its huge green copper dome one of the most conspicuous features of the Edinburgh skyline. The building for a long time (1811–1964) housed St. George's Church and was designed by Robert Reid. Not far away, at the western end of Princes Street and barely within the limits of the New Town, is **St. John's Church** *(443)*, serving an Episcopalian congregation and different from its contemporary neighbors in not adhering to the classical canon. Designed by William Burn, the style is more or less English Perpendicular with plaster fan-vaulting seemingly copied from St. George's Chapel, Windsor. It was built in the years 1816–1818. During the same years, at the other end of the New Town, for another congregation of the same denomination, Archibald Elliot planned the building now designated **St. Paul's and St. George's Episcopal Church** *(449)*, on the model of King's College, Cambridge.

By that time the New Town was outgrowing its original confines and pushing eastward toward **Calton Hill** *(445)*. On this prominent elevation, visible from all over the city, was beginning to rise a strange collection of monuments, mostly meant to be replicas of ancient Greek originals and much admired by the burghers, who boasted of their city as the "Athens of the North." Others apparently agreed, and Queen Victoria reported that even Albert "felt sure that the Acropolis could not be finer." Here is the National Monument, planned by the English architect C. R. Cockerell but built by William Playfair as a replica of the Parthenon and dedicated to those who had fallen in the Napoleonic wars. The foundation stone was laid during King George IV's visit of 1822, but within a short time the money ran out and only twelve Doric columns were completed. Nearby is the New Observatory (1818) also by Playfair—a cruciform, domed temple that was meant to replace the Old Observatory (1776) by James Craig—a rather bizarre neo-Gothic structure not to be expected of the man who planned the New Town at the bottom of the hill. Two other monuments by Playfair merit attention: the first built in 1818 and dedicated to his uncle, John Playfair, eminent Professor of Mathematics at Edinburgh University; the second, the Dugald Stewart Monument (1832), honoring that most popular of the university's philosophy professors. Not far away is the Burns Monument, completed by Thomas Hamilton in 1830—another Corinthian peristyle, this one of questionable appropriateness. Nelson's Monument is more so—an upended stone telescope recalling the famous incident at Copenhagen when he chose to disregard his superior's orders to break off action against the Danes. It was designed shortly after the hero's death at Trafalgar by Robert Burn, father of the more famous architect, William. Down the hill toward the New Town lies the **Calton Old Burial Ground** *(445)*, with its splendid circular memorial to David Hume by Robert Adam (1777) and, of special interest to Americans, a fine statue of Abraham Lincoln with a manumitted slave at the base (1893). Westward of here lies the classical **Regent Bridge** *(445)*, built in 1815 by Archibald Elliot, also as a war memorial. It spans Calton road and carries the same architect's Waterloo Place (the eastward extension of Princes Street) on to the foot of Calton Hill.

North of the New Town, in 1823-1836 William Burn built the **Edinburgh Academy** *(449)*, a rather plain, single-story Doric building with a domed elliptical hall. Along the same lines, though more grandiose, was his John Watson's School (1828) on Belford Road—now housing the **Scottish National Gallery of Modern Art** *(449)*. Better known academically than either of these institutions was the **Royal High School** *(445)*, opened in 1829—an enormous and splendid building looking like an oversized Doric temple. The architect was Thomas Hamilton.

But it was William Playfair, more than any other architect, who gave the New Town its Greek monumental look. His **St. Stephen's Church** *(449)* on St. Vincent Street is a huge octagonal building with a cavernous arched entryway, above which rises a high clock tower with corners of twin Doric pillars. The **Royal Scottish Academy** *(444)* (originally the Royal Institution), standing at the north end of the Mound on Princes Street, was completed in 1835—a massive Greek temple with fluted Doric columns and a profusion of carving on the pediments and architraves. Ten years later

Thomas Hamilton completed a home for the **Royal College of Physicians** *(447)* on Queen Street. Here is an unusual terraced frontage in the Corinthian order—a flat-topped portico supporting two large statues at its corners, and above that a pedimented portico enclosing a central window and topped by a third statue.

To the south of the Royal Mile too there was much building in the decades that straddled the turn of the eighteenth and nineteenth centuries. In the 1760s it appeared for a while that Brown Square and George Square would become the most fashionable parts of town, but the opening of the New Town shifted by 180 degrees the flow of rich escapees from the noise, stench, and congestion of the old city. Then, in June 1788, access to the south was greatly facilitated by the opening of the South Bridge, a high viaduct spanning the Cowgate. This, of course, gave birth to much construction activity in the area, of which the most notable early example was the erection of a new home for the city's university. This institution, though rapidly growing in both size and prestige, was still housed in the dilapidated quarters that Principal Robertson, in showing the premises to Dr. Johnson in 1773, had apologetically referred to as *"Hae miseriae nostrae."* To Robert Adam was awarded the commission for raising what is now called **Edinburgh University, Old College** *(435)*, on the corner of South Bridge and Chambers Street. The foundation stone was laid in November 1789, but Adam died before the building was completed. Then, owing to the outbreak of war with France in 1793, construction was stopped and the half-finished site lay empty until 1817, when William Playfair was commissioned to finish the job. Much of his predecessor's plan was retained. Except for the dome (designed in 1886–87 by Rowand Anderson), the great classical entrance front off South Bridge is pure Adam, as is the elevation within the court facing the main gate. Playfair's most notable contribution was the upper library, which, in the words of A. J. Youngson, is "one of the finest achievements of late classical architecture in Britain, and which can stand comparison, although in a quite different style, with the Wren Library at Trinity College, Cambridge." Playfair's second great architectural contribution to Edinburgh's "south side" was the Surgeon's Hall, now called the **Royal College of Surgeons' Hall and Museum** *(435)*, on Nicolson Street, today sadly obscured by the ugly neighboring buildings. Here the Ionic order was employed in a multicolumn hexastyle portico that fronts a massive building richly decorated with scrollwork. It was completed in 1832.

Although growing even faster than Edinburgh, and by 1821 outstripping it in size of population, Glasgow displays far fewer architectural relics of this great period of its history. The city's rising commercial prosperity was directly attributable to the Act of Union of 1707, which brought Scotland within England's Old Colonial System. Specifically, this meant that Scotland could share in the former monopoly of English shippers in the carrying trade of such important colonial raw materials as sugar, cotton, and tobacco and of English ports in the transshipment of these commodities abroad. The Clyde ports, closer by several hundred miles than any of their English competitors to the tobacco-growing colonies of America, were thus placed in a highly advantageous position. Although not until the early nineteenth century was the river channel deepened and straightened so as to permit oceangoing vessels to tie up at the city's own docks, Glasgow merchants managed the business and owned the ships that plied to and from the downriver ports of Greenock and Port Glasgow. Tobacco, though not the only colonial product to be imported, was the major one, accounting in 1772 for 80 percent of all Scottish imports from North America. By that time the so-called "Tobacco Lords" of Glasgow were importing as much as all the English ports combined, most of the product being re-exported to France under arrangements highly profitable to the middlemen. After the American War of Independence, this advantage of course disappeared, but Glasgow merchants quickly shifted to sugar and cotton and suffered only temporarily from the loss of the mother country's monopoly of the export of American products. The foundations of what was to become Britain's "second city" were thus firmly laid even before the Industrial Revolution had gone into full gear.

Glasgow's urban growth, in contrast to that of Edinburgh, was piecemeal. The city spread mostly to the north of the river, although across the Clyde arose a handsome Georgian village in the Gorbals, later to become the most notorious slum in Glasgow. Of the few surviving eighteenth-century buildings, probably the most impressive is the **Trades House** *(403)* on Glassford Street, designed by Robert Adam but not completed until after his death. The rusticated facade of the ground floor is topped by a pedimented portico with Ionic pillars—a fairly typical Adam production. Not far away is **Hutchesons' Hospital** *(404)* on the corner of Ingram and John Streets. Now headquarters for the National Trust for Scotland, this simple classical structure, with a steeple in the manner of Christopher Wren, was designed by a local architect, David Hamilton, and completed in 1805. **Blythswood Square** *(405)*, built in 1823–1829 to a plan of John Brash, comes closer in style to Edinburgh's New Town than do any of the other residential buildings in Glasgow. And like its prototype, the square attracted an upwardly mobile middle class intent on escaping the pollution of the burgeoning central city.

Another sign of the city's growing prosperity was the creation of the Royal Exchange for the convenience of its businessmen. David Hamilton was commissioned in 1827 to enlarge the mansion first built in 1780 by the rich Tobacco Lord, William Cunningham, and later taken over as the Glasgow office of the Royal Bank of Scotland. Opened in 1829, the exchange served not only the purposes for which it had been built but also as a reception hall for distinguished nineteenth-century visitors, including Confederate ex-President Jefferson Davis and Prince Kropotkin. Subsequently acquired as the home of Stirling's Library, the present site on Royal Exchange Square is designated **Glasgow Royal Exchange & Stirling's Library** *(403)*. This is a fine, handsome building, the stateliness of its massive Corinthian portico matched by the elegance of the barrel-vaulted coffered ceiling inside.

Of Glasgow's surviving churches dating from the period under consideration, only two (in addition to St. Andrew's, described above) are worthy of note. The first is **St. George's Tron Church** *(405)* on Buchanan Street, designed by William Stark and completed in 1807. Essentially baroque in character, the lower half of the tower reflects the influence of the English architect Nicholas Hawksmoor; the upper half, topped by a pretty miniature rotunda, resembles the work of Sir Christopher Wren. The second is **St. Andrew's Cathedral** *(401)* on Clyde Street opposite the river—designed by a prolific Scottish ecclesiastical architect, James Gillespie Graham, in a more or less English Perpendicular style. Though not originally a cathedral, this roomy church was built to serve Glasgow's growing Roman Catholic population. The worshippers at St. Andrew's in the early nineteenth century would have been predominantly Irish, recently settled in Glasgow. Their presence in such numbers as to warrant the building of such a church was the direct result of the city's rapid industrialization and its consequent growing need for a large supply of cheap labor.

The Industrial Revolution

That "rapid, cumulative, structural change" in the economy of Britain, which is Peter Mathias's definition of the Industrial Revolution, was taking place in Scotland as well as England in the late eighteenth and early nineteenth centuries, though perhaps lagging a few years behind. The antecedent conditions for the unprecedented expansion in the large-scale manufacture of goods for sale were the same on both sides of the border. Scottish infant industries, like those of Lancashire and Yorkshire, were blessed with a large pool of cheap labor—constantly filling to overflow with Irish immigrants and Highlanders, the latter sometimes driven south by the clearances. Thanks to improvement, domestic production of foodstuffs was sufficient to supply this labor force no longer engaged in agriculture. Scottish manufacturers enjoyed the same market advantages as the English from the overseas empire secured and maintained by British naval and military might. Thanks in part to the profits accumulated in Glasgow from the tobacco trade, capital was available for industrial investment, and Scotland had long had a sophisticated banking system, if anything, more responsive than England's to the needs of new and speculative enterprises. Basic raw materials for fabrication were on hand, as in the case of flax, or easily obtainable, as in the case of cotton. Water power was plentiful. The relatively high degree of literacy in Scotland created favorable conditions for the emergence of a native managerial class. Technical skills of a high order also seem to have been a by-product of the Scottish educational system. Lowland Scots were notoriously hard workers—partly from necessity, partly perhaps because of long exposure to Calvinist strictures on the sin of sloth. And, by the time that Scottish industry had reached what economists call "the point of take-off into self-sustained growth," Scotland had a network of internal communications capable of moving raw materials from their site of origin to their place of manufacture and of finished goods thence to their markets.

In respect to the last point, the Scottish Turnpike Act of 1750 and the enforcement of Statute Labor Acts had vastly improved and enlarged the network of roads leading between England and Scotland, between such Scottish towns as Edinburgh, Glasgow, Perth, and Dundee and between these places and their rural hinterlands. Nor was Thomas Telford's road work solely confined to the Highlands. He supervised the building of 184 miles of new roads in the Lowlands, including the one paralleled by the present trunk route from Carlisle to Glasgow (the A 74 and A 73). Above Lanark it crossed the Mouse Water over Telford's **Cartland Crags Bridge** *(411)*, 130 feet in height, with three tall arches, and very dramatic. Even more so is his **Dean Bridge** *(449)* over the Water of Leith in Edinburgh. Here are four arches, each of 90-foot span, and footpaths on either side supported on secondary arches. Telford's first bridge in Scotland was the pretty little **Tongland Bridge** *(383)*, spanning the Dee above Kirkcudbright. It still stands—with a crenellated parapet and a wide middle arch with three narrow pointed arches on each side.

Just as useful for purposes of industrial development were the new canals—not "going from nowhere to nowhere" as in the case of the Caledonian Canal, but connecting coal fields with factories, towns with towns, and industries with markets. The most important to survive is the **Forth and Clyde Canal** *(407)* which ultimately ran from Bowling on the west bank of the Clyde above Glasgow to the mouth of the Carron River at Grangemouth. The first sod was cut on 10 July 1768 under direction of the engineer John Smeaton, and on 18 July 1790, Smeaton's successor, Robert Whitworth ceremoniously poured a hogshead of Forth Water into the Clyde, thus opening the canal. The following month the sloop *Agnes* sailed from Leith on the Forth to Greenock on the Clyde. Today, there are still a number of visible sites related to this fine artificial waterway, thirty-five miles in length with thirty locks: the **Kelvin Aqueduct** *(407)* in Glasgow; the **Bowling Locks and Customs House** *(475)* on the Clyde southeast of Dumbarton; the **Cumbernauld Locks** *(474)*, just north of the town of that name; and the long series of **Falkirk Locks** *(476)* in the town center.

Still the Forth and Clyde did not enter Edinburgh. To correct the deficiency, work was commenced on the **Union Canal** *(427)* to run from Falkirk into the capital. It was completed in 1822 but, unlike the Forth and Clyde, was never a commercial success, largely owing to its having been built on the eve of Scotland's great railway boom, which would render all canals obsolete. At Falkirk the **Union Canal Tunnel** *(476)* can still be seen, and in West Lothian, between Broxburn and Kirkliston, is a series of **Union Canal Bridges** *(431)*. Better still is the **Canal Museum** *(427)* in Linlithgow, located on a stretch of the abandoned waterway and offering a half-hour's pleasure cruise on the *Victoria*, a replica of a nineteenth-century steam packet.

Even more than in England, the industrial revolution in Scotland was primarily a revolution in the manufacture of textiles. And the first textile to be primarily the product of mechanical processes that could be called "industrial" in the modern sense was linen. The Board of Trustees for Manufactures and Fisheries, established by Act of Parliament in 1727, did much to encourage the industry, and the Bounty Acts of 1742 and later fostered the development of a considerable trade with the sugar and tobacco colonies, especially the export of cheap cloth for slaves. Spinning was done mostly by women; weaving by men. In both cases they worked at home. Flax-spinning machinery remained primitive, and not until 1787 was the first Scottish water-driven mill for spinning linen thread opened in Kincardine. After 1825, when John Kay of Lancashire invented a technique for "wet spinning," which overcame the natural gumminess of flax fibers, spinning rapidly moved from fireside to water-powered factory. Weaving remained by and large a hand loom craft until about the same date. In general, the production of coarse linen for sails, sacking, tents, etc., was concentrated in Angus and Fife (Dundee, Kirkcaldy, and Dunfermline in particular); that of fine linens in the West, especially Glasgow and Paisley.

Without the experience built up in the linen trade, especially around Glasgow, it is doubtful if the cotton industry would have taken root there as early as it did. Beginning in the 1770s, the costs of raw cotton began to fall just as the price of flax was rising, and Eli Whitney's invention of the cotton gin in 1793 accelerated the process. Glasgow quickly began to build up an extensive cotton industry on the basis of the already existing manufacture of linens. The numerous hand loom weavers who had previously made fine linen cloths now found more rewarding work in the manufacture of cotton textiles. Wages (in the form of piece rates for woven cloth) were high, and the work could be performed at home. The **Weaver's Cottage** *(397)* in the village of Kilbarchan about eight miles southwest of Glasgow, now maintained by the National Trust for Scotland, dates from 1723 and is probably typical of such establishments. It, incidentally, houses a two-hundred-year-old loom, still in working order.

Technology advanced at an uneven pace. New inventions—originating in England—speeded up the spinning process, thus causing a bottleneck in weaving, in spite of John Kay's flying shuttle, which had made its appearance as early as 1733. James Hargreaves's spinning jenny, patented in 1770, used eight spindles, increased to eighty-four by 1784. It spun a fine weft but was unsuitable for warps. Richard Arkwright's water frame produced a much stronger thread for the warp and, unlike the jenny, could be driven by water power. This made it feasible to assemble the spinners in factories, at first always called "mills." Crompton's mule, introduced in 1775, was an improvement over Arkwright's invention and made possible the spinning of both weft and warp of sufficient strength to produce fine muslins. The first big water-powered mill to spin cotton was established at Rothesay on Bute in 1779, but it was not until the founding of **New Lanark** *(411)* in 1786 that cotton spinning in Scotland was organized on a large scale.

New Lanark was an industrial settlement built on the falls of the River Clyde by the English inventor and manufacturer Richard Arkwright in partnership with David Dale, a Glasgow linen merchant and banker. Arkwright hoped the site would become a "new Manchester." Instead, under the supervision of Dale and later of his son-in-law, Robert Owen, it became a model industrial village, the cynosure of progressives, socialists, labor sympathizers, and enthusiasts for the cooperative movement throughout the Western world. Dale built four mills plus tenements for the workers—as many as two thousand of them, including pauper children and a group of Highlanders, stormbound en route to Maryland, whom he diverted to his new enterprise. (A bell bearing the inscription "Haggars Town [Hagerstown, Maryland] . . . 1786" can still be seen here.) After the arrival of Owen, a Welshman who had prospered in the cotton-spinning business in Manchester, more buildings were added, including the Institute for the Formation of Character and a school for children under ten, which was the minimum age for millhands established by this unusually benign factory owner. Owen's advanced views on labor relations and his renowned paternalism paid dividends, as he himself was first to acknowledge. His profits from the enterprise were reckoned at only slightly under £400,000. Most of the buildings raised by Dale and Owen at New Lanark still stand, and the riverine setting of the village on the northeast bank of the upper

Clyde is still as beautiful as it must have been when Arkwright and Dale first settled on it as the site for their new Manchester. Now undergoing restoration, it promises to be, when properly developed to receive visitors, the premier industrial-archaeological site in Scotland.

Dale also established cotton mills at Blantyre, Lanarkshire, in partnership with James Monteith. Thanks to the fact that the famous Scottish medical missionary and African explorer David Livingstone was born on the premises, a portion of the workers' tenements has been preserved and converted into a museum. In the **David Livingstone Centre** *(398)* can be seen the furnished single-room apartment in "Shuttle Row" where he was born and spent his childhood—employed after the age of ten as a paid mill hand working from 6:00 A.M. until 8:00 P.M. Here too, in addition to a large collection of relics of Livingstone's African career, is the Blantyre Room with displays of spinning machinery and a model of the village and mill as it appeared in the early nineteenth century. No such efforts at preservation have been made, unfortunately, in connection with another of David Dale's projects. In the north, with the assistance of George MacIntosh, inventor of the raincoat, he established the **Spinningdale Mill** *(551)* on the Dornoch Firth east of Bonar Bridge. This four-story jenny factory was gutted by fire in 1809, and all that survives is the burnt-out shell.

In the weaving section of the cotton industry the factory system was much slower to develop, and as late as 1838 there were more than fifty-one thousand hand looms in the Lowlands, the great majority being engaged in cotton weaving. Wages, meanwhile, after 1800, had dropped precipitately, and the failure of a weavers' strike in 1812 had driven them down still further. Indeed it was low wages, especially in the area of Paisley, that induced an Edinburgh manufacturer in about 1805 to put weavers to work on the production of imitation Kashmir shawls. These intricately designed and colorful patterns quickly caught on, and "Paisley shawls" became immensely popular, even though many were woven (or stamped) elsewhere. After the 1830s, more and more were factory-made as power looms began to edge out the domestic industry. Even so, until the 1870s, when Paisley shawls suddenly went out of fashion, many continued to be woven in the old-fashioned manner. At the **Paisley Art Gallery & Museum** *(396)* is a fine exhibit of these once very popular items of apparel, arranged in chronological order of their manufacture, with informative placards relating the history of the industry.

Surprisingly, considering the number of sheep in Scotland, the Scottish woollen industry lagged behind cotton textiles, in both technological progress and quantity of production. The woollen and worsted mills of Yorkshire appear to have had for many years a pronounced competitive advantage over those of the Scottish Border counties, even to the extent that they absorbed a lion's share of the production of Scottish wool. Nevertheless, in the late eighteenth century Galashiels in Selkirkshire began to develop as a spinning center for woollen yarn, and by the 1790s mills were to be seen lining the banks of Gala Water and the River Tweed. Even as late as 1851, Border woollen mills derived 84 percent of their power from water—well after the cotton textile industry had gone over mostly to the steam engine. By the 1820s, weaving too was becoming factory-centered. In addition to manufacturing tartan, increasingly fashionable after King George IV's visit to Edinburgh in 1822, the Borders became famous for their production of tweed. The brand name dates from 1826, when a London clerk misread the word *tweel*—meaning "grays and drabs"—on an invoice from Scotland and labelled the goods after the name of the river that Sir Walter Scott had made so famous. By mid-century, travelling cloaks and fancy trousers of this material were very popular items of men's wear, especially the black and white pattern called "shepherd's check." The **Scottish Museum of Textiles** *(421)*, in the rear of Henry Ballantyne & Sons at Walkerburn, has a very informative series of exhibits illustrating the history of the local woollen industry. Another branch was hosiery knitting, which came to be centered at Hawick, where mechanical knitting frames were introduced as early as the 1770s. The story of this development can be followed at the **Hawick Museum and Art Gallery** *(412)* in Wilton Lodge Park on the north bank of the Teviot River.

After textiles, the mining and smelting of metal ore and the fabrication of products therefrom constituted the second significant ingredient of Scotland's Industrial Revolution. Lead mining and smelting in the Lowther Hills of Dumfriesshire date back to Roman times. In the seventeenth century the mines were owned and exploited by the Hope family, later to become Earls of Hopetoun, and in the eigtheenth and nineteenth centuries by the Dukes of Buccleuch. The open-air **Museum of Scottish Lead Mining** *(387)*, in the vicinity of Wanlockhead, contains an abandoned mine (opened in 1790), a smelting mill, a wooden beam engine (originally horse-powered) for pumping water from the mine shafts, and a miners' library, in addition to a small conventional museum of artifacts and exhibits associated with the industry.

The iron industry in Scotland, as elsewhere in Britain until the early eighteenth century, depended on charcoal as the highly carbonized fuel required to burn off impurities in the ore and produce a pig iron that could be hammered into wrought iron products or further heated and converted into cast iron. Charcoal was of course a wood derivative, and as Britain's supply of timber diminished, the production of iron by this process became more and more expensive. The constant search for new sources of timber drove the industry north into the Furness peninsula of Lancashire and thence into Scotland. At Taynuilt in Argyll a group of investors from Lancashire leased a large piece of well-wooded land from the Earl of

Breadalbane and Campbell of Lochnell. There in 1752 they built **Bonawe Furnace** *(473)* for the purpose of smelting ore brought up mostly from Lancashire by ship. The pig iron thus produced was then shipped back from the company's dock on Loch Etive close to the furnace. War with France brought prosperity even to such a high-cost enterprise, and it is perhaps not surprising that the workers of Bonawe raised the first monument in Britain to Lord Nelson, shortly after his death at Trafalgar. Today the remains of this establishment (blast furnace, charcoal houses, iron-ore sheds, workers' housing) constitute the best-developed industrial-archeological site in Scotland. That these buildings should have been so well preserved is doubtless due to the fact that the works continued in operation until as late as 1876.

Coke, however, not charcoal, was to be the basis of the major development of the iron industry in Britain. Coke is a coal derivative that Abraham Darby first succeeded in using to smelt iron in his furnace at Coalbrookdale in Salop, thereby freeing the industry from its dependence on timber. In 1759 the Carron Iron Works was established near Falkirk—the first in Scotland to use coke. It became quickly famous for the carronade, a large-caliber cannon of short range, especially suitable to the new type of close-in naval tactics favored by Horatio Nelson. Yet the Scottish industry was at a disadvantage because of the inferiority of the local coal, which seldom yielded as much coke as did that mined in England or Wales. True, the ironmaster David Mushet had discovered in 1801 that black-band ironstone, when mixed with raw coal before firing, would yield a satisfactory product. But it was not until 1828, with the patenting by James B. Neilson of the hot-blast process of smelting (i.e., preheating the furnace), that the Scottish iron industry became truly competitive. With an ample supply of both coal and black-band ironstone, especially in the Old Monkland parish just east of Glasgow, Scotland could produce pig iron of high quality at low cost, and after 1835 a boom in iron began. From having accounted for 5 percent of British production early in the nineteenth century, the Scottish iron industry increased its share to 25 percent by 1840 and maintained it at that level for at least two decades.

Without a steady supply of cheap coal, such a development would, of course, have been impossible. Coal there was aplenty in Scotland, but most of it was situated in deep underground seams accessible only by vertical shafts from the bottom of which galleries had to be driven horizontally. All these deep mines were subject to seepage, and keeping shafts and galleries clear of water was the most troublesome aspect of coal mining. In 1712 Thomas Newcomen, a Devon ironmonger, had perfected a pump that operated by alternately forcing steam into a cylinder and then condensing it with an injection of cold water, thus imparting an up-and-down motion to a piston that drove the simple mechanism for bringing water up out of a shaft. Useful as it was, the Newcomen engine was inefficient owing to the great thermal losses resulting from the cylinder's having to be reheated each time cold water was injected to condense the steam. It was a Scottish instrument maker who hit upon the means of correcting this deficiency and who is rightly considered the inventor of the steam engine—unquestionably the most significant technological breakthrough of the Industrial Revolution.

James Watt was born in Greenock, where the **Mclean Museum** *(396)* maintains a small collection of his personal belongings and tools. At the age of nineteen he went to London as an apprentice instrument maker and two years later returned home to be employed by the University of Glasgow. There he was asked to repair a Newcomen engine that was being used as a teaching aid by John Anderson, Professor of Natural Philosophy. Watt improved on it by installing a separate condenser, thus speeding up the motion of the piston by eliminating the need to reheat the cylinder after each injection of cold water. Simple as it was, the idea was revolutionary. Another Glasgow professor, Joseph Black, encouraged Watt to perfect the device and introduced him to Dr. John Roebuck, a cofounder of the Carron Iron Works who had leased **Kinneil House** *(425)* near Bo'ness with a view to working the local coal seams. Interested in the commercial possibilities of an improved steam engine, Roebuck sponsored Watt's patent application in return for a two-thirds share in the invention. When the patent was in fact granted in January 1769, Roebuck established Watt in a small outhouse on the Kinneil grounds to build a full-scale engine. This little building still stands, and in front of it is the cylinder of one of James Watt's first engines. Roebuck, however, went bankrupt in 1773, and his share in the invention was sold to Matthew Boulton of Birmingham, who, in partnership with Watt, was thereafter responsible for the production of the engine. Once Watt had discovered a method for converting the reciprocal movements of the steam-driven piston to rotary motion, his engine could be linked to a series of gears and shafts to drive machinery of almost infinite variety. Thus industry was freed from the water wheel; factories could be set up wherever convenient; steam could be employed to drive ships and, later, wheeled vehicles. The second phase of the Industrial Revolution was launched.

POLITICS

"The important point about eighteenth century [British] government attitudes toward Scotland," concludes the historian Alexander Murdoch, "is that they very seldom took the trouble to have one." This is to say that, so long as the sixteen Scottish Peers and forty-five Members of Parliament remained subservient to the wishes of the prevailing ministry in London, there was little government intrusion into the domestic affairs of Scotland. Subservience was assured, after The Forty-five as before, by assigning government patronage to a single "manager" who in return could guarantee to the ministry in power all, or most of, the votes of the Scottish representatives in both houses of Parliament. Until his death in 1761, this was Archibald Campbell, third Duke of Argyll, who in 1743 had stepped into the shoes of his brother, the second duke. Although Lord Hervey compared him to "a pedantic, dirty, shrewd, unbred fellow of a college," and Horace Walpole wrote that Argyll "had so little great either in himself or his views . . . that posterity will probably interest themselves very slightly in his fortunes," he was on the whole an effective manager and gave both the ministry in London and the Scottish nobility and gentry what they wanted. What the ministry chiefly wanted of Scotland, especially after William Pitt the Elder came into office, was soldiers. What the Scots wanted was a steady flow of army commissions and other lucrative government posts. Argyll served as friendly broker, to the satisfaction of both sides.

When George III ascended the throne in 1760, his chief minister was Argyll's nephew, John Stuart, third Earl of Bute. For the short time he was in power, Bute's deputy for Scottish affairs was his brother, James Stuart MacKenzie, who was made Lord Privy Seal for Scotland, so that, as Bute explained, "Scotch affairs will go on under the care of my brother as they did under my late uncle." But MacKenzie was dropped when George Grenville assumed the ministry in 1765, and for a number of years there was no autonomous manager of Scotland. Then a new star appeared on the horizon in the person of Henry Dundas, who made his political fortune by attaching himself to William Pitt the Younger.

Scion of a remarkable Edinburgh legal dynasty, Dundas served as Solicitor General for Scotland, Member of Parliament for Midlothian, and Lord Advocate; and, in London, as Pitt's Treasurer of the Navy, Home Secretary, President of the Board of Control for India, Secretary for War, and First Lord of the Admiralty. Sometimes referred to by contemporaries as "Harry the Ninth, uncrowned King of Scotland," Dundas, in the words of the historian William Ferguson, "at the height of his powers, straddled Britain like a colossus." Though generally well liked in Scotland for his bluff and friendly manner, he was burned in effigy by an Edinburgh mob in 1792 for the repressive measures taken against radical supporters of the French Revolution. Created Viscount Melville in 1802, he was impeached by the House of Commons for the alleged mishandling of treasury funds, acquitted in 1806 in the House of Lords, but kept out of office thereafter until his death in 1811. To his son, Robert Dundas, second Viscount Melville, fell the government's management of Scottish business.

But the reign of the Dundas dynasty was approaching its end. In 1829 Robert resigned, unable to stomach the Tories' reluctant agreement to repeal the political disabilities imposed on Roman Catholics. In Scotland a group of Whigs, dominated by Lord Advocate Francis Jeffrey and Solicitor General Henry Cockburn, moved into the vacuum left by the disintegration of the Dundas regime. Though far from radical in their social and political views, the Whigs advocated moderate electoral reform. At the general election of 1831 they won the majority of Scottish seats in the House of Commons. And in 1832 they helped to pass the great Reform Bill, to be followed the next year by the Burgh Reform Act. These two measures increased the number of Scottish voters in parliamentary elections from about forty-five hundred to sixty-five thousand, gave the municipal franchise to all £10 householders, and broke the power of burghal councils to perpetuate themselves. It was not democracy, but it did destroy the Dundas machine forever and made it possible for the Whigs and their successors of the Liberal Party to dominate Scottish politics for the rest of the nineteenth century and into the twentieth.

In the general election of 1831, Sir Walter Scott, then in the last year of his life, voted, of course, for the Tory candidate. On his way to the polls he was cursed and spat upon, and on his way home was jeered at with cries of "Burke him!" Death came none too soon for this romantic antiquarian, whose nostalgia for a fictitious past would have equipped him poorly for the future now at hand. A tinkering Glasgow instrument maker had turned the old order on its head. While Sir Walter dreamed of Jacobites and knights in armor, Scotland was becoming a modern industrialized society.

Chapter Nine

The Nineteenth and Early Twentieth Centuries

1832–1945

If Walter Scott was the chief popularizer of the nineteenth century's romantic vision of the Scottish Highlands, it was Queen Victoria mainly whose imprimatur made the region fashionable. "The English coast appeared terribly flat," wrote she on her return voyage from a visit to Scotland in the autumn of 1844. "Lord Aberdeen was quite touched when I told him I was so attached to the dear, dear Highlands and missed the fine hills so much." Her husband Albert concurred. On their first visit two years before, the Prince Consort had gone shooting with the Marquis of Breadalbane at Taymouth and in one day killed nineteen roe deer, several hares and pheasants, and three brace of grouse. "Oh! what can equal the beauties of nature!" Victoria later exclaimed. "Albert enjoys it so much; he is in ecstasies here."

In 1847 the royal couple came back, this time to tour the west coast. Then the Earl of Aberdeen (formerly Foreign Secretary and subsequently Prime Minister) showed them a set of watercolors done by a local artist, James Giles, of the ancient castle of Balmoral overlooking the River Dee in Aberdeenshire near Ballater. (One of these paintings still hangs at **Haddo House** *[539]*). On the strength of these views by Giles—plus a favorable report by the queen's physician on the climate of the Dee valley—Victoria and Albert leased, and later purchased, Balmoral; tore down the old building; and raised **Balmoral Castle** *(539)* as a royal residence. The architect was William Smith of Aberdeen, but the prince consort himself played an active role in drawing up the plans for the new house. Completed in 1855, it was a huge, sprawling neo-Gothic, crenellated and turreted mansion of a style that came to be known as Scottish Baronial. Victoria carpeted the floors, curtained the windows, and covered chairs and sofas with various tartan setts ascribed to the Royal House of Stuart from which she boasted her descent.

The queen was never happier than during her autumn visits to Balmoral. The royal family explored the neighboring countryside on ponyback, attended Church of Scotland services in the village of Crathie, and watched the hammer-throwing and caber-tossing at the annual Highland games in the vicinity of Braemar. And Albert bagged more deer and grouse.

Then, in December of 1861, the prince consort died of typhoid fever. Disconsolate, Victoria returned to Balmoral to find some comfort in the familiar hills and in the company of her head gillie, John Brown, a local man whose "good conduct and intelligence . . . attention, care, and faithfulness" the queen considered to be of the highest order. Her eldest son thought otherwise, and when he succeeded to the throne as Edward VII in 1901, removed or destroyed all the mementos of the gillie that his mother had preserved at Balmoral after Brown's death in 1883. (One of these—a huge portrait commissioned by the queen shortly before Brown died— survived, though in a damaged condition, and is now on display at the **Museum of Scottish Tartans** *[500]* in Comrie, Perthshire.) Slowly Victoria recovered her composure and took to travelling by railway as far southwest as Argyll and as far northwest as Sutherland. Yet for all the time she spent in the Highlands, there is no indication that the queen was ever made aware of the great economic and social upheaval that the region was undergoing during her reign, or of the dislocations and other hardships then being suffered by its inhabitants.

THE COUNTRYSIDE

Notwithstanding the unfavorable publicity attendant upon the Sutherland clearances, vast acreages in the Highlands continued to be converted to sheep raising. In the late 1820s and the 1830s many landlords in the western isles began to sell out. The little islands of Rhum and Muck were cleared. So was much of Skye, and the outer islands of Harris and Lewis. Between 1829 and 1840, the Duke of Hamilton arranged for the transportation to Canada of about seven hundred tenants from Arran. The departure of the first group of emigrants to board the brig *Caledonia* is commemorated by the **Lamlash Clearance Monument** *(394)*, a few miles south of Brodick. Erected by their Canadian descendants, this is a simple arrangement of three huge boulders, one bearing a bronze plaque on which is inscribed a line from "The Canadian Boat Song," an anonymous poet's well-known ode to the legendary homesickness of the Scottish emigrant:

> From the lone shieling of the misty island
> Mountains divide us, and the waste of seas—
> Yet still the blood is strong, the heart is Highland,
> And we in dreams behold the Hebrides.

In the 1840s the pace of clearance quickened. The most notorious case was that of the tenants of Glencalvie near Bonar Bridge in 1845. When given notice of eviction by the landlord's agent, James Gillanders, these people, abetted by their minister, placed an advertisement in an Edinburgh newspaper, *The Scotsman*, seeking a public subscription for their resettlement. Thus the press was alerted, and when eighty-three evicted tenants took refuge in the yard of **Croick Church** *(550)*, the incident was widely publicized. Today a pathetic reminder of the episode is preserved in the east window of the kirk, where some of the refugees scratched their names and recorded the fact that "Glencalvie people was in the churchyard here May 24 1845." Soon thereafter they were dispersed.

A year later another disaster hit the Highlands and Islands: the potato blight, which had already devastated Ireland, now arrived in Scotland. The primary food crop of the entire peasant population was attacked by a fungus known as *phytophtora infestans*, and in July and August 1846 the major part of the year's planting rotted on the vine, leaving nothing but shrivelled, blackened fruit and a hideous stench. Already experienced in dealing with the Irish famine, the government in Westminster acted quickly, placing an able administrator, Sir Edward Pine Coffin, in charge of relief and shipping tons of meal into the stricken areas. It was, however, not to be given away, for it was Westminster's policy that "next to allowing the people to die of hunger, the greatest evil that could happen would be their being habituated to depend on private charity." Hence food was distributed only in return for hard labor on such public projects as the Destitution Road (now the A 832) running from Poolewe to Corrieshalloch Gorge. It must be said, however, that the churches organized a number of relief projects, and some of the landlords gave generously. Of these the most noteworthy was Norman MacLeod of Dunvegan (twenty-fifth Chief), who spent an estimated £13,000 of his own money buying up meal for distribution among the people of Skye in the years 1846–1848.

Under these circumstances, it is not surprising that emigration escalated. In 1851 Parliament passed the Emigration Advances Act to facilitate "voluntary" departures, and during the next ten years at least sixteen thousand people left the Highlands and Islands for Canada, the United States, and Australia. Though some emigrated at their own expense, most were assisted by the government, by public subscriptions, or by their landlords. Sir John Matheson, owner of Lewis, gave financial aid to some seventeen hundred people to resettle in Canada, coupling the offer with a threat of eviction of those rent-delinquents who declined it. Over twenty-five hundred of Lord MacDonald's tenants on Skye were dispatched to Canada and Australia. Of the distress of these people, a visiting geologist, Sir Albert Geikie, has left a moving report:

> On gaining the top of one of the hills . . . I could see a long and motley procession winding along the road that led north from Suishnish . . . Everyone was in tears; each wished to clasp the hands that had so often befriended them, and it seemed as if they could not tear themselves away. When they set forth once more, a cry of grief went up to heaven, the long plaintive wail, like a funeral coronach, was resumed, and after the last of the emigrants had disappeared behind the hill, the sound seemed to re-echo through the whole wide valley of Strath in one prolonged note of desolation. The people were on their way to be shipped to Canada. . . .

Against such testimony, however, must be balanced the undoubted fact that many of the emigrants were glad to go. The "frenzy" for America that Dr. Johnson had noted in the 1770s had certainly not completely vanished, and it is noteworthy that, after Highland evictions had ceased altogether in the 1880s, far more people left the area of their own volition than had gone before. The romantic myth of the tradition-loving Gael clinging loyally to his native heath in spite of unspeakable poverty does less than justice to the enterprise of the thousands of Highland Scots who pulled up stakes for Canada, the United States, or Australia in search of a better life—which they usually found.

After about 1870, sheep farming began to lose its attractiveness in the face of mounting imports of wool and mutton from Australia and New Zealand and of mounting tariffs on woollen products imposed by the United States. Evictions diminished greatly, and there were no further wholesale clearances. Economic conditions for the crofters, however, did not improve significantly. In the early 1880s the potato crop failed, the grain harvest was disappointing, coastal fishermen were pulling up empty nets, and bad storms wrecked many of their boats. One result of the renewed threat of destitution was the so-called "Crofters' War" on Skye—an effort on the part of tenants to reverse the clearance process by reasserting old grazing rights lost to landlords years before.

In the autumn of 1881 a number of Lord MacDonald's tenants in the region south of Portree demanded the right to use Ben Lee as common pasture. When the landlord rejected their demand, they promptly refused to pay the rent. He responded with eviction notices; the crofters manhandled the sheriff trying to serve them; police reinforcements from Glasgow were called in; and at a place called The Braes on the Portree road (B 883) a skirmish took place, which the press promptly dubbed "the Battle of The Braes." The site of this fracas is marked by a small stone pedestal called **The Braes Memorial** *(523)* and in the **Skye Black House Museum** *(523)* at Colbost are posted numerous contemporary newspaper clippings of the affair.

The upshot of this and other instances of crofter resistance was the appointment by the government in Westminster of a royal commission headed by Lord Napier, which produced a massive factual report on Highland conditions and resulted in the passage in 1886 of the Crofters' Holdings (Scotland) Act. Though this legislation did not meet all the crofters' demands, it did guarantee them security of tenure, recognized their right to claim compensation for improvements made on their holdings, and, most importantly, set up a land court to fix fair rents.

For its time, the Crofters' Holdings Act was a very advanced piece of social legislation. But it did not restore arable land to the tenants, or enable them to become self-sufficient farmers. As before, they continued to occupy tiny plots of land, raise a few sheep and fewer crops (mostly potatoes), and eke out a living only by part-time employment. Their houses bore testimony to their poverty. Some of these were the traditional black houses, mostly made of unmortared stone, with thatched roofs, dirt floors, and central hearths. In plan, the "black house" was a nuclear arrangement of rooms to include under the same roof the kitchen and sleeping quarters of the family, the byre for the cattle, an entrance porch, and a barn for the storage of crops. Another common type was the linear-plan cottage, consisting of a kitchen with a fireplace built into the wall, a bedroom, and a byre for the cattle. A surprising number of these humble dwelling places still exist—many of them now converted into folk museums. On Skye, in addition to the already-mentioned **Skye Black House Museum** *(523)* at Colbost, there are the **Skye Cottage Museum** *(524)* at Kilmuir and the **Skye Crofter's House Museum** *(522)* at Luib near Broadford. In Caithness is the **Laidhay Croft Museum** *(553)* near Dunbeath; in Ross and Cromarty, the **Gairloch Heritage Museum** *(548)*; in Shetland, the **Shetland Croft House Museum** *(570)* at South Voe (Dunrossness) near Boddam; and on Lewis, the **Black House** *(557)* at Arnol.

Not very distant from the last named place occurred a much publicized postscript to the Crofters' War of 1881. In December of 1887 a gunboat with a force of marines aboard was dispatched to Stornoway to quell an uprising of crofters protesting against the conversion of the Park Estate into a deer forest. In the end the ringleaders were arrested, but their threats were serious enough to induce the island's major proprietress, Lady Mathieson, to abandon Lewis and take up residence in the South of France. The incident itself was of no great significance. But it did serve as a reminder of the ultimate irony of the Highland clearances—that sheep walks, which had replaced the settlements of the long established native tenants, were themselves to be swallowed up by deer forests devoted exclusively to serving the pleasure of a new breed of wealthy sportsmen.

The sport of deer-stalking did not originate with Prince Albert, but it was his enthusiasm for it that made it fashionable, especially among the newly rich industrialists of England and the Scottish Lowlands. After his first visit to Taymouth in 1842, the prince consort concluded that "without doubt deer-stalking is one of the most fatiguing, but it is also one of the most interesting of pursuits." In praising the sport to Victoria's half-brother Charles, Prince Leiningen, he explained: "There is not a tree, or a bush behind which you can hide yourself. . . . One has, therefore, to be constantly on the alert . . . crawling on hands and knees, and dressed entirely in grey."

Deer forests were not forests at all in the usual sense of the word, but mostly treeless moors where hunters could get a clear shot at a distant stag, whose antlers, it was hoped, would grace the great hall or billiard room of the patient and skillful marksman. Scotland had an ample supply of such barren wasteland, and by 1914 more than 3½ million acres (about 20 percent of all the country north of the Tweed) were devoted to deer forest.

Rich huntsmen also required appropriate living quarters, and thus sprang up all over the Highlands a host of shooting lodges of curious mock-Baronial design—none more so than Lord Abercorn's house of Adverikie. Here, according to Queen Victoria, "stag horns" adorned the building inside and out, and the walls of the drawing room and anteroom were "ornamented with beautiful drawings of stags by [Sir Edwin] Landseer"— her favorite painter. Small fortunes were spent on such luxuries, and Scottish architects—especially the Edinburgh firm of William Burn and David Bryce—were showered with commissions to build these "Scottish Baronial" fantasies now mostly torn down or converted to hotels or schools. One still standing, however, is **Torosay Castle** *(471)* on Mull—its crow-stepped gables and cone-capped turrets in a good state of preservation and its rooms still replete with antlers. It was built in 1858 to a design by David Bryce, and Sir Robert Lorimer laid out the terraced gardens.

On an even grander scale were some of the mammoth country houses of the mid–nineteenth century, of which the most illustrious example is **Dunrobin Castle** *(552)* near Golspie, Sutherland. Queen Victoria visited here in 1872, and her gilt four-poster bed is still on display. She described the house as having "a very fine imposing appearance with its very high roof and turrets, a mixture of an old Scotch castle and French château." The architect was Sir Charles Barry, who was also responsible for the design of the Houses of Parliament in Westminster. He was commissioned by the second Duke of Sutherland to rebuild the family's ancient tower-house, and the result stands today pretty much as Queen Victoria described it, except that the interior was later restored by Sir Robert Lorimer after a fire in 1915. Lorimer grew up in **Kellie Castle** *(491)* in Fife and had a hand in its restoration. He was also responsible for restoring **Earlshall Castle** *(495)*, near St. Andrews, in 1891. In 1905 he drew the plans for another Fife country house, **Hill of Tarvit** *(486)*, a surprisingly restrained exercise in neoclassic symmetry. More distinctly conforming to the neoclassical canon is **Manderston House** *(423)*, near Duns in Berwickshire. Built (or rather rebuilt on earlier foundations) in the years immediately following the turn of the century, this great neoclassical mansion is a monument to Edwardian opulence. It was designed by John Kinross for Sir James Miller, heir of a mercantile fortune, who distinguished himself chiefly by raising champion horses and marrying the fourth daughter of Lord Scarsdale of Kedleston Hall. It was this great house in Derbyshire, the creation of Robert Adam at the peak of his genius, that the architect of Manderston was instructed to duplicate at any price. The result is sumptuous to a fault, not so much a copy as a parody of Adam's refined taste. The best features of this place are the luxurious dairy-house and the superb formal gardens, laid out in the manner perfected by Victorian horticulturists and never since surpassed.

Though England and Scotland together had a long and distinguished gardening tradition, it was not until the nineteenth century that the rich and colorful horticultural abundance that typifies today's British garden became commonplace. For it was the Victorians who reintroduced flowers and flowering shrubs into the terraces and parks, from which they had been mostly excluded by the landscapers of the seventeenth and eighteenth centuries, and who discovered that all sorts of exotic plants and trees would thrive in the damp but moderate climate of Britain. Of the factors that contributed to this horticultural revolution of the nineteenth century, the most important were: (1) improvements in the construction of glass hothouses, especially the installation of cast iron water pipes that permitted the maintenance of a uniform level of warmth; (2) the importation of many new species by botanical expeditions dispatched to all parts of the British Empire and beyond; and (3) the professionalization of gardening, to which Scotland made a major contribution. Three types of gardens (with numerous variations) emerged from these developments: (1) the formal garden, often terraced, in which perennial flowers or hardy annuals of strikingly contrasting colors were arranged in tight geometric patterns; (2) the herbaceous border—a straight or curving bed or island of various species of flowers intermingled in such a way as to produce a riot of color; and (3) the woodland garden, usually consisting of an extensive layout of thickly planted trees and flowering shrubs crisscrossed with winding footpaths. The first two were made possible by the development of the technique of "bedding out," i.e., raising the plants from seed in hothouses and transferring them to flower beds only during their blooming season. The third was the product of long experimentation with non-native plants and their hybrids under various conditions of soil and climate.

Scotland, like the rest of Britain, is blessed with such a multitude of magnificent gardens that any selection of the most distinguished among them is bound to be arbitrary, if not capricious. Those mentioned here owe their present appearance mostly to work done originally in the nineteenth and early twentieth centuries. At **Balmoral Castle** *(539)*, Prince Albert himself, with the help of artist James Giles, laid out the gardens in 1855. Today, the most attractive features here are the tower garden on the east front; the rose garden to the west; the fountain garden, dating from 1920; and, above all, the hothouse, crowded with blooms of every hue from floor to rooftop. **Scone Palace** *(506)* in Perthshire has one of the finest collections of rare conifers in the country, started by the third Earl of Mansfield in 1848, although fourteen years earlier the first Douglas fir seeds were planted—named after David Douglas, botanist and world traveller who was born on the estate and had worked here as under-gardener. Here also is a woodland garden with fine stands of rhododendrons and azaleas. The great parterre of **Drummond Castle** *(501)* reputedly dates from as early as the seventeenth century, but the existing arrangement of beds and topiary was laid out in the nineteenth, probably about the time that Queen Victoria planted the still-standing copper beech in 1842. Equally or more impressive are the parterres lying between **Dunrobin Castle** *(552)* and the Dornoch Firth—one circular and two rectangular, now filled with roses but picked out with bedded plants in season when first installed, probably by the architect Sir Charles Barry.

The woodland garden is another Victorian invention, stimulated by the arrival from the Himalayas of several species of broad-leafed rhododendrons that lent themselves to hybridization and proliferation of new varieties. One of the early massive displays of these shrubs was at **The Hirsel** *(423)*, near Coldstream, Berwickshire. Here, about 1860, the Earl of Home began the planting of Dundock Wood, which is still famous for its rhododendrons and azaleas. At **Brodick Castle** *(393)*, on the Isle of Arran, the woodland garden planted in the nineteenth century had by the time of World War I grown into an impenetrable jungle of native *rhododendron ponticum*. In 1920 the Duchess of Montrose took charge and laid out new arrangements that today, under the administration of the National Trust for Scotland, comprise one of the most exciting woodland gardens in Britain. But the grandest of all is **Inverewe** *(549)* near Poolewe, Ross and Cromarty. Planting on this once bleak and barren promontory overlooking Loch Ewe began in 1864 at the hands of Osgood Hanbury Mackenzie, whose mother had given him the property. His first step toward the development of a great garden on this unlikely spot was the installation of shelter belts of Scots pine, Wellingtonia, rowan, larch, beech, Douglas fir, and *rhododendron ponticum*. This required the importation of soil, which had to be carried up the steep hillside in wicker creels strapped to his workers' backs. Fifteen years later, he began the planting of such exotic species as eucalyptus, tree fern, arbutus, and bamboo. Mackenzie died in 1922, but his daughter Mairi continued the work until her death in 1953, importing magnificent specimens of rhododendron and other species of shrubs and plants, native and non-native, too numerous to mention. Now under the care of the National Trust for Scotland, Inverewe is one of the horticultural wonders of the world.

Finally, note should be taken again of Scotland's two great public gardens, already mentioned in the previous chapter. Moved to its present site in 1820 to 1823, the one at Edinburgh expanded steadily throughout the nineteenth century and in 1889 came under the jurisdiction of the Crown and was renamed the **Royal Botanic Garden** *(450)*. In 1834 and 1858 it acquired its charming interconnected glass houses, the Tropical Palm House and the Temperate Palm House. Glasgow's botanical collections were moved to Kelvinside in 1842 and taken over by the city as the **Glasgow Botanic Gardens** *(409)* in 1887–1891. The splendid curved glass "Kibble Palace," originally built at Coulport, was moved here and reerected in 1873. It was not only a monument to the advance of botanical science but also, in its day, a great feat of civil engineering. Though not designed in Glasgow, Kibble Palace's final resting place overlooking the sprawling metropolis on the Clyde is a fitting symbol of the city's central role in the nineteenth-century industrial development of Britain.

INDUSTRY AND URBAN DEVELOPMENT

After James Watt, in partnership with Matthew Boulton, succeeded in perfecting and marketing an economically viable steam engine, industry in Scotland, as elsewhere, gradually shifted from water power to steam. The principal source of energy was therefore coal, of which Scotland had an ample supply, mostly located in two major fields—the region north and south of the Firth of Forth and the southwestern counties of Lanarkshire and Ayrshire. As the nineteenth century wore on, the center of gravity in the coal-extraction industry gradually shifted from east to west, and by the 1870s nearly 70 percent of the Scottish output came from the southwestern coalfields. The enormous increase in the productivity of the mines was made possible by the perfection of more efficient steam-powered drainage pumps. One of these, a "Cornish beam engine," manufactured in 1874, is still to be seen in its five-story engine-house at the **Prestongrange Mining Museum** *(453)* on the south shore of the Firth of Forth east of Edinburgh. The horizontal beam, measuring 33½ feet in length, operated on the same principle as that of a child's seesaw, with one end attached to a rod whose up-and-down motion pumped water up from the mine below through a deep shaft. The beam itself was set in motion by the reciprocal action of a rod attached to a piston encased in a huge cylinder into which steam was forced and then condensed. Today, with the mine defunct, the apparatus is operated by electricity for the edification of visitors.

One early by-product of the coal industry was the manufacture of coal gas for illumination. As early as 1832, the year of the first Reform Bill, most of the cities of Scotland, and many of the towns, had their main streets lit by gas, and it was not long before gas jets were to be a common sight in domestic dwellings as well. (Sir Walter Scott had Abbotsford equipped for gas in 1825.) Typical of the many nineteenth-century municipal gas-distributing plants is the **Biggar Gasworks** *(398)* in Lanarkshire, recently converted into a museum. Another source of illumination was paraffin (known in America as kerosene), a product of shale-oil deposits, mostly in West Lothian. Established in the 1850s as a result of the development of a patented process by James ("Paraffin") Young, the shale-oil industry flourished until the late 1870s, when the influx of natural petroleum from Pennsylvania began to undercut the market, although production continued until the discovery of Middle Eastern oil just before the First World War. Today, the **BP Information Centre** *(477)* on the northern outskirts of Grangemouth will provide guidance to travellers wishing to drive by car over the "Paraffin" Young Heritage Trail, a forty-mile trip through the Lothian villages of Pumpherston, West Calder, Winchburgh, Broxburn, and Bathgate, with numerous signposts pointing to sites connected with the shale-oil industry.

After coal, the next major ingredient in Scotland's industrial development was iron, of which there was plenty available, once David Mushet had discovered the value of black-band ironstone and John Neilson had perfected the hot-blast method for smelting it. The iron industry came to be divided into three main sections: the furnaces, where the ore was smelted to produce pig iron; the foundries where pig iron was remelted and cast; and the malleable or wrought ironworks, where plates, bars, etc., were made. It was in the foundries that the blacksmith work of forging was carried on, and here, in the manufacture of machine parts, Glasgow's great heavy engineering industry had its beginnings. By the 1870s the malleable ironworks were being threatened by the influx of foreign steel manufactured by the Bessemer or the Siemens-Martin process, neither of which could make use of the high-phosphoric ores of Scotland. Not until the 1880s, with the invention of the Gilchrist-Thomas process, was this deficiency remedied and Scotland's steel industry able to take off.

Throughout the nineteenth century a major market for iron, and later steel, was of course the railways with their seemingly insatiable demand for rails, girders, rivets, engines, engine parts, and so forth required to lay their tracks; build their bridges and viaducts; run their locomotives, wagons, and carriages (in America called freight cars and passenger cars); erect their stations and station hotels, etc. Although preceded by numerous short lines carrying both goods (chiefly coal) and passengers, the first major trunk line in Scotland—between Glasgow and Edinburgh—was opened in 1842. Thereafter, progress in railway construction was phenomenal. A total of 121 companies were at one time or another granted authorization by Act of Parliament to open lines. By the end of the Victorian era these had been consolidated into five: (1) the North British Railway, with lines running north and south from Berwick-upon-Tweed through Edinburgh to Perth and Dundee, west to Glasgow, southwest to Carlisle through Hawick, and north of Glasgow to Fort William and Mallaig; (2) the Caledonian Railway, with lines from Carlisle through Glasgow, north to Oban, and east and northeast to Edinburgh and Aberdeen; (3) the Glasgow and South Western Railway, with an intricate network of connections between the city and all the counties to the southwest of it; (4) the Highland Railway, which connected Aberdeen to Inverness, from which point lines ran north into Sutherland and Caithness and west to Kyle of Lochalsh; and (5) the Great North of Scotland Railway (the smallest of the "big five" in spite of its ambitious name), which ran west out of Aberdeen into the Grampians and on which Queen Victoria usually travelled en route to Balmoral.

Edinburgh and Glasgow were the two major rail centers of Scotland, and the latter's connection with the industry was reinforced by its becoming the prime site of locomotive manufacture. It is not inappropriate, therefore, that the best, or at least the best organized, collection of locomotives today in Scotland is at the **Glasgow Museum of Transport** *(480)*, which has on display six of these mighty engines, all made in Glasgow: two from the Caledonian Railway and one each from the North British, the Glasgow and South Western, the Highland, and the Great North of Scotland. Less well developed, though promising one day to become a major railway museum, is the **Scottish Railway Preservation Society Depot** *(476)* at Falkirk, which is linked with the **Scottish Railway Preservation Society Museum** *(425)* in Bo'ness—both open-air museums with locomotives and rolling stock, the latter offering regular steam-train rides during the summer months. Another operating line is the **Strathspey Railway** *(514)* in Inverness-shire, which runs regular excursions over five miles of track between Aviemore, formerly a junction on the Highland Railway, and Boat of Garten, whose station served the Great North of Scotland line. At Aviemore are situated an early passenger station and an engine shed, and some of the stock dates from the Victorian and Edwardian eras. The **Alford Transport and Railway Museum** *(537)* in Aberdeenshire contains a fair-sized collection of automobiles and other vehicles, but the railway section consists only of a restored passenger station. Unfortunately, Scotland can boast no railway museum comparable to the splendid English establishments at York and Swindon.

Of nineteenth-century railway bridges and viaducts, however, there remain a respectable number. Spanning this mountainous, watery, and corrugated country with a network of railways was no small engineering feat. Sharp bends, feasible for horse-drawn carriage traffic, would have been dangerous for fast-moving trains, and steep grades slowed down the engines and increased fuel consumption. The answer to both problems was the viaduct to carry the tracks across deep valleys or ravines. A particularly impressive example is the **Ballochmyle Viaduct** *(391)*, built in 1848 by the civil engineer John Miller for the Glasgow and South Western Railway to span the gorge of the River Ayr between Mauchline and Cumnock in Ayrshire. It was made of local sandstone. Concrete, however, was used in the equally spectacular **Glenfinnan Viaduct** *(516)*, built in 1898 on the Fort William-to-Mallaig line.

In the early days of Scottish railroading, the problem of crossing wide rivers or estuaries was solved by the roll-on-roll-off railway ferry—a cumbersome and expensive device for eliminating circuitous routing of the trains. To expedite traffic across the Tay estuary, the North British Railway commissioned Thomas Bouch to erect a slender, malleable-iron lattice-girder bridge mounted on high brick columns and running for two miles between Wormit on the south bank and Dundee on the north. It was opened for traffic in September 1877. Queen Victoria crossed here on the way to Balmoral and subsequently knighted the builder. Then, on Sunday 18 December 1879, about 7:30 P.M., the Tay Bridge collapsed, carrying into the water eighty-eight feet below the 4:15 train from Edinburgh with seventy-three passengers and four railwaymen aboard. All perished. Investigation by the Board of Trade revealed grave structural defects, especially the failure of the designer to make adequate allowance for the high winds common in the Tay estuary. Sir Thomas Bouch died in disgrace about ten months afterward. Meanwhile, his commission to build a similar span across the Firth of Forth was cancelled and the contract let to Sir John Fowler and Benjamin Baker of the Great Northern Railway to erect a massive cantilever bridge from South Queensferry, West Lothian, across to North Queensferry in Fife, using the little islet of Inch Garvie as a central base. To allow free passage to shipping, a vertical clearance of 150 feet had to be provided for. Work began in January 1883, and the bridge was ceremoniously opened on 4 March 1880 by the Prince of Wales, later Edward VII. Though fifty-seven workmen lost their lives during construction, the **Forth Railway Bridge** *(429)* was, and is, a spectacular feat of civil engineering—best viewable today from the harbor at South Queensferry or, better still, from the boat that plies regularly between there and Inchcolm Island.

Of the scores of railway stations and their adjacent hotels that once were such prominent features of the Scottish town and city scene, not much is left to remind today's traveller of their former grandeur. Where these buildings have managed to escape the iron ball of the demolition crews, modernization has mostly done away with the aura of Victorian or Edwardian opulence that once was theirs. **Central Station** *(403)* in Glasgow, opened in 1879 for passengers on the Caledonian Railway, retains its neoclassic interior facade, its curvaceous varnished stalls, and its roof of glass and steel girders, but the intrusion of a modern "travel centre" and other excrescences has destroyed most of its original richness of decor. Only the station hotel next door, designed by Sir Rowand Anderson in the Queen Anne style and opened in 1883, preserves a hint of the Victorian era, when this was the major hostelry of the "second city of the British Empire." **Waverley Station** *(444)*, the North British Railway's terminal on Waverley Bridge in Edinburgh, is even more disappointing, though again the station hotel (the North British) retains some of its original Victorian grandiosity. Because the tracks were laid in the deep bed of the old Nor' Loch between the old city and the New Town, the station, erected in 1874, never had an imposing facade, and the "modernized" interior is now not worth a second look. The same can be said for most of the other once-great city railway terminals and station hotels in Scotland. Only in a few small towns—Oban, Ayr, and Paisley, for example—have the little passenger stations retained any of their original charm, sometimes enhanced today with festive baskets of flowers hanging from the girders of their roofs.

Glasgow's prominence as a railway center and seat of a thriving locomotive industry was matched, and indeed excelled, by its position of world leadership in shipping and shipbuilding. From the year 1812, when Henry Bell launched the steam-powered *Comet* on the Clyde, until after the end of the First World War, Glasgow and its satellite communities up and down the river (Govan, Whiteinch, Dumbarton, Renfrew, Port Glasgow, and Greenock) were at or near the top in the production of ships of all sizes and descriptions. First to be built were vessels of wood, then iron, then steel; the earliest powered by reciprocating steam engines, then by steam turbines; and propelled through the water first by paddles, then by single screws (propellors), then twin and multiple screws. Clyde-built and/or Clyde-engined ships were the first to cross the open sea (from Greenock to Belfast) and the first to cross the Atlantic to New York—the *Sirius* in 1838, arriving a few hours before the Bristol-built *Great Western*. By the end of the nineteenth century, the Clyde launched not far short of one-fifth of the world's output of ships—more than the total production of either the United States or Germany. Among the foremost names of those local engineers and shipbuilders responsible for this phenomenal record are

David and Robert Napier, Charles Randolph, John Elder, William Denny, A. C. Kirk, and Charles A. Parsons. Among the companies they and others formed, the most prominent and prosperous were Napier and Sons; Barclay, Curle and Company; John Brown and Company; Beardmore and Company; William Denny and Company; and the Fairfield Shipbuilding and Engineering Company. The only place today where the interested traveller can acquire a firsthand appreciation of the great variety of the product of these and other Clydeside yards is in the Clyde Room of the **Glasgow Museum of Transport** *(400)*, containing over six hundred ship models, most of them Clyde-built. Most of the yards themselves are today shut down, and the river itself is sometimes wryly referred to by Glaswegians as "the redundant Clyde."

Not only shipbuilding, but shipowning and shipping stood high among Glasgow's preoccupations and were a major source of the city's nineteenth-century prosperity. Among the great inter-oceanic shipping firms of Glasgow origin were the Cunard line, formed in 1840 by a partnership between Samuel Cunard of Halifax, Robert Napier, and the Glasgow shipowners George Burns and David Maciver; Jardine Matheson and Company, begun in 1832 to trade with India and China; Mackinnon and Company, whose senior partner was William Mackinnon, founder also of the British India Steam Navigation Company, the Netherlands India Steam Navigation Company, and the Queensland Steam Shipping Company; and Burrell and Son, which brought to William Burrell the huge fortune spent in amassing the great **Burrell Collection** *(401)* of paintings and *objets d'art* that he subsequently willed to the city of Glasgow.

Notwithstanding the great advantages of steam power, the age of sail did not promptly fade away with the launching of Henry Bell's *Comet*. Where time in transit was not a major consideration and where distances were so great as to require frequent and expensive recoaling of steamships, sailing ships for the first seven decades of the nineteenth century still enjoyed significant economic advantages. This was especially true of those engaged in trade with the Orient and the Antipodes, at least until the opening of the Suez Canal in 1869, which rendered the long trip around the Horn of Africa unnecessary. Although Glasgow shipyards were among those to build some of the fastest sailing vessels (including the famous *Cutty Sark*), it was Aberdeen that won the palm in this regard. Sailing-ship design made a significant advance in 1839 with the launching by William and James Hall of the *Scottish Maid*, a small clipper schooner with a streamlined hull and raked "Aberdeen bow." In the early 1850s A. Hall & Company broke into the American monopoly of the China tea trade with their sleek tea clippers *Stornoway*, *Chrysolite*, and *Cairngorm*, to be followed by the record-breaking *Thermopylae,* built by Walter Hood & Company. Even as late as the 1880s, the Duthie family of Aberdeen was still turning out handsome sailing ships. One of the rooms in the **Aberdeen Maritime Museum** *(535)* commemorates their accomplishments with a reconstruction of their business office as of 1884. Other parts of this superb museum are devoted to various aspects of the town's shipbuilding and shipping industries.

As shipbuilding, marine and locomotive engineering, and the extractive industries assumed an ever-increasing share of Scotland's investment of capital and labor, the old cotton textile industry on which the industrial revolution had originally centered went into a gradual decline. The American Civil War, temporarily cutting off the supply of raw material, accelerated the process, but the root of the industry's decadence lay in the tardy mechanization of the weaving phase of production. In any case, by mid-century Manchester had clearly forged far ahead of Glasgow and its neighbors. Only Paisley throve, in spite of the collapse of the market for shawls in the 1870s. The spinning of cotton thread became its major industry, and by the end of the century the firm of Coats and Clark led the world. The manufacture of woollens, on the other hand, after a slow start in mechanization, made considerable headway with the introduction of steam-powered weaving machinery and power-driven spinning mules. Both the American Civil War and the Franco-Prussian War boosted the market for woollen uniforms, but by 1880 the boom was over. The American McKinley Tariff of 1890 placed a 90 percent duty on Scottish woollens, and this once very profitable market was effectively closed. The Border textile towns decayed: the population of Hawick declined by two thousand between 1891 and 1901 and that of Galashiels by a quarter. But one branch of the industry continued to prosper, namely, carpet making, especially in the West of Scotland. The leading firm here was James Templeton and Company, which eventually came to be the largest employer of industrial labor inside the city limits of Glasgow. In 1856 its factory was destroyed by fire, and in 1889 a new one was built facing Glasgow Green. Still standing, the **Templeton's Carpet Factory** *(402)*—a wondrous structure of polychrome brick meant to resemble the Doge's Palace in Venice—is one of the city's most interesting Victorian relics.

In the West of Scotland the linen industry followed pretty much the same course as cotton, but in the East, Dunfermline throve on the weaving of damasks and other fine cloths. The **Dunfermline Museum** *(488)* is largely devoted to the history of this craft, and the nearby **Andrew Carnegie Birthplace Memorial** *(488)* has been restored to represent a typical linen weaver's cottage as it would have been in the days when the great American millionaire philanthropist's father lived and worked here. Dundee maintained its lead in the production of coarse linen products such as sailcloth and tenting material and, with the coming of the American Civil War, enjoyed a booming prosperity in selling to both sides. Then, with the discovery of a process for softening Indian jute with whale oil, the city became the leading jute-producing area of the world at a time when there was a marked upturn in the demand for cheap bagging material. The Cox Brothers' **Camperdown Works** *(510)* in Lochee became the world's biggest jute factory. Its 282-foot-high chimney in the form of an Italian campanile is still the city's most prominent landmark. In the McManus Galleries of Dundee's **Central Museum and Art Gallery** *(510)* are demonstrations of aspects of the town's textile industry with a few relevant artifacts on display. Unfortunately for Dundee, by 1885 the boom was over, and thereafter Calcutta began to establish its own factories, which easily undercut the Scottish city's former monopoly. What jute was to Dundee, the manufacture of linoleum was to Kirkcaldy in Fife, and the town's small **Industrial Museum** *(490)* offers a nice display illustrating the history of this unusual industry.

A major reason for Dundee's easy conversion to jute was that the north shore of the Tay estuary had become the center of a prosperous whaling industry that sent out ships as far as the Davis Straits to the west of Greenland. **Broughty Castle** *(511)*, in the suburb of Broughty Ferry east of the city, contains a fine display of whaling relics and artifacts. Not the whale, however, but herring first and later cod, haddock, turbot, and halibut were the mainstays of the Scottish east coast fishing industry, which flourished in the nineteenth and early twentieth centuries as never before or since. Fishing in open undecked boats gave way in the 1870s to trawling in decked sailing smacks; to drift-trawling in paddle-propelled steamships in the 1880s; and to great-line fishing under steam at the turn of the century. Fishing communities were scattered all along the northeast coast of Scotland, from Wick down to the northern shore of the Firth of Forth and as far south as Eyemouth. Prominent among the Forth-shore ports was Anstruther in Fife, where the **Scottish Fisheries Museum** *(483)* contains a really splendid array of fishing gear, coopers' equipment, model ships, fisherman's domestic furnishings, and the like, as does the **Wick Heritage Centre** *(553)*; also the **Aberdeen Maritime Museum** *(535)* with a section devoted entirely to the town's once thriving fishing industry. Because of its central location, its good railway connections, and the foresight of the city fathers in promoting harbor development, Aberdeen between 1875 and 1896 became the leading center of herring fishing, its harbor handling as many as 395 boats in the summer of the latter year. In 1882 the first steam trawler, the *Toiler*, made an appearance in Aberdeen Bay, and by the year 1912 Aberdeen was sending out 230 of these sturdy vessels in search principally of cod and haddock, making the city the first fishing port in Scotland and the third largest in the United Kingdom. Starting about the turn of the century, great-line fishing for halibut, turbot, skate, cod, and ling came into fashion, and Aberdeen was credited with four-fifths of Scotland's catch in this branch of the industry. Then, with outbreak of the First World War and the disappearance of the German and Baltic market, the industry collapsed, never to recover its former greatness.

URBAN GROWTH: GLASGOW AND EDINBURGH

Although Aberdeen's population continued to grow throughout the nineteenth and early twentieth centuries, its rate of increase was a mere fraction of that of Scotland's central belt with the great conurbations of Glasgow and Edinburgh at either end. By 1901 the western Lowlands with Glasgow as its focus, contained some 2 million people, or 45.6 percent of Scotland's total population, while the eastern Lowlands, centered on Edinburgh, held a population of some 1½ million. By 1914 Glasgow alone had achieved the number of 1 million souls. For more than two decades it had been the second city, not only of Britain but of the British Empire.

When Queen Victoria and the prince consort visited here in 1849, Her Majesty reported the town to be "a handsome one with fine streets built in stone and many fine buildings and churches." As they crossed the river into the central city, Albert remarked that it "was very like Paris." Few visitors today would make the comparison, but in 1849 the city's large public park (Glasgow Green), wide streets, and amplitude of neoclassic architecture might well have merited the prince consort's praise. But "Victorian Glasgow," architecturally speaking, had yet to be created. To the second half of the nineteenth century belong the great majority of the buildings that mark this city still as the most typically Victorian of any in Britain. To say "typically Victorian" is not to imply any uniformity of style. Quite the contrary. Ancient Egypt, Greece and Rome, Gothic France, and Renaissance Spain and Italy all provided inspiration for the fascinating medley of neo-almost-everything with which imaginative architects devised the variegated cityscapes of late-nineteenth-century Britain, none more interesting than Glasgow's. Structurally, however, all these buildings were modern. Iron and glass were the chief ingredients that made them so. Camouflaged by antique facades, iron (later steel) beams spanned wide openings filled with factory-produced sheet glass. Working with these materials, Victorian architects had far more latitude than that enjoyed by any of their predecessors who had worked exclusively in stone and wood. Commercial buildings, public edifices, and churches were the chief products of their enterprise. Of these categories the last will be considered later in this narrative. Of the first two, there is such an abundance still surviving (though often in a begrimed state), that only a few samples can be mentioned here.

Probably the most eminent of Glasgow's architects at mid-century were Charles Wilson and Alexander ("Greek") Thomson. Wilson, the son of a local builder, had been apprenticed in David Hamilton's office. His chief contribution to the city center is the present **Christian Science Church** *(409)*—formerly known as Queen's Rooms—at 1 La Belle Place, erected in 1857. This is meant to resemble a classical temple, though the frieze and other exterior ornamentation have a Late Renaissance appearance, more or less Germanic in tone. Alexander Thomson followed Wilson as President of the Glasgow Institute of Architects, and his cognomen "Greek" does not imply a strict adherence to the architectural canon of Periclean Athens. Of his commercial buildings, four are especially worth mention. The **Buck's Head Building** *(402)* on the corner of Dunlop and Argyle streets (1849) was a highly original experiment, involving the setting of an almost continous glass screen on two sides of the top story behind a freestanding classical colonnade. The **Grosvenor Building** *(403)* on Gordon Street (1859–1861) and the **Grecian Building** *(404)* on Sauchiehall Street (ca. 1865) are the most conventionally neoclassical of all. The **Egyptian Halls** *(403)* on Union Street (1871–1873) was, like the Buck's Head Building, one of Glasgow's many warehouses. Here the two lower rows of pilasters are of classical provenance, but the colonnade that shields the continuous glass curtain along the top story is Egyptian in style—a typical Thomson touch in spite of his nickname.

Another warehouse was **Gardner's Iron Building** *(401)* on Jamaica Street, designed by the Glasgow architect John Baird in conjunction with R. McConnel, an iron founder. This structure, now occupied by Gardner's Cabinet-Making and Upholstery establishment, has still a graceful, airy look and is of great significance in architectural history for its pioneering use of wrought iron in its structural frame and of cast iron on the street facades. The **Ca d'Oro** *(403)* on the corner of Union and Gordon streets (1872) by John Honeyman was also originally a warehouse, another cast-iron-fronted building, somewhat marred by a top-heavy mansard roof added later. In an entirely different mode is the **Stock Exchange House** *(405)* on the corner of Buchanan Street and St. George's Place, built in 1875–1877 to the design of John Burnet, Senior. This is a Venetian Gothic fantasy, originally copied from the architect's unsuccessful entry in the competition for the London Law Courts.

Of all of Glasgow's central city buildings, none so aggressively asserts the self-confidence of the city's Late Victorian merchants and manufacturers as the **City Chambers** *(404)* on George Square, built in 1883–1888 to the design of William Young, a London-based Scot. The exterior is conventionally classical, if somewhat heavily so, but the interior is a marvel of grandiosity, with endless rooms and corridors finished in a yellowish Italian marble, carved oak and mahogany in abundance, lush velvet wallpaper, and heroic murals galore. Another equally pretentious public building, though of a later date and style, is the **Glasgow Art Gallery and Museum** *(407)*, erected in 1892–1900 to the design of Sir J. W. Simpson and Milner Allen for the Glasgow International Exhibition of 1901 in Kelvingrove Park. Built of red sandstone, the structure is meant to be Spanish Renaissance in style to match the pseudo-Moorish decor of the exhibition's temporary buildings, since torn down.

In an architectural class by itself is the central building of the **University of Glasgow** *(407)*, begun in 1866 to the design of the doyen of late Victorian English Gothicists, Sir George Gilbert Scott. In the seventeenth century the ancient university had been housed in what was then a new building on the High Street, to which handsome additions in a neoclassical style had been added in the succeeding century and a half. Then, in 1863, the university authorities agreed to sell this central city property to the City of Glasgow Union Railway Company, which wished to acquire the site as a "goods yard" and, on doing so, proceeded to tear down these fine historic relics. With £65,000 of the £100,000 received for the sale, the university bought forty-three acres on Gilmorehill and commissioned George Gilbert Scott of London to erect a new building—the largest such project to be undertaken in Britain since the Houses of Parliament. Scott himself described his production as following "simply a thirteenth or fourteenth century secular style with the addition of certain Scottish features." In 1870, though this huge double quadrangle was yet unfinished, the university took possession, and for the rest of the century additions continued to be made, mostly to the designs of the original architect's son, John Oldrid Scott, or of the Glasgow architect John J. Burnet. When completed, the main part of Glasgow's University—this "new and splendid edifice" in the words of a contemporary—was without question one of the finest of Victorian Gothic exercises in Britain.

In the final decade of the nineteenth century there appeared at last, out of the midst of Glasgow's talented but orthodox architectural fraternity, a true genius who proved to be the most original designer of buildings (and much else besides) to make an appearance in Britain since the Adam brothers. His name was Charles Rennie Mackintosh. Born in Glasgow in 1868, the son of a superintendent of police, he entered the prestigious architectural firm of Honeyman and Keppie in 1890 and six years later won a competition for the design of the **Glasgow School of Art** *(404)*, where he had been an evening pupil for several years. With a small group of other art students, including Frances Macdonald, whom he was later to marry, he had developed a novel approach to the decorative arts that bore the mark of such disparate influences as the English Pre-Raphaelite painters, the Arts and Crafts movement of William Morris, the art-for-art's-sake doctrines of the contemporary Aesthetic Movement, the Art Nouveau of Aubrey Beardsley, Japanese art as interpreted by James A. McNeill Whistler, and the still fashionable Scottish Baronial tradition. Much of Mackintosh's (and his wife's) work consisted of drawings, decorative panels, posters, and furniture, the latter typically severe and rectangular, relieved by the occasional long, sweeping curve and decorated with metal panels, ironmongery, or stencilled fabric. His architectural designs displayed some of the same characteristics, and his buildings, though somewhat bizarre by almost any conventional standard, never lack originality or interest. Indeed, if Mackintosh is to be faulted it all, it would be for his apparent tendency to cherish novelty for novelty's sake.

The **Glasgow School of Art** *(404)*, completed in two stages (1897–1899 and 1906–1909), is a bulky asymmetrical building displaying curious but attractive ornamentation outside and in, with well-lighted interior rooms of varied shapes, painted white and filled with uncomfortable but graceful high-backed or barrel-backed oaken chairs, unusual wrought iron fixtures, and other typically Mackintosh oddities. Words are inadequate to describe either this or his other buildings and decorative schemes. They must be seen to be believed. Included in his *oeuvre* are (1) the former **Willow Tea Rooms** *(405)* on Sauchiehall Street, designed for Miss Kate Cranston (along with several others since destroyed), now unfurnished but restored and incorporated within Daly's Store; (2) the **Scotland Street School** *(399)*, a rather Spartan exercise not up to the architect's usual virtuosity; (3) the very attractive reconstructed Mackintosh home in the **Hunterian Art Gallery** *(408)* on Hillhead Street across from the main buildings of the University of Glasgow; (4) **Queen's Cross Church** *(409)* on Springbank Street, now defunct but used as the headquarters of the Charles Rennie Mackintosh Society; and (5) the completely furnished **Hill House** *(476)*, a fascinating private residence built by Mackintosh in Helensburgh, restored and now maintained by the National Trust for Scotland.

It is a far cry from the ordered spaciousness of Hill House to the typical dwelling place of the average Glasgow workingman in the nineteenth and early twentieth centuries. In 1839 an investigator of housing in Great Britain reported to Parliament: "I have seen human degradation in some of the worst places, both in England and abroad, but I did not believe until I had visited the wynds of Glasgow that so large an amount of filth, crime, misery and disease existed in one spot in any civilized country." And there is small evidence that the situation was much improved a hundred years later. All of Scotland's cities were notorious for the overcrowding of their lower-class tenements, but Glasgow was the worst. Many of these slum dwellers, to be sure, were Irish immigrants or displaced Highlanders, accustomed from birth to cramped living quarters in their native huts and black houses and therefore presumably inured to the one- or two-room city apartment where typically whole families resided, often finding room for a lodger or two besides. The city authorities were alarmed at the situation, and made some efforts toward slum clearance and more toward enforcing minimum standards of occupancy. But to little effect. In the **People's Palace** *(401)* on Glasgow Green is a replica of a typical "single end" dwelling place of a sort prevalent as late as the 1920s. It consists of a tiny room with range, sink, box bed, dresser, and a couple of chairs. In the same museum are examples of "tickets" that, in the late nineteenth century, were placed by housing authorities outside the doors of these tenements, stating their cubic capacities and the number of people permitted by law to live within. The system was introduced by the Glasgow Police Act of 1866, and the typical ticket reads: "1200 cubic feet [roughly $10 \times 17 \times 7$] = 3 adults." In 1896 there were twenty-five thousand ticketed houses in Glasgow, and one in ten were thought to be illegally overcrowded.

Sanitary conditions were of course abominable and the cost to public health inestimable. One result of the overcrowding was that Glaswegians became notorious street dwellers—noisy, gregarious, combative, and always on the move. Small wonder that the most widely used public utility was the city's excellent and low-priced tramway system, which opened in 1872 with horse-drawn cars, was taken over by the Glasgow Corporation in 1894, and was converted to electricity in 1902. The tram works were at Coplawhill, and one of the buildings there is now the **Glasgow Museum of Transport** *(400)*, containing six of the city's now unused tramcars.

In Scotland, unlike in America, it must be remembered the word *tenement* does not connote a slum dwelling. Most Glaswegians, except for the wealthy and the upper middle class, lived in tenements. Those of the middling sort of people—well-paid artisans, clerks, and the like—were usually buildings of four or five stories, each floor containing one or more flats or "houses" of high-ceilinged and well-lighted rooms, situated on quiet streets close to the city center, with plenty of shops and other amenities nearby. A splendid relic of this style of living is the **Tenement House** *(405)* on Buccleuch Street, restored and maintained by the National Trust for Scotland. From 1911 to 1975 this nicely furnished first-floor three-room flat was owned and occupied, first by a widowed seamstress, Mrs. Agnes Reid Toward, and her daughter of the same name who worked as a typist for a shipping firm, then by the daughter alone after her mother's death in 1939. These two women lived frugally but not uncomfortably, and they apparently never discarded any object that ever came into their possession. Here then is a fascinating museum of middle-class urban living with an incredible assortment of memorabilia bound to evoke nostalgia in the heart of any viewer born before the Second World War.

Another reminder of the mutability of taste, though of a different order and from a different era, is the **Glasgow Necropolis** *(406)*, adjacent to and behind the medieval cathedral. First laid out in 1833, this is a marvelous outdoor atelier of sculptural virtuosity and extravagance. Elaborate grave-markers, mausoleums, statues, and miscellaneous other bric-a-brac of stone and marble offer silent but convincing testimony to the wealth and status of the many Glasgow merchants and industrialists who lie buried here. Especially noteworthy among this somewhat bizarre assemblage of memorials are the Egyptian Vaults (1836–1837), the Menteith Mausoleum (1842), the Moorish Kiosk (1849), and the Davidson of Ruchill Mausoleum (1851). Presiding over all is the pillared statue of John Knox (1825), with a panoramic view of the great city nestled in the river valley below. For all the Victorian grandiosity of its masonry and sculpture-work, this is a quiet and lovely spot—not to be missed.

The phenomenal growth of Glasgow in the nineteenth century tends to disguise the fact that Edinburgh too was burgeoning, if at a lower rate of increase. By the end of the century, its population was about half that of Glasgow's, but less than a third of these people were industrial workers. Here there were no textiles or heavy industries, only luxury crafts, breweries, publishers, papermakers, small factories, and the like. Ultimately, this concentration on consumer-oriented industry would save the city from the economic ruin that overinvestment in heavy engineering and shipbuilding brought to Glasgow, but, until the end of the First World War, Edinburgh appeared to be eclipsed by its more progressive neighbor to the west. Still, the ancient capital was the metropolis of the most productive agricultural region of Scotland, the residence of the law courts, the corporate home of Scotland's three major chartered banks, headquarters of the established Church of Scotland and of the other denominations that split off from it, seat of a great university, an important railway center, and, if Leith is included, a port and shipping center of no small importance. Its middle class was prosperous and growing. And its architects found a ready market for their skills.

For a while the neoclassical style continued to prevail—at least in the design of public and commercial buildings. To the New Town's George Street vista, David Rhind in 1847 added another temple to Mammon for the **Royal Bank of Scotland** *(447)*, with a Corinthian portico and a domed atrium of superimposed orders. In the same year, for the British Linen Bank, David Bryce built in St. Andrew Square a fine Roman facade with disengaged Corinthian columns, now owned by the **Bank of Scotland** *(447)*. The **Royal Scottish Museum** *(434)* on Chambers Street, begun in 1861 when the prince consort laid the foundation stone, had a neoclassical Italianate facade behind which lay a spacious exhibition hall of slender cast iron pillars and arches. It was authorized and financed by Act of Parliament to serve as an industrial museum for Scotland and was probably modelled on the Crystal Palace designed by Joseph Paxton for the Great Exhibition held in London in 1851 to celebrate Britain's scientific and industrial progress. But the finest and purest of all mid-century neoclassical buildings in Edinburgh was the **National Gallery of Scotland** *(444)*, designed by William Playfair and built in 1850–1857—noble composition in the Ionic style, more refined and delicate than its massive near-neighbor, the Royal Scottish Academy, executed by the same architect a decade earlier.

But Playfair, like most of his contemporaries, had already succumbed to the growing popular preference for medieval and postmedieval reproductions. His Tudoresque New College and Assembly Hall (to be described below) was built in 1846–1850, and roughly the same years saw the completion of his **Donaldson's School** *(449)* in Haymarket Terrace—an institution for the deaf designed to resemble a Tudor or Jacobean mansion. Playfair died in 1857, and none of his successors would leave quite so personal a mark on Edinburgh's cityscape. If the Scottish capital was indeed the "Athens of the North," then Playfair could justly claim to be its Callicrates. After him the neoclassical tradition, in its pure form, died out. Sir Robert Rowand Anderson, one of Edinburgh's most fashionable architects of the latter part of the nineteenth century, tended to find his inspiration in the Renaissance. The university's grandiose **McEwan Hall** *(434)* is a sort of Italianate version of Rome's Pantheon. On the other hand, Anderson's red sandstone building housing the **National Museum of Antiquities** *(447)* and the **Scottish National Portrait Gallery** *(448)* resembles the Doge's Palace in Venice. Situated at the east end of Queen Street, its corner towers, rising above niches filled with statuary, stand in marked contrast to cool classicism of its neighbors in the New Town. The eighteenth-century dream of a planned urban development of uniform architectural design was fast being eroded. Nowhere is this more evident than in the multitude of new churches to spring up in Edinburgh and other Scottish cities in the last half of the nineteenth century.

RELIGIOUS DEVELOPMENTS

Factionalism among Scottish Presbyterians was perhaps inevitable, given their stout belief in the supreme authority of such an ambiguous compendium of theology, history, law, and ethics as the Holy Bible, and given the fundamental Protestant tenet of the "priesthood of all believers." Without a Pope or even archbishop to pronounce with finality on matters of faith and doctrine, differences of scriptural interpretation led easily to friction within the Church of Scotland, then to schism and finally to secession. In the eighteenth century, as related in the previous chapter, the Original Secession Church broke away in 1733 and in turn splintered into smaller factions, while in 1761 the Relief Church hived off on the issue of lay patronage. Within the Church of Scotland itself, the same issue divided the dominant Moderate party from the Evangelicals, who denounced the right of lay patrons to "intrude" ministers unacceptable to their congregations and who also differed from their more latitudinarian brothers on questions of dogma and moral behavior. In the General Assembly of 1834 the Evangelicals succeeded in pushing through a "Veto Act" giving congregations the right to reject a minister presented to them by lay patrons. Both the Scottish Court of Session and the House of Lords declared this act invalid, and it soon became clear that the Moderates had enough votes in the General Assembly to rescind it. By the time that body convened in 1843, the Evangelicals had therefore decided to secede.

The deed was done on 18 May of that year, when the acknowledged leader of the Evangelicals, Dr. Thomas Chalmers, along with about 200 kindred spirits, walked out of the General Assembly during its opening session at the handsome kirk on George Street, Edinburgh, now called the **Church of St. Andrew and St. George** *(446)*. This event came to be known as "the Disruption." The dissidents then marched out of the New Town and down to the Canonmills, where a hall had been hired for the accommodation of a new General Assembly of the self-styled Free Church of Scotland. Next day, no less than 470 out of the 1,200 ministers of the Church of Scotland signed the "Act of Separation and Deed of Demission" by which they abandoned their livings, their churches, and their manses and sacrificed an annual revenue of more than £100,00. They did not abandon, however, their claim to be *the* true Church of Scotland and thus felt obliged to set up a parallel and competitive ecclesiastical establishment with their own kirks in every parish, their own schools, and their own colleges for the training of new clergy. Whatever the merits of their position, then, the seceders gave a decided boost to Scotland's architectural profession and building industry.

In Edinburgh a new divinity school and meeting place for the Free Church General Assembly was not long in coming. By 1850 the prominent edifice on the Lawnmarket facing the Princes Street Gardens and known as the **New College and Assembly Hall** *(438)* was ready for use. It was a Tudor-style building designed by William Playfair, more or less in imitation of an Oxford or Cambridge college of the sixteenth century. Later, David Bryce added the assembly halls to the north. Subsequently, a second Free Church theological college was established in Glasgow, now called **Trinity College** *(408)*, on Lynedoch Street. Designed by Charles Wilson in an Italianate style, its three tall towers would not look out of place on the plains of Lombardy. Of the many churches rapidly put up to house the seceding congregations, few were of enough architectural merit or interest to warrant inspection today. One exception, however, is **Barclay Church** *(450)* on Bruntsfield Place in Edinburgh, built in 1861–1864 to the design of Frederick Thomas Pilkington. An extreme example of the Victorian Gothic Revival, here is a fanciful conglomeration of pinnacles and turrets grouped around a spire that rises to a height of 250 feet and is still among the most prominent landmarks of the city.

As to the Church of Scotland, it had no need for additional kirks and indeed inevitably suffered from reduced attendance at those already in existence. This situation, coupled with the barnlike appearance of some of the houses of worship thrown up hastily by the Free Church, produced a popular jingle:

> The wee Kirk, the Free Kirk,
> The Kirk wi' out the steeple;
> The auld Kirk, the cauld Kirk,
> The Kirk wi'out the people.

Undaunted, the established church proceeded at once to provide its General Assembly with a new meeting place. This was **Tolbooth St. John's Church** *(437)* (originally called simply the Tolbooth Church) on the Lawnmarket, distinguished by having Queen Victoria herself lay the foundation stone on her first visit to Scotland in 1842. It is a splendid Gothic Revival building, designed by the Scottish architect James Gillespie Graham in collaboration with the eminent English gothicist A. W. N. Pugin, one of the architects of the Houses of Parliament in London.

Thus the two rival religious bodies, differing not at all in theology or in devotion to presbyterian principles of church government, maintained separate identities and separate headquarters opposite each other on the Lawnmarket. The original issue between them had been the question of lay patronage, restored by Act of Parliament in 1712. But when that act was repealed in 1874, it was too late to repair the breach. Meanwhile, a third Presbyterian denomination of significant size had appeared on the scene. This was the United Presbyterian Church, formed in 1847 by 518 congregations affiliated with one or another of the various groups that had hived off of the Church of Scotland in the eighteenth century. Concentrated in towns and cities, this was a one-class church, consisting mostly of hardworking, thrifty *petit bourgeoisie*, many of whom by mid-century had achieved considerable affluence. Their church buildings reflected their newfound prosperity, and in Glasgow especially the United Presbyterians, more than any other denomination, were responsible for the most grandiloquent essays in Victorian ecclesiastical architecture. "Greek" Thomson was one of their favorite architects, and his two surviving churches are among that city's most noticeable landmarks. These are the **Caledonia Road Church** *(399)* and **St. Vincent Street Church** *(402).* Both consist of spacious rectangular assembly halls with huge attached Ionic porticos standing on gigantic platforms of rusticated masonry. Alongside each is a conspicuous high tower, that of the Caledonia Road Church being of Lombardic inspiration, while St. Vincent Street's is part Greek, part Egyptian. A fire gutted the former in 1965, and it is now empty and boarded up; the latter currently serves a "Wee Free" congregation (see below). More conventionally Grecian is the **Trinity Duke Street Church** *(407),* formerly the Sydney Place United Presbyterian Church, built in 1857 by the firm of Peddie and Kinnear. Here the front pillars are Corinthian, topped by a pediment decorated with unusually fine stone carving. Two U.P. churches designed by the Glasgow architect John Honeyman are also worthy of note. **Lansdowne Church** *(409)* was built in 1863 on the then fashionable Great Western Road when its congregation decided to move out of the deteriorating neighborhood of Cambridge Street, its original location. Victorian Gothic in the Early English manner, it is distinguished by its high tower topped by an elegant open spire. **Barony North Church** *(407),* constructed in 1878 in Cathedral Square, is by contrast baroque in style with a pronounced Mediterranean look.

Notwithstanding their disparate architectural styles, all of these buildings were costly to build and expensively furnished—in keeping with the rising prosperity of their congregations. Since the Free Church drew its strength (and its financial support) largely from the same upwardly mobile middle class, it is not surprising perhaps that in 1900 these two denominations, minus a small group of fundamentalist holdouts known popularly as the "Wee Frees," amalgamated to form the United Free Church of Scotland with a total of seventeen hundred congregations. Finally, in 1929, the Church of Scotland and the United Free Church reunited, thus putting most Scottish Presbyterians again under the same ecclesiastical umbrella. But, true to Scottish tradition, there were dissidents who remained aloof from the union. These people, still known as "Wee Frees," maintain their own separate houses of worship—mostly in the Highlands and Islands.

While Presbyterians quarrelled and parted from each other's company, the former Jacobite and Hanoverian factions of the Scottish Episcopal Church reunited in the nineteenth century, to offer Protestants an attractive alternative to Presbyterianism and to become the haven of a growing number of wealthy, anglicized Scots. Long before the High Church movement in England became fashionable among Oxford dons and others, Scottish Episcopalians held true to the principles of Archbishop Laud, and even when they adopted the Thirty-nine Articles of the Church of England, took exception to those of a decidedly Calvinist twist. Through Victorian times the number of Episcopalian congregations grew steadily, though never approaching in size any of the principal Presbyterian denominations. Indicative of their progress was the erection in each of Scotland's two principal cities of a handsome cathedral, each dedicated to St. Mary and each designed by the great English gothicist, Sir George Gilbert Scott. **St. Mary's Episcopal Cathedral** *(409)* in Glasgow, erected in 1871–1874 on Great Western Road, is a mix of Early English and Decorated styles; **St. Mary's Episcopal Cathedral** *(449)* in Palmerston Place, Edinburgh (1873–1879), is pure Early English. Both are magnificent.

The fastest growing denomination in both nineteenth- and early-twentieth-century Scotland, however, was Roman Catholicism. This phenomenon was entirely due to the influx of Irishmen, especially into Glasgow and the Southwest. Between 1841 and 1851, 115,000 Irish immigrants arrived, and in each of the following three decades the number was never less than 45,000. Even as late as 1921, census records indicate a figure of 159,000 Scottish residents born in Ireland. In 1864 twenty-two Irish priests from the west of Scotland petitioned the Holy See for the reestablishment of a Roman Catholic hierarchy in Scotland, and in 1878 Pope Leo XIII provided for two archbishops, each with four suffragans—all, as in the Middle Ages, independent of English control. The first two dioceses were established, naturally enough, in Glasgow and Edinburgh.

Despite the resurgence of Episcopalianism and Catholicism, Scotland remained primarily a Presbyterian country, both in numbers of communicants and in the prevailing national ethos. Moreover, the worldliness, rationalism, and moderation that had once been dominant in the Church of Scotland tended to give way before the overwhelming tide of evangelicalism—conservative and even fundamentalist in theology; fearful of the scientific skepticism unleashed by the likes of Charles Darwin; strongly supportive of laissez-faire capitalism and of the Liberal Party; zealous to convert the heathen overseas, though inclined to indifference toward the spiritual life of the underprivileged at home; and strict in their adherence to a puritanical code of conduct that owed less perhaps to historic Puritanism than to the distaste of a complacent middle class for the earthy morals and disorderly habits of the poor.

Such attitudes permeated the pages of *The Witness*, the Edinburgh-published newspaper of the Evangelical party, edited after 1840 by Hugh Miller, a former stonemason whose rise to fame and a degree of fortune

followed the legendary pattern of the Scottish "lad o' pairts." Born at
Cromarty in the humble thatched **Hugh Miller Cottage** *(548)*—now maintained by the National Trust for Scotland—Miller became a stonemason
with an unusual interest in fossils, which he collected in large numbers and
whose features he recorded in detail. Thanks to the publication of a strong
letter opposing lay patronage in the Church of Scotland, he was appointed
editor of *The Witness,* for which he wrote a number of scientific articles
later assembled and published in his first and best-known book, *The Old
Red Sandstone.* Significantly, the book begins with a strong, if irrelevant,
appeal to workingmen to abandon radical democratic politics and satisfy
themselves with self-improvement on the model of the author. Most of
Miller's writings, however, aimed at reconciling the discoveries of modern
science with his deeply held religious convictions concerning Creation, the
Flood, and other biblical traditions. In the end, overcome by depression, he
killed himself. His scientific theories, once immensely popular, were
eventually discredited by the more solidly grounded and convincing studies
of Charles Darwin, Charles Lyell, et al.

Another "lad o' pairts" was David Livingstone, born in 1813 in a weaver's
cottage on the grounds of a cotton mill in Blantyre, now preserved as part
of the **David Livingstone Centre** *(398)* (see Chapter 8). Persuaded by his
missionary father-in-law, Robert Moffat, to go to Africa under the auspices
of the London Missionary Society, this intrepid Scot's journeys deep into
the interior of the Dark Continent convinced him that, before Christianity
could take root there, the slave trade had to be abolished, and for that to be
accomplished, the region must be opened up to legitimate commerce
managed by British traders. Thus, economic development would go hand in
hand with Christian conversion—an idea congenial to most European
Protestants and to none more than the Scottish Evangelicals. Africa was to
become the greatest of all Scottish mission fields. The Free Church was
active in Zululand and in Nyasaland, where it founded a station named
Livingstonia; the Church of Scotland established another 350 miles to the
south and named it Blantyre; the United Presbyterians opened missions in
Nigeria; and the Scottish Episcopal Church proselytized in Kaffraria.

At home, the two behavioral aberrations selected by the Evangelicals as
major social evils demanding instant eradication were Sabbath-breaking
and intemperance. In the Disruption Assembly of 1843, ministers of the
emerging Free Church paused from their creative labors long enough to
hold a lengthy debate on how to prevent the running of Sunday trains
between Glasgow and Edinburgh. It was not long before a threatened
boycott and stockholders' revolt persuaded the directors of the North British
Railway to discontinue the service. And it was late in the nineteenth century

before the Edinburgh Botanic Gardens were allowed to open their gates on Sunday, though that was the only day when most of the working population could visit them.

As to the crusade against strong drink, there was ample evidence that alcohol abuse was indeed a serious social problem in Scotland, especially after 1823, when the duty on spirits was greatly reduced and consumption more than tripled in the following two decades. A parliamentary investigation in 1851 revealed that Glasgow was the most drunken city in the United Kingdom—three times more so than Edinburgh, five times more so than London. Among the urban poor especially, habitual drunkenness was becoming a national scandal, leading to the formation of a host of temperance societies with a range of remedies running from education to total prohibition. Among religious denominations, the Free Church was the most outspoken and persistent in supporting temperance causes. Success was limited to an Act of Parliament in 1853, closing public houses on Sundays and after 11:00 P.M. on weekdays, and to the Temperance (Scotland) Act of 1913, providing for local option to impose strict controls on the sale and consumption of liquor. But though Evangelical Protestantism was in the forefront of the movement, it should be noted that most labor union leaders and early socialists were strongly supportive. Whether drunkenness was the major cause of sin, crime, and poverty as many of the Evangelicals claimed, or largely the product of the debasement of the working class by the capitalist system as some labor leaders contended, there was no disagreement that alcoholism was rampant in Scotland and was an affliction especially grievous among the urban poor.

WHISKY AND GOLF

If the crime rate in the industrial Lowlands rose as a result of the greater consumption of spirits made possible by the lowering of the whisky excise, for the same reason the incidence of law-breaking in the Highlands fell. Throughout the eighteenth and early nineteenth centuries, government efforts to tax the hundreds of illicit stills scattered throughout the remote areas of the country had largely failed. All this changed with the passage of the Act of 1823, which on the one hand reduced the tax to about one-third of its previous amount and on the other provided for a much more rigorous enforcement. Although illegal distilling did not thereafter disappear, it ceased to be a real problem to the excisemen. Whereas in the year before the passage of the act there were known to be about fourteen thousand illicit stills, by 1874 the official number had diminished to six. Tax revenues of course increased commensurately, and so did output. In 1822, 2,225,000 gallons paid the excise duty; by 1884, the figure had risen to more than 20 million.

The word *whisky* derives from the Gaelic *uisge-beatha*, meaning "water of life." Although an entry for *aqua vitae* is recorded in the Scottish Exchequer Roll of 1494–1495, it was not until the seventeenth century that it became a general drink in Scotland, replacing claret and ale. In 1746, when the bibulous Charles Edward Stuart was hiding in the Highlands after Culloden, the only spiritous liquor he could find was whisky—no great disappointment in his case. By the 1770s, Dr. Johnson was reporting that breakfast in the Hebrides was usually preceded by a glass of whisky.

Scotch whisky in its pure form is produced by the double distillation of fermented malted barley, and the stages of its manufacture have not essentially changed since the days when it was an illicit cottage industry. These are six in number: (1) malting the barley by soaking it in water until partial germination has taken place; (2) drying the malt in a pagoda-roofed kiln, preferably over a peat fire; (3) fermenting a mixture of dried malt and hot water (called "the wort") by the addition of yeast to produce a brew of about 5 percent alcohol by volume (called "the wash"); (4) first distillation of the wash by boiling it in a pear-shaped "pot still" and condensing the vapor in a water-cooled coiled copper pipe (called "the worm"); (5) by the same process, redistilling the "low wines" resulting from the first distillation to produce spirits of about 57 percent alcohol by volume; (6) diluting these spirits with spring water and aging them for at least three years in oaken casks, preferably barrels previously used for storing sherry, which imparts coloration to the final product.

This is the process employed in the manufacture of *malt* whisky. *Blended* Scotch whisky, as the name implies, is a mixture of malt whiskies, usually with the addition of grain spirits, most commonly distilled from maize (equivalent to American corn) in a "patent still" consisting of two linked copper columns forty or fifty feet high. All Scotch whiskies marketed today, unless otherwise indicated, are blended products, consisting of up to 80 percent grain (as distinct from malted barley) spirits. Tasty and effective as they may be, to the purist they are not *true* Scotch whisky, and the places where they are produced and bottled are nothing more than assembly plants and not worth visiting.

Malt whisky distilleries, on the other hand, with their unmistakable pagoda roofs and pear-shaped copper stills, are fascinating sights, and, fortunately for the traveller, many are open to the public. At all of those listed here, guided tours and sometimes audiovisual shows are provided by the management, as well as a complimentary ounce or two of the delicious product. Some of these places have been in continuous operation since the mid–nineteenth century, and all of them, with only minor variations, use the same old traditional types of equipment and techniques of manufacture.

There are more malt whisky distilleries in the valley of the Spey and its tributaries than anywhere else in Scotland. Along the "whisky trail" north of Tomintoul, the following are especially recommended: **The Glenlivet Distillery** *(533)* in Glenlivet, Banffshire; **Glenfarclas-Glenlivet Distillery** *(531)* in Ballindalloch, west of Charlestown of Aberlour, Banffshire; **Tamdhu-Glenlivet Distillery** *(530)* in Knockando, Moray; **Aberlour Glenlivet Distillery** *(532)* north of Dufftown, Banffshire; **Glenfiddich Distillery** *(531)* in Dufftown; **Convalmore Distillery** *(532)* also in Dufftown; **Glen Grant-Glenlivet Distillery** *(530)* in Rothes, Moray; and **Strathisla-Glenlivet Distillery** *(532)* in Keith, Banffshire. Others, scattered throughout Scotland, include **Glengoyne Distillery** *(477)* in Dumgoyne, Stirlingshire; **Glenturret Distillery** *(501)*, near Crieff, Perthshire; and **Highland Park Distillery** *(560)*, near Kirkwall, Orkney.

Second to whisky drinking, though probably of more ancient origin, the most distinctly Scottish recreational pastime is the wholly indigenous game of golf. Possibly owing its ancestry to the medieval Dutch game of *Het Kolven*, it was popular enough in Scotland by 1457 to warrant a royal decree by King James II to the effect that "the futeball and golfe be utterly cryed down and not be used." The reason for this and subsequent equally futile attempts to prohibit golf was that it sapped the martial spirit of the populace by diverting them from the practice of archery. By the sixteenth century, royalty itself had succumbed to the game's seductions: James IV, James V, and Mary, Queen of Scots, all were golfers, the last named being charged with playing at Seton within a few days of the murder of her husband, Darnley. James VI/I introduced the game into England (though it did not become popular there until the nineteenth century); Charles I is known to have played on the links of Leith during his visit to Edinburgh in 1641; and James VII, while Duke of York, played a famous match at Leith, which he won with the help of his partner, a mere shoemaker.

This last incident is usually cited as evidence that golf in Scotland has traditionally been a democratic, or at least classless, pastime. An even earlier indication of the same phenomenon is the license granted in 1552 by Archbishop John Hamilton confirming the right of the townsmen of St. Andrews to the common links for "playing at golff, futeball, schuteing at all gamis with all other maner of pastime . . . without ony dykin or closing of ony pairt thairof." No one, in short, was to interfere with the general public's right to use the town links for sport. The word *links* refers to any barren strip of sand and brush just inland of the seashore, and, in most coastal towns, at least in the east of Scotland, these appear to have been opened to golfers at an early date.

Modern golf began with the formation of gentlemen's societies or clubs in the mid–eighteenth century—the Honourable Company of Edinburgh Golfers originating in the establishment of an annual prize match on the links of Leith in 1744, to be followed ten years later by a similar arrangement at St. Andrews. Royal recognition of the St. Andrews society of golfers came in 1834, when King William IV authorized its change of name to the Royal and Ancient Golf Club of St. Andrews. Thus, the **Old Course** *(495)* in this ancient cathedral city, with its neoclassical building, erected in 1854 to house the Royal and Ancient Golf Club, can claim to have the longest history as the home of an organized golfing society occupying its original location. But though the members of this and other similar clubs played regularly on their home links, they did not have exclusive use thereof. Even today many of the famous links of Scotland—St. Andrews, Carnoustie, North Berwick, Prestwick, Turnberry, and Troon, for example—are open to the public, though, at the more popular sites, signing up well in advance of playing has become a necessary precaution, at least in the summer months.

The nineteenth century brought about the development of championship golf, beginning with an invitation match sponsored by the Prestwick club in 1857. By that time distinctions were being drawn between amateurs and professionals—the latter eventually being defined as any golfer who accepted prize money. Professionalism originated among men who hired themselves out as green-keepers or caddies or who became skilled craftsmen in the manufacture of clubs and golf balls. This latter industry flourished especially at St. Andrews, where as early as 1772 the English naturalist, Thomas Pennant, reported a prevalence of fatal consumption among the inhabitants owing to their making of golf balls "by stuffing a great quantity of feathers into a leathern case by help an iron rod, with a wooden handle, pressed against the breast." The sewn leather sphere stuffed solidly with feathers is indeed the earliest known form of golf ball. Not until the mid–nineteenth century was it succeeded by the invention (probably by a St. Andrews clergyman) of the "guttie"—a ball made of gutta-percha, a latex obtained from trees in Malaya that had been in commercial production for years. Later, from America, came the rubber-cored ball, mass-produced by the Goodrich Rubber Company. Some of this history is well illustrated with antique clubs and balls on display at the **Spalding Golf Museum** *(510)* in Camperdown House on the outskirts of Dundee. There is another good collection of golfing paraphernalia on exhibit at the **National Museum of Antiquities** *(447)* in Edinburgh.

In England, where there was no tradition of public links, golf tended to be the domain of those who could afford memberships in the exclusive clubs being laid out on expensive real estate on the outskirts and suburbs of the great cities. Hence, in late Victorian and Edwardian times, it tended to be equated with shooting and fishing as a pastime of the upper classes, especially prosperous business or professional men who found golf to be the most convenient sport to fit into a busy work schedule. In short, golf in England, unlike in Scotland, was a sport of fashion. But none was more responsible for making it so than that ardent and much publicized golfer, Arthur James Balfour, a Scot who became Secretary of State for Ireland in 1897 and Prime Minister of Great Britain in 1902.

POLITICS: 1832–1914

By the eve of World War I, the invasion of the high councils of British government by native Scots or men with strong Scottish connections or men elected to the House of Commons from Scottish constituencies had become an established fact of British politics. Before the prime ministership of Balfour, there had been the brief incumbency of Lord Rosebery in 1894. After Balfour came Sir Henry Campbell-Bannerman, another Scot; and after him Herbert Henry Asquith, whose second wife was a Scottish heiress and who sat for East Fife. But the greatest statesman of Scottish origin, though born and raised in England, was William Ewart Gladstone, leader of the Liberal Party and four times Prime Minister of Great Britain (1868–1874, 1880–1885, 1886, and 1892–1894).

Son of a Leith corn merchant, Gladstone's father, John Gladstones, had moved to Liverpool in 1781 and later dropped the s from the original family name. His mother was Anne Mackenzie Robertson, of pure Highland stock. John, before long, amassed a fortune and, at the age of sixty-five, moved back to Scotland after purchasing the estate of **Fasque** *(546)* in the Howe of Mearns in Kincardineshire. The originally modest eighteenth-century house here had already been heavily gothicized by the previous owner, and John Gladstone was to add a handsome new portico and numerous other improvements. By this time, his youngest son William was already a Member of Parliament, but it became his habit to spend parliamentary recesses at Fasque. Even after his marriage and rise to prominence, the young politician returned with some frequency to his father's home.

Thus Gladstone, despite a busy life in Westminster and later in the management of his wife's family estate of Hawarden in Montgomeryshire, kept alive his Scottish connection. Then, in 1879, he was persuaded to compete for the electoral seat of Midlothian and launched the first of his four successful campaigns in that county. It was during the first of these that he delivered his famous attack on the adventurism and aggressive imperialism of Disraeli and the Tory Party and spelled out an alternative policy for Great Britain of restraint, international cooperation, and antimilitarism. "It is deplorable," he pronounced, that "all manners of gratuitous, dangerous, ambiguous, impracticable, and impossible engagements are contracted for us in all parts of the world." Gladstone was an immensely energetic and popular campaigner. During his first Midlothian campaign, he addressed an estimated eighty-seven thousand people, often from the rear platform of his train—a new political technique to become widely copied by politicians everywhere. Between train trips and speeches, he rested at **Dalmeny House** *(429)*, home of his foreign minister and eventual successor, Lord Rosebery.

Gladstone's immense personal popularity is only a small part of the explanation of the unswerving loyalty of the majority of Scottish voters to the Whig and Liberal parties during the greater part of the nineteenth century. The Liberals, Gladstone especially, were completely in tune with the moral attitudes of Evangelical Protestantism, and for a long while there was an unspoken alliance in Scotland between the Liberal Party on the one side and the Free and the United Presbyterian churches on the other. Not until Gladstone espoused the cause of Irish Home Rule, thus raising the specter of a Roman Catholic regime in Britain's "other island," was the Liberal monopoly of the Evangelical vote broken, as many Scottish Presbyterians sought shelter among the Liberal-Unionists who split with Gladstone on this issue. But more than religion wedded the Scottish middle class to the party, par excellence, of free trade and *laissez-faire* capitalism. First enfranchised by the Whig Reform Bill of 1832, these prosperous merchants, industrialists, lawyers, and the like had every inclination to be grateful to the politicians most closely identified with the economic policies to which, in part, they ascribed their seemingly permanent prosperity.

Electoral reform did not end, of course, in 1832. Bills passed in 1867 and again in 1884 expanded the franchise to include almost every male adult in Britain, and the Ballot Act of 1872 gave to common men the additional protection of secrecy in voting. Thus, other segments of society, less enamored with the status quo than the middle class, began to emerge on the political scene toward the end of the nineteenth century. Poverty, low wages, long hours of labor, dangerous working conditions in factories and mines, bad housing, and the tyranny of employers over their workers were the concerns of an increasing number of trade union leaders and political activists who were beginning to make themselves heard.

Among these pioneers of the British labor movement, none was more eloquent or effective than James Keir Hardie of Lanarkshire, commemorated today by the **Keir Hardie Statue** *(390)*, a modest bust standing in front of the town hall of Cumnock, Ayrshire. Born a bastard in 1836, set to work in the coal mines at the age of ten, persecuted by mine owners as a labor agitator, Hardie was instrumental in organizing the short-lived Scottish Labour Party in 1888; was elected as a Liberal Member of Parliament for a working-class London constituency in 1892; and next year helped to found the Independent Labour Party in Bradford, which shortly absorbed the Scottish Labour Party. Of the "big four" of the I.L.P., three—Hardie, Bruce Glasier, and Ramsay MacDonald—were Scots. Parallel with these developments was the rise of political activism among the British labor unions. In 1897 the Scottish Trade Union Congress had been formed with this in mind, and together with the Independent Labour Party it organized the Scottish Labour Party. Shortly thereafter, this group merged with its English equivalent to become the modern Labour Party, which after the First World War was to play so prominent a role in British politics. Dying in 1915, Keir Hardie was not to witness this postwar burgeoning of British socialism whose intellectual forebears were Marx and Engels, modified by such British Fabians as Sidney and Beatrice Webb, H. G. Wells, and Bernard Shaw. Hardie was no intellectual, nor was he a Marxist. His socialism, if such it can be called, was derived mostly from the Holy Bible, Robert Burns, and Thomas Carlyle.

LITERATURE AND ART: 1832–1914

Carlyle's Birthplace *(385)* in Ecclefechan, Dumfriesshire, now maintained by the National Trust for Scotland, is a sturdy dwelling place built by his father and uncle, both stonemasons. Born in 1795, and educated at the University of Edinburgh, the soon-to-be celebrated essayist and historian left Scotland for good in 1834 and settled in Chelsea, where he lived until his death in 1881. Cosmopolitan in his worldview, profoundly influenced by Goethe and other German philosophers, Carlyle's writings nevertheless reflected to a degree the defiant egalitarianism of his Covenanting Scots forebears. Glorifying the dignity of labor, he deplored the social injustices spawned by the Industrial Revolution, condemned the "Mammonism" of the newly rich, and attacked the Benthamite philosophy of *laissez-faire*, which tended to view gross inequalities of wealth as the necessary price of economic progress. Rejecting the offer of an honored resting place in Westminster Abbey, Carlyle chose to be buried with his ancestors in Hoddam kirkyard, a few hundred yards from his place of birth.

But Thomas Carlyle is rightly known to history as the "sage of Chelsea," whose genius, notwithstanding the early essays collected under the title *Sartor Resartus*, did not come to flower until he moved to London. In Scotland itself, for some fifty years after the deaths of Walter Scott and James Hogg in the early 1830s, no literary work of any significance was produced. Then, in 1886, Robert Louis Stevenson of Edinburgh published *Kidnapped*, a lively novel of adventure that remains, and justly so, a well-read classic. Born in 1850, son and grandson of noted Scottish lighthouse engineers, sickly from childhood, a fanatical traveller, Stevenson's literary fame as author of novels for boys and poems for children (*Kidnapped, Treasure Island, Black Arrow,* and *A Child's Garden of Verses*) has somewhat obscured his true genius. Always preoccupied with the problem of moral ambiguity, some of his novels (*The Strange Case of Dr. Jekyll and Mr. Hyde, The Master of Ballantrae,* and the unfinished *Weir of Hermiston*) are masterpieces of psychological insight. But *Kidnapped* remains the most readable of his works, and a traveller in Scotland today, with a taste for Highland scenery, could do worse than to follow the itinerary of David Balfour and Alan Breck from Mull to Appin to Rannoch Moor to Ben Alder to Balquhidder and then to Edinburgh. Stevenson died in 1894 in Samoa. He is commemorated with a fine bronze bas-relief in **St. Giles Kirk** *(439)*, and some mementos of his life and work are on display (along with those of Burns and Scott) in **Lady Stair's House** *(438)* in the Lawnmarket. Like all great writers, though, his most impressive memorials are his own written words.

In the year that Stevenson died, Scotland saw the publication of a book, as insipid as it was popular, which set a new fashion in fiction, soon to be exploited by a group of Scottish writers known collectively as the "Kailyard School." The book was *Beside the Bonnie Briar Bush*; its author an English-born minister of Highland descent, John Watson, writing under the pen name of Ian Maclaren. The best-known exponent of Kailyard fiction was James Matthew Barrie, many of whose possessions and first editions are now on view in the **Barrie Birthplace** *(513)* in Kirriemuir, Angus. Before he became a successful London playwright, his best known fictional works were *A Window in Thrums* and *The Little Minister*. Barrie's and the other Kailyard authors' mawkish and sentimental versions of village life in contemporary Scotland were to be brutally satirized in another novel, *The House with the Green Shutters* by George Douglas Brown, whose *nom de plume* was simply George Douglas. Equally distorted in its vision, this was a shocking exposé of a fictional Ayrshire village where all the characters were unremittingly vicious, cruel, stupid, greedy, envious, or drunken. Travellers and students in search of a truer picture of rural and small-town life in late-nineteenth-century Scotland are better served by the several folk museums throughout the country that display a remarkable collection of artifacts from this era. Among the most noteworthy of those not mentioned elsewhere in this book are the **Gladstone Court Museum** *(398)* in Biggar, Lanarkshire; the **Museum of Islay Life** *(466)* in Port Charlotte, Islay; the **Fife Folk Museum** *(484)* in Ceres; the **Crail Museum** *(484)* in Fife; and the **Angus Folk Museum** *(512)* in Glamis.

As the literary critic Maurice Lindsay has pointed out: "One of the curious facts of the nineteenth-century Scottish novel is its reluctance to allow itself to be urbanized. . . . The fact that the central belt of . . . Scotland . . . had been turned into a vast industrial machine . . . could hardly be guessed at in the novels of the period." The same could be said of most of the works of contemporary Scottish painters. Following the lead of David Wilkie, many of them were "genre" painters of rural and village life, depicting anecdotally an Arcadian rusticity as remote from the real world of mine and factory and shipyard as were the idyllic scenes and quaint but lovable characters of the Kailyard school. Among the most popular of this stripe were Thomas Faed, William Allan, W. H. Lizars, George Harvey, and John Burr.

Scotland's glorious landscapes of course could not escape the attention of the painter's brush, and although none of the indigenous artists approached the popularity of Sir Edwin Landseer, some proved to be able technicians, if not great artists. Horatio McCulloch, George Chalmers, and William McTaggart fall into this category. Then there were the Scottish painters who fell under the influence of the English Pre-Raphaelites, with their curious combination of highly romantic or devout subject matter and almost photographic attention to detail. The most eminent of these was William Dyce, whose greatest work, commissioned by Prince Albert, was his painting of the frescoes in the House of Lords. Others included Sir Joseph Noel Paton (a favorite of Queen Victoria) and Robert Scott Lauder. Only a handful of artists of the "Glasgow School" (W. Y. MacGregor, James Guthrie, George Henry, and John Lavery), under the influence of Whistler and Millais, late in the century began to break away from the extreme literalness that characterized most Scottish painting before the First World War.

Scottish art galleries are well stocked with the works of all the artists cited—notably the **National Gallery of Scotland** *(444)*; the **Glasgow Art Gallery & Museum** *(407)*; the **Hunterian Art Gallery** *(408)*, Glasgow; the

Perth Art Gallery and Museum *(505)*; the Central Museum and Art Gallery
(510), Dundee; and the Aberdeen Art Gallery *(535)*. Though none of these
paintings would be said today to be of outstanding artistic merit, many are
worth examining from the point of view of social history. Here details of
costume, household furnishings, village architecture, and the like have been
forever captured in oil and canvas, and there can be no reason to doubt their
authenticity. There can be no doubt either that on these gallery walls hangs
the visual embodiment of the aesthetic and cultural values of the Victorian
and Edwardian eras. Like so much else in Britain, these too would be lost
forever in the holocaust of the Great War of 1914-1918.

WAR AND PEACE: 1914-1945

In the Royal Highland Fusiliers' Regimental Museum *(405)* on Sauchiehall
Street in Glasgow is a life-sized three-dimensional tableau of a young
Scottish soldier, garbed for battle, taking leave of his distraught wife as he
goes off to the trenches across the Channel. Set in the midst of a room full
of showcases holding the regimental plate and colors, honors won, and
medals awarded, this is a sharp reminder of what the First World War was
really like to those who fought it and to those who stayed at home.
Seventeen thousand officers and men from this single unit were killed in
action. The record is not untypical. Approximately 147,000 Scottish soldiers
were killed or died of wounds in the 1914-1918 war. This was close to 20
percent of the British total—far out of proportion to the ratio of Scotland's
male adult population to Great Britain's. In recognition of their ultimate
sacrifice, a great shrine was built close to the highest point of Edinburgh
Castle *(436)*. Designed by Robert Lorimer, with stained glass windows by
Douglas Strachan, each recess in the "gallery of honour" here is devoted to
a single Scottish regiment. And within each recess is a separate "roll of
honour"—a leather-bound folio listing the names of the regimental dead for
both World Wars. For the 1914-1918 war, the Gordon Highlanders' folio
contains 301 pages with more than thirty names per page; that of the Black
Watch, 296 pages, each with about the same number. Down the hill, in the
Castle esplanade, is the huge equestrian statue of General Sir Douglas (first
Earl) Haig who in December 1915 became supreme commander of British
forces in France. In Huntly House *(442)* on the Canongate there is a room
full of Haig mementos. Born in Edinburgh, he was buried in 1928 among
the ruins of Dryburgh Abbey *(418)*. Here his simple gravestone bears the

inscription "HE TRUSTED IN GOD AND TRIED TO DO RIGHT"—probably a fair estimate of the quality of Haig's uninspired military leadership. To those who died under his command, almost every Scottish town and village was also to raise a commemorative monument. None is more impressive than the **Inveraray War Memorial** *(464)* in the village park on the shore of Loch Fyne. Here, silhouetted against the loch, stands a stone statue of a kilted Scottish infantryman with these words inscribed on its base:

IN
MEMORY OF
THOSE
YOUNG LAMENTED
HERE
WHO DIED
IN THEIR COUNTRY'S SERVICE
1914–1918
"These are they which came out of great tribulation"

On the home front, Scotland prospered—especially Glasgow, Dundee, and other industrial cities. Shipbuilding in Glasgow had already hit a new high in the years immediately preceding the outbreak of war, thanks mostly to the Anglo-German naval race. In 1913, the Clyde set a record of 757,000 tons, more than a third of Britain's total for that year. The outbreak of hostilities in August 1914 brought still more business. After Germany resorted to submarine warfare, more British destroyers had to be built to counter this new underwater threat and more merchant ships to replace those sent to the bottom. Glasgow's metallurgical and heavy engineering industries were quickly converted to the manufacture of guns and shells. Dundee's jute factories turned out innumerable sandbags to line the endless trenches stretching across the fields of France. Textile workers turned their hands to the fabrication of army and navy uniforms. But by 1919 all this profitable business had come to an end.

As far as the West of Scotland was concerned, the war had only masked the instability and weakness of an economy too deeply committed to the production of capital goods—coal, steel, shipbuilding, and heavy engineering. It had also brought to a halt the region's tentative prewar moves toward diversification, such as the manufacture of the Argyll and Arroll-Johnston automobiles in Glasgow and Paisley respectively. (Models of both makes are at the **Glasgow Museum of Transport** *[400]*; but not at the **Doune Motor Museum** *(503)* in Perthshire—an omission perhaps symptomatic of Scotland's failure to sustain its early start in the automotive industry.) The fact is, to quote the economic historian S. G. Checkland, "it was impossible to generate within a heavy producer-goods industrial economy like Glasgow's radically new sectors of a more flexible and responsive kind. And as high prosperity faded [after the war], the capacity of the region to do new things declined."

By 1922 the wartime boom had turned to depression. Glasgow alone reported an unemployment figure of 80,000, and comparable statistics were registered for other industrial areas of Scotland (as well as for South Wales and the English regions of Tyneside, Cumberland, and Lancashire). In 1923 Clydeside shipbuilding was down to 180,000 tons from more than 750,000 ten years before. Ten years later the figure was 56,000. Unemployment soared. That of Scotland averaged 14 percent between 1923 and 1930—as compared to 11.4 percent for the United Kingdom as a whole. In 1931-1938 the ratio rose to 21.9 percent against a UK figure of 16.4. Emigration swelled proportionately. Between 1921 and 1931, nearly 400,000 people left Scotland, almost twice the average number of departures in any previous decade since 1881. In the same decade there were more Scots than English entering the United States, and in 1931 the number of Scots-born people in Canada was almost 280,000.

Not surprisingly, one result of all this economic distress was mounting labor unrest and a decided leftward swing in Scottish political affiliation. Even during the war, a small wave of strikes and a handful of radical agitators had alarmed conservative opinion in Britain to the point of labelling (or libelling) Glasgow and its industrial satellites as "Red Clydeside." Then, when the Labour Party won two-thirds of the city's parliamentary seats in the general election of 1922, the label stuck. That year Scotland at large returned twenty-nine Labour MPs and even one Communist. The Liberal Party's rapid loss of popularity between the wars was Labour's gain. The Scottish socialist Ramsay MacDonald's capture of the prime ministership in 1924 would have been impossible without his fellow countrymen's support. Clydesiders admired him particularly for his outspoken pacificism during World War I, as well as for his lifelong dedication to the cause of labor. And in 1933 Glasgow's city council was captured by the Labour Party, though the odds against finding a socialistic solution to a single city's problems in the midst of a worldwide depression were insuperable.

As hard times worsened, many north of the border laid the blame on England and turned to Scottish nationalism as an appropriate remedy. The movement had its antecedents in the mid–nineteenth century with the founding of the Scottish Rights Society, whose chief accomplishments were to finance the erection of the **Wallace Monument** *(480)* on Abbey Crag outside Stirling and to discredit the use of the word *Scotch* instead of

Scottish, notwithstanding the fact that both Burns and Scott had mostly employed the older form. In 1885 the British government had taken a small step in the direction of acknowledging Scotland's special status by creating the position of Secretary for Scotland, and after 1902 the incumbent secretary was always in the cabinet and the Scottish Office was given Dover House in London as its headquarters. Meanwhile, with Gladstone's conversion to home rule for Ireland, the Scottish Home Rule Association had come into being in 1886, and the concept of "Home Rule All Around" (including Scotland) gathered considerable momentum in Liberal Party circles until the coming of the war precluded any such divisive action.

From home rule and devolution to national independence seemed a logical progression to some Scots after the war, though many more would have settled for much less. The government's response was to upgrade the Scottish Secretary to a full Secretary of State in 1926 and a few years later to move various governmental functions from Whitehall to **St. Andrew's House** *(445)* in Edinburgh at the foot of Calton Hill. Devolution and home rule were taken up again by the National Party of Scotland, formed in 1928, and by the Scottish National Party, established in 1934, which aimed at something like Dominion status for Scotland within the British Empire. As in 1914–1918, the coming of the Second World War again put the quietus on Scottish nationalism, though it would rise once more and in greater strength than ever with the coming of the peace.

Closely associated with the agitation for restructuring the constitutional framework of the United Kingdom, to Scotland's presumed advantage, was a group of men of letters who claimed, in the period between the wars, to be the vanguard of a "Scottish Renaissance." If they had a leading spokesman, it was the Langholm-born Christopher Murray Grieve, who, writing under the pen name Hugh McDiarmid, espoused both political and cultural nationalism—and occasionally Communism as well. His best-known literary work is a long poetic monologue, *A Drunk Man Looks at the Thistle.* Hailed as a masterpiece in Scottish literary circles, it made only a slight impression elsewhere in the English-speaking world, doubtless because it is virtually unreadable without frequent reference to a glossary. The poem was written in a synthetic form of Broad Scots called "Lallans"— a language spoken by no one, nowhere, and at no time. Somewhat more successful in re-creating the rhythm of native Scots speech, without losing the reader in a morass of unfamiliar words, was Lewis Grassic Gibbon (pen name for J. Leslie Mitchell), born in Aberdeenshire in 1905 and dead thirty-four years later. His *Sunset Song*, the first volume of a trilogy of novels, called *A Scots Quair*, is arguably the most enduring literary product of the Scottish Renaissance—a work of outstanding lyricism, though based on a misconception of Scottish prehistory and somewhat muddled in its earthy mysticism. Even more concerned with exploring the mystical union between the primitive Celt and his native heath was the Caithness-born Neil Gunn (1891–1974), who produced a series of worthy novels, though somewhat flawed by their highly romanticized view of the indigenous culture of Gaeldom. It is surprising that, except for George Blake, author of *The Shipbuilders*, none of the major writers of the twenties and thirties paid much attention to Scotland's *urban* problems. As in the case of the much scorned Kailyard School before them, their preoccupation with rural and village life and their imaginings of an agrarian golden age were at bottom simply escapist.

It was no golden age that dawned on 1 September 1939, when Adolph Hitler's planes and troops launched their attack on Poland, thus bringing Britain again into a war of global dimensions. British—including Scottish—military casualties were far lower in the Second World War than in the first, owing largely to the abandonment of static infantry tactics, to the early British evacuation of the Continent after the fall of France, and to the overwhelming Allied superiority of arms during and after the Allied reinvasion of Europe and the Russian resurgence on the eastern front. But this time progress in air power had made the home front vulnerable, and Britain suffered immeasurably from repeated bomb and rocket attacks against its cities, factories, ports, and communications centers.

Scotland, however, was to escape the full brunt of Hitler's savagery, in spite of the fact that Glasgow served as Britain's chief port; was the point of entry for more than a million American and Canadian soldiers; worked its shipyards to full capacity in response to the Royal Navy's rising demands; and converted the nearby airfields at Renfrew and Prestwick into major military airports. Such an inviting target could not forever escape the attention of German bombers, however, and on 19 July 1940 the city felt its first aerial attack. It was a small daylight raid, with not much damage caused. In a night attack of 19 September the Germans dropped a stick of bombs on the city center and set a cruiser at Yorkhill docks on fire. Finally, in the spring of 1941, Glasgow began to receive the attention formerly paid to London and other English industrial cities. In mid-March over a thousand were killed and half again as many seriously injured in a single bombing raid. Other strikes, though somewhat less deadly, followed in April and May. The March strikes were directed principally against Clydebank; those in May against Greenock. The final air raid on Glasgow, a small one, occurred on the night of 23 March 1943. But not until France and the Low Countries were overrun in the summer and autumn of 1944 could British civilians feel relatively safe from the ever-present danger of terror from the sky or afford to relax a little from their daily precautions. Some faint idea of what life was like in this constant state of siege can be gleaned from the exhibit in Glasgow's **People's Palace** *(401)* of the gas masks, first-aid kits, Anderson shelters, etc., which became standard items of household equipment in every British city during the Second World War.

The most bizarre visit from the skies over Scotland, however, was not a bomber strike, but Rudolph Hess's parachute drop near the village of Eaglesham, Renfrewshire, on 10 May 1941. Hitler's Deputy Fuehrer had been convinced by the famous German exponent of geopolitics, Professor Karl Haushofer, and his son Albrecht that the anti-Churchill, appeasement wing of Britain's Conservative Party would welcome peace-feelers from Germany. Albrecht Haushofer had for some years been on friendly terms with the Duke of Hamilton, a well-known sportsman and Conservative MP, later to serve with the Royal Air Force. The duke was therefore selected as a likely go-between, and his estate of Dungavel in Lanarkshire was Hess's chosen destination. In fact, he dropped by parachute only a few miles from this target, before being apprehended and shipped off to London, where he spent the balance of the war incarcerated in the tower. The map he carried with him on his flight, with the site of Dungavel encircled in pencil, is now on view at **Lennoxlove House** *(457)*, the present ducal residence in East Lothian.

Britain, of course, was not prepared to withdraw from the war, as Hess had so foolishly imagined. In June 1944 the massive Anglo-American-Canadian landings on beaches in Normandy proved to be the prelude to total victory over Germany in 1945. Scotland had provided a major training ground for some of the special amphibious troops to be engaged in that and other such operations. The **Commando Memorial** *(524)* at Spean Bridge, Inverness-shire—a trio of life-sized sculptured soldiers—commemorates those men killed in World War II who learned their dangerous trade among these hills and lochs.

Far to the north, in Orkney, is another wartime memento—this one of the enemy. On the islet of Lamb Holm stands the quaint **Italian Chapel** *(561)*, a Nissen hut covered on the inside with colorful religious frescoes. It was thus decorated (and later restored) by Italian prisoners of war who had been set to work in the construction of the **Churchill Barriers** *(561)*, a concrete causeway connecting the main island of Orkney with the string of islets to the south. Now used as an interisland highway, it was originally designed to guard the great naval anchorage of Scapa Flow from German submarines approaching from the east.

This was not Churchill's only special gift to Scotland during the war. Early in 1941 he had appointed Tom Johnston, Labour MP for West

Stirlingshire, to be the Secretary of State for Scotland. It was a brilliant choice, and Johnston proved unquestionably to be the most effective statesman ever to hold that office. His greatest achievement probably was the establishment of the North of Scotland Hydro-Electric Board, later responsible for the construction of the fifty-six dams and fifty-four main hydroelectric power stations throughout the country. It was Johnston also who created a separate Scottish Tourist Board, thus anticipating, and to some extent creating, the great post-war boom in tourism, so important to Scotland's efforts to diversify its economy and free itself from a too long overdependency on heavy industry.

Today the Scottish Tourist Board is prepared to assist in myriad ways the thousands of annual visitors—coming mostly from England, the United States, and the former British Dominions—to discover Scotland. And, as this book has tried to indicate, there is much indeed to discover. Travellers in Scotland who ask for no more than the sound of bagpipes or the show of tartan kilts are cheating themselves. Here is a country rich in scenery and richer still in history. The Scots themselves have a strong sense of identification with their past, and, without some familiarity with it, no visitor can hope to comprehend, or even fully to enjoy, this "dear, dear land"—as Queen Victoria was wont to call it. For the land and its history and its traditions and its long record of the struggles of a proud and determined people are all commingled and inseparable. And no one knew this better than Robert Louis Stevenson, homesick in Samoa, where he penned that most poignant *cri de coeur* of the uprooted Scot:

> Blows the wind today, and the sun and the rain are flying,
> Blows the wind on the moors today and now,
> Where about the graves of the martyrs the whaups are crying,
> My heart remembers how!
>
> Grey recumbent tombs of the dead in desert places,
> Standing stones on the vacant wine-red moor,
> Hills of sheep, and the howes of the silent vanished races,
> And winds, austere and pure.
>
> Be it granted to me to behold you again in dying,
> Hills of Home! and to hear again the call;
> Hear about the graves of the martyrs the pewees crying
> And hear no more at all.

Stevenson did not return. But today's visitor to Scotland is privileged to walk the windy moors, to view the ancient monuments, and to sense, as did the poet, the ghostly presence of his country's past.

Part Two

Gazetteer

SOUTHWESTERN SCOTLAND
Wigtownshire
GLEN LUCE (DUMFRIES AND GALLOWAY)

* Glenluce Abbey *(148)*, 2 m. nw (82 NX 185 587); AM

About 1192, Roland, Lord of Galloway, founded this Cistercian monastery and brought monks here from nearby Dundrennan Abbey. Not much of the abbey church remains standing except for the walls of the First Pointed south transept built in the thirteenth century. The best feature of these ruins is the vaulted chapter house, probably a late-medieval replacement of the original. Foundations of the other claustral buildings are visible, indicating the usual Cistercian arrangement, with the frater jutting south from the south range instead of parallel to it.

Droughdad Motte *(83)*, 4 m. w; n of A 715, e of A 748, ¼ m. s of Dunragit (82 NX 148 569)

This is a well-preserved Norman motte, presumably dating from the twelfth century.

PORT PATRICK (DUMFRIES AND GALLOWAY)

Ardwell Motte *(83)*, 10 m. se; w of A 716 from 3 m. s of Sandhead (82 NX 107 455)

This is a well-preserved motte of probable twelfth-century date.

Ardwell Broch *(33)*, 11 m. se; 4 m. s of Sandhead (82 NX 066 466)

Here is a much ruined Late Iron Age broch, typically situated close to the sea, presumably for defense against pirates. The inside wall-face can be seen above the rubble. There are two narrow entrance passages, one facing the sea, the other on the landward side.

Port William (Dumfries and Galloway)

Barsalloch Point Fort *(29)*, 1½ m. se; n of A 747 (82 347 413); AM

This is a Late Iron Age promontory fort formed by two ramparts and a median ditch built across the neck of a headland overlooking Luce Bay.

Drumtroddan *(26)*, 2 m. ne; e of A 714 (83 NX 363 447); AM

Here on a flat rock-face are numerous Bronze Age incisions, including cup-marks and cups with concentric rings, some with radial grooves and connecting channels.

Druchtag Motte *(83)*, 2½ m. n; n of Mochrum village (82 NX 349 466)

Here is a high Norman motte, probably of twelfth-century date.

Big Balcraig *(26)*, 3 m. ne; n of B 7021 (83 NX 374 440)

Here are rocks with Bronze Age cup-and-ring marks.

Stranraer (Dumfries and Galloway)

* Castle Kennedy Gardens *(261)*, 3 m. e; n of A 75

The much ruined L-plan sixteenth-century castle of the Kennedy Earls of Cassillis is little more than a decoration-piece for this vast woodland garden laid out in the early eighteenth century by Field Marshal John Dalrymple, second Earl of Stair, who employed for the purpose the Royal Scots Greys and the Inniskilling Fusiliers. Avenues of trees converge on a giant lily pond like the spokes of a wheel on a hub. The avenues are named for famous battles fought against the French; e.g., Dettingen. In subsequent years, new stands of timber were planted—Norway spruce, monkey puzzle, etc., as well as a host of rhododendrons, azaleas, camellias, and magnolias.

* Kirkmadrine Crosses *(60)*, 9 m. s; 1 m. w of A 716 from 1½ m. s of Sandhead (82 NX 081 484); AM

Set in a glass-front recess in the outside wall of Kirkmadrine church are a number of Early Christian stones, of which the three most important date from the fifth and sixth centuries. The earliest of these bears a Chi Rho monogram (the first two Greek letters of the name of Christ) and the inscription "HIC JACENT S(AN)C(T)I ET PRAECIPUI SACERDOTES IDES VIVENTIUS ET MAVORIUS [Here lie the holy and chief priests, Ides, Viventius, and Mavorius]."

High Drummore Motte *(83)*, 16½ m. se; n of B 7041, ½ m. w of Drummore (82 NX 139 359)

Here is a typical Galloway Norman motte, probably dating from the twelfth century.

WIGTOWN (DUMFRIES AND GALLOWAY)

* Wigtown Parish Kirkyard *(247)*, town center

Here, behind an iron railing, are the graves of a number of persecuted Covenanters of the "killing time" of the 1680s, including that of Margaret Lachlan, who was reportedly put to death by drowning. About a hundred yards below the kirk toward Wigtown Bay is the **Martyr's Stake** *(247)*—a stone replica of the original—to which she is supposed to have been bound until the incoming tide covered her head. Whether the event actually took place is a matter of scholarly controversy. The fact that the stake today stands so far from the shoreline can be explained by the likelihood of subsequent silting.

** Torhousekie Stone Circle *(22)*, 3½ m. w; s of B 733 (83 NX 383 565); AM

This Bronze Age stone circle now contains nineteen stubby boulders set on a circumference of about sixty-five feet in diameter, inside of which is a line of three additional boulders.

* Cruggleton Church *(163)*, 10 m. s; e of B 7063 from 2½ m. s of Garlieston (83 NX 478 428)

This tiny Romanesque church, probably built in the twelfth century, is associated with the very ruined castle east of here. The key can be had at Cruggleton Farm about one-quarter mile north of the church.

Cruggleton Castle *(84)*, 10 m. s; e of B 7063 from 2½ m. s of Garlieston (83 NX 485 429)

Overlooking Wigtown Bay, here are the scant remains of a stone castle probably built by Walter Comyn, Earl of Menteith, in the early thirteenth century. Nothing but the foundations remains visible. The stone arch at the castle entrance is a folly installed in the late eighteenth century by the Marquis of Bute.

** Whithorn Priory *(59, 148, 159, 182)*, 10½ m. s; w of A 746 (83 NX 445 403); AM

The roofless building here was the nave of a Premonstratensian priory church, which also served as the cathedral of the Bishop of Galloway. A small portion of the existing walls dates from the twelfth century. So does the splendid Romanesque doorway relocated in the west end of the south wall. (These compass points are approximate only as the church, unconventionally, does not lie on a true east–west axis.) Most of the north wall and parts of the south were built in the thirteenth century, while the existing east and west walls date from a rebuilding of the eighteenth. East of this building is a crypt with a barred entry (access can be had by key obtainable at the site museum). This crypt formerly lay underneath a chapel extending east and south of the choir when the church was much longer than it now is. In the area immediately outside the east end of the church, excavations have revealed the existence of the foundations of a Dark Age church, which may have been St. Ninian's original establishment of the fifth century (*Candida Casa*) but are also possibly the remains of a seventh-century chapel dedicated to the saint by his successors at Whithorn.

The excellent site museum stands just outside the entrance to the churchyard. Here is a splendid collection of Early Christian stone monuments and crosses, all from Whithorn itself or from nearby St. Ninian's Cave. The earliest of these is the so-called Latinus stone, dating from the fifth century.

* St. Ninian's Chapel *(60)*, 14½ m. s, on Isle of Whithorn at southern terminus of A 750 (83 NX 479 362); AM

Situated on an islet connected with the mainland by an artificial causeway, the chapel is a simple rectangular, dry-stone building without a roof, dating probably from the thirteenth century. In all likelihood it was an oratory for pilgrims landing here to visit St. Ninian's shrine at nearby Whithorn Priory.

* St. Ninian's Cave *(60)*, 14½ m. s; 1 m. s of A 747 through Glasserton to Physgill house, down path to shoreline and west ½ m. up beach (83 NX 422 360); AM

This cave may have served as St. Ninian's solitary hermitage in the fifth century. Incised crosses still observable on the walls of the cave and on nearby boulders are thought to have been executed by pilgrims who came here after the saint's death. Other crosses from here are to be seen in the site museum of Whithorn Priory.

Kirkcudbrightshire

CASTLE DOUGLAS (DUMFRIES AND GALLOWAY)

*** Threave Castle *(113, 122, 128)*, 2½ m. w; 1½ m. nw of A 75 from 1 m. s of Castle Douglas; access by passenger ferry (84 NX 739 623); AM

Built probably by Archibald the Grim, third Earl of Douglas, soon after 1369, this five-story tower-house rises seventy feet above its island in the River Dee. In 1455 it was besieged by King James II; and though heavy artillery was used, including probably the famous "Mons Meg" (now in Edinburgh Castle), Threave surrendered only after its garrison had been bribed. In the early sixteenth century it was in the hands of Robert, fifth Lord Maxwell, who was probably responsible for the outer wall and gunports. During the Civil War an army of Covenanters led by John Home besieged the castle for thirteen weeks before its garrison surrendered. Partly dismantled at that time, it served again as a prison for French prisoners during the Napoleonic Wars and was thereafter allowed to fall into the ruin that is seen today.

A tiny passenger ferry brings the visitor to the foot of the "artillery wall," probably installed by the fifth Lord Maxwell. Both the wall and its mural towers are pierced with gunports of the inverted keyhole and dumbbell variety. Near the top of the tower-house, around three sides, runs a triple row of shallow square recesses that are probably putlog holes for timbers to support an overhanging *bretasche* for the defense of the wall-faces. Internally, the castle is constructed in the typical Scottish tower-house manner: vaulted storage basement: first floor kitchen; second floor hall; third floor solar (upper chamber) and bedroom; fourth floor sleeping quarters for the domestic servants and retainers. The main entrance is in the east wall of the first floor, but a gangway led to it from the floor above.

In spite of its rough handling over the centuries, the castle is a remarkably well-preserved ruin, splendid in its solitude and very handsome in its riverine setting.

* Orchardton Tower *(131)*, 5½ m. se; 1 m. se of A 711 from junction with B 736 (84 NX 817 551); AM

Here is the substantial ruin of a uniquely round (cylindrical) tower-house, built in the mid-fifteenth century by John Carnys. Above the rectangular vaulted basement, the circular first floor contains an aumbry and a stone piscina, indicating the use of this apartment as a chapel. This floor and those above are served by a mural turnpike stair terminating in a cap house leading to the parapet walk. The tower's barmkin wall remains standing.

Dalbeattie (Dumfries and Galloway)

* Mote of Urr *(80)*, 3 m. n, w of A 710; by footpath over iron bridge across Urr Water (84 NX 815 646)

This is the site of a twelfth-century motte-and-bailey castle. The present mound rises to a height of more than thirty feet with a diameter of about eighty-five feet at the summit. It is separated by a wide ditch from the surrounding bailey, which is itself demarcated by a still wider ditch across which a causeway leads to the original entrance.

Mote of Mark *(49)*, 7 m. s; 2 m. w of A 710 from Lochend (84 NX 845 540); NTS

Overlooking Rough Firth, this granite outcrop was the site of a Dark Age fortified settlement, possibly built over an earlier Iron Age hill-fort. On the inland side of the flat top are the scant remains of a vitrified rampart. Clay molds for making penannular bronze brooches have been found inside the fort, indicating Dark Age occupation. This was probably the stronghold of a British chieftain before the kingdom of Rheged was absorbed by the English of Northumbria. Local tradition associates it with King Mark of the Arthurian legend, though there is no evidence that this authentic Dark Age chieftain ever strayed this far north from his native Cornwall.

GATEHOUSE OF FLEET (DUMFRIES AND GALLOWAY)

** Cardoness Castle *(131)*, 1 m. sw; n of A 75 (83 NX 591 553); AM

This high-standing ruin is what remains of a tower-house built in the late fifteenth century by the McCulloch family. It is rectangular in plan and rises to three stories above the ground floor. The great hall, with its handsome Late Gothic fireplace, is on the first floor; the floors above are missing, but fireplaces and corbels indicate their location. Turnpike stairs and straight stairs lead to the upper rooms. A guard room adjoins the entrance passage; mural rooms served as garderobes (latrines).

From the upper stairway there is a good view of the River Fleet.

Boreland Motte *(83)*, 1 m. sw; s of A 75 (83 NX 584 551)

Here are the remains of a Norman motte built by the de Morevilles in the twelfth century.

* Trusty's Hill *(29)*, 2 m. w; ½ m. e of Anwoth (83 NX 588 561)

This is a small rectangular Iron Age hill-fort, the enclosing wall of which has been vitrified by fire. Outside the main walls, further down the hill, are the remains of outworks in the form of ramparts and ditches. To the east of the fort are two outcrops of rock, on one of which are carved three Pictish symbols: a monster, a double disc with Z-rod, and a circle with projecting horns containing a stylized human face.

* Cairnholy Chambered Cairns I and II *(12)*, 5 m. sw; 4 m. se of Creetown; ½ m. n of A 75 at end of Kirkdale Road (83 NX 518 541); AM

Both of these Neolithic chambered tombs belong to the Clyde group of gallery graves. Cairnholy I is the better preserved of the two, although mostly denuded of its original cairn material. The exposed tomb now consists of (1) the two portal stones of the original entry plus a recumbent stone that once stood upright to block passage into the chamber after the final burial; (2) a short arc of stones on each side of the portal, constituting the tomb's facade; (3) a line of curbstones on the south side which once served to hold the cairn material in place; and (4) the now roofless burial chamber, divided into two parts by a high septal stone.

A short distance up the hill lies Cairnholy II, also stripped of its original cairn. Here also two portal stones (now leaning toward each other) mark the entrance to the tomb. The burial chamber is bipartite, divided by a high septal stone. The front compartment is now roofless; that to the rear is still covered by its original capstone.

Castle Haven Dun *(33)*, 7 m. sw; 2½ m. w of Borgue (83 NX 594 483)

This is an Iron Age galleried dun, shaped like a **D**, with its straight edge hugging a cliff on the shore of Wigtown Bay. A secondary wall of a later date surrounds the dun. Typical features are the hollow walls, mural galleries, narrow doorways, and parts of a staircase projecting from the inner face of the wall. The dun has been partially restored and is now covered with ivy.

KIRKCUDBRIGHT (DUMFRIES AND GALLOWAY)

* Maclellan's Castle *(225)*, town center; AM

This roofless but well preserved ruined tower-house dates from 1582. It is an L-plan house with an extra projection at one corner. It was built by Sir Thomas Maclellan, using stones from the nearby defunct Franciscan friary. Defensive features are minimal. The main staircase and the fireplace in the great hall are impressive.

** Stewartry Museum *(8)*, St. Mary's Street

This is a fine small museum of archaeology and local history with excellent prehistoric holdings and a good collection of medieval weapons. Also of interest is the exhibit of eighteenth- and nineteenth-century Communion tokens.

Greyfriars' Church *(168)*, town center

This pleasant Scottish Episcopal chapel incorporates fragments of the town's medieval Franciscan friary.

*** Dundrennan Abbey *(144)*, 6½ m. se; e of A 711 (84 NX 749 475); AM

This was a Cistercian monastery founded by King David I in 1142 and colonized by monks from Melrose. The architecture of the church is Transitional, with both round and pointed arches. Entering through the round-headed (restored) west doorway, there is little to see of the nave whose walls have mostly disappeared. North and south transepts and the side walls of the choir stand high, however. In the south range of claustral buildings, the entrance facade of the chapter house displays fine First Pointed windows built in the late thirteenth century. The west range, normally reserved for lay brothers in a Cistercian abbey, was apparently used here as a *cellarium*, whose remains are fairly substantial.

NEW ABBEY (DUMFRIES AND GALLOWAY)

*** Sweetheart Abbey *(151)*, village center; e of A 710 (84 NX 965 633); AM

The last Cistercian foundation in Scotland, this abbey was founded by Devorguilla, wife of John Balliol of Barnard Castle and mother of King John of Scotland. Its name (*Dulce Core*) derives from its widowed founder's insistence on being buried here with the embalmed heart of her late husband. Though nothing is left of the claustral buildings, the monastic church is a substantial ruin. Built in the late thirteenth and early fourteenth centuries, it belongs to the last phase of the First Pointed period, when narrow lancet windows were giving way to traceried openings of greater width. Above the Gothic west door is such a window, flanked by lancets and surmounted by a great round wheel, above which is a trefoil opening just below the apex of the gable. The upper (clerestory) windows of the nave are especially fine: triple lights with trefoil arched heads and five-lancet windows fitted within semicircular arches. The central crossing stands to its battlements, and the north and south transept walls are complete almost to their roofs. In the south transept are a piscina and a wall press for altar furnishings; also doors leading to the sacristy and, at a higher level, to the monks' dorter. Here too is the reconstructed tomb of Devorguilla and, next to it, the decorated coffin lid of John, the first Abbot of Sweetheart, whose sworn fealty to King Edward I is probably what saved this church from the usual destruction visited upon Scottish abbeys by English armies. The east window of the choir has five narrow lights surmounted by five circles and above this, still another Gothic window with its tracery destroyed. Here also are another piscina and triple sedilia. Although there is little left of the cloister, the original precinct walls are in good condition.

Ingleston Motte *(83)*, 1 m. se; ¼ m. e of A 710 (84 NX 982 651)

The turf-covered remains of a Norman motte probably dating from the late twelfth century.

Tongland Bridge *(317)*, 2 m. n; e of A 711 (83 NX 693 534)

A pretty little parapeted bridge across the River Dee, it dates from 1737, when it was built by Thomas Telford.

Newton Stewart (Dumfries and Galloway)

* Bargrennan White Cairn *(12)*, 8 m. nw; ¼ m. w of Glentrool village (77 NX 353 784)

This is a Neolithic passage grave of the "Bargrennan group," small in number and found only in southwestern Scotland. The top of the cairn of rounded boulders has been removed to expose both burial chamber and passageway which run together without any clear distinction, though the latter narrows to a width of only one foot at the outer edge of the cairn. Two massive capstones remain in place, supported by split boulders about four feet in height. The chamber, with its capstones, is visible from above.

Dumfriesshire

DUMFRIES (DUMFRIES AND GALLOWAY)

** Dumfries Museum *(9, 66)*, The Observatory, Church Street

Founded in 1835 on the site of an eighteenth-century windmill as an observatory *cum* museum, this is now one of Scotland's better small museums of local history and archaeology. Worthy of note are the microliths from Luce Bay Sands; items from Trusty's Hill and the Mote of Mark; Roman finds from Birrens Fort; Early Christian crosses and grave-slabs, including several from St. Kentigern's monastery at Hoddam, long since disappeared; eighteenth-century Communion tokens; astronomical instruments; and a *camera obscura*, which projects the scene outside the building onto a horizontal circular plate within a darkened room (a curiosity popular in the early nineteenth century).

* Burns House *(302)*, Burns Street

This is the house where Robert Burns died on 21 July 1796 and where his widow, Jean Armour Burns, continued to live until her death in 1834. It has recently been restored and stocked with memorabilia relating to the poet.

Burns Mausoleum *(302)*, St. Michael's Churchyard

This elaborate monument was erected in 1815 to house the remains of Robert Burns, who was originally buried nearby in 1796.

Ellisland Farm *(302)*, 6½ m. nw; e of A 76

Robert Burns leased this farm from June 1788 until November 1791, when he moved to Dumfries. The granary contains some interesting Burnsiana.

* Lincluden College *(169)*, 1½ m. n; e of B 729 through Lincluden village (84 NX 966 779); AM

Founded in 1389 by Archibald the Grim, third Earl of Douglas, as a college for twelve canons and a provost, this house took the place of a suppressed Benedictine nunnery. Now situated in a rather unattractive housing development, the red stone ruins consist of the south transept of the collegiate church, choir, and sacristy, plus the undercroft of what was probably the provost's lodgings. The chief attraction here is the fine tomb of Margaret, wife to the fourth earl, daughter of King Robert III, and sister of King James I. This lies in the choir behind a handsome *pulpitum* of stone.

*** Caerlaverock Castle *(96, 104, 189)*, 7 m. s; s of B 725 (84 NY 026 656); AM

The original triangular courtyard castle of stone was built here about 1290. It exchanged hands several times between Scots and English during the War of Independence; was partially dismantled by order of King Robert Bruce in 1312; was rebuilt by Herbert Maxwell in the mid-fourteenth century; was partially destroyed again by the English in 1357; was rebuilt again in the sixteenth century and furnished with gunports; was modernized again in the seventeenth century, with the addition of a fine range of buildings in the Scottish Renaissance style; and finally was captured by a Covenanting army in 1640 and reduced to its present ruined condition shortly thereafter.

Today, the ruin is approached from the north by a causeway leading across its dry outer ditch and a bridge across the inner water-filled moat. The great twin-towered gatehouse stands at the apex of this uniquely triangular-shaped courtyard castle. The northwest tower (to the right on entering) dates mostly from the original thirteenth-century building, except for the machicolations added in the fifteenth. Also of the thirteenth century are the lower courses of the west curtain wall and the base of the southwest tower (Murdoch's Tower). The upper parts of this wall and tower, however, belong to the fourteenth century, and the machicolations at the top of Murdoch's Tower were added in the fifteenth. The early-fifteenth-century south curtain wall is almost completely ruined, as is the early-fourteenth-century southeast tower. The east curtain wall is a patchwork of restorations, while the northeast tower (to the left on entering) dates mostly from the early fifteenth century, except for the machicolations, added in the late fifteenth.

Above the entrance is a large sandstone plaque bearing the arms of the Maxwells. Two portcullis slots are still observable in the passageway. The range of buildings along the inside of the west curtain (to the right of the entry) dates from the second half of the fifteenth century. The remaining internal buildings (along the south and east sides) were built about 1634 and display fine Renaissance features, especially in the pediments above windows and doorway and the ornate fireplaces.

From every standpoint—site, silhouette, state of preservation, variety of architectural detail, and historic interest—Caerlaverock must be rated among the very best of Scotland's many ruined castles.

*** Ruthwell Cross (65), 9 m. se; ¼ n, e of B 724 (85 NY 101 682); AM

Although reconstructed and partially restored after having been broken up by Protestant zealots in the seventeenth century, this is the best preserved and most elaborately carved of all extant Anglian crosses in Britain. Well lighted and equipped with explanatory materials, the cross stands fifteen feet high inside the parish kirk of Ruthwell village. It dates from the late seventh or early eighth century. On one face are the sculpted figures of St. John the Evangelist; St. John the Baptist; Christ; Saints Anthony and Paul in the desert; the flight from Egypt; and the Nativity. On the other are an eagle; an archer; Mary Magdalene, washing Christ's feet; Christ, healing the blind man; the Annunciation; and the Crucifixion. The sides of the cross are decorated with running vine-scrolls inhabited by animals and birds. Along the edges of the two faces are runic inscriptions that, when translated, prove to be the first seventy-eight lines of "The Dream of the Rood," the first of the Early English religious poems.

ECCLEFECHAN (DUMFRIES AND GALLOWAY)

* Carlyle's Birthplace (362), village center

The great nineteenth-century essayist and historian Thomas Carlyle was born in 1795 in this stone house built by his father and uncle. The birth room has been restored, and there are other materials on display relating to the author's life and works.

* Burnswark Hill-Fort *(44)*, 2½ m. n (85 NY 187 788)

On the top of this conspicuous and very steep hill was an Iron Age hill-fort, possibly the *oppidum* of either the *Damnonii* or the *Novantae*. The original ramparts are barely observable, but just to the south lie the fairly well-preserved remains of a practice siege camp built by Roman soldiers from the nearby fort of *Blatobulgium* (Birrens). The entire rectangular circuit of the camp is discernible, as are the single gateways in the middle of the southern, eastern, and western sides of the ramparts. The three gateways on the northern side are shielded by huge earthen mounds that must have served as platforms to support the catapults used in training exercises against the native fort. Archaeologists are certain that these engines were used only in mock battles because the sixty-seven sling-bolts excavated at Burnswark were clearly fired *after* the fort had been dismantled. The ramparts of a smaller and earlier Roman fortlet can also be observed in the northeast corner of the camp.

Birrens Roman Fort *(44)*, 1½ m. e; 1 m. s of B 722 from Middlebie (85 NY 215 754)

Here was the important Roman fort of *Blatobulgium*, probably laid out by Agricola during his initial invasion of Scotland and continued in operation as late as A.D. 180. It lay on the main Roman road from Carlisle into southwestern Scotland. Of the original six concentric banks and ditches surrounding the fort, only those on the north side are clearly observable.

LANGHOLM (DUMFRIES AND GALLOWAY)

Gilnockie Tower *(190)*, 4 m. s; 1 m. n of Canonbie, e of A 7; admission by arrangement with owners (tel: Canonbie 245)

This is a sixteenth-century rectangular tower-house that belonged to John Armstrong of Gilnockie. It was probably from here that this famous Border reiver rode out in 1529 to meet his death by hanging at the hands of King James V. The tower has recently been completely restored as a very attractive private residence. It is clearly visible from the A 7, looking eastward.

LOCHMABEN (DUMFRIES AND GALLOWAY)

Lochmaben Castle *(96, 189)*, 1½ m. s; at south end of Castle Loch (78 NY 087 812)

This is a very ruined rectangular courtyard castle, seemingly without projecting mural towers. The entrance was in the middle of the landward (south) wall, and this side of the castle is protected by a series of four ditches and banks cut across the base of the promontory on which the castle is situated. The other sides were protected by the waters of the loch. The castle may have been erected in the late thirteenth century by Robert Bruce the Competitor. Access to the site is not signposted, and the interior of the castle is fenced off to protect would-be visitors from falling stones. The view of the lake from here is lovely.

SANQUAR (DUMFRIES AND GALLOWAY)

* Museum of Scottish Lead Mining *(321)*, 7 m. ne in Wanlockhead village on B 797

Here is a mining museum associated with an open-air museum, both relating to 250 years of lead mining at this place. The former contains machinery, tools, a model miner's living quarters, etc. The latter includes a visitable mine, worked from 1790 to 1860; the lead miners' library, founded in 1756; a beam engine; a smelt mill; and ruined workers' cottages. Two hours should be allowed for a thorough visit.

THORNHILL (DUMFRIES AND GALLOWAY)

Nith Bridge Cross *(65)*, ½ m. w; s of A 702 (78 NX 868 954)

Standing eight feet high in a field west of the bridge, this is an eighth-century Anglian cross. The cross arms have disappeared, and the stone is much weathered, but on both faces and sides are carved vine-scroll with animals.

*** Drumlanrig Castle *(254, 255, 257, 262)*, 3 m. n; ½ m. w of A 76

This magnificent pink sandstone Scottish Renaissance palace was built by William Douglas, first Duke of Queensberry, between 1679 and 1691. The architect was either James Smith or his father-in-law, Robert Mylne, though earlier plans by William Wallace for a house resembling his Heriot's Hospital in Edinburgh may have provided the inspiration for the builders. In plan the building is a rectangle laid around an inner courtyard. On the entrance (north) front, stalwart towers flank a neoclassical facade with an arcaded loggia, giant Corinthian pilasters, rows of pedimented windows, balustrades, a horseshoe staircase, and a baroque frontispiece topped by a clock tower over which rises the ducal coronet.

Inside, the entrance hall was originally an open loggia, later (1813) glazed in. Beyond the courtyard is a magnificent set of rooms, some with fine wood carving in the Grinling Gibbons style, all elegantly furnished. Of special interest are the oak-panelled staircase hall, the staircase gallery with its heavy silver chandelier (ca. 1680), and the room where Prince Charles Edward slept when his troops briefly occupied the castle on their way north from England in 1746 (and incidentally vandalized a portrait of King William [of Orange] by Sir Godfrey Kneller, which, though repaired, still shows the slash marks). The house contains a priceless set of paintings, including a Rembrandt, a Correggio, two Murillos, a Clouet, and portraits by Michael Dahl, Sir Godfrey Kneller, Sir Joshua Reynolds, and Allan Ramsay.

* Morton Castle *(129)*, 4 m. n; 1½ m. se of A 702 (78 NX 891 992); AM

These substantial ruins of an early-fourteenth-century Douglas hall-house consist of a rectangular hall over an unvaulted undercroft with an outsized arched doorway leading to the screens passage. A hooded fireplace is to be seen at the opposite (dais) end of the hall. Adjoining this room is a rounded tower containing bedrooms, latrines, etc. The house is situated on a promontory jutting into Loch Morton and is entered by way of a tall ruined twin-towered gatehouse.

The site is poorly signposted and difficult to find.

*** Durisdeer Parish Kirk *(262)*, 6 m. n, in Durisdeer village, e of A 702

This was originally a T-plan kirk with a school attached to the west end, but in 1713 a north aisle was added to house the remains of James Douglas, second Duke of Queensberry and owner of nearby Drumlanrig Castle. The "Queensberry Aisle" contains an extraordinarily elaborate baroque funeral monument to the duke and duchess—white marble effigies beneath a canopy of black and white, and a white marble baldachino of twisted columns rising from a black-and-white checkered floor. This amazing confection would not be out of place beneath the dome of St. Peter's in Rome.

Ayrshire

AUCHLINLECK (STRATHCLYDE)

Boswell Mausoleum and Museum *(281)*, village center; admission on application to G. P. Hoyle (tel: Cumnock 20757)

In the restored medieval parish kirk is a museum housing a miscellany of artifacts more or less associated with the family of Dr. Johnson's biographer, James Boswell. Underneath is the mausoleum added in 1754 by the latter's father, Lord Auchinleck, where five generations of the family are buried, including James and his wife. In the museum is a scale model of the house where Johnson and Boswell stayed in 1773, now derelict and off bounds to the public. The mandatory guided tour lasts about an hour and a half—much too long, especially considering the rather meager contents of the museum.

AYR (STRATHCLYDE)

*** Tam o' Shanter Museum *(302)*, High Street

This former brew house is replete with interesting Burns mementos and memorabilia, casually displayed in a manner more suitable to the poet's personality and lifestyle than in most of the overdressed shrines and museums dedicated to his memory.

*** Burns Cottage and Museum *(301)*, 2½ m. s, in Alloway on B 7024

Robert Burns was born on 25 January 1759 in this two-room ("but-and-ben") thatched cottage, built by his father William Burnes (sic). Here is the original bed where he first saw light, plus other contemporary furniture. The place is spotless and shiny—too much so to be an authentic reproduction of what an eighteenth-century village cottage must have looked like. Next door is the museum containing the Burns family Bible, numerous samples of the poet's writings and correspondence, many pictures of him, and a library of his collected works.

* Alloway Old Kirk *(301)*, 2½ m. s, in Alloway on B 7024

Across the road from the present nineteenth-century parish kirk, this is a roofless but fairly substantial ruin where William Burnes (sic), father of Robert Burns, was buried. It is also the site of the dance of the witches and warlocks featured in Burns's best narrative poem, "Tam o' Shanter."

Land o' Burns Centre *(302)*, 2½ m. s., in Alloway, Murdoch's Lane, opposite Alloway Parish Kirk

Here is an example of tourism at its worst. The exhibits and an audiovisual show do not compensate for the tasteless commercialism of this place, advertised as the first stop of the Burns Heritage Trail.

Burns Monument *(302)*, 2½ m. s, in Alloway, e of B 7074

A rotunda of Corinthian pillars, this monument was erected in 1823 on a lovely site overlooking the River Doon. Below it, spanning the river, is the

Brig o' Doon *(302)*, over which Tam o' Shanter barely escaped the witches' fury in Burns's famous poem.

CUMNOCK (STRATHCLYDE)

Keir Hardie Statue *(362)*, town center

This simple bust standing in front of the town hall is a too modest memorial to one of Britain's greatest nineteenth-century pioneers in the fight for improved wages and working conditions in factories and mines.

DALMELLINGTON (STRATHCLYDE)

* Loch Doon Castle *(97)*, 8 m. s; 7 m. s of A 714 (77 NX 484 950); AM

Near the shore of the loch are the ruins of a polygonal courtyard castle originally built in the late thirteenth or early fourteenth century on an offshore island and in the 1930s removed to the present site when the loch's waters were raised. The main entranceway is complete; the portcullis slot is clearly visible, though the chamber above it is gone. The postern entrance is in good condition. Also observable are the large kitchen fireplace and the smaller one in the great hall.

The road leading to the site is unusually bad for this part of Scotland.

KILMARNOCK (STRATHCLYDE)

** Dean Castle *(121)*, Dean Road, e of Glasgow Road (B 7038) (70 NS 435 394)

This was the seat of the Boyds of Kilmarnock, who rose to power temporarily during the minority of King James III. To the original tower-house, built about 1350, Robert Boyd added a "palace" and curtain walls to form a courtyard about 1460. The gatehouse is modern. The entire ensemble was restored and made habitable between 1908 and 1936.

On the ground floor of the original tower-house is an armory consisting chiefly of arms and armor of Continental origin. On the second floor is a fine collection of early European musical instruments. In the palace is a representative assemblage of seventeenth-century furniture. Surrounding the buildings is the Dean Castle Country Park with well-marked trails through extensive woodlands full of rhododendron, laurel, wildflowers, etc.

Burns Monument and Museum *(302)*, Kay Park; museum open only by arrangement (tel: Kilmarnock 26401)

Here is a tall statue of Scotland's favorite poet, executed in the heroic mode favored by Victorian taste.

KILWINNING (STRATHCLYDE)

* Kilwinning Abbey *(146)*, town center (63 NS 304 433); AM

This was a Tironensian house founded by Hugh de Moreville or his son Richard between 1162 and 1189. On the grounds of the parish kirk that overlies the original choir of the abbey church, the existing remains consist of part of the west end (next to the modern clock tower); the lower part of the south wall of the nave to the right of the entrance; the high south transept gable with three fine lancet windows topped by a small circular opening, indicating construction in the First Pointed style of the thirteenth century; and the ruined east range of the cloister (including a substantial portion of the chapter house) with several round-arched doorways, probably of twelfth-century provenance.

LARGS (STRATHCLYDE)

** Skelmorlie Aisle *(262)*, town center

This is a chapel added in 1636 to the parish kirk, which has since disappeared. It was built by Sir Robert Montgomery of Skelmorlie as a mausoleum for himself and his wife, and their remains still lie buried in the vault below, though their recumbent effigies are missing from the grand baroque tomb that rises out of a sunken well beneath one of the most elaborately painted ceilings in Scotland. Here are depicted the four seasons, the signs of the zodiac, the coats of arms of the twelve tribes of Israel, the temptation of Eve, Jacob and Esau, the Largs kirk, and the old castle of Skelmorlie.

MAUCHLINE (STRATHCLYDE)

* Burns House Museum *(301)*, Castle Street

The upper floor contains the room that Robert Burns took for Jean Armour in 1788. It still has some of the original furniture. Downstairs is a small collection of Burnsiana, intelligently displayed.

* Bachelors' Club *(301)*, 4½ m. w, in Tarbolton on B 730

This is the site of the literary and debating society founded in 1780 by Robert Burns and his friends. The furniture is contemporary, and from one of the windows can be seen Lochlea Farm, where the Burns family was living.

Ballochmyle Viaduct *(339)*, 5 m. s; w of A 76

Crossing a deep gorge of the River Ayr, this impressive viaduct was built in 1848 for the Glasgow and South Western Railway.

Maybole (Strathclyde)

*** Crossraguel Abbey *(149)*, 2 m. sw; s of A 77 (76 NS 525 627); AM

The original settlement here was a house of Cluniac monks from nearby Paisley Abbey on lands donated by Duncan, Earl of Carrick, about 1214. Almost nothing is left of the original buildings. The now roofless rectangular church replaced the original cruciform building. The rather simply constructed nave dates mostly from the fourteenth century. In the sixteenth century, for reasons unknown, a stone partition was put up to separate nave from choir. The latter is of fifteenth-century construction and has a polygonal apse. To the same period of construction belongs the fine vaulted chapter house in the Second Pointed style. The other claustral remains date mostly from the fourteenth century. So does the well-preserved abbot's house to the southeast of the main cloister. Next to it is a ruined tower house built in the sixteenth century, and from the same period is the well-preserved gatehouse at the other end of the precinct. To the south lie the lower courses of a range of cottages erected in the fifteenth century to house "corrodiars"; that is, old-age pensioners attached to the monastery.

* Souter Johnnie's Cottage *(302)*, 4 m. s, in Kirkoswald on A 77

This thatched cottage belonged to John Davidson, memorialized by Robert Burns as Souter Johnnie in the poem "Tam o' Shanter." Inside is a small collection of Burnsiana, and outside a curious set of larger-than-life-size statues of various characters in the poem.

*** Culzean Castle *(308)*, 5 m. w; w of A 719; NTS

Commissioned by David Kennedy, tenth Earl of Cassillis, to renovate the family's sixteenth-century tower-house, Robert Adam produced this elegant Italianate palace overlooking the Ayrshire coast and added to it the stable block with a central clock tower and the buildings of the home farm, now recently restored as a park center. The interiors are exquisite—among the best that Adam ever produced, though he died before the work was finished. The grounds are distinguished by the fountain court, a formal garden on the south side of the house; a fine walled garden; the "gothick" camellia house; swan pond; and a bounty of horticultural delights throughout. Thanks to his service in the Second World War, General Dwight David Eisenhower was awarded lifetime use of a flat within the castle. It now contains numerous mementos of the general, and here visitors may listen to recorded broadcasts relating to World War II, including speeches by Eisenhower and Churchill.

Troon (Strathclyde)

* Dundonald Castle *(115)*, 3½ m. ne, in Dundonald village; s of junction of A 759 and B 730 (70 NS 363 345); AM

This substantial ruin is that of a rectangular keep, possibly built by King Robert II and certainly his favorite castle. He died here in 1390. The fragmentary curtain wall probably belonged to a thirteenth-century castle that this building would have replaced. Although under the care of the Scottish Development Department, the grounds are unkempt and the interior of the castle is closed to the public.

Bute

Arran (Strathclyde)

(Access by car ferry from Ardrossan to Brodick, five times daily; and from Claonaig, Kintyre, to Lochranza, seven times daily.)

Brodick

*** Brodick Castle *(195, 241, 335)*, 1½ m. n of Brodick Pier; NTS

The oldest part of this now sumptuous, stately home dates probably from the late thirteenth century. In 1503 the castle and much of the island of Arran passed to James Hamilton, first Earl of Arran, who married the daughter of King James II. His son, the second earl and later Duke of Chatelherault, enlarged the building about 1558. During the Civil War the place was captured from the royalist first Duke of Hamilton by Archibald Campbell, Marquis of Argyll, and later occupied by Cromwell's troops.

A fortunate Hamilton marriage in the early nineteenth century brought the Beckford Collection of art treasures to Brodick. In the mid–nineteenth century the heir to the tenth duke commissioned the architect, James Gillespie Graham, well-known ecclesiastical architect in Scotland and leader of the Gothic Revival, to enlarge the house to more than double its then existing size. In the twentieth century the only daughter of the twelfth duke married the sixth Duke of Montrose. It was this Duchess of Montrose and her son-in-law, Major J. P. T. Boscawen, who were responsible for the installation of the magnificent woodland gardens on the property.

A tour of the castle leads first through James Gillespie Graham's "Gothic" additions; up the grand staircase to the landing leading to the Duchess of Montrose's dressing room, bedroom, and boudoir; through the long gallery on the first floor, which opens into the drawing room, old library, and dining room, the last two encased in the sixteenth-century part of the castle. At the extreme west end is a chamber miscalled "Bruce's Room," situated within what was the original thirteenth-century keep. For the edification of innocent tourists, it has been reconstructed as a prison, though whether it was ever actually used as such is doubtful. Downstairs is the old kitchen, restored in the Victorian manner. The way out leads through the tower constructed during the Cromwellian occupation. Throughout, the house is replete with fine English and European furniture, china, and miscellaneous objects of art; racing trophies and sporting pictures; portraits of various Hamiltons, etc.

The woodland garden, stretching from the house down to the shoreline, is one of the finest in Britain, noted especially for the tall stands of rhododendrons. It is largely a post-World War I creation of the Duchess of Montrose. The walled garden immediately below the castle consists of charming, if conventional, herbaceous borders. There is also a water garden and a rustic "Bavarian" summer house. Visitors to the castle should not neglect to explore these grounds—in some ways more enjoyable than the somewhat overstuffed ducal residence.

Lamlash Clearance Monument (329), 4 m. s; w of A 841

This is a memorial to the tenants of the Duke of Hamilton, who had to leave Arran for Canada in the years 1829-1840. It was erected by their Canadian descendants. Consisting of three huge boulders, marked by a bronze plaque, the monument stands across the road from a small turf-covered mound next to the sea—the site of these emigrants' gathering place to board the outbound brig Caledonia on 25 April 1829.

* Auchagallon Stone Circle (22), 7½ m. w; e of A 841; n of Machrie Road, 200 yards up footpath from telephone kiosk (69 NR 893 346); AM

This Bronze Age circle of fifteen standing stones surrounds a round cairn. The stones may originally have been freestanding, or they may have constituted the curb or peristalth set around the outer edge of the cairn to prevent slippage of the cairn material.

** Moss Farm Stone Circle and Machrie Moor Standing Stones (23), 10 m. w; ½ to 1 m. e of A 841 by footpath from Tormore, south of bridge (69 NR 900 326 to 910 324); AM

Along a line running roughly east and west along the south side of Machrie Water lies this interesting agglomeration of Bronze Age stone circles, cairns, and cists. The most complete is Moss Farm Road Circle, consisting of an inner circle of eight granite boulders surrounded by an oval of more granite boulders. Inside are the scant remains of a burial cairn. To the northeast, about half a mile along the footpath, are the remains of four more stone circles, which originally contained cists and burial cairns. The most complete of these consists of a circle of seven boulders within another circle of fourteen. Nearby is a setting of only four boulders, presumably all that remains of a second circle. The other two circles are formed by tall shaped stones up to twenty-five feet in height, now reduced to three stones in one and a single monolith in the other. Obviously, this area was the site of a Bronze Age religious center and cemetery.

Torrylin Cairn *(13)*, 10 m. sw; ½ m. s of A 841 from Kilmory (69 NR 955 211); AM

Of this much ruined Neolithic gallery grave of the Clyde group, all that remains are the two side walls of the long burial chamber and the three septal stones dividing it into four compartments.

ROTHESAY (STRATHCLYDE)

* Buteshire Natural History Society Museum *(8)*, Stuart Street

This is a typical small museum of local history and archaeology.

*** Rothesay Castle *(85, 98, 117)*, town center (63 NS 088 646); AM

Here are the remains of a circular courtyard castle, unique in Scotland. Built in the thirteenth century, no doubt to replace a timber motte-and-bailey castle, Rothesay was stormed by Norsemen in 1230 and again in 1263 during King Hakon's invasion, which ended with his defeat at the Battle of Largs. A hundred years later, it became a Stewart residence, and Robert III died here. His eldest son had been created Duke of Rothesay, a title thereafter enjoyed by the heirs apparent of the Scottish and subsequently British thrones. James IV and James V used the castle as a base of operations against the Lords of the Isles. Badly damaged during the Civil War, it was burned by the Earl of Argyll in 1685 and partially repaired by the Marquises of Bute in the nineteenth century.

The castle consists of a circular curtain wall, thirty feet high and nine feet thick, inside a water-filled moat, with four drum towers spaced at equal distances around the circuit. Of these, only the northwest tower is in a good state of preservation. The castle is approached from the north via an entryway that projects into the moat and served as a combination barbican and great hall. This was added to the original building by either James IV or James V in the fifteenth or sixteenth century. At the same time, the original thirteenth-century curtain wall was heightened by some six feet, and the original crenellations on each side of the entrance were sealed up, though their outlines are still visible. In the western quadrant, to the right of the entrance, is a postern gate. In the eastern quadrant there are signs that the wall has been rebuilt at the spot where, probably, Norsemen broke into the castle in 1230 or 1263. The chapel inside dates probably from the sixteenth century.

St. Mary's, Rothesay *(107)*, ½ m. s on A 845 (63 NS086 637); AM

In this roofless choir of the fourteenth-century Church of St. Mary lie the effigies of a knight and lady, the former probably John, third Earl of Menteith. He is wearing a bascinet and aketon of early-fourteenth-century design.

* St. Blane's Church *(62)*, 5½ m. s; 2½ m. s of Kingarth; ¼ m. e, along stone wall, from end of single-track road; signposted (63 NS 094 535); AM

This roofless church probably dates from the twelfth century. The nave is Romanesque with a fine carved round-arched door leading to the choir, the latter probably of thirteenth-century construction, judging by the two lancet windows in the east wall. Also in the east wall are an aumbry and a piscina. Below the churchyard is a second cemetery lying within a dry-stone wall that was probably the *vallum* of a monastery founded in the sixth century by St. Blane, a contemporary of St. Columba. Visible underneath the precipice west of the church are some fragmentary stone foundations that could be those of monastic cells dating from the eighth century.

Renfrewshire

GREENOCK (STRATHCLYDE)

McLean Museum and Art Gallery *(323)*, 9 Union Street

This is a rather uninteresting little local gallery, distinguished chiefly for its tiny collection of memorabilia relating to James Watt, inventor of the steam engine, born in this town.

PAISLEY (STRATHCLYDE)

*** Paisley Art Gallery and Museum *(9, 320)*, High Street

In this well-organized museum of local history, art, and archaeology, the exhibition of Paisley shawls is of outstanding merit. Those on view date from about 1775 to 1903 when the last shawl was made in Paisley.

*** Paisley Abbey *(396)*, town center

Founded in 1136 by Walter the Steward for Benedictine monks of the

Cluniac order, this monastery was very badly mauled by the English in 1307 and has since suffered serious damage by fire and neglect. What remains is now incorporated into the unusually handsome parish kirk. Of special interest are the First Pointed western end, including the main doorway; the restored fifteenth-century nave; the Romanesque processional door at the east end of the south wall of the nave; the rare medieval sculptured frieze in St. Mirin's chapel; and the gorgeous modern eastern window in the Second Pointed style. The "tomb" of Marjorie Bruce, King Robert I's daughter, who married Walter the Steward and thus founded the royal Stewart dynasty, is of doubtful authenticity. A guided tour is available but not mandatory.

* Weaver's Cottage *(319)*, 6 m. w, in Kilbarchan village; 1 m. sw of A 761; NTS

Built in 1723, this was a typical hand loom weaver's dwelling and now consists of several rooms with simple furniture from the eighteenth and early nineteenth centuries. In the basement is a working loom. Like other vernacular properties of the National Trust for Scotland, this is well organized and well presented, but somewhat overly picturesque.

Crookston Castle *(131)*, 4 m. e; e of A 754 (64 NS 525 627); AM

This very dilapidated ruin is all that remains of a tower-house built by Sir Alan Stewart of Darnley in the mid-fourteenth century. The central block of the tower typically rests on a vaulted basement. Above the first floor hall are bedrooms, solar, and garderobes. Untypically, to each corner of the central block is attached a square tower, with more rooms, garderobes, etc. This arrangement is unknown elsewhere in Scotland except at Hermitage Castle in Roxburghshire.

Port Glasgow (Strathclyde)

*** Newark Castle *(131)*, n of A 8, behind Ferguson Brothers building (63 NS 329 744); AM

The original tower-house and gatehouse were erected here by Sir George Maxwell soon after 1478. Sir Patrick Maxwell added the Scottish Renaissance mansion in 1597-1599. Though empty, the castle is roofed and in an excellent state of preservation.

The two-story gatehouse on the western side of what was once an enclosed barmkin has gunports and a guardroom with fireplace. The tower-house at the southeast corner is rectangular in plan and has the usual vaulted ground floor with hall above and bed chambers above that, reached by a spiral staircase. The large windows were inserted at a date later than the original construction. The late-sixteenth-century mansion, uniting tower and gate-house, has a cellar, kitchen, bakehouse, and buttery on the ground floor; a well-lighted hall with a fine fireplace on the first; and bedrooms on the floor above.

The castle stands on the south shore of the mouth of the River Clyde and enjoys a fine view of this once busy estuary.

Lanarkshire

BIGGAR (STRATHCLYDE)

Greenhill Covenanters' Museum *(246)*, town center, n of Biggar Kirk

In a seventeenth-century farmhouse moved to this site, this small and seemingly unfinished museum is devoted to local history with particular emphasis on the Covenanters of the late seventeenth century. The displays are informative, but there are few artifacts except for a number of Bibles and pamphlets and the press bed in which the Covenanting preacher Donald Cargill spent his last night before his capture and execution in 1681.

Biggar Gas Works *(337)*, town center; admission by arrangement (tel: 031-225-7534)

Here is a museum of the gas industry, housed in a now inoperative municipal gas works.

** Gladstone Court Museum *(364)*, town center

Here is an interesting collection of reconstructed shops, tradesmen's workplaces, private dwellings, a schoolroom, etc., designed to illustrate village life in the nineteenth century. The project has been carried out with great imagination and skill.

BLANTYRE (STRATHCLYDE)

** David Livingstone Centre *(320, 355)*, Hamilton Circle

On the site of Blantyre Cotton Spinning Works, founded in 1785 by David Dale and James Monteith, this interesting museum is dedicated to commemorating the life and works of the great African explorer and missionary Dr. David Livingstone, who was born here, son of a mill hand. In Shuttle Row—a workers' tenement complex—is the room of his birth, and in the Blantyre Room are relics of the early textile industry. Other parts of the museum include the library, with a collection of books and manuscripts relating to Livingstone; the Room of Adventure, with numerous paintings depicting his African career; the Livingstone Gallery of illuminated bas-relief sculptures; the Relic Section of African memorabilia; the Shrine; the Africa Pavilion; and the Social History Gallery.

CRAWFORD (STRATHCLYDE)

* Leadhills Library *(296)*, 8 m. sw, in Leadhills village at junction of B 797 and B 7040

Also called the Allan Ramsay Library after the well-known bookseller and poet who was born in the village, this was founded in 1741 as a subscription library for the Leadhills Miners' Reading Society. A number of the original books—now rarities—are on display. The building also houses the local office of the Scottish Tourist Authority.

DOUGLAS (STRATHCLYDE)

*** St. Bride's Chapel *(110)*, village center; AM; key obtainable at Number 2 Clyde Road, opposite churchyard gate.

This is the restored choir of a fourteenth-century church, of which the only other remaining feature is a short length of the ruined south wall and aisle, now outside the existing building. Here is the burial place of the Douglases. Inside are the embalmed and encased hearts of "the Good Sir James," Bruce's companion-in-arms, and Archibald ("Bell-the-Cat"), fifth Earl of Angus. Here also are the altar tombs and effigies of the Good Sir James; of Archibald, fifth Earl of Douglas and second Duc de Touraine; and of James, seventh Earl of Douglas. In the tower is a fifteenth-century clock still in working order.

GLASGOW (STRATHCLYDE)

South of River Clyde
(East to west; north to south)

Caledonia Road Church *(353)*, Caledonia Road

Now a burnt-out shell, this was one of the architectural *tours de force* of Alexander ("Greek") Thomson when built for a United Presbyterian congregation in 1856–1857. The portico is Ionic, and the assembly hall conforms more or less to the classical canon, but the ground-floor entrance doors are Egyptian and the high tower is vaguely Lombardic.

Scotland Street School *(347)*, 225 Scotland Street

Designed by Charles Rennie Mackintosh and completed in 1903, this is the least distinctive of his buildings, except for the glassed staircase towers, which are an interesting adaptation of the Scottish Baronial theme to modern functional uses.

*** Glasgow Museum of Transport *(338, 341, 348, 366)*, 28 Albert Drive; w of Pollockshaws Road (A 77) to Kilmarnock

Among this excellent museum's large and diverse array of objects pertaining to the history of Scottish transport, the special attractions are the Glasgow tramcars, the Glasgow-built locomotives, the antique autos of Scottish manufacture, and the great collection (six hundred altogether) of ship models, mostly of Clyde-built vessels.

** Govan Old Parish Church *(66)*, Govan Road; between Napier Road and McKechnie Street; key at Pierce Institute, Govan Road

Within this undistinguished late-nineteenth-century parish kirk is a notable collection of about two dozen Early Christian stones, including cross-shafts, "hogback" stones, and a fine carved coffin thought to have held the remains of the eighth-century St. Constantine, who founded a monastery here.

* Haggs Castle *(225, 260)*, e of B 768, 1½ m. s of A 737 from Govan (64 NS 563 627)

Originally an L-plan tower-house built in the 1580s by Sir John Maxwell, this castle has a projecting west wing added in the 1890s by the architects David MacGibbon and Thomas Ross. In the 1660s and again in the 1780s it was a center of Covenanting activity; otherwise its history is undistinguished. Today it is a children's museum with some good seventeenth-century furniture and costumes and numerous nineteenth-century artifacts such as typewriters and cameras. On the grounds are interesting reproductions of seventeenth-century gardens: a knot garden, an herb-and-vegetable plot, a cottage garden, and a raised border.

** Pollok House *(308)*, 2060 Pollokshaws Road (A 736)

Commissioned by John Maxwell of Blawarthill, William Adam began the construction of the original house in 1747. It was completed by his son John in 1752 and enlarged in 1890 under the direction of Sir Robert Rowand Anderson. The house now contains the fine Stirling Maxwell Collection of paintings, mostly by distinguished European artists, especially Spanish. At the rear is a beautiful formal garden and on the grounds a "demonstration garden."

** **Burrell Collection** *(341)*, Pollok Park; n of Pollokshaws Road (A 736), near Pollok House

Opened in 1983, this museum of red sandstone, timber, and glass houses an immense collection of paintings and *objets d'art* given to the city of Glasgow by Sir William Burrell, former partner in the great shipping firm of Burrell and Son. Although Burrell was at one time a patron of the "Glasgow School" of artists, most of the paintings here are of European provenance, including works of Rembrandt and Bellini, and several by Degas. An avid, if not always discriminating, collector, Burrell accumulated an amazing assortment of Near Eastern antiquities, Chinese ceramics, Japanese prints, Persian and Turkish carpets, Northern European tapestries, medieval stained glass, armor, furniture, sculpture-work, and more besides. It is all here, packed in a very modern building with a mazelike arrangement of walls and partitions that makes it easy for visitors to get lost as they wander among this plethora of antique curiosities.

North of River Clyde
(West to east; south to north)

CITY CENTER

* **Gardner's Iron Building** *(345)*, 36 Jamaica Street

In this former warehouse, built in 1855–1856, the architect John Baird and the iron-founder R. McDonnell made architectural history by the use of structural wrought iron in the basic frame and cast iron on the facade. Making the facade of metal rather than stone permitted a much greater expanse of window glass, thus giving the building far more interior light than usual and imparting to its exterior a delicate appearance not normally found in Victorian architecture. It is still a good-looking building and would not look out of place in the most modernistic of urban settings.

** **St. Andrew's Cathedral** *(316)*, 172 Clyde Street

Built in 1816 to the design of James Gillespie Graham, the style is English Perpendicular. The first Roman Catholic church of significant size to be erected in Scotland since the Reformation, it was needed to serve the large population of Irish immigrants who were flooding into Glasgow to be employed in the city's rapidly expanding industrial establishment.

*** **People's Palace** *(348, 370)*, Glasgow Green

Opened in 1898, this is a most unusual and fascinating repository of the artifacts produced by centuries of urban life, along with photographs, paintings, etchings, and much more. The collection can best be described as "vernacular," that is, representative of the more mundane aspects of history that are normally not to be found anywhere except in folk museums. Exhibits change frequently. Among the most interesting are those illustrating tenement life among the poor in nineteenth century Glasgow. Also, there is a good collection of the gear employed by civilians in World War II to protect themselves against bombing raids.

* Templeton's Carpet Factory (342), Glasgow Green

Erected in 1889 to the design of William Leiper, this ornate building was meant to resemble the Doge's Palace in Venice. Though now vacant, it once contained the largest number of industrial workers under one roof in Glasgow. Because of its protected situation, it has survived in better condition than most nineteenth-century industrial sites and is one of the great Victorian landmarks of the city.

Buck's Head Building (345), Dunlop and Argyle streets

Originally a warehouse, erected in 1849 to the design of Alexander ("Greek") Thomson, this was a pioneer experiment in the use of plate glass as a major element in the construction of building facades.

*** St. Andrew's Parish Church (307), St. Andrew's Square

Construction of this building, designed by Allan Dreghorn, was begun in 1739 but not competed until 1756, owing to the interruption of the rebellion of 1745. In the interim, on the occasion of his unwelcome visit to Glasgow, Prince Charles Edward Stuart stabled his horses in the unfinished nave. A noble classical building with magnificent interior plasterwork, it was modelled on James Gibbs's church of St. Martin-in-the-Field on Trafalgar Square, London.

** St. Vincent Street Church (353), St. Vincent Street

This is Alexander ("Greek") Thomson's most conspicuous contribution to Glasgow's cityscape. Built in 1859 on the side of the steep hill rising from Bothwell Street to St. Vincent Street, it contains an auditorium that rests on a high rusticated podium, and the Ionic columns, front and back, conform to the classical canon for which the architect was famous. But the high tower is more Egyptian in appearance than anything else, as is the decor of the interior. Originally housing a congregation of the United Presbyterian Church (after the "Disruption" of 1843), it has, since 1971, been occupied by a Free Church congregation.

Central Station and Central Station Hotel *(340)*, entrances on Hope and Gordon streets

Built in 1879 as the Glasgow terminal of the Caledonian Railway, the station was extended in 1899 and reconstructed in 1901–1906. The station hotel was designed by Sir Robert Rowand Anderson, opened in 1883, and enlarged in 1901–1906 to designs by James Miller. Although much modernized, both retain a hint of their original Victorian splendor, especially the hotel, with its wrought iron balustrading and great staircase winding from the ground to the top floor.

Grosvenor Building *(345)*, Gordon Street

Another warehouse designed by Alexander Thomson, this one was built in 1859–1861 and rebuilt in 1865–1866 after a fire.

Egyptian Halls *(403)*, 94–100 Union Street

Glass windows behind freestanding columns on the top floor of this building, erected in 1871–1873, betray the identity of the architect— Alexander ("Greek") Thomson. In this case, the columns derive from Thebes, not classical Athens.

Ca d'Oro *(403)*, 120–126 Union Street

Originally a furniture warehouse, designed by John Honeyman and built in 1872, this structure has cast-iron-fronted upper floors. The heavy mansard roof is a later addition.

** Glasgow Royal Exchange & Stirling's Library *(316)*, Royal Exchange Square

The inner core of this building consists of a mansion built in 1780 for William Cunningham, one of Glasgow's most eminent "Tobacco Lords," and used later to house the Royal Bank of Scotland. It was enlarged in 1827–1829, under the direction of the Glasgow architect David Hamilton, and put to use as the city's mercantile exchange. Later it became the home of Stirling's Library. It is a magnificent neoclassical building with a fine pedimented porch with Corinthian columns. Inside, the barrel-vaulted coffered ceiling is of outstanding merit.

* Trades House *(315)*, 85 Glassford Street

Designed by Robert Adam and completed in 1794, this house features a facade that is a fine exercise in neoclassical design, though the interior has been completely remodelled.

** Hutchesons' Hospital *(315)*, corner of Ingram and John streets

Built in 1802–1805 to the design of David Hamilton, this is a very attractive small neoclassical building topped by a Wren-like steeple. The statues of the Hutcheson brothers date from 1649. It is now the Glasgow headquarters of the National Trust for Scotland.

*** City Chambers *(346)*, George Square

Designed by William Young and completed in 1888, this building captures better than any other the civic pride and self-confidence that characterized Glasgow at the height of its prosperity in the late nineteenth century. The facade is mixed neoclassical and baroque, and the interior is a supreme example of Victorian decorative grandiosity. Here are seemingly endless rooms and corridors finished in Italian marble, alabaster and porcelain, carved oak, mahogany, and lush velvet wallpaper and filled with heavy furniture and still heavier chandeliers.

Guided tour of about thirty minutes. Not to be missed by lovers of Victoriana.

Blythswood Square *(315)*, bounded by George, Douglas, Regent, and Blythswood streets

Except for the east side, which has been reconstructed, these rows of buildings surrounding a central garden were built in 1823–1829 as a suburb to attract Glasgow's prosperous citizens away from the pollution of the central city. More or less an imitation of Edinburgh's New Town, this place retains a pleasant air of quiet dignity.

Grecian Building *(345)*, 336–356 Sauchiehall Street

The freestanding columns in front of the glazing on the top floor of this building, constructed about 1865, are typical of the architect, Alexander ("Greek") Thomson.

*** Glasgow School of Art *(346, 347)*, 167 Renfrew Street

This is Charles Rennie Mackintosh's masterpiece—built in two stages (1897–1899 and 1907–1909). The south facade of the building is reminiscent of the Scottish Baronial style; the north, with its huge windows and wrought iron finials, has a modern, functional appearance. Inside, furnishings and decor are vaguely Art Nouveau in style but are better described as "pure Mackintosh," which is to say unique. Visitors should note especially the chairs, desks, and lamp fixtures, particularly in the library and board room.

Willow Tea Rooms *(347)*, 199 Sauchiehall Street

Within Daly's Store are the restored rooms designed by Charles Rennie Mackintosh for Miss Kate Cranston, the highly successful proprietress of a string of Glasgow tearooms, several of which were decorated by Mackintosh and his wife. This one was finished in 1904.

**Royal Highland Fusiliers' Regimental Museum *(289, 290, 365)*, 518 Sauchiehall Street

This is a conventional regimental museum containing uniforms, medals, honors, plate, and other memorabilia of this unit, which is an amalgamation of the Royal Scots Fusiliers, originating in 1678; the 73d (71st) Highlanders (Lord MacLeod's Regiment, first recruited in 1778); and the 74th Highland Regiment, organized in 1787. Here also is a touching life-sized tableau of a First World War soldier saying good-bye to his wife before going back to the trenches of France.

*** Tenement House *(348)*, 145 Buccleuch Street; NTS

This is a perfectly preserved three-room, first floor flat occupied for sixty-four years (1911–1975) by Mrs. Agnes Reid Toward, a seamstress, and/or her daughter Miss Agnes. Respectable and frugal, these two women must not have discarded any of the nonperishable goods they ever bought or were given. The house is therefore essentially a museum, chock-full of the domestic miscellany of more than a half century's accumulation—a pedal-operated sewing machine, carpet beaters, medicine bottles and pillboxes, kitchen utensils, even a 1906 calender with the leaf for December not yet torn away. Nothing could illustrate better the lifestyle of lower-middle-class Glaswegians in the first half of the twentieth century.

Stock Exchange House *(345)*, Buchanan Street and St. George's Place

Constructed in 1875–1877 to the design of John Burnet, senior, the building's style is more or less Venetian Gothic—fussier than most of Glasgow's inner-city buildings of the Victorian era.

* St. George's Tron Church *(316)*, Buchanan Street; church closed except for services

Built by William Stark in 1807, this prominently situated church is more or less baroque in style, reminiscent of both Sir Christopher Wren and Nicholas Hawksmoor. The interior is unattractive.

* Provand's Lordship *(157)*, Cathedral Street

This is reputed to be the oldest house in Glasgow, built in 1471. It is thought to have been the living quarters of a cathedral prebend or some other functionary. Mary, Queen of Scots, is thought to have stayed here briefly. The house is in the process of being furnished and converted into a museum.

*** Glasgow Cathedral *(157, 234)*, Cathedral Street

Dedicated to St. Kentigern (Mungo) and built in the thirteenth century on the presumed site of his early Celtic church, this is the most authentic and complete large-scale early medieval building in mainland Scotland. The builder was Bishop William de Bondington; the style mostly First Pointed. Because of the contour of the land here it was built on two levels, its separate stories now referred to as "upper church" and "lower church." The western facade has been deprived of its two great towers. The entrance on this side is a double door, but the main entrance now in use is the south door of the nave. The nave displays compound piers with deeply molded capitals and high narrow lancets. Between nave and choir is a late-fifteenth-century stone screen or *pulpitum*, a very rare survival. The choir to the east is distinguished by its fine window of four lights. Opening off the choir is the fifteenth-century sacristy. There are no transepts as such, but from a stairway leading down to the lower level from the south aisle of the nave one comes into Blacader's Aisle, built in the fifteenth century and probably intended to be the lower story of a south transept, though the upper story was never added. This is perhaps the prettiest part of the cathedral—a fan-vaulted chapel with brightly colored bosses. In the lower church is the site of the long-gone shrine of St. Kentigern. East of it is the fine Chapel of the Blessed Virgin; and still further east and down another level is the Chapel of the Four Altars. On the north wall of the Chapel of St. Andrew is the recumbent stone effigy of Bishop Robert Wishart, who was one of Robert Bruce's chief supporters, in spite of papal excommunication. North of here, an elaborately carved doorway leads into the chapter house begun by Bishop de Bondington and finished in the fifteenth century. Noteworthy here are the seats reserved for the dean and canons of the cathedral chapter.

** Glasgow Necropolis *(349)*, entrance from Cathedral Street

Laid out in 1833, this vast cemetery became the burial ground of some of Glasgow's richest and most prominent citizens in the Victorian era. Its funereal monuments are therefore most imposing, in the grandiose style to be expected. Prominent are the Catacombs, the Egyptian Vaults, the Menteith Mausoleum, the Moorish Kiosk, and the Davidson of Ruchill

Mausoleum. With a view stretching across the city, John Knox's monument by Thomas Hamilton (1825) slightly predates the cemetery itself.

Barony North Church *(353)*, Cathedral Square

Designed by John Honeyman and built in 1878 as a United Presbyterian Church, this church is Italian baroque in style, which was unusual for this denomination or for this architect.

Trinity Duke Street Church *(353)*, 176 Duke Street

A fine neoclassical building, erected in 1857 by the architectural firm of Peddie & Kinnear, this originally served the Sydney Place congregation of the United Presbyterian Church.

OUTSKIRTS

Kelvin Aqueduct *(318)*, Maryhill

Built in 1787–1790 to carry the **Forth and Clyde Canal** *(318)*, into the city of Glasgow, this was then the largest canal aqueduct in Britain.

*** Glasgow Art Gallery and Museum *(7, 66, 273, 346, 364)*, Kelvingrove Park

Completed in 1900, to the design of Sir J. W. Simpson and Milner Allen, in time for the opening of the following year's International Exposition, this ornate red sandstone pile is meant to be Spanish Renaissance in style to conform to the motif of the exposition's temporary buildings. This is one of Britain's major municipal museums and art galleries. Its Archaeology Gallery includes a good representative collection of Mesolithic, Neolithic, Bronze Age, and Iron Age artifacts. At one end of the main gallery is a cast of the Kildalton Cross. The superb display of Scottish weapons includes fifteenth- to seventeenth-century two-handed swords with quillons (hand-guards) typically slanting toward the point; seventeenth- and eighteenth-century basket-hilt swords; sixteenth-century claymores; eighteenth- and nineteenth-century flintlocks and percussion guns. The Scott Collection of Arms and Armour includes good examples of seventeenth-century date. Scottish painters represented in the Art Gallery include Henry Raeburn, Alexander Nasmyth, Allan Ramsay, Gavin Hamilton, Horatio McCulloch, William McTaggart, James Guthrie, William Q. Orchardson, Noel Paton, and William Dyce.

** University of Glasgow *(346)*, Gilmorehill

The great, sprawling main building of the university was designed by Sir

George Gilbert Scott, doyen of the Victorian Gothic Revival. Ready for occupation in 1870, the style is more or less Early Decorated, which in Scotland is called Second Pointed, but in the crowstepped gables and cone-capped towers there is a strong element of Scottish vernacular. The architect's son, John Oldrid Scott, added Bute Hall and finished the main tower in 1887. Other buildings were added as late as 1967.

* Hunterian Museum *(7, 45, 299)*, Glasgow University, University Avenue

This is Glasgow's oldest museum, founded in 1807 by the generous bequest of Dr. William Hunter, who had left Glasgow to become an eminent London physician. The contents were moved to the present location within the University of Glasgow in 1870. Of major historical importance is the Roman collection, which contains the great majority of distance slabs as well as other material found on the line of the Antonine Wall and other Roman sites in Scotland.

*** Hunterian Art Gallery *(347, 364)*, Gilmore hill, opposite main buildings of the University of Glasgow

Opened in 1980, here is perhaps the most unusual art gallery in Britain. In addition to having a good representation of Flemish and Dutch paintings of the seventeenth century (including a Rembrandt), and of such British painters as Stubbs, Reynolds, Ramsay, and Romney, the Hunterian owns the best collection of the works of James McNeill Whistler in the world, with the possible exception of the Freer Gallery in Washington, DC. This consists of nearly eighty paintings, over a hundred pastels, and several hundred prints and drawings. (Glasgow was more hospitable to the artist than London; it had been the first city to purchase one of his works for its public collection, and the university gave him a degree in 1903.) In addition to this priceless holding, the gallery also has the world's largest single collection of the works of Charles Rennie Mackintosh—over sixty pieces of furniture; more than six hundred drawings, watercolors, and designs; and numerous *objets d'art*. The best of these are contained in the four rooms brought here and reconstructed when Mackintosh's house on Southpark Avenue was torn down and in another reconstructed room from a house in Northampton designed by the same artist. In addition, there is a good collection of Scottish artists of the late nineteenth century, including William McTaggart and James Guthrie.

Trinity College *(352)*, Lynedoch Street

Built in 1856–1861 to the design of the Glasgow architect Charles Wilson, this somewhat Lombardic-looking building first served as a college for the Free Church after the "Disruption" of 1843.

Christian Science Church *(345)*, 1 La Belle Place

Formerly known as the Queen's Rooms, this elegant Italianate templelike building, built in 1857, is the handiwork of Charles Wilson, leading mid-century architect of Glasgow.

* St. Mary's Episcopal Cathedral *(354)*, Great Western Road at Holyrood Crescent

The great English neo-Gothicist Sir George Gilbert Scott designed this fine Early Decorated Gothic Revival church, built in 1871–1874. The architect's son, John Oldrid Scott, completed the building, adding the tower in 1893.

* Queen's Cross Church *(347)*, 866 Garscube Road

Built in 1896–1899 to the design of Charles Rennie Mackintosh, the church can roughly be described as "Art Nouveau Gothic." The interior contains the usual Mackintosh novelties. No longer in use for services, it now houses the Charles Rennie Mackintosh Society.

Lansdowne Church *(353)*, Great Western Road at Kelvin Bridge

Built in 1863 to the design of John Honeyman for a congregation of United Presbyterians, the church is Early English Gothic Revival in style, with an unusual high open spire.

*** Glasgow Botanic Gardens *(298, 336)*, Great Western Road (A 82)

Moved here from a site at the west end of Sauchiehall Street in 1842, and maintained by the City of Glasgow since 1891, this is one of Britain's eminent botanical gardens. Kibble Palace was moved here from Coulport in 1873 and is perhaps the most impressive example of Victorian glass house construction still in existence. It contains a unique collection of tree ferns and other tropical plants and is joined by modern glass exhibition wings housing a host of exotic flora. On the grounds, the most interesting horticultural displays are the Herb Garden, the Systematic Garden, and especially the Chronological Border in which plants are arranged in beds, one for each century from the sixteenth to the twentieth.

Provan Hall *(158)*, Auchinlea Road (b 806) off M 8, 4 m. e of city center; NTS

This unpretentious stone house of fifteenth-century vintage was a summer residence of the Bishops of Glasgow. Now located in the midst of rather dismal housing developments, it is difficult to find.

HAMILTON (STRATHCLYDE)

*** Cameronians (Scottish Rifles) Regimental Museum *(246, 248, 289),*
129 Muir Street, adjacent to Hamilton District Museum

This is a fascinating small museum containing not only mementos and memorabilia of the regiment known as the Cameronians (Scottish Rifles) but of the insurgent Covenanters, who were crushed by the Duke of Monmouth at nearby Bothwell Brig in June 1679. The regiment was formed in 1881 by combining the 90th Perthshire Light Infantry with the 16th Cameronian Regiment. The latter, made up chiefly of ultrapresbyterian Covenanters, was originally raised in May 1689 under the colonelcy of the nineteen-year-old James Douglas, Earl of Angus. In actual command was Lieutenant Colonel William Cleland, who was killed at Dunkeld later in the year while leading the Cameronians in combat against a Jacobite force raised by John Graham of Claverhouse, Viscount Dundee (Bonnie Dundee). "Bluidy Clavers," as the Covenanters called Graham, had already been killed at Killiecrankie, and the rout of his Highland army at Dunkeld effectively finished whatever chance James VII/II may have had to recapture the thrones of which he had been deprived by the Revolution of 1688–89.

*** Bothwell Castle *(97, 104, 113),* 3 m. nw; ¾ m. sw of Uddingston (64 NS 688 593); AM

These magnificent red sandstone ruins in their lovely sylvan setting on the east bank of the upper Clyde are those of a thirteenth-century courtyard castle probably built by Walter de Moravia (Moray). Held by English sympathizers at the outbreak of the War of Independence, it was captured by the Scots in 1289; recaptured by Edward I in a famous siege in 1301; surrendered to Edward Bruce after the Battle of Bannockburn in 1314; dismantled by order of King Robert I; again occupied by the English in 1336 as King Edward III's headquarters; recaptured by its Scottish owner, Sir Andrew of Moray; dismantled by him to prevent future English use; reoccupied about 1362 by Archibald the Grim, third Earl of Douglas, and restored by him; forfeited to the Scottish Crown in 1455, after which it passed into the hands of Archibald ("Bell-the-Cat") Douglas, fifth Earl of Angus; partially demolished by its owner in the late seventeenth century; and inherited by the Home (now Douglas-Home) family in the mid-nineteenth century.

The plan is rectangular, except for the west side, which is an obtuse triangle, terminating in the great half-destroyed circular *donjon*. The entrance is on the long northern side of the rectangle, but it is now only a wide gap in the curtain wall built by Archibald the Grim in the late fourteenth century. To the right (west) are the remains of the ninety-foot-high circular *donjon* separated from the castle yard by a deep and wide ditch partly hewn out of living rock. Only the inner half of the *donjon* remains standing, the rest having been torn down by Sir Andrew de Moray. The portcullis and drawbridge chamber over its entrance are worth close examination. Next, moving counterclockwise along the inside of the courtyard, is the so-called prison tower, polygonal in shape and rising to three stories; then the latrine tower, the south curtain wall, and the southeast tower enclosing a chapel—all built in the early fifteenth century, probably by the Douglas Duc de Touraine, Archibald the Grim's son. Set against the late-fourteenth-century east curtain wall is the great hall dating from the fifteenth.

In the words of the official guidebook: "The noble castle of Bothwell . . . takes rank among the foremost secular structures of the Middle Ages in Scotland."

LANARK (STRATHCLYDE)

*** New Lanark *(319)*, 1½ m. s

This is the best-preserved industrial village in Britain. Most of the buildings were put up shortly after 1786, when Richard Arkwright and David Dale set up cotton-spinning mills here on the falls of the upper Clyde. In 1800 Dale sold out to his son-in-law Robert Owen, who continued to work the mills and run the village until 1825. The buildings dating from the period of Dale's management are: Mill Buildings, Nos. 1, 2, and 4; the "New Building" (with bellcote); the rows of workers' tenements; and the two houses occupied respectively by Dale and Owen. The latter's contributions were Mill Building No. 3; the "Institute for the Formation of Character"; the school; and the workshops. It was chiefly during Robert Owen's paternalistic regime that the village achieved world renown as a model industrial community.

Undergoing restoration, with an uncertain date of completion, the streets can be explored and the buildings observed, but there are few signposts or other visual aids to guide visitors. Nevertheless, the village itself is a sight worth seeing. Situated as it is on the banks of the upper Clyde, it enjoys a scenic ambience of surprising beauty, considering that this was a mill town.

Cartland Crags Bridge *(317)*, 4 m. nw on A 73 (72 NS 868 445)

This triple-arched bridge, 130 feet high above Mouse Water, was built by Thomas Telford in 1822.

*** Craignethan Castle *(191, 195)*, 4½ m. nw; 1 m. w of A 72 through Crossford (72 NS 815 463); AM

The ruined, though well-preserved, rectangular tower-house and its adjacent courtyard and fortifications were built in 1532 by James Hamilton of Finnart, illegitimate son of the first Earl of Arran. It became royal property after Finnart's execution by King James V in 1540, but two years later was acquired by the second Earl of Arran, subsequently elevated to the French Dukedom of Chatelherault, who served as Governor of Scotland during the early minority of Mary, Queen of Scots. It was he who laid out the outer courtyard to the west of the castle proper. The house at the southwest corner of this enclosure was erected by the Covenanter Andrew Hay, who bought the property in 1659. Craignethan is thought to have been the inspiration for Tillietudlem Castle in Sir Walter Scott's *Old Mortality*.

From the gatehouse leading to the outer courtyard, by which today's visitors enter the castle precinct, Andrew Hay's house lies to the right. Proceeding straight across the protective ditch (by way of a modern bridge), the path leads through the scant ruins of a western rampart, once pierced with gunloops. To the right (extending across the south end of the ditch) is a *caponier* (unique in Britain) with three loops for handguns. Ahead, the ruined tower house still stands to the wall-heads. The absence of gunloops here and the generous windows indicate that it was not meant to be defensible. Unusually, the great hall is on the ground floor, with a basement underneath. Of the four original corner towers of the barmkin wall surrounding the tower, only that on the southeast is in a good state of preservation. It has widemouthed gunloops set high in the wall just below the parapet.

SOUTHEASTERN SCOTLAND
Roxburghshire

HAWICK (BORDERS)

* Hawick Museum and Art Gallery *(9, 321)*, Wilton Lodge Park

This is a good small museum of art, archaeology, natural history, and local history, with representative Roman finds, a fine collection of Victoriana, and an interesting section devoted to nineteenth-century hosiery-knitting machines.

Hawick Mote *(80)*, Mote Park, Loan Street

This turf-covered mound, about twenty-five feet high and forty feet across at the summit, overlooks the town of Hawick and the valley of the River Teviot. It was probably raised in the twelfth century to support a timber motte-and-bailey castle.

*** Hermitage Castle *(131, 189, 208)*, 14 m. s; ½ m. w of B 6399 (79 NY 497 961); AM

This splendid, high-standing, roofless ruin is as formidable in aspect as any medieval castle in Scotland. It is in fact a tower-house, with an atypical inner courtyard, built in the late fourteenth century, probably by William, first Earl of Douglas, on the foundations of an earlier manor house erected here about forty years previously by a prominent English Border family, the Dacres. In 1492 Hermitage was taken out of the hands of Archibald ("Bell-the-Cat") Douglas, fifth Earl of Angus, and given to Patrick Hepburn, first Earl of Bothwell, in exchange for Bothwell Castle in Lanarkshire. It was still in the Hepburn family in 1566 when Mary, Queen of Scots, rode here from Jedburgh to give comfort to the wounded James Hepburn, fourth Earl of Bothwell, whom she later married. When the fifth earl was attainted in 1594, the property reverted to the Crown but was later made over to the Scotts of Buccleuch. Under both the Hepburns and Scotts, it was the headquarters of the Keepers of Liddesdale, charged with the almost hopeless task of maintaining order in this particularly lawless part of the Borders.

Viewed from the outside, the castle is formidable and magnificent. The high rectangular tower is joined at four corners by smaller towers of equal height. On the east and west sides the recess between the corner towers was filled in at the top with added masonry, so as to permit the continuation of a straight row of putlog holes to support timber hoardings for defense of the walls beneath. Underneath each hole is a stone corbel, and above is a row of rectangular doors through which the overhanging wooden gallery could be entered. From a distance, it looks as if these two facades of the castle were pierced by giant doorways with pointed arches reaching almost to the roofline. This is an illusion, for, in fact, behind these arches is solid wall, and they really form the bottom edge of the added masonry between the towers. On the north and south sides of the building the corner towers jut out in a normal manner. Inside, the courtyard, entered through a small arched doorway on the south side, is the oldest part of the building, its four sides having been part of the original manor house.

Above the peaceful moorland, now dotted with grazing sheep, this great stronghold standing against the sky is a grim reminder of the Border region's bloody past.

JEDBURGH (BORDERS)

*** Jedburgh Abbey *(145, 197)*, High Street; AM

One of King David I's many foundations, this was a house of canons of the Augustinian Order. The style of architecture of this impressive ruin is Transitional. The late-twelfth-century west end of the church, opening onto the street, is almost intact and has a fine Romanesque round-arched recessed doorway. The heavy round columns separating nave from aisles stand high, but the exterior walls are badly damaged, though in part restored. The crossing, transepts, and south presbytery chapel were rebuilt in the fifteenth and early sixteenth centuries following English depredations. Part of the north transept is reroofed to house the burial vault of the Earls of Lothian. The choir is mid-twelfth-century Romanesque at the west end and Transitional at the east. A fine round-arched doorway leads from the south aisle into the cloister, where the ruins are slight, though well marked by the Scottish Development Department, which has made the monastic ground plan easy to follow. There is a good site museum near the southwest corner of the church.

** Mary Queen of Scots' House *(208)*, town center

This is a sixteenth-century "bastel house," built like a pele tower or Border tower-house and serving the same defensive purpose. It is four stories high and rectangular in plan with a wing projecting from the center of the eastern side, and it belonged to the Kerrs of Ferniehurst, one of the two major families of the East March. Queen Mary stayed here in 1566 while on "justice ayre" in Jedburgh, and it was from here that she rode to Hermitage Castle to visit the wounded James Hepburn, Earl of Bothwell, whom she later married.

The house is now a well-maintained museum devoted chiefly to mementos of the queen. Among other interesting objects to be seen are the Breadalbane Portrait of Queen Mary by George Jamieson, a portrait of Bothwell, miniatures of the queen, her death mask (painted), her Communion service, one of her gowns, her seal, and pictures of the mummified remains of Bothwell, preserved in Denmark where he died in prison.

* Pennymuir Roman Camp *(44)*, 8½ m. se; s of A 68 through Edgerton (80 NT 755 138)

Just south of Pennymuir village on the east side of the lane leading to Tow Ford and Woden Law is the best preserved of Roman temporary camps in Scotland. The original camp enclosed an area of forty-two acres inside earthen ramparts laid out as a rectangle with rounded corners, in the manner typical of Roman fortifications. Of this rampart, the north and west sides are fairly well preserved, standing up to 4½ feet high alongside an exterior ditch 4 feet deep and 12 feet wide. The gaps in the earthworks represent the camp's gateways. In the southeast corner is a smaller and later camp, the east and west sides of which are clearly visible.

Woden Law *(43)*, 10¼ m. se; 6½ m. e of A 68 through Edgerton; 1½ m. s of Pennymuir through Tow Ford (80 NT 768 125)

At the summit of this high hill are the remains of a Late Iron Age hill-fort consisting of a single stone wall reinforced by two outer ramparts with a ditch in between. Inside this enclosure is another earthen rampart faced with large boulders, which was probably erected in the Late Roman or the Dark Age period. On the slopes below the summit, on all sides except the west, is a well-preserved earthwork consisting of two banks and three ditches. These represent Roman siege lines, as do the other ramparts and ditches still observable further down the hill. Archaeologists believe that these earthworks were built after the hill-fort had been evacuated by its native defenders, the *Selgovae*, and that Woden Law was thereafter a practice ground for Roman soldiers stationed at nearby Pennymuir Camp.

KELSO (BORDERS)

*** Kelso Abbey *(143, 197)*, Bridge Street

Though much denuded, this is one of the most beautiful monastic ruins in Scotland—a splendid example of the Romanesque style of architecture. Virtually all that is left, after the English invasions of the sixteenth century coupled with years of neglect and local depredations, is the west end of the monastic church, built some time after a colony of Tironensian monks came here in 1128 after first having settled in Selkirk on the invitation of King David I. The western doorway is almost gone, but the Galilee porch and the two western transepts of this once double-transepted church stand high with a beautiful display of round-arched window openings and arcades. Claustral buildings have all but disappeared.

Roxburgh Castle Mound *(125)*, 1 m. sw; s of A 699 (74 NT 716 338)

Approachable by an unmarked footpath, but best viewed from the Rennie Bridge across the River Tweed, this high mound, with a few fragments of masonry, is all that remains of the castle and royal burgh that stood in the main path of English invading armies and was a major strategic objective of both Scots and English in their almost constant warfare of the fourteenth and fifteenth centuries. Here James II was killed by the explosion of one of his own guns while besieging the castle in 1460. Shortly thereafter, the Scots captured the place and destroyed both castle and town. The present village of the same name a few miles to the south dates from a later period.

** Floors Castle *(254, 258, 306)*, 2 m. nw, w of A 6089

The central block of this sprawling, palatial, very stately home was built for John Ker, first Duke of Roxburghe, between 1721 and 1726. The architect may have been William Adam, although there is some evidence that his role was secondary to that of Sir John Vanbrugh. In any case, the original work was greatly enlarged by William Playfair after 1838. He added flanking pavilions to the main block, increased the number of rooms, and adorned the roof with a multitude of pepper pots and castellated parapets, so that the building as seen today is a strange mixture of Georgian and pseudo-Jacobean styles.

The interior is lavishly furnished, though more in the French than in the British mode. Portraits include those by Sir Godfrey Kneller, Sir Joshua Reynolds, Gilbert Stuart, Thomas Gainsborough, John Hoppner, and Sir Henry Raeburn. There is also a room devoted to nothing but stuffed birds. A short bus ride will take the visitor to the garden center, a commercialized flower-and-shrub emporium of no distinction.

Hume Castle *(189)*, 6 m. n; w of B 6364 in Hume village

This was the family seat of the Earls of Home. The foundations and lower courses date from the thirteenth century, but after much destruction by Cromwell's forces it was allowed to go to ruin until converted, at the end of the eighteenth century, into a "folly" by superimposing a battlemented parapet on the crumbling walls. The results of this surgery are somewhat freakish.

* Smailholm Tower *(225, 303)*, 7 m. w; sw of B 6397 from Smailholm village (74 NT 738 347); AM

This is a five-story rectangular tower–house standing on a prominent rocky outcrop overlooking the Tweed valley. It dates mostly from the early sixteenth century, and David Pringle was probably the builder. In the mid-seventeenth century it came into the possession of the Scotts of Harden and Merton, ancestors of Sir Walter Scott, who visited here as a small boy and was much influenced by the romantic wildness of the by then ruined "castle." Adjacent to the tower are the ruins of an outside kitchen, dating from about 1650.

*** Mellerstain *(308)*, 8 m. nw; w of A 6089

The foundations of this great house were laid in 1725 under the direction of William Adam, who completed the two flanking wings by 1738 when the owner, George Baillie, died. Thereafter, nothing more was done until the second half of the eighteenth century, when the builder's grandson George Baillie-Hamilton engaged Robert Adam to join the two wings with the central block and decorate the interior. Thus the house as it appears today is mostly the work of the younger Adam. The exterior is vaguely Georgian Gothic—rather plain and symmetrical in plan, but with castellated parapets. Inside, the elegant plasterwork, chimneypieces, friezes, cornices, and some of the furnishings are among the best of Robert Adam's many splendid works.

* **Greenknowe Tower** *(225)*, 9 m. nw; n of B 6105, 12 m. w of Gordon (74 NT 639 428); AM; key from custodian, G. H. Forsyth, West End, Gordon

Here is the well-preserved ruin (complete to the wall-heads) of a five-story, L-plan tower-house, built in 1581 by Sir James Seton. The original yett guards the front doorway.

MELROSE (BORDERS)

*** **Melrose Abbey** *(117, 143, 197)*, town center; AM

This is among the most beautiful and, thanks partly to Sir Walter Scott's *Lay of the Last Minstrel*, certainly the most famous of Scotland's many ruined abbeys. It was the first monastery of the Cistercian order in Scotland, founded by King David I in 1136 and colonized by monks from Rievaulx in Yorkshire. Very little of the twelfth-century buildings remains, owing to the destruction wrought by the invading armies of Edward II in 1322 and Richard II in 1385. Most of the present remains date from the century after this latter visitation. Richard II himself sent masons from York to do most of the work in the east end of the choir in the English Perpendicular style of architecture, otherwise rarely seen in Scotland. Later, the south transept of the church was built under the direction of a Parisian mason, Jean Moreau, which accounts for the flamboyant tracery of its windows, done in a manner closer to that of the Ile de France than to the English Curvilinear Decorated style which it also resembles. The west end of the nave was never finished. The abbey was ravaged again by the English in 1544–1545, and, though for a while used as a parish church, it thereafter became the victim of neglect by its lay commendators as well as prey to local pilferers.

Starting at the east end of the church's interior, the most distinctive feature is the splendid Perpendicular east window and the other windows of the presbytery in the same style. Proceeding clockwise to the south transept, here is the marvelous flamboyant window designed by Jean Moreau. In the nave, west of the crossing, stands the almost complete choir screen (*pulpitum*), which separated the monks' choir from that part of the church allotted to the lay brothers. West of here the windows of the south wall of the nave are also flamboyant, though most of the tracery has disappeared. The west end of the nave is represented by foundations only, and the north wall is a mere fragment. The church fabric is alive with fascinating stone carvings—decorative bosses, gargoyles, carved corbels, pinnacled flying buttresses, and the like.

The claustral remains are in a much greater state of ruin than the church, though the outline of the cloister and its adjacent buildings can be observed in well-marked foundation stones. Here is a typical Cistercian arrangement, except for the fact that the cloister lay not to the south of the church but to its north, in order to provide for drainage into the River Tweed, which runs on that side. Moving out from the north transept, we come first to the rectangular chapter house with its original tile floor. Underneath here may lie the heart of King Robert Bruce, though it may have been buried beneath the high altar in the choir. Next in line in the east range of claustral buildings comes the monks' dayroom, above which was their dorter or sleeping quarters. Turning left along the north range, we pass the site of the monks' warming house, frater (refectory), and kitchen. The west range of buildings was assigned to the lay brothers, who had their own warming house, frater, and dorter, and a separate cloister still further to the west. Across the great drain on the north, in a separate building, was the commendator's house. Built originally in the fifteenth century, it was much altered in the sixteenth by James Douglas, last of the abbey's lay commendators. (His predecessor was the bastard son of King James V.) The house is now the site of the abbey museum.

*** Dryburgh Abbey *(146, 197, 365)*, 3½ m. se; ¾ m. e of A 68 through Newtown St. Boswells (74 NT 591 317); AM

In its sylvan setting on the south bank of the River Tweed, this may well be the loveliest of all of Scotland's ruined Border abbeys. Founded by Hugh de Moreville in 1140, it was the first of the country's Premonstratensian houses. The west entrance to the church is a round-arched doorway, built in the fifteenth century when this by then archaic style had come back into fashion in Scotland. Like the other Border abbeys, Dryburgh was badly treated by the English during the "Rough Wooing" of 1544–1545. Not much is left of the nave, but transepts and choir, erected in the late twelfth and early thirteenth centuries, are Transitional, with both round-headed and pointed arches. Sir Walter Scott and Earl Haig are buried in the north transept. The claustral remains are more complete, especially the eastern range, which is entered through a fine Romanesque recessed processional doorway from the east end of the nave. Library, vestry, parlor, chapter house, and warming room stand high and are roofed. Of the south range, only the undercroft and the west gable of the frater remain in evidence. The west side of the cloister was enclosed not by another residential range, as was customary, but by a simple straight wall. These grounds are exceptionally well marked by the Scottish Development Department, so that Dryburgh presents the best opportunity of any ruined abbey in Scotland for the visitor to comprehend the layout of a medieval monastic house.

Eildon Hill, North *(43)*, 1 m. se; by footpath from B 6359 at southern edge of Melrose (73 NT 555 328)

This is the site of the largest Iron Age hill-fort in Scotland, occupied in

Roman times by the *Selgovae*. Roman soldiers from nearby Newstead apparently drove the natives out, and about all that remains to be seen here are the faint traces of three concentric ramparts; a shallow circular ditch just west of the summit where the Romans raised a signal station in the first century A.D.; and a number of barely discernible "hut circles"—flat, round, earthen platforms for primitive dwelling places probably built some time after the hill-fort had been demilitarized.

*** Abbotsford *(267, 303, 309, 337)*, 8 m. w; s of B 6360, ¼ m. sw of A 7

Sir Walter Scott began construction here in 1822, and the present building, with the exception of the west wing added in 1855, can be attributed entirely to this greatest of romantic novelists and his sympathetic architect, William Atkinson. Outside and in, it is an odd mixture of pseudo-medieval, pseudo-Tudor, and pseudo-Jacobean, which manages to reflect perfectly both the historical predilections and the literary style of the owner.

Although Queen Victoria found it "rather gloomy," most visitors are captivated by the storybook atmosphere of this place, and especially by the fascinating miscellany of historical relics that Scott managed to collect and store here. Among these are: Rob Roy's purse, sporran, sword, and dirk (also his portrait); a lock of Bonnie Prince Charlie's hair; a pocketbook worked by Flora MacDonald; Bonnie Dundee's pistol; Montrose's cabinet captured after Philiphaugh; two Highland swords found on the battlefield of Culloden; and (built into the fountain in the center of the south court) the bowl of Edinburgh's mercat cross, which ran with wine on the occasion of Charles II's restoration in 1660.

Selkirkshire

SELKIRK (BORDERS)

* Halliwell's House Museum and Gallery *(194, 238)*, town center

This is a fine new museum of local history housed in a row of restored eighteenth-century houses. Of particular interest among its holdings are the "Flodden Flag," allegedly captured from the English during that famous battle, and numerous weapons recovered from nearby Philiphaugh, scene of Montrose's defeat in September 1645 by David Leslie and his Covenanters.

*** Bowhill *(246, 306, 309)*, 3 m. w; s of A 708

This palatial house, essentially Georgian Gothic in style, was built mainly in 1812 to the plans of William Atkinson (Sir Walter Scott's architect at Abbotsford) but substantially modified later in the nineteenth century at the hands of the architects William Burn and David Bryce. Its owners were, and are, the Dukes of Buccleuch and Queensberry, descended from Anne

Scott, Countess of Buccleuch, and her husband James, Duke of Monmouth, illegitimate son of Charles II and commander-in-chief in Scotland, who defeated rebellious Covenanters at Bothwell Brig in June 1679. It is this connection that accounts for the "Monmouth Room," which contains the duke's cradle, saddle, and other memorabilia, including the shirt he wore at his execution after the suppression of the Monmouth Rebellion against James VII/II in 1685.

The furnishings and *objets d'art* here are extraordinarily fine and the collection of paintings is one of the best in private hands in Scotland. It includes outstanding works by Sir Joshua Reynolds, Thomas Gainsborough, Sir Thomas Lawrence, Sir Henry Raeburn, David Wilkie, and several Italian masters, including Leonardo da Vinci. There is also a fine collection of miniatures, including an unfinished portrait of Oliver Cromwell by Samuel Cooper, and representations of Queen Mary Tudor by Hans Eworth, Queen Elizabeth I by Nicholas Hilliard, and Catherine Howard by Hans Holbein, the younger.

Newark Castle *(238)*, 6 m. w; 2 m. from A 708 past Bowhill (73 NT 420 285)

This much ruined tower-house (closed to the public but clearly visible from the minor road running west of Bowhill) was the scene of the massacre of numerous prisoners of war and camp followers of the Marquis of Montrose's army, defeated at nearby Philiphaugh on 13 September 1645. The perpetrators of the atrocity were General David Leslie's Covenanting soldiers, egged on by bloodthirsty Presbyterian clergymen.

James Hogg Monument *(303)*, 16 m. sw; 1 m. w of B 7009 from Ettrick village

This monument marks the birthplace of the "Ettrick Shepherd," James Hogg (1770–1835), author of *The Private Memoirs and Confessions of a Justified Sinner.*

Peeblesshire

INNERLEITHEN (BORDERS)

*** Traquair House *(23, 238, 277)*, ½ m. s from A 72

The oldest part of this charming country house is the north end of the main block (to the left on entering), which was a typical Scottish Border tower house, probably dating from the fourteenth century. Most of the remainder was added in the early seventeenth century by John Stewart, first

Earl of Traquair, Lord Treasurer of Scotland under Charles I. It was he who barred the front door to the fugitive Marquis of Montrose after his defeat by General David Leslie at Philiphaugh in September 1645. The side wings enclosing the front courtyard were built by Charles Stewart, the fourth earl, in the late seventeenth century. It was he who employed the architect James Smith to install the iron gates and screen, the terrace, and the two little pavilions with ogee roofs on the east front. Later the earl joined the Jacobite rising of 1715 and was afterward imprisoned in the Tower of London. The Bear Gates were erected in 1737–1738. Tradition has it that they were closed permanently when Bonnie Prince Charlie left the house after a brief stay in 1745, but the known evidence indicates that the prince was never at Traquair.

A Roman Catholic house since the conversion of John Stewart, second earl, Traquair has a seventeenth-century chapel (the "priest's room") and another more elaborate one built in the nineteenth century. It also has a fine collection of Jacobite relics, including miniature paintings of both Old and Young Pretenders; Princess Clementina Sobieska Stuart, Prince Charles Edward's mother; and Prince Henry Stuart, Cardinal York, his younger brother. Here too is an interesting array of Jacobite glassware.

** Scottish Museum of Textiles *(321)*, 2 m. e, in Walkerburn on A 72

Behind Henry Ballantyne & Sons is this excellent small museum demonstrating the manufacture of woollen textiles from cottage industry to factory. The visual aids are especially cogent.

PEEBLES (BORDERS)

* Cross Kirk *(163, 168)*, off Cross Street, north of town center

This is a ruined mid-thirteenth-century church that, in the fifteenth century, was turned over to the Trinitarian (Red) Friars. The western tower stands high, as do the west, north, and south walls of the nave. The eastern wall was added in the seventeenth century, when the church became a Protestant kirk. To the east of this the original choir is reduced to mere foundations. Some very fragmentary remains of the friars' cloister can be seen north of the building.

** Neidpath Castle *(132)*, 1 m. w; s of A 72 (73 NT 238 404)

This was originally a tower-house built in the early fourteenth century by the Hays of Yester, one of whose descendants, the second Earl of Tweeddale, remodelled it in the seventeenth century. In the eighteenth, the Douglas Earls of March made additional alterations to the tower and courtyard buildings. One of these owners was the third Earl of March, who was denounced by William Wordsworth as "Degenerate Douglas! Oh the unworthy lord!" for selling off an ancient stand of timber from the estate— a "brotherhood of venerable trees."

The castle is an L-plan tower-house rising some sixty feet from a rocky outcrop above the River Tweed and set at the west end of a courtyard surrounded by walls and cottages of mixed dates. The main block has six stories with the top floor missing, while the west wing has only two surviving floors, with a pit prison underneath the lower one. The first floor hall is now divided by a transverse wall and has panelling and plaster ceilings of the seventeenth century. In the upper floors are bedrooms. The slate roof is of more recent construction. A delightful public park lies below the castle on its river side.

* Stobo Kirk *(220)*, 6 m. sw, on B 712

This small and much restored church has both Norman and fifteenth-century features—round arches in the south doorway and north window opposite; Second Pointed windows in the east end. Originally it was a typical medieval rectangular church with a west tower and belfry and a chancel slightly narrower than the nave, but later a mortuary aisle was added to the north side, converting the building into a T-plan church, which made it quite suitable to Protestant worship after the Reformation. Seats of some kind were then placed in the north aisle, a laird's loft installed in the west end, and a pulpit erected in the middle of the south side, where it still stands. Another interesting post-Reformation feature is the set of jougs now displayed under glass in the south porch. These iron collars, secured to the church wall, were used to restrain offenders against church discipline and to punish them by public exposure.

*** Dawyck House Gardens *(295)*, 8 m. sw; e of B 712

In spite of great destruction caused by gales in 1968 and 1973, this is one of Britain's greatest examples of sylviculture on a large scale. Starting with Sir James Naesmyth in the early eighteenth century, and continuing down to the present, the owners of the Dawyck estate have been in the forefront of scientific forestry. The marvelous variety of trees here is the result. Also the gardens are noted for their rhododendrons, and, in the spring, for the great spread of daffodils.

* Dreva Craig Hill-Fort *(30)*, 10 m. sw; 1 m. se of A 701 from Broughton (72 NT 126 353)

Two ruined stone walls of this Iron Age hill-fort enclose an area measuring 190 feet by 140 feet. Outside, to the southwest, are the remains of a *cheveaux de frise* type barricade, presumably intended to break up cavalry charges and otherwise impede attacks against the main gate of the fort. Today the barricade consists of about two hundred boulders, half of them still earthfast. Such devices were fairly common among Celts on the Continent but, judging from surviving evidence, rare in Britain.

Berwickshire

COLDSTREAM (BORDERS)

Coldstream Museum *(242)*, Market Place

This was General George Monck's headquarters before he left Scotland in 1660 to bring about the restoration of Charles II with the help of a regiment later known as the Coldstream Guards. Uniforms and other regimental memorabilia comprise the greater part of the museum's collection. As regimental museums go, this one suffers from amateur management.

* The Hirsel *(335)*, 2 m. w; e of A 697, n of junction with A 698

Dundock Wood on this estate was first planted by the Earl of Home in the 1860s and is still one of Scotland's superior woodland gardens, best known for its rhododendrons and azaleas. The Exhibition Centre provides guides and maps around the nature walks and contains as well an interesting agricultural museum.

* Ladykirk (Kirk o' Steill) *(164)*, 7 m. ne; ¼ m. n of B 6470 from 3 m. e of Swinton

This is a cruciform parish kirk, situated on the north bank of the Tweed just across the border from England. Legend has it that King James IV was its founder—out of gratitude for having been rescued from drowning in a steill (pool) in the river during the last decade of the fifteenth century. Building is known to have begun in 1500, and a fair amount of the original Second Pointed fabric survives.

DUNS (BORDERS)

** Manderston House *(334)*, 2 m. e; n of A 6105

Built in the first decade of the twentieth century by John Kinross for Sir James Miller, this immense mansion is the epitome of Edwardian opulence—some would say vulgarity. Modelled on Robert Adam's masterpiece, Kedleston Hall in Derbyshire (home of Baron Scarsdale, Miller's father-in-law), Manderston falls short of the original in taste, though not in extravagance. Of considerable interest, however, are the servants' quarters, stables, and marbled dairy-house. The most attractive feature of this place are the gardens, formal in style, in the best Victorian and Edwardian manner.

* Edinshall Fort *(29)*, 5½ m. n; 1½ m. n of junction of B 6266 and B 6355 (67 NT 772 603); AM

This Iron-Age hill-fort consists today of an ovoid double rampart with external ditches in front of each embankment. Inside are the remains of a Late Iron Age circular broch with walls as high as five feet. This building displays door-checks, guard cells leading from the entry, and three mural cells opening from the central court, as well as the remains of a stone staircase. In the western half of the hill-fort are a number of circular hut foundations of a probable postbroch (Dark Age) date.

EARLSTON (BORDERS)

Haerfaulds Hill-Fort *(30)*, 8 m. n; s of Blythe, 1½ m. n of A 697 from Cambridge (74 NT 574 500)

This Iron Age hill-fort now consists of an oval of strewn stone rubble, all that remains of what must have been a massive wall. Inside it are a number of circular stone hut foundations, probably dating from the Roman period of occupation after the hill-fort had been dismantled.

EYEMOUTH (BORDERS)

* Coldingham Priory *(142)*, 1 m. w; n of A 1107 (67 NT 904 659)

Here the remains of a Benedictine monastery colonized from Durham on land granted by King Edgar in the last years of the eleventh century are incorporated into a lovely parish kirk of pink stone. Of the thirteenth-century Transitional priory church, the most noteworthy relics are the north and east walls of the choir, with fine lancet windows above round-arched arcading on the outside and pointed arched arcades on the interior.

LAUDER (BORDERS)

* Lauder Kirk *(264)*, town center

This little kirk is built on the Greek-cross plan, unusual in Scotland, especially for the late seventeenth century when it was put up by Sir William Bruce while he was engaged in enlarging and beautifying nearby

Thirlestane Castle for the Duke of Lauderdale. Over the crossing is an octagonal steeple; pews and galleries face the central pulpit on all four sides, so that the sermon could be more easily heard—a matter of great importance in the reformed service of the Church of Scotland.

*** Thirlestane Castle *(212, 258, 264, 295)*, ½ m. ne of A 68

The original keep here may date back to the Middle Ages, but the present mansion is largely the product of two builders: John Maitland of Thirlestane and his grandson, John Maitland, Duke of Lauderdale. The former was chancellor to James VI and in the 1590s built here a great rectangular tower-house with round towers on the four corners (best seen now from the garden in the rear of the castle). In the late seventeenth century the Duke of Lauderdale, Charles II's Secretary of State for Scotland, employed William Bruce to add the wings flanking the entrance on the west front, thus creating a T-plan building, which was given further emphasis when the wings were extended in the nineteenth century.

The rooms are graced with numerous portraits of the Maitlands (including those by George Romney, George Jamesone, Sir Joshua Reynolds, John Hoppner, and Thomas Lawrence), plaster ceilings, fine seventeenth- and eighteenth-century English and French furniture, and the usual number of objects of art found in British stately homes. Prince Charles Edward Stuart is believed to have stayed here following the Battle of Prestonpans in 1745, and the room in which he allegedly slept is proudly on display, though furnished anachronistically with a nineteenth-century sleigh bed. Within the castle is the relatively new Border Country Life Museum—very well organized, with emphasis on the history of Lowland agriculture.

West Lothian

BO'NESS (CENTRAL)

Scottish Railway Preservation Society Museum *(338)*, off Union Street

Here are the beginnings of an ambitious open-air railway museum, linked with a similar enterprise at Falkirk. A train shed and a nineteenth-century station, brought from Wormit at the south end of the Tay railway bridge, have been reerected on this site. Tickets are sold here for excursion trips by steam train.

** Kinneil House *(195, 323)*, ½ m. w; s of A 904 (65 NS 983 806); AM

Here is an interesting conventional Scottish rectangular tower-house to which was attached a more elegant palace wing. The builder was James

Hamilton, second Earl of Arran and Duke of Chatelherault, Governor of Scotland during the early minority of Mary, Queen of Scots. Reroofed and refloored in this century, Kinneil is in an unusually good state of preservation. The tower is five stories in height; the palace three. Surviving shot holes indicate that it was meant to be defensible. The main attraction here, however, are the wall paintings in the palace, dating from the sixteenth and seventeenth centuries—among the best of their kind in Scotland.

On the grounds are the remains of a workshop used by James Watt in 1769–1773 to build a full-scale steam engine under an agreement with John Roebuck of the Carron Ironworks. An upright steam boiler commemorates the largely unsuccessful experiment. Nearby also is the local museum illustrating the social and industrial history of Bo'ness.

LINLITHGOW (LOTHIAN)

*** Linlithgow Palace *(128, 184, 195)*, town center; AM

This lovely ruined palace of gray and yellow sandstone stands on a promontory on the southern shore of Linlithgow Loch. It has four sides surrounding a courtyard. Between 1425 and 1435, King James I built the great hall and kitchen tower, now comprising the east range, at the then considerable cost of £4,518. James IV made some minor improvements, and his queen, Margaret Tudor, spent most of her married life here. James V (1513–1542), who was born here, converted the palace into its present quadrangular form and shifted the main entrance from the east to the south side. In 1607 the north side of the quadrangle collapsed and had to be entirely rebuilt. William Wallace, working for James VI, was responsible for the restoration. All the fifteenth- and sixteenth-century monarchs of Scotland, starting with James I, sojourned here frequently, and Mary, Queen of Scots, also was born here. The palace was occupied by Cromwell in 1650–1651. In 1746 soldiers of the Duke of Cumberland, fresh from defeat by the Jacobites at Falkirk, set it on fire, after which it was abandoned.

The palace is approached through a turreted outer entryway of the sixteenth century surmounted by a parapet added in the nineteenth. The inner entry is through the south facade built by James V, who also installed the beautiful Gothic/Renaissance fountain in the center of the court. On the right lies the sixteenth-century chapel with five lofty round-headed windows. Moving counterclockwise, the east range of buildings consists of the great hall and adjoining kitchen tower—the original palace of James I. Also called the "Lyon Chalmer," the hall is entered from the inner court through a round-arched doorway topped by three canopied niches, and from the outside by its twin, flanked by canopied and corbelled niches and surmounted by a carved panel containing the arms of the royal house. The room is lighted by five rectangular windows and has a splendid tripartite fireplace at the dais end. The north range of buildings, put up in the reign of James VI (1567–1625), is chiefly remarkable for William Wallace's neoclassical windows opening onto the inner court. Inside, on the first floor, are the king's bedchamber, the presence chamber, and a room called "His Majesties Hall." The west end of the south facade (as far as the main entrance) is occupied by still another hall.

*** St. Michael's Church *(173)*, town center, in front of palace

This is one of Scotland's showpieces, a largely fifteenth-century cruciform church built on earlier foundations, expanded in the sixteenth century, neglected in the seventeenth and eighteenth, and restored to serve as a parish kirk in the nineteenth. There was a church here before King Edward I occupied Linlithgow, and parts of it, including the great tower, were incorporated when rebuilding began in the fifteenth century—to which most of the present fabric is owed. The predominant style is Second Pointed, though the three windows in the apse, added to the east end about 1531, are among the few examples in Scotland of the English Perpendicular style. The strange-looking "crown" of aluminum was emplaced on the square tower (by helicopter) in 1964—an entirely gratuitous desecration.

When the kings and queens of Scotland were in residence at the palace up the hill, St. Michael's served as a royal chapel, and the doorway in the north wall was apparently inserted especially for their use. In 1540 the church was bestowed on the burgh by a royal charter that provided for the election of a provost, making it in effect collegiate.

In plan it is cruciform, although the transepts are unusually short. The western tower, through which the main entranceway leads, contains a fine set of bells, including one dating from the year 1490. Just west of the south porch is a fifteenth- or sixteenth-century stone statue of St. Michael—a rarity, somehow missed by the iconoclasts of the Reformation.

Of special note inside the church are the flamboyant window tracery in the nave, the Burne-Jones window in the south wall, the stone-carved retable in the vestry, the fine vaulting in the aisles, and the three aumbries, one on each side of the west entrance and one in the south transept.

* Canal Museum *(318)*, s of town center

At the edge of the **Union Canal** *(318)*, completed in 1822, this small museum, housed in a building once used as a stable for canal horses, displays numerous photographs, artifacts, etc., associated with the waterway. Visitors may also enjoy a short trip on the canal itself aboard the *Victoria*, a replica of a nineteenth-century steam packet.

* The Binns *(245)*, 2 m. ne; e of B 9109, ½ m. n of A 904; NTS

This is a seventeenth-century mansion, enlarged in the two succeeding centuries to form the present U-plan building with a battlemented neo-Gothic facade. Its most distinguished occupant was General Thomas (Tam) Dalyell, who joined Charles II's invasion of England in 1651, was imprisoned after the Battle of Worcester in September of that year, escaped from the Tower of London, entered the service of Czar Alexis Michaelovitch of Russia, and returned to Scotland in 1666 to be put in command of His Majesty's Forces in the restored Charles II's northern kingdom. In this capacity he was active in the repression of the Covenanters, was in command of government forces at the Battle of Rullion Green, and won the title of "Bluidy Muscovite" for his severity against the ultra-Presbyterian rebels of the Southwest. In 1681 he organized a new cavalry regiment, the Royal Regiment of Scots Greys, which held its first muster in this house.

The house is attractively, though not remarkably, decorated and furnished, mostly with eighteenth-century pieces. There are two fine plaster ceilings of seventeenth-century date. The mandatory guided tour lasts about forty-five minutes and is not especially informative.

** Blackness Castle *(214, 241, 245)*, 4½ m. ne; from end of B 903 (65 NT 055 803); AM

The main tower here was built in the fifteenth century, the enclosing wall in the sixteenth, and the spur at the west end was added in the seventeenth as a gun platform. The castle passed back and forth frequently between the Crown and prominent nobles (Crichtons, Stewarts, Livingstons), and while under royal control frequently served as a prison. Prominent prisoners included Cardinal Beaton in 1543, the Earl of Angus in 1544, a handful of Highland chiefs in 1608, and a number of Covenanters in the 1660s. The castle was turned over to the French in 1548 and was taken for Cromwell by General George Monk in 1654. Today, it is almost intact. The contours of the enclosing wall have the appearance of a ship, with the bow pointing northeastward toward the Firth of Forth, thus offering a splendid view across to Fife.

QUEENSFERRY (LOTHIAN)

** Priory Church of St. Mary of Mount Carmel *(168)*, town center

Still in use as a Scottish Episcopal church, this is the restored church of a Carmelite friary founded in 1441 by James Dundas on condition that perpetual prayers be said for "the souls of the grantor and his wife, his ancestors and successors"—a stipulation still being honored, though not according to the rites of the Roman Catholic Church. Of the original building, the tower, south transept, and vaulted choir survive, though of course restored. Piscina, aumbry, and sedilia are still in evidence. The church is located close to the south bank of the Firth of Forth, and from its yard can be obtained a fine view of the two great modern bridges leading into Fife.

* Forth Railway Bridge *(339)*, e of town center

Best viewed from Hawes Inn or the town harbor (or from the passenger ferry to Inchcolm), this spectacular cantilever bridge was completed in 1890 to carry the North British Railway line from Edinburgh north across the Firth of Forth. The architect/engineers were Sir John Fowler and Benjamin Baker. The bridge was formally opened by the Prince of Wales, later Edward VII. Because of the previous collapse of the Tay Bridge, extra precautions were taken here in construction: 54,000 tons of steel were used; 6½ million rivets, 740,000 cubic feet of granite, 46,300 tons of rubble masonry, and 21,000 tons of cement. Slightly more than 1.5 miles in length, the bridge is 361 feet tall from the top of the main towers to the high-water mark.

*** Dalmeny House *(306, 309, 361)*, 3 m. e; 1 m. ne of A 90

This great many-turreted mansion was built after 1815 by Archibald Primrose, fourth Earl of Rosebery, in conscious imitation of an East Anglian Tudor manor house. The architect was William Wilkins of London, but the style was the owner's. Although the facade facing the Firth of Forth is symmetrical, the entrance front, with its contrived asymmetry, is more typically Tudor, as are the octagonal turrets, mullion windows, and innumerable chimney pots. So are the fan vaulting in the corridor, the plaster hammerbeam ceiling in the hall, and the Flemish stained glass windows.

Paintings include portraits by Thomas Gainsborough, Sir Joshua Reynolds, Sir Thomas Lawrence, and Sir Henry Raeburn. In the drawing room is the sumptuous Mentmore Collection of French furniture and objects of art, brought here when the Rothschild estate at Mentmore was broken up. In the Napoleon Room is a fascinating collection of Bonaparte mementos, gathered together by the fifth earl after he had retired as Liberal Prime Minister in 1895 and turned to writing books, including a biography of the former French emperor. In the hall is a bust of W. E. Gladstone, who was Lord Roseberry's guest here during the Midlothian campaigns.

*** Dalmeny Church *(162)*, 1 m. e; ½ m. s of B 924 in Dalmeny village

This is the best-preserved Romanesque church in Scotland. It has a rectangular nave, a slightly narrower and shorter rectangular choir, and a semicircular apsed east end. Both choir and apse are vaulted. The west tower is a restoration of 1930; otherwise the church mostly retains its original twelfth-century appearance. One entrance is on the south—a tall, round-arched door with two decorated orders; the other is at the east end. The round arches between nave and choir and between choir and apse are heavily decorated with chevrons in the typical Romanesque fashion. On the south wall outside is a fine round-arched interlaced arcade. As in many medieval churches converted to Protestant use, a laird's loft was added north of the nave—in this case to accommodate the Roseberry family, owners of nearby Dalmeny House.

*** Hopetoun House *(258, 262, 305, 306, 307)*, 1½ m. w; n of A 904

The original building here was designed for Charles Hope, first Earl of Hopetoun, by Sir William Bruce and put up in the years 1699 to 1703. In 1721 William Adam was engaged to make substantial alterations, which, along with interior remodelling, were completed by his sons Robert and John in 1767. In spite of the long period of construction and the different architectural styles of the builders, Hopetoun House retained an essential aesthetic unity and for sheer grandeur cannot be surpassed in Scotland.

Bruce's work—neoclassical and French Renaissance in mode—can best be seen from the garden side of the house. The Adams were responsible for the entrance front, where the baroque influences of Sir John Vanbrugh are evident in the ponderous top story, the giant Corinthian pilasters, the round-headed windows, and the curved bays. Inside, the contrast is just as noticeable as the visitor moves from room to room. The serenely classical entrance hall is typical of the Adam brothers, Robert and John; so are the libraries. The garden parlor, which formed the entrance hall from the garden of the original house, is equally typical of Bruce's work; next to it the writing closet contains a selection of documents relating to Bruce; the front stairs were also installed by him in their present form, as were the west wainscot bedchamber and anteroom. The magnificent yellow drawing room and red drawing room were done by the Adams; so was originally the state dining room, but about 1820 it was redecorated in Regency style.

The paintings here are of no great distinction, though there are portraits by John Wooton, Daniel Mytens, David Allan, Allan Ramsey, George Jamesone, and Sir Henry Raeburn, who was knighted at Hopetoun during a visit by King George IV in 1822. Of all the great houses in Scotland, this is perhaps the most accommodating to the interests and convenience of the visiting public—courteous and well-informed staff, informative hand-cards available in every room, and *no* mandatory guided tour. The grounds sweeping down to the Firth of Forth are lovely.

* Abercorn Church *(262)*, 1½ m. w; n of A 904, at entrance to grounds of Hopetoun House

The most interesting feature of this tiny kirk is the laird's loft, built by Sir William Bruce in the early eighteenth century for the first Earl of Hopetoun for whom he also designed nearby Hopetoun House. This is a colorfully painted gallery that was also provided with an adjoining suite of panelled rooms to which the earl and his family could repair between morning and afternoon services.

Union Canal Bridges *(318)*, 6 m. s; from 1½ m. s of Broxburn to 3 m. s of Kirkliston (65 NT 080 710 to 117 710)

Along this stretch of the **Union Canal** *(318)*, completed in 1822, are eight bridges (Nos. 19–22 and 30–33).

TORPHICHEN (LOTHIAN)

* Torphichen Preceptory *(145)*, ½ m. n; e of B 792 (65 NS 969 725); AM

This was the principal settlement in Scotland of the Knights Hospitallers of the Order of St. John of Jerusalem and was chartered by King David I in 1153. Only the transepts, crossing, and a small fragment of the north wall of the preceptory church remain. The ruins date from the twelfth century with thirteenth-, fourteenth-, and fifteenth-century modifications. Of major interest here is the excellent museum in the tower, devoted to the history of the military orders in Scotland.

*** Cairnpapple Hill *(19)*, 1½ m. se (65 NS 987 717); AM

Sitting high on a hilltop with magnificent views in all directions, this is one of Scotland's most notable prehistoric sites. There is evidence here of occupation from Neolithic through Iron Age times. Because of frequent reconstruction, the site is difficult to interpret. Today, its centerpiece is a Bronze Age rock-cut cist underneath a concrete dome in the care of the Scottish Development Department. Nearby are the remains of a Neolithic stone circle and four Iron Age cists. The site museum (not always open) contains explanatory material—more needed here than at most prehistoric sites.

Midlothian

DALKEITH (LOTHIAN)

* Dalkeith Parish Church *(169)*, town center

Lying just to the east of this much restored building are the ruined choir and apse of the Collegiate Church of St. Nicholas, founded in the early fifteenth century by Sir James Douglas of Dalkeith. Here is the recumbent effigy (in civilian attire) of his grandson, James Douglas, first Earl of Morton, and of his wife Joanna, the mute daughter of King James I.

** Borthwick Castle (132, 208, 209), 7 m. s; 1 m. e of A 7 through North Middleton (66 NT 371 597)

Borthwick has been described by the architectural historian Stewart Cruden as "the epitome of fifteenth-century classical tower house building." It was erected some time after 1430 by the local laird, Sir William Borthwick. Mary, Queen of Scots, was here in 1567 before her capitulation at Carberry Hill; and in 1650 Cromwell laid siege to the castle but did only minor damage before it was surrendered.

The building consists of a high machicolated rectangular block with a jamb extending from each end of the west side. It stands within a curtain wall pierced with wide gunports and entered through a single-towered gatehouse with gunports and originally a portcullis and drawbridge. The main entrance to the house is on the north side of the first floor and is approached by a high bridge leading from the curtain wall. The first floor hall has a splendid hooded fireplace, mural cupboards, and a minstrel's gallery. The three floors above contain solars and bedrooms and, on the second, an oratory with piscina and aumbry.

Now a luxurious hotel and conference center, the castle grounds and interior can be viewed only on application or by booking for dinner or lodging (tel: Gorebridge 20514).

*** Crichton Castle (120, 208, 213), 7 m. se; ½ m. sw of B 6367 from Crichton village (66 NT 380 612); AM

This splendid castle, now ruined, was built in three stages: (1) the original tower-house raised by Sir John de Crichton in the reign of King Robert III (1390–1406); (2) the gatehouse keep added by Sir William Crichton, Chancellor of Scotland under James II (1437–1460); and (3) the Renaissance-style north range installed by Francis Stewart, Earl of Bothwell, in the reign of James VI (1567–1625). Sir William Crichton was responsible for the "Black Dinner" at Edinburgh Castle, where the young Earl of Douglas and his brother were murdered in 1440. Francis Stewart was a cousin of James VI and a notorious brawler suspected of witchcraft, but withal a cultivated nobleman who imported an Italian architect to renovate his castle.

The central portion of the east front (to the right of the entrance) is a typical fourteenth-century rectangular tower-house with a vaulted basement and first floor hall, though the top story has been removed. To the left of the entrance is the gatehouse keep built by Sir William Crichton. Its original entrance on the south front has been blocked up. This structure is rectangular in plan and three stories in height with an oversailing machic-olated parapet. The first and second floor halls are graced with hooded fireplaces and other architectural embellishments. The western front of the castle, another three-story building, was added in the late fifteenth century. The north range is Francis Stewart's. It is Italianate in design, and the faceted stonework on the face of the piazza suggests that it may have been inspired by the Palazzo dei Diamanti in Ferrera.

Crichton Collegiate Church *(170)*, at entrance to castle grounds

Built in the fifteenth century by Chancellor Sir William Crichton, the church consists of choir and transepts only. It now serves as a parish kirk, and the public is admitted during services. A caretaker, living next door, has a key but is not always willing to share it with visitors.

EDINBURGH (LOTHIAN)

South Edinburgh

Flodden Wall *(194)*, The Vennel, West Port, above the Grassmarket

Here is the best preserved portion of the battlemented town wall begun in the early sixteenth century, possibly in panic after the disastrous defeat of James IV's army by the English at Flodden in 1513.

Magdalen Chapel *(165)*, Cowgate, off the Grassmarket; admission by arrangement with the Scottish Reformation Society, 17 George IV Bridge (tel: 031-225-1836)

In this sixteenth-century chapel are the only pre-Reformation stained glass windows in Scotland. These consist of four circular medallions, one of which bears the royal arms of Scotland, another the arms of Marie de Guise. The building itself is small, dark, and shabby.

** Greyfriars Kirk *(221, 234, 246)*, Candlemaker Row; open during services only, except by arrangement (tel: 031-225-1900)

The original Protestant Kirk of the Greyfriars was built here in 1601–1620 on the site of the defunct Franciscan friary, which had been converted to a town burial yard. After an explosion of gunpowder in 1718, the west end was rebuilt, and, after a fire in 1845, so was the east end, so that the present First Pointed Gothic building (restored again in the 1930s) incorporates very little of the original, except for its foundations.

It was on this site in 1638 that the great National Covenant was signed, and in the existing session house is an original copy of that document, as well as a good collection of nineteenth-century Communion tokens. The kirkyard is, if anything, more interesting than the kirk. Here Covenanters captured at the Battle of Bothwell Brig were confined. Here also are a number of splendid funereal monuments, including the tombs of the architects John Mylne (d. 1667), William Adam (d. 1748), James Craig (d. 1795), and James Gillespie Graham (d. 1855); the clergyman Alexander Henderson (d. 1646), one of the framers of the National Covenant; Duncan Forbes of Culloden (d. 1747); and many others. In front of the church, commemorating the dog that loitered for many years at the grave of his master, John Gray (d. 1858), is a replica in stone of "Greyfriars Bobby"—a notable monument to Victorian sentimentality.

** Heriot's Hospital *(257)*, Lauriston Place

This is perhaps the finest extant example of what is known as the Scottish Renaissance style of architecture—classical in its symmetrical courtyard plan, Scottish Baronial in the four solid corner towers, and Gothic in the shape of its chapel windows. Founded by George Heriot in the reign of James VI for the education of "puir fatherless bairns," the building was begun under the direction of William Wallace in 1628 and finished by Robert Mylne, who added the clock tower and George Heriot's statue in 1693.

Visitors will be shown around the college by one of the porters on request.

McEwan Hall *(350)*, Teviot Place

Part of the University of Edinburgh, this grandiose Italianate building, completed in 1897, was designed by Sir Robert Rowand Anderson.

*** Royal Scottish Museum *(349)*, Chambers Street

Designed by Captain F. Fowke of the Royal Engineers, more or less on the model of London's famous Crystal Palace of 1851 (now gone), the building's foundation stone was laid in 1861 by the prince consort. Behind an Italianate exterior, the glazed roof and slender cast iron columns and arches were products of the most advanced principles of mid-Victorian engineering and architecture. Intended as a monument to nineteenth-century industrial and scientific progress, the museum is still distinguished for its exhibitions of natural history and geology, as well as technology and the decorative arts. In the Hall of Power and the Shipping Hall are an early Watt and Boulton steam-powered beam engine, a large industrial water wheel, ship models, and machinery associated with coal mining, shipbuilding, and general engineering. The Civil Engineering gallery contains materials relating to Scotland's lighthouses. Other exhibits include collections of ship models, locomotive models, electrical appliances, sewing machines, gramophones, cameras, typewriters, microscopes, barometers, clocks, armor, etc.

*** Edinburgh University, Old College *(222, 287, 314)*, South Bridge

Classes began meeting in this spot soon after the university (the fourth oldest in Scotland) received its charter in 1582. In 1617 King James VI conferred on it the name of "The College of King James." In 1789 the foundation stone of a new college was laid to a design prepared by Robert Adam. Before the architect's death in 1792, however, only the Triumphal Arch leading from South Bridge was completed, though the dome above was designed by R. Rowand Anderson in 1886–1887 as an enlargement of Adam's original plan. Building stopped during the Wars of the French Revolution and Napoleon, and it was not until 1817 that construction of the present quadrangle was recommenced under the guidance of William H. Playfair, who mostly followed Adam's design. His Upper Library, with its splendid barrel-vaulted coffered ceiling, has been called "one of the most imposing neoclassical interiors in Scotland." It is open to visitors by arrangement with the porter on duty.

* Royal College of Surgeons' Hall and Museum *(314)*, Nicolson Street

Completed in 1832 to the design of William Playfair, this is a fine example of Greek Revival style—a massive temple with an Ionic hexastyle portico and much decorated with scrollwork. The museum (admission on application) contains an interesting collection of eighteenth- and nineteenth-century surgical instruments, including bleeding lances and cups, amputation saws, etc., as well as many bottled specimens of diseased human organs. For strong stomachs only.

* Arthur's Seat *(49)*, Holyrood Park

This volcanic hill overlooking the central city from the southeast is 822 feet high. The eastern approach is easily climbed and well worth the effort for the magnificent view from the top. Here, and on the Salisbury Crags immediately to the west, are traces of stone ramparts of probable Dark Age date. Although there is some evidence that the legendary King Arthur may have fought one of his twelve battles in Scotland, there is no proof of his having any personal connection with this particular place. Its name, however, does reflect the persistent legend that King Arthur played a role in the Dark Age history of Scotland.

Restalrig Collegiate Church *(170)*, Restalrig village; n of Regent Road on Restalrig Road, South

This parish kirk was formerly the Collegiate Church of the Holy Trinity and Blessed Virgin Mary, erected in 1457 by King James IV. It was practically destroyed in 1560 as a "monument of idolatrie." Restored in 1837, it has since served as a parish kirk. No admission to church or churchyard except during services.

The Royal Mile
(West to east)

***Edinburgh Castle** *(106, 112, 122, 128, 136, 184, 207, 210, 231, 241, 243, 288, 365)*, Castle Hill

The castle, on its high basaltic rock overlooking the city has served as a fortress, a royal palace, a treasury, a repository of government records, a place of Christian worship, and a prison. Its history is almost inseparable from that of Scotland as a whole. The rock was probably the site of an Iron Age hill-fort and later (seventh century A.D.) of a stronghold of King Edwin of Northumbria. In the eleventh century Malcolm Canmore and his queen, Saint Margaret, lived here. From 1296 to 1313 the castle was held by the English during the first phase of the War of Independence. It was then captured by the Scots through the clever and daring strategem of Sir Thomas Randolph, nephew of Robert Bruce, who led a team of rock-climbers up the north face of Castle Rock, took the garrison by surprise, and then razed the stronghold to prevent its use by Bruce's enemies. The first rebuilding took place in the reign of David II. In 1440 Sir William Crichton murdered the youthful Earl of Douglas and his brother here on the occasion of the infamous "Black Dinner"—an incident that gave the castle a sinister reputation for a long time thereafter. Here Mary, Queen of Scots, gave birth to James VI, later James I of England. Cromwell took the castle in 1651. Bonnie Prince Charlie failed to take it in 1745, though he occupied the City of Edinburgh. Today, there is no grander sight in Britain, especially at night, when floodlights capture the full majesty of this ancient citadel. During the late summer, when thousands gather in Edinburgh for the annual festival, the castle is the scene of the famous Tattoo—a spectacular performance of martial music, marching bands, and gymnastic feats.

From the west end of the Royal Mile, the visitor enters the Esplanade. To the right (north) stands an equestrian statue of Field Marshal Douglas Haig, who commanded the British Expeditionary Forces in the First World War. Ahead looms the towering Half Moon Battery erected by the Regent Morton in the sixteenth century. The path upward passes through the much restored Portcullis Gate, also installed by Morton. It lies beneath Argyll's Tower, so-called because it was allegedly the place of imprisonment of Archibald Campbell, eighth Earl of Argyll, before his execution in 1661. From this point the path steepens and leads up past eighteenth-century buildings to the Royal Scots Museum, a typical collection of regimental memorabilia. Just beyond are the prisons that housed French captives during the Napoleonic Wars. In one of these cells is "Mons Meg," a 6½-ton artillery piece manufactured in the fifteenth century—now painted bright orange, allegedly its original color.

Coming back from the French prisons, the path leads up again to the highest part of the citadel. Here is St. Margaret's Chapel, probably built about 1100. To the southeast of it are the upper parapets of the Regent Morton's Half Moon Battery, which enclose the remains of David's Tower, built by Robert Bruce's son King David II (1329–1371) and largely demolished by Morton in 1573. West of here is the Palace Yard, also called The Close or the Crown Court. On its north side was an eighteenth-century barracks now replaced by the Scottish National War Memorial, designed by Sir Robert Lorimer, dedicated in 1927 and commemorating Scots forces who served in both World Wars. On the east is a building known as the King's Lodging, first constructed in the fifteenth century and restored and "classicized" in the seventeenth by William Wallace, master mason to James VI and Charles I. Within it are (1) the Crown Chamber housing the Regalia and other royal jewels of Scotland; (2) a room containing part of the collection of the Scottish United Services Museum; and (3) Queen Mary's Apartments, where James VI was born in 1566. The south side of the Palace Yard is occupied by the Great Hall, built in the early sixteenth century by James IV and now displaying a fine collection of arms and armor. Finally, on the west side of the yard is an eighteenth-century barracks building, now housing the Scottish United Services Museum, noted for its collection of Highland weapons. The museum of the Royal Scots is maintained separately.

Cannonball House (222), Castle Hill

This is a seventeenth-century house, dating certainly from as early as 1630, with an eighteenth-century three-gabled facade. The name derives from the cannonball embedded in the west gable.

Outlook Tower (222), 549 Castle Hill

The lower stories of this house date from the seventeenth century; the upper portion from 1853, when a *camera obscura* was installed. On clear days the profile of the city can still be viewed on this device—very popular in the nineteenth century.

* Tolbooth St. John's Church (352), Lawnmarket

Designed by James Gillespie Graham and A. W. N. Pugin and built in 1842–1844, this first served as the meeting place of the General Assembly of the Church of Scotland, following the "Disruption" of 1843 and the formation of the Free Church. The foundation stone was laid by Queen Victoria during her first visit to Scotland. On Sunday afternoons the services are in Gaelic, owing to the amalgamation of this congregation with that of Edinburgh's Highland Church.

Mylne's Court (255), 513–523 Lawnmarket

Designed and built by Robert Mylne in 1690, this restored eight-story tenement is the earliest large courtyard residential building on the Royal Mile.

* New College and Assembly Hall (351), Lawnmarket

Overlooking Princes Street Gardens and one of the city's most prominent landmarks, this Tudor-style building, designed by William Playfair and erected in 1846–1850, served originally as a divinity school and meeting place of the General Assembly of the Free Church of Scotland, built soon after the "Disruption" of 1843, and now houses the Church of Scotland General Assembly.

Numbers 3 and 5 James Court (255, 280), 501 Lawnmarket

This restored tenement was built in 1725–1727 by James Brownhill. It was very fashionable in the eighteenth century, and James Boswell lived in one of the flats, where he entertained Dr. Samuel Johnson in 1773.

*** Gladstone's Land (222), 483–489 Lawnmarket; NTS

This is a narrow, two-gabled, six-story tenement, "modernized" by Thomas Gladstanes in 1617–1620. Restored and maintained by the National Trust for Scotland, with its fine original fireplaces and painted walls, this is one of the handsomest urban interiors of any antiquity in Scotland.

* Lady Stair's House (223, 363), 477 Lawnmarket

The seventeenth-century (1622) house was restored and "Gothicized" in the late nineteenth century by George Shaw Aitken. It now serves as a literary museum devoted to Robert Burns, Sir Walter Scott, and Robert Louis Stevenson.

* Bailie MacMorran's House (223), Riddle's Close, 322 Lawnmarket

This very rare sixteenth-century town house, with magnificent interior ceilings, was restored in 1893 and again in 1964.

Numbers 312–318 Lawnmarket (255)

This is a six-story row of tenements built between 1726 and 1752 and partially restored.

Bank of Scotland *(310)*, The Mound

The original building, designed by Robert Reid and erected in 1802–1806, was of conventional neoclassical style, later modified into something approaching the baroque by the addition of the present dome and other decorative features by David Bryce in 1865–1870. Inside is an attractive panelled ceiling.

* **City Chambers** *(310)*, 249 High Street

Built in 1753–1756 to a design of John Adam, this was originally the Royal Exchange, intended as a center for the city's mercantile activities. As such it was a failure and was later converted to house the Edinburgh Council. The council room, installed about 1899, is visitable on request, as is an earlier room dating from about the time of the building's construction.

* **Parliament House** *(232, 233, 310)*, Parliament Square

Built by order of Charles I in 1632–1639, the 122-foot-long hall boasts one of the most magnificent hammerbeam roofs in Britain—dating from the original construction. Not only did the Scottish Parliament meet here (until 1707), but so did "the Tables" in 1637–1638; i.e., the unofficial committees of nobles, lairds, burgesses, and clergy who organized the Presbyterian rebellion against Charles I. In 1807–1810 the parliament building and the **High Court of Judiciary** *(310)*, attached to it were given a neoclassical face-lift at the hands of the architect Robert Reid, thereby substituting a rather uninteresting facade for what appears to have been an attractive example of Scottish vernacular architecture.

*****St. Giles Kirk** *(172, 204, 210, 217, 232, 233, 240, 243, 245, 363)*, High Street

All that remains of the twelfth-century cruciform church, after its burning by King Richard II in 1385, are the four massive central pillars. In the rebuilding that followed, the cruciform ground plan mostly disappeared, as aisles (i.e., chapels) were inserted in the angles of the crossing. After further restoration in the nineteenth century, the exterior of the building was squared off and encased in new masonry. The net effect of all these changes was to reduce the cruciform to a rectangle, which is basically the present shape of the church. In elevation, it is mostly Second Pointed Gothic. The stained glass in the flamboyant traceried windows is, of course, modern. The oldest of the chapels is the Moray Aisle, where lies buried the Regent Moray, Mary, Queen of Scots' half-brother; next the Albany Aisle; then the Preston Aisle, named after Preston of Gorton, who donated the armbone of St. Giles in 1454. The choir was lengthened, the roof heightened, and the upper (clerestory) windows added by Mary of Guelders, widow of James II (d. 1460). In 1467, with papal approval, St. Giles was made a collegiate church by James III. In 1560 John Knox became minister to the Protestant congregation here, and, after his death in 1572, he was buried in the churchyard. Under Charles I, the kirk was elevated to cathedral status with a bishop and rites approximating those of the Church of England. In protest against the introduction of a new prayer book, a riot occurred during a service held on 23 July 1637 after one Jenny Geddes is alleged to have thrown her stool at the dean. This incident sparked the protest movement that led to the signing of the National Covenant and rebellion against the king. During the Civil War, Cromwell's troops (Protestant but not Presbyterian, as the Church of Scotland had become) worshipped here. After the Restoration, the remains of the beheaded Marquis of Montrose were buried in the Chepman Aisle where his effigy now lies. Not long afterward, a similar monument to his mortal enemy, the Marquis of Argyll, was erected on the opposite side of the church. After the battle of Rullion Green in November 1666, about eighty Covenanters were imprisoned in "Haddo's Hole" above the north porch. After the visit of King George IV to Edinburgh in 1822, further reconstruction took place, both inside and out. In 1911 the Thistle Chapel at the southeast corner was completed to a design of Sir Robert Lorimer in a synthetic late medieval style, more English or French than Scottish and ornate to a fault in any case.

Entering the church through the north door from the High Street and moving right (counterclockwise), the visitor first encounters the Argyll monument, then the Albany Aisle with its twentieth-century war memorial, both along the north wall of the nave; next, crossing to the south wall, comes the Moray Aisle with a bas-relief of Robert Louis Stevenson; then, beyond the crossing and south of the choir is the Chepman Aisle, with Montrose's memorial and a copy of the National Covenant; and, before coming back to the starting point, the Thistle Chapel (admission fee).

The best way to view the church and appreciate its majestic quality is to attend Sunday services, which are spectacular. With the great booming organ; the choir garbed in scarlet robes, brilliant against the smoky gray walls of the ancient building; the slow and stately processional; the clergy clothed in colorful vestments—it is altogether a thrilling performance. One hates to think, however, how Jenny Geddes would have reacted to all this Presbyterian pomp.

Tron Kirk (232), High Street

The original kirk was built in 1633 by order of Charles I to a design by John Mylne. It was shortened in 1785–1787 to accommodate the construction of South Bridge, received a new steeple in 1829; and in 1973 had its interior gutted. No longer in use, the church is locked.

Number 199 High Street (255)

This is a recently restored seven-story tenement on the corner of Cockburn Street, originally built in the early eighteenth century.

Adam Bothwell's House (223), Byer's Close, 373 High Street

This tall thin house with its apsidal front was built in the seventeenth century.

Mowbray House (223), 53 High Street

This is a sixteenth-century house built on a still earlier base.

John Knox's House (223), 45 High Street

This sixteenth-century house belonged to James Mossman, goldsmith to Mary, Queen of Scots. That John Knox ever lived here is unlikely, but it now serves, in a manner of speaking, as a museum devoted to the great Reformer.

Tweeddale House (255), 14 High Street

This is a sixteenth-century house with seventeenth-century additions designed by Sir William Bruce, which was reconstructed in the eighteenth for the Marquis of Tweeddale who, said Daniel Defoe in 1724, "has a good City House, with a plantation of lime trees behind it instead of a garden."

Moray House (223, 240, 241), 174 Canongate

Built about 1628, this was at one time the most elegant mansion in Edinburgh, an L-plan three-story building with splendid Renaissance plaster ceilings. Behind its windows in 1650 Archibald Campbell, eighth Marquis of Argyll, watched his enemy, the Marquis of Montrose, being carted to the scaffold. Soon thereafter, Oliver Cromwell chose this house as his headquarters during his occupation of Edinburgh. It now contains the Moray House College of Education.

*Canongate Tolbooth (223, 269), 163 Canongate

This is the Canongate town hall, built in 1592 and restored in 1879. The turreted steeple is typical of Scottish tolbooth architecture. Inside, on the ground floor, is a small and not very impressive museum devoted to the history of the burgh of Canongate. Upstairs is an exhibit of eighteenth- and nineteenth-century tartans.

** Huntly House *(223, 365)*, 146 Canongate

Built about 1570, this fine town house now serves as the local museum of Edinburgh history. Its holdings include prehistoric and Roman finds and much else besides. One room is devoted to mementos of General Douglas Haig.

*** Canongate Kirk *(248)*, Canongate

This is a very handsome cruciform church designed by James Smith by order of King James VII/II when he converted the Holyrood Abbey church into a Roman Catholic Chapel in 1685. The south front has a Flemish (curly) gable and above it a set of antlers meant to commemorate the miracle of the Holy Rood. The interior is aisled, with a shallow apse at the north end—an unusual construction in the seventeenth century, when most new Protestant churches were without either aisles or chancels. In the church-yard, from which there is a splendid view of the Royal High School and Calton Hill, are the graves of a number of distinguished people associated with the Scottish Enlightenment, including Adam Smith, Dugald Stewart, John Ballantyne (Scott's publisher), and Mrs. James M'Lehose (Robert Burns's "Clarinda").

Queensberry House *(255)*, 64 Canongate

This is a large mansion originally designed in 1682 for the first Duke of Queensberry by James Smith, who was also probably responsible for the duke's great country palace of Drumlanrig.

White Horse Close *(280)*, 31 Canongate

This is a picturesque enclave of restored houses around a courtyard that once contained Boyd's Inn, where Dr. Johnson lodged in 1773. The original buildings date to the seventeenth century.

*** Palace of Holyroodhouse *(73, 183, 193, 204, 207, 243, 257)*, e end of Canongate

In plan the palace is a square, built around an inner court, with a wing projecting forward from each corner of the entrance facade facing west. The northwest wing (on the left facing the entrance) is the oldest part of the building. It was begun by King James IV between 1498 and 1501 and completed by his son, James V. The original building was a freestanding rectangular tower four stories high, with circular towers affixed to the corners. The rest of the palace, including the matching southwest tower, was erected by order of King Charles II, beginning in 1671. His architect was Sir William Bruce of Balcaskie; his builder, Robert Mylne, the king's master mason. The facade joining the two towers is neoclassical with a Doric gateway in the center. Behind it is a courtyard, also neoclassical, faced with Doric pilasters surmounted by others of the Ionic and Corinthian orders, in that sequence. This is, in short, a Renaissance palace built upon a sixteenth-century Scottish tower house.

A mandatory guided tour (about forty minutes) leads today's visitor through (1) the State Apartments, still used by the reigning sovereign; (2) the Picture Gallery, with the mostly imaginary likenesses of 111 kings of Scotland from the legendary Fergus to James VII/II, all but the last commissioned by Charles II and painted by Jacob de Wet; (3) the Darnley Rooms on the first floor of the northwest (James IV) Tower; and (4) the Mary Queen of Scots Suite on the floor above. The latter consists of an audience chamber and bedroom, a dressing room, and a supper room. The audience chamber was the scene of some of Queen Mary's unhappy interviews with John Knox in the 1560s. Here also is a brass plate marking the alleged spot where the queen's secretary, David Riccio, was stabbed to death in 1566, although in fact the floor levels in this part of the building were changed when the palace was restored by Charles II. The ceiling in this room may date from the reign of Mary's father, King James V; the embroidered panels on the wall are thought to be the work of the queen and Bess of Hardwick, Countess of Shrewsbury, done while Mary was a prisoner in England.

* Holyrood Abbey *(144, 197, 248)*, e end of Canongate, next to palace

Here is the site of a house of Augustinian canons established by King David I, now much ruined. Nothing is left of the claustral buildings. The western facade is mainly in the Transitional style of the early thirteenth century. The English did considerable damage here in the 1540s, after which a new east window was inserted, probably in its present position at the east end of the nave. The northwest tower was restored in the seventeenth century. The choir to the east of the nave is gone, but the nave itself served as the parish church of the Canongate until James VII made it a Roman Catholic chapel for the order of the Thistle. In the eighteenth century the building collapsed under the weight of a new roof, so that now about all that is left are the walls of the nave.

New Town
(West to east)

St. John's Church *(312)*, Princes Street

An Episcopal church built in 1816 to the design of William Burn, the style is English Perpendicular and the fan vaulting is thought to have been modelled on that of St. George's Chapel, Windsor.

*** National Gallery of Scotland *(124, 306, 350, 364)*, The Mound

A splendid testimonial to the Greek Revival in Edinburgh ("the Athens of the North"), the building was designed by William Playfair and erected between 1850 and 1857. For all its size it is a graceful Greek temple adorned with Ionic columns and topped with a roofline balustrade. It houses a fine representative collection of Continental and English Great Masters, as well as the Trinity Altarpiece, with portraits of James III and Queen Margaret by Hugo van der Goes (1440-1482). Here also is the best single collection of Scottish paintings, including *The Porteous Mob* by James Drummond (1816-1877); *The Hind's Daughter* by Sir James Guthrie (1859-1930); *The Ordination of Elders in a Scottish Kirk* by John Henry Lorimer (1856-1936); *Inverlochy Castle* by Horatio McCulloch (1805-1867); *The Young Fishers* and *The Storm* by William McTaggart (1835-1910); *Master Baby* by Sir William Quiller Orchardson (1832-1910); *Sir John Sinclair of Ulbster, Colonel Alastair Macdonell of Glengarry*, and *Mrs. Scott Moncrieff* by Sir Henry Raeburn (1756-1823) (but probably not *Reverend Robert Walker Skating on Duddingston Loch*, though attributed to Raeburn); *The Painter's Wife* and *Jean-Jacques Rousseau* by Allan Ramsay (1713-1784); and *Pitlessie Fair, The Letter of Introduction, Distraining for Rent*, and *The Irish Whiskey Still* by Sir David Wilkie (1785-1841).

* Royal Scottish Academy *(313)*, Princes Street

This massive Greek temple with fluted Doric columns and a profusion of stone carving was built in 1832-1836 to a design by William Playfair for the joint use of the Royal Society of Edinburgh, the Society of Scottish Antiquaries, the Institution for the Encouragement of the Fine Arts, and the Board of Trustees for Manufactures and Fisheries. It now houses changing exhibitions of contemporary art.

Waverley Station *(340)*, Waverley Bridge

Built in 1874 for the North British Railway, the low facade is undistinguished, and the once attractive neoclassical interior has been unfortunately modernized. The station hotel (the North British) is still grand.

*** Scott Monument *(304)*, Princes Street

Designed by George Meikle Kemp, an obscure "country joiner" who won the commission in an open architectural competition, the monument was completed in 1844, and the statue to Sir Walter Scott by Sir John Steell was installed two years later. A hundred eighty feet in height and crowded with arches, pillars, pilasters, and pinnacles meant to bear some similarity to Melrose Abbey, this fantastic Gothic mélange is a most suitable tribute to the supreme romanticist it commemorates.

** Register House *(311)*, Princes Street

Designed by Robert Adam and his brother James to house the National Records and largely completed between 1784 and 1788, this is considered by some to be the finest neoclassical building in Edinburgh. The ground floor is rusticated, the central block fronted by a Corinthian portico, and the flanking pavilions pierced with fine Venetian windows. The domed interior of the Legal Services Room is most impressive. In the foyer are changing exhibits of Scottish historical documents.

Regent Bridge *(313)*, Waterloo Place

Designed by Archibald Elliot in 1815 as a memorial to those fallen in the Napoleonic Wars, this large semicircular span graced with a Corinthian arch and Ionic screens carries Waterloo Place over Calton Road.

** Calton Old Burial Ground *(313)*, Waterloo Place

In this solemn and dignified burial ground the outstanding monuments are Robert Adam's memorial to David Hume (1777) and the statue of Abraham Lincoln (1893) by George Bissett.

Royal High School *(313)*, Regent Terrace

This huge Doric temple with flanking pavilions was built in 1825–1829 to a design by Thomas Hamilton.

St. Andrew's House *(368)*, Waterloo Place

This heavy and unattractive building houses offices of the Secretary of State for Scotland, moved here shortly before the outbreak of World War II.

*** Calton Hill *(312)*, e of Waterloo Place

On this high hill overlooking the central city from the east is situated the splendid collection of monuments that gave to Edinburgh the claim of being the "Athens of the North." Included are the National Monument (1822) by C. R. Cockerell and William Playfair, an unfinished replica of the Parthenon; Dugald Stewart's Monument (1832) and John Playfair's Monument (1826), both by William Playfair; the Old Observatory (1776) by James Craig, planner of the New Town; the New Observatory (1818) by William Playfair; and Nelson's Monument (1816). The climb to the top is worth it for the view alone.

*** West Register House *(110, 234, 312)*, Charlotte Square

This building, with its conspicuous green-copper dome, was originally St. George's Church, Charlotte Square, designed by Robert Reid and opened for worship in 1814. In 1964 it was converted into a branch repository of the Scottish Record Office. The front hall usually displays an exhibit of documents illustrating Scottish history, all under glass and accompanied by succinct written explanations of the historical significance of each. Among others here are David I's charter to the monks of Melrose; the Treaty of Edinburgh/Northampton; the Declaration of Arbroath; a copy of the National Covenant signed by James Graham, Earl of Montrose, and more than eighty nobles, lairds, and others from the district of Carrick; a copy of the Articles of Union; and the Deed of Demission, signed by Thomas Chalmers and others in 1843 separating themselves from the established Church of Scotland.

An hour spent here will afford the intelligent traveller a good, brief introductory course in the history of Scotland from the twelfth century to the present. Indeed, this is as good a place as any to commence a tour of the country's historic sites.

*** Georgian House *(312)*, 7 Charlotte Square; NTS

This house and those surrounding it on the north side of Charlotte Square were designed by Robert Adam, though mostly unfinished by the time of his death in 1792. Under the care of the National Trust for Scotland (whose headquarters are at No. 5 nearby), the interior has been authentically restored and furnished in the high style of the late eighteenth century and is of surpassing elegance.

*** Church of St. Andrew and St. George *(312, 351)*, George Street

Built in 1784 to the design of Major Andrew Frazier (except for William Sibbald's high steeple added in 1789), this is a fine oval-shaped building with a large Corinthian portico fronting on George Street. Inside, the ceiling plasterwork is reminiscent of that of Robert Adam, though the modern stained glass windows are a mistake. It was here that the great "Disruption" of the Church of Scotland began when Thomas Chalmers walked out of the 1843 meeting of the General Assembly, taking with him about two-fifths of the members to form the Free Church of Scotland.

Royal Bank of Scotland *(307, 311)*, 14 George Street

Built in 1847 to the design of David Rhind, this is a good example of Victorian neoclassicism. The portico is Corinthian, the domed atrium of superimposed orders.

** Royal Bank of Scotland *(349)*, St. Andrew Square

The original neoclassical building here was designed by the London architect Sir William Chambers for Sir Lawrence Dundas and was the first to go up in Edinburgh's New Town (in 1772-1774). The fine cast iron dome with its glazed star-shaped coffers was added in 1858 and endowed the house with one of the most elegant interiors in Edinburgh. Visitors are welcome during banking hours.

Bank of Scotland *(349)*, 38-39 St. Andrew Square

With its splendid facade, rooftop statuary, and free-standing Corinthian columns on the upper stories, this is another example of Victorian neoclassicism. It was originally the British Linen Bank, built in 1851-1852 to the design of David Bryce. The interior contains a noble staircase and soaring granite columns.

Royal College of Physicians *(314)*, Queen Street

Designed by William Hamilton and completed in 1845, this marked the final phase of the Greek Revival in Edinburgh. Its most interesting external feature is the double Corinthian portico adorned with statues of a size disproportionate to the rest of the building.

*** National Museum of Antiquities of Scotland *(7, 9, 19, 28, 40, 43, 45, 47, 51, 54, 58, 63, 66, 211, 220, 234, 263, 273, 350, 359)*, Queen Street

This is the Scottish equivalent of the British Museum and the National Museum of Wales, though not so handsomely arranged as either. Designed by Sir Rowand Anderson, and modelled on the Doge's palace in Venice, this much-pinnacled building of red sandstone (also incorporating the Scottish National Portrait Gallery) was erected in 1886-1890. Its somewhat cluttered exhibits include the following:

Ground Floor: three "Stirling Heads," carved relief portraits from Stirling Castle, including those of King James V and Queen Mary of Guise; a room full of Pictish and Early Christian crosses and grave-slabs, including the Birsay Stone, the Kilchoman Cross, a cast of the Kildalton Cross, and one of "St. Constantine's coffin" from Govan Church; a copy of the National

Covenant; Communion tokens from the seventeenth and eighteenth centu-
ries; a late-sixteenth-century pulpit; a "stool of repentance" from Greyfriars
Kirk, Edinburgh; a seventeenth-century laird's loft ("the Reay Loft") from
the parish kirk of Tongue; a good collection of Scottish swords, spearheads,
Doune pistols, and guns; "the Maiden," a beheading machine made in
Edinburgh and used in the execution of the Regent Morton (1581), the first
Marquis of Argyll (1661), and the ninth Earl of Argyll (1685), among others;
implements used in the woollen textile industry; eighteenth-century costumes and early tartans; eighteenth-century bagpipes; nineteenth-century
golf clubs and golf balls; and the Monymusk Reliquary, thought to have
contained a relic of St. Columba and to have been carried by Abbot Bernard
de Linton at the Battle of Bannockburn (1314).

First Floor: Mesolithic microliths from Morton Farm, Fife, the Oban Caves,
the Oronsay Shell Mounds, and Lealt Bay, Jura; late Neolithic stone balls;
Neolithic, Bronze Age, and Iron Age weapons, implements, and pottery;
Bronze Age and Iron Age personal ornaments of gold and jet; the St.
Ninian's Isle Treasure; Viking burial goods, including brooches, armlets,
and necklaces; Pictish chains; the Torrs Chamfrein; Iron Age cauldrons; the
Traprain Law Treasure, and sundry artifacts from Jarlshof.

Second Floor: Roman finds from the Antonine Wall, Newstead, Birrens, and
other forts; a relief of the Goddess Brigantia; Roman weapons, armor,
implements, and pottery; and the model of a Celtic two-wheeled, horse-
drawn chariot such as might have been used by the native British against the
Roman invaders.

*** Scottish National Portrait Gallery *(306, 350),* Queen Street, adjacent
to the National Museum of Antiquities

Here is an impressive collection of portraits of important historical
personages in Scotland, including James VI; Mary, Queen of Scots (the
Cogham Portrait by Pierre Oudry); Bonnie Prince Charlie; Flora MacDon-
ald; John Maitland, Duke of Lauderdale (by Lely); Charles I (by Mytens);
Charles, Prince of Wales—later Charles II (by William Dobson); Alexander
Henderson (by Van Dyck); James Graham, Marquis of Montrose; John
Campbell, fourth Duke of Argyll (by Gainsborough); James VII/II (by
Lely); King George IV (by David Wilkie); David Hume (by Allan Ramsay);
Professor Dugald Stewart and William Creech (by Sir Henry Raeburn);
James Keir Hardie; Ramsay MacDonald; and W. E. Gladstone. There is also
a fascinating contemporary painting of the execution of Charles I, allegedly
by an eyewitness.

Among the Scottish artists represented here are Sir Henry Raeburn, Allan

Ramsay, Gavin Hamilton, and Sir James Guthrie. Guthrie's portraits of the *Statesmen of the Great War*, including Lloyd George, Winston Churchill, Arthur Balfour, Viscount Grey, Herbert Henry Asquith, Bonar Law, and Admiral David Beatty, hang in a separate room.

* St. Paul's and St. George's Episcopal Church *(311)*, York Place and Broughton Street

The nave of this church was built in 1816-1818 to the design of Archibald Elliot, modelled on King's College Chapel, Cambridge. The chancel was done by Kinnear and Peddie in 1892.

St. Stephen's Church *(313)*, St. Vincent's Street; closed except for services

This huge octagonal church, with its oversized arched entry and tall clock tower, was built in 1827 to the design of William Playfair.

Edinburgh Academy *(313)*, Henderson Row

Designed by William Burn and built in 1823-1836, the main building is an austere Doric temple of one story only.

Outer Edinburgh

* Dean Bridge *(317)*, Queensferry Road

Built by Thomas Telford in 1829-1831, this splendid quadruple-arched span carries the road to Queensferry high over the Water of Leith and offers a good view of the mills and cottages of Dean Village below.

** St. Mary's Episcopal Cathedral *(354)*, Palmerston Place

The greatest example of the Victorian Gothic Revival in Edinburgh, this enormous church was built in 1873-1879 to the design of Sir George Gilbert Scott. The style is Early English, modelled somewhat on Ely Cathedral in Cambridgeshire.

** Scottish National Gallery of Modern Art *(313)*, Belford Road

Designed by William Burn and built in 1828, this was originally John Watson's School. Recently it has been restored and put to use as a gallery of modern art with a large and diverse collection of twentieth-century paintings and sculpture, Continental, British, and American.

* Donaldson's School *(350)*, Haymarket Terrace

Built in 1842-1854 and one of the largest public buildings erected in

Edinburgh in the nineteenth century, this was originally a school for the deaf. The architect was William Playfair, and the style is English Tudor or Jacobean—a departure from the neoclassicism of most of his contributions to Edinburgh's cityscape.

*** Royal Botanic Garden *(298, 336)*, Inverleith Row

This is one of the great botanical gardens of the world and should not be missed by any traveller with even a modicum of interest in horticulture. It was moved here (its third site) after 1820 from Leith Walk, and subsequently much expanded. The small octagonal Palm House, with its charming cast iron spiral staircases, was installed in 1834; the larger iron and glass Palm House in 1858; and the very modern glasshouses in 1965. Scattered throughout the grounds are a number of fine specialized gardens: heather garden, rock garden, woodland garden, peat garden, demonstration garden, etc. The herbaceous borders are outstanding.

* Barclay Church *(352)*, Bruntsfield Place

Designed by the English architect F. T. Pilkington and built for a Free Church congregation in 1864, this is one of the best examples in Edinburgh of the Victorian Gothic Revival.

Environs

*Duddingston Kirk *(220)*, Old Church Lane, Duddingston Village; key at manse next door

The oldest parts of this small kirk are Norman, but the style in general is Gothic, though frequently rebuilt over the years. At the time of the Restoration, the interior was much altered and a pulpit installed against the south wall, as it still is. At the entrance to the churchyard is an iron collar chained to the wall. This is a jougs collar used in the sixteenth and seventeenth centuries for restraining and publicly humiliating members of the community judged guilty of adultery and like offenses against the laws of God.

*** Craigmillar Castle *(123, 208)*, 3½ m. se of city center; Craigmillar Castle Road, n of A 68 and s of A 6095 (66 NT 385 710); AM

The original and most substantial part of this large ruined castle on the outskirts of Edinburgh is the L-plan tower-house built by Sir Simon Preston in 1374. The main rectangular block (now facing south toward the A 68) consists of a vaulted basement, a first floor great hall, and a loft beneath the hall vault. Entrance to both tower and main block was originally by way of a doorway in the reentrant angle of the L. In the jamb projecting slightly forward from the east end of the main block is the kitchen on the first floor with private rooms above. The kitchen was later converted into a living room, and it is thought that this was the apartment occupied by Mary, Queen of Scots, in November 1566 when she sojourned briefly at Craigmillar after a serious illness and where she learned of the "Craigmillar Bond" among her chief advisors to get rid of her husband, Lord Darnley.

In 1427 a massive quadrangular curtain wall was added to enclose the tower-house on all sides but the south. This was crenellated and machicolated and guarded by round towers on each corner, that on the northeast being pierced with inverted keyhole loops for cannon and still larger gunports higher up. This was possibly the first artillery battery to be seen in Scotland. Wall and towers both stand to their original height.

In 1544 the Earl of Hertford burned the castle. Subsequently, a range of buildings (now roofless and dilapidated) was built against the east curtain wall within the courtyard. About the same time, an outer curtain was installed—again on all sides but the south. It was not crenellated and was provided with only one mural tower, later converted into a dovecote. This new wall enclosed a sixteenth-century chapel, still partially standing. In 1661 a new owner, Sir John Gilmour, added another range of buildings (now ruined) against the inside of the western inner courtyard wall, thus giving the castle its final form as seen today.

Craigmillar is a very complex structure, likely to baffle today's visitors, partly because they must enter the premises not by way of the original front doorway but rather by entrances through the two curtain walls on the back (north) side of the building. Once past the second of these doorways, visitors find themselves in the inner courtyard. To the right is the west range built by Sir John Gilmour in the seventeenth century; to the left are the remains of the east range constructed after Hertford's destruction in 1544. Ahead lies the main block of the fourteenth-century tower-house with its great hall distinguished by an enormous hooded fireplace at the west end. From the opposite (southeast) corner, a doorway leads into Queen Mary's Room on the first floor of the jamb of the L. From here a circular stone staircase leads to the roof, from which can be obtained a marvelous view of Edinburgh, Arthur's Seat, and the Firth of Forth in the distance.

* Lauriston Castle *(309)*, Cramond Road North, 1 m. n of A 90

To the late sixteenth-century T-plan tower-house, erected by Sir Archibald Napier, the architect William Burn added (1827) a large Jacobean range on the north, only slightly modified in the late nineteenth century. Between 1903 and 1919, the then owner, William Robert Reid, filled the house with fine furniture and decorated it in the high Edwardian fashion for which it is now much admired. Mandatory guided tours of about forty-five minutes.

* Corstorphine Collegiate Church *(170)*, 4 m. w of city center; s of A 90
in Corstorphine village; open only Wednesday mornings and during
services

This is a restored fifteenth-century collegiate church with a square tower
and an unusual proliferation of chapels and aisles. It now serves as the
parish kirk.

* Cramond Roman Fort *(46)*, in Cramond village; 6 m. w of city center, 1
m. n of A 90 from Braepark (65 NT 195 770)

First established about A.D. 142 as an adjunct to the Antonine Wall, the
fort here was rebuilt in the early third century to be used as a supply depot
for the campaigns of the Emperor Severus in Scotland. Although excavations are still in progress, about all that can be seen today of the original fort
is a single stretch of wall next to the parish church. The outlines of the other
buildings have been marked out on the ground with stones, so that the
visitor can get a clear picture of the ground plan of the Severan fort.

The village of Cramond, which lies on the banks of the little Almond
River where it flows into the Forth, is one of the prettiest in Scotland and is
well worth a visit for its own sake.

Loanhead (Lothian)

*** Rosslyn Chapel *(172)*, 2½ m. s; e of Roslin village at end of B 7006

Founded as a collegiate church in 1446 by Sir William Sinclair, third Earl
of Orkney, but never completed beyond the existing choir and lady chapel,
this is the most ornate of Scotland's surviving medieval houses of worship.
The window tracery is more French flamboyant than anything else, but the
very intricate stone carving inside and out is unique in Scotland and not
traceable to any particular architectural influence. Within this crowded
scene of lapidary virtuosity, the most elaborate single feature is the
"Apprentice Pillar," so named by Sir Walter Scott after a fictitous episode
involving the murder of the youthful carver by his master in a fit of jealousy
over the superiority of the former's workmanship. Actually, it was originally called the "Prince's Pillar" after the Earl of Orkney, who preferred to
be called "prince."

This little church is an architectural *tour de force* of sorts, though
whether it is more grotesque than charming is a matter for argument.
Currently, it serves a congregation of the Scottish Episcopal Church.

MUSSELBURGH (LOTHIAN)

* **Prestongrange Mining Museum** *(336)*, 1 m. e; s of B 1348

On the site of a defunct coal mine, the former colliery generating-station houses a large collection of mining equipment and machinery. The chief feature of this place is the Cornish beam engine, installed in 1874, for pumping water out of the mines below. It is the only one of its kind left in Scotland. Formerly steam-powered, the engine (minus pump) now runs by electricity. Demonstrations are frequent, and the custodian is very knowledgeable about mining history.

East Lothian

DIRLETON (LOTHIAN)

*** **Dirleton Castle** *(97, 103, 241)*, village center, s of A 198 (66 NT 516 839); AM

These ruins rise from a rocky knoll next to a charming garden in one of Scotland's prettiest villages. The original stone castle, including the three high towers at the southwest corner, was built in the third quarter of the thirteenth century, probably by Alexander de Vaux. During the War of Independence, it was captured for King Edward I by Anthony de Bec, Bishop of Durham, and garrisoned by the English until 1311, when it fell to the Scots and was probably dismantled by order of King Robert I. By the mid-fourteenth-century, the castle was in the hands of the Halyburton family, who were responsible for much restoration and reconstruction. In 1515 it passed to the Ruthvens, who later became Earls of Gowrie. After an alleged attempt against the life of King James VI (the "Gowrie Conspiracy"), when the third Earl of Gowrie and his brother were killed, their properties were forfeited, and Dirleton was given by the Crown to Sir Thomas Erskine. During the Cromwellian occupation of Scotland, the castle was captured from Royalist "moss troopers" and used as a hospital for Commonwealth soldiers.

The ground plan here is roughly rectangular, except for the south side, which is a sort of triangle with its apex at the southwest corner marked by the three thirteenth-century towers. These are almost the sole remains of the original courtyard castle, which was surrounded by curtain walls with an additional round tower at both the southeast and northeast corners. (Only the bases of these remain.) The main entrance, marked by two massive jambs projecting outward from the south curtain wall, is approached by a bridge over a dry ditch (formerly by a drawbridge). The entry is barrel-vaulted with a round *meurtrière* in its ceiling. To the west (left) of the entry is the great round *donjon* to which are connected, in a sort of cluster, a rectangular tower and still another round tower—all belonging to the original castle. Back of them is the Ruthven Lodging, a sixteenth-century building three stories high. All the construction to the east and north (right) of the entry was part of the Halyburton restoration of the fifteenth century. Especially noteworthy are the chapel on the ground floor at the extreme northeast corner and the now roofless great hall, which takes up the entire east side of the castle. The north and west curtain walls, which originally enclosed the other two sides of the courtyard, have all but disappeared. To the north is a sixteenth-century dovecote in the shape of a beehive.

DUNBAR (LOTHIAN)

Dunbar Castle *(90, 111, 207, 208, 209)*, harbor front

Here are the very fragmentary red sandstone remains of a once formidable thirteenth-century castle that featured prominently in medieval Scottish history and later. In 1296 it was besieged and captured by King Edward I. In 1339 it was the scene of Black Agnes's successful defiance of the English army. At the invitation of the second Earl of Arran (Governor of Scotland during the minority of Mary, Queen of Scots), a French army occupied it briefly; it survived the town of Dunbar's sacking by the Earl of Hertford in 1544; under the custody of the fourth Earl of Bothwell, it became a refuge for Mary, Queen of Scots, both before and after her marrriage to the earl; and was destroyed by the Regent Moray after the Battle of Carberry in 1567.

* Dunbar Parish Kirk *(217, 262)*, town center

The most interesting feature here is the funereal monument of white, black, and various-colored marbles erected to George Home, first Earl of Dunbar, in 1611. It shows the earl garbed in his Garter robe, kneeling at prayer under a classical arch embellished by knights in armor and allegorical figures of Justice and Peace.

The Chesters *(30)*, 4 m. sw; 1½ m. sw of Spott (67 NT 660 739); AM

This is perhaps the best preserved of Iron Age hill-forts in southern Scotland, though not easy to find. Here, two massive earthen ramparts, as high as seven feet and bordered by exterior ditches, surround an enclosure measuring about 350 feet in diameter. The original entrance can be observed in the gap in the embankments on the east-southeast side.

* Preston Mill *(293)*, 5½ m. w; in East Linton, n of A 1; NTS

With few interruptions, this water mill has been in continuous operation since the seventeenth century. Very picturesque with its kiln, conical roof, wind vane, and eighteenth-century iron wheel (probably cast at the Carron foundry near Falkirk), this is a unique survivor of what was once a common sight in Lowland Scotland.

*** Tyninghame House Gardens *(261, 295)*, 6 m. w; e of A 198

Though Tyninghame House (restored by William Burn in 1829) is off bounds to the public, the extensive gardens, representing several centuries of horticultural endeavor, are open. The oldest feature on the grounds is the ruined Norman church of St. Baldred, which is approached by an avenue of lime trees installed by Thomas Hamilton, sixth Earl of Haddington, in the early eighteenth century. A pioneer arboriculturist in a country then noted for its treelessness, Haddington also planted the Long Avenue to the north of the house and extensive woods lying to the north and east. Antedating these is a charming walled garden with fine yew hedges dating from about 1660. Near the house is a parterre installed in 1818, as well as a rose garden and herbaceous borders.

** Collegiate Church of St. Mary, Dunglass *(169)*, 7 m. se; s of A 1, 1 m. n of Cockburnspath through Bilsdean village to private estate road (67 NT 767 719); AM

Here is the well-preserved, roofed, though windowless and doorless, ruin of a collegiate church built by Sir Alexander Hume in 1450. It is constructed of a pinkish stone, is cruciform in shape, has a square (now roofless) tower over the central crossing, high pointed barrel vaults, and Second Pointed windows with some tracery still extant. In the choir is a portion of the circular basin of the piscina, well-preserved triple sedilia, and an aumbry. There is a small sacristy north of the choir. Signs posted by the Scottish Development Department are very helpful.

* St. Mary's, Whitekirk *(164, 182)*, 6½ m. nw; w of A 198

This parish kirk is a much restored version of a late medieval church, once famous for its holy well visited by many pilgrims, including King James IV. Part of the west end of the nave dates from the mid-fourteenth century; the choir from about 1439. In 1914 the church was burned by suffragettes, and marks of the fire are still visible on the vaulted ceiling on the north side of the choir. In general appearance, the style is Second Pointed.

** Hailes Castle *(97, 268)*, 9 m. w; 1½ m. sw of A 1 from East Linton (67 NT 575 758); AM

The earliest part of this much ruined castle was built in the thirteenth century, probably by an Earl of Dunbar and March, and enlarged late in the fourteenth by the Hepburns, who owned it for two hundred years until 1567. Though not involved in the War of Independence, it was in later years not infrequently besieged by invading English armies or by Scottish rivals of the Hepburns. The last of that name to own it was James, fourth Earl of Bothwell and third husband of Mary, Queen of Scots. The queen stayed here at least once—in April 1567 en route to join Bothwell at nearby Dunbar. Cromwell dismantled the castle in 1650.

The remaining parts of the thirteenth-century construction consist of the lower courses of the central rectangular keep, the curtain wall extending eastward from it, and the vaulted stairway leading to a well. A second tower to the west is of fourteenth-century date. The building between the towers was put up in the fourteenth and fifteenth centuries and has a vaulted bakehouse in the basement and a chapel with a piscina on the floor above. Each of the towers has a pit prison, now accessible by ladder leading down from hinged hatch covers.

Traprain Law *(43)*, 10 m. w; 2 m. s of East Linton (67 NT 581 746)

This huge isolated hill rising abruptly from the East Lothian plain was the site of occupation and fortification from the Bronze Age well into the Dark Age. In Roman times it was the capital, or *oppidum* of the *Votadini*, whom the Romans pacified and to some extent civilized. The northern side of the hill has been eaten away by quarrying, and there is no clearly marked path leading to the summit, which is on private property. About all that can be seen there in any case is a turf wall, twelve feet wide and faced on either side with stone. This is situated on the western slope of the hill and was probably built late in the fourth century, just before the final collapse of Roman authority in North Britain.

HADDINGTON (LOTHIAN)

** St. Mary's, Haddington *(173)*, town center, near Nungate Bridge

The fabric of this large cruciform church was built in the late fourteenth and early fifteenth centuries. The square tower over the crossing, once known as the "Lamp of Lothian," originally supported an open-crown spire, similar to that of St. Giles, Edinburgh. In 1548 Haddington was captured by an English army that held it against Scots and French for eighteen months, during which time the church suffered great damage, much of which was not repaired, although the west end came to be used as a parish kirk after the Reformation. In 1811 and again in 1892 the nave was radically altered; choir, tower, and transepts have been restored since 1973, so that the entire church is now be used for Church of Scotland services, as well as for concerts. A small vestry projects north from the choir. It was restored in the sixteenth or seventeenth century as a burial vault for the Maitland family and, about 1670, was furnished with an imposing memorial monument to the Duke of Lauderdale (hence the name "Lauderdale Aisle"). In the adjoining vault are buried, among others, William Maitland of Lethington, John Maitland of Thirlestane, and the donor himself, John Maitland, Duke of Lauderdale.

*** Lennoxlove House *(206, 209, 370)*, 1½ m. s; e of A 6137

Originally called Lethington by the Maitland family, who built it about 1345, the oldest part of this stately home is an L-plan tower-house. Here, in the sixteenth century, lived William Maitland of Lethington, Secretary of State to Mary, Queen of Scots. The house was enlarged in the seventeenth century by John Maitland, Duke of Lauderdale, Secretary of State for Scotland under Charles II. From him it passed to Frances Stewart, Duchess of Lennox, one of that king's many favorites and the model for the figure of "Britannia" on British coins. It was she who was responsible for having the place renamed Lennoxlove after her deceased husband. After an occupancy of more than two hundred years by the Blantyre Stewarts and their descendants, Lennoxlove was sold to the fourteenth Duke of Hamilton, and many of its present contents came from the now defunct Hamilton Palace.

A tour through the house begins in the seventeenth-century wing built by the Duke of Lauderdale. The interior here is mostly of eighteenth-century provenance. Portraits in the Blue Room include three by Sir Henry Raeburn. In the Petit Point Room is an inlaid tortoiseshell writing cabinet, the gift of Charles II to the Duchess of Lennox—"La Belle Stewart." Portraits by Van Dyck and Lely grace the Yellow Room. Passage into the anteroom leads to the original tower house. On the wall here is the map carried by Rudolph Hess on his 1941 flight to Lanarkshire to establish personal contact with the fourteenth Duke of Hamilton. In the barrel-vaulted great hall can be seen smoke holes above what was originally a mid-chamber hearth. Sir Robert Lorimer restored this room. Here also is a death mask of Mary, Queen of Scots, and a silver casket said to have contained the original "Casket letters" allegedly written by the queen to the Earl of Bothwell.

*** Yester Kirk *(263, 299)*, 4 m. s in Gifford village center

This is a fine little T-plan kirk built in 1708–1710, possibly to a design of James Smith, who was the architect for the Marquis of Tweeddale's nearby Yester House. In the short upright arm of the T, facing the pulpit in the center of the long south side of the kirk, is the Tweeddale gallery entered by a separate stairway from the outside. Near the foot of the stairway is the grave of James Witherspoon, the first minister to occupy this pulpit and father of John Witherspoon, President of the College of New Jersey at Princeton, first Moderator of the Presbyterian Church of America, and signer of the American Declaration of Independence in 1776. His birthplace was in the long-gone manse across the road, now commemorated by a bronze plaque attached to the garden wall.

** Pencaitland Church *(263)*, 6 m. sw, in Easter Pencaitland, s of A 6093, w of junction with B 6355

This is an interesting T-plan kirk, with the northeast angle of the T occupied by the chantry (the Winton Aisle) of the medieval church that stood on this spot before the existing sixteenth- to seventeenth-century building was erected on earlier foundations. The seventeenth-century pulpit (with baptismal basin bracketed to it) stands in the center of the south wall facing the Saltoun Aisle (the upright of the T), while at the west end is a gallery entered by a stairway from the outside. Next to it, secured to the church wall, is the chain to which was attached a set of jougs; i.e., an iron collar formerly used to bind wrongdoers and expose them to public humiliation, much in the manner of village stocks in Puritan New England.

NORTH BERWICK (LOTHIAN)

*** Tantallon Castle *(114, 122, 123, 124, 191, 241)*, 3 m. e; e of A 198 (67 NT 596 850); AM

The first known occupant, and probable builder, of this great red sandstone stronghold (now ruined) was William, first Earl of Douglas, whose bastard son was George, first of the "Red Douglas" Earls of Angus. From the latter, ownership descended to Archibald, fifth Earl of Angus, known as "Bell-the-Cat" for his alleged part in the hanging of King James III's favorites at Lauder Brig in 1482. Angus was besieged in Tantallon in 1491 by King James IV, but later he returned to royal favor and became Chancellor of Scotland. His grandson, Archibald, the sixth earl, married Margaret Tudor, sister of King Henry VIII and widow of James IV. Because of Archibald's treasonous dealings with the English, James V laid siege to the castle in 1528 and a year later, after a successful siege by the fourth Earl of Argyll, took possession of it. For most of the following two reigns, Tantallon was in the hands of the Crown. It was besieged and captured by General Monk in 1651. Thereafter, it was allowed to fall into decay.

The castle is situated on a promontory jutting into the Firth of Forth. Its first line of defense was a great dry ditch dug across the base of the promontory. At the east end of the ditch can be seen the scant remains of the sixteenth-century gate, flanked by walls pierced with widemouthed gun-ports. Ahead is still another ditch. Across it lies the great gatehouse or Mid Tower, flanked by high curtain walls stretching across the promontory and terminating in a tower at each end—all built in the fourteenth century. In the sixteenth the Mid Tower was reinforced by foreworks protruding out from the main entry. The two end towers are now in a very dilapidated state, but the Mid Tower and the crenellated curtain walls on either side of it still stand to their original height. Behind the west (Douglas) tower lies a fairly substantial range of building. No curtain walls were required to guard the north and east sides of the courtyard from which precipitous cliffs drop down to the sea. The foundations of a seagate that once led down to the shore remain standing.

Not far offshore lies the Bass Rock, a high volcanic island peak, site of an Early Christian hermitage, a medieval fortress, a prison for Covenanters, and a Jacobite stronghold.

PRESTONPANS (LOTHIAN)

** Seton Collegiate Church *(170)*, 2½ m. e; n of A 198 (66 NT 418 751); AM

Originally intended as a cruciform church, the nave here was never finished, so that this fifteenth-century Second Pointed building consists of an octagonal or "broach" tower (rare in Scotland) covering the area meant to be the crossing, north and south transepts, and a choir with a small sacristy leading from it. Construction was commenced by George, third Lord Seton, who died about 1478; continued by his son, the fourth lord until his death in 1508, then by the fifth lord who fell at Flodden (1513); and finished, though not completed, by his widow. The church was made collegiate in 1492 and endowed to support a provost, six prebendaries, two singing boys, and a clerk. Today it is a well-preserved and roofed ruin maintained by the Scottish Development Department. Noteworthy is the monumental stone carving inside: in the north transept an ornate seven-teenth-century Renaissance mural monument of James Ogilvie of Birnes, who married into the Seton family; in the south transept another of the same vintage of James, Earl of Perth, likewise a Seton in-law; in the choir a tomb recess contains the recumbent effigies of a plate-armored knight and his lady; and in the sacristy a large memorial slab commemorates George, seventh Lord Seton, who died in 1585. Piscinas are scattered here and there, and in the choir are fine triple sedilia. The flamboyant window tracery is especially good. Outside, under a roof, are some well-carved coats of arms from the extinct Seton Palace. To the southwest of the church lie founda-tions and lower courses of the collegiate lodgings.

WEST CENTRAL SCOTLAND
Argyll

BALLACHULISH (HIGHLAND)

Glen Coe and North Lorn Folk Museum *(251)*, 1½ m. e, in Glen Coe village; n of A 82

This is a small unkempt museum containing a few mementos of the MacDonalds of Glen Coe and other Jacobite relics.

Glen Coe Visitor Centre *(251)*, 3 m. e; n of A 82

Here are a few Jacobite mementos and some explanatory posters concerning the nearby massacre of 1692, but most of the space is devoted to a souvenir shop.

*** Tioram Castle *(99)*, 34 m. w; 6 m. n of A 861 from north end of Shiel Bridge, on road signposted to Dorlin (40 NM 663 725); accessible only at low tide; inquire locally for tidal information.

Located near the eastern neck of the Ardnamurchan Peninsula, this splendid ruin rises dramatically from a rocky outcrop at the seaward end of a long spit jutting into Loch Moidart. It was built either in the reign of Alexander II (1214–1249) or of Alexander III (1249–1286), possibly in connection with those kings' efforts to pacify the western Highlands. At an early date, however, it came into the possession of the MacDonald chiefs of Clan Ranald.

Of typical western Highland construction, the castle is polygonal in shape, with walls eight feet thick and thirty feet high, and on the seaward side, rising sheer from the edge of the rock, it reaches a height of sixty feet above the water. The wall-head is crenellated, and below the crenellations appear projecting water spouts and putlog holes for timbers to support hoardings. The entrance is on the north side: crudely arched and furnished with stone corbels to support a *bretasche*. Inside the courtyard is a massive, rectangular four-story keep, also with putlog holes for hoardings. Against the south wall is a high tower with corbelled angle turrets, erected about 1600.

As elsewhere in the Highlands, the surrounding scenery is breathtaking.

*Mingary Castle *(98, 185, 237)*, 38 m. w; ½ m. s of B 8007 from ½ m. e of Kilchoan village (47 NM 502 631)

Situated near the west end of the Ardnamurchan Peninsula overlooking the Sound of Mull, this is a typical western Highland courtyard castle, polygonal in plan, with walls six feet thick and thirty to forty feet high. Its history is uncertain, but Stewart Cruden, Scotland's leading expert on castles, thinks it was probably built either after Alexander II's reduction of Argyll in 1222 or after the Battle of Largs in 1263 and the Treaty of Perth (1266).

In any case, by the early fourteenth century it was in the possession of the MacDonald Lords of the Isles. After the forfeiture of the fourth lord by King James IV in 1493, the castle became Crown property, and it was here that he received the submission of the leading island chiefs of the former lordship. In 1644 it was seized by the Irish ally of the Marquis of Montrose and used as a base for terrorizing the Campbells and other dependents of the Marquis of Argyll.

The high curtain wall rises from the edge of the rocks on the seaward side and is cut off from the landward approach by a dry ditch. The landward (northwest) entrance was covered by a machicolated timber *bretasche*, whose supporting stone corbels are still in position. The entrance passage is nine feet in length. The parapet is crenellated, and beneath it on the outside of the curtain are putlog holes for hoardings. There is a second entrance on the seaward (south) side with a set of rock-cut steps leading from it down to the water. The building within the courtyard is an eighteenth-century barracks that probably replaced a medieval hall. The corner turrets are also a later addition.

Since it is remote and not easy to reach, visitors will be disappointed after a long and difficult drive to find the castle's interior closed to the public. The view of the Sound of Mull, however, is rewarding.

CAMPBELTOWN (STRATHCLYDE)

* Campbeltown Museum *(8)*, Hall Street

Located within the town library, the museum houses a good collection of Mesolithic microliths; Neolithic, Bronze Age, and Iron Age weapons, implements, and pottery; finds from Kildonan Dun; a fine jet necklace said to be "one of the most complete prehistoric jet necklaces found in Britain"; and various items of local history, including a well-preserved *cas chrom*, a primitive foot plow in common use in the Scottish Highlands until as late as the nineteenth century.

* Campbeltown Cross *(166)*, Old Quay Head, town center

Dedicated to Andrew MacEachern, priest of Kilchoman, this late-fifteenth-century disc-headed sculptured cross stands about ten feet high overlooking the town park and harbor. It is beautifully carved in the western Highland manner with figures of St. Mary and St. John, St. Michael slaying the dragon, various mythical animals, and typical foliation.

Kildonan Dun *(33)*, 6½ m. ne; e of B 842 (68 NR 780 277)

Here is the fairly well-preserved ruin of an Iron Age dun overlooking Kilbrannan Sound. It is oval in shape with such typical features as door-checks, bar-hole and socket, and mural rooms.

Saddell Abbey *(148, 166)*, 8 m. n; w of A 842 (68 NR 784 320)

Very little still stands of this, the only Cistercian monastery in the western Highlands, probably founded by Somerled or his son Reginald. Indeed, the site would not be worth inspecting but for the presence here of a good collection of sculptured stones housed under a roof. These include the lower part of a fifteenth-century cross, three knightly effigies with fourteenth-century armor, two effigies of ecclesiastics, and miscellaneous grave-slabs carved with swords and galleys.

COLONSAY (STRATHCLYDE)

(Access by ferry from Oban, three times weekly; 2½ hours)

Oronsay Priory *(151, 166)*, accessible at low tide only from southern tip of island

Here are the ruins of an Augustinian house, probably founded in the early or mid fourteenth century by John, first Lord of the Isles. The walls stand mostly as high as the roof, and there are lancet windows at the east end of the priory church. The most significant feature of this site, however, is not the priory, but the fine collection of western Highland sculptured stones, including a splendid standing cross, two other restored crosses, and some thirty effigies, grave-slabs, and cross fragments situated in a building known as the prior's house. It is most unfortunate that this place is so hard to get to from the mainland—not because of the waters that separate Oronsay from Colonsay, but because of the infrequency of ferries from Oban to the latter.

GARVELLACH ISLANDS (STRATHCLYDE)

(Access by boat from Easdale on Seil [tel: Balvicar 317] or from Cullipool on Luing [tel: Luing 282])

Eilach-an-Naoimh Monastery *(62)* (55 NM 640 097); AM

On this little island, the southernmost of the Garvellachs in the mouth of the Firth of Lorne, are well-preserved remains of an Early Christian monastery, consisting of a chapel, three round dry-stone beehive cells, and a grave called Eithne's Grave after St. Columba's mother. (The saint himself is alleged to have visited here frequently.) The beehive cells are similar to those more commonly found in Ireland.

INVERARAY (STRATHCLYDE)

*** Inveraray Castle *(187, 255, 259, 267, 281, 306)*, ½ m. n of town center

Archibald Campbell, third Duke of Argyll, began construction of this elegant stately home in 1744. Interrupted by the Jacobite uprising of the following year, work on the house was not completed until 1768, seven years after the death of the builder. Under the direction of William Adam and his sons Robert and John, Roger Morris was the original architect. He produced a Gothic Revival mansion, much modified after a fire in 1877 when George Campbell, the eighth Duke, commissioned Anthony Salvin to raise the roof, add gabled dormers, and cap the corner towers with conical turrets. The interior arrangements are mostly the handiwork of John Campbell, fifth Duke of Argyll, employing Robert Mylne as decorator. It is this duke (who, incidentally, was host to Johnson and Boswell in 1773) who was responsible for the exquisite eighteenth-century French furniture, Beauvais tapestries, and wall paintings by Girard and Guingard. Fortunately, these elegant trappings were not destroyed by a second fire at Inveraray (in 1976), and the interior has been restored with meticulous fidelity to the original.

Family portraits include those by Allan Ramsay, Thomas Gainsborough, and Sir John Medina. The Victorian room reflects the taste of Queen Victoria's daughter, Princess Louise, wife of John Campbell, the ninth duke. On the walls of the Armoury Hall is a good collection of sixteenth- to nineteenth-century weapons, and among the Highland military accoutrements on display are the sporran, belt, and dirk handle of Rob Roy.

Travellers lucky enough to visit here in the third week in July can also take in the annual Inveraray Highland Games, a full day devoted to piping contests, caber-tossing, hammer-throwing, Highland dances, etc. This too is the occasion for the annual Campbell Clan Gathering hosted by the present Duke of Argyll.

Old Town House *(285)*, town center

Now the office of the local authority, this was originally the Custom House, built by Robert Mylne in 1753.

* Inveraray Parish Kirk *(285)*, town center

Built by Robert Mylne in 1794–1806, this church features a central wall that divides the interior, thus splitting it into a Gaelic-speaking church and an English-speaking church. The former is now used as an arts and crafts center; the latter still serves its original purpose and has a laird's loft for the use of the Duke of Argyll and his family. Unfortunately, the original steeple was removed during the Second World War.

*** Inveraray War Memorial *(366)*, town park

Silhouetted against Loch Fyne stands this life-sized statue of a kilted Scottish soldier dressed in the uniform of the First World War. It is representative of the countless other monuments in the towns and villages of Scotland dedicated to the men killed in 1914–1918. Below it are listed the names of about seventy such casualties from this single and not very populous small parish. Underneath are eleven additional names of those killed in the Second World War.

*** Auchindrain Museum of Country Life *(282, 285)*, 5½ m. sw; e of A 83

This is an open-air museum consisting of a central building with excellent displays illustrating the history of Scottish agriculture, with special reference to the township of Auchindrain, which maintained the run-rig system of communal tillage and pasture until well into the nineteenth century. Adjacent are partially restored tenants' houses and out-buildings dating from the late eighteenth and the nineteenth centuries. As of 1985, restoration of the township is incomplete, but enough has been accomplished to give the visitor a unique view of the looks of a Highland clachan before improvement had consolidated the scattered holdings of the tenants or before clearance had eliminated them altogether. To date, the restorers have resisted the temptation to prettify this place, and, as it stands, it conveys an authentic impression of the poverty and squalor typical of these communities.

** Kilchurn Castle *(132, 187)*, 13 m. n; nw of junction of A 85 and A 819; 1 m. w of Dalmally (50 NN 133 276); AM

Standing at the north end of Loch Awe is the romantic ruin of a fifteenth-century rectangular tower-house built by Colin Campbell of Glenorchy and enlarged in 1693 by John Campbell, first Earl of Breadalbane, who added a courtyard enclosed by curtain walls with round corner towers pierced with gunports. Following the rebellion of 1745, the castle served as headquarters for government troops.

ISLE OF IONA (STRATHCLYDE)

(Access by passenger ferry, frequently from Fionnphort, Mull, and twice weekly from Oban)

*** **Iona Abbey** *(57, 63, 107, 137, 148, 159, 166, 281, 287),* n of pier

This is the site of St. Columba's famous monastery, founded in 563. Coming up the road leading north from the ferry landing, the first building encountered is the substantial ruin of a Benedictine nunnery, dating from about 1200 with thirteenth-century additions; then comes the tiny medieval parish kirk dedicated to St. Ronan; next to it is the eleven-foot-high **MacLean's Cross** *(166)*, dating from the fifteenth century; and on the left is an eighteenth-century "parliamentary church" designed by Thomas Telford. Then comes St. Oran's Chapel and Cemetery. The chapel is Romanesque in style and is alleged to have been built by order of Queen Margaret about 1080. The cemetery was the reputed burial ground of Dark Age kings of Scotland, Ireland, and Norway, as well as those of numerous Highland chieftains in the Middle Ages and later. Most of the ancient gravestones are of late medieval date and are now housed in the nearby site museum. Among the more impressive are the effigies of Bricius MacKinnon and Prioress Anna MacLean. The cathedral is the much restored and renovated church of the Benedictine monastery dating mostly from the fifteenth century. The church received its brief status as a cathedral in 1498. In front of it stand three Early Christian stone crosses dedicated respectively to St. Martin, St. Matthew, and St. John. St. John's Cross is a replica. Fragments of the original are in the site museum. Of St. Matthew's Cross, only the lower part of the shaft survives—decorated with figures of Adam and Eve and key-pattern ornament of Anglian style. St. Martin's Cross, more than fifteen feet high and dating from the tenth century, is almost complete, lacking only the ends of the arms. Its intricate carvings are a mix of Northumbrian and Celtic styles. The front face depicts the Virgin and Child, Daniel in the lion's den, and sundry angelic, human, and animal figures; the back is ornamented with Celtic spiralwork and Anglo-Saxon interlace patterns. Overlooking the cathedral from the west, on a low hill called Tor Abb, are the scant remains of a small dry-stone cell that may have been Columba's sleeping place. The cloister and the other monastic buildings abutting the church are modern.

Johnson and Boswell came here in 1773, and today's visitor will find it hard not to share the former's conclusion: "That man is little to be envied, whose patriotism would not gain force upon the plain of Marathon, or whose piety would not grow warmer among the ruins of Iona."

ISLAY (STRATHCLYDE)

(Access by car ferry from Tarbert [Kennacraig] to Port Ellen and Port Askaig, twice daily—two hours; by air from Glasgow, twice daily.)

Bowmore

Kilchoman Cross *(166)*, 12 m. w (60 NR 216 633)

Inside the village churchyard stands this fine disc-headed cross, a good example of fifteenth-century western Highland stone carving, with fine foliation and interlace and the figure of a knight on a rearing charger on the front of the shaft.

Port Askaig

Finlaggan Castle *(114)*, 3 m. w, 1 m. nw of A 846 (60 NR 388 682)

Visible from the north shore of Loch Finlaggan, but closed to the public, this ruined island hall house was a chief administrative center of the Lords of the Isles in the fourteenth and fifteenth centuries.

Port Charlotte

** Museum of Islay Life *(364)*, village center

In this well-stocked museum of local history and archaeology are numerous prehistoric artifacts, agricultural implements of the nineteenth century, and reconstructed rooms portraying various aspects of domestic life on the island.

Port Ellen

Dunyveg Castle *(114)*, 2½ m. e, s of A 846 (60 NR 407 455)

This ruined coastal tower was a fourteenth-century stronghold of the MacDonald Lords of the Isles.

** Kildalton Cross *(65)*, 7 m. ne; 3½ m. ne of Ardbeg village; e of unnumbered road (60 NS 458 508); AM

Although not easy to reach, this is one of the best preserved and handsomest of the Early Christian monuments of Scotland. It is a complete wheel cross of the eighth century, standing nine feet high in the churchyard. Richly carved with Celtic curvilinear decoration as well as Anglian interlace, the cross also displays several biblical scenes: David (or Sampson) wrestling with a lion; the sacrifice of Isaac by Abraham; and the Virgin and Child. Life-size copies may be seen in the National Museum of Antiquities in Edinburgh or the Glasgow Art Gallery and Museum.

LISMORE (STRATHCLYDE)

(Access by car ferry daily from Oban [Strathclyde]; and by passenger ferry every two hours from Port Appin)

* **Tirefour Broch** *(33)*, e of B 8045, 3½ m. n of Achnacroish ferry landing, 3 m. s of Port Appin–Lismore ferry landing

Overlooking the Lynn of Lorn, this ruined broch stands about twenty feet at its highest point. The original entry has disappeared and the interior is turf-covered.

Lismore Parish Kirk *(159)*, w of B 8045; 3 m. n of Achnacroish ferry landing, 3½ m. n of Port Appin–Lismore ferry landing

Incorporated within this small and quite pretty church are the foundations and walls of the choir of the thirteenth- or fourteenth-century cathedral church of the Bishops of Argyll, probably built after the see was separated from the episcopal jurisdiction of Dunkeld. The original altar would have stood under the present loft where a door has been cut into the east wall. Noteworthy are the sedilia and piscina; also the modern stained glass in the east window (observable in the loft). To the west of the church, the foundations of the nave can be discerned, though now covered with turf. Even in its heyday, this was obviously a very small cathedral.

LOCHALINE, MORVERN (HIGHLAND)

Ardtornish Castle *(114)*, 6 m. ne and then se around shore of Loch Aline by road and footpath (49 NM 691 427)

This was the principal mainland stronghold of the Lords of the Isles in the fourteenth and fifteenth centuries. It was probably built by John, first of the MacDonalds known to have used the title. He died in 1360. Here is a rectangular tower, seventy-five by fifty feet, much reduced from its original height, standing at the narrowest part of the Sound of Mull. It is hard to imagine this place as the scene of the Celtic festivities described in such detail by Sir Walter Scott in *The Lord of the Isles*. The castle can be viewed at a distance from Lochaline Pier or from the McBrayne ferries to and from Oban.

Lochgilphead (Strathclyde)

Keills Chapel *(166)*, 16 m. sw; 10 m. sw of Crinan at end of B 8025 (62 NR 690 806); AM

Next to a ruined and roofless chapel stands a good fifteenth-century stone cross, carved on one side only with a boss and three small discs in the center, mythical animals, and a figure probably representing Daniel in the lion's den. The sculpture work is unusual in not having any foliated or interlace design. Beautifully situated on a point of land between Loch Sween and the Sound of Jura, the site can be reached only over a rough and narrow track that leads nowhere else.

* Castle Sween *(81, 187)*, 17 m. sw; 12 m. s of B 841 from Bellanoch (62 NR 713)

On the eastern shore of Loch Sween, now within the grounds of a private caravan park, this ruin is either the oldest or the second oldest (after the Castle of Old Wick) castle in mainland Scotland. It was probably built in the early twelfth century by a Highland chief named Dougall, from whom ownership passed to the MacSweens in the thirteenth century, the Campbells in the fourteenth, and the MacNeills in the fifteenth. Although it appears at first glance to be a courtyard castle enclosed by a forty-foot wall, it may, on the other hand, have been a spacious keep whose floors and roof have disappeared. This at least is one explanation offered for the deep channel running horizontally around the inside face of the thick wall—the supposition being that it could have housed the timber ends of a floor that covered the entire space within the walls. The round-arched entrance on the south side and a sea gate on the west are the only apertures in the wall. The northeast corner tower is a thirteenth-century addition; the tower rising from the northwest corner probably dates from the sixteenth.

Entry into the castle has been barred to the public on grounds of danger. It can, however, be closely inspected from the outside, though whether such a limited view is worth the long and difficult ride to this remote spot is questionable.

* Kilmory Knap Chapel *(108, 166)*, 18 m. sw; 3 m. s of Castle Sween (62 NR 703 753)

This is a roofless thirteenth-century chapel containing a good collection of western Highland sculptured stones, mostly dating from the fifteenth century. The group includes Macmillan's Cross (AM), a disc-headed rood with the Crucifixion on one side and a hunting scene on the other; several grave-slabs decorated with swords, two with swords and galleys; four knightly effigies, two life-sized and equipped with bascinet, aventail, aketon, and sword; and one recumbent effigy of a churchman.

* Kilberry Sculptured Stones *(108, 166)*, 22 m. sw; w of B 8024 (62 NR 710 643); AM

Housed in a shed, this is a good collection of sculptured grave-slabs, mostly decorated with a single medieval broadsword. Two slabs have knightly effigies wearing the usual late medieval armor: bascinet, aventail, and aketon.

* Achnabreck *(26)*, 2 m. n; n of Achnabreck village (55 NR 856 906); AM

Here is one of the largest groups of cup-and-ring marks in Scotland, incised on contiguous exposed rock-faces. Included are simple cups, cups with from one to seven rings, cups with radial grooves, and a double spiral.
Inquire in village for directions.

* Cairnbaan *(26)*, 2½ m. nw; n of junction of A 816 and B 841; by footpath leading up steep hill behind Cairnbaan Motor Inn (55 NR 838 910); AM

These Bronze Age rock carvings are protected by a railing installed by the Scottish Development Department. Incised on flat rocks are several small cup-marks and large cup-and-ring marks with up to four rings.

* Crinan Canal *(287)*, 1 to 4 m. nw along B 841 from Cairnbaan to Bellanoch

Here is the best view of the canal built in 1793–1801 across Knapdale between the Sound of Jura and Loch Fyne. It is today used chiefly by pleasure craft.

Kilmichael Glassary *(26)*, 4 m. n; in Kilmichael Glassary village, ½ m. ne of A 816 from Bridgend (55 NR 858 935); AM

Here are unusual rock carvings, presumably of Bronze Age date, consisting of large deep cups, some paired in dumbbell shape and others contained in incisions shaped like keyholes or horseshoes.

*** Dunadd *(51)*, 5½ m. n; ½ m. w of A 816 (55 NR 837 936); AM

This high craggy rock with its twin peaks rising out of the drained marshland of the Crinan Moss was the Dark Age site of the capital of the kingdom of the Dalriadic Scots who emigrated here from Northern Ireland about the end of the fifth century. On the lower (southernmost) of the two peaks stands the citadel, protected by a dry-stone wall twelve feet thick. On the terrace below are other enclosing walls, thus making this what archaeologists call a "nuclear fort." Just outside the entrance to the citadel beside the steps leading up to it is a flat rock bearing the carvings of a cuplike depression, a human footprint, and the incised figure of a boar. These are thought to be connected with the inauguration ceremonies of the kings of Dalriada. The boar, however, was a common Pictish symbol, and this one may date from a period of Pictish occupation of the site, most likely after 736 when Fergus, King of the Picts, besieged and captured this Scotic capital.

The view from the top across the Crinan Canal, the Sound of Jura, and eastward toward Loch Fyne is truly spectacular.

Dunchraigaig Cairn *(19)*, 6½ m. nw; w of A 816 (55 NR 833 968); AM

This is a Bronze Age circular cairn of loose stones alongside a large cist constructed of boulders, with a huge capstone thirteen feet in length.

Ri Cruin Cairn *(19)*, 7 m. nw; w of B 8025 (55 NR 825 972); AM

This is a dilapidated Bronze Age circular cairn of loose stones containing three cists.

Ballygowan *(26)*, 7½ m. nw; 1½ m. sw of A 816 from ½ m. s of Kilmartin, by road, dirt track, and footpath (55 NR 816 977); AM

Here is a flat rock incised with Bronze Age cup-and-ring marks, radial grooves, an oval, and a horseshoe. Though surrounded by a fence installed by the Scottish Development Department, there are no signs pointing to this remote site, and local inquiries are essential.

* Temple Wood Stone Circle *(19, 23)*, 7½ m. nw; ¼ m. w of A 816 (55 NR 826 979); AM

This is a Bronze Age cist inside a circle now consisting of thirteen standing stones.

*** Nether Largie, South *(13)*, 7½ m. nw; w of A 816; ¾ m. s of Kilmartin (55 NR 829 974); AM

This is the largest tomb in the Neolithic and Bronze Age linear "cemetery" stretching for almost three miles north and south in the Kilmartin valley. The cairn of rounded boulders has been partially restored by the Scottish Development Department. The tomb underneath is a gallery grave of the Clyde group. A door leads into the burial chamber, which is twenty feet long and four feet wide beneath a giant capstone seven feet above the present floor. Three low septal slabs, now no higher than sills, divide the chamber into four compartments.

* Nether Largie Mid Cairn *(19)*, 8 m. nw; w of A 816 (55 NR 830 983); AM

Here is a Bronze Age circular cairn of loose stones under which are buried two cists.

** Nether Largie, North *(19)*, 8½ m. nw; w of A 816 (55 NR 831 985); AM

This is a large circular Bronze Age cairn of rounded stones, containing a single cist. It can be entered by a ladder from the top. The underside of the cist's capstone bears cup-marks and representations of flat bronze axes.

** Kilmartin Church *(108, 166)*, 8 m. n; w of A 816

Inside this undistinguished parish kirk stand an Early Christian cross-slab, the shaft of a fifteenth-century cross, and the shaft and one arm of an early-sixteenth-century cross with the Crucifixion carved in front and Christ in Glory on the back. Within the mausoleum in the adjoining churchyard is a really fine collection of carved western Highland grave-slabs, mostly dating from the fourteenth and fifteenth centuries. Here are several knightly effigies with armor, but the most typical are those carved simply with a medieval broadsword covering the full length of the slab.

** Carnasserie Castle *(205)*, 9 m. n; w of A 816, 1½ m. n of Kilmartin (55 NM 838 009); AM

This ruined but well-preserved sixteenth-century tower-house attached to a commodious hall house was the property of John Carswell, Protestant Superintendent of Argyll and later Bishop of the Isles in the reign of Mary, Queen of Scots. He is famous for having translated Knox's *Book of Common Order* into Gaelic in 1567—the first book of any kind to have been printed in that language. The castle was taken and partly blown up by the ninth Earl of Argyll during the Monmouth/Argyll rebellion of 1685.

MULL (STRATHCLYDE)

(Access by frequent car ferry from Oban to Craignure)

Craignure

*** Torosay Castle *(333)*, 1 m. s; e of A 849

Completed in 1858 to the design of David Bryce, this is the best surviving visitable example of the Scotch Baronial style for which he was famous. The fine terraced gardens were laid out by Sir Robert Lorimer. The house served as a shooting lodge, as indicated by the large number of antlers still decorating the entrance hall. The furnishings are typically Edwardian and opulent. In the boudoir is a large painting of the Loch Ness monster and other materials relating to this legendary beast. Since shortly after the completion of the building, it has been owned by the Guthrie family.

** Duart Castle *(185, 305)*, 3 m. se; 1 m. e of A 849

There was a castle on this strategic site overlooking the conjuncture of the Sound of Mull, Loch Linnhe, Loch Etive, and the Firth of Lorne, possibly as early as the thirteenth century, but no later than 1390. By the later Middle Ages it was occupied by the MacLeans. Despite feuds with the MacDonalds of Islay, disputes over property rights with the Campbells of Argyll, and the recurring disfavor of the Scottish Crown, the family held on to their lands until 1691, when the MacLean estates were forfeited. Their castle fell gradually into ruin until bought and restored in 1911 by Colonel Sir Fitzroy MacLean, twenty-sixth Chief of Clan MacLean, who undertook extensive reconstruction, so that it is once again habitable. It also serves as a clan memorial and museum.

Although it is furnished and open to the public, there is not really very much to see inside the present restored building. Among the mementos on exhibit are a small Spanish cannon recovered from the wreck of a galleon of the Spanish Armada that sank in Tobermory harbor in 1588; numerous Highland weapons; a bureau that belonged to the poet William Wordsworth; Crimean War uniforms; MacLean portraits; and an exhibition tracing the history of the Boy Scouts since 1907—installed by Sir Charles MacLean, eleventh baronet and twenty-seventh chief, who served as Chief Scout of the Commonwealth.

Tobermory

* Old Byre Heritage Centre *(282, 291)*, 8 m. se; 1 m. s of Dervaig village

This is essentially a wax museum with sound effects. Two tableaux are to be seen: one, of the interior of a Highland black house of about 1840, before the clearances; the other of a shepherd's cottage of the 1890s. A half-hour audio presentation describes the life of the occupants of each. The message seems to be that there was a vast improvement in the quality of life over this fifty-year span, though the fact that the black-house dwellers had to be evicted before the shepherds could come in is glossed over.

Oban (Strathclyde)

*** Dunstaffnage Castle *(98, 106, 164, 242)*, 3 m. n; 1 m. n of A 85 from 1 m. n of Oban (49 NM 883 345); AM

This ruined rectangular courtyard castle, with curtain walls thirty feet high, is perched on a rocky knoll on a promontory projecting into Loch Etive. It was built in the early thirteenth century, probably by Ewen MacDougall, Lord of Lorn and great-grandson of Somerled. In 1308 it was surrendered by Alexander MacDougall to Robert Bruce after the Battle of the Pass of Brander. Later, King Robert I awarded the property to a branch of the Campbell family, and it later came into the possession of the Earls of Argyll. In 1652 it was turned over to Cromwell's government by Archibald Campbell, first Marquis of Argyll, and garrisoned by Protectorate troops until 1660.

The castle is entered today by a wooden stairway leading up to an arched entrance passage in the southeast corner, above which rises a tower house built in the seventeenth century. Diagonally across from the entrance, in the northwest corner of the courtyard, is a three-story rounded tower that served as the *donjon*. In the northeast corner is another tower, round on the outside and square where it faces inward. In the north and east curtain walls are pairs of First Pointed lancet windows that date the castle to the early thirteenth century. About two hundred yards to the west is a roofless chapel, also with lancet windows in the First Pointed style.

Ardchattan Priory *(125, 150)*, 10 m. ne; 5 m. e of A 828 from n end of Connel bridge across Loch Etive (49 NM 971 349); AM

Here are the very scant remains of one of the three Valliscaulian monasteries in Scotland. (The other two are Beauly Priory, Inverness-shire, and Pluscarden Abbey, Moray.) All were founded in the thirteenth century—Ardchattan by Duncan MacDougall in 1230. The monks' refectory has been incorporated into the adjacent private house. Of the priory church, only fragments of the choir remain standing, including parts of the east and north walls, each with an aumbry and an arch surmounting a piscina. Of major interest here are the two effigies of fifteenth-century knights, Somerled and Alan MacDougall, father and son. The former is clothed in mail and wears a bascinet, typical of the fourteenth century and therefore old-fashioned at the time of the wearer's death. Alan's armor, by contrast, is of plate, in keeping with the changing style of the late fourteenth and fifteenth centuries.

The road to this remote place is narrow and rough, and the site itself probably not worth the trip were it not for the marvelous views of Loch Etive en route.

*** Bonawe Furnace *(322)*, 12 m. e; ½ m. n of A 85 from Taynuilt; AM

One of the few well-developed industrial-archaeological sites in Scotland, these are the substantial remains of a charcoal-fired iron furnace and associated buildings, established here in 1752. The ore was shipped north from Furness, Lancashire, and the pig iron back by way of Loch Etive. The extant buildings consist of the furnace, charging house, iron-ore shed, charcoal sheds, and workers' houses. At the custodian's office, informational material is available, and the site is well marked.

TARBERT (STRATHCLYDE)

Tarbert Castle *(109, 187, 242)*, town center, by steep footpath from behind police station (62 NR 868 687)

This much ruined, ivy-clad stone castle was probably built, or perhaps rebuilt, by Robert Bruce as the headquarters of the sheriffdom of Kintyre. After abolishing the Lordship of the Isles in 1493, James IV repaired and garrisoned the castle in order to assure royal domination of the Kintyre Peninsula to the south. It was subsequently assigned to the custody of the Campbell Earls of Argyll. In 1652 Archibald Campbell, first Marquis of Argyll, turned it over for occupation by a Cromwellian garrison. Only one corner of the original keep survives.

** Skipness Castle *(98, 164, 187)*, 12 m. s; ¼ m. e of B 8001 from Skipness village (62 NR 908 577); AM

The original building here was a long rectangular hall house erected in the first quarter of the thirteenth century, perhaps just after Alexander II's successful expedition into the western Highlands. Late in the century this house was incorporated into a massive courtyard castle with high curtain walls and towers at each corner—now a well-preserved ruin.

The entrance is on the south side. A pointed arched doorway leads to a passageway with a small portcullis chamber above. The west curtain consists of the outer facade of a late-thirteenth-century hall, adjoining (to the north) the western gable of the original early hall house. This side is pierced with a row of crosslets, narrow on the outside and splayed on the interior. The tower at the northeast corner (now reroofed) is a sixteenth-century addition.

About sixty yards to the southeast, overlooking Kilbrannan Sound, is an early-thirteenth-century church dedicated to St. Columba, with a fine double-lancet window in the east end.

Dunbartonshire

CUMBERNAULD (STRATHCLYDE)

Cumbernauld Locks *(318)*, 4 m. n; e of A 80

This is a good place to view the **Forth and Clyde Canal** *(317)*, completed in 1790.

DUMBARTON (STRATHCLYDE)

*** Dumbarton Rock and Castle *(48, 200, 214, 241, 269)*, 1 m. se of town
center; s of A 814 (64 NS 400 745); AM

The Rock, an isolated volcanic plug standing 240 feet above the north
shore of the River Clyde, is a spectacular sight with a spectacular view from
the top. It was probably occupied by the *Damnonii* in the Late Iron Age and
was certainly the capital of the Dark Age Strathclyde Britons until 1018.
Nothing remains, however, of this early occupation except for two gravestones of a probable tenth-century date, now in the Guard House of the
Castle.

During the Middle Ages, there was an important royal castle here, though
very little of it is left. After the Battle of Pinkie in 1547, the infant Mary,
Queen of Scots, was brought here before her escape to France; and during
the troubled years of her reign, the castle was held by the queen's supporters
until 1571, when it was surprised and taken by Thomas Crawford in a
daring feat that gave the lie to the citadel's alleged impregnability. Cromwell's forces held it from 1652 until the Restoration. Thereafter, it was
renovated and modernized from time to time, the most active periods of
reconstruction being during General George Wade's tour of duty in Scotland after the Jacobite uprising of 1715 and again in response to the
invasion scares during the Napoleonic Wars.

Today's visitor must climb a steep set of steps before passing through the
nineteenth-century outer gate to reach King George's Battery and the
adjacent governor's house, both built by order of General Wade in 1735.
West of here, the ancient wall may be a surviving part of the medieval hall.
It leads to the Spur Battery, built in the late seventeenth century, beyond
which are the Spanish Battery and the Bower Battery, both designed by the
military engineer Captain John Romer, under the command of General
Wade. Up another flight of steps past the sixteenth-century guard house and
through the fourteenth-century portcullis arch, the visitor can digress to the
circular foundations of the medieval white tower; then return to the arch,
proceed up the path past the so-called French prison of late-eighteenth-
century date, and on to the Duke of York's Battery, the Duke of Argyll's
Battery, and the Prince of Wales's Battery—all built or reconstructed during
the Napoleonic Wars. The first named of these incorporates the basement of
a medieval building called the Wallace tower, though it is improbable that
William Wallace was actually imprisoned here as is alleged.

Bowling Locks and Custom House *(318)*, 4 m. e; s of A 82

This was the western terminus of the **Forth and Clyde Canal** *(317)*, opened
in July 1790.

HELENSBURGH (STRATHCLYDE)

*** Hill House *(347)*, Upper Colquhoun Street; NTS

Designed and furnished by Charles Rennie Mackintosh, and built in the first years of the twentieth century, this was the home of the publisher, W. W. Blackie. Overlooking the Clyde estuary, it consists of two wings (one for the children and servants), and the style is a vaguely Scottish baronial. Inside, Mackintosh had free rein, and the results are as novel as might be expected of this highly inventive artist and decorator. The walls are white, the panelling dark; the chairs are high-backed and uncomfortable; the same checkerboard motif is duplicated on chairs, carpets, and wallpaper; and there are plenty of windows to give the rooms the brightness that Mackintosh tried to achieve in all his buildings.

Stirlingshire

FALKIRK (CENTRAL)

Falkirk Locks *(318)*, city center

These were built to serve the **Forth and Clyde Canal** *(317)*, completed in 1790.

Union Canal Tunnel *(318)*, city center

This was built to carry the **Union Canal** *(318)*, completed in 1822.

Scottish Railway Preservation Society Depot *(338)*, Wallace Street

Associated with the Scottish Railway Preservation Society Museum in Bo'ness, here are twenty-one steam locomotives and a large number of now antique coaches and wagons (passenger and freight cars).

* Antonine Wall *(44)*

* Watling Lodge *(45)*, 2 m. w; S of B 816, 1 m. sw of junction with A 803 (65 NS 862 798); AM, NTS

Here is a good stretch of the huge ditch that guarded the Antonine Wall on its northern side. It still measures some forty feet wide by twelve feet deep, which is close to the original dimension.

* Rough Castle *(45)*, 3 m. w, s of A 803; 2 m. s of Bonnybridge, n of B 816 (65 NS 843 799); AM, NTS

This is the best preserved of the eighteen or nineteen original wall-forts along the Antonine Wall. Earthen rampart and ditches are in good condition on all sides, especially the northern, which was formed by the wall itself. Inside the fort are a few traces of excavated stone buildings. North of the fort beyond the ditch is a series of pits, called *lilia* by the Romans, in which pointed stakes were concealed to serve as an ambuscade against attacks from that direction.

* **Seabegs Wood** *(45)*, 5 m. w; 1½ m. sw of Bonnybridge, s of B 816 (65 NS 814 793); AM, NTS

A short section of the Antonine Wall can be observed here, as well as a longer section of the ditch to its north. Both are well preserved. The area is thickly wooded—surprisingly so considering the intense industrialization of the surrounding region.

GRANGEMOUTH (CENTRAL)

BP Information Centre *(337)*, w of B 9143, 1 m. n of M 9 from Exit 5

This is the starting point of the "Paraffin Young Heritage Trail," a forty-mile course through the Lothian villages where the nineteenth-century shale-oil industry flourished, thanks to the discoveries of James ("Paraffin") Young. (Paraffin is the same as American kerosene.) Guide-books and other information available at the center; signposts along the way.

KILLEARN

** **Glengoyne Distillery** *(358)*, 1½ m. s, in Dumgoyne

Lying almost precisely on the Highland Line, this malt whisky distillery has been in business since at least 1833. Open to the public, here is a fine exhibit of the distilling process, very popular with visitors because of its convenient location in one of the most frequented parts of the Highlands.

STIRLING (CENTRAL)

*** **Stirling Castle** *(104, 106, 108, 122, 171, 183, 213, 214, 241, 260, 266, 290)*, town center

The nodal point of Scotland from time immemorial, the high rock on which the castle stands dominates the most important land passage from the south of Scotland into the Highlands. There was a wooden castle here at least as early as the reign of Alexander I (1107–1124). The site changed hands between Scots and English several times during the War of Independence, and siege operations here precipitated the Battle of Bannockburn in 1314. After the English garrison surrendered, Robert Bruce, as was his custom, razed the castle to prevent its use by the English or their Scottish allies. The earliest extant building on the ground dates probably from the reign of James IV (1488–1513) and the other major construction from the reigns of James V (1513–1542) and James VI (1587–1625). Following the Revolution of 1689–1690, a seven-gun battery was installed on the wall-walk, and the danger of a French invasion on behalf of the Old Pretender in 1708 led to the construction of new outer defenses.

Today, the castle is entered from the Esplanade on its south side, through a system of eighteenth-century outer defenses surrounding the guardroom square, then on to the forework built by James IV in the early sixteenth century. This is a crenellated wall extending across the full width of the Castle Rock and is pierced by a twin-towered gatehouse that is the main entrance to the castle precincts. Once past the gatehouse, the visitor finds himself in the lower square, with the great hall dead ahead and the palace to the left. He should proceed at once up the road between these two buildings to the upper square, which is the heart of the castle. The west side of the square is occupied by the King's Old Building, mostly rebuilt in the nineteenth century and now housing the excellent Museum of the Argyll and Sutherland Highlanders, an amalgamation of the Argyll Highlanders (98th/91st Regiment of Foot), first organized in 1794, and the Sutherland Highlanders (93rd Regiment), recruited in 1799. Proceeding clockwise, the north side of the square is occupied by the Chapel Royal, established in 1501 as a college of secular priests by King James IV and rebuilt in a neoclassical style in 1594 by James VI (on or near the same site) to celebrate the birth of his first son, Prince Henry. To the east lies the great hall, built in the reign of James IV. Now under restoration by the Scottish Development Department, this large, rectangular, well-lighted building is one of the grandest medieval halls in Britain. Finally, on the south side of the upper square, we come to the palace, a four-sided building set up around an inner court (the "Lion's Den") built in the sixteenth century by James V. Externally, it is perhaps the most splendid example of Renaissance architecture in Scotland, with its neoclassical windows alternating with cusped-headed niches containing a fascinating array of statuary. Inside, the big attraction is the display of "Stirling Heads," beautifully carved roundels from the ceilings of the king's apartment, now gracing the walls of the queen's apartment but eventually to be reinstalled in their original position.

The wall-walk along the parapets on the north side of the main castle enclosure offers marvelous views of the surrounding countryside. Near the northwest corner is the Douglas Garden into which the corpse of the eighth Earl of Douglas was allegedly thrown after his murder by James II in 1452. West of the upper square is a section of the parapet known as the "Lady's Hole." From here can be seen a turf-covered octagonal mound representing the remains of a formal garden called the "King's Knot" laid out in the seventeenth century. Most of the gun batteries and casements scattered here and there date from the eighteenth century, by which time the castle had ceased to be a royal residence.

Mar's Wark *(210)*, Broad Street, below castle

Here is the ruined facade of what was meant to be a Renaissance palace built by John Erskine, first Earl of Mar, who served briefly as Regent of Scotland during the infancy of King James VI.

Argyll's Lodging *(231)*, Castle Wynd

Now housing a youth hostel, this was originally an elegant quadrangular town house mostly built (on preexisting foundations) in the 1630s by Sir William Alexander, first Earl of Stirling. The handsome screen wall with the entrance doorway was added by Archibald Campbell, ninth Earl of Argyll, who resided here in the 1670s. The ornamentation is typical of the Scottish Renaissance style.

** Church of the Holy Rude *(171, 210)*, Castle Wynd

In this collegiate church the infant James VI was crowned according to Protestant rites in which John Knox took part. The nave with a good open timber roof dates probably from the early fifteenth century. The choir with its fine three-sided apse was added in the early sixteenth. Both are in the Second Pointed style.

* Cambuskenneth Abbey *(124, 145)*, 1 m. e (57 NS 809 939); AM

Little survives of the monastery, founded in 1147 by King David I as a house of Augustinian canons regular, except for the Gothic western doorway of the church and a complete detached campanile unlike any other medieval tower in Scotland. It is roofed, stands sixty-seven feet high over a vaulted basement, and is pierced by single- and double-lancet windows in the First Pointed style of the thirteenth century.

King James III (1460–1488) and his Danish Queen Margaret were buried beneath the high altar of the church. In 1864 the remains of the royal tomb were uncovered and later reinterred by command of Queen Victoria, their great-great-great-great-great-great-great-great-great-great granddaughter.

*** Bannockburn Heritage Centre *(107, 108)*, 2 m. s; w of A 872 (57 NS 794 905); NTS

Near the spot where Robert Bruce is thought to have established his command post on the eve of the Battle of Bannockburn (23–24 June 1314), the National Trust for Scotland has built a rotunda and raised an equestrian statue of the king, looking eastward toward the site of the main battlefield which was probably located near the outskirts of the present village of Bannockburn. Nearby is the visitors' center, which contains, among other things, an audiovisual theater where a film is run every fifteen minutes to explain the battle.

Stirling Bridge *(103)*, Barnton Street, on north edge of town

This is a stone footbridge built about 1400, known locally as the "Old Bridge." It is downstream from the site of its wooden predecessor, where William Wallace won his famous victory in 1297.

* Wallace Monument *(102, 367)*, 1½ m. ne; n of junction of A 9 and A 907 (57 NS 812 956)

Built in 1861–1869 in the pseudomedieval style known as "Scottish Baronial," this freestone tower, financed by the Scottish Rights Society, a mid-nineteenth century nationalist organization, rises 220 feet above the summit of the Abbey Craig overlooking the town of Stirling. It is topped by an open stone "lantern," more or less an imitation of the spire of St. Giles Kirk, Edinburgh. At the southwest corner of the 36-foot-square building is a bronze statue of William Wallace to whom the monument is dedicated. Inside, on the ground floor, is a painting meant to represent the Battle of Bannockburn (fought after Wallace's death); on the first floor above is the Hall of Arms, containing a collection of weapons; on the second floor is the Hall of Heroes, with busts of eminent Scots. Here also is the sword purportedly taken from Wallace's side at the time of his capture. In fact, two-handed swords of this type (known as the "claymore") were not known in Scotland until the late fifteenth or early sixteenth century.

The view from the parapet is worth the climb.

EAST CENTRAL SCOTLAND
Clackmannanshire
ALVA (CENTRAL)

Menstrie Castle *(231)*, 2½ m. w, in Menstrie village; NTS

This restored sixteenth-century tower-house was the birthplace in 1567 of Sir William Alexander, first Earl of Stirling, courtier, poet, and founder of the ill-fated Scottish colony in Nova Scotia. In the Nova Scotia Commemoration Room are the coats of arms of forty-five baronets of Nova Scotia to whom Charles I awarded their titles in consideration for their financial backing of the scheme.

CLACKMANNAN (CENTRAL)

Clackmannan Tower *(132)*, ½ m. w of town center; s of A 907 (58 NS 906 919); AM

This is a fourteenth- to fifteenth-century L-plan tower-house with a Renaissance doorway added a century later. Partially collapsed, it is fenced off and observable from the outside only.

DOLLAR (CENTRAL)

*** Castle Campbell *(187)*, 1 m. n (58 NS 961 993); long walk by footpath from car park at end of unmarked road; AM

The well-preserved and roofed four-story tower-house at the northeast corner of this ruined courtyard castle dates from the late fifteenth century and was erected by Colin Campbell, first Earl of Argyll. It was initially called Castle Gloom, occupying a commanding position between precipitous ravines through which run streams called the Burn of Sorrow and the Burn of Care. The great hall, as usual, is on the first floor above ground level, and from this level also a floor hatch opens onto a pit prison below. Bed chambers and garderobes occupy the floors above. The turnpike stairway was added in the sixteenth century, as were the buildings around the courtyard to the south and west of the tower. Late in that century, or possibly early in the seventeenth, the vaulted entrance gateway flanked by two gunports was added, and the eastern range embellished with a handsome loggia. The castle was a stronghold of Covenanters during the Civil War and was so damaged by royalist enemies of the Campbells that it ceased to be a viable residence after about 1654.

Kinross-shire

KINROSS (TAYSIDE)

** Kinross House Garden *(258)*, town center, behind Salutation Hotel

This is a very handsome formal garden of rose beds, herbaceous borders, and shaped yew trees (topiary) built around a central pool and fountain. The present arrangements date from the early twentieth century. The view from here of Loch Leven is entrancing. A handsome avenue of trees leads to

Kinloss House designed by the great seventeenth-century architect Sir William Bruce for his own use. Though it is not open to the public, the classical exterior, with its Ionic pillars and Corinthian pilasters, makes an elegant backdrop to the garden.

*** **Loch Leven Castle** *(132, 209)*, ½ m. e; in Loch Leven; access by passenger ferry from town pier (58 NO 138 018); AM

This island castle is an almost square, five-story tower-house built in the late fourteenth century and standing to its original height. Here Mary, Queen of Scots, was imprisoned for ten months in 1567–1568 before her escape by boat. The ground floor is a barrel-vaulted storage basement; the first floor, a kitchen; second floor, the great hall: and the upper floors, bedrooms. The main entrance led to the second floor and was reached by a forestair, since gone. A turnpike staircase connected the hall with the upper chambers and with the kitchen below. The present stair connecting kitchen and basement is an insertion. Originally, communication between them was through a small floor hatch. A barmkin wall, parts of which may date from as early as the thirteenth century, surrounds the castle on three sides. The round mural tower at its southeast corner is a sixteenth-century addition.

The setting is notably picturesque—even for Scotland.

* **Burleigh Castle** *(133)*, 2½ m. ne; n of A 911; ½ m. e of Milnathort (58 NO 130 047); AM

This ruined fifteenth-century tower-house of the Balfour family is joined by a fragment of barmkin wall to a late-sixteenth-century gatehouse, which is roofed and remarkably well preserved. The gatehouse is circular, with a polygonal room on top, and is well supplied with shot-holes for artillery and shut-holes (i.e., shuttered windows) for ventilation.

Fife

ABERDOUR (FIFE)

** **Aberdour Castle** *(210)*, near town center, s of A 92; AM

This place was a Douglas stronghold, from 1342 until it was partially destroyed and abandoned in the eighteenth century. In 1458 James Douglas, fourth Lord Dalkeith, was granted the earldom of Morton, which included Aberdour with its castle, which then consisted of a simple tower-house built probably in the previous century. All that survives of this building (at the northwest corner of the existing complex) is the basement and a substantial portion of the east wall. In the fifteenth century this tower was rebuilt and expanded, and in the sixteenth, James Douglas, the fourth earl and Regent of Scotland in the minority of King James VI, added the central range. The L-shaped eastern range was built in the early seventeenth century by William Douglas, the sixth earl, who dissipated a large part of his fortune supporting the cause of Charles I during the Civil War.

Though ruined, the buildings have been partially reroofed and are in a good state of preservation.

* St. Fillans, Aberdour *(162)*, s of A 92; near town center; AM

On the grounds of the castle, this tiny restored church dates from the twelfth century. Part of the west gable, most of the north wall, and the small flat-ended choir are original; the south porch and south aisle are thought to date from the fifteenth century.

*** Inchcolm Abbey *(142)*, 1½ m. s, in Firth of Forth; accessible by boat (the *Maid of the Forth*) daily from Hawes Pier, South Queensferry, West Lothian (round trip: 2¼ hours); (66 NT 190 826); AM

This was an Augustinian house founded by King Alexander I about 1123, though, except possibly for the beehive "hermit cell" beyond the west end of the abbey church, the extant buildings date mostly from the thirteenth to the fifteenth century. Because of the monastery's protected location on an island in the Firth of Forth, it escaped destruction by the English and so survives in an unusually good state of preservation.

The modern pathway leads the visitor to the southeast corner of the abbatial complex, with the ruined hospital range on the left and, on the right, the octagonal chapter house, fully roofed and standing to its original height. The monastic precincts are entered from the east side of the vaulted cloister-walk, above which is the monks' dorter. The south and west cloister-walks are also covered, the former by the frater and kitchen, the latter by the guest hall. This arrangement of cloister-walks underneath sleeping and eating quarters is unique in Britain. Along the north side of the cloister is the abbey church in the usual position. The east end and the transept are reduced to foundations only, though here is a thirteenth-century tomb bearing the painted figures of seven ecclesiastics (now headless)—also a unique survival. The central tower of the church stands to its original height and is roofed. The west end (nave) was converted into the abbot's lodging and survives in part in that form.

ANSTRUTHER (FIFE)

*** Scottish Fisheries Museum *(343)*, Harbourhead

In this outstanding museum, every aspect of east-coast fishing receives loving and intelligent attention. Included are fine displays of fishing gear, navigation instruments, models of fishing boats, a simulated wheelhouse, the interior of a typical fisherman's house, and an aquarium containing examples of fish caught in Scottish waters.

The White House *(224)*, The Esplanade

This L-shaped group of eighteenth-century buildings was restored as part of the Little Houses Improvement Scheme of the National Trust for Scotland.

BURNTISLAND (FIFE)

*** St. Columba's, Burntisland *(221)*, south of town center; key at Manse off Cromwell Street

This was the first Protestant church to be erected in Scotland after the Reformation (1592). It was the meeting place of the General Assembly convened by James VI in 1601. The church is square in plan with a centrally located pulpit and galleries added in 1613 and assigned to separate guilds. The octagonal tower was built in 1749 and rests on four semicircular arches on square piers. Although the pulpit is a modern replacement, the woodwork in the galleries and the rear pews is original. The curious "Magistrates' Pew" was erected in 1606 by Sir Robert Melville for his own use.

CERES (FIFE)

** Fife Folk Museum *(364)*, village center

This restored weigh house contains a small and very good museum commemorating village and agricultural life in Fife, with special emphasis on the nineteenth century. The exhibits contain a great variety of material, including agricultural implements, household goods, costumes, etc.

CRAIL (FIFE)

* Crail Museum *(364)*, town center

Next to the town tolbooth bearing the model of a fish (the "Crail Capon") as a weathervane, this small museum of local history is devoted especially to fishing, knitting, and woodworking, all occupations important to the community in the nineteenth century. Down the street are a number of dwelling places restored under the Little Houses Improvement Scheme of the National Trust for Scotland.

Customs House *(224)*, town harbor

This late-seventeenth-century building with crowstepped gables and an interesting ship motif on the lintel over the main door has been restored and converted into a dwelling house.

* Crail Parish Church *(163)*, town center

Founded in the second half of the twelfth century, the church was raised to collegiate status in 1517. John Knox preached here in June 1559. In 1587 King James VI granted the church to the town council. The nave and west tower date from the thirteenth century, but the arch between nave and choir and some of the walling are Romanesque. Immediately to the left of the entrance is a good sculptured Pictish cross-slab dating from the eighth century.

CULROSS (FIFE)

*** The Palace *(223, 262)*, town center; NTS

Built by Sir George Bruce in 1597–1611, this is a unique example of a merchant's house of this period. The builder, knighted by James VI, was a highly successful entrepreneur, responsible for the development of a flourishing coal-mining industry in this region. The house consists of two separate buildings joined by walls. Inside are some of the finest wall and ceiling paintings in Scotland.

Bessie Bar's Hall *(224)*, town center

This gabled building with its forestair was a malt house, belonging to one Bessie Bar in the late sixteenth and early seventeenth centuries.

* Culross Town House *(224)*, town center; NTS

This was the burghal tolbooth built in 1626. The clock tower was added in 1783. It is now the local center of the National Trust for Scotland, which has been instrumental in the restoration of this unique and remarkable seventeenth-century mercantile and mining community.

** The Study *(224)*, town center; NTS

Next to the palace, this is the grandest house in Culross. It was built about 1630 and is believed to have been occupied in the late seventeenth century by Bishop Leighton of Dunblane. The outlook tower offers splendid views of the River Forth.

Culross Abbey *(149, 262)*, nw of town center

Up a steep hill leading northwest from the town center is the parish kirk, now incorporating the few remains of an abbey founded by Malcolm, Earl of Fife, in the early thirteenth century and colonized by Cisterican monks from Kinloss. The nave of the monastic church has disappeared, and so have all but a few fragments of the claustral buildings. The central tower and vaulted choir are preserved in the present church, which is entered from the west through a door that once served as the passage through the *pulpitum* between choir and nave. In the north transept is the splendid ornate Jacobean tomb of Sir George Bruce of Carnock, developer of the coal seams beneath the River Forth and builder of Culross Palace, knighted by James VI. Beneath the recumbent effigies of Sir George and his wife are the kneeling figures of their three sons and five daughters in an attitude of prayer.

CUPAR (FIFE)

Hill of Tarvit *(333)*, 2½ m. sw; e of A 916; NTS

Built in the early twentieth century to the design of Sir Robert Lorimer, this house is vaguely neoclassical with a French provincial twist. The interior is sumptuous in the Edwardian manner. Of special interest are the kitchen and laundry.

* Scotstarvit Tower *(226)*, 3 m. s; w of A 916; key at Hill of Tarvit, e of A 916; AM

Built between 1550 and 1579, this is a well-preserved five-story rectangular tower-house with a tiny jamb in one corner containing the turnpike stair, which rises to the roof where it ends in a cap house topped by a conical stone turret (a rarity). The rectangular windows are small. Although the original floor between the basement and the entresol is missing, all the other floors are in place, as is the roof. The parapet, originally crenellated, is now plain. The house is unfurnished, but otherwise whole, and is one of the most complete surviving examples in Scotland of a sixteenth-century laird's tower. The original barmkin, however, has disappeared. The name was affixed to the house by Sir John Scot, who bought it in 1611, a minor essayist who published a collection of tracts under the title *Scot of Scotstarvet's Staggering State of the Scots Statesmen.*

Norman's Law Hill-Fort *(30)*, 5½ m. nw; 1 m. n of A 913 from point 2½ m. e of Lindores through Denmuir (59 NO 302 203)

The summit of the hill here is enclosed by a ruined stone wall of Iron Age date. Further down the hill runs another longer wall, no doubt the hill-fort's outer defense. To the southwest is an oval enclosure that probably dates from the Scottish Dark Age, as do the circular hut foundations inside and on top of the ruined ramparts.

DUNFERMLINE (FIFE)

*** Dunfermline Abbey *(110, 137, 230)*, Monastery Street; AM

Nothing remains above ground of the church established here by Saint Margaret about 1070, though its foundations can be seen through gratings in the floor of the nave. Of the Benedictine Abbey church built by David I about 1150, only the nave still stands. With its round arches and massive cylindrical piers, decorated with incised chevrons and spiral curves, this is one of the finest Romanesque interiors in Scotland. The impressive west door, with its five diminishing rings of chevron-decorated arches, is part of the original twelfth-century construction, as is the north door. The northwest tower was the work of Abbot Bothwell in the mid-fifteenth century. The vaulted porch on the north side and the external buttresses were installed in the reign of James VI. The present parish church on the site of the choir and crossing was built in the nineteenth century to a design by William Burn. Here beneath the pulpit is the tomb of King Robert Bruce, marked today by a memorial brass. Outside the church, at the east end, are the foundations of the shrine of St. Margaret, where she and King Malcolm III are believed to have been buried.

Nothing remains of the east or west sides of the abbatial cloister, but the south side has partially survived in the ruined early-fourteenth-century frater (refectory), which is connected by an arched tower to Dunfermline Palace across the road. Once the monastic guest house, this became a favorite royal palace, where a few kings of Scotland were born, the last being Charles I. After being burned by Edward I in 1303, it was restored by James IV in 1500. The abbot's house to the east of the church, with its crowstepped gables and tiny turrets, was built in the late sixteenth century. For a while it was the home of a lay commendator with the title of Lord Dunfermline, but has recently been converted into a community center managed by the Dunfermline Carnegie Trust.

* Pittencrieff Park *(73)*, Monastery Street; entrance opposite west door of Abbey church.

This is a handsome public park with beautiful gardens, the gift of Andrew Carnegie to the town of his birth. On a high mound about a hundred yards west of Dunfermline Abbey, a stone fence encloses fragments of masonry thought to be the site of King Malcolm's Tower, a favorite residence of Malcolm Canmore and Queen Margaret. This is the spot presumably alluded to in the famous ballad, *Sir Patrick Spens*:

> The king sits in Dunfermling toune,
> Drinking the blude-red wine. . . .

* Dunfermline Museum *(342)*, Viewfield

Exhibits of linen damask and other artifacts connected with the linen industry are the distinguishing features of this museum of local history and archaeology.

* Andrew Carnegie Birthplace Memorial *(342)*, Moodie Street

The small cottage where the great Scottish-American industrialist and philanthropist was born has been restored and arranged as the typical home of a Dunfermline linen-weaver, which was the occupation of Andrew Carnegie's father.

FALKLAND (FIFE)

*** Falkland Palace *(163, 194, 260)*, town center; NTS

About the year 1500 King James IV commenced the building of a new palace here on the foundations of an early medieval castle used primarily as a royal hunting lodge. The plan was for a three-sided building set around an inner courtyard with the main entrance through a twin-turreted gate-house at the southwest corner. Of this structure, the north range (the oldest part of the building) has been reduced to foundations only, largely as the result of an accidental fire set by Cromwell's troops in 1653. The east range stands only in part but contains the much restored king's bed chamber furnished in the style of the early sixteenth century. The gatehouse and south range (facing the street) are fully habitable, as restored in the nineteenth century by the third Marquis of Bute.

In 1537 King James V, in preparation for the arrival from France of his first wife, Madeleine, embellished the south and east ranges—especially on the courtyard side. There, on the south facade, the elegant upper windows separated by decorative neoclassical pilasters and carved roundels are probably the handiwork of French masons—"a two dimensional exercise in Renaissance design" (Stewart Cruden). Unfortunately, entry into the inner courtyard is now prohibited, so that today's visitor gets only a distant view of this elegant stonework.

James V apparently so loved this place that he chose to return here to die after the defeat of his army at Solway Moss—leaving his second wife, Marie de Guise, at Linlithgow to give birth to the child who became Mary, Queen of Scots.

The interior of the south wing is now mostly furnished and decorated according to the neo-Gothic fashion favored by the third Marquis of Bute. The original great hall has been converted to a chapel for Roman Catholic services. The garden—a post–World War II creation distinguished especially for its herbaceous borders—is a delight. Beyond it is a building housing the royal tennis court—erected by James V in 1539, and therefore the second oldest (after Hampton Court) of such edifices in Britain.

INVERKEITHING (FIFE)

Inverkeithing Museum *(168)*, town center

This small and typical local museum is housed on what is thought to be the *hospitium* of a medieval friary, probably Franciscan, though signposted as Dominican.

KIRKCALDY (FIFE)

* Industrial Museum *(343)*, Abbotshall Road

This is an instructive small museum dedicated to the industrial history of Fife, with special emphasis on Kirkcaldy's linoleum industry.

*** Ravenscraig Castle *(127, 128)*, n of town center; s of A 955 in Ravenscraig Park (59 NT 291 925); AM

The first castle in Scotland designed from the outset for artillery defense, Ravenscraig was begun in 1460 by King James II for occupation by his wife, Mary of Guelders, and sufficiently advanced to permit her to move here in 1461, the year after the king's death. After Queen Mary died, James III awarded the castle to William Sinclair in partial exchange for his surrendering his rights in the earldom of Orkney to the Crown. Construction continued throughout the sixteenth and into the seventeenth century.

Built on a promontory jutting southward into Kirkcaldy Bay, all of the castle's formidable defenses face the landward (northern) approach. The frontal range of buildings consists of a rectangular block flanked by two massive D-shaped towers. The central building is entered through a barrel-vaulted passage, and over it extends an artillery platform open to the sky and formerly guarded on the landward side by a high parapet with widemouthed gun embrasures. Both central block and flanking towers are pierced with inverted keyhole gunports. The seaward (southern) end is unprotected except by a wall against which kitchens and other offices (now much ruined) are attached. Living quarters for Mary of Guelders were built into the western tower, to the right of the entrance. The eastern tower housed the garrison.

Pan Ha', Dysart *(224)*, 2 m. ne on A 955

Just above the shoreline in the tiny village of Dysart is this fascinating group of little houses built in the sixteenth to the eighteenth centuries and then occupied by functionaries attached to this once flourishing port.

NEWBURGH (FIFE)

Lindores Abbey *(148)*, ½ m. e; n of A 913 (59 NO 243 185)

Here are the very scant ruins of a Tironensian abbey founded in 1191 by David, Earl of Huntingdon, grandson of King David I and younger brother of Malcolm IV and William the Lion. It was, until the Reformation, one of the most celebrated monasteries in Scotland. In 1543 the abbey was sacked by zealous Protestants and the monks temporarily expelled.

Nothing is left of this once notable establishment, situated beside a private farmhouse whose buildings were obviously constructed out of stones taken from the abbey, except for an archway, part of a tower, and scattered pieces of masonry.

NEWPORT-ON-TAY (FIFE)

Balmerino Abbey *(149, 197)*, 5 m. w; 2½ m. w of B 946 from ½ m. s of Wormit (59 NO 359 247)

Founded in 1226 by Queen Ermengarde, widow of King William the Lion, this was a Cistercian house colonized by monks from Melrose. It was badly savaged by the English in 1547, and very little remains except for the vaulted chapter house and adjoining parts of the eastern range of the cloister—here, as at Melrose, on the north side of the monastic church.

PITTENWEEM (FIFE)

Kellie Lodging *(224)*, High Street

This is a substantial town house built about 1590.

Gyles House *(224)*, harbor front

This is a restored two-story sea captain's house built in the seventeenth century.

** Kellie Castle *(228, 333)*, 3 m. nw; ½ m. n of B 9171; NTS

To the original tower-house, built in the mid-fourteenth century by the Oliphant family, a new tower was added in the sixteenth century, and in the early seventeenth the two separate parts of the now stately residence were joined by additional buildings, thus creating a T-plan mansion. Later in the seventeenth century, handsome plasterwork was added to the interiors. Much restoration work was carried on in the late nineteenth century by Professor James Lorimer, father of the famous architect Robert Lorimer, who assisted in the undertaking. The interior is filled with fine furnishings, plasterwork, and ceiling paintings. The walled garden is charming—herbaceous borders at their best.

ST. ANDREWS (FIFE)

*** St. Andrews Cathedral *(66, 153)*, The Pends

This was the prime cathedral of Scotland and, after 1472, seat of its first archbishop. The cathedral church was the largest in the country and one of the largest in Britain. Founded in the mid-twelfth century by Bishop Robert, who had brought Augustinian canons here from Scone, this was one of two cathedrals in Scotland served by regular clergy (the other was at Whithorn). Building began about 1160 and was completed in 1238, but the church was so severely damaged by fire that it had to be rebuilt about 1280 with a shortened nave. After surviving Edward I's ill usage, the church was again destroyed by fire in the 1370s and rebuilt over a period of seventy years. Protestant zealots during the Reformation did away with most of the altars, statuary, and other "popish" embellishments, but the present ruined condition of the church and claustral buildings is chiefly the product of neglect and pillage by the local townspeople.

The best-preserved part of the abbey and cathedral precinct is the surrounding sixteenth-century wall built over fourteenth-century foundations and the fine entrance gateway through it, called the Pends, also dating from the fourteenth century. Of the west front of the church, only the late-thirteenth-century door and a single adjacent tower survives. Much less remains of the nave, except for the south wall, which offers an instructive contrast between the Transitional and First Pointed architectural styles—the windows of the six western bays are twin-lighted and pointed-arched; those of the four eastern bays are round-arched. The fragmentary remains of the south transept, including part of the night stairs leading once into the canons' dorter, were built in the fifteenth century. The eastern gable, the highest section of the ruin, belongs to the twelfth-century period of construction, as indicated by its three round-arched windows. The wide Gothic opening above them is an insertion of the fifteenth century.

Of the claustral remains, only the east range survives to any extent. Here, in what was once the warming house, is the site museum, which contains a very important collection of Early Christian sculptured stones, including more than fifty fragments of eighth-to tenth-century cross-slabs of mixed Celtic and Anglian styles. The single most interesting item is the so-called sarcophagus of St. Andrew, possibly made in the eighth century to house the relics of Scotland's patron saint, though more likely dating from the tenth. Carved on the front is a scene of King David and the lion, while the end panels have interlaced serpents. Also in the museum are a fine head of Christ dating from the thirteenth century, two fragments of a bishop's effigy, and an interesting collection of episcopal seals.

*** Church of St. Rule (Regulus) *(136)*, cathedral precinct

This Anglo-Saxon-style church was built in the eleventh century and dedicated to St. Rule (Regulus), who was believed to have brought relics of St. Andrew to this place in the eighth century. This is the legendary origin of the cult of St. Andrew, which eventually elevated him, the brother of St. Peter, to the status of Scotland's patron saint. Also to the legend that he was crucified on a diagonal cross (X-shaped) is owed the origin of Scotland's national flag, the white saltire on a blue field.

The church consists of a choir about 24 feet long with a 108-feet-high square tower attached to the western end. It is a steep climb to the top, but the view of the city of St. Andrews and the coast of Fife is worth it.

** St. Andrews Castle *(154, 199)*, Castle Street

This handsomely situated but badly ruined castle was the residence of the bishops and archbishops of St. Andrews from the time of its earliest construction about 1200 until the abolition of episcopacy in the seventeenth century. During the War of Independence it changed hands several times between Scots and English and suffered considerable damage on each occasion; was almost destroyed in 1337 when the Scots under Sir Andrew Moray drove out the English supporters of Edward Balliol; was rebuilt at the end of the fourteenth century; was restored in the early sixteenth by Cardinal David Beaton; and was rebuilt again in the second half of the sixteenth century, after it had been severely damaged by the French. Here in 1546 Protestant rebels captured and killed Cardinal David Beaton and strung his corpse from the battlements of his own castle in retaliation for his part in the burning of George Wishart, which had taken place in front of the building. The insurgents, joined by John Knox, then occupied the castle for a year until forced to surrender to besieging forces assisted by a French fleet—after which Knox and his fellows were consigned to French galleys or prisons. Archbishop John Hamilton thereafter made some much needed repairs, but only in time to have the castle taken over by the Crown in 1587, though it was thereafter occasionally the residence of the archbishops.

After so much savaging by so many people over such a long period of time, it is not surprising that the ruins are hard to comprehend from an architectural viewpoint. The present foretower, the fourth version, is part of the English restoration of 1336 before Moray took the castle "and to the erd syn dang it doun." It incorporates, however, a part of the original building now represented by the cross-wall in the existing foretower. To the left, after entering by way of a modern bridge across the protective ditch, most of the south and west walls, including the sea tower, are of late-fourteenth-century construction. In the chambers on each side of the entrance are pits dug by the Protestant defenders in 1546–1547 to block the efforts of the besiegers to sink mines underneath the castle walls. The sea tower at the northwest corner contains a "bottle dungeon" hollowed out of solid rock, where George Wishart and other Protestants were incarcerated by Beaton. The north range hugging the coast is of late-sixteenth-century construction, but the kitchen tower at its eastern end belongs to the fourteenth, as does most of the eastern and southeastern wall leading back to the foretower.

Church of St. Mary's on the Rock (169), n of cathedral precinct

Here are the bare foundations of the nave of a mid-thirteenth-century collegiate church built on the site of a much earlier Culdee foundation. It is the first church in medieval Scotland to have received a collegiate charter. Nice view from here of the harbor of St. Andrews and the coast of Fife.

*** The University of St. Andrews (174, 297, 298), town center

*** College of St. Salvator (174, 198), North Street

The chapel to the right of the main entrance is, though somewhat restored, the original collegiate church founded by Bishop James Kennedy in 1450 and built shortly thereafter. Here still are the founder's splendid tomb, the mace he donated to the college, and the pulpit from which John Knox is alleged to have preached when it was in Holy Trinity Church a short distance away. The quadrangle of residential buildings of the combined College of St. Salvator and St. Leonard was built in the nineteenth century in the Jacobean style. The adjoining garden court is of twentieth-century construction. In front of the main gate is the spot where the

Protestant martyr Patrick Hamilton was burned in 1528.

*** St. Mary's College (175), South Street

Today the prettiest and most peaceful spot in this busy university city, St. Mary's was founded as a college for the study of theology by Archbishop James Beaton in 1525. Of the existing buildings, those on the north and west sides of the quadrangle date to about the time of the founding. A legend of doubtful authenticity attributes to Mary, Queen of Scots, the planting of the hawthorn tree still on the college grounds.

* St. Leonard's Chapel (175), e of Abbey Street, in grounds of St. Leonard's School

This attractive little chapel is the only surviving relic of St. Leonard's College, founded in 1512 as a "college of poor clerks" attached to the neighboring Augustinian priory and part of the University of St. Andrews. Inside, the most interesting feature is the tomb of Robert Stewart, Bishop of Caithness, and uncle of James VI.

** University Museum (7, 238), Parliament Hall, South Street

Originally built in 1643 as a library and hall for graduations and other university ceremonies and called the "Public School," this was the scene of a meeting of the Scottish Parliament in 1645, owing to the ongoing plague in Edinburgh. The chief business of the session was the trial and condemnation of supporters of the Marquis of Montrose. Much remodelled, the present building serves as a small but very good museum containing, among other things, a representative collection of prehistoric artifacts found in Fife, rare books from the university library, seventeenth-century archery medals, university maces, and elegant silverware and leatherwork from St. Mary's College and St. Leonard's College.

* Holy Trinity Kirk (202, 245), South Street

The central tower here dates from the fifteenth century, but the rest of the structure has been rebuilt so frequently that little remains of the actual fabric of the kirk where John Knox preached his first public sermon in 1547 and to which he returned in 1559 when the Lords of the Congregation had occupied St. Andrews. (Knox's pulpit is in the chapel of nearby St. Salvator's College.) The chief object of interest inside is the elaborate marble monument to Archbishop James Sharp who was murdered at Magus Muir by a band of Covenanters in 1679.

Blackfriars Chapel *(168)*, South Street

Here are the very fragmentary remains of a church built probably in the early sixteenth century by Dominican friars.

The Old Course *(359)*, n of town center

Here is the most famous golf course in Scotland, open to the public most of the year. The clubhouse, built in 1854, is for the exclusive use of members (and guests) of the Royal and Ancient Golf Club, founded in 1754.

* Dairsie Kirk *(221)*, 7 m. w; 1 m. s of A 91 from Dairsie or Osnaburgh

This interesting little kirk was built in 1621 by Archbishop John Spottiswoode at a time when he and King James VI were trying to move the Church of Scotland toward greater conformity with the Church of England. This may account for the simulated Gothic style, especially the cinquefoil plate window tracery, and certainly would explain the original presence of a chancel screen, since disappeared along with all the other church furnishings. The building is now in the custody of St. Andrews University.

** Leuchars Parish Church *(162)*, 6 m. n; e of A 919, in Leuchars village

Although the nave of this pretty little church is modern, the choir and apse, with their original round-arched chevron-decorated doorways, are pure Romanesque of late-twelfth-century date. The outer wall is graced with some excellent round-arched arcading on two levels.

* Earlshall Castle *(266, 333)*, 6 m. n; e of A 919 from Leuchars village

This is a five-story Z-plan tower-house built in 1546 by Sir William Bruce. The attached smaller house may have been of slightly earlier construction. Earlshall was restored by Robert Lorimer late in the nineteenth century and is now displayed as a stately home. Noteworthy are the splendid gallery, with its seventeenth-century painted ceiling depicting the arms of the principal families of Scotland; the large collection of basket-hilted swords; and the garden with topiary shaped like chessmen.

ST. MONANCE (FIFE)

** Church of St. Monan *(164, 168)*, s of A 917, near town center

Dramatically situated overlooking the coast of Fife, this is a mid-fourteenth-century church, established by King David II, later turned over to Dominican friars, and in the nineteenth century converted to use as a parish kirk. The style is good, though simple, Second Pointed. The original sedilia, piscinas, and aumbry are still to be seen. The fully rigged ship's model is modern, as are the whitewashed walls of this quite charming little kirk.

West Shore *(224)*, town harbor

Hugging the shoreline is this charming row of mostly eighteenth-century little houses restored by the National Trust for Scotland.

Perthshire

ABERFELDY (TAYSIDE)

Wade's Bridge *(271)*, B 846, n of town center

Built in 1732 by General George Wade to carry his Crieff-to-Dalnacardoch road across the River Tay, this bridge now serves the same purpose for the B 846, though only wide enough for one-way motor traffic. It is the longest of the Wade bridges (four hundred feet), is constructed of ashlar, and is ornamented with four obelisks. William Adam was the architect, which accounts for the bridge's unusually graceful appearance.

* Black Watch Memorial *(268)*, w of B 846 at south end of Wade Bridge

In a park on the south bank of the River Tay stands this larger-than-life-size statue of a Highlander of the Black Watch, wearing the standard belted plaid (which would have been of black, green, and blue tartan) and equipped with basket-hilted sword, musket, bayonet, etc., which were regulation gear for 1740, the date of the regiment's formation at Aberfeldy. The statue was raised in 1887, and, though somewhat excessively heroic in the Victorian manner, well worth examining because of the faithful rendering of the original uniform and equipment of this famous regiment.

** Castle Menzies *(225, 305)*, 1 m. nw; n of B 846

Built by Sir James Menzies in 1571-1577, this is a Z-plan tower-house to the back of which an additional wing was added in the nineteenth century. There are gunports at the ground level, decorated dormer windows above, and stepped gables and corner turrets on the rooftop. Already in a good state of preservation, the house is in the process of further restoration as a Clan Menzies center and museum. Most of the furniture is Victorian. Here too, almost inevitably, is a room where Bonnie Prince Charlie is supposed to have slept. In this case, solid documentation supports the claim that Charles Edward Stuart stayed here the night of 4-5 February 1746, in spite of the fact that the then owner, Sir Robert Menzies, was a Hanoverian sympathizer.

Wade's Tummel Bridge *(271)*, 16 m. nw, B 846

Next to the iron bridge carrying the B 846 is Wade's bridge of 1733, which carried his Crieff-to-Dalnacardoch road across the River Tummel.

ABERFOYLE (CENTRAL)

*** Inchmahome Priory *(107, 151, 199)*, 4½ m. e; by ferry from Port of Menteith on B 8034 (to signal for ferry, turn signal board on dock so that white side faces the island) (57 NN 574 005); AM

Beautifully situated on an island in the Lake of Menteith, this ruined Augustinian priory was founded in 1238 by Walter Comyn, fourth Earl of Menteith. The rectangular church was built in the First Pointed style, and the high-standing east gable still contains five lancets with double-lighted windows on each side. The western door is flanked by blind twin lancets with trefoil and quatrefoil openings in the spandrels. The tower at the northwest corner was added in the sixteenth century. Triple sedilia stand against the south wall of the choir. The claustral buildings are fragmentary, except for the barrel-vaulted warming-room and the rectangular chapter house, which is complete and contains the effigy of John Drummond (d. 1372), armed and armored in the style of the early fourteenth century. Mary, Queen of Scots, stayed here very briefly as a child before being shipped to France to marry the Dauphin.

ABERNETHY (TAYSIDE)

* Abernethy Round Tower *(67)*, e side of town center; ¼ m. s of A 913; AM

This solitary round tower, seventy-four feet high, is one of two of this type in Scotland, both displaying Irish architectural influence. The lower portion probably dates from the tenth century, but the upper part, with its early Norman belfry windows, was probably added in the twelfth. Unlike the other round tower at Brechin, this one is bare of any sculptural decoration.

AUCHTERARDER (TAYSIDE)

* St. Serf's, Dunning *(137)*, 4 m. e; n of B 8062, in Dunning village

The early medieval Romanesque rectangular tower (eleventh-century) is attached to the west end of a much restored parish kirk with a fine Second

Pointed arch mounted on round Romanesque columns and an early round-arched north doorway.

BLAIR ATHOLL (TAYSIDE)

*** Blair Castle *(234, 249, 274, 275, 277, 295)*, ½ m n, on minor road n of A 9

Even for a Scottish castle, the history of Blair is marvelously complex. Although the attractive white-harled stately home now appears to be all of one piece, it is in fact the product of about six hundred years of building and rebuilding. The main tower, traditionally known as Cumming's Tower, was erected in the mid-thirteenth century by John Comyn of Badenoch on ground that lay within the earldom of Atholl. During the War of Independence the earldom was forfeited to the Crown, then in 1457 conferred on Sir John Stewart of Balvenie, whose male descendants held it until 1629, when it passed to John Murray, Master of Tullibardine, through his mother Dorothea Stewart. This is how the Murray family came to own Blair Castle. In the intervening years another tower had been built south of Cumming's Tower, and the space between filled with a rectangular block containing the great hall. During the interregnum the castle was garrisoned by Cromwell's troops, then restored to the earl, who was elevated to the rank of marquis by Charles II. While this second marquis sided with King William after the Revolution of 1689–1690, his castle was seized by Jacobites, and General Hugh MacKay's effort to recapture it resulted in the inconclusive battle at nearby Killiecrankie Pass. The second marquis was made first Duke of Atholl in 1703, but, because of the defection of his eldest son to the Jacobites in 1715, the dukedom passed to the second son, James.

It was this James, second Duke of Atholl, who began making extensive alterations to Blair Castle, only to be interrupted by The Forty-five uprising, during which time his house was first occupied by Jacobites, then garrisoned by the Duke of Cumberland's troops, and finally unsuccessfully besieged by the owner's younger brother, Lord George Murray, who had joined forces with Charles Edward, the Young Pretender. Not until the final crushing of the rebellion at Culloden was the second duke able to complete the task of remodelling Blair into the Georgian mansion that it still remains, at least on the inside. On the outside, however, an attempt was made by the seventh duke to recapture the castle's medieval appearance by hiring the architect John Bryce to recastellate the building in 1869.

Except for the baronial entrance hall (1872), with its stuffed stags and wall-mounted weapons, and the Stewart Room, which contains some rare seventeenth-century furniture, most of the interior is decorated and furnished in the elegant fashion of the eighteenth century. Among the interesting objects on display are an original copy of the National Covenant of 1638, a number of Jacobite relics, and contemporary portraits of James V and Marie de Guise; Mary, Queen of Scots, and her son James VI; John, first Duke of Atholl, by Jacob de Wet; Charles II (as Prince of Wales) and Charles, Lord Stanley, by Sir Peter Lely; the third Duke and Duchess of Atholl and their children, by Johann Zoffany; and Prince Charles Edward, by Giles Hussey. Throughout, the panelling and plaster ceilings are exquisite. The grounds are especially distinguished for their heavy and extensive growth of larch and Scots pine—varieties especially favored by the fourth Duke of Atholl, who, between 1744 and 1747, planted about four thousand acres of commercial woodland here.

Killiecrankie Visitor Centre *(249)*, 4 m. se; w of A 9; NTS

Here are well-written posters describing the Jacobite uprising of 1689 and the battle that took place nearby between the forces of Viscount Dundee and Hugh MacKay. A footpath leads to the "Soldier's Leap," where a government trooper named Donald MacBean jumped, according to his own report, eighteen feet across the River Garry to avoid capture by pursuing Jacobites.

Clan Donnachaidh Museum *(305)*, 4 m. w, in Bruar; n of A 9

This is a small and rather attractive museum devoted to memorabilia associated with the clan and its affiliated septs: Robertsons, Reids, MacRoberts, and others. Not always open as scheduled.

Wade's Road *(270)*, 4 m. nw; n of Calvine from junction of A 9 and B 847

A steep one-quarter-mile climb by footpath opposite the point where the B 847 turns off the A 9 (signposted Kinloch Rannoch) leads to a long stretch of the Dunkeld-to-Inverness road built by General George Wade in 1728–1729. With some interruptions, this runs northwest for more than a mile until blocked by the A 9 near Clune's Lodge.

Wade's Stone *(270)*, 10½ m. nw; e of A 9, 7 m. nw of Calvine

At the side of the southbound (east) lane of the dual carriageway stands one of General Wade's marker stones, which were put up after the completion of his roads so that travellers would not lose their way during heavy snowfalls. This one is eight feet in height and bears the date 1729. It was moved to this spot when the present road was laid down.

BLAIRGOWRIE (TAYSIDE)

Inchtuthil *(42, 43)*, 6½ m. sw; 1 m. s of junction of B 947 and A 984 (53 NO 125 297)

At the end of a bumpy road and on private property are the scant remains of the great Roman fortress begun by Agricola about A.D. 83 and dismantled three or four years later. There is very little left to see, except for a ditch that lay outside the eastern rampart of the fortress and the now grass-covered southern rampart.

CALLANDER (CENTRAL)

Balquhidder Kirkyard *(267),* 12 m. n; 1½ m. w of A 84 from 3 m. s of Lochearnhead

Here behind a railing are the graves of the famous outlaw Rob Roy MacGregor (d. 1734), his wife, and two sons. The kirk itself is of nineteenth-century construction and is undistinguished, though it does house two interesting Gaelic Bibles and the Early Christian "St. Angus Stone."

COMRIE (TAYSIDE)

*** Museum of Scottish Tartans *(269, 305, 329),* town center

This is an excellent small museum devoted exclusively to the history of the Scottish tartan. Here are thirteen hundred specimens of tartan, the largest collection anywhere, and well-written posted explanations concerning the manufacture and use of this peculiarily Scottish material. The information provided is refreshingly free of the romantic nonsense so frequently associated with this subject. A prize feature is a huge restored contemporary portrait of Queen Victoria's beloved servant, John Brown, wearing a very somber kilt. The painting is believed to have been deliberately damaged by the resentful King Edward VII when he was cleaning out Balmoral Castle after his mother's death. It is located in the "Balmorality corner," where mild fun is made of the queen's uninformed enthusiasm for tartans. Outside is a reconstructed weaver's cottage with a "cruck-frame" roof; also a wild dye plant garden growing the materials traditionally used in the Highlands for dying tartans before their manufacture was taken over by Lowland textile mills using chemical dyes.

COUPAR ANGUS (TAYSIDE)

Pitcur Souterrain *(36),* 3 m. se; e of A 923 (53 NO 253 374)

Here are the remains of a post–Iron Age *souterrain* with a main passage 190 feet long and a side passage of about 60 feet. Most of this trenchlike structure is roofless, but about a quarter of the main passage is still covered by its original lintels.

** Meigle Museum *(54, 66)*, 4 m. ne, in Meigle, on A 94; AM

This is an outstanding collection of thirty-four Pictish stones, mostly belonging to Class II or Class III. Those worth special attention are numbered 1, 2, 4, and 5.

Key to the museum is at custodian's cottage next to the red telephone kiosk in the village square.

CRIEFF (TAYSIDE)

*** Glenturret Distillery *(358)*, 1½ m. n; n of A 85

Occupying the premises of a distillery established in 1775 and in continuous operation until American Prohibition forced it temporarily to close its doors, this is a relatively small establishment and therefore closer in character than most to the early stills of Scotland before whisky making became such a giant industry. There is a good audiovisual show explaining the distillation process, followed by a well-conducted guided tour and a free drink of excellent malt whisky at the end.

*** Drummond Castle Garden *(260, 335)*, 3 m. s; w of A 822

In the valley behind the much altered fifteenth-century tower-house (not open to the public) lies this spectacular Italianate parterre, which can be entered by a steep set of stone steps leading down from the balustrade. In the center is a multifaceted sundial dated 1630 and designed by John Mylne. The garden itself was laid out in the form of St. Andrew's cross in or about 1842, the year Queen Victoria planted the great copper beech in the parterre. The best place for viewing this great work of horticultural art is from the terrace above.

* Muthill Church *(137)*, 3 m. s; e of A 822 in Muthill village

Attached to a much ruined fifteenth-century church is a high square Romanesque tower of eleventh-century date, in both appearance and age comparable to the Church of St. Rule in St. Andrews.

* Innerpeffray Chapel and Library *(171)*, 3 m. se; sw of B 8062 (58 NN 902 185); AM

This small rectangular chapel was founded as a collegiate church by Sir John Drummond in 1508. The original altar stone and painted ceiling are still to be seen. The adjacent library was founded in 1691 by David Drummond, third Lord Maderty, and operated as a lending library, used by all conditions of people from 1747. It contains a rare and fascinating collection of books, some dating from the sixteenth century.

* Fowlis Wester Stone *(54)*, 5 m. e; ½ m. n of A 85 from New Fowlis (58 NN 928 241); AM

In the village square stands a much eroded ninth-century Class II Pictish stone, twelve feet in height. The arms of the cross project slightly from the slab—a unique feature. On the back is an interesting array of horsemen, foot soldiers, animals, and Pictish symbols. Inside the nearby parish kirk, on the north wall, is an eighth-century Class III slab, five feet high and carved on one face only with a cross flanked by fabulous animals and other figures.

** Tullibardine Chapel *(170)*, 6 m. se; n of A 823 (58 NN 909 135); AM

Unoccupied, but unaltered and structurally complete, is this small cruciform collegiate church, founded by Sir David Murray in 1446. The choir dates from the original founding, the nave and transepts probably somewhat later. The Scottish Development Department has posted excellent wall placards. A key can be obtained from the neighboring farmhouse.

Wade's Road *(270)*, 5-7 m. n; nw of A 822 from Faulford Inn; signposted to Connachan Lodge

Veering left from the A 822 about fifty yards north of Faulford Inn is a good two-mile stretch of the Crieff-to-Dalnacardoch Road built by General George Wade in 1730. At the north end the old road rejoins the A 822.

Wade's Road *(270)*, 11-12 m. n; nw of A 822 from n of Almond River Bridge

A few yards north of the bridge over the River Almond, a section of Wade's 1730 road from Crieff to Dalnacardoch leaves the A 822 on the left and continues for about a mile before rejoining it.

Wade's Road *(270)*, 13-14 m. n; w of A 822, between Corrymuchloch and Amultree

Where the A 822 bends to the northeast at Corrymuckloch a mile-long section of Wade's road from Crieff to Dalnacardoch goes straight north to rejoin the modern road at Amulree.

DOUNE (CENTRAL)

*** Doune Castle *(115)*, village center; 8 m. nw of Stirling on A 84 (57 NN 721 011)

Erected before 1400 by Robert Stewart, first Duke of Albany and brother to King Robert III, the castle became its builder's chief residence while Governor of Scotland during the captivity of James I in England. Along with the title, it was inherited by Albany's son Murdoch, later executed by James I after his return to Scotland.

Still in an excellent state of preservation, this is a courtyard castle with its defensive strength concentrated in the gatehouse keep at the main entrance. This consists of a three-story rectangular building with a single projecting corner tower. The entrance passage to the courtyard contains a fine specimen of a typical Scottish yett. On the first floor above is the great hall, with a double fireplace at the dais end and a restored screen and minstrels' gallery at the other. Above the hall is the solar or withdrawing room, a small oratory, and other domestic apartments. The portcullis was operated from a window embrasure in the hall. This room was entered by a door into the screens passage reached by a walled stairway leading from the courtyard. On the same floor as the great hall is the common hall, but the present doorway between them is a modern insertion. Originally there was no direct communication between the lord's living quarters and those reserved for his retainers—possibly a deliberate precaution on the builder's part against the contingency of mutiny. The common hall is a large chamber with a high timber roof and open hearth in the middle of the floor. It is attached to the kitchen and service accommodations, which are contained in a separate building to the side. Behind this impressive range of towers lies a rather unimpressive curtain wall enclosing the courtyard. It is possible that this part of the castle was still unfinished when Murdoch met his death.

** **Doune Motor Museum** *(366)*, 1 m. nw of town center; n of A 84

Here is a fine collection of English and European automobiles, the oldest being a 1905 Rolls Royce.

DUNBLANE (CENTRAL)

* **Dunblane Cathedral** *(158, 165)*, town center

The oldest part of the medieval cathedral is the lower section of the square tower attached to the west end of the church. The lower four stories date from the eleventh century. The rest of the church (mainly thirteenth-century in origin) is the product of two restorations: the first in the nineteenth century by Sir Robert Rowand Anderson who succeeded in recreating the Early Pointed appearance of the major part of the church fabric; the other, later, by Sir Robert Lorimer, who introduced a more elegant, and not especially appropriate, late Gothic flamboyant element. Noteworthy are the misericord stalls attributed to the mid-fifteenth-century Bishop Ochiltree. The building now serves as a parish kirk.

** **Ardoch Roman Fort** *(46)*, 7 m. ne; 1 m. n of Braco village (Tayside) 3 m. e of A 822 (58 NN 839 099)

This is the best preserved of all Roman fortifications in Scotland. Though no stonework remains visible, there is a well-preserved system of earthen ramparts and ditches on both the northern and eastern sides of the fort. It was founded by Agricola, but the present remains date from about A.D. 142 when Ardoch was reinforced to serve as an outpost for the Antonine Wall.

DUNKELD (TAYSIDE)

** **Dunkeld Cathedral** *(115, 155, 165, 249)*, High Street; AM

In its lovely setting beside the River Tay, this was the site of a Culdee monastery in the ninth century and of an episcopal see of about that date and later. Of the cathedral, built in various stages between the thirteenth and fifteenth centuries, the restored eastern end now serves as the parish kirk, while the nave is roofless. The architectural styles of some parts of the building are eccentric and atypical of their respective dates of construction. The ruined nave was built mostly in the early fifteenth century. The great window in the west gable is not truly centered, and the few fragments of its tracery hint of a French flamboyant influence. Inside, the huge round pillars suggest a reversion to the Romanesque style of the twelfth century, as do the round-arched windows in the north and south walls. Above these are other traceried windows, more or less in the Second Pointed style contemporary to their construction. The well-preserved tower at the northwest corner dates from the late fifteenth century, as does the chapter house extending north of the choir. Within the former, on the ground floor, are two rare, though dimly visible, wall paintings. The fabric of the choir is the oldest part of the building and was erected in the thirteenth and fourteenth centuries. It has undergone several restorations, which have made possible its continued use since the sixteenth century as a parish kirk. At the east end is the recumbent armored effigy of a knight, believed to be Alexander Stewart, the "Wolf of Badenoch."

In 1689 the cathedral witnessed a terrible battle between the Jacobites and government forces in the aftermath of the Jacobite victory at Killiecrankie. The government troops (Cameronians) drove out the rebels by setting fire to the town, but not before their commander, Lieutenant Colonel William Cleland, was killed. His gravestone can be seen in the southwest corner of the ruined nave.

* **Dunkeld Bridge** *(287)*, on A 923 at south end of town

This graceful stone bridge of five arches across the River Tay was built by

Thomas Telford in the early nineteenth century and still carries the main road leading south from town. The best view is from the grounds of the cathedral.

Dunkeld Little Houses *(249)*, town center; NTS

These charming rows of tiny dwellings lining both sides of Cathedral Street and The Cross were built to replace the houses burned in 1689 when Jacobites fought a regiment of Cameronians raised to defend King William (of Orange) and the Protestant interest in Scotland. The houses were restored by the National Trust for Scotland and the Perth County Council.

PERTH (TAYSIDE)

** St. John's Kirk *(202)*, St. John Street

This is a fine fifteenth-century double-aisled cruciform church with a central tower completed in the early sixteenth century, modified in the nineteenth by James Gillespie Graham and others, and restored in the 1920s, at which time also Sir Robert Lorimer designed the War Memorial Shrine commemorating the 3,670 Perthshire men who died in combat in World War I. (A second memorial chapel at the east end of the choir commemorates the World War II dead—far fewer in number.)

It is here that John Knox preached his inflammatory sermon on 11 May 1559, touching off a wave of iconoclasm against Roman Catholic "idolatry" and sparking the revolution that ended in the establishment of the Protestant religion in Scotland. In 1598 the building was divided into two kirks and, for a time, after 1773, into three—in keeping with the Presbyterian preference for an intimate connection between preacher and congregation. The interior partitions were removed in the twentieth century, and the building now serves only one congregation of the Church of Scotland.

* Perth Art Gallery and Museum *(9, 365)*, George Street

This is a typical municipal museum of archaeology and local history plus an art gallery featuring the genre paintings, landscapes, etc., of nineteenth-century Scottish artists.

*** Black Watch Museum *(268, 289)*, Balhousie Castle, Hay Street, opposite North Inch Park

Here are four floors of Black Watch mementos and memorabilia dating from 1740 to the present; also a room devoted to "allied regiments" from Australia, Canada, New Zealand, and South Africa and another to volunteers and Territorials from Angus, Dundee, Fife, and Perthshire. This is the largest and most complete regimental museum in Scotland—and also the finest. No military buff should miss it.

*** Scone Palace *(72, 142, 262, 308, 335)*, 2 m. n; w of A 93

The property, containing the Moot Hill of Scone and the ancient abbey (destroyed), has been in the Murray family since 1604, when it was given by King James VI to Sir David Murray, later first Viscount Stormont, whose splendid alabaster monument can be seen in the tiny chapel atop Moot Hill. One of its eighteenth-century owners was William Murray, first Earl of Mansfield, Chancellor and Lord Chief Justice, deservedly famous for his decision in the Somerset case (1771) outlawing Negro slavery in Great Britain. The present house was built in 1802–1813 by the Lord Chief Justice's great-nephew, the third Earl of Mansfield. The present owner is William David Murray, eighth earl.

The house was designed by James Wyatt's pupil, William Atkinson, later Sir Walter Scott's architect at Abbotsford. It is a huge rectangular building of local red sandstone enclosing three inner courtyards. The roofline is battlemented, while square and polygonal towers appear regularly along all four facades, thus giving the house its "Georgian-Gothic" attributes. The interior decor combines plasterwork in the style of Robert Adam with pseudomedieval vaults and chandeliers.The lavish furnishings are more French than British, owing to the second earl's having served as ambassador to the Court of Louix XVI. English and Scottish paintings include portraits of George III and Queen Charlotte by Allan Ramsay; of the first earl of Mansfield by Joshua Reynolds, and Lady Elizabeth Murray by Johann Zoffany; and a well-known painting by Sir David Wilkie—*The Village Politicians*

Here also is a famous pinetum, begun in 1848 by the third Earl of Mansfield. Nearby are Douglas firs grown from seed sent to Scone in 1827 by a former subgardener, the famous arborist, David Douglas.

*** Huntingtower Castle *(211)*, 2½ m. w; n of A 85 (58 NO 084 252); AM

This is a completely roofed and floored "palace" consisting of two three-story tower-houses linked by a square hall. It belonged to the Ruthven family, the senior member of which, William, Lord Ruthven, was created Earl of Gowrie in 1581. It was he, in league with other Protestant nobles, who a year later kidnapped the teenaged King James VI and held him prisoner for ten months. Gowrie was subsequently beheaded, and after the frustration of another alleged conspiracy by the third earl in 1600, James VI confiscated all the family's properties and changed the name of this place from Ruthven to Huntingtower. The castle remained in Crown hands until

1643, when Charles I gave it to William Murray, Earl of Dysart and Lord Huntingtower.

The oldest section of this tripartite building is the eastern tower, parts of which are of fifteenth-century provenance. From here a passage opens on to the central hall, built mostly in the seventeenth century. On the ceiling and walls of the first floor are some fine paintings in tempera—the earliest of their kind in Scotland. The western wing is L-shaped, and in a first floor room are the remains of a painted coat of arms, also of seventeenth-century date.

** Elcho Castle *(225)*, 3 m. se; e of M-85 (58 NO 164 211); AM

On the south side of the Tay, this roofed and well-preserved tower-house was built about 1550 by John, Earl of Wemyss. The ground plan is somewhat unusual, consisting of two corner square towers or jambs at one end, a round tower at an opposite corner, and a small round tower in the middle of one side. The interior is fairly typical: a vaulted ground floor containing the kitchen; great hall and withdrawing room on the first floor; bedrooms with fireplaces and garderobes on the upper two floors. Good view from here of the River Tay.

* St. Madoe's Stone *(55)*, 5 m. e, on A 85 in Glencarse (58 NO 197 212)

Under cover in the churchyard is this fine Class II Pictish stone, with a cross surrounded by fabulous beasts on the front, and on the back three cloaked horsemen and a good selection of typical Pictish symbols.

PITLOCHRY (TAYSIDE)

* Dunfallandy Stone *(55)*, 1½ m. s, outside of churchyard near
Dunfallandy Hotel (52 NN 946 565); AM

This is a fine Class II Pictish stone with a sculpted cross flanked by various animals and beasts, and on the back two enthroned men with a cross between them, as well as fishtailed serpents, a horseman, "swimming elephants," and a variety of typical Pictish symbols.

Angus

ARBROATH (TAYSIDE)

*** Arbroath Abbey *(147)*, High Street

This was a Tironensian house founded by King William the Lion in 1178. It was dedicated to St. Thomas of Canterbury, the martyred English archbishop. Approached from the street through an arch guarded by a late-thirteenth-century gatehouse, the western facade of this well-preserved ruin is entered through a deeply recessed Romanesque doorway above which was a tribune or Galilee porch. On each side stands the remains of a massive tower. The major remaining parts of this once great cruciform church are a section of the east gable with three lancet windows; the vaulted sacristy; the south nave wall; and, of particular note, the south transept built in the First Pointed Style, with immense lancets and a very large circular window under the eaves of the southern gable. This is the famous "O of Arbroath," which sailors once used as a navigational aid. The cloister range has disappeared, except for a late-twelfth-century undercroft at the west end of the south range, above which at a later date the abbot's house (now the site museum) was erected. In a chamber above the gatehouse arches, reached by a turnpike stair within the northwest tower, is a fine exhibit of the history of the abbey.

** St. Vigeans Museum *(54, 66)*, 1 m. n; ½ m. w of A 92; AM (key available at cottage next door)

Here is a collection of thirty-two Pictish sculptured stones, all found in the neighborhood of the parish kirk. The best known is the Class II "Drosten stone," with three Pictish names spelled out in late-ninth-century Irish letters. Another worth noting is Stone #7, a Class III stone that combines Celtic curvilinear decoration and Anglian interlace motifs.

BRECHIN (TAYSIDE)

** Brechin Cathedral and Round Tower *(67, 159)*, town center

The cathedral, built originally in the thirteenth century, suffered badly from post-Reformation neglect as well as misguided restoration in the early nineteenth century. The present building is mostly the product of another restoration carried out in this century in an effort to recapture the looks and style of the original. The restored nave retains intact most of the features of the early-thirteenth-century construction. The choir, including the splendid lancet windows, has been almost completely rebuilt, as have the unmatching transepts. The square cathedral tower was probably built in the late fourteenth century and, except for its spire, retains much of its original appearance. The various fragments of Early Christian stones inside the church have been imported here from elsewhere.

The round tower adjacent to the church is one of two in Scotland and reflects architectural influences derived from Ireland. It was built probably late in the tenth century, except for the spire, which was added in the fourteenth, stands eighty-six feet high, and is made of blocks of red sandstone. The doorway is six feet above ground—obviously for defensive purposes. Above its arch is a sculpted figure of the crucified Christ with uncrossed legs—another indication of Irish influence. On each side of the door is a relief of two hooded clergymen, probably bishops, below whom crouch two grotesque beasts.

The tower, which is under guardianship of the Scottish Development Department, cannot be entered. The cathedral now serves as the parish kirk.

*** White Caterthun and Brown Caterthun *(31)*, 5 m. nw; 3 m. nw of Little Brechin (44 NO 548 660 and 555 668); AM

These are the most impressive Iron Age hill-forts in Scotland. The southernmost of the two (the White Caterthun) consists of five concentric defense-works of ramparts and adjacent ditches. The three outer ramparts are much eroded. The summit of the hill is encircled by an oval ring of scattered stones representing the remains of the two inner walls of the fort, which presumably collapsed after the decay of the interlaced timbers of the original construction. The smaller Brown Caterthun has three encircling ramparts, now covered with turf. The most interesting features of this site are the many entranceways piercing the two outer embankments. The outlines of the Brown Caterthun are best viewed from the White Caterthun, which stands on a higher elevation.

* Edzell Castle and *** Garden *(227, 260)*, 6 m. n; 1 m. w of B 966 from Edzell village (54 NO 585 691); AM

This is a sixteenth-century L-plan tower-house to which a large rectangular courtyard mansion was added about 1580 and, still later (1604), a spacious walled garden or "pleasance" with a summer house and bathhouse attached. The last was the handiwork of Sir David Lindsay, Lord Edzell, and it is this feature, maintained by the Scottish Development Department, that is the main attraction of this ruined castle.

The main entrance (from the west) leads into the unfinished 1580 mansion; to the right rises the earlier four-story tower-house. On the south side of this building is the pleasance, surrounded on three sides by a garden wall pierced with niches arranged in a checkerboard fashion so as to reproduce the arms of the Lindsays. Within each niche are boxes, ordinarily filled with blue and white flowers alternately, which, together with the red sandstone of the walls, reproduce the family's armorial colors. Between the niches are carved panels illustrating the cardinal virtues, the liberal arts, and the planetary deities. Although the bathhouse at the northwest corner is reduced to mere foundations, the summer house at the opposite corner is in a good state of preservation. "Taken as a whole," reads the official guidebook, "the pleasance with its sculptured wall and adjuncts forms one of the most remarkable artistic monuments that Scotland can show."

DUNDEE (TAYSIDE)

* Central Museum and Art Gallery *(7, 343, 365)*, Albert Square

This is a good conventional museum of local history, archaeology, natural history, and geology. The art gallery contains a respectable collection of British and European masters. Among the Scottish artists represented are John Petty, Thomas M. Dow, Robert MacGregor, John Blake MacDonald, Frank Holl, and Thomas Faed. In the McManus Galleries are relics of Dundee's famous jute industry and other materials relating to the industrial history of the city.

* Spalding Golf Museum *(359)*, in Camperdown House, Camperdown Park

In this early-nineteenth-century mansion is an interesting exhibit of old golf balls, clubs, golfing photographs, and other materials relating to Scotland's national game. The history of the sport is lucidly told in the accompanying placards.

Camperdown Works *(343)*, Methven Street, Lochee

Beneath the 282-foot-high chimney, designed to resemble an Italian campanile, is the factory that made Dundee famous in the nineteenth century as the world's leading manufacturer of jute.

Rossie Priory Stone *(55)*, 8 m. w; 1 m. n of A 85 (53 NO 292 308)

Inside the church here is a fine carved Class II Pictish stone, unusual in that it has a cross on both faces. Fabulous beasts and Pictish symbols adorn either side.

** Fowlis Easter Church *(165, 171)*, 6½ m. w; 2 m. sw of A 923 from Muirhead; key at cottage across road

This fifteenth-century church is distinguished above all others in Scotland for its surviving medieval artwork, especially the original carved oak door and several paintings on oak panels dating from the fifteenth and sixteenth centuries. These include a splendid Crucifixion scene and an Entombment.

*** Claypotts Castle *(226)*, 4 m. e; s of A 92 on Broughty Ferry Road (54 NO 453 318); AM

Built by Sir John Strachan, probably between 1569 and 1588, this is the most interesting of Scotland's many Z-plan tower-houses. As is common with this design, two circular towers project from diagonally opposite corners of a rectangular block. Claypotts is unusual, however, in that the corner towers are topped by rectangular, crowstepped gabled houses. There are ten gunports inserted in the walls at ground level, which together provide complete enfilade fire along all sides of the castle. Considerations of comfort, however, more than defense probably determined the size and shape of the building.

** Broughty Castle *(199, 343)*, 5 m. e; St. Vincent Street, Broughty Ferry, s of A 930

This is a typical fifteenth-century tower-house, built by George Douglas, fourth Earl of Angus, about 1454 and soon thereafter occupied by the Gray family. It was captured by the English in 1547 during the invasion of Scotland by the Duke of Somerset. After being retaken by a Franco-Scottish force in 1550, it was enlarged. During the civil wars General Monck occupied the castle, but in the eighteenth century it fell into disrepair. In 1854, during the Crimean War, the castle was bought by the British government and later converted into a coastal artillery fortress. It now serves as a local museum, featuring the history of the fishing and whaling industry. One room contains a good collection of medieval through eighteenth-century weapons.

Tealing Souterrain *(36)*, 5½ m. n; ¼ m. w of A 929 (54 NO 413 382); AM

This semicircular stone-lined trench, about ninety feet in length and about five feet in depth, represents the remains of a post–Iron Age *souterrain*. There is a very well-preserved late-sixteenth-century dovecote nearby.

FORFAR (TAYSIDE)

** Restenneth Priory *(65, 146)*, 1½ m. e; n of B 9113 (54 NO 482 516); AM

The lower part of this forty-five-foot tower dates from the early eighth century and was part of a *porticus* built by Northumbrian masons imported by the Pictish King Nechtan to build a stone church *juxta morem Romanorum*; i.e., in the Romanesque style then being adopted by the Anglo-Saxon Church. Early in the twelfth century the *porticus* was raised into a lofty tower. The graceful octagonal broach spire was not added until the fifteenth century. In the mid-twelfth century the church became the property of an Augustinian priory. It was the canons of this order who began the nave of a new church (now reduced to its bare foundations) and who, in the thirteenth century, built the beautiful but now roofless choir with its First Pointed lancet windows. (Nave and choir were thus separated by the tower, which served them as a choir screen, obstructing the view from the nave of the celebration of the Mass.) Of the canons' chapter house to the south of the choir, only the foundations survive. The high wall, which encloses the southern and western sides of the cloister garth, is of a later date than the other buildings.

Here is a scene of charming quiet pastoral beauty, well tended by the Scottish Development Department.

Finavon Hill-Fort *(31)*, 4 m. ne; 1 m. sw of A 94 from Finavon (54 NO 506 556)

This is a rectangular Iron Age hill-fort, its tumbled walls vitrified by fire. Projecting from the south end of the wall is a horn-work, and inside is a rock-cut well.

** Aberlemno Stones *(55)*, 5½ m. ne, se of B 9134 (54 NO 523 555 and 559); AM

In the parish churchyard stands a particularly fine Class II Pictish stone, sculpted on one face with a decorated cross flanked by intertwined beasts and on the other with a battle scene accompanied by Pictish symbols. About a quarter of a mile to the northeast, on the south side of the B 9134, standing within an enclosure, is a Class I stone with a variety of incised Pictish symbols and a Class II cross-slab with a wheel cross flanked by angels on the front and a hunting scene with Pictish symbols on the rear.

*** Glamis Castle *(191, 256)*, 5½ m. sw; n of A 94; in Glamis village; mandatory guided tour of no less than 45 minutes

The core of this very stately home (a childhood residence of the present queen mother and birthplace of the Princess Margaret) is a fourteenth-century L-plan tower-house built by Sir John Lyon, who married a daughter of King Robert II and became the first Lord Glamis. It was seized by James V in 1540 from the then Lady Glamis (a sister of the Earl of Angus), who was burned at the stake in Edinburgh. Subsequently, it was returned to its original family owners, who, in the seventeenth century, became Earls of Strathmore and Kinghorne. Patrick, the third earl (1643–1695), was responsible for converting the medieval tower into a stately country home. In the eighteenth century the ninth earl married a very rich Durham heiress, Mary Eleanor Bowes, after which the family name become Bowes-Lyon. The castle was much expanded and altered again around 1800, and once more in the Victorian era, so that from the outside the original tower-house is almost indiscernible among the multitude of wings, turrets, and battlements that encase it.

The Dining Room, through which today's visitor enters, is decorated in Victorian Tudor style, and beyond it is the tunnel-vaulted medieval crypt displaying armor and hunting trophies. Above the crypt is the Drawing Room, with a fine early-seventeenth-century plaster ceiling. Similar plaster-work of about the same date adorns King Malcolm's Room (Malcolm II is believed to have died at Glamis, though certainly not in this house). The late-seventeenth-century chapel has panels painted by Jan de Wet, who did the series of monarchical portraits for Charles II in the Palace of Holyrood-house. Much of the furniture is also of a Jacobean or Carolean date. Two formal gardens (the Dutch Garden and the Italian Garden) were laid out in the nineteenth and twentieth centuries respectively in the immediate vicinity of the house, but the park through which the visitor enters was initially planted in the 1770s in the mode made popular by the English landscape gardener Lancelot "Capability" Brown.

Glamis Manse Stone *(55)*, 6 m. sw, on A 94 in Glamis village, near Angus Folk Museum (54 NO 386 467)

In front of the manse opposite the parish church at the east end of the village, this Class II Pictish stone stands nine feet high. It has a good cross carved in relief on the front and incised Pictish symbols on the back.

** Angus Folk Museum *(364)*, 6 m. sw, n of Glamis village center

In this row of interconnected cottages is contained a very attractive and well-organized museum of village life, with emphasis on nineteenth-century domestic equipment, spinning and weaving implements, school-room furnishings, etc.

* Eassie Cross Slab *(55)*, 8½ m. sw; n of A 94 (54 NO 352 473); AM

Under a shed in this now ruined and roofless parish kirk is a fine Class II Pictish stone with a richly decorated cross on one face and processional scenes and barely discernible Pictish symbols on the other.

KIRRIEMUIR (TAYSIDE)

* Barrie Birthplace *(363)*, town center

This two-story cottage, where the novelist and playwright James M. Barrie was born in 1860, is now a museum containing a great variety of materials pertaining to his life and works: his christening robe, settee, desk, academic gowns, theater programs, etc.

Kirriemuir Pictish Stones *(55)*, in cemetery n of town center (54 NO 387 544)

Housed under a roof at the top of the cemtery are five Pictish stones, three belonging to Class II, with interlace ornament and human figures on one side and Pictish symbols on the other; the other two to Class III, with crosses but no symbols.

MONIFIETH (TAYSIDE)

Laws Hill-Fort *(30)*, 2 m. n; ¼ m. s of B 961 from Drumsturdy (54 NO 493 349)

This oval Iron Age hill-fort has a rubble wall faced with stone blocks showing evidence of vitrification by fire. The two ends of the fort are contained by similar walls, with a third at the southwest end. Inside are the scanty remains of a Late Iron Age broch.

Ardestie Souterrain *(36)*, 1½ m. n; n of A 92, 100 yards w of junction with B 962 (54 NO 502 344); AM (no parking)

This now roofless curved stone-lined trench, ninety-five feet long, was a post–Iron Age *souterrain*. Next to it are the foundations of three or four contemporary huts.

Carlungie Souterrain *(36)*, 3 m. n; 12 m. n of A 92 from ½ m. e of junction with B 962 (54 NO 511 359); AM

Here is a long roofless stone-walled U-shaped trench, with an ancillary passageway leading to the bottom of the U. Maximum depth is about four feet. These are the remains of a post–Iron Age *souterrain*.

NORTHERN SCOTLAND
Inverness-shire
AVIEMORE (HIGHLAND)

* Strathspey Railway *(338)*, w of A 95, n of B 970

In the summer, regular steam train excursion trips run on the Strathspey Railway from Aviemore's attractive antique passenger station (moved here from Dalnaspidal) north to Boat of Garten. Also at Aviemore are an engine shed and miscellaneous nineteenth- and early-twentieth-century rolling stock.

CARRBRIDGE (HIGHLAND)

* Landmark Visitors' Centre *(291)*, village center

The chief attraction here, outside of the souvenir shop, is the excellent audiovisual show on the history of the Highlands.

FORT AUGUSTUS (HIGHLAND)

** Great Glen Exhibition *(291)*, town center

This is an ambitious, relatively new museum, contained in four buildings and exhibiting a variety of artifacts and geological specimens illustrating the history and natural history of the Great Glen, with an audiovisual show to simplify things. One building contains a smithy; another is devoted to evidence, chiefly photographic, of the Loch Ness Monster.

Wade Bridge *(271)*, 9 m. ne, on A 862 at Whitebridge

Just upstream of the presently used bridge is another built by General George Wade in 1732 to carry his Great Glen road connecting Inverness with Fort Augustus and Fort William.

FORT WILLIAM (HIGHLAND)

*** West Highland Museum *(250, 273, 277)*, town center

Here is a fascinating array of exhibits and artifacts, including a furnished room from the dismantled Governor's House of old Fort William; a reproduction of a nineteenth-century crofter's house; fine collections of eighteenth-century Highland weapons; eighteenth-century army uniforms; Communion tokens, both Presbyterian and Episcopalian; and numerous Jacobite relics, including miniature portraits of Bonnie Prince Charlie, his embroidered silk jacket and tartan trews, locks of his hair, and an anamorphic painting of Charles Edward so contrived that his features are reflected in a polished metal cylinder placed on top of what appears to be a black surface with random brushstrokes in red, blue, green, and yellow.

** Neptune's Staircase *(287)*, 2 m. nw; n of A 830

This is a series of eight locks built by Thomas Telford in the early nineteenth century to carry the **Caledonian Canal** *(000)*, uphill from Loch Linnhe at its southern end. From this point the canal remains visible as far as the southern end of Loch Lochy; there are other locks at Fort Augustus; and a sea lock at Inverness, the northern terminus of the waterway.

* Inverlochy Castle *(99, 106, 237)*, 2 m. ne; s of B 8006, ¼ m. w of A 830 (41 NN 122 756)

This is a quadrangular courtyard castle with round corner towers, the one in the northeast corner being larger than the others and therefore presumably the *donjon*. The two entrances, plain, pointed-arched openings, are opposite each other in the north and south sides of the curtain wall. That on the north was a watergate, leading to the River Lochy. The other three sides are surrounded by a wide ditch and outer bank.

The castle was built probably in the last quarter of the thirteenth century and was the property of John Comyn of Badenoch until King Robert Bruce captured it in 1308. In 1431 it was the scene of a decisive defeat of a royal army under King James I by a band of rebel Highland chiefs led by Donald Balloch of Islay. In 1645 Archibald Campbell, eighth Earl of Argyll, and his Covenanting army were defeated near here and the castle captured by the Marquis of Montrose fighting in the name of King Charles I.

Despite its important historical connections, the castle is not under guardianship of the Scottish Development Department and is consequently in a poor state of preservation. Approaches are poorly signposted. Would-be visitors should not confuse this site with the Inverlochy Castle Hotel, which lies west of the A 82 and more than a mile to the northeast.

* Glenfinnan Monument and **Visitors' Centre** *(272)*, 18 m. w, on A 830; NTS

Overlooking Loch Shiel, this tall pillar of stone is topped by a statue representing a Highlander dressed and accoutred in the manner of Prince Charles Edward's troops, who fought in The Forty-five uprising. It was near this spot that he raised the standard of revolt on 19 August 1745. Across the road, the Visitors' Centre displays informative placards relating objectively the history of the rebellion, and an audio program that does the same, only in terms somewhat more sympathetic to the prince.

Glenfinnan Viaduct *(339)*, 18 m. w; 1 m. n of A 830 from Glenfinnan Monument (40 NM 910 813)

Built in 1898 for the West Highland Railway line from Fort William to Mallaig, this is a spectacular feat of civil engineering.

GLENELG (HIGHLAND)

* Bernera Barracks *(270)*, 1 m. n

This substantial, though roofless and floorless ruin stands four stories high with gunports facing the seaward side looking toward the Sound of Sleat across to the Isle of Skye. It was built as part of the British government's scheme for pacifying the Highlands after the uprising of 1715, though it was never of much importance, and General Wade did not see fit to tie it into his defensive scheme by laying a road to it. Today's single-track road from the Shiel Bridge to Glenelg is a hair-raising experience for the motorist.

** Dun Telve *(34)*, 3 m. se (33 NG 829 173); AM

Although called a dun, this is in fact the second best preserved (after Mousa in Shetland) of all Scottish Iron Age brochs. Its circular wall rises as high as 33½ feet. Except for the fact that it is located inland rather than on the shoreline, this broch displays all the typical features of its genre: narrow entranceway, stone staircase, mural cells and galleries, plus the unusual feature of a second ledge above the first, running around the interior face of the broch wall. This was presumably a roof support, while the lower ledge probably held a floor.

** Dun Troddan *(34)*, 3¼ m. se (33 NG 834 073); AM

Like its neighbor, Dun Telve, this is an Iron Age broch, not a dun. The third best preserved among all brochs in Scotland, its wall rises to a maximum height of twenty-five feet. Typical broch features are the narrow entrance passage, mural cells and galleries, a stone staircase, and an inner ledge to support a roof.

Dun Grugaig *(33)*, 4 m. se; ½ m by footpath from road's end (33 NG 852 159)

Hugging a steep cliff overlooking the burn of Ghlinne Bhig, here is a much ruined D-shaped Iron Age galleried dun with a thick hollow wall rising in places to a height of eight feet. Typical features are the mural chambers, door-checks, bar-hole, and a ledge around the inner wall-face.

INVERNESS (HIGHLAND)

* Inverness Museum and Art Gallery *(9)*, Castle Wynd

This is a good modern museum of archaeology, natural history, and local history, though somewhat sparse in artifacts.

Craig Phadrig Hill-Fort *(53, 62)*, 2 m. w; n of Upper Leachkin village, ¼ m. ne of Craig Phadrig Hospital (26 NH 640 453)

Although this was originally an Iron Age hill-fort, sufficient evidence of Dark Age occupation has been discovered here to suggest that it was a Pictish capital, possibly the site of King Bridei's court, which was visited by St. Columba in the sixth century. The fortifications consist today of a well-preserved, turf-covered, vitrified, rectangular, dry-stone wall standing nearly twelve feet high and an outer wall, also vitrified but in a more ruinous condition. Although the grounds are maintained by the Forestry Commission, the site itself is hard to locate.

** Beauly Priory *(150, 242)*, 8½ m. w; in Beauly village (26 NH 528 466); AM

Founded by Alexander II in 1230 as one of the three Valliscaulian houses in Scotland (Pluscarden and Ardchattan priories were the others), the red sandstone monastic church, though roofless, is very well preserved. Architecturally, it is a mixture of several styles and periods—thirteenth-century First Pointed, fourteenth- and fifteenth-century Second Pointed, and sixteenth-century restoration in imitation of both. The most unusual feature is the shape of some of the nave windows, which are in the form of curved equilateral triangles with cusped trefoils. The lancet windows, some of which were late-medieval insertions, are wider than is typical of the First Pointed style. The claustral buildings have disappeared altogether.

*** Culloden Battlefield and Visitor Centre *(276)*, 5 m. e, on B 9006; NTS

The site of the justly famous battle of 16 April 1746 between Prince Charles Edward Stuart's Jacobite army and the government forces led by William Augustus, Duke of Cumberland, lies astride of the B 9006 in the vicinity of the Visitor Centre. It is currently in the process of being cleared of trees, so that, when the stumps are uprooted, it will presumably again take on the appearance of the moorland it was when the engagement took place. Markers have been erected to indicate the position of the various units on both sides along the lines of battle drawn up at the beginning of the action. Other earlier placed stones mark the presumed sites of the mass graves of those killed in action—particularly on the Jacobite side. The tiny stone "Old Leanach Cottage" still stands where it did on the day of the battle and now serves as a museum.

The guided tour over the battlefield is not very instructive, and, before exploring the site, an inspection of the maps available at the Visitors' Centre is advisable. Here the National Trust for Scotland has arranged exhibits and placards that describe, with a fair degree of objectivity, the battle and the events leading to it and following from it. There is also an audiovisual show lasting fifteen minutes, which is only mildly Jacobite in tone and does make clear that some of Cumberland's forces were also Highlanders and that a significant number of the most important Highland clans did not support

Bonnie Prince Charlie at this or any other time during The Forty-five.

*** **Balnuaran of Clava Cairns** *(14, 36)*, 6 m. e; 1 m. se of Culloden
Battlefield Visitor Centre on B 9006, s of Clava Lodge Hotel (27 NH 757
445 to 756 433); AM

Here are three Neolithic cairns in a row, running roughly southwest to
northeast. **Balnuaran of Clava, Southwest**, is a passage grave of the Clava
type and today consists of (1) an enclosing stone circle of ten monoliths, the
highest reaching seven feet; (2) a circular curb of smaller stones; (3) the
remains of a cairn of water-worn stones: (4) an entrance passage facing
southwest in line with the two highest stones of the circle; and (5) a roofless
oval-shaped burial chamber. There are Bronze Age cup-marks on the second
stone west of the entrance. **Balnuaran of Clava, Centre**, is a ring cairn with
the central burial ground surrounded by a ring of boulders and pebbles
through which there is no passageway. Like the two neighboring passage
graves, this is surrounded by a stone circle (nine now standing) inside of
which is a circular curb of low flat slabs. **Balnuaran of Clava, Northeast**, is
another passage grave of the Clava group, consisting of (1) an oval of eleven
standing stones; (2) a curb of boulders inside the standing stones; (3) a
covering cairn of pebbles and small boulders; (4) a long, low narrow
passageway entered from the southwest; and (5) a roughly circular roofless
burial chamber of about thirteen feet in diameter. There are several cup-
marks on various boulders.

*** **Fort George** *(276, 280, 290)*, 15 m. e; on Ardersier Point at end of B
9006, 3 m. n of A 96; AM

Situated at the end of a peninsula jutting into the Moray Firth east of
Inverness, this was the major fort built to keep the Highlands in order after
the quelling of Bonnie Prince Charlie's uprising of 1745. It was designed by
the British Army engineer, William Skinner, was begun in 1748 by John
Adam (son and brother of the more famous architects William and Robert),
and finished in 1769. Johnson and Boswell visited here in 1773. In plan it
conformed to the latest eighteenth-century military-architectural standards,
i.e., a ditch-encircled, star-shaped rampart with arrowheaded and polygonal
bastions around the edges so as to permit guns to fire at all angles. By the
time it was completed, it was already unneeded for the purpose for which it
was built, and, with the development of rifled naval ordnance in the
nineteenth century, it became obsolete as a coastal artillery base, though still
useful as a military depot.

Today it is a splendid sight. Grounds, north casements, chapel, and
museum are open to the public. Housed in the latter are uniforms, plate,
medals, and other memorabilia of the Queen's Own Highlanders, formed by

an amalgamation of the Seaforth Highlanders, the Ross-shire Buffs, and the Queen's Own Cameron Highlanders, all regiments having their origins in Britain's wars of the late eighteenth century.

Wade's Road *(270)*, 8–20 m. s; B 852

At Dores, 8 m. s of Inverness, the B 852, a single-track motor road, overlies Wade's road of 1732 for about twelve miles south to the junction of the B 852 with B 862. The road hugs the southeast shore of Loch Ness, and the scenery is therefore spectacular. At Inverfarigaig and at Whitebridge, **Wade's Bridges** *(270)* cross the Rivers Farigaig and Fechlin respectively, upstream of the present bridge.

** Urquhart Castle *(106, 109)*, 15½ m. s; on A 82, 2 m. se of Drumnadrochit (26 NH 531 286); AM

On the western shore of Loch Ness, this much ruined castle stands on a promontory just off the main road between Inverness and Fort Augustus. The first known owner, and probably the original builder, was Alan Durward, brother-in-law of King Alexander II (1214–1249). Upon his death it passed to the Comyn family, Lords of Badenoch; it was seized by Edward I in 1296, taken by the Scottish rebel Sir Andrew Moray soon thereafter, recaptured by Edward, then seized by Robert Bruce in 1308 and thereafter granted to his nephew, Thomas Randolph, Earl of Moray. In the fifteenth century the castle was mostly in the hands of the MacDonald Lords of the Isles, in the sixteenth it came into possession of the Grants, and after the Jacobite rising of 1689 it was deliberately slighted by government troops and never since restored.

Across the ditch dividing the promontory from the mainland, the early-sixteenth-century gatehouse survives only in its lower story. To its right stand the wall foundations of what was probably the curtain built in the thirteenth century around an earlier Norman motte. Straight ahead from the gatehouse and to the left along the water's edge are the scanty remains of the castle's domestic buildings attached to the thirteenth-century curtain. To the extreme left (north) is the keep, a sixteenth-century tower built over a fourteenth-century basement.

Needless to say, the view of Loch Ness from this vantage point is unrivalled.

** Corrimony Chambered Cairn *(14)*, 21 m. sw; 8 m. w of Drumnadrochit: ½ m. sw of A 831 (16 NH 381 304); AM

This is the best preserved of the Clava group of Neolithic passage graves. It consists of (1) an enclosing circle of standing stones; (2) a circular curb of upright slabs and boulders designed to hold the cairn material in place; (3)

a cairn of rounded boulders and pebbles, complete except for the top; (4) a low narrow passageway from the edge of the cairn to the center; and (5) a round, corbelled central burial chamber about twelve feet in diameter, the roof of which has been removed so as to permit a view from above. The original capstone now lies on top of the cairn and shows Bronze Age cup-marks.

KINGUSSIE (HIGHLAND)

*** Highland Folk Museum *(282)*, Duke Street

This is an outstanding folk museum, founded by the distinguished historian of the Highlands, the late Dr. I. F. Grant. In addition to the showcases in the reception building which are full of artifacts well selected to illustrate Highland life, there is a reconstructed black house and a water-driven "clack mill" with horizontal paddles, in common use in the Norse-settled regions of the northern islands and the Outer Hebrides. This one came from Lewis.

** Ruthven Barracks *(269, 274)*, ¾ m. s; n of B 970 (35 NN 765 997); AM

This well preserved but roofless stone fortress was begun in 1717 after the Jacobite uprising of 1715 and enlarged by General George Wade in 1727 as part of his ambitious scheme for pacifying the Highlands. It was success-fully besieged and then burned by the Young Pretender's troops in 1746.

Wade's Road *(270)*, 12½ m. sw; A 889, ½ m. n of Dalwhinnie

Where the A 889 takes a sharp left turn north of Dalwhinnie, a section of Wade's Dunkeld-to-Inverness road (1728–1729) runs straight ahead.

NEWTONMORE (HIGHLAND)

Clan MacPherson House & Museum *(305)*, Main Street

This small museum is devoted to Clan memorabilia with a few relics associated with Bonnie Prince Charlie.

SKYE (HIGHLAND)

(Access by car ferry from Kyle of Lochalsh to Kyleakin or from Mallaig to Ardvasar)

Armadale Pier

Clan Donald Centre *(185, 280, 305)*, 3 m. n; w of A 851

Situated in the restored north wing of Armadale Castle, built in 1815 to replace an earlier house of the MacDonalds of Sleat (visited by Boswell and Johnson in 1773), here is a small museum devoted to the history of Clan Donald. Actually, the exhibits consist mostly of explanatory placards, with only a few appropriate artifacts. Surrounding the place is a very handsome woodland garden.

Dunscaith Castle *(185, 187)*, 33 m. nw; 27 m. nw of A 851 from Ostaig House

This very ruined fifteenth-century keep overlooking Loch Eishort was the original stronghold of the MacDonalds of Sleat, though captured in the early sixteenth century by Alasdair Crotach, Chief of Clan MacLeod, hereditary enemy to the MacDonalds. It lies beyond the end of a very rough and narrow road.

Broadford

** Skye Crofter's House Museum *(332)*, 6 m. w; s of A 850 in Luib

This is a late-nineteenth-century thatched crofter's cottage (not a black house) of three rooms, the kitchen with fireplace and chimney. Contemporary furnishings and agricultural implements are in good supply. Wall placards explaining crofting are instructive.

Dunvegan

*** Dunvegan Castle *(185, 205, 281, 306)*, ½ m. n; w of A 863

The seat of the MacLeods of Dunvegan since the thirteenth century, here is a stately home of great antiquity that has seen some sort of building alteration in every century since about 1270, when the first chief of Clan MacLeod built the curtain wall and sea gate that still stand to the west of the castle. Today, the approach to the house is from the east by way of an entrance front erected in the mid-eighteenth century. To the right is first the medieval keep of the fourteenth century with a pit prison underneath, and beyond and behind it a wing built in 1790 by General Norman MacLeod, the twenty-third chief. To the left is "Rory Mor's House," added in 1623 by the fifteenth chief, and beyond is the "Fairy Tower," put up by the eighth chief, Alasdair Crotach, about 1500. Behind it is "Ian Breac's Work," dating from about 1690, and running north of it to General MacLeod's wing is a corridor added in the mid-nineteenth century.

Of the many objects of interest inside the house, the most noteworthy are family portraits by Allan Ramsay, Sir Henry Raeburn, and Johann Zoffany; a copy of Sir Joshua Reynolds's portrait of Dr. Samuel Johnson, who paid an extended visit here in 1773; the Dunvegan cup, a tenth-century Irish wooden drinking vessel encased in silver in 1493; Rory Mor's silver drinking horn, holding nearly two bottles of claret, which each new chief is expected to drain; the "Fairy Flag," woven probably in the seventh century—a MacLeod talisman thought to bring certain victory in three successive battles; rare late medieval coats of mail; miscellaneous Highland weapons; and Clan MacLeod memorabilia. From the sea wall at the rear of the house is a fine view of Loch Dunvegan.

*** Skye Black House Museum *(331, 332)*, 4½ m. nw; w of B 884 in Colbost

This is a typical thatched black house of the nineteenth century, now a museum containing sundry items of crofting equipment: a *cas chrom* (crooked spade), peat cutter, potato dibber, threshing machine, etc., as well as household furnishings. The floor is of packed earth, the interior dark, and a peat fire still burns on a central hearth, with smoke escaping through the thatch. Less prettified than many of Scotland's cottage museums, this is the most authentic of them all. On the walls are newspaper clippings concerning the Crofter's War of the early 1880s.

Dun Hallin *(34)*, 8 m. n; ½ m. e of Hallin village; 3 m. n of end of B 886 (23 NG 257 593)

In its bleak moorland setting, this ruined Iron Age broch measures thirty-six feet in diameter with a wall eleven feet thick and standing twelve feet high in places. Still visible are two mural cells and the foot of the stairway. The site is on private property and is badly signposted.

** Borreraig Piping Centre *(186)*, 9 m. nw; in Borreraig village

Near the site of the college of piping founded in the sixteenth century by the MacCrimmons, pipers to the chiefs of Clan MacLeod, here is a neat and compact museum dedicated to the history of the bagpipe and its music. Recorded pibroch music can be heard on demand, and the exhibits are highly informative. Lovers of piping should not miss this.

Portree

The Braes Memorial *(331)*, 6 m. s; e of B 883

This small stone pedestal marks the approximate site of the "Battle of the Braes" on 19 April 1882, a confrontation between crofters and police, occasioned by Lord MacDonald's attempts to evict tenants who refused to pay their rent except on condition of regaining ancient grazing rights.

* Dun Beag *(34)*, 11 m. w; ¼ m. n of A 863 from junction with road to Ullinish Lodge (23 NG 339 386); AM

This is the best surviving broch on Skye. It measures thirty-six feet in diameter inside a wall fourteen feet thick and in places twelve feet high. Mural cells are well preserved. The broch stands on a high hill overlooking Loch Bracadale and is reached by way of a well signposted footpath leading from the road.

Uig

** Skye Cottage Museum *(332)*, 4½ m. n; e of A 855 in Kilmuir

Here is a well-constructed and relatively roomy nineteenth-century thatched crofter's cottage (not a black house) of two bedrooms and a kitchen with fireplace, not central hearth. The simple furnishings are typical, as is the very good collection of agricultural implements, including a *cas chrom* (crooked spade) and various peat-cutting tools. On the grounds are three other cottages: a weaving house with live demonstrations of the hand loom; a smithy; and a "ceilidh house" with an interesting collection of crofters' photographs dating from the early twentieth century.

Flora MacDonald Monument *(277)*, 5 m. n; e of A 856 in Kilmuir Kirkyard

This twenty-five-foot-high modern wheel-headed cross was erected as a memorial stone to Flora MacDonald, who helped the fugitive Prince Charles Edward Stuart escape capture by bringing him to Skye, disguised as her Irish maid. After emigrating to North Carolina with her husband, she later returned to Skye and is buried in this kirkyard.

Duntulm Castle *(185)*, 8 m. n; w of A 855

Standing high on a rocky headland overlooking Score Bay, this romantic castle ruin was the stronghold of the MacDonalds of Sleat from the fifteenth century until about 1730.

SPEAN BRIDGE (HIGHLAND)

* Commando Memorial *(370)*, 1 m. w; n of B 8004

This monument to those commandos who received their training in this area and were killed in World War II consists of a larger-than-life-sized statue of three soldiers accoutred for the hazardous duties of their profession. Very impressive.

Wade's High Bridge *(271)*, 2 m. nw ; 1 m. n of A 82 from 1 m. w of Spean Bridge, on minor road signposted Brackletter

After the bridge at Aberfeldy, this is the most impressive of Wade's bridges, although now in a state of disrepair. Built in 1736 to carry the Great Glen road from Inverness to Fort William across the deep gorge of the River Spean, it is now impassable.

Nairnshire

NAIRN (HIGHLAND)

*** Cawdor Castle *(187)*, 5 m. sw; s of B 9090

This is a late-fourteenth-century tower–house expanded into a stately home by the addition of several wings, most dating from the seventeenth century. The entire complex is surrounded on three sides by a moat (now dry but still crossed by a drawbridge) and on the fourth by Cawdor Burn.

The central tower was probably begun about 1370 by the third Thane of Cawdor, although royal permission to crenellate was not given until the mid-fifteenth century by King James II. In 1498 the eighth thane died, leaving a posthumous daughter who was abducted by the Earl of Argyll and subsequently married off to his son, John Campbell, who then became thane. The earldom of Cawdor (still a Campbell possession) dates from the late eighteenth century.

Interesting features of the house include the ancient tree trunk in the Thorn Tree Room, the yett brought here from the Moray stronghold of Lochindorb in 1456, family portraits by Sir Thomas Lawrence and Sir Joshua Reynolds, and a fine collection of tapestries. On the grounds is a gorgeous herbaceous garden; also a wildflower garden and nature trails.

* Cawdor Kirk *(221)*, village center; s of B 9090

This is a T-plan church with a high central pulpit against the south side, galleries at the east and west ends, and pews facing the pulpit from three directions. It was built in 1619, but later enlarged. The battlemented south tower and Gothic windows are typical examples of the Scottish tendency toward architectural anachronism.

Moray

ELGIN (GRAMPIAN)

** Elgin Museum *(9, 53)*, High Street

This is a better-than-average local museum of natural history and archaeology with a good collection of Neolithic and Bronze Age artifacts, stone slabs from nearby Burghead, incised with Pictish representations of bulls ("the Burghead bulls"), and a very interesting and unusual collection of mementos and memorabilia of British imperial rule in Africa and Asia.

*** Elgin Cathedral *(115, 155)*, North College Street; AM

The episcopal see of the Bishops of Moray was moved here from nearby Spynie in 1224, and soon thereafter the new cathedral was consecrated. It was an aisled cruciform church built in the First Pointed style with two western towers and a central tower over the crossing. In 1270 the cathedral was burned, and in the rebuilding the church was enlarged to its present dimensions; a chapter house was added north of the choir; the nave was widened by the addition of a second aisle on each side; choir and presbytery were doubled in length. In 1390 the cathedral was burned again, this time by Alexander Stewart, Earl of Buchan, known as the "Wolf of Badenoch." In the ensuing rebuilding, the western gable was raised and provided with a large traceried window; the crossing and mid-tower were reconstructed; new tracery was made for the wheel window in the east gable; and the chapter house was provided with a central stone pillar and rib-and-panel (lierne) vaulted ceiling. After the Reformation the cathedral was not converted to Protestant use, as the town had an adequate parish church. In 1567, under the Regency of Queen Mary's half-brother James Stewart, Earl of Moray, the roofs were stripped of their lead, which was then sent to Holland. In the seventeenth century some of the interior church furnishings were removed by local Covenanters, while Cromwell's troops defaced some of the monuments and destroyed the tracery of the west window. In 1711 the central tower collapsed, leaving the rest of the church in its present state of ruination.

Three major styles of architecture are discernible among the substantial ruins. The two great western towers, still standing almost to their original height, are in the First Pointed style of the thirteenth century, as is the fine western portal. The inner screen of this portal, with its two doorways, is in the Second Pointed style and was built after the fire of 1390. The western window was enlarged in the fifteenth century. Most of the nave walls collapsed with the fall of the central tower in 1711. The transepts are the oldest part of the building and have both round- and pointed-arched windows, indicating the Transitional style of architecture. The northern wall of the choir is also Transitional. The presbytery at the extreme east end of the church is First Pointed, with a double row of lancet windows in the east gable. The overhead vault of the First Pointed chapter house is of outstanding architectural merit.

Across the street is the so-called Bishop's Palace, which was in fact the precentor's manse. Not much is left of it: a couple of walls, a fireplace, and the arms of Bishop Patrick Hepburn in stone relief.

** Church of the Greyfriars Monastery *(168)*, Abbey Street; ring convent bell for admission to church

This rectangular fifteenth-century Franciscan church was restored in the nineteenth century by that busy amateur medievalist, the third Marquis of Bute. It is thought to be an authentic reproduction of the interior of a typical small medieval church. The barrel roof and rood screen are particularly fine. It now serves as the church of the adjoining convent of the Sisters of Mercy.

Birnie Church *(163)*, 3½ m. s; ½ m. e of B 9010 on unmarked road

Here is a small Romanesque church consisting of a square tower, nave, and choir with typical round arches, said to be the oldest parish church in continuous existence as such in Scotland. Not signposted and hard to find.

** Pluscarden Abbey *(150)*, 6 m. sw; 5 m. sw of B 9010 on unmarked road from Pittendreich (28 NJ 144 575)

This was originally a Valliscaulian priory founded by King Alexander II in 1230. It was restored somewhat in the nineteenth century by the third Marquis of Bute and shortly after World War II reoccupied by a colony of English Benedictines, so that it is today a genuine "working abbey." The abbey church consists of a central tower and two transepts (no nave) with a tiny lady chapel leading off the south transept. The choir is ruined but will probably be restored. To the south lies the restored east range of the claustral buildings now occupied by the Benedictines but closed to the public.

Craigellachie Bridge *(287)*, 12 m. se; w of A 941 at n end of Craigellachie village

This restored cast iron bridge across the River Spey was originally built by Thomas Telford in 1815.

* Spynie Palace *(156)*, 2 m. n; ¼ m e of A 941 (28 NS 230 658); AM

Although the see of Moray was moved from Spynie to Elgin in 1224, the bishops kept this place as their residence and over the years enlarged and fortified it extensively. Especially active in the militarization of the palace was Bishop David Stewart (1461–1476), who was at constant odds with the neighboring Earls of Huntly. To him is owed the powerful gatehouse and "David's Tower," still standing to the wall-head. The last bishop, Patrick Hepburn (1535–1573), installed most of the ground-level gunports. The adjacent buildings around the courtyard are in a very ruined condition. Still undergoing repair by the Scottish Development Department, the grounds can be entered and the castle inspected at close quarters.

*** **Duffus Castle** *(81)*, 3 m. nw; ½ m. w of B 9012 from 1 m. s of Duffus village (29 NJ 189 673); AM

Here is a very well-preserved Norman motte—a high truncated cone surrounded by a ditch and constructed in the twelfth century to support the timber castle of Freskin, a Flemish immigrant from Lothian who became the founder of the de Moravia (Moray/Murray) family. About 1300 a new Lord of Duffus, Reginald le Chen, built the now ruined three-story stone keep on the site of the original motte-and-bailey castle. The weight of the stonework eventually caused the motte to sink and the castle to split apart and partially collapse. To the east of this building are the ruins of a great hall erected in the fifteenth century. An outer ditch, now water-filled, enclosed the castle bailey, which was surrounded by a curtain wall of stone, still standing in part.

FORRES (GRAMPIAN)

*** **Sueno's Stone** *(56)*, 1 m. ne; w of B 9011 (27 NJ 047 595); AM

This is the most elaborate Dark Age sculptured stone in Scotland, excluding some of the Early Christian crosses. Dating probably from the ninth century, it stands twenty feet high beside the road and is a Class III stone (without Pictish symbols). On the front is a sculpted wheel-headed cross with interlace, and on the back are four much weathered panels depicting battle scenes. The monument is believed to be a cenotaph commemorating a Pictish victory over invading Vikings somewhere in this neighborhood.

Kinloss Abbey *(144, 242)*, 2½ m. ne; s of B 9011, s of Kinloss village (27 NJ 065 616)

Very little is left of this Cistercian abbey founded by King David I and colonized from Melrose. The fragmentary remains, situated within a churchyard, represent only part of the wall and foundations of the cloister and abbot's house.

** **Darnaway Castle** *(206, 213)*, 3½ m. w; s of A 96; minibus from Darnaway Estate Visitor Centre; mandatory guided tour (about 1 hour); open Wednesdays and Sundays only.

When the earldom of Moray was bestowed by Mary, Queen of Scots, on her half-brother, James Stewart, the fifteenth-century castle of Darnaway became his principal seat in the North. The earldom and its castle were later inherited through marriage by James Stewart of Doune, the "Bonnie Earl of Moray," murdered at Donibristle, Fife, in 1592 by George Gordon, sixth Earl of Huntly. Of the castle known to these sixteenth-century earls, only the much modified great hall with its splendid oak hammerbeam roof remains. It is incorporated into a Gothic Revival mansion of pinkish sandstone built in 1802–1812 by the ninth Earl of Moray. Of the internal contents, the most interesting items are Hans Ewart's famous portrait of Henry Stuart, Lord Darnley, and his younger brother; portraits of the Regent Moray and his wife, attributed to Ewart; and, best of all, a painting on wood of the corpse of the "Bonnie Earl" with blood still gushing from his many wounds.

* Brodie Castle *(226)*, 4 m. w; n of A 96

Originally a Z-plan tower-house built in the 1560s, the castle was greatly expanded in the seventeenth and again in the nineteenth century, so that its early appearance has been all but swallowed up in the extensive additions to the north and east of the tower. Now displayed as a stately home, much of the plasterwork dates from the seventeenth century, but the elaborate furnishings are mostly of nineteenth-century provenance. The exterior of the tower is embellished with a parapet and fake stone cannon in the pseudomilitary style of the late sixteenth and seventeenth centuries.

GRANTOWN-ON-SPEY (HIGHLAND)

Castle Roy *(99)*, 4 m. s; w of B 970, 1 m. n of Nethybridge, Inverness-shire (36 NJ 005 219)

In the midst of a fenced cow pasture lies this much ruined castle, probably built in the thirteenth century, as one of the several strongholds of the Comyns. It is a square courtyard castle bounded by high curtain walls with a single rectangular corner tower that presumably served as the *donjon*. The entranceway is now nothing more than a gap in the wall. A chase cut into the interior wall-face presumably held in place a floor, or possibly the roof, of a courtyard building.

Lochindorb Castle *(99)*, 10 m. n; 2½ m. sw of A 939 from 7½ m. n of Grantown-on-Spey or from ¼ m. s of junction with 940 (27 NJ 975 364). Visible from shore; for boat transport, inquire at Scottish Tourist Board Information Center, 54 High Street, Grantown-on-Spey, or at Angus Stuart's Fishing Tackle Shop nearby (tel: 0479-2612).

This is a much ruined courtyard castle built in the late thirteenth century on an island in Lochindorb. The curtain walls are thin and the corner towers slight. At one end is a second enclosure entered through a portcullis gate. The castle belonged to John Comyn of Badenoch at the end of the thirteenth century and was visited by King Edward I in 1303. It was slighted in 1455–1456 by order of King James II.

Rowboats (without motors) are available for anyone wanting to see the site at close quarters (above), but most travellers should be satisfied with the clear view of the ruin from the eastern shore of Lochindorb.

KNOCKANDO (GRAMPIAN)

** Tamdhu Glenlivet Distillery *(358)*, village center; s of B 9102

This malt-whisky distillery was founded in 1896 and is open to the public as a regular stop on the "Whisky Trail."

LOSSIEMOUTH (GRAMPIAN)

Burghead Fort *(53, 62)*, 7 m. w; nw terminus of B 9089 (28 NJ 110 692); AM; key at cottage #81

Before being mostly destroyed by port construction in the nineteenth century, the original Dark Age promontory fort here was divided into two parts by a solid stone rampart running east and west. This rampart can still be observed rising behind the steps leading down to a rock-cut square-sided well, which could be Roman, Dark Age, or early medieval. The discovery within the fort of about two dozen stones bearing incised drawings of bulls (three of them now in nearby **Elgin Museum** *[9, 53]*) indicates occupation by Picts. It is possible that this was the stronghold of Pictish King Bridei, who was visited in the sixth century by St. Columba, although a more likely candidate for the honor is Craig Phadrig, closer to Inverness.

ROTHES (GRAMPIAN)

*** Glen Grant-Glenlivet Distillery *(358)*, town center

One of the most attractive in appearance of the malt-whisky distilleries on the "Whisky Trail," this one was founded in 1840 and is open today to the public, who will be treated with hospitality, a guided tour, and a free shot of the product.

Banffshire

BANFF (GRAMPIAN)

** Duff House *(259)*, east of town center; s of A 98

Built by William Adam in the years following 1730, this is the most

Palladian of the architect's many houses in Scotland. It was designed for William Duff, later Earl of Fife, but, because of Adam's perfectionism, costs of construction mounted to the point where Duff was unwilling to allow him to continue. The result is a single, tall, central block minus the flanking curtains and pavilions originally planned. Thus the house, though conforming to the Palladian canon so far as it goes, betrays a verticality unusual in neoclassical buildings. It is identical, back and front, except for the fine double-curved stairway at the front entrance. Not presently furnished and in a bad state of disrepair inside, Duff House is being currently restored by the Scottish Development Department, perhaps for eventual use as a museum of fine furniture.

CHARLESTON OF ABERLOUR (GRAMPIAN)

*** Glenfarclas Glenlivet Distillery *(358)*, 4 m. sw; s of A 95

First licensed in 1836 and bought by John Grant in 1865, this splendid malt-whisky distillery is still family-owned. Open to the public, it offers a guided tour and the usual free taste of whisky at the end.

CULLEN (GRAMPIAN)

*** Cullen Kirk *(171, 221)*, on grounds of Cullen House, south of town center

Dedicated to St. Mary and made collegiate in 1543 under the patronage of Sir Alexander Ogilvy, this very pretty cruciform church is chiefly distinguished for the magnificent tomb erected in memory of the founder, who died in 1554, and the fine laird's loft installed in 1602, believed to be the oldest in Scotland. The north transept was not added until the late eighteenth century.

DUFFTOWN (GRAMPIAN)

*** Glenfiddich Distillery *(358)*, n of town center

One of the best known of the malt-whisky distilleries on the "Whisky Trail," it is open the public, who will be treated to a short audiovisual show before being conducted on the very instructive guided tour, capped with a free taste of the product.

** Balvenie Castle *(99)*, 1 m. n; e of A 941 (28 NJ 326 408); AM

This is a spacious ruined courtyard castle—a quadrangular *enceinte*, 150 feet by 130 feet, surrounded by a curtain wall, 7 feet thick and over 25 feet high. On the south and west sides the castle is bordered by a wide stone-lined ditch separated from the curtain by a berm. All of the above belongs to the original construction of the late thirteenth century, when the property belonged to the Comyn family.

The castle is entered through an inconspicuous arched doorway (not the original medieval gate) located in the center of the eastern facade. It is guarded by a yett. Above the entrance and to its right, as far as the splendid drum tower at the northeast corner, are the well-preserved ruins of a Renaissance dwelling place erected in the late sixteenth century by John Stewart, fourth Earl of Atholl. Ground-level gunports guard this part of the castle. The remnants of buildings along the other three sides of the courtyard are of fifteenth- and early-sixteenth-century vintage.

During the War of Independence, when the Comyns owned the castle, it was visited by King Edward I. Another visitor—in 1562—was Mary, Queen of Scots. During the Jacobite rebellion of 1689, it served for a while as headquarters for government troops, but after the battle of Killiecrankie the rebels took possession. The estate passed to the Crown in 1715 and thereafter gradually fell into ruin.

** Convalmore Distillery *(358)*, s of town center

Open to the public, this is another well-organized malt-whisky distillery on the "Whisky Trail."

** Aberlour-Glenlivet Distillery *(358)*, 3 m. ne; e of A 941

Founded in 1826 on the banks of the River Lour by James Grant and rebuilt in 1880, this fine malt-whisky distillery is open to the public.

KEITH (GRAMPIAN)

** Strathisla Distillery *(358)*, w of town center

Founded in 1786 and therefore perhaps the oldest working distillery in Scotland, this one produces a fine single malt that may be tasted after the guided tour.

TOMINTOUL (GRAMPIAN)

** Corgarff Castle *(227, 276)*, 9 m. se, in Aberdeenshire; w of A 939; AM

This whitewashed, harled four-story L-plan tower-house was built in 1537 by Thomas Erskine, Earl of Mar, but was in the custody of the Forbes family in 1571 when it was besieged by Adam Gordon, who set fire to it, burning to death Margaret Forbes and twenty-six members of her household. It was briefly occupied by the Marquis of Montrose in 1645 and figured in the Earl of Mar's Jacobite uprising in 1715. After the defeat of Prince Charles

Edward Stuart's forces at Culloden in 1746, this became one of the key government fortresses, along with nearby Braemar Castle, in the pacification of the northeastern Highlands. It was therefore remodelled about 1748; wings were added to each gable wall of the tower; and a star-shaped curtain wall was installed for defense against gunfire.

*** The Glenlivet Distillery *(358)*, 9 m. n; e of B 9136

Founded in 1821 by George Smith, this is one of the most distinguished of the malt-whisky distilleries on the "Whisky Trail"—open to visitors, with a guided tour of about thirty minutes and a free shot.

Aberdeenshire

ABERDEEN (GRAMPIAN)

*** St. Machar's Cathedral *(158, 165)*, The Chanonry, Old Aberdeen

On the site of a Romanesque church dedicated to St. Machar, believed to have been a companion of St. Columba, Bishop Henry Cheyne (1282–1328) raised a cathedral, which, like its predecessor, has all but disappeared. Under Bishop Alexander Kinninmund II (1355–1380), still another church went up, a remnant of which survives in two cylindrical sandstone pillars (now at the east end) that once supported a central tower. The present structure is mostly the work of Bishop Henry Lichton (1422–1440), though in the seventeenth century his central tower collapsed and destroyed the original east end and transepts, so that all that remains of his cruciform granite church are the nave and the west end. Bishop Elphinstone (1483–1514) added the belfry and spire to the central tower; Bishop Dunbar (1518–1532) added spires to the western towers and installed the fine heraldic ceiling in the nave.

Although authentically medieval, the church is architecturally so eclectic as to suggest a Victorian imitation. Certainly it conforms to no set style and, like other Scottish buildings of the fifteenth century, includes several anachronistic features harking back to an earlier period of construction. The great square western towers are machicolated like castle parapets, though certainly no military function was intended. The great western window is unique—seven round-headed lancets of equal height, all in a row. The nave's pillars and arches are Romanesque in appearance—cylindrical and round. The colorful ceiling, painted with forty-eight heraldic devices, presents a striking and felicitous contrast to all this granite massiveness. Outside the church can be seen the foundations of the earlier choir. Neither it nor the transepts were replaced, so that the existing ground plan is a simple rectangle.

* University of Aberdeen *(175)*, Old Aberdeen

In 1494 Bishop William Elphinstone obtained from Pope Alexander IV a bull establishing a university in this cathedral city and from King James IV a charter to the same effect. Of the original buildings, only King's College Chapel survives (see below). On the university grounds the Round Tower dates from 1525 and the Cromwell Tower from 1658. The west front of the quadrangle dates from 1825 and is a good example of Scottish Baronial. The rest of the buildings are Victorian or twentieth-century.

*** King's College Chapel *(165, 175, 183, 297)*, Old Aberdeen

This was a collegiate church founded by Bishop William Elphinstone in connection with his newly established University of Aberdeen. Building began in 1500, and the style is generally Second Pointed, with French or Flemish flamboyant features. The exterior is distinguished by the open-crown spire, similar to that of the Kirk of St. Giles in Edinburgh. In ground plan the church is rectangular with a three-sided apse. Here is the best display of medieval woodwork to have survived in Scotland: the great oaken screen, the stalls with misericords, the wooden vaulted roof with gilded ribs and bosses, and the pulpit, formerly belonging to St. Machar's Cathedral.

** Church of St. Nicholas *(221, 307)*, Back Wynd, off Union Street

Of the medieval church building (once the largest parish kirk in Scotland), all that remains to be seen are the north transept (Collison's Aisle), the round-headed arches in the crossing, the effigies in the north transept, and St. Mary's crypt under the east end. After the Reformation (in 1596), the church was partitioned so as to accommodate two separate congregations, and the structural division between West Kirk and East Kirk remains. The former was rebuilt in the prevailing neoclassical style of the mid-eighteenth century to a design by James Gibbs, a native of Aberdeen. Its original furnishings are almost intact. The central pulpit is faced on all four sides by galleries in the approved Protestant manner. The East Kirk, by contrast, though dating mostly from 1836–1838, has a Gothic appearance with its stained glass windows and lectern and Communion table at the east end. The central tower and spire were erected in 1874–1876 after a fire had destroyed the medieval steeple.

*** Provost Skene's House *(223)*, off Broad Street behind St. Nicholas House

This is a sixteenth-century town house to which the east wing was added in the 1670s by Sir George Skene, wealthy merchant and later Provost of

Aberdeen. Today it houses a superb local museum, which contains, among other things, a series of rooms furnished respectively in Jacobean, Cromwellian, Restoration, Georgian, Regency, and Victorian styles. Here also is a fine group of religious paintings in tempera on the timber vault of the long gallery.

** Provost Ross's House (223), Shiprow off Castlegate; NTS

Built about 1594, this town house came into the possession of Provost John Ross in 1702. Under the care of the National Trust for Scotland, some of the original interior has been preserved or restored. The building now houses the *** Aberdeen Maritime Museum (342), a superb repository of artifacts, paintings, ship models, and exhibits illustrating the history of the development of Aberdeen harbor, the Arctic whaling trade, local shipbuilding, maritime trade, the fishing industry, and the development of North Sea oil and gas.

* Aberdeen University Anthropological Museum (9), Marischal College, Broad Street

Here is a good collection of archaeological finds, including an unusual group of Beaker skeletons.

** Aberdeen Art Gallery (365), Schoolhill

Here is the best collection, outside of Edinburgh and Glasgow, of the works of Scottish nineteenth-century artists, with heavy emphasis on genre paintings and landscapes.

* Gordon Highlanders Museum (290), Viewfield Road

This is a conventional military museum, displaying the uniforms, medals, plate, honors, scrapbooks, etc., of the Gordon Highlanders, organized in 1794, and of the 75th (Highland) Regiment of Foot (1787) with which it was amalgamated in 1882.

* Dyce Stones (55), 8 m. nw; 4 m. nw of Dyce village on Pitmedden road (36 NJ 875 154); AM

Here are two Pictish stones standing inside the ruined St. Fergus Church. One belongs to Class I and is incised with the "swimming elephant" and other Pictish symbols; the other is a Class II stone sculpted on one side only with a wheel-headed cross flanked by a variety of Pictish symbols.

** Drum Castle (109), 10 m. sw; 3 m. w of Peterculter, 1½ m. w of A 93

(38 NJ 796 007); NTS; mandatory guided tour of about 1 hour

This is an exceptionally well-preserved granite tower-house built in the late thirteenth or early fourteenth century, on land bestowed by King Robert Bruce on William de Irwin, his armor bearer. It is rectangular in plan, seventy feet in height, with rounded corners and a battlemented parapet. Two pointed stone vaults above the barrel-vaulted basement were each divided horizontally by wooden floors, thus providing five stories in all: storage basement, first floor hall, second floor solar, and two floors of bedrooms. Entrance to the tower was originally by way of a wooden ladder to the first floor. Windows are few. A good arched fireplace graces the hall.

Adjacent to the tower-house is a fine seventeenth-century mansion. The property was occupied by the Irvine family until recently, when it was turned over to the National Trust for Scotland. The house is filled with fine furnishings, mostly of eighteenth- and nineteenth-century provenance, though the guided tour through it is unnecessarily long.

* Cullerie Stone Circle *(24)*, 11 m. w; ½ m. se of B 9125 near junction with B 9119 (38 NJ 785 043); AM

This was originally an almost perfect megalithic circle, thirty-two feet in diameter. It consists today of eight rather squat undressed boulders. Inside are eight small circular cairns that originally covered cremation interments of a later date than the surrounding Bronze Age stone circle.

Barmekin of Echt *(24)*, 14 m. w; 1¼ m. nw of B 9119 from Echt (38 NJ 725 070)

This is an elaborate Iron Age hill-fort with five concentric ramparts, though only the two inner walls of tumbled stones are observable to any but the most practiced archaeological eye. The climb over the surrounding moorland is steep and rough, and only the very hardy will want to attempt it.

*** Castle Fraser *(228, 306)*, 15 m. w; 2 m. nw of A 944 from Dunecht

This is a Z-plan tower-house with additional wings, built by Sir Michael Fraser and his son between 1575 and 1636. The outside is adorned with such pseudodefensive features as blind machicolation and stone cannons projecting from the walls. The well-furnished interior is beautifully laid out and intelligently displayed. Most of the furnishings are of eighteenth- or nineteenth-century vintage. The paintings are undistinguished, except for one of General Alexander MacKenzie by Raeburn. There is no guided tour, but hand placards that provide all the information necessary to understand the house and its contents are distributed generously. There is a "laird's lug," correctly described as a strongroom and not, in the traditional fashion of romantic fiction, as a secret listening post. (This latter myth seems to have originated with Sir Walter Scott and is perpetuated by tour guides in Scottish stately homes and castles in much the same manner as the fictitious identification of "priest holes" in their English counterparts.)

ALFORD (GRAMPIAN)

Alford Transport and Railway Museum *(338)*, town center

Here is a collection of antique automobiles and other vehicles, but the railway portion of the museum at present consists only of a restored passenger station.

*** Craigievar Castle *(228)*, 6 m. s; w of A 980; NTS; mandatory guided tour of about 45 minutes.

Built between 1600 and 1626 by William Forbes, a merchant of Aberdeen (nicknamed "Danzig Willie" or "Willie the Merchant"), this tall, pink granite, much turreted and gabled L-plan tower-house is considered by the National Trust for Scotland to be the "apotheosis" of Scotland's traditional native architecture of the Jacobean period. The interior is distinguished by elaborately molded plasterwork and pine paneling.

*** Kildrummy Castle *(99, 105, 115, 163, 267)*, 11 m. w; w of A 97 (37 NJ 455 164); AM

This is the noblest early medieval castle ruin in northeastern Scotland. It is also an architectural oddity—combining the features of a heavily defended gatehouse keep at the front entrance with a massive *donjon* at the rear. The original *enceinte*, probably built by Gilbert de Moravia, Bishop of Caithness in the early thirteenth century, was polygonal with its back (northwest) side guarded by a deep ravine and the other sides by a wide dry ditch.

It was entered from the southeast through a twin-towered gatehouse, probably built after 1306, when an English army under Prince Edward of Caernarvon (later King Edward II) captured the castle from Neil Bruce by suborning its blacksmith to set the place on fire. Today this gatehouse (possibly designed in imitation of contemporary Welsh models) is badly ruined, standing at its greatest height to no more than six feet. To its left, the south curtain wall and the southwest D-shaped mural tower are fairly well-preserved. The late-thirteenth-century circular *donjon* at the west corner is reduced to about the same height as the gatehouse. Against the inner face of the northwest curtain wall are the fairly substantial remains of a great hall and its associated domestic range, all dating probably from the second half of the thirteenth century, though partially reconstructed in the sixteenth. At the north corner stands the best-preserved part of all—a high drum tower (called the "Warden's Tower") built to match the *donjon*, though not quite so spacious. Along the northeast curtain wall, and slightly projecting from it, is a square-ended chapel with three fine lancet windows in the east gable. This was probably inserted in the mid-thirteenth century. Next, to the southeast, comes another D-shaped mural tower, and then the southwest curtain wall leading back to the gatehouse. Finally, having finished inspecting the interior, the visitor should walk around the outside of the castle to get an idea of its exterior dimensions and formidable defensive features.

After its repossession by the Scots in the early fourteenth century, the castle had a lively history. In 1333 King Robert Bruce's sister, Christian, successfully withstood its siege by the Earl of Atholl on behalf of Edward Balliol. In 1361 King David II captured the castle from the Earl of Mar. In 1404 the Countess of Mar was at Kildrummy when she was seized by, and forced to marry, Sir Alexander Stewart, a natural son of the "Wolf of Badenoch." For the next 250 years the property passed back and forth between royal and private hands until it finally came into the possession of the Erskine Earls of Mar. During the Civil War it was captured for Cromwell in 1654. In 1715 it was the headquarters of the Earl of Mar, who organized the Jacobite uprising of that year. When the rebellion collapsed, his earldom was forfeited, and Kildrummy Castle was dismantled.

* Auchindoir Church *(163)*, 10½ m. nw; 2½ m. s of Rhynie, s of B 9002, ½ m. w of A 97 (37 NJ 476 245)

Here is a well-preserved though roofless ruin of a rectangular church of the late twelfth or early thirteenth century. There is a fine Romanesque doorway on the south side. The other doorways and the square windows are later insertions.

** Glenbuchat Castle *(227)*, 14 m. w; w of A 97 (37 NJ 398 149); AM

This is a typical Z-plan tower-house, built in 1590 by Sir John Gordon. It was a center of Jacobite activity during the 1715 uprising and, after the rebellion of 1745, was briefly garrisoned by government troops. Its present ruined condition is owed to abandonment in the nineteenth century, not to military action. Restored by the Scottish Development Department, Glenbuchat is one of the finest examples in Scotland of the Z-plan tower-house, in this case a rectangular central block with square towers at diagonally opposite corners. The building is liberally supplied with gunloops.

BALLATER (GRAMPIAN)

** **Balmoral Castle** *(328, 335),* 8 m.w; w of A 93 from Crathie

This grandiose turreted and castellated mansion, exemplar of the nine-teenth-century Scottish Baronial style, was built by Queen Victoria and Prince Albert in the mid-fifties and became the royal family's permanent Scottish residence thereafter. The architect was William Smith of Aberdeen, but the Prince Consort exercised strict supervision over both planning and building. Only the grounds are open to the public, and then not while royalty are in residence. The tower garden and the rose garden were laid out by the prince; the fountain garden by Queen Mary in 1920. The hothouse, with its abundant floral display, is especially attractive.

** **Braemar Castle** *(276),* 15½ m. w, n of A 93, ½ m. n of Braemar village

This is a modified L-plan tower-house first built in 1628 by John Erskine, second Earl of Mar. During the Revolution of 1689–1690, it was burned by the Jacobite Farquharsons to prevent its use by General MacKay in his campaign against Bonnie Dundee (Graham of Claverhouse). Thereafter it remained a blackened shell until restored in 1748 to house a garrison of government troops sent north after The Forty-five to maintain law and order in the northeastern Highlands. At that time the castle was owned by John Farquharson of Invercauld, who leased it to His Majesty for ninety-nine years. John Adam (son of William, brother of Robert) was the architect in charge of the rebuilding. In the nineteenth century the castle was returned to the Farquharsons, and the twelfth Lord Invercauld converted it into the attractive Victorian home that it still is.

Doune of Invernochty *(80),* 15 m. n; n of B 973, ¼ m. w of Bellabeg (37 NJ 352 129)

Here are the remains of a twelfth-century motte, now about 60 feet high and 250 feet across at the summit. A deep ditch surrounds the earthworks. Girdling the summit is a stone wall, now mostly turf-covered—the remains of a medieval shell keep that replaced the original timber palisade. Inside are the scant remains of later medieval buildings.

ELLON (GRAMPIAN)

** **Haddo House** *(259, 328),* 7½ m. nw; s of B 9095; NTS

Although enlarged and modified in the nineteenth century by the addition of the courtyard and clock tower beyond the south wing, a front porch, new front steps, and a chapel, Haddo House is essentially Palladian in style, as designed in 1731 by William Adam, working under the direction of Sir John Clerk of Penicuik. Thus, typically, the severely classical central block is flanked by two pavilions connected by curving curtains (as at Hopetoun House). The first occupant was William Gordon, second Earl of Aberdeen, and among his descendants who lived here was George Gordon, fourth earl, who served as British Foreign Secretary under both the Duke of Wellington and Sir Robert Peel and, from 1851 to 1855, as Prime Minister. Another was John Gordon, seventh Earl and first Marquis of Aberdeen (d. 1934), who served as both Viceroy of Ireland and Governor-General of Canada.

The interior is predominantly Victorian in decor. Indeed, one of the bedrooms was specifically furnished for Queen Victoria when she visited the house in 1857. Here also is a watercolor by James Giles of the old castle of Balmoral, which was subsequently torn down by Queen Victoria and Prince Albert after they had built their new Highland residence there. Haddo's chapel was designed in 1881 by Sir George Street, leading English ecclesiastical architect of the Gothic Revival and responsible for the ultra-neo-Gothic Law Courts in London. One of its windows is by the Pre-Raphaelite Edward Burne-Jones. In short, for lovers of Victoriana, this is a treasure-house. The mandatory guided tour lasts a full hour but is well done.

FRASERBURGH (GRAMPIAN)

* **Memsie Cairn** *(19)*, 3 m. s; s of B 9032, ¼ m. e of A 981 (30 NJ 976 620); AM

This is an exceptionally well-preserved Bronze Age cairn of loose stones more than twenty feet in height.

HUNTLY (GRAMPIAN)

*** **Huntly Castle** *(122, 189, 213)*, town center (29 NJ 532 407); AM

On the site of the twelfth-century "Peel of Strathbogie," an L-plan tower-house was erected in the late fourteenth or early fifteenth century, though only its bare foundations are to be seen today on the north side of the present ruined castle. Later in the fifteenth century, Alexander Gordon, first Earl of Huntly, began the construction of a hall house, an oblong structure with a round tower at its southwest corner. Between 1551 and 1554, George Gordon, fourth Earl of Huntly, rebuilt this house from the ground floor upward and added a vaulted range adjoining it, as well as another range on the north side adjacent to the original tower house. Parts of these buildings were blown up by order of James VI in 1594 as a result of the fifth earl's plotting rebellion. Later forgiven and made first Marquis of Huntly, it was the same George Gordon who restored the hall house and converted it into an elegant palace in the style of the contemporary château at Blois. An east range was added or restored about the same time. During the Civil War the castle was occupied by Covenanting troops. It was probably at this time that the chapel inside the courtyard was converted into a stable. The Huntlys ceased to occupy the castle thereafter, and in the eighteenth century it served as a.quarry for the rebuilding of nearby Huntly Lodge.

The only well-preserved portion of the castle is the beautiful palace of sixteenth- and seventeenth-century construction rising from the foundations of the fifteenth-century hall house. Above its entrance at the northeast corner is a splendid carved "frontispiece" of heraldic symbols done in the early seventeenth century. On the opposite (south) side of the building is a lovely row of oriel windows installed about the same time and probably inspired by Blois. Equally impressive is the great heraldic mantelplace in the main upper stateroom, which also dates to this period of reconstruction by the first marquis. Of the buildings on the east, north, and west sides of the courtyard, nothing substantial remains.

Tap o' Noth Hill-Fort *(31)*, 10½ m. s; ¾ m. n of A 941 from point 1 m. e of Rhynie (37 NJ 485 293)

On a high conical hill sits this Iron Age hill-fort, now consisting of a single wall, heavily vitrified and covered with turf and heather. The loose boulders to the north and east may be the remains of an outer wall. Difficult climb.

INVERURIE (GRAMPIAN)

Bass of Inverurie *(80)*, 1 m. s; n of B 993 (38 NJ 783 205)

Here, in a cemetery beside the River Don, is a well-preserved Norman motte, about fifty feet high with a diameter of about sixty feet at the summit.

Kinkell Church *(119)*, 1½ m. s; s of B 993

Within this roofless ruin of a small early-sixteenth-century church is the upright grave-slab of Gilbert de Greenlaw, slain at the Battle of Harlaw in 1411. On the face of the slab is the incised figure of an armored knight.

* Brandsbutt Stone *(55)*, 1¼ m. nw; w of A 96 (38 NJ 760 225); AM

This is a reconstructed undressed Class I Pictish stone, incised on one side with miscellaneous Pictish symbols and with a line of Ogam markings— unfortunately untranslatable. The site is somewhat obscured by the surrounding cottages of a modern housing development.

* Easter Aquhorthies Stone Circle *(25)*, 3 m. w, on unmarked roads past Newbigging Farm (38 NJ 733 208); AM

This is a Bronze Age recumbent stone circle with nine undressed stones plus two flankers standing in an almost perfect circle about sixty feet in diameter. The recumbent stone, a huge dressed block, lies on the south side between the two flankers, which are the highest uprights in the circle.

** Loanhead of Daviot *(25)*, 5 m. nw; ⅓ m. nw of Daviot (38 NJ 748 288); AM

This Bronze Age recumbent stone circle of nine stones is set in a circle about sixty-five feet in diameter. The recumbent stone lies on the south side between the highest stone of the circle and a tenth megalith just inside. At the circle's center is a ring of smaller stones that probably served as the outer curb of a ring cairn.

Maiden Stone *(55)*, 6 m. nw; 1 m. se of A 96 from Mill of Garden (38 NJ 703 247); AM

This is a Class II Pictish stone with a cross on front, flanked by panels of sculpture, including a representation of Jonah and the whale; and on the back, Pictish symbols carved in relief.

KINCARDINE O'NEIL (GRAMPIAN)

* Peel of Lumphanan *(80)*, 4½ m. n; ½ m sw of A 980 from Lumphanan (37 NJ 577 037); AM

These remains of a twelfth- or thirteenth-century motte-and-bailey castle consist of a circular flattened earthen mound (motte) about thirty feet high surrounded by a ditch and bank that once surrounded the bailey. Both castle and palisades would originally have been built of timber, of which nothing of course now remains. The earth-covered rectangle on top of the mound is all that is left of the foundations of a fifteenth-century house.

It was near this place that (Shakespeare to the contrary) Malcolm Canmore finally caught up with Macbeth and killed him, though it is not likely that any castle stood here at that time.

Culsh Souterrain *(36)*, 11 m. nw; 7 m. n of Aboyne; 2½ m. ne of Tarland, s of B 9119 (37 NJ 505 055); AM

This turf-covered subterranean passage was a post–Iron Age *souterrain*, better preserved than most. A flashlight (electric torch) can be obtained at the neighboring farm for would-be explorers of this underground tunnel.

* Tomnaverie Stone Circle *(25)*, 9 m. nw; 4 m. nw of Aboyne, 1 m. se of Tarland; s of B 9094 (37 NJ 478 034); AM

This is a somewhat dilapidated Bronze Age recumbent stone circle with the standing stones set in a circle fifty-six feet in diameter and a huge uncut recumbent stone lying on the southwest. Inside is a ring of smaller stones that probably served as a curbing for a ring cairn.

OLDMELDRUM (GRAMPIAN)

** Tolquhon Castle *(226)*, 6 m. w; e of B 999 (38 NJ 874 286); AM

This is a Forbes family stronghold begun as a rectangular tower house in the fifteenth century and expanded into a Z-plan courtyard castle in the late sixteenth. In front of the main entrance on the north side is a forecourt flanked by triple gunloops, so angled as to allow fire in three directions. The twin-towered gatehouse is embellished with more triple gunloops, carved figurines, and coats of arms. The courtyard facades reveal numerous architectural refinements not normally found in the classic Scottish tower house. To the left (east) of the entranceway is the much ruined Preston's Tower, the original keep. The east range of buildings is equally ruinous. The principal apartments of the palatial sixteenth-century house occupy the south side of the quadrangle opposite the entrance. The southeast tower contains a pit prison and next to it the bakehouse. Along the west side, on the first floor, was a long gallery. The round tower at the northwest corner contained bedrooms. Gunloops are plentiful throughout.

*** Pitmedden Garden and **Museum of Country Life** *(260)*, 5 m. e; n of A 920; NTS

This is arguably the handsomest formal garden in Scotland and among the best in Britain. It was first laid out by Sir Alexander Seton and his wife Dame Margaret Lauder about 1675 and may have been copied from the parterre at Holyroodhouse Palace, installed by Charles I in the French style made fashionable by André le Nôtre, designer of the gardens at Versailles. It was restored in 1952 by the National Trust for Scotland, using as a model the Holyroodhouse garden depicted in a print of a bird's eye view of Edinburgh, dated 1647.

Best viewed from the balustrade above the sunken parterre, here is a set of intricately designed patterns composed of box hedge, annuals, and herbaceous borders. Twin pavilions flank the garden, one of them containing information on the history of gardening in Britain.

On the same grounds, the Museum of Farming Life is housed in several buildings and adjacent yards. It includes a farmhouse furnished in late-nineteenth-century style, a stable, a one-man bothy or chaumer, and a large selection of nineteenth- and early-twentieth-century farm machinery and implements. Of Britain's several agricultural museums, this is one of the very best.

PETERHEAD (GRAMPAIN)

** **Slains Castle** *(266, 280)*, 8 m. s; ½ m. e of A 975 from n end of Cruden Bay via Castle Road; not signposted.

Built against the edge of a high cliff descending abruptly to the North Sea, this is a fine ruin of the family seat of the Earls of Errol, erected in 1664 to take the place of an ancient castle demolished by King James VI because of the rebellion of the Roman Catholic ninth earl (Francis Hay). In April 1707, John Hay, twelfth earl, conspired here with the Jacobite agent, Nathaniel Hooke, to assist a French invasion of Scotland, which was in fact launched the following year in the name of the Old Pretender, but failed to achieve its purpose. On 24 August 1773 Dr. Samuel Johnson and James Boswell visited here on their way from Edinburgh to Skye. (The resident owner at the time was the son of William Boyd, fourth Earl of Kilmarnock, one of the two peers executed for their participation in The Forty-five.)

Johnson thought the view from here to be "the noblest he had ever seen," but Boswell complained that the roar of the sea outside his bedroom window kept him awake. "The windows," he explained, "look upon the main ocean, and the King of Denmark is Lord Errol's nearest neighbor on the north-east."

Today the ruins of what must then have been a magnificent mansion are still extensive, though untended and unblessed with a site museum or any other aids to the puzzled traveller. The style of this seventeenth-century building is an anachronistic form of Scottish Baronial, with a twin-towered gatehouse, crenellation, etc. That it was not built for defense, however, is evident in the huge rectangular windows (resembling modern picture windows) facing the sea. Sipping tea and coffee, Johnson and Boswell revelled in the view through one of these, while the doctor recited the ode *jam satis terris*.

Deer Abbey *(149)*, 10 m. w; s of A 950, n of B 9029, ½ m. w of Old Deer (30 NJ 969 481); AM

This Cistercian monastery, founded by William Comyn, Earl of Buchan, in 1219 and colonized from Kinloss, has all but disappeared. There is nothing left of the church except for the foundations, and only the south range of the cloister (originally housing frater and kitchen) and the abbot's house stand to any significant height.

TURRIFF (GRAMPIAN)

*** **Fyvie Castle** *(217)*, 8 m. s; ½ m. n of Fyvie village; e of A 947; NTS; opening scheduled for 1986

This magnificent palace, looking more like a French château than a Scottish castle, is a recent acquisition of the National Trust for Scotland. Its medieval beginnings are obscure, but by 1395 it appears to have been a typical late medieval courtyard castle with rectangular towers at each end of the south front and twin rounded towers guarding the main entrance at the center. In the final years of the sixteenth century, Alexander Seton, who was soon to be made Earl of Dunfermline and Chancellor of Scotland by King James VI, converted this grim fortress into a Renaissance palace, heightening the towers and adding turrets, carved finials, molded string courses, and other such embellishments. Inside, he remodelled the west range, adding the splendid wide turnpike stair, and emblazoned the walls with the Seton arms. In the late seventeenth century, the fourth Earl of Dunfermline added ornate plasterwork to many of the ceilings. In the eighteenth the house came into the possession of General William Gordon, who converted the mansion into something like a Georgian Gothic country house by crenellating both north and south facades and building a tower at the northwest corner to provide a semblance of symmetry. In 1889 the estate was bought by Alexander Forbes-Leith (later Lord Leith), an Aberdeen-born emigrant to the United States who had amassed a fortune in steel. He added another tower to the west of the Gordon Tower, more pepper-pots, and a clock tower in the courtyard side of the south range. More importantly, he filled the house with new panelling, tapestry, chimney pieces, enriched plasterwork, armor, rich furnishings, and an enormous collection of paintings, including such British masters as George Jamesone, Sir Peter Lely, Sir Anthony Van Dyck, Sir Godfrey Kneller, Sir Joshua Reynolds, George Romney, John Hoppner, and Sir Henry Raeburn.

Fyvie today is much as Lord Leith left it—a great medieval castle, Renaissance palace, Georgian country house, and late Victorian connoisseur's creation.

Kincardineshire

BANCHORY (GRAMPIAN)

*** **Crathes Castle** *(227, 261)*, 2 m. e; n of A 93; NTS

This fine early-seventeenth-century tower-house, built by Alexander Burnett of Leys, was expanded in the eighteenth into one of the most attractive of Scottish stately homes. The doorway retains its original yett, but the fake *bretasche* and stone cannon indicate that this was never meant to be a defensible castle, but a country home. Inside are some superb painted ceilings. Here also are about six acres of walled gardens subdivided by vast yew hedges, the latter dating from 1702. Mostly the handiwork of recent owners, there is no prettier horticultural display in the United Kingdom.

FETTERCAIRN (GRAMPIAN)

*** Fasque *(360)*, ½ m. n

This gothicized eighteenth-century house was bought in 1830 by the wealthy Liverpool merchant, John Gladstone, father of Prime Minister William Ewart Gladstone, who visited here frequently. The white-painted interior is very handsome, especially the curving double staircase rising from the main hall. Also of interest are the master bathroom, the business room where the owner kept his accounts, and the bedroom of the prime minister's youngest sister Helen, an opium addict who eventually left this house for a quasi exile on the Continent, where, to the family's chagrin, she converted to Roman Catholicism (which proved to be the means of arresting her addiction).

STONEHAVEN (GRAMPIAN)

*** Dunnottar Castle *(241, 247)*, 1½ m. s; e of A 92

Arguably the most spectacular ruined castle in Scotland, this was originally an L-plan tower-house built in the fourteenth century by Sir William Keith, first Earl Marischal, on top of a high cliff projecting into the North Sea and, except for a single knifelike passage, cut off from the mainland by a deep ravine. In the sixteenth century new defensive outer-works were added by later earls, and in the late sixteenth and early seventeenth centuries a courtyard palace with an adjoining chapel was built on the northeast end of the rock. To this was appended in the late seventeenth century another wing, the lower story of which is known as the "Whig's Vault."

Although the castle was visited frequently by Scottish royalty and other important personages from its beginnings through the sixteenth century, its chief historical interest begins in 1652, when it was besieged and eventually taken by Cromwell's troops. Some time during the siege the private papers of Charles II, as well as the Regalia of Scotland, were secreted out of the castle by the wife of the minister of nearby Kinneff Church, where they remained hidden until the Restoration. In May 1685 almost 170 Covenanters, men and women, taken before and during Argyll's Rebellion, were imprisoned here in the "Whig's Vault" under inhuman conditions. A few escaped (miraculously, it would seem, considering the precipitous drop to the sea and the high sheer cliffs that lead down to it); many died; all earned a high place in Scots Presbyterian martyrology.

Today's visitor must climb a steep path from the bottom of the ravine, entering the enclosure through the outer-works installed in the sixteenth century. To the right of the entrance, and still further uphill, is the ruined fourteenth-century tower-house, still standing to the wall-heads. Beyond is a range of outbuildings—storeroom, smithy, and stables. At the top of the rock and occupying its northeastern corner is the two-story palace with three residential wings and a chapel built around a central courtyard, though not quite enclosing it. These buildings date from the late sixteenth and early seventeenth centuries and display a degree of elegance conspicuously absent from the earlier tower. In the late seventeenth century an additional rectangular block was projected from the northeast corner of the palace quadrangle. It was into the basement and subbasement floors of this wing (the "Whig's Vault") that the Covenanters were herded in 1685.

** Dunnottar Kirkyard *(247)*, 1 m. w; ½ m. n of A 94 from 1 m. sw of junction with A 92

Here are buried a number of Covenanters who died in the overcrowded prison of nearby Dunottar Castle in 1685. Above their grave is a simple memorial stone, crudely carved with the names (if known) of these men and women "who died prisoners in Dunnottar Castle anno 1685 for their adherence to the Word of God and Scotland's covenanted work of Reformation." Of Scotland's many religious shrines, this is perhaps the most moving. Admirers of Lewis Grassic Gibbon's novel, *Sunset Song*, will remember Chris Guthrie's bitter thoughts evoked by her reading of this inscription.

** Kinneff Church *(241)*, 10 m. s; 2 m. ne of A 92, 1½ m. n of Inverbie

This T-plan kirk, built in 1738 on earlier foundations and enlarged in 1876, replaced the still smaller church where, in the autumn of 1651, the minister, James Grainger, and his wife buried the Regalia of Scotland, which Mrs. Grainger had helped to smuggle out of Dunnottar Castle where they had been stored for safekeeping but which were now in danger of capture by Cromwell's army. Over and above its historical association, this is a very pretty little kirk.

* Muchalls Castle *(228)*, 4 m. n; w of A 92 (on narrow road, not well signposted); short mandatory guided tour

This L-plan tower-house was built in two stages between 1619 and 1627 by Alexander Burnett and his son Thomas. Much simpler than nearby Crathes Castle (built also by Alexander Burnett), the castle has a rather plain exterior that stands in contrast to the superb Jacobean plasterwork of four of the ceilings within.

Ross and Cromarty

CROMARTY (HIGHLAND)

* Hugh Miller Cottage *(355)*, town center; NTS

Dating from about 1711, this modest stone cottage was the birthplace in 1802 of Hugh Miller, stonemason turned amateur geologist and editor of the Free Church journal *The Witness*. In addition to typical nineteenth-century furnishings, it houses a number of Miller's geological specimens and copies of his writings.

FORTROSE (HIGHLAND)

Fortrose Cathedral *(159, 242)*, town center

Nothing remains of the red sandstone cathedral church built in the Second Pointed style as the seat of the Bishops of Ross except the ruined and roofless south aisle of the fourteenth-century nave and a polygonal bell tower and turret of the fifteenth century. It is believed that George Monck robbed the building of most of its stones in the 1650s to build a new fort at Inverness.

GAIRLOCH (HIGHLAND)

* Gairloch Heritage Museum *(332)*, village center

This well-organized folk museum contains a nineteenth-century crofter's cottage, appropriately furnished and appointed.

KYLE OF LOCHALSH (HIGHLAND)

** Eilean Donan Castle *(188, 268, 305)*, 8½ m. e; s of A 87

In its romantic island setting at the foot of Loch Duich, this reconstructed medieval keep is perhaps the most photographed castle in Scotland. There was probably a tower here in the mid-thirteenth century, later owned by the Mackenzies of Kintail. In 1509, as this clan moved its center of operations northward, Eilean Donan was assigned to the MacRaes, who then occupied the castle as constables. In May 1719 a small Spanish expeditionary force, dispatched to support an unsuccessful Jacobite uprising on behalf of the Old Pretender (James VIII), set up headquarters here. British frigates bombarded the stronghold, captured the defenders, and left the castle in ruins. In 1912–1932 it was rebuilt by Lt. Col. John MacRae-Gilstrap and has ever since served as a center for Clan MacRae.

Only two rooms are open to the public: the billeting room and the banqueting hall. Their contents include some fine eighteenth-century furniture; numerous portraits of the MacRaes and other paintings; miscellaneous Clan MacRae memorabilia: a well-preserved yett; and mementos of Bonnie Prince Charlie, though he never visited here. At the base of the castle wall on the loch side is a bronze tablet commemorating all the MacRaes (including Canadians and Australians) who died in World War I. Approximately five hundred names are listed.

POOLEWE (HIGHLAND)

*** Inverewe (335), 1 m. n; e of A 832; NTS

Here, in probably the most magnificent of all of Scotland's many fine woodland gardens, planting was begun in 1864 by Osgood Hanbury Mackenzie, was continued by his daughter Mairi until her death in 1953, and is maintained today by the National Trust for Scotland. On this inhospitable, rocky promontory, where much of the soil had to be imported and special shelter belts of conifers grown as a preliminary to other planting, stands today such a profusion of rhododendrons, primulas, meconopses, celmisias, azaleas, and a great variety of other specimens as to boggle the mind. The grounds are interlaced with well-planned walks, and maps are provided at the visitors' center. Not to be missed either are the rock garden, the herbaceous borders in front of the house, the walled garden, and the American garden.

TAIN (HIGHLAND)

* St. Dutho's, Tain (171, 182), town center

This much restored rectangular collegiate church was initially constructed in the Second Pointed style about 1360. Noteworthy is the five-lighted east window, although the very handsome stained glass is not original. St. Dutho's was one of Scotland's most famous medieval places of pilgrimage, and James IV, among others, came here many times. At the time of the Reformation the Regent Moray donated the pulpit (now much restored), which still stands against the south wall. This church replaced a twelfth-century chapel, now much ruined and located in a cemetery about a mile to the northeast of town near the golf course.

Dunskeath Castle (83), 10 m. s; 1 m e of B 9176 from Nigg Ferry, across Cromarty Firth from Cromarty (21 NH 809 688)

This turf-covered mound is probably the motte of the timber castle erected here by William the Lion in 1179.

Sutherland

BETTYHILL (HIGHLAND)

*** **Strathnaver Museum** *(292, 305)*, village center

This is a fascinating small museum, organized in an amateurish fashion, but full of interesting relics, chiefly connected with the Sutherland clearances. It is housed in a former eighteenth-century church and still contains the pulpit from which the Reverend David MacKenzie announced the names of the local people scheduled for eviction. Around the walls are posters, lettered by schoolchildren, describing the clearances of 1810–1819. One cabinet contains relics of broken pottery, glass, etc., excavated from nearby Rossal Township. Here too is a portrait of the notorious Patrick Sellar, who was indicted for murder in connection with his allegedly setting fire to the huts of evicted tenants. Upstairs is a small Clan MacKay museum.

* **Rossal Township** *(292)*, 17 m. s; w of B 871, 1 m. s of Syre (by footpath for about 2 miles south of Forestry Commission car park near east end of River Naver bridge from Syre; well signposted)

These scattered stones, marked by good explanatory signposts, represent the remains of a preclearance township that contained thirteen families evicted in 1813 by Patrick Sellar, agent for the Duke of Sutherland. The site was excavated by archaeologists of the University of Glasgow in 1962. Getting here requires an arduous drive and a long walk, and there isn't much to see on arrival, but the site is one of the few easily identifiable as a visible relic of the Sutherland clearances.

BONAR BRIDGE (HIGHLAND)

** **Croick Church** *(287, 330)*, 12 m. w; 11 m. w of A 9 from Ardgay

This is a T-plan, harled, whitewashed little kirk with a high canopied pulpit on the north side and a long Communion table lying east-west almost the full width of the church. It was one of the forty-odd "parliamentary churches" built to the design of Thomas Telford in the early nineteenth century, but is more famous in connection with the clearance of nearby Glencalvie in 1845 to make way for sheep. Some of the tenants, evicted by James Gillanders, factor to Major Charles Robertson, took refuge in the churchyard here until new homes could be found. The pathetic record of their visit is scratched on panes in the east window: "Glencalvie people was in the churchyard here May 24 1845" and "The Glencalvie tenants visited in May 24 1845."

Spinningdale Mill *(320)*, 5 m. e; s of A 9

Here are the gaunt and high-standing remains of a cotton-spinning mill founded in 1785 by David Dale, George MacIntosh, and George Dempster. Burned out in 1809, it was never restored and stands as a romantic ruin on the shore of Dornoch Firth. On private property, it is quite visible from the roadside.

DORNOCH (HIGHLAND)

** Dornoch Cathedral *(159)*, town center

Incorporated within the existing parish kirk are the remains of the thirteenth-century cathedral of the see of Caithness, built originally by Bishop Gilbert de Moravia. Much damaged in 1570 during a feud between the Murrays and MacKays, it was rebuilt in the seventeenth century, restored in the nineteenth and again in the twentieth. Nevertheless, the pillars, arches, tower, choir, and east walls of the transepts all belong to the period of original construction and are in the Transitional style of architecture. The nave was built in the nineteenth century, and the stained glass windows are of both nineteenth- and twentieth-century provenance. Across the street the sixteenth-century bishop's palace has been converted into a luxurious hotel.

The Mound *(287)*, 8 m. n. on the A 9

This artificial embankment was built by Thomas Telford in the early nineteenth century to carry his Bonar Bridge–to–Wick road across the narrows of Loch Fleet—a purpose it still serves.

*** St. Andrew's, Golspie *(263)*, 10 m. n; n of A 9 in Golspie village center

This very pretty little cruciform church was built in 1738 by the Earl of Sutherland, whose residence was at nearby Dunrobin Castle. It was enlarged in 1754 with the addition of the south aisle opposite the Sutherland aisle, the latter containing the laird's loft and retiring room. The high canopied central pulpit has its original baptismal bracket, and there are additional galleries at the east and west ends.

*** Dunrobin Castle *(333, 335)*, 11 m. n; 1 m. e of Golspie, s of A 9

Charles Barry, chief architect of the Houses of Parliament in Westminster, rebuilt the thirteenth-century castle of Dunrobin in the 1840s for the second Duke of Sutherland. The style is mostly French Renaissance, with an admixture of Scottish Baronial. After a fire in 1915, Sir Robert Lorimer redecorated the interior. A portion of the medieval castle is still visible from the "Queen's Corridor," but otherwise this imposing pile is a Victorian creation. Victoria herself stayed here in 1872, and her four-poster gilt bed is on display. The furnishings are as sumptuous as could be expected of one of the richest families in Britain. Family portraits include those by Allan Ramsay, John Hoppner, Sir Thomas Lawrence, Sir Joshua Reynolds, and Sir Edwin Landseer. The formal garden below the castle on the seaward side is a masterpiece of mid-nineteenth-century landscaping.

Durness (Highland)

* Dun Dornadilla *(34)*, 28 m. se; 10 m. s of A 838 along eastern shore of Loch Hope on single-track road to Altnaharra (9 NC 457 451)

In spite of the name, this is a ruined circular Iron Age broch. Part of the outer skin of the once hollow wall stands to a height of twenty feet. An unusual feature is the massive triangular lintel still in position over the entrance passage. Entry to the broch is blocked, and the interior is filled with earth.

Lochinver (Highland)

Ardvreck Castle *(240)*, 11 m. e; w of A 837, s of junction with A 894 (15 NC 240 237)

This gaunt and tumbled ruin overlooking the north shore of Loch Assynt was the site of the alleged betrayal of the Marquis of Montrose in 1650. The castle's owner, Neil MacLeod, to whom Montrose had appealed for shelter after losing the battle of Carbisdale, is said to have taken him into custody and delivered him to General David Leslie for the price of 25,000 pounds Scots. On private property, the ruin is clearly visible from the A 837.

Tongue (Highland)

St. Andrew's Kirk *(263)*, village center

This is a rather plain little T-plan church, built in 1680 by Donald MacKay, Lord Reay, and rebuilt in 1729. The pulpit and reader's table are located in the center of the crossbar of the T, facing the pews and a laird's loft in the upright bar.

Caithness

DUNBEATH (HIGHLAND)

** Laidhay (Caithness) Croft Museum *(332)*, ½ m. n; e of A 9

Here is a restored early-nineteenth-century thatched crofter's "long house" of three rooms and a byre laid out in linear arrangement. Inside are many mementos of crofting life—domestic utensils, farm tools, kitchen ware, two box beds, etc. Next door is the barn with a well-preserved cruck roof.

THURSO (HIGHLAND)

* Reay Parish Kirk *(220, 263)*, 9½ m. w; n of A 836 in Reay village center

This is a simple and quite attractive T-plan, whitewashed kirk built in 1740. The canopied pulpit (probably original) is in the middle of the south side, as was customary in Protestant churches after the Reformation. Facing it is the laird's loft, situated in the upright bar of the T. In front of it is the elders' pew, and in front of that a long Communion table of a type once common in Scotland but now rare.

Strathy Parish Kirk *(287)*, 15½ m. w on A 836 in Strathy village

This small and undistinguished village kirk was one of the forty-odd "parliamentary churches" designed by Thomas Telford in the early nineteenth century.

WICK (HIGHLAND)

** Wick Heritage Centre *(286, 343)*, Bank Row

Here, clustered around the harbor built by Thomas Telford in 1810, are fishermen's cottages, outbuildings, a kippering kiln, and other relics of the herring fisheries that flourished here in the nineteenth century.

* Castle of Old Wick *(81)*, 1 m. se; ½ m e of A 9 (not signposted; accessible by side road east of A 9, south of cemetery) (12 ND 369 489); AM

This rectangular tower vies with Castle Sween in Argyll for being the oldest castle in mainland Scotland. It is probably Norse in origin and twelfth century in date. Much ruined, it rises to a height of some thirty to forty feet on a rocky promontory between two deep ravines leading to the sea. For added protection there was a deep ditch on the landward side. There are few window openings and no observable door; presumably the main entry lay in the now destroyed east wall of the castle and was reached by a tall ladder to an upper level. Beam holes and scarcements for supporting wooden floors of this four-story building can be seen on the interior wall-faces.

* Cairn of Get (Garrywhin) *(15)*, 7 m. s; ½ m. nw of A 9 from Ulbster (12 ND 313 411); AM

Here is a short, horned passage grave of the Orkney-Cromarty-Hebridean group with a turf-covered cairn standing to eight feet. The burial chamber underneath consists of a rectangular outer compartment and a circular inner compartment with a corbelled roof. Both are mostly visible.

** MidClyth Stone Rows (Hill o' Many Stanes) *(25)*, 9 m. sw; ½ m. ne of A 9 (11 ND 294 384); AM

Here is a curious fanlike setting of 250 stubby stones (some upright, some fallen) laid out in twenty-two rows with an average of eight stones in each. The date is probably Bronze Age, but the reason for the arrangement is unknown.

*** Grey Cairns of Camster *(15)*, 16 m. sw; 5 m. n of A 9 from 1 m. e of Lybster on road to Watten, 8 m. s of A 882 from ¼ m. e of Watten (11 ND 260 442-440); AM

Here are two restored Neolithic passage graves of the Orkney-Cromarty-Hebridean group. The northernmost cairn is a long (125 feet) mound of rocky material, "horned" at both ends. The horns consist of stepped projections of flagstones that probably served as some sort of stage for burial rites. There are two burial chambers underneath this cairn, one polygonal and the other stalled into three compartments. Both open onto the long southeast side of the cairn. Both can be entered through long, low, dark passageways. The chambers themselves are lighted from a glassed-over hole cut in the top of each cairn. About 200 yards to the south lies the second cairn—round and consisting of loose stones, virtually intact, with a segmented burial chamber underneath, also accessible by way of a low passageway from the east and also lighted from a hole in the top. The circular stone wall between the two cairns is a modern sheepfold.

* **Achavanich Standing Stones** *(24)*, 18 m. sw; 4 m. nw of A 9 from ¼ m. w of Lybster (11 ND 188 417)

This is a U-shaped setting of about forty standing stones, the tallest about six feet in height. The date of construction is probably Bronze Age. The remains of a cist stand against the most northerly stone in the setting. The site lies near the south shore of tiny Loch Stemster.

OUTER HEBRIDES
Barra

(Access by car ferry from Oban and Lochboisdale, South Uist, four times weekly; passenger ferry from Ludag, South Uist, twice daily; plane from Glasgow, daily)

CASTLEBAY

** **Kisimul Castle** *(99, 185)*, access by boat from Castlebay pier, Wednesdays and Saturdays; inquire at Scottish Tourist Information Centre, Castlebay

This is a typical western Highland polygonal courtyard castle, dating probably from the twelfth and thirteenth centuries, although there is no record of its existence before the fifteenth, when it was the residence of the Chief of Clan MacNeil. Legend has it that, when the chief was in residence, a trumpeter would mount the battlements after dinner every day to announce that, since The MacNeil had dined, the rest of the world could now feel free to do likewise.

The castle occupies the whole of a rocky islet in Castlebay harbor, its walls rising sheer from high-water mark to battlemented parapets below, which are putlog holes to support hoardings. In the southeast sector of the enclosure, next to the entrance, rises a great rectangular square keep, four stories high, with battlements and putlog holes below. This may antedate the thirteenth-century curtain wall. The other buildings inside the walls date from the seventeenth and eighteenth centuries. The castle was restored in the twentieth century by the late Robert Lister Macneil, an American.

Since visiting hours are very restricted, most travellers may have to content themselves with a view of the castle from the opposite shore in Castlebay or from the ferry that passes very close to the island.

South Uist

(Access by car ferry from Oban four times weekly)

LOCHBOISDALE

Howmore Parish Kirk *(220)*, 12 m. n; w of A 865

This simple undistinguished kirk contains a rare specimen of a long Communion table of the sort installed in most Scottish churches immediately after the Reformation. The table stretches the full length of the central aisle and is enclosed by partitions containing hinged doors for the admission of communicants.

North Uist

(Access by car ferry, daily from Uig, Skye; twice weekly from Tarbert, Harris)

LOCHMADDY

* Barpa Langass *(15)*, 5¼ m. sw; s of A 867 (18 NF 837 656)

This is a fairly well-preserved Neolithic passage grave of the Orkney-Cromarty-Hebridean group. The cairn itself is a circular pile of stones measuring eighty feet in diameter with a setting of flat curbstones around the circumference. The ovaloid burial chamber measures nine feet by six feet and is up to seven feet in height, capped by three large lintels. The interior can be observed from the outside, although to enter it would require crawling over a litter of loose boulders to get inside. Though poorly signposted, the site is clearly visible from the road.

Harris

(Access by car ferry, daily from Uig, Skye; twice weekly from Lochmaddy, North Uist)

TARBERT

** St. Clement's, Rodel *(55, 185)*, 14 m. s; w of A 859 (18 NG 047 832); AM; key at Rodel Hotel, ¼ m. s of church on A 859

Situated at the southern tip of Harris, this is a much restored late-fifteenth-century cruciform church with a battlemented west tower. Inside, the chief attraction is the recessed wall-tomb of Alastair Crotach (Alexander MacLeod), eighth chief of Clan MacLeod of Dunvegan *(Siol Tormod)*, who died about 1547. His well-preserved stone effigy shows him wearing plate armor with a bascinet and aventail and grasping a two-handed sword (claymore). The tomb on which it rests is beautifully sculpted; among other figures are a castle, a fine hunting scene, an intricately carved galley, and representations of the twelve apostles. In another recessed wall-tomb is the effigy of Alexander's son William (d. 1551) garbed in mail, though not so well sculpted. Along the opposite wall of the nave lies still another tomb— of an unknown armored knight.

Lewis

(Access by car ferry, twice daily from Ullapool; by air, daily from Inverness and Glasgow)

STORNOWAY

*** Callanish *(23)*, 13 m. w; ½ m. w of A 858, ¼ m. s of Callanish village (8 NB 213 220); AM

After the English sites of Stonehenge and Avebury, this is the most interesting and elaborate Bronze Age stone circle in Britain. Its basic pattern is (1) a flattened circle of megaliths, near the center of which stands the tallest stone of the ensemble next to the remains of a Neolithic chambered tomb; and (2) four avenues of standing stones leading from the center toward the circumference of the circle. The most complete of the avenues today is the one pointing to the north-northeast. It consists of two parallel rows of stones, now numbering nineteen. A line of four stones pointing east-southeast probably represents the remains of one side of another avenue. Similarly, the line of five leading due south must have been part of the western side of a third avenue, the eastern side of which is represented by a single stone. Another line of four running due west is all that is left of the fourth avenue. A single stone standing south-southwest of the center of the circle may be the sole remnant of an outer circle.

Although the compass orientation of the circle and its avenues indicates that the stones were originally set with some consideration paid to the rising and setting of celestial bodies, the claim that Callanish was some sort of prehistoric astronomical observatory is farfetched. It is more likely that this was a great outdoor temple dedicated to the worship of the gods of the sea or of the water, with elaborate rites involving processions to and from the center by way of the four avenues.

About a mile to the east, just south of the A 858, are the remains of two smaller stone circles. The area was obviously an important religious center of some sort.

** Black House *(332)*, 15 m. nw; n of A 858 at Arnol; AM

This is a restored, typically nucleated, Hebridean black house, dating from the nineteenth century. Walls are of unmortared stone. Kitchen (with central hearth), bedroom, byre, and barn are contained under the same thatched roof. Furnishings and farm gear are contemporary. Well organized as a museum, this place is a bit too clean and tidy to seem really authentic.

* Trushel Stone *(25)*, 13 m. nw; ¼ m. nw of A 857, se of Balantrushel village (8 NB 375 537)

This twenty-foot-high monolith, presumably of Bronze Age date, is the tallest of its kind in Scotland. Its original purpose, if any, is unknown.

Steinacleit Cairn *(15)*, 13 m. ne; se of A 857 (8 NB 396 540); AM

This is a much ruined Neolithic passage-grave of the Orkney-Cromarty-Hebridean group. The most noticeable feature of the site is the circular setting of ten upright slabs originally constituting the curb or peristalth designed to hold the cairn material in place. Inside is a litter of stones that must have been part of the covering cairn and three uprights that were apparently part of the burial chamber underneath. Surrounding the peristalth is an oval setting of stubby stones of unknown purpose.

** Dun Carloway *(34)*, 15½ m. nw (8 NB 189 412); AM

Here are the substantial ruins of a typical Iron Age broch (not a dun, in spite of the name). The circular wall rises to a maximum height of thirty feet, and the site has the usual broch features: low entrance passage (with lintel), guardroom, mural cells and galleries, stone staircase, and a ledge running around the interior of the wall-face.

NORTHERN ISLANDS
Orkney

(Access daily by car ferry from Scrabster and John o'Groats; by air once or twice daily from Glasgow, Edinburgh, Aberdeen, Inverness, and Shetland)

MAINLAND

Kirkwall

** Tankerness House *(9, 58)*, Broad Street

In this well-restored sixteenth-century merchant's house is the local museum, which contains a fine collection of prehistoric and historic materials, including finds from Orkney's many chambered tombs and from Skara Brae, the Pictish "Burrian Stone," the Viking St. Magnus reliquary, and miscellaneous items illustrating Orcadian agriculture, industry, commerce, and fishing.

*** St. Magnus Cathedral *(160)*, town center

Here, in the author's opinion, is the handsomest church interior in Scotland. Construction of the cathedral began in 1137, when Earl Rognvald, nephew of the murdered St. Magnus, ordered his uncle's bones, along with the seat of the bishopric of Orkney, to be transferred here from the Brough of Birsay (see below). Masons from Durham were apparently imported to do the job; the basic building material was a local red sandstone—later pieced out by white, thus giving the exterior a somewhat mottled appearance in places. Since repairs and reconstruction continued throughout three centuries, the church displays three distinct architectural styles—Romanesque, Transitional, and Early Gothic—all easily detected. In its impact on the viewer, the Romanesque predominates.

The western facade and the three west bays of the nave are of thirteenth-century construction as modified in the fifteenth. The middle section of the nave is thirteenth-century Gothic. The eastern third of the nave is Transitional (late twelfth century); the crossing is both Transitional and Romanesque; the transepts and western section of the choir are Romanesque; the eastern end of the choir is thirteenth-century Gothic; the square tower was added in the fourteenth. Noteworthy features are the interlaced round-arched arcading on the north wall of the nave; the pillars in the choir inside of which are the remains of St. Magnus and Earl (St.) Rognvald; and the fine Romanesque doorway to the north transept.

Church of Scotland services are held here every Sunday, and attendance is the best way for the visitor to savor fully the awesome magnificence of this building.

** Bishop's Palace *(86, 160)*, town center; AM

The original palace on this site was built in the twelfth century, probably at the same time as the nearby St. Magnus Cathedral. It was in this place that the Norwegian King Hakon died in 1263 after his defeat at the Battle of Largs. Here also, in all probability, the Maid of Norway died in 1290 on her way to being inaugurated as Queen of Scots.

Of the present substantial ruin, only the lower courses of the exterior walls and the undercroft can be dated to this early period. The three enormous buttresses on the entrance (west) facade of the existing building were erected by Bishop Robert Reid in the mid-sixteenth century, as was the three-story tower on the northwest corner. The great hall above the undercroft was also his work, though it was later (about 1600) partitioned and remodelled into four rooms by Earl Patrick Stewart, who also added the southern extension with large oriel windows on either side.

*** Earl's Palace *(215)*, town center, south of cathedral

One of the finest examples of Renaissance architecture in Scotland, this well-preserved ruin was built originally by Patrick Stewart, Earl of Orkney, between 1600 and 1607, though never quite completed according to plan. It consists of two long, now roofless, stone buildings set at right angles, with a square tower projecting from the northwest corner of the eastern range. The main entry is in the angle where the south and east ranges join. The great hall on the first floor of the eastern range is described in the official guidebook as "one of the noblest state rooms of any private castle in Scotland." It is distinguished for its oriel and bow windows and its magnificent fireplace.

** Highland Park Distillery *(358)*, 1 m. s on A 691

This single-malt whisky distillery, founded in 1798, is perhaps the most traditional of all Scottish distilleries in that it still uses local peat to dry the malt and a mixture of peat and coke to bring about vaporization prior to distillation. Open to visitors.

** Wideford Hill Chambered Cairn *(17)*, 4 m. w; s of A 965 (6 HY 408 121); AM

This is a Neolithic passage grave of the Maes howe group. The circular cairn is reinforced by three concentric retaining walls, parts of which are visible today, thus giving the exterior of the mound a stepped appearance. The burial chamber, reached by a long, low passage, is rectangular in shape with corbelled walls rising to a modern concrete roof installed by the Scottish Development Department. Three side chambers lead off the main chamber through apertures at floor level.

* Grainbank Earth House *(36)*, 1 m. nw; n of A 985 (6 HY 442 117); AM

This well-preserved post–Iron Age *souterrain* is possibly of Viking provenance. It consists of a subterranean chamber lined with dry-stone walling and roofed with flat lintels supported by four stone pillars. It is entered, with difficulty, through a sloping, curved passage.

* Rennibister Earth House *(36)*, 4 m. w; n of A 965 (6 HY 397 127); AM

Situated in the middle of a farmyard, this is a post–Iron Age *souterrain*. Its polygonal chamber, about eleven feet by eight feet in dimension, is lined with dry masonry and stone slabs and is roofed with overlapping lintels supported by four stone uprights. Entry today is by a trapdoor instead of via the original long, low, covered passageway.

** Cuween Hill Chambered Tomb *(17)*, 7 m. w; s of A 965 (6 HY 364 127); AM

A Maeshowe type of Neolithic passage grave, this grass-covered cairn has a diameter of 55 feet and a maximum height of 8½ feet. Entrance to the chamber is by way of a long, low passageway, negotiable only by the agile visitor. The main burial chamber is rectangular, with walls reaching 7½ feet to a modern roof maintained by the Scottish Development Department. Four corbelled side chambers lead off the central area.

Churchill Barriers *(370)*, 9-12 m. s on A 961

This is a causeway between Mainland, Orkney, and the islands of Burray and South Ronaldsay to the south. It was built by Italian prisoners during World War II to prevent German submarines from entering the great Royal Navy anchorage at Scapa Flow from the east.

* Italian Chapel *(370)*, 9 m. s on Lamb Holm, e of A 961

This ordinary Nissen Hut was handsomely decorated on the inside by Italian prisoners during World War II to serve as a Roman Catholic chapel. The frescoes would not look out of place in a hill town in northern Italy. After the war, returning prisoners restored the paintings. Very charming.

** Broch of Gurness *(34)*, 14½ m. n; 1 m. n of A 966 from juncture with B 9057 (6 HY 383 267); AM

Here is a ruined Iron Age broch, typically located in a coastal position overlooking Eynhallow Sound. Its circular wall rises to a maximum height of fifteen feet and is surrounded by a rock-cut ditch. The broch displays the usual features: narrow entrance passage with door-checks, two guard cells, a mural gallery, stairway, and ledge around the inner wall-face. Inside and outside the broch itself are the foundations and walls of a postbroch (presumably Dark Age) settlement.

Brough of Deerness Monastery *(63)*, 13 m. e; 1½ m. n of Skaill (6 NY 596 088)

Up a steep and narrow path leading to this rocky sea-washed promontory, the forms of nineteen rectangular buildings can be seen under the turf around a ruined stone chapel with walls five feet thick. This was probably the site of a seventh- or eighth-century monastic foundation. It is not easy to reach.

Stromness

* Orphir Round Church *(163)*, 10 m. se; ½ m. e of A 964 from Myre (7 HY 334 043); AM

Dedicated to St. Nicholas and situated on a beautiful site overlooking Scapa Flow, this is the only medieval "round church" in Scotland. Modelled, like other British churches of this type, on the Church of the Holy Sepulchre in Jerusalem, it is believed to have been built by Earl Hakon Paulsson about 1120 after his return from a pilgrimage to the Holy Land taken as penance for his murder of St. Magnus in his church on Egilsay three years earlier. Originally this building was twenty feet in diameter with a semicircular apse on the east, but now all that is left are the ruins of the apse and enough of the attached foundations to indicate the church's roundness. Next to it are the foundations of a Norse hall known as the Earl's Bu.

** Onstan (Unstan) Chambered Cairn *(16)*, 3 m. ne; n of A 965 (6 HY 282 117); AM

This is a Neolithic passage grave of the Orkney-Cromarty-Hebridean group, restored and maintained by the Scottish Development Department. The turf-covered circular cairn is held in position by two retaining walls (peristalths). Underneath, and visible through a window in the modern concrete roof, is a long burial chamber divided (stalled) into five pairs of compartments by upright slabs projecting from the side walls. A small side chamber opens from the center of the west wall.

* Ring of Stenness *(24)*, 4½ m. ne; n of A 965 (6 HY 306 125); AM

All that is left of the original Bronze Age henge here is an arc of four standing stones out of a probable thirteen, the highest measuring seventeen feet. The enclosing ditch has all but disappeared. The stone bench is a modern intrusion.

** Ring of Brodgar *(23)*, 6 m. ne; sw of B 9055 (6 HY 294 134); AM

This is a Bronze Age henge consisting of a stone circle surrounded by a ditch broken by two opposing causeways. It is the largest stone circle in Scotland, with a diameter of 350 feet. Out of the original sixty upright stones, twenty-seven survive to a maximum height of almost 16 feet.

*** Maeshowe Chambered Cairn (17), 7½ m. ne; n of A 965 (6 HY 318 127); AM; key at cottage across the road

This is the most impressive of all the many surviving Neolithic chambered tombs in Scotland and among the best in all Europe. A ditch surrounds the large, dome-shaped, circular, turf-covered cairn. The entrance into the mound consists of a long, lintelled, dry-stone and slab passageway. It leads into the main burial chamber, which is roughly fifteen feet square beneath a high corbelled roof now capped by a concrete dome installed and maintained by the Scottish Development Department. The four corners of the roof are supported by dry-stone buttresses, each faced with a massive upright stone slab. Three small side chambers lead off the central space, each connected with it by a rectangular aperture near the floor, originally sealed by a stone block. The three blocks now lie on the floor in front of the openings. The tomb was broken into in the twelfth century by Norsemen in search of hidden treasure. Evidence of their depredation is to be seen in the runic inscriptions on several stones in the main chamber and in the pictoral engravings of a dragon, a walrus, and a serpent knot. The site is very well maintained by the Scottish Development Department. The keeper of the key in the cottage across the road also conducts short and informative guided tours.

*** Skara Brae (9), 6½ m. n; w of B 9056 (6 HY 321 188); AM

Here, on the edge of the Bay of Skaill, are the well-excavated ruins of a late Neolithic village, consisting of a cluster of seven (possibly eight) tiny roofless stone huts, each containing various pieces of stone furniture (beds, dressers, shelves, and limpet boxes) and a central hearth. The village was evidently deserted during a sandstorm that covered it completely until 1850 when another storm partially revealed its existence. The Scottish Development Department maintains an excellent site museum on the well-kept premises with a guide on duty to answer questions.

Earl's Palace, Birsay (215), 13 m. n; at w end of A 966 (6 HY 364 128); AM

This is the much ruined palace of Robert Stewart, Earl of Orkney, built before 1574. It originally consisted of four narrow ranges built around a central court. The earl was the bastard half-brother of Mary, Queen of Scots, and, along with his son Patrick, ruled the northern islands for forty years.

*** Brough of Birsay (58, 160), 13½ m. n; n of w terminus of A 966 (6 NY 239 285); AM

This tiny promontory on the northwest corner of Mainland, Orkney, approachable only at low tide, is the site of one of the most interesting Dark Age settlements in Britain. After climbing the steep pathway from the causeway, the visitor should first stop at the site museum, where the custodian can be counted on for an informative lecture on the adjacent ruins. To the right, in front of the museum, is the cemetery, containing Norse graves as well as an earlier series of Pictish graves marked by slabs set on end. (One of these, the famous Birsay Stone, now resides in the National Museum of Antiquities in Edinburgh, though there is a replica on the site.) Beyond the cemetery are the walls of a church built in the eleventh century by Thorfinn the Mighty, Earl of Orkney, on the site of an earlier Celtic religious establishment probably dating from the seventh century. Thorfinn's church consists of a small rectangular nave and a narrower round-apsed choir, both in ruins. Adjacent to the southwest corner of the cemetery are the remains of a group of twelfth-century buildings, thought to have served as a clerical residence. East of the cemetery are the foundations of buildings that probably served as the great hall and associated domestic quarters of the Earls of Orkney. On the slope to the north of the cathedral are a number of separate buildings, including the foundations of two Norse farmhouses, possibly of a ninth-century date.

The view of the coastline from here is splendid, the grounds are well tended by the Scottish Development Department, the custodian is unusually helpful, and the excitement of the place is enhanced by the visitor's natural anxiety that an incoming tide might prevent his returning to the mainland.

HOY

(Access by air from Kirkwall daily; by sea from Stromness to Moness Pier, three times daily)

** **Dwarfie Stane** *(18)*, 3 m. s of Moness Pier (7 HY 243 005); AM

A rock tomb cut out of a large solid block of red sandstone, this is the only Neolithic grave of its type in Britain. The central burial chamber is a rectangle in plan, about seven feet by three feet, and almost three feet high. The opening into it is both narrower and lower. Small cells with rounded roofs flank the chamber. Outside the entrance is a huge slab that fits the contours of the aperture leading into the tomb. It was obviously a sealing stone.

WYRE

(Access by passenger ferry from Tingwall Pier, Mainland, twice daily; from Kirkwall, once weekly)

* **Cubbie Roo's Castle** *(81)*, 1 m. sw of pier (6 HY 442 264); AM

This is the oldest datable castle in Scotland, built 1143–1148 by a Norseman named Kolbein Hruga. It is a ruined miniature stone keep, only twenty-five feet square, with walls five feet thick and now no more than seven feet in height. There is no entrance to the ground floor, which has, however, two slit windows. A well is sunk into the rock floor inside. The castle is enclosed by ramparts and ditches, probably of a later date. There is a small ruined twelfth-century church nearby, consisting of nave and narrow chancel.

Visitors unwilling to spend the better part of the day on this tiny island can get a fairly good, though distant, view of this castle from the passenger ferry plying between Tingwall Pier and nearby Rousay Island.

EGILSAY

(Access by passenger ferry from Tingwall, twice daily by arrangement [tel: Rousay 203]; from Kirkwall, once weekly [tel: Kirkwall 2044])

* **St. Magnus Church** *(163)*, ¼ m. e of Skaill Pier (6 HY 466 304); AM; key at neighboring farmhouse

This is a well-preserved ruin of an eleventh-century church, which may be the building where St. Magnus was murdered by Earl Hakon Paulsson in 1117. Its most distinctive feature is the tall round tower at the west end, still standing almost fifty feet in height. The ruined nave—about thirty feet long—is rectangular, as is the smaller and narrower choir, which has a chamber over it. There are two good round-arched doorways, one of them blocked.

ROUSAY

(Access by sea from Tingwall Pier, Mainland, twice daily; from Kirkwall, once weekly; no cars; bicycles for hire near pier)

** **Taversoe Tuack Chambered Cairn** *(16)*, ¾ m. w of Rousay Pier, n of B 9094 (6 HY 426 276); AM

This is a rare two-story Neolithic passage grave of the Orkney-Cromarty-Hebridean group, with a trapdoor in the floor of the upper story provided by the Scottish Development Department. The burial chamber lies beneath a circular turf-covered cairn edged by a curb of flat stones. The lower, subterranean chamber is rectangular in shape and divided into four compartments of upright septal slabs. The upper chamber, now reroofed with a concrete dome, consists of two compartments with rounded ends and a small cell opposite the entrance between the two. Just beyond the edge of the cairn is a tiny oval-shaped underground chamber of unknown date and purpose.

** Blackhammer Chambered Cairn *(16)*, 1½ m. w of Rousay Pier, n of B 9064 (6 HY 414 276); AM

Here is another Neolithic passage grave of the Orkney-Cromarty-Hebridean group. Under a rectangular turf-covered cairn is a long burial chamber originally partitioned (stalled) by six pairs of projecting slabs, of which four have been removed. The chamber is visible from a hole cut in the roof by the Scottish Development Department.

** Knowe of Yarso *(16)*, 2½ m. w of Rousay Pier; ¼ m. n of B 9064 (6 HY 404 281); AM

The westernmost of a string of three Neolithic passage graves of the Orkney-Cromarty-Hebridean group, the rectangular cairn has been returfed and reroofed by the Scottish Development Department. Underneath, the burial chamber is divided into three main compartments by upright slabs measuring four feet high and projecting from side walls standing up to six feet.

*** Midhowe Chambered Cairn *(16)*, 5 m. nw of Rousay Pier, w of B 9064 extension (6 HY 371 306); AM

Here is a Neolithic passage grave of the Orkney-Cromarty-Hebridean group now housed under a shed maintained by the Scottish Development Department, with raised gangways for viewing. The cairn is rectangular with rounded corners, more than a hundred feet in length, and bounded by two concentric curbs. Inside, the long narrow burial chamber is divided by pairs of transverse slabs into twelve compartments, making this the longest stalled cairn in Scotland. One side of the chamber is lined with benches on which were found the bones of twenty-three people buried here.

** Midhowe Broch *(34)*, 5 m. nw of Rousay Pier, w of B 9064 extension (6 HY 371 307); AM

This is a typical ruined Iron Age broch with a circular wall, now reaching as much as fourteen feet in height. It is surrounded by a thick wall with a ditch on either side. Between broch and outer wall are the foundations of a later settlement. The broch itself displays the usual features: door-checks, bar-holes, mural cell and galleries, and stone staircase.

SANDAY

(Access by air from Kirkwall, twice daily; by sea from Kirkwall, three times weekly)

* **Quoyness Chambered Cairn** *(18)*, south shore, 2 m. sw of Roadside (5 HY 676 378); AM

The cairn of this Neolithic passage grave of the Maes howe type is more or less pear-shaped and is faced by partially exposed retaining walls. The main burial chamber is rectangular with a corbelled roof thirteen feet high. There are six small cells leading from the central area, two along each side and one at each end. The interior of the tomb can be entered by crawling through the passageway leading from the outer retaining wall.

WESTRAY

(Access from Kirkwall by air, twice daily; by ferry, three times weekly)

* **Cross Kirk (Westside Church)** *(163)*, 1 m. e of B 9067 from Langskaill, 5 m. s of Pierowall (5 HY 455 432); AM

This twelfth-century Romanesque church has a rectangular nave and a square-ended choir. Though roofless, its walls stand to 7½ feet in height. The round choir arch is well preserved.

** **Noltland Castle** *(216)*, ½ m. n of Pierowall (5 HY 429 488); AM

This is a very well-preserved Z-plan tower-house built some time after 1560 by Gilbert Balfour, one of the murderers of Cardinal Beaton at St. Andrews Castle and later of Lord Darnley at Kirk o' Field, Edinburgh. In 1592 the castle was besieged and captured by Patrick Stewart, Earl of Orkney. Altogether seventy-one gunloops pierce the castle's outer walls, and the Z-plan arrangement (a central rectangular block with square towers at diagonally opposite corners) made it possible to protect any side of the building with enfilade fire. The inside is distinguished for its splendid stone stairway and well-lighted great hall.

PAPA WESTRAY

(Access by air from Kirkwall, twice daily; by sea from Kirkwall, three times weekly)

* **Holm of Papa Westray Chambered Cairn** *(18)*, on islet of same name, e

of Papa Westray; boats usually available on inquiry at island co-op (5 HY 509 518); AM

This is an unusual Neolithic passage grave of the Maes howe group. The long cairn has been turfed over by the Scottish Development Department, which has also covered the chamber with a concrete roof pierced by manholes through which access can be gained into the interior. The main chamber is sixty-seven feet long by five feet wide with oversailing walls as high as eight feet. Toward each end, cross-walls subdivide the chamber into three sections. Fourteen mural cells open off the central area.

Shetland

(Access by car ferry three times weekly from Aberdeen; by air frequently from Aberdeen, Birmingham, Glasgow, and Edinburgh)

MAINLAND

Lerwick

** Shetland Museum *(9, 58, 63)*, Lower Hillhead

Here is a good collection of materials illustrating Shetland's prehistory and history, including finds from Jarlshof and Clickhimin Broch, replicas of the St. Ninian's Isle Treasure, Early Christian stones, ship and boat models, agricultural implements, including a *cas chrom* (crooked spade), and items salvaged from the wreck in 1588 of a ship of the Spanish Armada.

** Clickhimin Broch *(35)*, 1 m. sw; n of A 970 (4 HU 465 408); AM

This ruined Iron Age broch, surrounded by an outer wall, stands no more than fifteen feet in height. It displays interesting mural cells and a mural staircase that does not reach the floor. Between broch and outer wall is a blockhouse, probably of Iron Age date, as well as a Bronze Age courtyard house, probably the oldest building on the site. Within the broch are the remains of a wheelhouse, with radial piers, built some time after the broch fell into disuse and occupied perhaps as late as the ninth century A.D. by Viking immigrants to Shetland.

** Scalloway Castle *(215)*, 6 m. w; s of A 970 (4 HU 405 393); AM

Built in the early seventeenth century by Patrick Stewart, Earl of Orkney, this is the substantial ruin of an L-plan four-story tower-house with corbelled turrets at all angles except one. Shot-holes for hand guns occur in the breasts of the windows, and ornamental false shot-holes in the eastern turrets between the corbels. The interior construction is typical: vaulted ground floor, well-lighted hall with fireplace on the first, and bedrooms with fireplaces and garderobes on the upper stories.

*** **Mousa Broch** *(35)*, 14 m. s (4 HU 457 236); AM; access by boat from Sandwick. Inquire at co-op in Sandwick village or at Scottish Tourist Information Centre in Lerwick.

On the islet of Mousa, just off the east coast of the Mainland of Shetland, stands the finest and best preserved of all of Scotland's ruined Iron Age brochs. Its tapered circular wall reaches a maximum height of forty-three feet. Here are the usual broch features, but better observable than in most other sites of the same sort: door-checks, bar-hole, mural cells, galleries, stone staircases, and two ledges running around the inner wall-face to support a floor and a roof.

Although this is not easy to get to—and virtually impossible in bad weather—visitors to Shetland should bend every effort to see this remarkable site. Passengers on the Lerwick-Aberdeen ferry may get a good view of the broch whenever their ship proceeds through Mousa Sound on leaving Lerwick.

* **Stanydale** *(10)*, 8 m. nw; 1½ m. se of Bridge of Walls; follow black and white striped poles from edge of road across moorland (3 HU 285 503 and 288 502); AM

The most interesting feature of this site is the so-called temple of Neolithic or Early Bronze Age date. It is oval-shaped and measures about 40 feet by 20 feet, with six shallow recesses in the east wall and sockets for two spruce uprights, presumably to support a roof. (Spruce was unknown in Scotland until the sixteenth century, so the original timbers must have been imported from Scandinavia or perhaps were driftwood from North America.) A short distance to the west are the scant remains of a contemporary village of nine huts, the best preserved of which measures 30 feet by 15 feet with a wall reaching a maximum height of 2½ feet.

Sumburgh Airport

*** **Jarlshof** *(26, 35, 58, 215)*, ½ m. s; w of A 970 (4 HU 397 096); AM

Here can be seen evidence of the longest sequence of occupation of any archaeological site in Scotland (with the possible exception of Cairnpapple Hill, West Lothian): Late Bronze Age and Early Iron Age settlements; an Iron Age broch; a postbroch wheelhouse settlement; a village of Viking long-houses; a medieval farmstead; and, finally, the late-sixteenth-century home of the Stewart Earls of Orkney, rechristened "Jarlshof" by Sir Walter Scott in his novel, *The Pirate.*

From the entrance, today's visitor follows a path along the shore, past the half-eroded broch on the left. North of this ruin are the remains of Late Iron Age wheelhouses. East of the broch are the foundations and ruined walls of the Stewart earls' house, built in the late sixteenth and early seventeenth centuries. Opposite this to the east are the foundations of six Iron Age and Bronze Age huts, of which the Bronze Age "Dwelling III" at the north end of the group is the best preserved and can be viewed from a wooden platform. Heading north from here, we come to the foundations of a medieval farmstead. Farther on, and much more extensive, are the remains of a ninth- to eleventh-century Viking settlement, of which the foundations of at least eight houses can be seen.

Before undertaking any of this tour, visitors are advised first to inspect the site museum, where wall charts will assist them in making their way through the confusing ruins.

Ness of Burgi *(31)*, 2 m. s; 1 m. s of A 970 from Scord hamlet (4 HU 388 084); AM

This Iron Age promontory fort now consists of a substantial ruined wall flanked by ditches running across the tip of a rocky headland. Inside is a ruined blockhouse, which is probably of Late Iron Age date and served to guard the single entrance to the fort. There are no signposts, and the route from the end of the road to the site across moorland and huge rocks is not for the timid.

** Shetland Croft House Museum *(332)*, 4½ m. n; e of A 970 in South Voe (Dunrossness), 1 m. s of Boddam

Here is a nineteenth-century thatched stone cottage consisting of kitchen, bedroom, byre, barn, and corn-drying room with a covered fireplace. Furnished with boxbeds and other contemporary pieces, the museum also contains a good collection of agricultural implements—a Shetland spade for plowing, peat cutter, flails, etc.

St. Ninian's Isle *(63)*, 8 m. nw; 1 m. w of B 9122 through Bigton village (4 HU 369 208)

After crossing the strip of sand from Bigton and climbing the steep and barely visible footpath to the right, the visitor will see the ruined chapel off to the left of the point where the path reaches the summit. It consists of the walls of the nave and chancel of a church built about 1150. Underneath it are the foundations of a pre-Norse church, presumably of the eighth century. It was here that St. Ninian's Isle Treasure was discovered—a priceless hoard of ornamented silver pieces now in the National Museum of Antiquities in Edinburgh, though replicas can be seen in the Shetland Museum in Lerwick. Whether these pieces belonged to a Pictish chief or to the church where they were discovered is a matter of argument. In either case they were most probably buried to save them from Viking marauders.

UNST

* Muness Castle *(216)*, 10 m. s of Haroldswick, 1 m. e of A 968 (1 HP 629 013); AM

This is the northernmost castle ruin in Britain. Built in 1598 by Laurence Bruce, half-uncle to Patrick Stewart, Earl of Orkney, it is a three-story Z-plan tower-house, with circular towers at diagonally opposite corners of the main rectangular block. The internal arrangement is typical: vaulted ground floor, first floor with hall, bedrooms with garderobes on the second floor and in the corner towers.

Appendix A
The Best of Scotland

THREE-STAR SITES AND MUSEUMS

Prehistoric, Roman, and Dark Age Sites

Balnuaran of Clava Cairns *(519)*, nr. Inverness, Inverness-shire
Brough of Birsay *(563)*, nr. Stromness, Mainland, Orkney
Cairnpapple Hill *(431)*, nr. Torpichen, West Lothian
Callanish *(557)*, nr. Stornoway, Lewis, Outer Hebrides
Dunadd *(469)*, nr. Lochgilphead, Argyll
Grey Cairns of Camster *(554)*, nr. Wick, Caithness
Jarlshof *(569)*, nr. Sumburgh Airport, Mainland, Shetland
Maeshowe Chambered Cairn *(563)*, nr. Stromness, Mainland, Orkney
Midhowe Chambered Cairn *(566)*, Rousay, Orkney
Mousa Broch *(569)*, nr. Lerwick, Mainland, Shetland
Nether Largie, South *(470)*, nr. Lochgilphead, Argyll
Skara Brae *(563)*, nr. Stromness, Mainland, Orkney
Sueono's Stone *(528)*, nr. Forres, Moray
White Caterthun and **Brown Caterthun** *(509)*, nr. Brechin, Angus

Ruined Castles and Tower Houses

Bothwell Castle *(410)*, nr. Hamilton, Lanarkshire
Caerlaverock Castle *(384)*, nr. Dumfries, Dumfriesshire
Castle Campbell *(481)*, nr. Dollar, Clackmannanshire
Craigmillar Castle *(450)*, nr. Edinburgh, Midlothian
Craignethan Castle *(411)*, nr. Lanark, Lanarkshire
Crichton Castle *(432)*, nr. Dalkeith, Midlothian
Dirleton Castle *(453)*, Dirleton, East Lothian
Doune Castle *(502)*, Doune, Perthshire
Duffus Castle *(528)*, nr. Elgin, Moray
Dunnottar Castle *(546)*, nr. Stonehaven, Kincardineshire
Dunstaffnage Castle *(472)*, nr. Oban, Argyll

Earl's Palace *(560)*, Kirkwall, Mainland, Orkney
Hermitage Castle *(413)*, nr. Hawick, Roxburghshire
Huntingtower Castle *(506)*, nr. Perth, Perthshire
Huntly Castle *(540)*, Huntly, Aberdeenshire
Kildrummy Castle *(537)*, nr. Alford, Aberdeenshire
Linlithgow Palace *(426)*, Linlithgow, West Lothian
Loch Leven Castle *(482)*, Kinross, Kinross-shire
Newark Castle *(397)*, Port Glasgow, Renfrewshire
Ravenscraig Castle *(489)*, Kirkcaldy, Fife
Rothesay Castle *(395)*, Rothesay, Bute
Tantallon Castle *(458)*, nr. North Berwick, East Lothian
Threave Castle *(378)*, nr. Castle Douglas, Kirkcudbrightshire
Tioram Castle *(460)*, nr. Ballachulish, Argyll

Habitable Castles, Palaces, and Tower Houses

(See also **Stately Homes**)

Claypotts Castle *(510)*, nr. Dundee, Angus
Dumbarton Castle *(475)*, Dumbarton, Dunbartonshire
Edinburgh Castle *(436)*, Edinburgh, Midlothian
Falkland Palace *(488)*, Falkland, Fife
Fort George *(519)*, nr. Inverness, Inverness-shire
Palace of Holyroodhouse *(442)*, Edinburgh, Midlothian
Stirling Castle *(477)*, Stirling, Stirlingshire

Churches

Canongate Kirk *(442)*, Edinburgh, Midlothian
Church of St. Andrew and St. George *(446)*, Edinburgh, Midlothian
Cullen Kirk *(531)*, Banffshire
Dalmeny Church *(429)*, nr. Queensferry, West Lothian
Dunfermline Abbey *(488)*, Dunfermline, Fife
Durisdeer Parish Kirk *(388)*, nr. Thornhill, Dumfriesshire
Glasgow Cathedral *(406)*, Glasgow, Lanarkshire
King's College Chapel *(534)*, Aberdeen, Aberdeenshire
Paisley Abbey *(397)*, Paisley, Renfrewshire
Rosslyn Chapel *(452)*, nr. Loanhead, Midlothian
St. Andrew's Parish Church *(402)*, Glasgow, Lanarkshire

St. Columba's Burntisland *(484)*, Fife
St. Giles Kirk *(439)*, Edinburgh, Midlothian
St. Machar's Cathedral *(533)*, Aberdeen, Aberdeenshire
St. Magnus Cathedral *(559)*, Kirkwall, Mainland, Orkney
St. Michael's Church *(427)*, Linlithgow, West Lothian
Yester Kirk *(457)*, East Lothian

Ecclesiastical Ruins

Arbroath Abbey *(507)*, Arbroath, Angus
Crossraguel Abbey *(392)*, nr. Maybole, Ayrshire
Dryburgh Abbey *(418)*, nr. Melrose, Roxburghshire
Dundrennan Abbey *(382)*, nr. Kirkcudbright, Kirkcudbrightshire
Elgin Cathedral *(526)*, Elgin, Moray
Inchcolm Abbey *(483)*, nr. Aberdour, Fife
Inchmahome Priory *(497)*, nr. Aberfoyle, Perthshire
Iona Abbey *(465)*, Isle of Iona, Argyll
Jedburgh Abbey *(413)*, Jedburgh, Roxburghshire
Kelso Abbey *(415)*, Kelso, Roxburghshire
Melrose Abbey *(417)*, Melrose, Roxburghshire
Ruthwell Cross *(385)*, nr. Dumfries, Dumfriesshire
St. Andrews Cathedral and Church of St. Rule *(492)*, St. Andrews, Fife
St. Bride's Chapel *(399)*, Douglas, Lanarkshire
Sweetheart Abbey *(382)*, New Abbey, Kirkcudbrightshire

Educational Institutions

Edinburgh University, Old College *(435)*, Edinburgh, Midlothian
Glasgow School of Art *(404)*, Glasgow, Lanarkshire
The University of St. Andrews, St. Andrews, Fife
    St. Mary's College *(494)*
    College of St. Salvator *(493)*

Monuments and Public Buildings

City Chambers *(404)*, Glasgow, Lanarkshire
Inveraray War Memorial *(464)*, Inveraray, Argyll
Scott Monument *(444)*, Edinburgh, Midlothian
West Register House *(446)*, Edinburgh, Midlothian

Stately Homes

Blair Castle *(498)*, Blair Atholl, Perthshire
Bowhill *(419)*, nr. Selkirk, Selkirkshire
Brodick Castle *(393)*, Brodick, Arran, Bute
Castle Fraser *(536)*, nr. Aberdeen, Aberdeenshire
Cawdor Castle *(525)*, nr. Nairn, Nairnshire
Craigievar Castle *(537)*, nr. Alford, Aberdeenshire
Crathes Castle *(545)*, nr. Banchory, Kincardineshire
Culzean Castle *(392)*, nr. Maybole, Ayrshire
Dalmeny House *(429)*, nr. Queensferry, West Lothian
Drumlanrig Castle *(387)*, nr. Thornhill, Dumfriesshire
Dunrobin Castle *(552)*, nr. Dornoch, Sutherland
Dunvegan Castle *(522)*, Dunvegan, Skye, Inverness-shire
Fasque *(546)*, nr. Fettercairn, Kincardineshire
Fyvie Castle *(545)*, nr. Turriff, Aberdeenshire
Glamis Castle *(512)*, nr. Forfar, Angus
Hopetoun House *(430)*, nr. Queensferry, West Lothian
Inveraray Castle *(463)*, Inveraray, Argyll
Lennoxlove House *(457)*, nr. Haddington, East Lothian
Mellerstain *(416)*, nr. Kelso, Roxburghshire
Scone Palace *(506)*, nr. Perth, Perthshire
Thirlestane Castle *(425)*, nr. Lauder, Berwickshire
Torosay Castle *(471)*, nr. Craignure, Mull, Argyll
Traquair House *(420)*, nr. Peebles, Peeblesshire

Town and City Houses

Georgian House *(446)*, Edinburgh, Midlothian
Gladstone's Land *(438)*, Edinburgh, Midlothian
Hill House *(476)*, Helensburgh, Dunbartonshire
The Palace *(485)*, Culross, Fife
Provost Skene's House *(534)*, Aberdeen, Aberdeenshire
Tenement House *(405)*, Glasgow, Lanarkshire

Parks and Gardens

Brodick Castle Gardens *(393)*, Brodick, Arran, Bute
Calton Hill *(445)*, Edinburgh, Midlothian
Cawdor Castle Garden *(525)*, nr. Nairn, Nairnshire

Crathes Castle Garden *(545)*, nr. Banchory, Kincardineshire
Culzean Castle Garden *(392)*, nr. Maybole, Ayrshire
Dawyck House Gardens *(422)*, nr. Peebles, Peebleshire
Drummond Castle Garden *(501)*, nr. Crieff, Perthshire
Dunrobin Castle Garden *(552)*, nr. Dornoch, Sutherland
Edzell Castle Garden *(509)*, nr. Brechin, Angus
Glasgow Botanic Gardens *(409)*, Glasgow, Lanarkshire
Inverewe *(549)*, nr. Poolewe, Ross and Cromarty
Pitmedden Garden *(543)*, nr. Oldmeldrum, Aberdeenshire
Royal Botanic Garden *(450)*, Edinburgh, Midlothian
Tyninghame House Gardens *(455)*, nr. Dunbar, East Lothian

Industrial Sites

Bonawe Furnace *(473)*, nr. Oban, Argyll
Glenfarclas Glenlivet Distillery *(531)*, nr. Charlestown of Aberlour,
    Banffshire
Glenfiddich Distillery *(531)*, Dufftown, Banffshire
Glen Grant-Glenlivet Distillery *(530)*, Rothes, Moray
Glenlivet Distillery, The *(533)*, nr. Tomintoul, Banffshire
Glenturret Distillery *(501)*, nr. Crieff, Perthshire
New Lanark *(411)*, nr. Lanark, Lanarkshire

Museums and Galleries

GENERAL

Glasgow Art Gallery and Museum *(407)*, Glasgow, Lanarkshire
National Museum of Antiquities of Scotland *(447)*, Edinburgh, Midlothian

ART GALLERIES

Hunterian Art Gallery *(408)*, Glasgow, Lanarkshire
National Gallery of Scotland *(444)*, Edinburgh, Midlothian
Scottish National Portrait Gallery *(448)*, Edinburgh, Midlothian

FOLK, ARCHAEOLOGY, AND LOCAL HISTORY

Highland Folk Museum *(521)*, Kingussie, Inverness-shire
Museum of Scottish Tartans *(500)*, Comrie, Perthshire
Paisley Art Gallery & Museum *(396)*, Paisley, Renfrewshire
People's Palace *(401)*, Glasgow, Lanarkshire

Skye Black House Museum *(523)*, nr. Dunvegan, Skye, Inverness-shire
Strathnaver Museum *(550)*, Bettyhill, Sutherland
West Highland Museum *(575)*, Fort William, Inverness-shire

INDUSTRY, TRANSPORT, FISHING, AND AGRICULTURE

Aberdeen Maritime Museum *(535)*, Aberdeen, Aberdeenshire
Auchindrain Museum of Country Life *(464)*, nr. Inveraray, Argyll
Glasgow Museum of Transport *(400)*, Glasgow, Lanarkshire
Pitmedden Museum of Country Life *(534)*, nr. Oldmeldrum, Aberdeenshire
Royal Scottish Museum *(434)*, Edinburgh, Midlothian
Scottish Fisheries Museum *(483)*, Anstruther, Fife

LITERARY

Abbotsford (Scott) *(419)*, nr. Melrose, Roxburghshire
Burns Cottage and Museum *(389)*, Alloway, Ayrshire
Tam o' Shanter Museum (Burns) *(389)*, Ayr, Ayrshire

MILITARY

Bannockburn Heritage Centre *(479)*, nr. Stirling, Stirlingshire
Black Watch Museum *(505)*, Perth, Perthshire
Cameronians (Scottish Rifles) Regimental Museum *(410)*, Hamilton, Lanarkshire
Culloden Battlefield and Visitor Centre *(518)*, nr. Inverness, Inverness-shire
Edinburgh Castle *(436)*, Edinburgh, Midlothian
     Royal Scots Regimental Museum
     Scottish National War Memorial
     Scottish United Services Museum
Fort George *(519)*, nr. Inverness, Inverness-shire
     Queen's Own Highlanders (Seaforth and Camerons) Regimental Museum
Stirling Castle *(477)*, Stirling, Stirlingshire
     Argyll and Sutherland Highlanders Regimental Museum

Appendix B
Selected Readings

Guide Books

Doak, A. M., and McLaren Young. *Glasgow at a Glance*. Rev. ed. London: Robert Hale, 1977.

Fedden, Robin, and John Kenworthy-Browne. *The Country House Guide*. New York: W. W. Norton & Company, 1979.

Macnie, Donald Lamond, ed. *The New Shell Guide to Scotland*. London: Edbury Press, 1977.

McKean, Charles, and David Walker, eds. *Edinburgh: An Illustrated Architectural Guide*. Edinburgh: RIAS Publications, 1982.

Museums and Galleries in Scotland. Edinburgh: Scottish Tourist Board, 1981.

Nicholson, Robert. *Nicholson's Guide to Scotland*. London: Robert Nicholson Publications, 1981.

Prebble, John. *John Prebble's Scotland*. London: Secker & Warburg, 1984.

Prentice, Robin, ed. *The National Trust for Scotland Guide*. New York: W. W. Norton & Company, 1977.

Scotland's Distilleries: An Illustrated Visitors' Guide. Alexandria, Dunbartonshire: Famedram Publishers, 1984.

Scotland: 1001 Things to See. Edinburgh: Scottish Tourist Board, 1983.

Simpson, W. Douglas. *The Highlands of Scotland*. London: Robert Hale, 1976.

Tindall, Jemima. *Scottish Island Hopping: A Handbook for the Independent Traveller*. New York: Hippocrene Books, 1981.

Tomes, John. *Blue Guide to Scotland*. London: Ernest Benn, 1975.

General Histories

Dickinson, W. Croft, and George Pryde. *A New History of Scotland*. 2 vols. London and New York: Thomas Nelson, 1962.

Donaldson, Gordon. *Scotland, The Shaping of a Nation*. London: David and Charles, 1974.

_____ , and Robert Morpeth. *A Dictionary of Scottish History*. Edinburgh: John Donald, 1978.

Fry, Plantagenet and Fiona Somerset. *The History of Scotland*. London: Boston, Melbourne, and Henley, Routledge & Kegan Paul, 1982.

Glover, Janet R. *The Story of Scotland*. London: Faber and Faber, 1977.

Grant, Isabel Frances. *The Economic History of Scotland*. London, New York, and Toronto: Longmans, Green and Co., 1934.

Lythe, S. G. E., and J. Butt. *An Economic History of Scotland, 1100–1939*. Glasgow & London: Blackie, 1975.

Mackie, J. D. *A History of Scotland*. Harmondsworth, Middlesex: Penguin Books, 1978.

Maclean, Fitzroy. *A Concise History of Scotland*. London: Thames and Hudson, 1970.

Mitchison, Rosalind. *A History of Scotland*. London: Methuen & Co., 1970.

Orel, Harold, Henry L. Snyder, and Marilyn Stokstad, eds. *The Scottish World: History of the Culture of Scotland*. New York: Harry N. Abrams, 1981.

Smout, T. C. *A History of the Scottish People: 1560–1830*. Glasgow: William Collins & Sons, 1969.

Topical Studies

Browning, Robert. *A History of Golf: The Royal and Ancient Game*. New York: E. P. Dutton & Company, 1955.

Burleigh, J. H. S. *A Church History of Scotland*. London, New York, Toronto: Oxford University Press, 1960.

Butt, John. *The Industrial Archaeology of Scotland*. Newton Abbot: David & Charles, 1967.

Caldwell, David H., ed. *Scottish Weapons and Fortifications, 1100–1800*. Edinburgh: John Donald Publishers, 1981.

Cant, Ronald Gordon. *The University of St. Andrews: A Short History*. Edinburgh & London: Scottish Academic Press, 1970.

Collinson, Francis M. *The Bagpipe: The History of a Musical Instrument*. London: Routledge & Kegan Paul, 1975.

Cox, E. H. M. *A History of Gardening in Scotland*. London: Chatto & Windus, 1935.

Daiches, David. *Scotch Whisky*. New York and Glasgow: Fontana/ William Collins & Sons, 1976.

Donaldson, Gordon. *The Scots Overseas*. London: Robert Hale, 1966.

——————— . *Scotland: Church and Nation Through Sixteen Centuries*. Edinburgh: Scottish Academic Press, 1972.

——————— . *Scottish Kings*. London: B. T. Batsford, 1967.

Dunbar, John G. *The Architecture of Scotland*, rev. ed. London: B. T. Batsford, 1978.

Dunbar, John Telfer. *History of Highland Dress*. London: B. T. Batsford, 1979.

Forman, Sheila. *Scottish Country Houses and Castles*. Glasgow and London: Collins, 1967, 1971.

Franklin, Thomas B. *A History of Scottish Farming*. London and New York: Thomas Nelson and Sons, 1952.

Graham-Campbell, David. *Scotland's Story in Her Monuments*. London: Robert Hale, 1982.

Grant, Isabel Frances. *Highland Folk Ways*. London and Boston: Routledge & Kegan Paul, 1961.

_____ . *The MacLeods: The History of a Clan, 1269–1956*. London: Faber and Faber, (Spurbooks Reprint, 1981).

_____ . *The Lordship of the Isles*. Edinburgh: The Moray Press, 1935 (James Thin Reprint, Edinburgh: The Mercat Press, 1982).

Hay, George. *Architecture of Scotland*. Stockfield, Northumberland: Oriel Press, 1969.

Hesketh, Christian. *Tartans*. London: Octopus Books, Ltd., 1972.

Horn, D. B. *A Short History of the University of Edinburgh, 1556–1889*. Edinburgh: The University Press, 1967.

Kermack, William Ramsay. *The Scottish Highlands: A Short History*. Edinburgh and London: W. & A. K. Johnston & G. W. Bacon, 1957.

Lindsay, Maurice. *History of Scottish Literature*. London: Robert Hale, 1977.

McDowell, R. J. S. *The Whiskies of Scotland*. London: John Murray, 1971.

Mackie, John Duncan. *The University of Glasgow, 1451–1951*. Glasgow: Jackson, 1954.

MacLeod, Dawn. *The Gardener's Scotland*. Edinburgh: William Blackwood & Sons, 1977.

Munro, R. W. *Scotland: Land of Kin and Clan*. London: Johnston and Bacon, 1980.

Oakley, C. A. *The Second City*. Glasgow and London: Blackie & Son, 1967.

Petzsch, Helmut. *Architecture in Scotland*. London: Longmans, 1971.

Scarlett, James D. *The Tartans of the Scottish Clans*. Glasgow and London: William Collins Sons and Co., 1975.

Symon, J. A. *Scottish Farming Past and Present*. Edinburgh and London: Oliver and Boyd, 1959.

Verney, Peter. *The Gardens of Scotland*. London: B. T. Batsford, 1980.

Wittig, Kurt. *The Scottish Tradition in Literature*. Edinburgh: The Mercat Press, 1958.

Prehistoric, Roman, and Dark Age Scotland

(Chapters 1 and 2)

Breeze, David J. *Roman Scotland: A Guide to the Visible Remains.* Newcastle-upon-Tyne: Frank Graham, 1979.

Cruden, Stewart. *The Early Christian & Pictish Monuments of Scotland.* Edinburgh: H.M.S.O., 1964.

Feacham, Richard. *A Guide to Prehistoric Scotland.* London: B. T. Batsford, 1963.

——————. *The North Britons: The Prehistory of the Border People.* London: Hutchinson of London, 1965.

Henderson, Isabel. *The Picts.* London: Thames and Hudson, 1967

Henshall, Audrey Shore. *The Chambered Tombs of Scotland.* 2 vols. Edinburgh: Edinburgh University Press, 1963, 1972.

Lacaille, Armand D. *The Stone Age in Scotland.* London, New York, and Toronto: Oxford University Press, 1954.

Laing, Lloyd. *Orkney and Shetland: An Archaeological Guide.* Newton Abbot, London, North Pomfret, VT., Vancouver: David & Charles, 1974.

Mackie, Euan W. *Scotland: An Archaeological Guide.* London: Faber, 1975.

Piggott, Stuart. *Scotland before History.* London, Edinburgh, Paris, Melbourne, Johannesburg, Toronto, and New York: Thomas Nelson and Sons, 1958.

Piggott, Stuart, and W. D. Simpson. *Illustrated Guides to Ancient Monuments.* Vol. VI. Edinburgh: H.M.S.O., 1970.

Richmond, Ian A., ed. *Roman and Native in North Britain.* Edinburgh, London, and Melbourne: Thomas Nelson and Sons, 1958.

Simpson, William Douglas. *The Ancient Stones of Scotland.* London: Robert Hale, 1965.

Smyth, Alfred P. *Warlords and Holy Men: Scotland AD 80–1000.* The New History of Scotland, vol. I. London: Edward Arnold, 1984.

Thomas, Charles. *The Early Christian Archaeology of North Britain.* London: Oxford University Press, 1971.

Wainwright, Frederick T., ed. *The Problem of the Picts.* Edinburgh, London, Melbourne, and Cape Town: Thomas Nelson and Sons, 1955.

Medieval Scotland

(Chapters 3, 4, and 5)

Barrow, G. W. S. *Kingship and Unity: Scotland 1000–1306.* The New History of Scotland, vol. II. London: Edward Arnold, 1981.

_____ . *The Anglo-Norman Era in Scottish History*. Oxford: The Clarendon Press, 1980.

_____ . *The Kingdom of the Scots: Government, Church and Society from the Eleventh to the Fourteenth Century*. New York: St. Martin's Press, 1973.

_____ . *Robert Bruce and the Community of the Realm of Scotland*. Berkeley and Los Angeles: University of California Press, 1965.

Bingham, Caroline. *The Stewart Kingdom of Scotland: 1371–1603*. London: Widenfeld and Nicolson, 1974.

Brown, Jennifer M., ed. *Scottish Society in the Fifteenth Century*. New York: St. Martin's Press, 1977.

Coulton, G. G. *Scottish Abbeys and Social Life*. Cambridge: University Press, 1933.

Cowan, Ian B., and David E. Easson. *Medieval Religious Houses, Scotland*. London and New York: Longmans, 1976.

Cruden, Stewart. *The Scottish Castle*. Edinburgh: Spurbooks, 1981.

_____ . *Scottish Abbeys*. Edinburgh: H.M.S.O., 1960.

Duke, John A. *History of the Church of Scotland to the Reformation*. Edinburgh: Oliver & Boyd, 1957.

Duncan, Archibald A. M. *Scotland: The Making of the Kingdom* The Edinburgh History of Scotland, vol. I. Edinburgh: Oliver & Boyd, 1975.

Grant, Isabel Frances. *The Social and Economic Development of Scotland before 1603*. Edinburgh: Oliver & Boyd, 1930.

Mackenzie, W. Mackay. *The Medieval Castle in Scotland*. London: Methuen & Co., 1927.

MacLean of Dochgarroch, Loraine, ed. *The Middle Ages in the Highlands*. Inverness: Inverness Field Club, 1981.

Nicholson, Ranald. *Scotland: The Later Middle Ages*. The Edinburgh History of Scotland, vol. II. Edinburgh: Oliver & Boyd, 1974.

Richardson, James S. *The Medieval Stone Carver in Scotland*. Edinburgh: The University Press, 1964.

Simpson, William Douglas. *Scottish Castles*. Edinburgh: H.M.S.O., 1959.

Street, K. A., and J. W. M. Bannerman. *Late Medieval Monumental Sculpture in the West Highlands*. Edinburgh: H.M.S.O., 1977.

The Sixteenth, Seventeenth, and Early Eighteenth Centuries

(Chapters 6 and 7)

Bingham, Caroline. *James V, King of Scots*. London: Collins, 1971.

_____ . *The Making of a King: The Early Years of James VI and I*. London: Collins, 1968.

Cowan, Ian B. *The Scottish Reformation*. New York: St. Martin's Press, 1982.

——————. *The Scottish Covenanters, 1669–1688*. London: Victor Gollancz, 1976.

——————, and Duncan Shaw, eds. *The Renaissance and Reformation in Scotland: Essays in Honour of Gordon Donaldson*. Edinburgh: Scottish Academic Press, 1983.

Daiches, David. *The Last Stuart: The Life and Times of Bonnie Prince Charlie*. New York: G. P. Putnam & Sons, 1973.

Donaldson, Gordon. *James V–James VII*. The Edinburgh History of Scotland, vol. III. Edinburgh: Oliver & Boyd, 1978.

——————. *Mary, Queen of Scots*. London: The English Universities Press, 1974.

——————. *The Scottish Reformation*. Cambridge, London, New York, New Rochelle, Melbourne and Sydney: Cambridge University Press, 1979.

Dow, F. D. *Cromwellian Scotland, 1651–1660*. Edinburgh: John Donald Publishers, 1979.

Ferguson, William. *Scotland: 1689 to the Present*. The Edinburgh History of Scotland, vol. IV. Edinburgh: Oliver & Boyd, 1978.

Fraser, Antonia. *Mary, Queen of Scots*. New York: Delacorte Press, 1969.

——————. *King James VI of Scotland, I of England*. New York: Alfred A. Knopf, 1975.

Fraser, George MacDonald. *The Steel Bonnets*. New York: Alfred A. Knopf, 1972.

Hay, George. *The Architecture of Scottish Post-Reformation Churches, 1560–1843*. Oxford: Clarendon Press, 1957.

Lee, Maurice, Jr. *James Stewart, Earl of Moray*. New York: Columbia University Press, 1953.

——————. *John Maitland of Thirlestane*. Princeton, N.J.: Princeton University Press, 1959.

——————. *Government by Pen: Scotland under James VI and I*. Urbana, Chicago and London: University of Illinois Press, 1980.

Lythe, S. G. E. *The Economy of Scotland, 1550–1625*. Edinburgh and London: Oliver & Boyd, 1960.

McRoberts, David. *Essays on the Scottish Reformation, 1513–1625*. Glasgow: Burns, 1962.

Mitchison, Rosalind. *Lordship to Patronage: Scotland 1603–1674*. The New History of Scotland, vol V. London: Edward Arnold, 1983.

Prebble, John. *Glencoe*. Harmondsworth, Middlesex: Penguin Books, 1968.

——————. *Culloden*. Harmondsworth, Middlesex: Penguin Books, 1967.

Ridley, Jasper. *John Knox.* New York and Oxford: Oxford University Press, 1968.

Riley, P. W. J. *King William and the Scottish Politicians.* Edinburgh: John Donald Publishers, 1979.

Speck, W. A. *The Butcher: The Duke of Cumberland and the Suppression of the 45.* Oxford: Basil Blackwell Publisher, 1981.

Stevenson, David. *The Scottish Revolution, 1637-1644: The Triumph of the Covenanters.* New York: St. Martin's Press, 1973.

——————. *Revolution and Counter-Revolution in Scotland, 1644-1651.* London: Royal Historical Society, 1977.

Wormald, Jenny. *Court, Kirk, and Community: Scotland 1470-1625.* The New History of Scotland, vol. IV. London: Edward Arnold, 1981.

The Late Eighteenth, Nineteenth, and Early Twentieth Centuries

(Chapters 8 and 9)

Butt, John, ed. *Robert Owen: Prince of Cotton Spinners.* Newton Abbot: David & Charles, 1971.

Campbell, Ian. *Kailyard: A New Assessment.* Edinburgh: The Ramsay Head Press, 1981.

Campbell, R. H. *The Rise and Fall of Scottish Industry, 1707-1939.* Edinburgh: John Donald Publishers, 1980.

——————, and Andrew S. Skinner, eds. *The Origins and Nature of the Scottish Enlightenment.* Edinburgh: John Donald Publishers, 1982.

Checkland, Sidney G. *The Gladstones: A Family Biography, 1764-1851.* Cambridge: University Press, 1971.

——————. *The Upas Tree: Glasgow, 1875-1975.* Rev. ed. Glasgow: University of Glasgow Press, 1981.

——————, and Olive Checkland. *Industry and Ethos: Scotland 1832-1914.* The New History of Scotland, vol. VII. London: Edward Arnold, 1984.

Chitnis, Anand C. *The Scottish Enlightenment: A Social History.* London: Croom Helm, 1976.

The Curious Diversity: Glasgow University on Gilmorehill: The First Hundred Years. Glasgow: University of Glasgow, 1970.

Daiches, David. *Robert Louis Stevenson.* Norfolk, CT: New Directions Books, 1947.

——————. *The Paradox of Scottish Culture: The Eighteenth-Century Experience.* London: Oxford University Press, 1964.

——————— . *Robert Burns*. Edinburgh: Spurbooks, 1966.

——————— . *James Boswell and His World*. New York: Charles Scribner's Sons, 1976.

——————— . *Sir Walter Scott and His World*. New York: The Viking Press, 1971.

Drummond, Andrew L., and James Bulloch. *The Scottish Church, 1688-1843*. Edinburgh: The Saint Andrews Press, 1973.

——————————————— . *The Church in Victorian Scotland, 1843-1874*. Edinburgh: The Saint Andrews Press, 1975.

Duff, David, ed. *Queen Victoria's Highland Journals*. Exeter, England: Webb & Bower, 1980.

Fleming, John. *Robert Adam and His Circle*. London: John Murray, 1962.

Gray, Malcolm. *The Highland Economy, 1750-1850*. Edinburgh: Oliver & Boyd, 1957.

Haldane, Archibald R. B. *The Drove Roads of Scotland*. Newton Abbot: David & Charles, 1973.

Hamilton, Henry. *The Industrial Revolution in Scotland*. London: Frank Cass & Co., 1966.

Hanham, H. J. *Scottish Nationalism*. London: Faber and Faber, 1969.

Hardie, William. *Scottish Painting, 1837-1939*. London: Cassell, 1976.

Harvie, Christopher. *No Gods and Precious Few Heroes: Scotland 1914-1980*. The New History of Scotland, vol. VIII. London: Edward Arnold, 1981.

Hunter, James. *The Making of a Crofting Community*. Edinburgh: John Donald Publishers, 1976.

Irwin, David and Francina. *Scottish Painters at Home and Abroad, 1700-1900*. London: Faber and Faber, 1975.

Kellas, James G. *Modern Scotland*. Rev. ed. London: George Allen & Unwin, 1980.

Lauber, John. *Sir Walter Scott*. New York: Twayne Publishers, Inc., 1966.

Lenman, Bruce. *An Economic History of Modern Scotland, 1660-1976*. London: B. T. Batsford, 1977.

Lindsay, Maurice. *Robert Burns*. London: MacGibbon & Kee, 1971.

Macdonald, Finlay J. *A Journey to the Western Isles: Johnson's Scottish Journey Retraced by Finlay J. Macdonald*. London and Sydney: Macdonald & Co., 1983.

Macleod, Robert. *Charles Rennie Mackintosh: Architect and Artist*. Rev. ed. London and Glasgow: William Collins Sons and Co., 1983.

Marwick, William Hutton. *Scotland in Modern Times: An Outline of Economic and Social Development since the Union of 1707*. London: F. Cass, 1964.

Murdoch, Alexander. *The People Above: Politics and Administration in*

Mid-Eighteenth Century Scotland. Edinburgh: John Donald Publishers, 1980.

Orr, Willie. *Deer Forests, Landlords and Crofters.* Edinburgh: John Donald Publishers, 1982.

Prebble, John. *The Highland Clearances.* Harmondsworth, Middlesex: Penguin Books, 1969.

——————. *Mutiny: Highland Regiments in Revolt, 1743-1804.* Harmondsworth, Middlesex: Penguin Books, 1975.

Richards, Eric. *A History of the Highland Clearances.* London and Canberra: Croom Helm, 1982.

Rolt, Loral T. C. *Thomas Telford.* London, New York, and Toronto: Longmans, Green and Co., 1958.

Shenker, Israel. *In the Footsteps of Johnson and Boswell.* Boston: Houghton Mifflin Company, 1982.

Taylor, William. *The Military Roads of Scotland.* Newton Abbot; David & Charles, 1976.

Webb, Keith. *The Growth of Nationalism in Scotland.* Glasgow: The Molendinar Press, 1977.

Wendt, Allen, ed. *Samuel Johnson, "A Journey to the Western Islands of Scotland" and James Boswell, "The Journal of a Tour to the Hebrides with Samuel Johnson, L.L.D."* Boston: Houghton Mifflin Company, 1965.

Youngson, Alexander J. *The Making of Classical Edinburgh, 1750-1840.* Edinburgh: University Press, 1966.

——————. *After The Forty-Five.* Edinburgh: Edinburgh University Press, 1973.

Index

Page numbers in **bold type** refer to Gazetteer.

About the Author

Philip A. Crowl was born in Dayton, Ohio, in 1914. After graduating from Oakwood High School in that city, he was educated at Swarthmore College (A.B. with Highest Honors in History, 1936), the University of Iowa (M.A. in History, 1939), and the Johns Hopkins University (Ph.D. in History, 1942). He has taught history and related subjects at Princeton University, the U.S. Naval Academy, Swarthmore College, the University of Nebraska, Stanford University, and the U.S. Naval War College. Between 1942 and 1945 he served as an officer in the U.S. Navy, mostly in the Pacific, and between 1957 and 1967 as an intelligence officer in the Department of State in Washington. His publications include *Maryland During and After the American Revolution* (1943), *The U.S. Marines and Amphibious War* (with J. A. Isely—1951), *Seizure of the Gilberts and Marshalls* (with E. G. Love—1955), *Campaign in the Marianas* (1960), and, most recently, *The Intelligent Traveller's Guide to Historic Britain* (1983), to which this present volume is the sequel.

Since his retirement in 1980 from the chairmanship of the Department of Strategy at the Naval War College, he and his wife have lived in Annapolis, Maryland, where he gardens and sails occasionally between visits abroad, mostly to the British Isles.

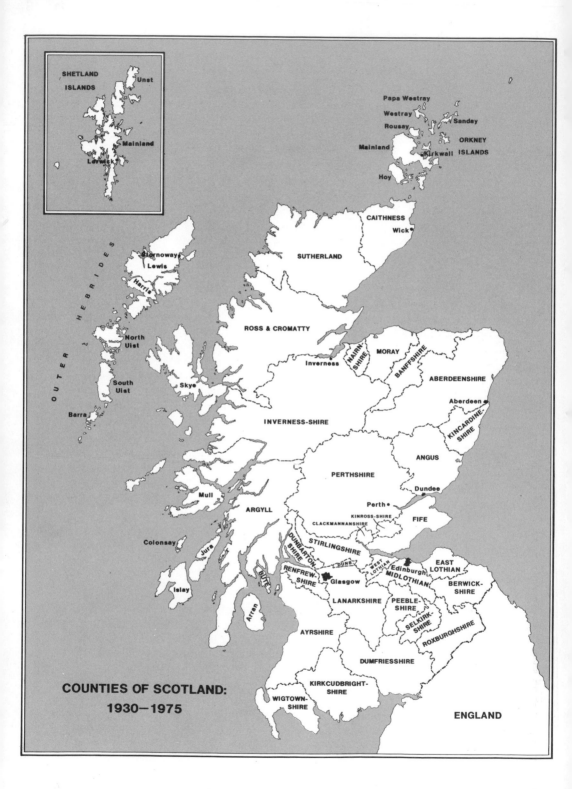

SHETLAND
ISLANDS
Unst

Mainland

Lerwick

Papa Westray
Westray
Rousay   Sanday
Mainland   ORKNEY
        Kirkwall ISLANDS

Hoy

CAITHNESS
Wick

Stornoway
Lewis
Harris

SUTHERLAND

O
U
T
E
R

H
E
B
R
I
D
E
S

North
Uist

ROSS & CROMATTY

Skye

NAIRN- MORAY
SHIRE

BANFFSHIRE

Inverness

ABERDEENSHIRE

South
Uist

Barra

INVERNESS-SHIRE

Aberdeen

KINCARDINE-
SHIRE

ANGUS

Mull

PERTHSHIRE

Dundee

ARGYLL

Perth

KINROSS-SHIRE

FIFE

CLACKMANNANSHIRE

Colonsay

STIRLINGSHIRE

Jura

DUNBARTON-
SHIRE

DUNB.

WEST
LOTHIAN

Edinburgh

EAST
LOTHIAN

Islay

BUTE

RENFREW-
SHIRE   Glasgow

MIDLOTHIAN

BERWICK-
SHIRE

Arran

LANARKSHIRE

PEEBLE-
SHIRE

SELKIRK-
SHIRE

ROXBURGHSHIRE

AYRSHIRE

DUMFRIESSHIRE

COUNTIES OF SCOTLAND:

1930—1975

KIRKCUDBRIGHT-
SHIRE

WIGTOWN-
SHIRE

ENGLAND